Light at the End
of the Tunnel

A Vietnam War Anthology

Light at the End of the Tunnel

A Vietnam War Anthology

Edited by
Andrew J. Rotter
Colgate University

St. Martin's Press

New York

Senior editor: Don Reisman
Project management: John Fancher, Publication Services
cover art: Tom McKeveny
cover photo: UPI/Bettmann Archives

For information write:
St. Martin's Press, Inc.
175 Fifth Avenue
New York, NY 10010

ISBN 0-312-04529-8

To Lorraine and J. C. Kaimal

Preface

"Vietnam Vietnam we've all been there," wrote Michael Herr at the conclusion of his book, *Dispatches*. It is a chilling incantation, and it has great meaning for those who matured intellectually during the 1960s. The war in Vietnam surrounded Americans from 1965 to 1973. The war was on television, at school, in the streets. It came in the mail, it was opposed or memorialized on walls, and it was featured in popular music. Herr got it right: even if you did not go to Vietnam, you went.

Much of this puzzles today's college students, for whom this book is primarily intended. Seniors graduating in the spring of 1989 were born perhaps in the year of the Tet offensive. Most of today's freshmen, conceived in the early 1970s, were not yet literate when Saigon fell. Not surprisingly, students use third person pronouns when they refer to Vietnam veterans and antiwar protestors. Vietnam is not a place where they have been or are going: it is history, as remote from their experience as the Thirty Years War or the origins of the New Deal.

This does not mean that students are not interested in the Vietnam War. Indeed, despite efforts by some politicians in the 1970s to erase all memory of the war and its consequences, curiosity about Vietnam seems rather to have intensified recently. The number of college courses on the war has grown spectacularly in the last few years, at large and small four-year schools and at community colleges as well. Enrollment in these courses is often as large as the registrar will allow; the University of California at Santa Barbara has a course with 900 students and the State University of New York at Stony Brook enrolls 800. The popularity of these courses shows no sign of diminishing.

At the same time, American culture today bears at least the faint mark of the Vietnam War era. Here one must be cautious; the current infatuation with tie-dyed shirts, for example, probably reflects nothing more than a hazy nostalgia for the 1960s, unburdened by any feeling about Vietnam one way or another, but although the war did not cause the rise of the New Left or the emergence of the drug culture, rock music, or the women's movement, it surely contributed to the growth of these things.

The stubborn defense by Presidents Johnson and Nixon of the increasingly disastrous war led to the erosion of political authority and encouraged more sweeping challenges to "the establishment." The act of protest itself was profoundly liberating for many young people. Having rejected the foreign policy of the authorities, many protestors were tempted to reject generally accepted styles as well, as some argued that smoking marijuana was hardly a criminal act when compared to U.S. policy in Vietnam, and others made the same claim for defacing property. Even the hippies, many of whom professed indifference to the war, were nevertheless affected by it. At an antiwar rally in Berkeley in 1965, Ken Kesey, leader of the countercultural Merry Pranksters, urged his listeners to turn their backs on the war and irreverently played "Home on the Range" on his harmonica. Humor and surrealism, however, did not make the war go away. Kesey and others could not finally ignore its presence.

Several vestiges of culture of the Vietnam War era remain, or have been rediscovered. Some current styles in clothing may be references to Vietnam. Professionals who came of age in 1960s have patronized a store called Banana Republic, a purveyor of jungle wear for the sedately upscale. The store sells shirts with epaulets, khaki pants with multiple pockets, maps, pith helmets, and jungle boots. The Banana Republic catalogue does not refer explicitly to Vietnam, but the appeal of the place seems obvious; imperialism—the American in jungle clothing—is benign, even chic. This is not combat garb, fashionable in the 1960s. Now Americans can go back into the bush and not get killed.

There is also evidence that a connection exists between curiosity about Vietnam and popular music. Along with the civil rights movement, Vietnam helped inspire protest music. Today, rock 'n' roll and folk artists continue to write lyrics and espouse causes that are politically charged. The Clash made a critically successful album called *Sandinista*. More recently, U2 and Bruce Springsteen have raised money for Amnesty International, an organization dedicated to the protection of human rights, and politically engaged singers such as Joan Baez and Tracy Chapman have performed before enthusiastic audiences. I recall discussing Frances Fitzgerald's book *Fire in the Lake* with a perplexed student, trying to impress him with the subtlety and complexity of Fitzgerald's argument. I told him that the book rewarded careful reconsideration, whereupon he brightened and said, "Like the Beatles' *White Album!*"

Television executives and filmmakers have rediscovered Vietnam. Public television produced *Vietnam: A Television History*, a thirteen-part series that won widespread acclaim. Two of the major networks have launched dramatic series on the war. Since the mid-1970s, Vietnam has been a favorite theme of filmmakers. Two of the best movies about the war are documentaries: *Hearts and Minds*, a powerful indictment of the war, and *The War at Home*, a mostly sympathetic look at the antiwar movement in Madison, Wisconsin. Commercial films about Vietnam have generally done well with critics and audiences. Several came out in the late 1970s:

Francis Ford Coppola's extraordinary *Apocalypse Now* ("I love the smell of napalm in the morning," says an officer played by Robert Duvall. "It smells like... victory"); *Coming Home*, which offered a sensitive portrait of a handicapped veteran but depicted another vet as dangerously unstable; and *The Deer Hunter*, a powerful movie that took considerable liberties with the historical record. Recently, there has been a second wave of Vietnam movies. *Platoon* won an Oscar as the best picture of 1986. It was well received in part because of its apparent realism, and in good part because it hinted the United States might have won the war if its soldiers had fought as cleverly as the "good" sergeant depicted in the movie. Stanley Kubrick's *Full Metal Jacket*, released in 1987, offered a harrowing representation of boot camp and a blackly comic view of military journalism. *Good Morning Vietnam* featured Robin Williams as a manic army disc jockey in wartime Saigon. During 1989, *Casualties of War*, *In Country*, and *Born on the Fourth of July* appeared, the last to an especially strong critical reception.

The symbolic locus of the new curiosity about Vietnam is the Vietnam Veterans Memorial in Washington, D.C. Dedicated in 1982, the Wall, as it has come to be called, was initially opposed by some conservatives, who found it a morbid reminder of failure rather than a celebration of accomplishment (and who insisted that a more conventional sculpture of soldiers be placed alongside it). Millions of Americans visit the Wall each year, and few leave unmoved. The Wall is made of enormous slabs of black granite, in which are carved the nearly 58,000 names of the dead and missing in action. Visitors walk down an incline to begin reading the names—it is like going into a bunker. When the Wall is polished and the sun is right, visitors see themselves reflected in the granite. The Wall requires a discourse with the dead: "Vietnam Vietnam we've all been there."

All of which brings me to this anthology. I made the decision to edit this collection when I taught an undergraduate course on the United States in Vietnam. I wanted to introduce my students to a variety of topics on the war and a number of interpretations of U.S. intervention. I found I could do this only by assigning whole monographs, which reduced the number of books I could use, or by assigning excerpts from the monographs, which was frustrating and expensive for the students. I decided that a substantial anthology, one that offered coverage and depth, would solve these problems.

The result is this book. As the table of contents indicates, it is divided into eleven chapters. The first four chapters offer a chronological survey of the American War in Vietnam; each chapter contains two or three excerpts from scholarly or journalistic accounts of the war and one passage from the account of a participant. Part Two—chapters five, six, and seven—more closely describes the war itself, examining the Vietnamese who fought the Americans, the battlefield, and the U.S. military. Chapters eight through ten treat the consequences of the war. They cover, respectively, the scholarly controversy over the sources of the war, the impact of Vietnam on American society, the role of the media in representing the conflict, and the legacy of the war.

Chapter eleven, an "Afterward," is an excerpt from a book by a Vietnamese woman named Le Ly Hayslip. I have included it not only because it is a moving piece of writing, but in order to leave the reader with the testimony of someone who lived in Vietnam. This collection has as its focus the United States' experience in Vietnam, for which I make no apology. But we misunderstand the nature of that experience if we look upon Vietnam as a venue for war, rather than a country with a history and a culture. I have tried at least occasionally to point this out, in the introduction and in my selection of readings, and I urge readers to keep it in mind.

Beyond that, I have worked to choose readings that are diverse, interesting, provocative, and intellectually responsible. Teachers may, of course, edit the collection themselves by assigning only certain selections or reorganizing the book to suit their needs. I suggest that this book be used alongside one of the several fine documentary collections on the war, such as Gareth Porter, *Vietnam: A History in Documents*, or William Appleman Williams et al., *America in Vietnam: A Documentary Collection*. Mostly, though, I hope the book is useful to students, who may find that, in looking behind them at the Vietnam War, they are really looking ahead.

ACKNOWLEDGMENTS

I am grateful for the help of Abigail Scherer, Heidi Schmidt, and especially Don Reisman at St. Martin's, and I appreciate very much the suggestions of five scholars who read the manuscript for the press: Virginia M. Harrington, Cornell University; Andrea McElderry, University of Louisville; Chester J. Pach, Jr., The University of Kansas; and John R. W. Smail, University of Wisconsin—Madison. Thanks of course, to the authors and publishers who granted permission to use the material reprinted here. Finally thanks, as always, to Padma.

Contents

Introduction · 1

PART ONE

**A CHRONOLOGY OF UNITED STATES
INTERVENTION 27**

**CHAPTER 1
Getting In, 1945-1950 · 29**

1 · Ho Chi Minh: The Untried Gamble · 31
Robert Shaplen

2 · Moving toward Commitment, 1949 · 48
Robert M. Blum

3 · An Encounter with Ho Chi Minh · 68
Archimedes L.A. Patti

**CHAPTER 2
Fighting Shy, 1950-1961 · 75**

4 · Eisenhower, Dulles, and Dienbienphu:
"The Day We Didn't Go to War" Revisited · 77
George Herring and Richard Immerman

5 · Geneva, 1954: The Precarious Peace · 101
Ellen J. Hammer

6 · An American Boost for Ngo Dinh Diem · 114
Edward Geary Lansdale

CHAPTER 3
Digging In, 1961-1968 · 123

7 · No "Non-Essential Areas": JFK and Vietnam · 125
Herbert S. Parmet

8 · LBJ Goes to War · 137
George C. Herring

9 · The Tet Offensive · 152
Larry Berman

10 · A Dissenter in the Government · 165
George W. Ball

CHAPTER 4
Getting Out, 1968-1975 · 177

11 · Nixon's War · 179
Stanley Karnow

12 · The Failure of Force · 190
Gareth Porter

13 · The Secret Bombing of Cambodia · 206
William Shawcross

14 · In Defense of the Nixon Policy · 220
Henry Kissinger

PART TWO
IN COUNTRY 235

CHAPTER 5
The American Enemy · 237

15 · The Making of a Revolutionary · 239
Truong Nhu Tang

16 · The Communists' Road to Power · 253
Douglas Pike

17 · The People and the Americans · 266
Konrad Kellen

18 · The National Liberation Front and the Land · 274
Tom Mangold and John Penycate

CHAPTER 6
The Battlefield · 281

19 · At the Edge of Sanity · 283
Michael Herr

20 · Getting Hit · 291
Philip Caputo

21 · "They Did Not Know Good from Evil" · 297
Tim O'Brien

22 · A Black Man in Vietnam · 305
Wallace Terry

CHAPTER 7
The Military · 313

23 · Assessing the Army's Performance · 315
Bruce Palmer, Jr.

24 · Military Mismanagement · 330
Loren Baritz

25 · The Question of American War Guilt · 346
Guenter Lewy

PART THREE

**CONTROVERSIES AND CONSEQUENCES
OF AMERICAN INVOLVEMENT 375**

CHAPTER 8
Interpreting the War · 377

26 · A Clash of Cultures · 379
Frances FitzGerald

27 · A Bureaucratic Tangle · 400
James C. Thomson, Jr.

28 · A Capitalist Imperative · 411
Gabriel Kolko

29 · A Defense of Freedom · 423
Norman Podhoretz

30 · A Systematic Success · 436
Leslie Gelb

CHAPTER 9
The War at Home and the Media • 455

31 · The Draft and Who Escaped It · 457
Lawrence M. Baskir and William A. Strauss

32 · The SDS and Vietnam · 475
Nigel Young

33 · Women at the Barricades, Then and Now · 493
Myra MacPherson

34 · The Number One Story · 504
Michael J. Arlen

35 · Covering the Gulf of Tonkin · 514
Daniel Hallin

CHAPTER 10
The Legacy of War • 531

36 · The Aftermath of Communist Victory · 533
William J. Duiker

37 · A Deserter and His Family · 550
Gloria Emerson

38 · Agent Orange, and the Wall at Home · 556
Bobbie Ann Mason

CHAPTER 11
Afterword • 567

39 · Letting Go · 569
Le Ly Hayslip

APPENDIX
A Chronology of the Vietnam War, 1945-1975 • 579

Glossary · 587

Light at the End
of the Tunnel

A Vietnam War Anthology

Introduction

For years, most westerners who studied Vietnam depicted it as a geopolitical empty space, into which periodically came migrants or invaders from bigger places. The Vietnamese, scholars claimed, got their religion, their notions about statecraft and economics, their system of agriculture, and their art and architecture from China and India, whose peoples "diffused" into Southeast Asia or imposed their culture through conquest. The Vietnamese thus created nothing; they simply absorbed the ideas their neighbors brought.

Recent investigations by historians and anthropologists have pointed to different conclusions. Although there is no question that traditional Vietnamese culture was syncretic—that is, blended from various forms, some of them external to Vietnam—the country was not simply a cultural sponge, indiscriminately soaking up every idea with which it came in contact. For example, sometime in the first century A.D., a kingdom called Funan was established in southern Vietnam, near the delta of the Mekong River. It was a strong and prosperous place; 200 years after Funan's founding, a Chinese visitor noted the kingdom's walled cities and grand palaces and, according to G. C. Bentley, observed that Funan's people "paid their taxes in pearls, gold, and perfumes." Scholars have determined that Funan's political and religious institutions were indigenous, not the products of other people's cultures. Religious rituals and political practices elsewhere in Vietnam were also based on internally created forms.

Historically, most Vietnamese have lived in small villages and grown rice. Because they rely on the land for sustenance, peasants are powerfully bonded to the soil, to a particular place. Peasants define themselves according to their position in their families, presenting themselves not as "I" but as "my parents' second son" or "your father's sister," a participant in a kinship network. Respect for one's elders and one's social betters is the source of stability for the family, the village, and the state. At the same time, however, respect is a reciprocal obligation. Those who are socially and politically powerful must demonstrate qualities of leadership—they must live virtuously, worship the gods properly, and protect villages and families from harm. In other words, they must be effective and behave

1

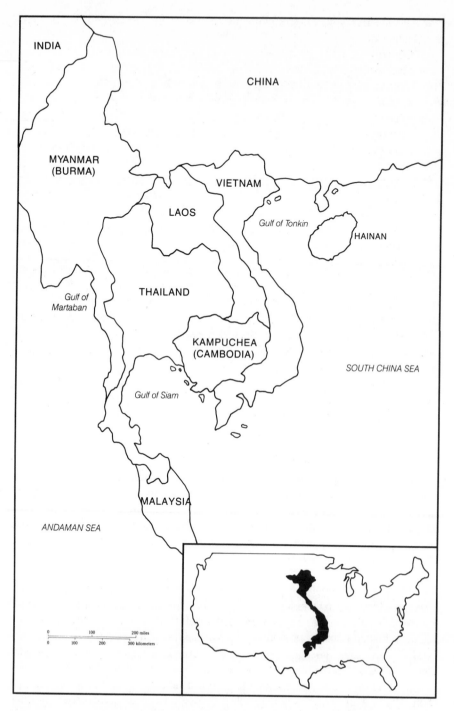

Figure 1. Southeast Asia; (*insert*) Vietnam in scale with United States.

themselves. Inability or unwillingness to do these things are grounds for popular dissatisfaction.

Comfortable with their culture and their place in the cosmos, the Vietnamese have never suffered invasion gladly. The Chinese were the first to discover this. They came to northern Vietnam late in the third century B.C., and ultimately the Han Dynasty (206 B.C.–A.D. 222) extended its control into what is today central Vietnam. For centuries, the Vietnamese gave their conquerors no peace. Vietnam gained its independence in 967 and fought off repeated Chinese efforts to repossess it, only to be reabsorbed once more late in the fourteenth century, when Vietnam was weakened by its own bullying of its smaller neighbors. The end of Chinese rule came finally in 1428, after the emperor Le Loi decisively defeated Chinese forces near Hanoi. The Chinese slunk home; the Vietnamese, to be safe from future invasions, agreed to pay a yearly tribute to China.

The independence of Vietnam was not threatened again for over 400 years. By the nineteenth century, Vietnam, weakened by internal warfare, again fell prey to outsiders. The interlopers this time were French. They came because they had a *mission civilisatrice*—they claimed they would lift the shroud of heathenism that covered the Vietnamese and replace it with the gilded robe of Christianity— because they hoped to protect their position in the emerging China market to the north and to secure Vietnamese resources, and because in the last half of the nineteenth century the prestige of a nation was measured by the number of dependencies it held. The French divided Vietnam into three states: Tonkin, in the north; Annam, in the narrow waist of the country; and Cochin China, encompassing the Mekong River delta in the south. The last they made a colony in 1867; in 1884 they established a protectorate over Tonkin and Annam. The French improved sanitation and started new schools. They also institutionalized the production and consumption of opium (despite the *mission civilisatrice* this was good money), insulted the Vietnamese with their arrogance, threw the social structure into chaos, and horribly mistreated the Vietnamese who worked for them on their rubber plantations, in their factories, and in their mines. The French frequently disrupted time-honored patterns of authority in the villages, where most Vietnamese lived, and they created an educated urban elite, many of whom would come to oppose the control of their country by another. As the old order came unstuck, the people were left angry and confused and the way was opened to resistance. By the early twentieth century, sporadic tax revolts indicated an incipient Vietnamese nationalism.

The man who would finally give direction to the anti-French feeling in the country was Ho Chi Minh. A man of many pseudonyms and nearly as many identities, Ho traveled widely, possibly to the United States and certainly to great Britain and France. It was in post–World War I Paris that Ho experienced political epiphany. Rejected by the Allies when he pleaded that Woodrow Wilson's idea of self-determination should apply to the Vietnamese, Ho moved quickly through the halfway house of European Socialism and became a Communist. The reason for this affiliation was simple: the Communists were unequivocally anticolonialist, and they alone, with their base in Moscow, might help him remove the French from his country. (Years later, U.S. foreign policymakers would sneer at the claim made by

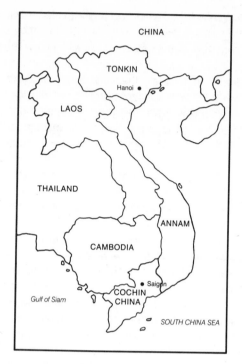

Figure 2. French Indochina, showing 3-part division of Vietnam.

American liberals that Ho was a nationalist first and a Communist second; in fact, the claim was literally true.) Ho went to the Soviet Union and China. In 1929, he founded the Indochinese Communist Party.

In Vietnam resistance to the French had intensified. A variety of organizations sought in their own ways to mobilize the Vietnamese. The Vietnam Nationalist Party, called the Viet Nam Quoc Dan Dang (VNQDD), staged an abortive revolt in 1930. There were persistent rebellions by dislocated farmers and strikes by unhappy workers. A quasireligious sect, the Cao Dai, gained the support of thousands of poor peasants and became a powerful force in the south, but it was politically unpredictable. By the late 1930s, the Communists were in the best position to rally the nationalists. Early in 1941, Ho Chi Minh returned to Vietnam and announced the formation of the Vietnam Independence League, or Vietminh. All nationalists were to join it; the Communists would lead it; and Ho was its General Secretary.

At this point, Japan forcefully entered Southeast Asian political affairs. Intent on creating an Asian empire euphemistically called the Greater East Asian Co-Prosperity Sphere, the Japanese had seized Manchuria in 1931 and six years later expanded the conflict to China proper. By late 1939, when the war in Europe broke out, the Japanese were bombing targets in south China and thinking seriously about the raw materials of Southeast Asia, including tungsten, tin, rubber, and, above all, oil. French Indochina—Laos and Cambodia, as well as Vietnam—was a gateway to these natural riches. When France surrendered to Germany in June

1940, the Japanese asked the French collaborationist, or Vichy, government for permission to place military observers in Hanoi; in July they demanded the right to build military bases throughout Indochina. The French were not in a position to refuse.

The Japanese threat to Southeast Asia caught the attention of the United States. In 1940 few Americans knew where Vietnam was, and few felt any motivation to find out. The level of sophistication in government circles was scarcely higher: some years later, when a State Department officer wrote a profile of "Ho Chi Mink," the error went undetected. The Americans, however, came to see the connection between the colonial economies of Southeast Asian nations and the fighting capabilities of the colonies' European owners. Specifically, they understood that the British, who faced Nazi Germany virtually alone after the summer of 1940, would be in deep trouble if Japan cut off their supply of Malayan rubber and tin and their oil from the Dutch East Indies. The United States decided to draw the line against Japanese expansion at Indochina. When the Japanese moved to construct military installations in Indochina in July 1940, the State Department embargoed exports of aviation fuel and high-quality scrap iron and steel to Japan. Negotiations between the two powers over the next year proved fruitless, and the Japanese, running out of fuel for their war machine, demanded in July 1941 that the Vichy regime permit Japanese troops to occupy southern Indochina. This decision apparently resulted from Japanese misapprehension of American concern for Southeast Asia, and it cost Japan dearly. The Americans then embargoed all exports to Japan save those of food and cotton and froze Japanese assets in the United States, a move immediately imitated by Great Britain and the Dutch East Indies. These steps persuaded Japanese militants that their country was trapped and that the only way out was military action. On December 7 the Japanese attacked Pearl Harbor. The same day they moved against the Philippines, Hong Kong, and Malaya.

The Japanese quickly conquered most of Southeast Asia. They occupied Vietnam, but they decided to leave the Vichy French government in place and rule through it. This meant the Vietminh had two different colonial powers to battle. Ho Chi Minh directed what military efforts he could against the Japanese; the two sides skirmished frequently until 1945. The Vietnamese leader also planned for the eventual independence of his nation. He drafted a platform calling for representative government, a "balanced" economy, the eight-hour day, and a minimum wage. In March 1945, in retreat throughout Asia and witnessing the liberation of France, the Japanese overthrew the Vietnamese Vichy government and took control. When the Japanese themselves surrendered in August, the way seemed open at last for the Vietminh. On September 2, 1945, Ho Chi Minh, speaking to a cheering crowd in Hanoi, declared Vietnam independent. "We hold these truths to be self-evident: that all men are created equal," he began. He believed this to be true. He also knew that France would want his country back and that only the United States could prevent Vietnam from being reclaimed.

Ho had some reason to hope that the Untied States would support him. In August 1941 President Franklin D. Roosevelt had endorsed (with a reluctant Winston Churchill, the British Prime Minister) the Atlantic Charter, a statement that declared, among other things, that people had the right to determine their own form of government. Even though Roosevelt himself died in April 1945, the Vietnamese continued to take this declaration seriously. In the last days of the war, operatives of the U.S. Office of Strategic Services (OSS), among them Archimedes L. A. Patti, had worked with Ho in the Tonkin jungle. In return for help finding downed American pilots, some of the OSS officers preferred advice and support. The Americans on the scene believed Ho was sincerely interested in their assistance and thus could be influenced by the United States. "We had Ho Chi Minh on a silver platter," Patti said later.

Roosevelt's views on colonialism are worth considering, largely because both the OSS men and the Vietminh turned out to be naive about the president's intentions. In an ideal world, FDR felt, all nations would be democracies and would trade with each other freely and openly. But the postwar world would be a troubled place, not instantly susceptible to utopian solutions. Although it was good to have the Atlantic Charter on the books, defining as it did the ideal world, it would be necessary temporarily to compromise its philosophy to achieve peace and stability. This conclusion had particular implications for colonialism. Not all nations were ready for independence. Places such as Algeria, Palestine, and Vietnam might for some time require tutelage by a great power, instruction in the practices of liberalism and capitalism. FDR imagined a world divided into four blocks, each one overseen by a powerful "policeman": the United States, Great Britain, the Soviet Union, and China. Gradually, the president hoped, the blocks would dissolve and a world system based on the principle of self-determination would emerge, but until that time nationalist aspirations threatened order and so must be put on hold.

Roosevelt concluded that Vietnam, Laos, and Cambodia were not ready for self-rule. At the same time, France did not figure prominently in the president's plans for the postwar system. The French, FDR told British officials, were "hopeless." They were bad colonialists, both cruel and shortsighted. They had capitulated to Germany with shocking speed and then had collaborated much too easily with the Germans and the Japanese to be considered trustworthy. FDR was suspicious of even the courageous French resistance movement, for it was led by Charles DeGaulle, whom Roosevelt regarded as an arrogant opportunist. Instead of reverting to French control, then, Indochina should be given in trust to China, under the leadership of Generalissimo Chiang Kai-shek (Jiang Jieshi).

Those who consider Franklin Roosevelt a realist might ponder the practicality of this plan. Certainly there were many at the time who believed it was unworkable. The British feared that FDR's hostility to French colonialism might soon come to rest on them. (The British Ambassador to the United States worried that "one of these days" FDR "might have the bright idea that the Netherlands East Indies or British Malaya would go under international trusteeships.") British officials were also skeptical that China would become a great power—and a worthy policeman—after the war. (Even Chiang Kai-shek had doubts about tutoring Indochina.) The Vietnamese would object, to put it mildly. Most compelling, though, was the opposition to the Chinese trusteeship scheme by officials in the Roosevelt administration. By 1944 most State Department experts anticipated trouble with the Soviet Union in Europe. Because defeated Germany would not provide a bulwark against Soviet expansion into western Europe, it was essential that France be made strong enough at least to forestall a Soviet invasion. To strip France of its Indochina colony would shatter French pride, weaken the French economy, and destroy the French will to resist Soviet incursions. State Department officials, joined by military leaders, pressured Roosevelt to give up the scheme altogether.

Early in 1945 FDR changed his mind. The first indication of this shift came at the Big Three (Roosevelt, Churchill, and Josef Stalin) conference at Yalta in February, when FDR reluctantly agreed that nations need not place their colonies under trusteeships unless they wanted to. Even more revealing was a conversation the president had with an adviser in mid-March, in which he expressed concern for "the brown people in the East" and said that the United States' "goal must be to help them achieve independence." When the adviser asked specifically about Indochina, FDR "hesitated a moment and then said'—well, if we can get the proper pledge from France to assume for herself the obligations of a trustee, then I would agree to France retaining these colonies with the proviso that independence was the ultimate goal.' " By the time of Roosevelt's death on April 12, hopes for self-determination had not quite disappeared from U.S. policy toward Indochina, but they had been shouldered aside by the return of French colonialism.

This was the policy left to Harry S. Truman, a former senator from Missouri who had been vice-president for only two and a half months when he became president. Truman's experience with foreign affairs was limited, and like most Americans, he didn't know who Ho Chi Minh was. Relations with French Indochina were handled largely by Truman's secretaries of state—James F. Byrnes (1945–47), George C. Marshall (1947–49), and Dean Acheson (1949–53)—and their staffs in the State Department, with assistance from civilian and military officials in other departments. The president, however, provided the fundamental principles of U.S. foreign policy and set its tone. Truman came to believe that the Soviet Union was determined to spread communism across the globe through military and political means. Only the United States, acting in concert with other free nations, could prevent Soviet expansion. Truman likened the Soviets to the Nazis: "There isn't any difference in totalitarian states," he said. "I don't care what you call them, Nazi, Communist or Fascist." The administration implemented the containment strategy in an effort to stop the Russians. With the Truman Doctrine speech in March 1947, the president divided the world into two armed camps, one for the Communists and the other for everyone else, and offered economic and military assistance to Turkey and Greece, two anticommunist governments with no claim to democracy. Less than three months later, Secretary of State Marshall announced the plan that would bear his name: a massive grant of economic aid to the war-devastated countries of western Europe. The Marshall Plan was designed to restore economic stability to western Europe to provide the United States with trade partners and diminish the appeal of communism. Then came the signing of the North Atlantic Treaty in April 1949, which created a military alliance between the United States, Canada, and various Atlantic and western European nations. These policies left no room for accommodation with Communists such as Ho Chi Minh.

In Vietnam, meanwhile, matters had taken a serious turn. The great powers ignored Ho's declaration of independence and fabricated instead a stunted version of Roosevelt's trusteeship plan. Vietnam was divided at the sixteenth parallel, with China occupying the north and great Britain the south. All parties acknowledged that this scheme would soon give way to French repossession of both sectors. Indeed, that is what happened: in September 1945 the British military commander in Saigon obediently armed 1,400 French troops who had been imprisoned by the Japanese. The soldiers, acting with appalling brutality, forced the Vietminh government to flee and recaptured Saigon. In the north, Ho Chi Minh managed to get the Chinese out by accepting, under duress, an agreement to make Vietnam a free state within the French Union—not an independent nation—and the return of French troops to Vietnamese soil. This was March 6, 1946.

The French soon demonstrated their determination to keep Vietnam in the fold. In negotiations they dithered or threatened; outside the conference room they gathered their forces. The March 6 agreement was never implemented. During the summer of 1946 Ho went to France seeking greater French flexibility. He came away with the Fontainebleau agreement of September, which offered, again, almost nothing. In the meantime the French separated Cochin China from the rest of Vietnam and placed it by fiat under the French Union. Ho, feeling rising pressure to act from more radical members of the Vietminh, begged the French to make concessions that would give him "a weapon against the extremists." The French were unyielding.

Ho and the Vietminh were not dewy-eyed pacifists. They were quite capable of brutality and shrank not at all from the use of military means to gain their objectives. By the fall of 1946 there was open warfare in the south, and tensions ran high in the northern cities of Hanoi, where the Vietnamese Assembly convened in late October, and especially Haiphong, where there were armed clashes in early November. The French bore primary responsibility for starting the violence. On November 23, French artillery opened up on the Vietnamese quarter of Haiphong, killing at least 6,000 people. Ho pleaded for calm, but it was no good: on the night of December 19, 1946, the Vietnamese in Hanoi, probably acting without Ho's orders, attacked the French with a full array of weapons. Fighting erupted throughout the countryside, and by the dawn of the western new year there was no turning back. "Before all, order must be reestablished," said the French premier, Leon Blum. "The war will be long and difficult," said Ho Chi Minh.

The French soldiers who fought the Vietminh soon came to appreciate Ho's words. Confident of quick victory, French authorities discovered instead that the Vietnamese desire for independence would not be easily denied. They decided, therefore, to fabricate a new Vietnamese government that would prove more cooperative; for its leader they selected the former emperor and erstwhile collaborator with the Japanese, Bao Dai. It took some doing to persuade Bao Dai to take the job. The former emperor was not without sympathy for the nationalists' position, and in 1947 he was leading a safe and comfortable life, dividing his time between Hong Kong and the French Riviera. The French cajoled him with various promises of self-government, and Bao Dai ultimately found the attractions of partial power irresistible. In April 1949 he returned to Vietnam as head of state "within the French Union."

The Bao Dai government held no interest for the Vietminh or for the majority of Vietnamese, who correctly regarded the new regime as a sham. The war intensified. The French, for their part, introduced their protégé around, in particular to the Americans, who alone had the wherewithal to bankroll the former emperor. When Bao Dai returned to Vietnam, the French formally asked the Truman administration to offer diplomatic recognition and financial and military assistance to the new government.

The Americans hesitated. There were many questions about Bao Dai. Did he have popular support? Assuming he did not, could he get it if the United States helped him? Was he essentially a playboy, involved in politics only for prestige or financial gain? What was his relationship with the French? Was he merely their stooge, a useful way for the French to maintain colonial control? Or was he another Chiang Kai-shek, the Chinese leader whose government was at that moment crumbling before the Communists? The evident answers to these questions were not reassuring to policymakers. Many of the Asian experts in the administration counseled caution. At least, these experts warned, the French should promise that they were moving toward independence for Vietnam.

But 1949 and 1950 were years of crisis in U.S. foreign policy, and patience became increasingly difficult to find in Washington. America's allies were still struggling to recover from the war. Japan and Germany—really the Allied occupation zone in the western part of Germany—had moved quickly from being enemies to being friends, but both nations depended heavily on U.S. economic aid, and West Germany seemed an imperiled frontline state in the Cold War tension between western and eastern Europe. The economy of Great Britain had shown signs of life in 1948, the first year of the Marshall Plan, but by the summer of 1949 British exports and dollar reserves dropped dramatically, and officials in London pleaded for help. The French economy staggered, too. Production and wages remained depressed, burdening French workers especially, and many turned to communism. The French government claimed it could do little to help labor because of the country's costly obligations in Vietnam. To make all of this worse, the Other Side, the Communist world that most believed was monolithic, seemed by the end of 1949 to be enjoying remarkable success. Communist parties had political clout in Italy and France. Ho Chi Minh had the French on the run in Vietnam. Late in the summer the Soviet Union detonated its first atomic bomb, years before Western experts believed the Soviets would have such capability. In October, the Chinese Communist leader Mao Tse-tung (Mao Zedong) announced the formation of the People's Republic of China, and Chiang Kai-shek retreated to Taiwan soon after.

The Truman administration tried to regain the initiative both militarily and diplomatically. It pressed forward with efforts to ensure the recovery of its allies in Europe and the Pacific. In January 1950 the president authorized a program to build a hydrogen bomb and asked for a reassessment of U.S. "objectives in peace and war" and "the effect of these objectives on our strategic plans." The result was the National Security Council (NSC) document number 68, which called for an enormous increase in defense spending. Policymakers talked of arming West Germany. Of lesser magnitude but equally profound implications, in the spring Truman decided to give $10 million in military aid and a small quantity of economic assistance to the French-backed Indochina governments. The administration hoped that the limited commitment represented by the aid would strengthen the anti-communist forces in Southeast Asia, secure regional markets for the Japanese, protect key British investments in Malayan raw materials, and offer some relief to the French, who had domestic problems (and now German rearmament) to worry about. It was much to expect of a little over $10 million—too much, as it turned out. Outside of a small group of statespersons and area specialists, few noticed the outlay had been made.

On June 25 Communist North Korea attacked non-Communist South Korea, its peninsular neighbor south of the thirty-eighth parallel. Though North Korea was a Soviet client and likely had Josef Stalin's permission to launch the assault, the timing and nature of the invasion had more to do with Korean politics than Cold War conditions. The Truman administration was convinced, however, that the North Korean attack represented a Soviet thrust by proxy and in the week following the invasion sent American forces (under United Nations auspices) to defend the besieged ally. Ultimately, the Americans stemmed the tide, pushed the North Koreans back across the thirty-eighth parallel, then joined South Korean troops in a drive to liberate North Korea. This move came to a halt in the late fall of 1950, when the Chinese intervened and forced the Americans to retreat south. By mid-1951 the Americans had rallied and stabilized their lines near the thirty-eighth parallel. On the battlefield a bloody stalemate ensued, while acrimonious negotiations between the two sides dragged on fruitlessly.

The Korean War had important implications for U.S. policy in Southeast Asia. For one thing, it became for policymakers a model of how Asian conflicts broke out during the Cold War: small communist states, acting on behalf of the Soviet Union or the People's Republic of China, invaded their weak, noncommunist neighbors. Regarding Indochina this was a misplaced analogy, for it assumed the two states in question were equally legitimate, which was never the case in Vietnam. Immediately following the North Korean attack, the Americans, who along with the French expected the next major communist thrust to come in Vietnam, significantly increased their aid for Indochina, and by 1952 were covering nearly one-third of the cost of the conflict. This support partly bolstered French confidence, but it also made the French wary of displacement by the United States; this was, after all, still a French fight. To show their mettle, the French now decided to take the offensive against the Vietminh. In late 1953 the French commander in Vietnam, General Henri Navarre, decided to try to lure the enemy into a set-piece battle in the northwest part of Vietnam, near the village of Dienbienphu. The Vietminh general Vo Nguyen Giap accepted the challenge. By early 1954 the French garrison, ensconced in a valley, found itself surrounded by Vietnamese soldiers and artillery. Disaster loomed for the French. They now urgently requested U. S. military intervention to rescue Dienbienphu.

There was a new administration in Washington by then: the Republican Dwight D. Eisenhower had been elected president in 1952. Eisenhower certainly allowed himself to be represented as a tough-minded realist on the Cold War, a president who would not shrink from confronting the Russians and the Chinese.

Eisenhower's secretary of state, John Foster Dulles, a gimlet-eyed lawyer from upstate New York, rejected the containment strategy as "futile and immoral" and proposed instead the "liberation" of communist countries by any means. Dulles also endorsed a policy of "massive retaliation" against perceived aggressors, a term with patently awful implications.

Because Eisenhower never publicly repudiated Dulles' pronouncements, most assumed that he shared them. But recent scholarship on the Eisenhower period has demonstrated that the president's thinking about foreign policy was not nearly as virulent as Dulles' statements might suggest. The president was not the passive, rather slow-witted bungler that liberals labeled him, but rather a shrewd man who played the foreign policy bureaucracy with the precision of a concert pianist. Eisenhower used Dulles' public posture to ensure for the administration the support of the Republican right wing. Some have even argued that the hopelessly tangled sentences Eisenhower offered up during press conferences were deliberately designed to confuse or mislead the public. Massive retaliation, which effectively replaced expensive conventional weapons with a few efficient nuclear missiles, was a cost-cutting measure. Eisenhower's crooked grin and his golf swing concealed a mind of energy and subtlety.

Unlike his immediate predecessors, President Eisenhower had been a career military man. As commander of the Allied forces in Europe during World War II, Eisenhower had conducted war, and he understood its horrors and its limitations. He believed the stalemate in the Korean War was a disaster, so he had brought the conflict to a speedy conclusion in 1953—in part by threatening privately to drop atomic bombs on China. When the French approached the administration seeking military help at Dienbienphu, Eisenhower was dubious. He allowed the proposal a serious hearing by the Joint Chiefs of Staff and mused out loud about the possibility of a U.S. air strike against Vietminh positions, as long as the planes were disguised as French. In the long run, however, because the president believed U.S. military intervention would serve no useful purpose, he made it conditional on congressional acquiescence, the cooperation of the British, and French willingness to accept the eventual independence of Vietnam. It was unlikely that even one of these conditions would be met; that all three would be met was impossible, as Eisenhower surely knew. Despite some embarrassing public blustering by Dulles and Vice President Richard Nixon, Eisenhower kept his "hidden hand" firmly on the decision-making process, and when Dienbienphu fell on May 7, 1954, it did not take American prestige with it.

Even before the debacle, the French sensed that their time in Vietnam was growing short. They had already asked for discussion of the Indochina problem at a conference on Far Eastern issues that opened in Geneva in late April. If the French had any leverage when the conference began, their influence disappeared with the collapse of Dienbienphu. On June 17 a new French government, led by the Socialist premier Pierre Mendes-France, promised to resign unless it could reach a negotiated solution to the war within thirty days.

At last, Ho Chi Minh must have thought, the years of struggle would be rewarded by diplomatic victory over France. It was not to be, for the great powers had their own interests to pursue in Vietnam. Josef Stalin had died the previous year, creating a tumult in the Russian political elite but removing a major obstacle to change in Soviet foreign policy. The British worried that persistent instability in Indochina, or a communist triumph there, would jeopardize their position in the economically valuable and unstable colony of Malaya. The Chinese, for whom the Vietnamese had no love, hoped that the annoying upheaval on their southern frontier would not bring U.S. intervention—the truce in Korea was not yet a year old—and therefore sought a political solution in Vietnam that would not humiliate the West. Just offstage the Americans glowered, as if daring the Vietminh to appear intractable.

The result was a remarkable arm-twisting session in the last hours before Mendes-France's self-imposed deadline, in which V. M. Molotov, the Soviet foreign minister, and the Chinese premier, Chou En-lai (Zhou Enlai), forced the Vietminh to accept a series of proposals that seemed to disregard the Vietminh's superior military position on the ground. A cease-fire was proclaimed for Vietnam, Laos, and Cambodia. (Communist forces enjoyed a military advantage in the latter two states as well.) Vietnam was partitioned at the seventeenth parallel. The northern part of the country, the Democratic Republic of Vietnam, would be governed by the Vietminh, and the south, called the State of Vietnam, would remain under the nominal control of Bao Dai, backed by the French, who would remain in place. The two zones were by no means to be permanent: elections were to be held throughout Vietnam in 1956 to choose a single government for the country. The elections would be overseen by an international commission that would guarantee their fairness.

The Vietminh had hoped for more territory and sooner elections, but Ho was willing to wait for the 1956 referendum, certain that he and his political allies would win. Thousands of southern Vietminh fighters were summoned north of the seventeenth parallel to await reunification. Ho meanwhile tried to whip the northern economy into shape—no easy task, given that most of Vietnam's food was grown in the south—and carried out a land reform policy in which thousands of landlords were killed. In the south, Bao Dai found himself outmaneuvered politically by Ngo Dinh Diem, whom Bao Dai had appointed prime minister in June 1954. Diem was a Catholic mandarin who was in his own mind a patriot and a would-be despot. Westerners who met Diem found him a fascinating bundle of contradictions, alternately puzzling, magnetic, and infuriating as he talked compulsively about Vietnamese philosophy and statecraft. Whatever Diem was, he had more backbone than Bao Dai. With the help of the American colonel Edward G. Lansdale, head of the U.S. Military Mission in Saigon, Diem asserted himself against the powerful Vietnamese sects and his other political rivals. By early 1955 he had established himself in American circles as a Vietnamese George Washington. The French could not abide him, and by the spring of 1955 they had pulled out of Vietnam.

That left the United States as Vietnam's sole outside support. The Eisenhower administration was hostile to the agreements reached at Geneva, believing the French had conceded too much by allowing the Vietminh to control the area north of the seventeenth parallel. U.S. representatives had difficulty understanding the complexities of Vietnamese politics—at Geneva, Undersecretary of State

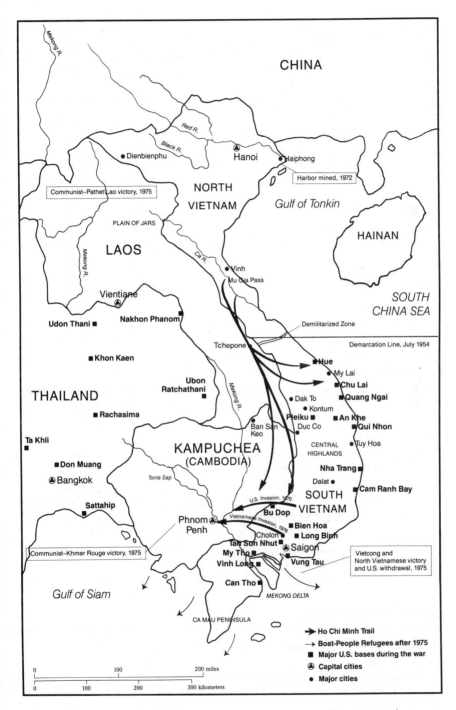

Figure 3. Vietnam partitioned 1954, with major cities of battle, Ho Chi Minh trail.

Walter Bedell Smith said that "$\frac{1}{3}$ of the Vietnamese people supported Bao Dai, $\frac{1}{3}$ supported Ho Chi Minh, and $\frac{2}{3}$ were on the fence"—but the Americans were resolved to prevent the Vietminh from taking control of all of Vietnam. The administration decided to support diem as head of government in a South Vietnam that was not just an artificial construct created as an expedient at Geneva but a nation with an independent future. Dulles found a way to tie South Vietnam to a regional defense association called the Southeast Asia Treaty Organization (SEATO), though this arrangement was specifically prohibited by the Geneva accords. The U.S. backed Diem when he refused to hold the 1956 elections and by 1961 had subsidized his regime to the tune of $1 billion. Under the foreboding rubric "black psywar," U.S. intelligence agents and their Vietnamese trainees conducted subversive operations against the Vietminh in the north. Typical activities included gun running, distributing phony leaflets, and pouring sugar into the gas tanks of North Vietnamese trucks. Occasionally things got out of hand: the *Pentagon Papers*, a secret Defense Department study of the war written in the late 1960s, disclosed that an alleged Communist prisoner was "interrogated by being handcuffed to a leper, both [men were] beaten with the same stick to draw blood, [the prisoner was] told he would now have leprosy, and both [were] locked up in a tiny cell together." Repression was rampant in South Vietnam.

Though these policies enraged Ho and the government in Hanoi, they resisted making a response to Diem's actions. Not so the Communist Party members who had remained in the south, in their home villages, after 1954. They and their families were the victims of intimidation, arrest, torture, and murder by the Saigon government. Restrained by Hanoi's policy of patience, the southern Party, according to Gabriel Kolko, lost at least two-thirds of its membership to arrest and death during 1957–58. Many struck back. The chief tactic of the southern Vietminh was to assassinate Diem's officials and uncooperative village leaders. Finally, in January 1959, the North Vietnamese government acceded to its southern allies; by the middle of the year arms and advisers had begun to flow south. The National Liberation Front (NLF), a collection of Communists, angry peasants, and disgruntled former sectarians, was formed in 1960 to carry out the armed struggle. The NLF was called by Diem the Viet Cong, or Vietnamese Communists.

In the United States, President Eisenhower was succeeded by the Democrat John F. Kennedy, who defeated Richard Nixon in 1960 after a hard-fought campaign. As a senator from Massachusetts JFK had been a champion of Diem, and during the presidential campaign he had attacked the Eisenhower administration for letting the communists push the United States around, especially in Cuba and two islands off the coast of China, Quemoy and Matsu. The Republican strategy of massive retaliation—the threat of nuclear attack—Kennedy charged, had paralyzed American foreign policy, robbing it of the flexibility it needed to respond to small conflicts in the so-called Third World. It was not always credible to threaten a country with nuclear annihilation because nuclear weapons were inefficient in rural areas, unable to discriminate between soldiers and civilians, and provocative, to say the least. JFK's solution to this strategic conundrum was "flexible response," which promised to fashion for policymakers an instrument that was somewhere between the penknife of CIA subversion and the battleax of atomic weaponry.

Everything about John Kennedy suggested motion. Eisenhower played golf; Kennedy and his brothers played touch football, with undisguised brio. During the campaign JFK had said, "It's time to get the country moving again." Where the country was to move and why movement was important were not so clear. It was a bit like a dialogue from Jack Kerouac's "beat" novel *On the Road*: "We gotta go and never stop going till we get there." "Where we going, man?" "I don't know, but we gotta go." Or, more to the point, as a Kennedy staffer put it: "The United States needs a *Grand Objective*. We behave as if ... our real objective is to sit by our pools contemplating the spare tires around our middles.... The key consideration is not that the Grand Objective be exactly right, it is that we *have* one and that we start moving toward it." In fairness, it must be said that JFK pointed toward "a new frontier," one with a variety of dimensions. Among them was Southeast Asia.

Kennedy was determined to "oppose any foes," as he put it in his inaugural address, and very quickly he found an opportunity to do that. Cuba had a Communist government led by Fidel Castro. From the Eisenhower administration JFK had inherited a plan mandating an invasion of Cuba by a group of anti-Castro exiles, trained in Guatemala by the CIA. Kennedy gave the scheme the go-ahead, and on April 16 the attack began. The invaders never had a chance: they were vastly outnumbered, American air support was inadequate, and the people of Cuba, most of them reasonably content with their lot, failed to rise against the government when the exiles splashed ashore at the Bay of Pigs. Everyone knew, or soon found out, that the CIA had been involved in the scheme. Kennedy blamed "the experts" for giving him bad advice, and he fired Allen Dulles, head of the CIA and brother of the late John Foster. But it was the president who suffered the humiliation of failure. He had swung hard at communism and missed.

Laos offered another chance. When Eisenhower briefed Kennedy on Southeast Asia in January 1961, he warned the incoming president that serious trouble was brewing in Laos, where an insurgency threatened to topple the Royalist government of Phoumi Nosavan. It might be necessary, Ike suggested, to intervene unilaterally to salvage the situation. (About Vietnam Eisenhower said little, though it must have been clear that prospects were not encouraging.) Phoumi's regime was in good part the creature of the CIA, which was one of the largest employers in the country, and was financed by a vigorous opium trade. It was besieged by a coalition of parties that ran the gamut from moderate (a group led by Prince Souvanna Phouma) to Communist (the Pathet Lao). The coalitionists seemed close to victory by early 1961.

Even before the Bay of Pigs fiasco, Kennedy's inclination was to use military force to protect the Royalist government in Laos. Robert McNamara, the new secretary of defense, suggested air strikes. The Joint Chiefs of Staff went further, calling for an invasion of Laos by 250,000 American troops, with tactical nuclear strikes held in reserve. It seemed likely that the United States would intervene. Then in late April, the administration's "roving ambassador," W. Averell Harriman, weighed in strongly for a negotiated solution to the conflict. At the eleventh hour Harriman and others, especially John Kenneth Galbraith, the ambassador in India, achieved a cease-fire in Laos and an agreement by both sides to reconvene the Geneva conference to discuss a joint Laotian government. It was a victory for diplomacy, some would argue, but on one level the president was disappointed. Negotiations with Communists were neither vigorous nor "manly," both important values in Kennedy's Camelot. JFK had started a second swing against communism, then checked it and fouled one off.

The third swing came in Vietnam. When JFK entered office, the United States was committed to Diem. Most of the $1 billion South Vietnam had received from the United States had gone to the military. There were over 1,500 American military advisers in Vietnam, and the CIA was still conducting its psywar north of the seventeenth parallel. In the late spring, following the Bay of Pigs and the decision to negotiate in Laos, Kennedy took several small but symbolically meaningful steps toward greater involvement in the war. He sent in 100 more advisers and recalled the ambassador, Elbridge Durbrow, who had urged the administration to make further aid to Diem conditional on genuine social reform; Durbrow was replaced by Frederick Nolting. Most critically, JFK secretly sent 400 Special Forces troops to teach the South Vietnamese to fight guerrilla warfare. The Special Forces, the best known of whom were the Green Berets, were avatars of flexible response and great favorites of the president. The Special Forces were not combat troops in the technical sense, but they often found themselves on the front lines anyway because of the realities of counterinsurgency warfare and the inexperience (or cowardice) of their South Vietnamese hosts.

Kennedy did not do as much as some in the administration would have liked. He wasn't sure how many soldiers it would take to defeat the Communists, and he was aware that if he sent thousands of troops to Vietnam, as adviser Walt W. Rostow urged, they would surely take casualties and involve the United States further in the war. Still, retreat was unthinkable. The "defeats" in Cuba and Laos drove Kennedy to seek victory in Vietnam. The president was also convinced that Nikita Khrushchev, the Soviet premier who had emerged from the power struggles following Stalin's death, respected only toughness: the Russian baited JFK mercilessly during their first summit conference, at Vienna in June 1961. And there was the commitment itself. Kennedy believed that American credibility was at stake in Vietnam. If the United States abandoned its charge, no one, friend or enemy, would ever again respect America's word.

The decision to deepen the American commitment collided with the increasing popularity of the NLF in the countryside, the willingness of the North Vietnamese to fight indefinitely for the unification of the country on their terms, the persistence of Soviet and Chinese support for the Communists, and most of all, the alarming degradation of the Diem government. Diem was a poor administrator, incapable of incisiveness and grudging on the matter of delegating authority, except to members of his immediate family. He was personally unsuited for leadership, and as his self-doubts increased, he more and more allowed himself to come under the influence of his opium-addict brother, Ngo Dinh Nhu, and Nhu's peculiar wife, Madame Nhu. The main reason for Diem's failure was his lack of a political base outside of certain neighborhoods in Washington. He was not of the people. When South Vietnamese voted for him in periodic desultory elections, it was because there was no choice, or he was no worse than anyone else on the ballot, or he hated communism, or they felt scared not to vote for him. Frances

Fitzgerald called Diem "the sovereign of discord" and observed that peasants defined his government by the behavior of its representatives, the " 'arrogant' officials who took bribes" and the soldiers who "drank too much, stole food, and raped the village girls." Diem hoped he had secured the Confucian "Mandate of Heaven." It was his only hope, for he ruled without the true consent of the governed.

A crisis involving South Vietnam's Buddhists led to Diem's downfall. Buddhist leaders believed that Diem, a Catholic with a quasi-Confucian ideology, had no respect for their religion, a view apparently confirmed on May 8, 1963, when government soldiers fired on a Buddhist gathering in Hue. The following month, in protest, a Buddhist monk sat down in an intersection in Saigon and allowed himself to be burned to death. The world was shocked, but the Diem government responded harshly. Madame Nhu spoke sadistically of "bronze barbecues," and in August the regime's own version of the Special Forces, trained by Americans, raided Buddhist pagodas throughout the country and carted protesting citizens off to jail. There were many injuries and some deaths.

The Kennedy administration now decided that Diem must go. Using the latest ambassador in Saigon, the strong-minded Henry Cabot Lodge, to lead the effort, the administration flashed a green light before a group of Diem's disgruntled generals who were known to be planning a coup. The generals, led by Duong Van ("Big") Minh, were a skittish bunch who sought guarantees of American support for their efforts. The administration responded by tightening ever so slightly the aid conduit to Diem. This was signal enough. The coup took place on November 1, 1963. Diem and Nhu, left friendless, escaped to a Catholic church. They surrendered early the following morning, having been promised safe passage, but Big Minh had them both killed. (He later claimed the brothers had committed suicide, though he could not explain the multiple entry wounds, some of them made with a knife.) Kennedy was appalled by the murders, and may have experienced a flicker of doubt about his Vietnam policy. We will never know. Just three weeks later, ironically and tragically, he himself was assassinated in Dallas.

In later years, many of the slain president's advisers did indeed claim that he was contemplating withdrawal from Vietnam before the killings of Diem and Nhu. Some pointed to a White House policy statement of October 2, 1963, that described the planned withdrawal of 1,000 men by December and implied that the rest would be home by the end of 1965. Read closely, however, the statement explains that withdrawal would be contingent on victory, which the authors of the statement assumed would be at hand within two years. It is also true that most of Kennedy's key advisers on Vietnam—Robert McNamara, Walt Rostow, Secretary of State Dean Rusk, and national security adviser McGeorge Bundy—stayed on with the next administration, which increased the U.S. commitment. We know only that in November 1963 there were 16,000 U.S. troops in Vietnam and that seventy Americans had died there.

Kennedy's successor, Lyndon Baines Johnson, was a shrewd politician from Texas. There is evidence that Johnson was insecure in his new office. He hated to be alone or understimulated, so he surrounded himself with televisions, spent hours on the telephone cajoling members of Congress to support one bill or another, and even briefed aides while he sat on the toilet. Added to this apparent insecurity was the burden of his predecessor's legacy. Kennedy's luster grew brighter with his death, and LBJ never escaped the feeling that he was a usurper, an awkward southerner who had rudely stumbled into the sanctum of the Harvard Club and who would not be forgiven for having done so.

Vietnam—"that bitch of a war," in LBJ's colorful parlance—would come to obsess the president. As vice president, Johnson had been to Vietnam, and he had returned with the conclusion that the United States must fight communism in Southeast Asia or face a threat to American security. Like his predecessors, and like most Americans, LBJ feared and loathed communism. He also believed in the importance of the American commitment to South Vietnam. Beyond that, Johnson came to regard Vietnam as a personal test of manhood. He likened the war to a hunt—a rite of passage for southern men. With victory in Vietnam, he said, he would "nail the coonskin to the wall." Defeating the enemy would stop communism, reassure the allies, and establish LBJ's reputation as president and as a man.

Johnson had the misfortune to take office as the military situation in Vietnam was worsening. Following the overthrow of Diem, Vietnam "went on an emotional binge," in Douglas Pike's phrase. Big Minh and his generals proved incompetent; the government ceased to govern. The NLF took the offensive in the countryside, and when North Vietnamese regulars joined their comrades in the south in ever-increasing numbers the killing escalated. In January 1964 there was another coup in Saigon, this one led by General Nguyen Khanh and a group of young officers. Khanh tried to walk the line between U.S. demands for stability and pacification of the countryside and the expectations of his people for peace and justice, and ended up pleasing no one. Khanh was an anticommunist general, not a national leader. By the end of 1964, the Americans deduced, the NLF controlled forty percent of the territory and fifty percent of the population in South Vietnam, estimates that were probably conservative. Khanh had resigned, to be replaced by a months-long power struggle.

From Lyndon Johnson's viewpoint, this turmoil simply would not do. Frustrated below the seventeenth parallel, the president contemplated carrying the war to what the administration believed was its source. Early in the summer of 1964, LBJ's advisers drew up plans for U.S. bombing attacks on targets in North Vietnam. To implement these plans would require a good deal of discretionary power for the president, who felt he could not consult Congress each time a bombing sortie seemed necessary. Johnson got his opportunity in August, when a series of dubious incidents in the Tonkin Gulf—well described in this volume by George Herring—brought from an obedient Congress a resolution authorizing the president to take "all necessary measures to repel any armed attacks against the forces of the United States and to prevent further aggression." It was not a declaration of war, but for years it was the functional equivalent. (What actually happened in the Gulf that dark August night was—and is—unclear. "For all I know," said the president privately, "the navy could have been shooting at whales out there.")

The administration stayed its hand, but not for long. On February 6, 1965, the NLF attacked the barracks at Pleiku, in the central highlands, killing nine Americans. That evening, Johnson ordered retaliation bombings north of the seventeenth parallel. Four days later, the president decided reprisals weren't enough, and a systematic program of bombing called "Rolling Thunder" was begun. (Actually, it joined a program of bombing in Laos called "Barrel Roll," already in progress.) The bombing was, naturally, the brainchild of the U.S. Air Force, and particularly of General Curtis LeMay, who was famous for the ruthless effectiveness of U.S. strategic bombing in World War II. LeMay promised "to bomb them back to the Stone Age."

The rejoinder to this was that the Vietnamese were still in the Stone Age, a culturally arrogant reply, but one that contained a germ of truth. The bombings, although terribly destructive, failed to demoralize the North Vietnamese or dislodge them from their purpose. The closed system in which bombing times and targets were selected leaked badly: "It was uncanny," wrote General Bruce Palmer, Jr., "how the Viet Cong and the North Vietnamese were able to defeat our security precautions." The North Vietnamese also responded with alacrity to the bombing. As quickly as bridges or roads were destroyed, mass labor reconstructed them. And the North Vietnamese economy was readily decentralized, denying the Americans large, tempting targets. Within a couple of years, the pilots in their powerful B-52s were often reduced to targeting bicycle repair shacks in the Vietnamese jungle.

Johnson made another fateful decision later in February 1965: responding to a request from General William Westmoreland, commander of U.S. forces in Vietnam since the middle of 1964, the president sent two marine battalions—about 3,500 men—to defend the U.S. air base at Danang. They arrived March 8. These were neither advisers nor "support troops," as their predecessors were called, but plain combat troops whose job description called for them to kill Viet Cong. As some predicted, the presence of the marines in Vietnam made it easy to justify the military's requests for more, if only to protect those who were already there. LBJ authorized 40,000 additional troops in April. By December there were 185,000 American soldiers in Vietnam; two years later the total was a half million, and the generals were clamoring for 200,000 more. But growing U.S. troop strength failed to bring stability to the government of South Vietnam. From the power struggle of early 1965 emerged a rakish air marshal named Nguyen Cao Ky. Like his predecessors, Ky tried hard to live up to the image his American backers fashioned for him, and like them he failed. Ky was deeply involved in the lucrative heroin trade and association with him was embarrassing for the Americans. He was eased aside in September 1967 in favor of Nguyen Van Thieu, who won a rigged election—with Ky as his running mate.

The decisions to bomb and send combat troops in early 1965 brought indignation and anger from many Americans, especially college students. There were rallies, marches, and "teach-ins," in which faculty members and students discussed the history of the war and its implications. Disturbed (if not yet alarmed) by the unrest on campus, LBJ dispatched administration "truth squads" to many universities, hoping to set the record straight. Confrontations occurred frequently. Some protestors saw Vietnam as the latest and most brutal exercise in American imperialism, and they demanded fundamental change in the political and economic system so as to make imperialism impossible. Many who opposed the war were veterans of the black civil rights movement, who instinctively mistrusted the liberal administration's commitment to social change and in some cases felt racial solidarity with the Viet Cong. The leading radical organization for white college students was the Students for a Democratic Society, or SDS. At its national convention in June 1965 the SDS decided to take up the antiwar cause. From that point on the movement grew: 100,000 people marched on the Pentagon (and a few tried to levitate it) in October 1967; in November 1969 more than a half million came to Washington to protest, thus constituting the largest demonstration ever in the capital.

Despite what many on the left said of him, Lyndon Johnson did not revel in the expanded war. Between 1965 and 1968 he did flirt occasionally with the possibility of negotiations. LBJ continued to insist, however, on attaining goals in Vietnam that were incompatible with the aspirations of the North Vietnamese, the NLF, and their peasant supporters. Johnson viewed the war as a case of aggression by the North Vietnamese against a legally constituted state in the south. Thus, before there could be peace, the North Vietnamese would have to withdraw NLF troops from South Vietnam and recognize the legitimacy of the South Vietnamese government. The Communists and their allies countered that the Americans, not the Vietnamese, were aggressors, that it was absurd to talk of removing indigenous forces (the NLF) from South Vietnam, and that the government of South Vietnam was a fabrication of the United States and had no popular support. Potential talks were further complicated by Thieu, the South Vietnamese president, who gambled that his hawkish sponsors in the United States would support him even if he objected to sitting down with Communists. For a time, he was not far wrong.

Then came Tet 1968. Beginning on the night of January 30, 1968—the night of the lunar new year, or Tet—thousands of NLF and North Vietnamese troops attacked U.S. strongholds throughout South Vietnam. The provincial capital of Hue was taken, followed by the horrific slaughter of civilians by the Viet Cong. Just outside Saigon, the Tan Son Nhut air base, the world's busiest airport, came under intense fire. Most shocking to the Americans, a handful of Viet Cong entered the compound of the U.S. embassy in Saigon. They killed two guards and held the yard for six-and-a-half hours.

In the ensuing days, every Communist thrust was parried. Hue was retaken in bloody, house-to-house fighting. Tan Son Nhut did not fall. Every Viet Cong who entered the embassy compound was slain; the building was secured in time for business the morning after its siege. The North Vietnamese command confessed to making serious mistakes in planning and executing the Tet offensive, and the NLF, whose soldiers had been used as shock troops by Hanoi, was badly damaged. But Tet did not seem like a victory to politicians, opinion makers, and ordinary people in the United States. It is possible, as Peter Braestrup has argued, that the media unfairly represented Tet as a military defeat for the United States and South Vietnam. More to the point, however, the administration had raised hopes that the enemy was on its last legs and presumably incapable of launching such a powerful assault as the Tet offensive. Victory "lies within our grasp—the enemy's hopes are bankrupt," Westmoreland had said on a visit to the United States the previous

November. The offensive also seemed to exhibit, and exacerbate, the special ugliness of the war. Americans witnessed the summary execution of a suspected V.C. terrorist by the chief of South Vietnam's national police. The officer, America's ally, placed his pistol to the prisoner's head and squeezed the trigger; a photographer caught the death grimace. Walter Cronkite, anchor of the CBS evening news and to many the most trusted man in America, was visibly shaken by the events of Tet and soon became a doubter.

Johnson's Vietnam policy had been tottering near the abyss, and the Tet offensive pushed it in. Defense Secretary McNamara, disillusioned by his own failures, had already announced his intention to resign and actually left within a month of the Tet offensive. His replacement was Clark Clifford, a political veteran and confirmed hawk. Within days, however, Clifford had reached the conclusions McNamara had: despite its insatiable appetite for more soldiers, the military could not promise that increased force would bring success in Vietnam. Clifford thus refused to endorse a request for 200,000 more troops, a position consistent with that of the apostate McNamara. On March 12, the president, bidding for reelection, suffered a stunning blow in the New Hampshire Democratic primary, when the antiwar Senator Eugene McCarthy came within a few hundred vote of defeating him. Johnson had had enough. On March 31 he told the American people that he unilaterally had stopped the bombing of most of North Vietnam and that he sought negotiations toward a peace settlement. He closed with a surprise: he would not seek another term as president. The Democratic party split wide open. The "peace candidate" McCarthy was shouldered aside by Robert Kennedy. When Kennedy was assassinated in June, on the night of his victory in the California primary, George McGovern tried to take up his mantle. During a tumultuous convention in Chicago, in which peace demonstrators were confronted by Mayor Richard Daley's ill-tempered police and lost, Vice President Hubert Humphrey secured the nomination. He showed touching loyalty to LBJ by refusing to criticize the administration's Vietnam policy, but Humphrey's discretion was not the best politics. Although he did become more dovish as the campaign went along, it was too late to save the Democrats. The Republican Richard Nixon, unsuccessful in previous campaigns for president and for governor of California and now rising like the phoenix from the political ash heap, narrowly defeated Humphrey and inherited the war.

What all this meant for those actually fighting in Vietnam was unclear. The North Vietnamese put a brave face on the Tet offensive and were pleased by the dramatic shift in American public opinion, but admitted their strategy had "many deficiencies and weak points" that "limit our successes." The death of Ho Chi Minh in September 1969 was also sobering. The troops of South Vietnam—the Army of the Republic of Vietnam, or ARVN—had frequently fought well during the Tet engagement. Nevertheless, the ranks continued to suffer high rates of corruption and desertion. The strain was beginning to show on the Americans, too. Eager volunteers like future author Philip Caputo, who came ashore at Danang in March 1965, increasingly were replaced by draftees. These men, who were disproportionately poor, black, and undereducated, were sent to the "front"—really on patrols into the jungle and rice paddies. Derided by other military units and too often treated as cannon fodder by their officers, these "grunts" turned sullen and dangerous. By 1969 the troops routinely dulled their fears by using drugs, and the incidence of "fragging," or killing one's own officer, climbed steeply.

Nixon promised to end the suffering. The new president was a vengeful and profane man, given to secrecy and duplicity; yet he had some advantages his predecessors had not enjoyed. Nixon's credentials as an anticommunist were impeccable. He had cut his political teeth on the sensational Alger Hiss case in the late 1940s, in which Hiss, a former high-ranking official in the State Department, had been found guilty of lying about his past associations with the Communist party. Nixon hated bureaucracy and had no compunction about circumventing it, openly or with stealth, and he was not constrained by annoying scruples about morality in international affairs. Following his national security adviser, Henry Kissinger, the president believed himself a realist. It did no good to pursue a moralistic foreign policy, he argued, because morals were relative: one nation's morality was another nation's high crime. Above all, Kissinger and Nixon agreed that stability among the great powers was essential for the maintenance of world peace. Different ideologies, presumably based on different perceptions of morality, should not stand in way of dialogue between nations. This meant that the Nixon administration would open serious talks with the Soviets and make an astonishing overture to the Chinese Communists. Because it prevented détente, a measure of understanding between the great powers, the war in Vietnam must be liquidated, one way or another.

What followed was an exercise in contradiction. On one hand, Nixon and Kissinger moved to reduce American troop commitments. Without waiting for change in Hanoi's position, the president began to order withdrawals: 65,000 in 1969, 140,000 in 1970, and 160,000 in 1971. This was consistent with the Nixon Doctrine, announced in July 1969, which implied that Asians should fight Asians, albeit with help from their great power patrons. The administration also moved to revitalize negotiations with the other side. Initiated by the Johnson administration, the Paris peace talks had thus far proved unproductive. In the summer of 1969, Kissinger began secret negotiations with North Vietnamese representatives. At first as fruitless as the Paris discussions, these "back channel" negotiations ultimately achieved some success: by the spring of 1971, Kissinger and Hanoi's Le Duc Tho were snarling and hissing toward a kind of accommodation.

The other side of the Nixon-Kissinger policy was the intensification of the war. Vietnamization meant arming the ARVN to the teeth to protect the retreating Americans and to hold up the Thieu government once the Americans were gone. South Vietnamese troops were augmented by over fifteen percent, and the South Vietnamese air force was made the fourth largest in the world. The Nixon administration also expanded the war to Cambodia and Laos. Both nations provided sanctuaries, without enthusiasm, to the NLF and North Vietnamese. The leaders of both countries, Prince Norodom Sihanouk in Cambodia and Prince Souvanna Phouma in Laos, desperately hoped to avoid a wider war. They could not. Early in 1969, during the first months of his administration, Nixon authorized the bombing of enemy sanctuaries in Cambodia. These attacks, which continued for over a year, were concealed from Congress and the American people, though they were of course no secret to the Cambodian peasant families they decimated and displaced. In April 1970, U.S. and South Vietnamese troops invaded Cambodia. Laos had been bombed for years; its turn for invasion came in February 1971, when the ARVN crossed the border in the first serious test of the Nixon Doctrine, known locally as Vietnamization. The invasion was a disaster, with the ARVN taking casualties at a rate of fifty percent. All the while, American planes dropped their bombs on targets inside North Vietnam.

Nixon's dual policy of sweet reason and deadly force failed to placate the antiwar movement at home. Some, it should be said, were mollified by the troop withdrawals. On the whole, however, the left mistrusted Nixon and Kissinger, and protestors correctly pointed out that the killing in Vietnam had not diminished under the Nixon Doctrine. The demonstrations grew larger and angrier. The invasion of Cambodia in the spring of 1970 sent thousands into the streets. On college campuses across the country, students denounced the invasion and the institutional complicity of their universities in the war. At Kent State University the Ohio National Guard killed four students on May 4; later that month, two students were slain at Jackson State, in Mississippi. The ranks of the demonstrators were swelled by housewives who had been touched by the war, blacks angered by the conflict's racism, disgruntled veterans, even high-school and grade-school students. Public opinion polls frequently indicated widespread disenchantment with Nixon's policy. Nixon called the protestors "bums" and instructed his subordinates to spy on his critics, a decision that led to the Watergate scandal and Nixon's undoing.

In Vietnam the North Vietnamese had been rather subdued since the failures of the Tet offensive, content, it seemed, to harass the departing Americans and blunt any ARVN initiatives. In the spring of 1972, however, the Communists launched a massive offensive. If the Communists hoped the attacks would end U.S. support for the Thieu regime, they were disappointed. But the Easter offensive achieved several other objectives. It exposed once more the folly of Vietnamization. The ARVN, writes James William Gibson, "went into immediate shock," taking 140,000 casualties and surrendering hundreds of allegedly secure villages. Again, as in the Tet offensive, an American-inspired counterattack rolled back the northern forces. A furious Nixon warned the Soviet Union that détente would be jeopardized unless the Russians could get their clients to behave and then escalated the war. B-52 bombers were unleashed to pound the enemy in the north and south. The president established a naval blockade of North Vietnam and authorized the mining of Haiphong Harbor.

The new bloodshed seemed to have a sobering effect on both sides, and in May there were at last signs of movement in the talks. Speaking for Hanoi, Le Duc Tho proposed a tripartite coalition government for the south, to include representatives of North Vietnam, the NLF, and the existing Saigon regime, though Thieu himself was unacceptable. Kissinger rejected the idea of coalition, but sensed flexibility on the Communist side and bore down. By September the North Vietnamese had dropped their demand that Thieu be replaced and transformed the coalition scheme into an all-parties council that would administer free elections in the south. Both sides squabbled and fine-tuned a bit; then, on October 11, they achieved substantial agreement on the text of the peace agreement. Kissinger was triumphant and flew off to Saigon to get Thieu's approval.

No one should have been surprised when Thieu balked at the agreement. He had previously objected to a number of the provisions to which Kissinger had just agreed, and he argued that the language of the treaty was sufficiently vague to permit the Communists dangerously wide latitude in interpreting it. Kissinger raged at Thieu, threatening to halt U.S. aid for his government and even hinting that the United States might make peace without him. He then returned home and announced: "We believe that peace is at hand."

Nixon was not as willing as his national security adviser to abandon Thieu. A week after he was overwhelmingly reelected to the presidency—his opponent, the dovish George McGovern, won only seventeen electoral votes—Nixon reassured Thieu of his full support and told Kissinger to take Thieu's objections to the North Vietnamese. Reluctantly, Kissinger did so. Le Duc Tho was indignant, and after a month of pointless bickering between the sides, he broke off the talks and went home. This was Nixon's signal to renew the air war over North Vietnam. Thirty-six thousand tons of bombs were dropped there during the 1972 Christmas season, more than had been dropped in the period from 1969 to 1971. The pilots did not try to hit civilians, but with all the ordnance, precision was impossible: a bomb fell on Hanoi's Bach Mai hospital, killing eighteen people and wounding dozens more. The North Vietnamese air defense took its toll on the Americans, who lost twenty-six planes and had ninety-three fliers killed or captured. The administration's critics reacted with anger. It was a bleak and ghastly time for everyone. It did, however, usher in the final phase of the war. An apparently chastened Nixon now decided to press Thieu to go along with the Paris accords. Without the president's backing Thieu felt he had no choice, and so at last he acquiesced. Smiling tightly, Kissinger and Le Duc Tho signed on January 27 what was substantially the same agreement they had made the previous October.

There followed what Gareth Porter has called "the cease-fire war" as both sides jostled for advantage. The Nixon administration claimed the Communists were responsible for most of the violations, but it didn't look that way to outsiders, who recorded numerous ARVN transgressions and pointed out that the Communists seemed more aggressive because their moves were more successful. Nixon tried hard, within the constraints placed on him by the Paris agreement and an impatient congress, to bolster Thieu by providing extensive aid, moral support, and threats directed at the North Vietnamese. Ultimately, none of it worked. Congress cut off funds for U.S. military activity in or over Indochina as of August 15, 1973. By that time Nixon had been implicated in the Watergate affair, and his power to pursue an unpopular foreign policy dropped dramatically as he fought to keep his office. Kissinger, now secretary of state, moved into the breach, reviving the argument that the allies would be demoralized if the United States let South Vietnam go. Congress refused to accept this claim. The North Vietnamese sensed their time had come, and early in 1975 they began a massive offensive, which they hoped would bring victory by the following year. It would not take that long.

South Vietnam fell during the brief presidency of Gerald Ford, who had succeed Nixon on the latter's resignation in August 1974. Ford was widely regarded as a decent man, but there wasn't much he could do about the situation in Southeast Asia. Alarmed at the collapse of ARVN forces during the spring of 1975, the president asked Congress for more military aid for Thieu, perhaps hoping that his own obvious integrity would change some minds on Capitol Hill. The efforts were unavailing. Thieu resigned on April 21 and left the country four days later. By the 29th the Communists had reached the outskirts of Saigon and were making plans to share their rice with starving Saigonese, if necessary. Amid the panic of those South Vietnamese who had worked closely with the United States and who feared what was to come, the last Americans departed by helicopter. The next day the Communists captured the presidential palace, and for the Americans, the war was over.

The end of the war did not instantly have a profound effect on the United States. There was a vigorous debate about what came to be called by conservatives "the Vietnam Syndrome," the alleged reluctance of the U.S. government to assert itself in foreign policy for fear of public criticism. The controversies over Americans still missing in action in Southeast Asia, the treatment of veterans, the construction of the Vietnam Veterans' Memorial in Washington, and the meaning of the war for American culture would emerge in the 1980s.

In Vietnam, the problems were greater and more immediate. Hundreds of thousands had been killed, millions bore wounds, and millions more were refugees. The land was devastated and the economy was wrecked. Relations with neighboring nations quickly soured: Vietnam invaded Cambodia in 1978, overthrowing its atrocious and truculent Communist government; early the following year Vietnam itself was attacked by China, which had supported the Cambodian regime. Domestically at least, Hanoi's rigid policies prevented reconciliation between north and south. Industry was nationalized, agriculture collectivized, and southerners who had opposed the revolution were subjected to rigorous political "reeducation." Millions of southerners, many of them ethnic Chinese, fled Vietnam; many settled in the United States. On the other hand, there was no bloodbath in Vietnam, and by the early 1980s grain production and industrial output had increased. Today, as the revolutionary generation grows older, there are signs of some economic and political reform, roughly analogous to a similar movement in the Soviet Union and Eastern Europe. At this writing, Vietnam's future is unclear, but one can say this: once more, as in traditional times, Vietnam has been restored to itself. It is no longer a cockpit of empires.

ONE

A CHRONOLOGY OF UNITED STATES INTERVENTION

September, 1945. Vo Nguyen Giap (left), who provided military leadership for the Vietnamese Communists with Ho Chi Minh, the ideological and political leader of the movement. AP/WIDE WORLD PHOTOS

CHAPTER 1

Getting In,
1945–1950

Though American involvement in Vietnam began before 1945, Franklin Roosevelt's decision early in that year to permit the return of French colonialism to Indochina provides a convenient starting point for this account. The readings in this section focus on the United States' handling of the Communist-nationalist leader Ho Chi Minh during this period. Robert Shaplen, the distinguished reporter who covered Vietnam for the *New Yorker* for many years, describes Ho's efforts to cultivate American representatives of the Office of Strategic Services (OSS) during the mid-forties. Historian Robert Blum follows with a survey of events in postwar Southeast Asia and a close look at Vietnam decision-making in the State Department in the critical spring and summer of 1949. The first-hand account in this chapter comes from Archimedes L.A. Patti, a major with the OSS. He describes his meeting with Ho in September 1945, just after the Vietminh established its provisional government in Hanoi. Shaplen and Patti clearly believe the United States missed a chance to work with Ho in establishing an independent Vietnam. Blum points out that some American officials were willing to consider this possibility as late as 1949.

1
Ho Chi Minh: The Untried Gamble

ROBERT SHAPLEN

If the relationship between the Americans and the Vietminh in Cochin China was never more than a tentative one, it was much closer in the north, both in the months preceding the end of the war and in the period immediately afterward. There are moments in history when certain events, however obscure and fragmentary they may seem in retrospect, nevertheless serve as an endless source of speculation: *if* they had been approached in another way, *if* they had been allowed to run their course, would the whole chain of events that followed have perhaps been different? There is certainly some reason to believe that this might have been true about the relations between Ho Chi Minh and a number of Americans in 1945 and 1946, and, more significantly, about Ho's relations with a small group of French politicians and diplomats. It is easy now to dismiss these events and their meaning as unimportant if one assumes that the Communists, and Ho in particular, never had any other intention than to create a Communist state in Vietnam. However, in the opinion of those who, with varying degrees of political sophistication, lived through this early postwar period and helped form part of its history, such broad assumptions are over-simplifications of what was a highly tenuous and complicated set of political circumstances.

I have always shared the belief of many, if not most, observers who were in Indochina at the time that a serious mistake was made by both the French and the Americans, especially by the dominant French policymakers in Paris, in not dealing more realistically with Ho in 1945 and 1946, when there was a strong possibility that he might have been "Titofied" before Tito and Titoism were ever heard of; that the whole course of events might thereby have been altered and a great deal of bloodshed averted; and that today a unified Vietnam, even under some form of left-wing leadership, might have been the bulwark of a neutral bloc of Southeast Asian states seeking, above all, to avoid Chinese Communist domination. Some of the highest American officials have privately told me, in recent years, that they now believe the gamble with Ho should have been taken; in fact, a considerable number of them are again talking about Vietnam becoming a Southeast Asian Yugoslavia, a possibility that seems to me now rather remote. History, contrary to the popular belief, seldom does repeat itself, and second chances are seldom offered. It is one of the particular tragedies of American postwar policy that so many first chances have been missed.

There are many facets to the story of Ho's relations with the West during and after the Second World War. Let us start with the somewhat naïve but at the same time revealing account of a former young lieutenant in the United States Army—I shall have to refer to him only as John—who in May, 1945, parachuted into Ho's jungle headquarters near the village of Kim Lung in northern Tonkin on a mission to establish an underground that would help Allied personnel escape to freedom. Kim Lung lies on the edge of a heavy rain forest, thickly underlaid by brush. Amid sugar-loaf formations of mountains lie tiny valleys, and it was in one of these, near a small stream halfway up a tall hill, that Ho Chi Minh's camp, consisting of four huts, lay sequestered. Each of the huts was twelve feet square, set four feet off the ground on bamboo stakes, and Ho's was as bare as the others.

In this crude revolutionary cradle, deep in Japanese territory, John had the unique experience of living and working with Ho for several months. He found Ho completely co-operative in lending the support of his guerrillas for scouting and raiding parties, including one to rescue some French internees near the China border. John used his portable radio to put Ho in preliminary touch with French negotiators who were in Kunming, China, and who would soon be debating Indochina's postwar future with Ho in Hanoi, but John himself played a more immediate role in Vietnamese affairs by informally helping Ho frame a Declaration of Independence.

"He kept asking me if I could remember the language of our Declaration," John says. "I was a normal American, I couldn't. I could have wired up to Kunming and had a copy dropped to me, of course, but all he really wanted was the flavor of the thing. The more we discussed it, the more he actually seemed to know about it than I did. As a matter of fact, he knew more about almost everything than I did, but when I thought his demands were too stiff, I told him anyway. Strange thing was he listened. He was an awfully sweet guy. If I had to pick out one quality about that little old man sitting on his hill in the jungle, it was his gentleness."

He and John exchanged toasts and shared stewed tiger livers. John now admits his naïveté in being ready to believe that Ho was not a Communist. But even if he was, John felt certain that Ho was sincere in wanting to co-operate with the West, especially with France and the United States. Some of Ho's men impressed John less. "They go charging around with great fervor shouting 'independence,' but seventy-five per cent of them don't know the meaning of the word," he wrote in his diary. John still has two letters in English Ho sent him in the jungle. One of them, written soon after the Japanese surrender, when the Vietminh was about to seize control of the nationalist movement, reads as follows:

Dear Lt. [John],

I feel weaker since you left. Maybe I'd have to follow your advice— moving to some other place where food is easy to get, to improve my health.
. . .

I'm sending you a bottle of wine, hope you like it.

Be so kind as to give me foreign news you got.

. . . Please be good enuf to send to your H.Q. the following wires.

I. Daiviet [an anti-Vietminh nationalist group] plans to exercise large terror against French and to push it upon shoulder of VML [Vietminh League]. VML ordered 2 millions members and all its population be watchful and stop Daiviet criminal plan when & if possible. VML declares before the world its aim is national independence. It fights with political & if necessary military means. But never resorts to criminal & dishonest act.

Signed—NATIONAL LIBERATION COMMITTEE OF VML

2. National Liberation Committee of VML begs U.S. authorities to inform United Nations the following. We were fighting Japs on the side of the United Nations. Now Japs surrendered. We beg United Nations to realize their solemn promise that all nationalities will be given democracy and in-dependence. If United Nations forget their solemn promise & don't grant Indochina full independence, we will keep fighting until we get it.

Signed—LIBERATION COMMITTEE OF VML

Thank you for all the troubles I give you. . . . Best greetings!

Yours sincerely, Hoo [*sic*]

What spells the difference between 1945 and 1965, between John's jun-gle love feast with Ho Chi Minh—the vast prestige America then enjoyed in Asia—and the complex tragedy of the war in Vietnam today, in which Americans are engaged in bombing Ho's country? Those who insist that we should have tried to win Ho to our side maintain this even though they were aware of the fact that he had never wavered from a straight Marxist-Leninist course. Despite his orthodox ideological convictions (or perhaps because they were so orthodox), and because Indochina was a long way from Stalin's Moscow, Ho had already written his own unique revolutionary case history. He was, at this time, less a potential apostate than a kind of old Bolshevik maverick, a last Marxist Mohican in the anti-colonial wilder-ness of Southeast Asia. If it appears that he simply bewitched a handful of Americans in an atmosphere of dangerous and rollicking camaraderie late in the war and the months afterward, there is considerable more ev-idence than John's alone to substantiate the theory that Ho meant what he said, that he very much wanted the friendship of liberal Americans and liberal Frenchmen, with whose help he hoped to steer a moderate course to Vietnamese freedom. Was it only a game he was playing, as a superb actor, and did he just use this small group of foreign friends to further his own burning cause in Moscow's image? There is enough proof of his sincerity to doubt this over-simplified conclusion. Not only was Moscow far off, with a record of having done little to help Ho concretely in the—

difficult years gone by, but, significantly, Communist China did not yet exist. Who, then, more than the Americans, professing themselves to be ardently against colonialism in the projected postwar world, were in a position to help him win liberty from France and simultaneously ward off Chinese penetration?

Official wartime American policy had been alternately positive and vague about Indochina. President Roosevelt had obtained the tentative approval of Stalin and Chiang Kai-shek for a postwar Indochina trusteeship, though both had expressed themselves as favoring ultimate independence for the Vietnamese. Churchill's reaction to the trusteeship proposal had been negative, and Roosevelt had chided him as an old imperialist. Roosevelt had been somewhat ambivalent himself, however, when it came to doing anything to pave the way for Vietnam's independence. In October, 1944, he had told Secretary of State Cordell Hull that "we should do nothing in regard to resistance groups in Indochina," and when a Free French mission to Kandy, Ceylon, sought help from the Allied Southeast Asia Command, Roosevelt gave orders that "no American representatives in the Far East, whether civilian or military, are authorized to make any decisions on political questions with the French or anyone else."

The "anyone else" presumably included Ho Chi Minh, although Roosevelt may never even have heard of him. Ho had long been a man of mystery and many names. For the moment, one need only go back to 1939, when Ho was still known as Nguyen Ai Quoc (Nguyen, the Patriot). In that year, following the fall of the Popular Front in France, the Indochina Communist Party Ho had welded together was disbanded and went underground. When the Japanese swept into Tonkin in September, 1940, the Communists and the non-Communist nationalists launched uprisings against both the French and the Japanese, but they were quickly crushed. In May, 1941, after the Japanese had established their puppet regime of Vichy Frenchmen, Ho and other Vietnamese Communists met with other nationalists at Tsin-li, just across the Tonkinese border in China. They reorganized their scattered ranks into the Vietnam Doc Lap Dong Minh—Vietminh for short—and the guiding spirit, the man selected as General Secretary, was bearded little Nguyen Ai Quoc, who had unexpectedly shown up at the meeting, though many had thought he had died of tuberculosis years before in the jungle. Without any flexing of Communist muscles, Ho and his friends concentrated on creating a common nationalist front to continue the fight against both Japan and France and to gain Vietnamese freedom.

At the end of 1941, Nguyen Ai Quoc was arrested by the Kuomintang secret police. They knew he was a Communist but chose to describe him as "a French spy" and threw him into jail at Liuchow. Eying Tonkin, as the Chinese had for many years, the Kuomintang had its own plans to build an anti-French "independence" movement around picked pro-Chinese Vietnamese. They soon discovered, however, that it was Nguyen Ai Quoc's Communist guerrillas of the Vietminh front who had the only real experience in Indochina. No one else, with one exception, had a network of agents there. The exception, oddly enough, was a civilian group headed by a dozen Allied businessmen, each of whom had his private organization of French, Chinese, and Vietnamese operatives; their original purpose had been to do what could be done to protect Allied assets and property in the Far East, and after Pearl Harbor this unique group had started working with Ho's guerrillas to gather intelligence for Allied air forces based in China and in India.

Early in 1943, Nguyen Ai Quoc sent a message from his prison cell to the southern Chinese warlord, Chang Fa Kwei, who, while an important leader of the Kuomintang, had frequently fought for power with Chiang Kai-shek and had his own ideas about Indochina. Nguyen Ai Quoc told Chang Fa Kwei that if he were set free, he would re-gather his intelligence network in Indochina and, presumably, work in Chang's behalf. Chang thereupon ordered his release from the Liuchow jail, and did so without telling Chiang Kai-shek. It was at this point that Nguyen Ai Quoc adopted the name Ho Chi Minh (He Who Shines), primarily to hide his identity from Chiang Kai-shek's secret-police chief, Tai Li. As Ho, he became the directing head of the umbrella organization of Vietnamese revolutionary groups called the Dong Ming Hoi, which the Kuomintang was sponsoring and of which the Communist-dominated Vietminh was at first simply a part.

Ho received and disbursed a hundred thousand Chinese Nationalist dollars a month to carry on espionage and sabotage in Indochina. During 1943 and 1944, the Vietminh built up its own political strength at the expense of the other Dong Minh Hoi organizations, and by the end of 1944 it had an independent army of ten thousand rebels under the command of the young lawyer and teacher, Vo Nguyen Giap, who had already begun to demonstrate a remarkable military talent. Inevitably, as a result of the Vietminh's growing independence, relations between Ho and the Kuomintang in Chungking and Kunming became strained; under the circumstances, there was little his guardian angel, Chang Fa Kwei, could do about it. Equally unhappy about Ho were both the Vichy and the Free French, who buried their differences long enough to exchange secret information about him.

In the second half of 1944, Ho began to look to the Americans; what took place over the next two years, including the strange jungle romance between Ho and young soldiers like John, had overtones of comic opera, although the story had a sad ending. Ho, on four separate occasions, came secretly to the office of Strategic Services in Kunming, late in 1944 and early in 1945, seeking arms and ammunition in return for intelligence, sabotage against the Japanese, and continued aid in rescuing shot-down Allied pilots. He was rejected each time. According to Paul E. Helliwell, who was O.S.S. intelligence chief in China at the time and who has since denied that O.S.S. in any way "managed" Ho, "O.S.S. China was at all times consistent in its policy of giving no help to individuals such as Ho, who were known

Communists and therefore obvious postwar sources of trouble." At the same time, however, and despite President Roosevelt's expressed policy of hands off the Indochina resistance movement—Helliwell says he was personally unware of any direct orders—the decision not to help Ho was principally based, he adds, on Ho's refusal to pledge that any arms he received would be used only against the Japanese and not against the French.

Ho kept on trying. Helliwell finally gave him six .38-caliber revolvers and twenty thousand rounds of ammunition, but this was simply a token of appreciation for Vietminh assistance in bringing out three American pilots. Later, Ho wrote to Richard Heppner, who was chief of O.S.S. in China late in the war, requesting the help of the United States, which had already pledged the Philippines their freedom, in pressuring the French to grant Indochina independence. The fact is Ho did get some assistance from O.S.S. and from other American and Allied agencies over and above Helliwell's six pistols, although the material aid he received was not as great as the inspirational encouragement he was unofficially accorded. As a subsequent American intelligence chief in the Far East put it, "Ho offered to be our man, and we never grabbed his hand because we couldn't bankroll him."

Ho tried several Allied sources. Major General Claire Chennault, head of the 14th Air Force, who was warned by his Kuomintang friends to steer clear of him, at one point unwittingly had Ho introduced to him as "an old Vietnamese guide." Nothing came of that, but the British were some-what more helpful and dropped some supplies to Free French and Viet-minh guerrillas in November, 1944, after Ho had secretly moved back into Tonkin with about two hundred of his Vietminh followers. With him came a representative of the civilian group of former American businessmen in Indochina, who had for some time been co-operating with Ho's men. This hush-hush group had been under the wing of the O.S.S. at first but was now unofficially attached to another American Army group, the Air Ground Aid Service (AGAS). The arms that Ho and his handful of Vietnamese car-ried with them into Tonkin at this point are known to have come partly from O.S.S. supplies, although they had not been initially distributed for that purpose, and partly from some other American arsenals.

In the northern Tonkin jungle, in a mixed-up area where Chinese bandits, Free French and American paratroopers, and various groups of nationalists were all active, Ho Chi Minh set up his revolutionary head-quarters. Vietminh troops, under young Giap, successfully harassed the Japanese, proselytized in behalf of Vietnamese freedom, and helped res-cue additional Allied pilots. An American who was with Ho at his for-est headquarters during this period remembers above all "his strength of character and his single-mindedness." His appraisal of Ho was as follows: "You've got to judge someone on the basis of what he wants. Ho couldn't be French, and he knew he could fight the French on his terms. He was afraid of the Chinese, and he couldn't deal with them because they'd always demand their pound of flesh. Moscow, so far away, was good at blowing up bridges, but not much good at building them again. If it weren't for the war, of course, Ho wouldn't have had a chance against the long background of French colonialism. But now he was in the saddle, although it wasn't clear what horse he was riding. For the moment, surely, he was helping us, on the ground. We and the French were in a position to help him in the future. I think he was ready to remain pro-West."

HO DICKERS WITH FRANCE

In the light of the above summary of Ho's career as a long-time trusted worker in Communist vineyards, let us return to the jungle and to the months, just before the end of the war in 1945, when he sounded out the French in Kunming over the radio of the young American lieutenant, John.

The messages John sent out for Ho reached Léon Pignon, a political career man of the French who was later to be High Commissioner of Indochina, and Major Jean Sainteny a Free French Army officer who became the chief French representative in North Vietnam. After reading Ho's demands for guaranteed independence from France in five to ten years, Pignon and Sainteny replied that they were willing to negotiate, but no time or place was set. The Americans by this time were posing a new problem for the French. When Roosevelt's orders against helping the underground in Indochina were lifted, early in April, the Office of Strategic Services had begun to retrain and equip some two thousand French soldiers who had made their way to Kunming after the Japanese take-over. The plan was to drop Franco-American teams back into Indochina, with supplies to follow if guerrilla resistance bands could be organized. In point of fact, while willingly taking any material help they could get, the French wanted to avoid any direct American involvement. Helliwell, the former O.S.S. intelligence head, later said: "It was perfectly obvious by June of 1945 that the French were infinitely more concerned with keeping the Americans out of Indochina than they were in defeating the Japanese or in doing anything to bring the war to a successful conclusion in that area."

Not too many Americans did get into Tonkin, but several O.S.S. teams were dropped into the jungle, and with their help Ho's forces managed to augment their supplies with a small number of tommy guns and carbines. At the war's end, replenishing their arsenal with captured or surrendered Japanese equipment, Vietminh troops moved swiftly to carry out Ho's orders of a general insurrection. All over Indochina, there was rising support for the independence movement. Under Giap, now a self-styled General, the Vietminh troops moved into Hanoi on August 17, 1945. A week later, Major Sainteny parachuted into the city from a Free French bomber, with Major Archimedes Patti, of the O.S.S. Patti's mission was to liberate war prisoners, for which he had to obtain the co-operation of the Japanese, since the Chinese occupation forces had not yet arrived. Sainteny found himself immediately hamstrung by the Vietminh and by the Japanese, who, with Patti's apparent blessing, completely restricted his movement, on the grounds of his personal safety, and kept several hundred French citizens virtually locked up in the Hotel Metropole. Sainteny was incensed, and five days after his arrival he telegraphed Calcutta: "We are before a collusive Allied maneuver with the purpose of throwing the French out of Indochina." He had a point, but it was far more accidental than collusive.

Within a period of weeks, other American officers arrived in Hanoi, among them some top officers of the China Combat Command. At the same time came a number of American correspondents. Their open sympathies, in typical American fashion of supporting the underdog, were clearly with the Vietminh, and especially with Ho. Major Patti made no bones about favoring Vietnamese independence; French sources say he even offered to help Ho get arms, and that an American general on the scene indicated he had some business connections back home that would sell the new regime heavy equipment for rebuilding the country. That Ho needed help was obvious. My *Newsweek* associate, Harold Isaacs, saw Ho in November, and Ho expressed his readiness to permit the French to maintain their economic position in Vietnam if they recognized Vietnamese independence. "Why not?" Ho asked. "We've been paying out our life's blood for decades. Suppose it costs us a few hundred million more piastres to buy our freedom?"

Recalling his long struggles, his years in Chinese and British prisons, Ho was full of humility and neither looked nor played the part of a head of government. He wore a faded khaki jacket and trousers, a white shirt, and old slippers. "They call me 'Excellency.' Funny, eh?" he remarked.

The sympathy Americans had for Ho late in 1945 and early in 1946 found expression in the formation of the Vietnam-American Friendship Association. Its first meeting in Hanoi was attended by an American general and his officers. After listening to Vietnamese professions of esteem and fondness for America, the general returned the compliments and looked forward to such things as student exchanges. Major Sainteny, who had suffered the further indignity of being arrested by the Japanese while riding in his jeep, which carried a French flag, and having an American colonel obtain his release, later referred to the Americans' "infantile anticolonialism, which blinded almost all of them." Despite his dismay, it was Sainteny who, more than any other Frenchmen, was to sympathize with Ho Chi Minh and try to promote a real policy of co-operation with him.

After two meetings with Ho, late in September and early in October, Sainteny felt that he was "a strong and honorable personality." Subsequently, in his book, *The Story of a Lost Peace, 1945–1947*, Sainteny wrote that "this ascetic man, whose face revealed at once intelligence, energy, cleverness, and fineness, was a personality of the highest order who would not be long in placing himself in the foreground of the Asian scene." Pignon, who was more interested in building up other nationalists than in adopting Ho, was also impressed but was less sure of his sincerity. From the outset, Pignon had no illusions about "Ho's Communist face" and considered him "a great actor." Nevertheless, both Frenchmen regarded Ho as "a man of peace," and Pignon's reservations about Ho's honesty did not include skepticism about Ho's preference for moderation and for compromise over killing. The two French negotiators differed most strongly perhaps on their assessment of Ho's humility and pride: Sainteny was always impressed with the first; Pignon flashed warning signals about the second.

Sainteny did most of the negotiation with Ho that led to the agreement of March 6, 1946, whereby the Republic of Vietnam was recognized as an independent part of the French Union, with French troops permitted to return to Tonkin. During the period of the negotiations, Sainteny has written, Ho "aspired to become the Gandhi of Indochina." Ho is quoted as saying: "While we want to govern ourselves... I need your professional men, your engineers, and your capital to build a strong and independent Vietnam." Ho, says Sainteny, wanted the French Union to be constructed with "a Vietnamese cornerstone.... He wanted independence for his country, but it was to France herself that he wanted to owe it.... It is certainly regrettable that France minimized this man and was unable to understand his value and the power he disposed of." Sainteny points out that China was Vietnam's age-old enemy, that Ho's overtures to the Americans had already proved "rather disappointing," and that, "against the wishes of an important faction of his party," Ho was not inclined to look for aid in Moscow, "which he knew too well." Sainteny, nevertheless, was realistic enough to admit that Ho's preference for French backing was partly predicated on the expectations of a Communist victory in France.

When the Communists in France lost out, Sainteny says, Ho felt he needed the support of French liberals and moderates more than ever if he was successfully to "muzzle his opposition" in Vietnam, which had begun to cause him some trouble. This particularly included some of the old Chinese Dong Minh Hoi groups, which Ho had subjugated in the late-war jungle days, when the Vietminh had become the dominant part of the underground front. The Chinese in Hanoi sought to reactivate these organizations, notably the Dong Minh Hoi and the more important Vietnam Quoc Dan Dang (VNQDD), the leading Vietnamese national party; they specifically wanted Ho to include representatives of these groups in his government.

The Chinese in the northern part of Vietnam had several objectives. In the first place, they were there for profit, if not for outright loot, and they succeeded—by inflating the Chinese dollar at the expense of the Indochina piastre; by making off with huge amounts of opium, which they seized both in Laos and in Vietnam; and by engaging in heavy black-market operations in Hanoi and Haiphong, where there was a large Chinese mercantile population. In the second place, the Chinese had no use for the French or the Vietnamese, and they did not hesitate to terrorize the local French and Vietnamese citizens. The fact that many of their occupation troops were more ragtail than professional encouraged this, and in the winter of 1945 things became so bad that Sainteny cabled Paris to ask for a United Nations investigation of the conduct of the Chinese forces; both the British and the American representatives in Hanoi supported him. As events turned out, this was not necessary, since the French finally managed to get the Chinese out of the north by renouncing their extraterritorial and other rights in China and by granting numerous concessions to the Chinese in Vietnam, including a free zone for Chinese goods at Haiphong and certain customs exemptions for goods shipped in over the railroad from Kunming.

Though the Chinese agreed to leave by Mid-March, 1946, they actually didn't pull out the bulk of their troops until the summer. In the meantime, they kept up their political offensive, and they obtained some advantage from the fact that initially the Vietminh's strength was largely concentrated in Hanoi itself and in a few other cities but not yet in the countryside, where both the Dong Minh Hoi and the VNQDD had previously built up considerable support, especially in the areas near the Chinese border. Much of the Vietminh's support, despite its Communist leadership, came from non-Communist Vietnamese, whose passionate desire for independence was a powerful factor in enabling Ho Chi Minh to form his original broad front in his own dynamic image. In order to stress his nationalist feelings more than his Communist background and doctrine, and also as a result of the orders that had come from the French Communist Party, Ho, in mid-November, 1945, dissolved the Indochina Communist Party in the north. (A small group of Communist extremists, including Giap and Dang Xuan Khu—better known today as Truong Chinh, the strongest pro-Peking man among the Hanoi Communists—formed what they called Marxist Study Groups, which later became the nucleus of the Laodang, or Workers, Party, the successor of the old Communist Party in Indochina.)

To obtain the support of as many groups as possible for the agreement he was about to sign with Sainteny, Ho selected the chief of the Dong Ming Hoi to be his Vice-president, and he gave three top Cabinet jobs to VNQDD men, including the Ministry of Foreign Affairs. At the same time, to pacify the Chinese further, he dropped Giap and one other leading Communist from the Cabinet. As the Vietminh began organizing People's Committees to replace the old Councils of Notables in the villages, it made further temporary concessions to the Chinese parties, promising the VNQDD fifty seats and the Dong Minh Hoi twenty out of a total of three hundred and fifty in the assembly elections that were to be held in January, 1946. The vote took place on a limited basis only, in some parts of the country, and about half of those elected, as it turned out, were non-political-party people, though the Vietminh did well by controlling the vote in many villages, and in Hanoi Ho received an alleged ninety-eight percent of the ballots. Ho had other reasons for wanting to go slow politically. He had an extremely difficult economic situation on his hands. There had been a famine early in 1945, followed by floods that had swept over the broken dikes of the Red River Delta. Then came a severe drought.

The breakdown of the Vietnamese transportation system had made it impossible to ship rice from the south, which was having its own troubles. In 1945 and through the early part of 1946, it was estimated that a million Vietnamese died of starvation in the north.

MODUS VIVENDI IS SIGNED

In the face of all these difficulties, Ho's eagerness in wanting to conclude the March, 1946, agreement with Sainteny can better be understood. When he signed it, he made a direct and dramatic appeal to the Vietnamese people at a big outdoor meeting in Hanoi. "Fellow countrymen, who have followed me up to now," he asked, "follow me once more. I would prefer death a hundred times to betraying my country."

Two months later, as the French were doing their best to sabotage Ho by holding the separatist conference at Dalat, in the south, and by getting ready to set up their independent puppet regime in Cochin China, Ho left for France with a small delegation to negotiate what he hoped would be a full implementation of the March contract he had made with Major Sainteny. During the summer, while he was away, and with both Sainteny and Pignon out of Hanoi, too, the extremist group among the Communists, led by Giap and Dang Xuan Khu, rode roughshod over the non-Communist nationalists. As in the south, terror also struck the country, and many pro-French Vietnamese as well as Frenchmen were assassinated. There are those who say that this was all part of the game, that Ho went to France and remained there as the pretender of peace, tortuously seeking an agreement, while the extremists were given a free hand back in Vietnam. Sainteny, among others, vehemently denies that this was the case.

In Biarritz, where he first rested, in Paris and then at the conference in Fontainebleau, Ho enjoyed huge personal success. He charmed everyone, especially the press. He distributed roses to women reporters, signed his name in blood for an American male correspondent. He was widely compared to Confucius, to the Buddha, to St. John the Baptist, to anyone's doting grandfather, and it was noted that he was an ascetic, since, among other things, he refused to take a drink. Everywhere he went, whether to the opera, to a fancy reception, to a picnic, or to a press conference, he appeared in his simple, high-buttoned linen work suit. "As soon as one approaches this frail man, one shares the admiration of all men around him, over whom he towers with his serenity acquired from wide experience," wrote one reporter. Noting his "tormented face and his eyes of blue which burn with an inner light," another declared that he "hides a soul of steel behind a fragile body." His wit, his Oriental courtesy, his *savoir-faire*, his mixed profundity and playfulness in social intercourse, his open love for children, above all his seeming sincerity and simplicity, captured one and all.

Unfortunately, in point of accomplishment Ho's trip was far less successful. The fault, now generally admitted, was chiefly that of the French, who, while the conference went on, continued to violate its spirit by further fostering the idea of the separate south and central federation in Indochina. In Paris, the shakiness of the national government delayed the start of the sessions with Ho. He stayed at Biarritz to wait and go fishing. "The conference was fishy from the start," one of his delegates remarked. Sainteny later wrote that Ho was "reticent and nervous," but after playing pelota, roaming the countryside, and visiting Lourdes, he "found his smile again" and was "as affable and simple as before." When three leading Communists, including the Minister of Air, paid him a visit and commented, for propaganda purposes, about the "indescribable conditions" in which Ho was quartered at Biarritz, Ho announced that, on the contrary, he was "enchanted" by his stay on the Basque coast.

When he and Sainteny finally flew up to Paris for the start of the talks, Sainteny described him as "pale, eyes brilliant, and tight-throated," and he quoted Ho as saying, when the plane was settling down, "Above all, don't leave me, whatever you do." As the conference dawdled in the shadow of defeat, by now the result of the activities of the Vietminh extremists in Hanoi as well as of the French maneuvers in Cochin China, Ho grew more and more restless. Sainteny agreed he ought to return to Hanoi as soon as possible. "What would I be able to do if I went home empty-handed?" Ho asked. "Don't let me leave this way," he begged Sainteny and Marius Moutet, the Socialist Minister of Overseas Territories. "Arm me against those who would seek to displace me. You will not regret it." It was a significant plea, as significant as what Ho said on another evening to Sainteny and Moutet, "If we have to fight, we will fight. You will kill ten of our men and we will kill one of yours, and in the end it will be you who will tire of it."

At midnight on September 14, 1946, the frail figure of Ho Chi Minh, in its military tunic, walked out of the Hotel Royal-Monceau in Paris (the Fontainebleau sessions had ended) and strolled to Moutet's house nearby. There Ho and Moutet signed a *modus vivendi*, which, while it underlined Vietnamese (and some French) concessions for safeguarding French rights in Indochina, only postponed agreement on basic political questions; it at least placed upon the French the responsibility for restoring order in Cochin China. This was nothing more than had been agreed to in the spring and been vitiated since, but Ho publicly called the *modus vivendi* "better than nothing." He murmured to a security officer who accompanied him back to the hotel early in the morning, however, "I have just signed my death warrant."

Despite the failure of his mission, Ho, in his true cosmopolitan fashion, had enjoyed his stay in Paris, a city he had always loved. Years before, standing on a bridge across the Seine, he had remarked to a Communist comrade, "What a wonderful city, what a wonderful scene!" When his friend had replied that Moscow was also beautiful, Ho had said, "Moscow is heroic, Paris is the joy of living." During the 1946 conference, Ho had revisited some of his former haunts and, mixing socially with several foreign correspondents, had talked freely about himself and his politics. "Everyone has the right to his own doctrine," he had said. "I studied and chose Marx. Jesus said two thousand years ago that one should love one's enemies. That dogma has not been realized. When will Marxism be realized? I cannot answer.... To achieve a Communist society, big industrial and agricultural production is necessary.... I do not know when that will be realized in Vietnam, where production is low. We are not yet in a position to meet the conditions."

Ho's self-analysis, in relation to Indochina's development, is a markedly honest one, in Marxist terms. From the outset, Marxism was far more than a blueprint for him. It was a *logique*, and as one of the keenest Indochina scholars, Paul Mus, has pointed out, it was acquired by Ho as a vital Western weapon, an arsenal in fact, with which, as an Asian, he could combat his French masters. Ho, as a Marxist, was quick to appreciate how his country was being robbed, kept in economic penury by a purposefully unimaginative colonial power. While the French took out rubber or rice or whatever else they wanted and sold it in the world market at a high profit, the Vietnamese lived under a system in which only human labor and not money, in any international sense, counted; goods were in effect bartered for subsistence. Such an economic condition became the fulcrum of Ho's anger and drove him way back, almost inevitably, to Marxism and thence to Communism. "Ho had to build on what every Asian must build *per se*," Mus says, "a Western logic to deal with us Europeans. Whether it be a profession such as the law or medicine or what have you, an Asian must find this *logique* or be lost. Ho found it first in Marxism and he became a Leninist, since Lenin was faced in Russia with the same problem of the vacuum at the village level. Ho was successful because he remained true to Leninism and Marxism. In this sense, straightforward according to *his* view, he belongs to a proper fraternity."

Along with Sainteny, Mus is one of those Frenchmen who admit that France and the Western world missed a proper opportunity with Ho in 1946. Mus himself, as a French negotiator, met Ho a year later, and he has the same queer fondness for him most men who knew him have retained. "I have no reason, as a Frenchman, to like Ho for what he has done," Mus told me long afterward, "but still I like him. I am not afraid to say so. I like him for his strong mind. Although he is a great actor— one cannot afford to be naïve with him—he does not go back on his word. He believes in the truth as he sees it. *But* he is a Marxist, and that is where we part company." He quotes Ho as telling him, in 1947, "My only weapon is anger.... I won't disarm my people until I trust you." Ho's willingness to deal with the French, Mus believes, was largely predicated on his need for French advice, above all for financial advisers. "Marxist doctrine calls for the proletarian state to use, at least temporarily, the accountancy of the bourgeois-capitalist countries," Mus says. Because of the inbred economy imposed by the Bank of Indochina, Ho knew that Vietnam could not stand on its own feet, either in terms of money or trade. He also knew he could not rely on the colonial French. His political approach was through metropolitan France. He wasn't convinced that this was his only chance, but he was determined to play the possibilities. He wavered between his affection and regard for France, which had given him his self in the Marxist image, and his new disillusion of 1946. "If we had supported him more strongly then," Mus added, "we might have won.... We thought we could crush him if it came to war. We did not appreciate how hard he could fight. But we must not forget that he really wanted an agreement with France at the time of Fontainebleau because it would have served him. That part of his motivation afterward died, of course, but we should understand that it existed at the time and that he was truly disappointed."

When Ho returned to Vietnam from France at the end of that sad 1946 summer, he was confronted with a difficult internal political situation. While the conflict between himself and the extremists was perhaps exaggerated, there is no doubt that the younger men around Ho, especially Giap and Dang Xuan Khu, had disapproved of his moderation and patience at Fontainebleau. They almost certainly wanted to move on to violence at once. Considerable conjecture about Ho's troubles with this group soon arose, and then shifted to speculation that ranged from rumors of Ho's retirement into mere figurehead status to the increasingly heard report, of which the French sporadically claimed proof, that he was dead. It is a fact that for many months he was not seen and was hardly mentioned, but what seems to have happened was this:

Ho became quite ill when he arrived back in Hanoi. He stayed in bed for several weeks. During this period, he may have been under some protective form of house arrest (British sources insist this was so); apparently he was surreptitiously moved in and out of a nearby jungle headquarters. Various elements within the Vietminh and out—among them the old pro-Chinese groups, for their own obvious purposes—openly accused Ho of having sold out to France with the *modus vivendi*, and tracts distributed in the Hanoi area bitterly attacked him. "When a man remains in foreign countries for a long while, he becomes their slave," one of them read. These were probably nothing more than the dying gasp of the pro-Chinese Vietnamese leaders, some of whom had already fled to China when Giap, with the departure of Chinese Troops, unrestrainedly cracked down on them.

If Ho was temporarily and perhaps deliberately kept in the background, his eclipse did not last long. His policy of moderation was surely in evidence once more in the fall of 1946, when a constitution of surprising temperance, by Communist terms, was adopted. Two months later, in December, following the incident over customs control in Haiphong harbor and the outbreak of Vietminh terror and French Army reprisals in Hanoi, the war between the French and the Vietminh began. Both sides by then seemed not only ready but anxious to fight. Ho and his government fled into the jungle. However, by April, 1947, Ho's position as the commanding figure in the Vietminh was again supreme. It was in that month that Paul Mus traveled through the forest as a French emissary to meet Ho and offer him what amounted to terms of unconditional surrender. When Ho asked Mus if he—were he in Ho's place—would accept them, Mus admitted he wouldn't. "In the French Union there is no place for cowards," Ho then declared. "If I accepted those conditions, I should be one." Mus says it was completely obvious to him that Ho was running his own show, and that he had the power to reject the French offer without even having to consult the Tong Bo, the five-man Vietminh "politburo."

Even if Ho had had trouble with the extremists, if he had still at that time been a moderate hoping for a *rapprochement* with France, this would not have meant that he was not also, as he always has been in the final analysis, Moscow's man; the two Ho's were not incompatible, and much of what has since happened in the postwar world would seem to corroborate this. Moscow, as a matter of fact, may very well have intervened secretly to restore fully Ho's power and prestige; in substantiation of this theory is the belief that some of the other Vietminh leaders, notably Dang Xuan Khu, have always been under the influence of the Chinese Communists rather than Moscow-orientated. If Ho was torn, within himself and with relation to his followers, a little Moscow glue may have put him together again.

An interesting comment on Ho came at this time from none other than Bao Dai, whose brief tenure as Ho's adviser ended when he fled to Hong Kong, from which place the French would soon resurrect him to head an opposition government in the south. "During the few months I was in Hanoi as Supreme Counselor," Bao Dai said, "I saw Ho Chi Minh suffer. He was fighting a battle within himself. Ho had his own struggle. He realized Communism was not best for our country, but it was too late. Ultimately, he could not overcome his allegiance to Communism."

After Paul Mus's 1947 visit, no non-Communist Westerner is believed to have seen Ho in the jungle until late in 1954. On several occasions, however, he replied telegraphically to questions sent him by Western correspondents. What gradually evolved was a somewhat altered version of him. While he became more cynical and coy, he also became more folksy. "Uncle Ho," the patriarch, emerged. And as he increasingly became more anti-American, he hewed closer than ever to the Communist line, as handed down by Moscow and later by Peking as well. He continued, however, to speak the truth about himself, in his own peculiar lights. "When I was young, I studied Buddhism, Confucianism, Christianity, as well as Marxism," he once told a United Press questioner. "There is something good in each doctrine." Asked his opinion of American intentions in Asia, Ho snapped back, "Marshallization of the world." The Russians, he said, were "against Marshallization of the world." In the next breath, with sad truth, he declared that American aid "is a good thing if it goes directly to the people," thereby touching a sore spot inasmuch as the United States aid to the Vietnamese became a sensitive issue with the French in the south. Ho denied vehemently that Vietnam was or could become Russia's or anyone else's "satellite." He kept insisting he could remain neutral, "like Switzerland," in the world power struggle. "If the Chinese Communists offer you artillery and heavy mortars, would you accept them?" he was subsequently asked. Ho fell back on coyness. "What friendly advice would you give us in that case?" he wired back to his questioner. To a Siamese journalist who inquired, "Is there any truth in the rumors that Mao Tse-tung and you have set up a close relationship and that you favor Communism of the Moscow kind," Ho replied—with an odd quality of dishonesty vis-à-vis his Asian questioner—"What is astonishing is that many intelligent foreigners believe these French slanders."

Events themselves belied Ho's last answer. There was no doubt that after 1950 he moved swiftly and snugly into the Moscow-Peking ideological camp.

As it evolved, the Vietminh emphasized the dominant role of the working class, in accordance with the decisions of the Asian and Australian Trade Union Conference held at Peking in November and December, 1949. Ho and Mao exchanged cables at that time, and soon thereafter eight hundred Vietnamese labor leaders met in rebel Indochina territory and, among panoplied pictures of Stalin, Mao, and Ho, demonstrated their total allegiance to Communism. Titoism was attacked, although when Yugoslavia quickly recognized Ho's regime, along with Soviet Russia and China, Ho had some embarrassing moments; he solved them typically, by pointing out that he had announced his readiness to establish relations with "any government" while at the same time continuing to blast Tito on the Vietminh jungle radio.

Early in 1951, when the Communists resumed their open leadership of the Vietminh movement, Ho lapsed into another period of silence. It was then that rumors of his death in the jungle again were heard. From time to time, Dang Xuan Khu, who became General Secretary of the new party, or someone else in the hierarchy, would publicly extol him. The tone grew reverential; a Ho myth in the milder image of a Stalin myth was reared, and a much tougher, more rigid Ho than he had ever made himself out to be slowly emerged. In 1953, Joseph Starobin, correspondent of the *Daily Worker* in New York, met Ho in the Tonkin jungle. He was not unexpectedly charmed by "the legendary president" who wore such simple peasant clothes and who knew so much about the world. Starobin rhapsodized: "As we sat there that first evening, these facets of the president's personality emerged. He was the world traveler, in whom each recollection of a crowded past was still vivid. He was the old-timer, the Communist leader of an older generation, for whom the lamps of memory needed only the reburnishing of conversation to become shiny and bright. There was also the Uncle Ho who works his own garden, types his own messages, teaches the four virtues—"industriousness, frugality, justice and integrity—to the youth." Starobin was with Ho when Stalin died. He described the rapt jungle scene: "Crude benches illumined by candles set in a makeshift candelabra made out of bamboo; at the front was a portrait of Stalin wreathed in flowers...two violins played softly."

This touching bit of pastoral Stalinoidism was real enough in the context of the time, or real enough, at least, for so stalwart a Stalinist as Starobin; but it seems somehow doubtful that Ho took it quite so seriously or regarded it so poignantly. He was far too clever for that, and he had seen far too many of his old comrades purged by Stalin to render such an unqualifiedly touching response to the old tyrant's death. Nevertheless, it was certainly true that by this time the die had been cast, and that Ho, rejected by the West, no longer had any option—if one may assume that he had one earlier—but to attach himself firmly to the Communist camp. The wandering minstrel of Southeast Asia was home again, but there were to be many moments in the future when his relationship to the Communists, especially after the Sino-Soviet split, would once again be tenuous and difficult to define. Perhaps no one anywhere in the world would be called upon to perform such a unique balancing act between Moscow and Peking as the adroit old guerrilla, Nguyen Ai Quoc. For the moment, however, it is sufficient to re-emphasize "what might have been" in that crucial year between August, 1945, when the big war ended, and July–September, 1946, when the abortive conference at Fontainebleau preceded by a few months the start of the Indochina war. This was the first important turning point in the unfortunate history of Indochina, and this, perhaps more than any other time, was when "the lost revolution" was actually lost.

2
Moving toward Commitment, 1949
ROBERT M. BLUM

On 3 March 1949, the day the president and the NSC adopted three policy papers on China, the State Department's Policy Planning Staff discussed yet another Asian document: "U.S. Policy Toward Southeast Asia." Designated "PPS-51," the study represented a departure from the department's traditional view of the region, which concentrated on policies toward individual countries. The planning staff's effort to win department-wide approval for its paper—and a carefully considered Southeast Asian policy—would prove to be an impossible task.

POSTWAR BACKGROUND

The planning staff examined a region of the world that the fall of the Japanese empire left in shambles. Japan did two things that broke European colonialism in Southeast Asia. First, it quickly defeated the European colonists at the war's outbreak and, in the process, destroyed the myth of the West's invincibility. Japan also stimulated Asian nationalism in some of its conquered colonies by granting the native populations a larger degree of self-rule than they had experienced under European masters; while Asian nationalists quickly soured on their Nipponese liberators, they did not lose their taste for independence. Left in the wake of Japan's defeat were former colonies unwilling to accept the reimposition of European rule.[1]

Some metropolitan powers coped with postwar Asian nationalism more gracefully than others. The United States, fulfilling a prewar promise, granted the Philippines political independence on 4 July 1946. American economic, political, and military interests, however, continued in the islands after independence and, through 1948, the United States poured in over a billion dollars of economic and military assistance to keep the country's conservative government oriented toward the West. By 1949, the Philippines were politically stable, by Asian standards, but suffered from inept rule and a small communist insurgency.[2]

Britain, after initial hesitation, granted most of her South and Southeast Asian colonies independence after the war. The consequences of

Reprinted from *Drawing the Line, The Origin of the American Containment Policy in East Asia,* by Robert M. Blum, by permission of the author and W. W. Norton & Company, Inc. Copyright © 1982 by Robert M. Blum.

decolonization were mixed. An independent Burma lapsed into a state of chronic civil war. After a period of initial conflict between India and Pakistan, the successors to British India observed an uneasy truce while quarreling over boundaries. The British chose not to withdraw from the multiracial Malaya where nationalism was diffuse among the country's heterogenous population. In all of these countries Communist elements were usually one part of a larger pattern of confusion. In chaotic Burma, the Communists were divided and fought among themselves as well as with other political factions; in Malaya, Communists in the Chinese community rebelled in 1948 but did not gain widespread support.

Siam, renamed Thailand in 1949, did not require a postwar grant of independence to be free. Although never a colony, it nonetheless suffered from internal political strife as well as problems with the French over the Siam-Indochina border. From the American perspective, Siam was stable but considered unreliable; the "wily" Thais were not a dependable bulwark against Chinese Communist expansion. As Dean Acheson explained to the Senate Foreign Relations Committee, the "Siamese are not very stouthearted fellows" and could not be counted on to put up "rugged resistance" to Communist subversion.[3]

The two largest problems in postwar Southeast Asia were Indonesia and Indochina, where the Dutch and French attempted to reimpose colonial rule. Between the end of the Pacific war and the beginning of 1949, the Netherlands reasserted their control of the East Indies by a mixed policy of force and negotiations. After lengthy discussions with a native Republican government, the Dutch attacked the non-Communist regime in December 1948, disregarding both United Nations resolutions and an American-backed truce reached in January 1948. After this "police action," the Netherlands' folly quickly became evident despite their capture of key Republican leaders. World opinion quickly turned against the Dutch, and even the United States Congress, which rarely noticed events in Southeast Asia, expressed its disapproval.[4]

FRENCH INDOCHINA

The French, with active assistance from Britain and the approval of the United States, also reimposed colonial rule on their former colony. Initially, they only reoccupied southern Indochina, the center of prewar French economic interest. In accordance with a wartime agreement, the Allies gave China the task of restoring order in the north. In the process of implementing their mandate, the Chinese occupying army encountered the hastily erected native government of President Ho Chi Minh's "Democratic Republic of Vietnam" (DRV). Based in Hanoi, Ho's regime enjoyed widespread support in the north and was backed by a coalition of political parties known as the Viet Minh. The party's key leaders, including Ho, were Communists, but they claimed to be only nationalists interested in independence from France. The Chinese tolerated the DRV's existence because of the political leverage it gave them against France and allowed Ho's government to operate under its watchful eye.

In February 1946 the Chinese agreed to turn over North Vietnam to the French, a decision that left Ho with the choice of either fighting or negotiating with France. On 6 March 1946, Ho signed an agreement with French authorities allowing colonial troops to enter the north in return for French recognition of the Vietnam Republic as a "free state having its own government, parliament, army and finances, and forming part of the Indochinese Federation and the French Union." In May 1946 Ho and a Vietnam delegation went to France to negotiate a settlement. After the talks broke down, Ho signed a temporary agreement that looked toward future discussions at an unspecified date. When French forces in the north built up to a point that its commanders thought would allow them to liquidate the Vietnam Republic, they began to use military force. In December 1946 the Viet Minh, aware of what was coming, launched a brief attack against the French in Hanoi and then retreated to the jungle to begin a long war for independence and dominance by the Viet Minh.[5]

By the end of 1948, Indochina was in a state of siege, with French and pro-French Vietnamese forces controlling the major urban areas, and the Viet Minh, concentrated in the north, controlling the countryside. It was evident to American diplomats that France was losing.[6] Since the French received economic assistance through the Marshall Plan, the Indochina war also indirectly drained American resources. According to the State Department's Far East Office the cost "of continued disruption of the Indochina economy" was estimated at $900 million over a four-year period. The importance of this sum was increased by the probability that it would not "purchase peace but would represent an indefinite drain upon French resources."[7]

The French attempted to retrieve their declining position in Vietnam through greater military power. They sought Vietnamese political support by fostering a "genuine nationalist movement" under the sponsorship of the thirty-six-year-old former Vietnamese emperor, Bao Dai; Ho's nationalist movement was "false" since it was tainted with Communists. The major problem with the "Bao Dai experiment," as the French frankly called it, was that both they and Bao Dai approached it halfheartedly. After two failed attempts to strike an agreement with France, the ex-emperor (he had abdicated to Ho in 1945) signed an agreement with the French president in the Elysée Palace on 8 March 1949, defining the new relationship between the French and Vietnam. The agreement gave a "Republic of Vietnam" only a semblance of nationhood "within the French Union." The meaning of the French Union, which was never precisely defined, was suggested by the powers that France reserved to itself in the agreement: control of Vietnam's foreign policy, finance, and national defense. The French government also promised to ask Parliament to pass a bill that would reintegrate Cochin China with the northern provinces of Vietnam (France had separated this southern province from Annam and Tonkin in 1945).[8]

The 8 March accord was flawed in several ways. The French government that signed it was weak and several strong elements in the French Assembly opposed the agreement. In Indochina it faced opposition from colonials who did not want Vietnam granted independence, no matter how denatured. Non-Communist Vietnamese, on whose behalf Bao Dai signed the agreement, greeted it with apathy. Part of the problem was the man on whom its success depended. In 1932, at the age of nineteen, Bao Dai assumed the throne of a dynasty that had been in power for three centuries. An accommodating attitude toward any force that appeared to be dominant marked his reign. Under the prewar French he urged his people to work in "close and confident collaboration with the protectorate government." When Japan took over Indochina in 1940, he quickly adjusted to the new order and was kept on as a puppet. After the war he abdicated, briefly cooperated with Ho Chi Minh's government in Hanoi, and in 1946, returned to the French Rivieria; where he pursued his interest in sports cars, gambling, and the good life.[9] Even after Bao Dai signed the 8 March agreement, many observers in Paris, Washington, and Saigon doubted he could lead a Nationalist movement with the enthusiasm necessary to compete with Ho Chi Minh. Consequently, the Elysée accord remained unratified for many months in Paris and unimplemented in Vietnam. In the interim, the Viet Minh increased their strength in the countryside.

France pursued the Bao Dai experiment in the face of strong opposition and apathy because it needed American support. The United States, the French knew, would not endorse an effort simply to reassert colonial rule in Indochina and wanted evidence that France was pursuing some higher purpose. A Bao Dai government, however, feeble, gave the Americans something they could construe as a genuine nationalist movement; the only alternative was rule by Ho Chi Minh.

AMERICAN PERCEPTION

The State Department, almost exclusively responsible for American Southeast Asia policy in the late 1940s, was slow to turn its attention to the region in the postwar years; its only major diplomatic effort undertaken in the area before 1950 was to mediate the Dutch-Indonesian conflict. The department was concerned about the region's deteriorating condition, its impact on the strength of Western Europe, and possible Soviet encroachment, but it was also disinclined to involve the United States in a major effort to reverse the course of events. Policy Planning Staff Director George Kennan expressed the dominant view when he wrote in February 1948 that the United States was "greatly over-extended in [its] whole thinking about what we can accomplish, and should try to accomplish" in Asia. American power should instead be projected in Japan and the Philippines, "the cornerstone of a Pacific security system."[10] Kennan's strategic offshore philosophy was the prevailing view, not only in the State Department but also throughout the administration. The concensus was that an American "defensive perimeter" ran along a line from the Aleutians, to Japan, to the Ryukyus, to the Philippines, to New Zealand, and Australia. Few, if any, senior officials within the Truman administration believed that the containment line should be drawn across the mainland of Asia.[11]

As 1948 progressed, the State Department's concern over Russian influence in Southeast Asia increased along with the general rise in tension in the Cold War. By late summer, Charles Reed, chief of the department's Division of Southeast Asian Affairs (SEA), saw "every indication that Moscow is turning more and more attention to the Far East, particularly in Southeast Asia."[12] On 13 October, the department sent a memorandum to American diplomatic missions in Asia echoing this worry: the single goal of Soviet policy in the region, it held, was to substitute Russian influence for that of the West "in such manner and degree as to ensure Soviet control being assurely installed and pre-dominant as in satellite countries behind the Iron Curtain."[13] In December, the CIA characterized the situation in the Far East as being "favorable" to the Soviets; the American "ability to check and reverse this trend is presently hampered by the US being in a middle position between the demands of Asiatic nationalism and the policies of Western European states."[14]

Some observers studying the Communist threat saw a pattern of events dating back to a "signal" the Soviet Union sent to Southeast Asia and other regions of the world in September 1947. The forum was a European Communist party conference held in Wiliza Gora, Poland; the messenger was Andrei Zhdanov, a high Kremlin official and ideologue. The signal was a speech calling on comrades around the world to oppose imperialism. The world, Zhdanov said, was divided into two camps. On one side stood the "imperialists and antidemocratic" forces headed by the United States whose purpose was to establish dominance and "smash democracy." On the other side stood the people's democracies led by the Soviet Union. It was the duty of the democratic forces to close ranks and oppose the antidemocratic forces. In many Western minds, confirmation of the speech's sinister nature came when the conference created the "Communist Information "Bureau" or "Cominform," a successor to the prewar Comintern that had spread Communist revolution.[15]

Events following Zhdanov's speech suggested coordination between the Soviet Union and Communist movements around the world. In December 1947, E. M. Zhukov, another Soviet theoretician, published an article applying Zhdanov's two-camp thesis to Asia. Three months after this article, a Communist-dominated "Southeast Asian Youth Conference" convened in Calcutta that went on record endorsing the two-camp thesis and condemning American imperialism. Not long after that conference, Communist-led insurrections occurred in Malaya, Burma, Indonesia, and somewhat later, the Philippines. State Department analysts saw the conference as an occasion for Moscow to pass along the Zhdanov-Zhukov doctrine and, they assumed, instructions to begin revolutionary violence in Southeast Asia. Whether or not the revolutionary activity could be traced directly to Soviet orders or from local assessments of opportunities to seize power, or both, the sequence of events, coupled with the pending Communist victory in China, forced the State Department to consider doing more to check Communist expansion in the region.[16]

The State Department's strongest advocate for a more active Southeast Asian policy was Charles Reed's SEA division. Yet, even Reed's recommendations for positive steps remained modest. The strongest counter-measure he proposed to meet the increased Soviet challenge in August 1948 was an intensified propaganda effort, supplemented by American business, missionary, medical, and educational activity. In addition, the division urged that the United States "publicize our readiness to loan technical experts in the fields of economic and social endeavor" (and thus anticipated Truman's "Point IV" program by several months).[17]

One potential force checking a bolder American policy in the region was FE director Butterworth. While he often acted vigorously on matters pertaining to his jurisdiction, Butterworth more frequently directed his energies toward blocking rather than encouraging American action on the Asian mainland. "The conduct of foreign affairs," he said in a March 1949 speech on Asian policy, "is a marginal operation, of persuasion, of the offer of benefit, at times the exertion of pressure in hope of changing the direction to suit our national interest." The greatest force operating against communism and the West in Southeast Asia was nationalism. He had "great confidence" in this force; it had "overcome any super-force to date" and its spirit was "the most essential characteristic of Southeast Asia today."[18] He was not opposed to modest measures of support for friendly or potentially friendly states like Siam or Indonesia, but he lobbied against a "Marshall Plan" for Asia or American stimulations of a "Pacific Pact" similar to the North Atlantic Treaty.[19]

Butterworth and Reed did not have sole control of Southeast Asian policy within the State Department. At least three geographic offices, and five divisions and independent units interested in economic policy, intelligence, and military assistance claimed an interest in the region. The major cause of disharmony in this system was a traditional rivalry between FE and the European office (EUR); the reason for conflict was usually either policy toward Indonesia or Indochina. Since these countries were at once European colonies and aspiring southeast Asian nations, both offices and their constituent divisions, SEA and the Western European Affairs Division (WE), had joint jurisdiction over all policy recommendations going to senior department officials as well as all cables going to the field.*

---

* Before the State Department reorganized on 3 October 1949, a geographic office was divided into divisions. The divisions of FE were CA (China), SEA (Southeast Asia), NA (Northeast Asia), and PI (Philippines). EUR had six constituent units. After 3 October, the regional offices became "bureaus" and the divisions became "offices." For a description of the department's organization, see U.S. Department of State, *Register of the Department of State, April 1, 1948* (Washington, D.C.: GPO, 1948) and later editions.

The division led to frequent conflict at what was called the department's "working level." EUR and WE argued that Dutch and especially French orientation toward the West was of such importance to American security that the United States should not risk alienation by pushing them too hard to free their colonies. FE and SEA held that more, not less, pressure should be applied to the metropolitan powers to encourage their accommodation to Asian nationalism. By the beginning of 1949, FE was making some headway on the Dutch-Indonesia question; the United States cut off economic aid to the Netherlands after the "police action" in December and threatened to exclude the Dutch from the Military Assistance Program if they did not back away from the confrontation.

FE had less success with Indochina. It wanted a "wait and see" approach buttressed with occasional efforts to pressure France to back Bao Dai more forcefully. The office preferred to hold back support for the doubtful experiment until it demonstrated a more certain chance for success. EUR wanted to leaven FE's aloof policy with expressions of American sympathy for France's predicament and not apply much pressure on the grounds that the French government was granting as many concessions as it could in Indochina; the American embassy in Paris went so far as to recommend that the United States openly back the experiment on the grounds that it would fail without American support.[20]

By late spring 1949, the European and Asian offices reached a general agreement on Indochina policy. In a 17 May meeting, senior officials in WE and SEA agreed "that the US should not put itself in a forward position in the Indochina problem since there appeared to be nothing we could do to alter the very discouraging prospects."[21] The department had already expressed the essence of this policy in cables to American diplomats in Paris and Saigon stating that the United States was willing to give Bao Dai diplomatic, economic, and arms support if France granted him the necessary concessions. The cable also noted that an aid program of "this nature would require Congressional approval."[22] Beyond this agreement, the two divisions argued vigorously over what constituted the necessary concessions and how hard the department should press France to make them. During departmental discussion of the Policy Planning Staff's paper on Southeast Asia, the consensus appeared to support the Far Eastern Office's hard-line view.

THE TROUBLED CAREER OF PPS-51

Perhaps because of orders from higher up, or a simple desire to earn their pay as shapers of policy, the Policy Planning Staff began drafting a Southeast Asia paper in February 1949. The study was a logical followup to the China paper that predicted the Chinese Communists would soon directly menace the subcontinent.

The "problem" PPS-51 identified was to "define U.S. policy toward Southeast Asia, including Indonesia, Indochina, Burma, Malaya, Siam and the Philippines." The "analysis" listed the characteristics that divided and united the region: many religions and varying degrees of political independence and political instability as opposed to a common racial background, economic backwardness, and the certainty "that SEA as a region has become the target of a coordinated offensive plainly directed by the Kremlin." The area was important because of its raw materials and its presence at a crossroads in global communication. If Southeast Asia were "swept by communism we shall have suffered a major political rout, the repercussions of which will be felt throughout the rest of the world, especially in the Middle East and in a then critically exposed Australia." With China falling to Communism, "SEA represents a vital segment on the line of containment, stretching from Japan southward around the Indian Peninsula." Japan, India, and Australia were the major non-Communist "base areas in this quarter of the world" and their security depended on Southeast Asia's denial to the Kremlin. The study identified "militant nationalism" as the most potent force in Asia. The problem facing the West was that the colonial-nationalist struggles in Indonesia and Indochina obscured the real enemy of Southeast Asia, Russian imperialism. With the Dutch and French following irrational colonial policies, the West had become its own worst enemy.

Given the great stakes involved in the success of non-Communist forces in Southeast Asia that were suggested in the analysis, the steps the report concluded the United States should take were modest. While it called for increased American activity in Southeast Asia, it contained no bold prescriptions for an American containment policy backed by large amounts of money, arms, technical assistance, or prestige; it suggested using all four, but only selectively and in small amounts. For the region, there should be multilateral consultation between the United States and the major friendly countries of South and Southeast Asia with India and the Philippines taking the lead. Economic interdependence between Southeast Asia, Japan, and the West should be encouraged along with American cultural and informational programs.

A two-page summary prepared for an under secretary's meeting on PPS-51 highlighted the paper's recommendations for individual countries: The United States should encourage Indonesian independence at the earliest feasible moment and "aid non-communist nationalist leaders to retain their supremacy and foster political and economic stability"; no dollar amount of aid was mentioned. With respect to Indochina, Washington "should frankly tell the French what we think about Southeast Asia," consult with the British and Indians, and "attempt to have the French transfer sovereignty in Indochina to a non-communist indigenous regime." There was no mention of material aid for the French or Vietnamese. For Burma, the department should consult with Britain and India and "wait until the smoke clears." In Siam, the United States should support the country's "resistance to Soviet and Chinese encroachment, and cultivate it as a center of stability and U.S. influence." Malaysia should be left to the British to worry about. The Philippines should be encouraged to play an active role in combating communism, be aided in developing its economy, and have benefit of a "major cultural and informational program." The summary also recommended that PPS-51 be forwarded to the NSC "for information" and that parts of it be shown to the Economic Cooperation Administration and the British.[23]

The planning staff presented the draft policy paper to an under secretary's meeting on 6 April with a misleading note stating that it had the "general approval" of seven bureaus and offices, including FE and EUR.[24] The staff had indeed written it in consultation with a number of offices, but the draft by no means pleased everyone. SEA chief Charles Reed was on record as objecting to the recommendations on Indonesia, complaining that they set forth operational steps best left to the discretion of the department's geographic offices. He disliked a paragraph calling for consultation with only the British and Indians on Indochina; the Philippines and Siam, he thought, should be consulted too. He also suggested a slight modification of the paragraph on Siam to allow for the possibility that "a Vietnam which is neither of a Soviet nor a Chinese inspiration" might encroach upon it.[25]

The paper fell flat in the meeting. Counselor Charles Bohlen, a man generally more concerned with European than Asian policy, argued against unilateral American efforts at encouraging nationalist movements in the area. He emphasized the need to work directly with Western powers and pointed out the "unwisdom of bringing the Australians, Indians, Pakistanis, *et al.*" in at the initial stages. The department's intelligence spokesman questioned the "timing factor" but suggested no specific changes. Butterworth had 'no objection to it," provided a paragraph on Indonesia did not restrict American support of an interim government. Paul Nitze of the Policy Planning Staff thought the paper gave insufficient emphasis to the difficulty of creating orderly and effective native governments. Despite the reservations, the group decided to send the paper to Acheson, approved it "for general guidance in the Department," and ordered that FE proceed to implement its conclusions.[26]

At some point after the 6 April meeting, FE and other offices in the department raised further objections to PPS-51. After a discussion of general Southeast Asian policy in the secretary's morning meeting on 29 April, the planning staff altered two paragraphs in favor of FE's views of the proper policy. One change outlined the importance of inducing the Dutch and French "to adopt their policies to the realities of the current situation in Southeast Asia" and stated that "our first step should be, in conjunction with the British, to set forth to the Dutch and French in candor, detail, and with great gravity our interpretation of the situation in and intentions with regard to SEA." The other stated that "determination of future [American] policy toward Indochina should await the outcome of the [recommended] demarché."[27]

These changes, however, did not placate all of the critics, and George Kennan made a special plea to Acheson. Contrary to what the secretary had heard about it, Kennan said that the "paper *does* contain concrete suggestions for action at this time with respect to Southeast Asia." He urged Acheson to discuss its contents with the British and French in Paris and to approve it "as broad guidance to Departmental thinking on the subject as a strategic concept from which tactical planning by the operational offices should flow."[28] The secretary left Washington for the Paris Foreign Ministers Conference several days later without taking Kennan's advice.

INDOCHINA POLICY AND THE JUNE DEMARCHÉ

In the absence of a departmental statement on Southeast Asia, the formulation and execution of policy fell to the querulous geographic offices. SEA chose to implement the portions of PPS-51 it agreed with and ignored the parts it found objectionable. One aspect of the paper it dismissed without hesitation was the notion of a "regional approach." The only "universal cement" Charles Reed could find for the region was the "preoccupation of certain non-communist Asiatic countries with the danger of an eventual communist dominated SEA." Reed also thought that the United States should give up on Indochina and focus on strengthening Siam. His doubts about Indochina developed from service as American consul in Hanoi and Saigon before and after the war, and as SEA chief since April 1948. The two earlier French efforts to implement a Bao Dai "solution" left Reed unimpressed and he distrusted the renewed experiment in 1949. "Merely because [Bao Dai] offers at present the only possible non-Communist solution in Indochina is no reason, in view of his very dubious chances of succeeding, in committing the United States at this time to his support," he wrote in April 1949.[29] A month later he informed Butterworth that "The chances of saving Indochina" were "slim." The United States "should look to a strengthened Siam as a base from which to contain communism."[30]

   Most American diplomats shared Reed's pessimism to some degree, but few were willing to write off Indochina without making an effort to save it. Butterworth and Reed's deputy in SEA were willing to support Bao Dai on the condition that France gave him a fair chance. Reed never pushed his argument very vigorously and accepted FE's conditional willingness to support the experiment by early summer. The key question in American policy thus became how hard to push France to give the ex-emperor his chance.[31] Since PPS-51 called for a stiff demarché to France on Indochina, FE concluded that it had a mandate to press hard.

   The logical pressure point was the 8 March accord. The State Department saw it as only the beginning of a process leading to real Vietnamese independence. Yet, as of June 1949, the French Assembly had only recently taken the preliminary step of rejoining Cochin China with the northern provinces, and the government still had not submitted the agreement for ratification. Responding to the tepid French followup to the agreement with Bao Dai, the Southeast Asian Division sought the approval of its European counterpart in the department to send the French government a frankly worded interpretation of the agreement and its implications for American policy. SEA, after a surprising clearance from WE for the strongly worded document, sent it to the American embassy in Paris on 6 June. Covering instructions, which Butterworth signed "for the Acting Secretary of State," requested that either Ambassador David Bruce or Charles Bohlen, then in Paris with Acheson for the Foreign Ministers Conference, present the demarché to the French Foreign Ministry as a statement of the department's thinking.

The fifteen-page note warned the French that they were playing into the hands of the Communists by not making the "requisite concessions" to nationalist demands in Vietnam. The accord's implementation, furthermore, would be only a first step; more concessions would be needed later if the United States were to view the effort with favor. Any American decision to support the Vietnam government would depend on "the extent to which the French Government has itself provided that Government with the political advantages upon which its appeal to the Vietnamese must be based."[32]

SEA attempted to alert the Paris embassy that the demarché was on its way and stress its importance as a cornerstone in American policy, but WE killed the warning cable.[33] As a result, the demarché and accompanying instructions arrived in Paris by courier without forewarning and the American embassy revolted. Ambassador Bruce, according to an aide, cried "poppycock" and, with the unanimous backing of the embassy's political section, sent his guest, Dean Acheson, the demarché, Butterworth's instructions, a draft cable Bruce proposed to send to Washington, and a cover note. In the note, Bruce expressed regret about bothering the secretary on matters unrelated to the Foreign Ministers Conference, but said that the presentation of the department's memorandum "would do a great deal of harm precisely at the time when encouragement rather than criticism is needed." Before this package reached the secretary, one of Acheson's aides showed it to Charles Bohlen, who attached a note to the growing pile of documents stating that he "entirely agreed" with Bruce. While he was for doing something "appropriate to bring the French attitude in line with that of the United States," Bohlen could not support a "holier than thou" lecture coupled with suggestions that France was not about to follow.

Acheson instructed Bruce to send his draft cable to Washington protesting the demarché.[34] Sent 13 June, Bruce's cable requested that the department allow him to convey its "general views" in an oral resume. He explained that the presentation of the document would be counterproductive. The French government had gone as far as it could go and would not renegotiate the Elysée agreement. To lend weight to his "request," Bruce noted that the secretary of state had read the cable and concurred.[35]

The Paris embassy also scored another coup while Dean Acheson was its guest. In early June it learned that the French were planning to exchange instruments with Bao Dai in the near future that would put the 8 March agreement into effect; following this step, the ex-emperor would announce formation of a provisional government and France planned to notify foreign powers of this event and of Vietnam's ability to receive foreign recognition. The sequence of events did not indicate a departure in existing French policy, only a paper transfer of limited powers and a quest for foreign approval. It failed to constitute the vigorous backing of the experiment that SEA deemed necessary for Bao Dai to succeed. As a result, the division did not see it as an occasion for the United States to speak out in support of Bao Dai. From his vantage point in Paris, however, Dean Acheson decided that the department should issue a statement welcoming the creation of the new government. The statement, released on 21 June, fell short of the full diplomatic recognition that Ambassador Bruce desired, but did move closer to association with the questionable experiment. It called the formation of the Vietnam state a "welcomed development" and expressed hope that the 8 March agreement would "form the basis for the progressive realization of the legitimate aspirations of the Vietnamese people."[36]

According to Charlton Ogburn, one of SEA's senior officers, his division's Indochina policy had been "junked." In a 28 June memorandum to Reed, he complained that "FE is being put in an extremely vulnerable position" since nothing was being done to promote a non-Communist solution in Indochina. He mentioned a column Joseph Alsop had written attacking FE for its halfhearted Indochina policy and credited WE with responsibility for planting the story. The recent reverses were "the culmination of three years of consistent effort on the part of WE to set aside all considerations of our position in Asia and to keep a free hand for the French." Consideration of the French government's weakness had "gagged" the State Department "beyond all reason in so many contexts that the thing has become joke." Ogburn assumed that WE had all along anticipated that the Paris embassy would scrap the demarché.[37]

SEA's policy of watchful waiting coupled with pressure on France to support Bao Dai was not yet fully junked, as Ogburn feared, but it had taken a measurable step closer to the scrap heap. In an effort to define policy in the wake of Acheson's "captivity" in Paris, Ogburn drafted a memorandum outlining five policy alternatives for Indochina. The choices were: (1) to continue the wait and see policy; (2) to give tepid support to the Bao Dai government; (3) to promote a compromise with Ho; (4) to give "utmost" support to Bao Dai; and (5) to "follow a compromise course, endeavoring to give encouragement to the Bao Dai solution without committing the United States to support of the 8 March agreement or the Vietnamese government envisaged in it, and at the same time preparing for the time when it might be expedient to reveal publicly why we were unable to do more to save Indochina." Ogburn recommended the fifth option for lack of a better alternative. Drafted at Butterworth's request, SEA sent the options memorandum to its counterpart in EUR who refused to cosign it as a statement of policy.[38] Indochina policy would linger in this confused, half-committed state until the United States Congress stimulated the department to adopt Ogburn's option number four.

THE UNEXPLORED ALTERNATIVE

When the State Department moved closer to endorsing Bao Dai on 21 June, it took one more step away from a rapprochement with Ho Chi Minh. By 1949 the department's attitude toward Ho was rigid. From evidence British and French intelligence provided in 1945, it knew that Ho had helped found the French communist Party after the First World War, had studied in Moscow's "Toilers of the East" university in the 1920s, and had operated in Asia as a Comintern agent in the interwar years. With this background, the Vietnamese leader fit the stereotype of an international Communist agent.

There was, however, strong evidence suggesting that Ho was also a nationalist. In 1919, for example, he had approached the American delegation at the Paris Peace Conference in an effort to present Secretary of State Robert Lansing a petition requesting independence for the Vietnamese people. During and after the Second World War he had sent Western leaders a stream of appeals for postwar Vietnamese independence. He made a special effort to court the United States and, to his own advantage, cooperated with American OSS officers in northern Vietnam in the last months of the war. Throughout his wartime and early postwar quest for Vietnam's independence, Ho brushed aside questions about his political ideology. All he sought, he said, was his country's independence. Ho's ambiguous record disturbed some American observers, but not enough for the State Department to have serious reservations about how to classify him. The department considered nationalism and Communism to be mutually exclusive and, by 1947, for the purpose of designing an Indochina policy, it considered him a Moscow-directed Communist.[39]

Doubts about Ho's true intentions nonetheless persisted and the Viet Minh leader would himself frequently add to the confusion. After he went underground in late 1946, Ho continued to seek American good will in the hope that the United States would not support the French effort to reoccupy Vietnam. In early 1948, he requested that an official American observer visit his camp, presumably to allow Ho to demonstrate his revolution's benign international intentions. SEA was not enthusiastic about the idea. If an American were to accept the invitation, one official reasoned, he might either find evidence that Ho was indeed a Moscow puppet and that past professions of friendship for the United States were a "hoax" or that Ho was an independent nationalist. If the observer verified the first possibility, "it would not change the policy of this government as our basic assumption seems to be that we cannot afford to assume that Ho is anything but Moscow-directed." If evidence were found to support the second possibility, it was unlikely that such a single report "would change the basic assumption of this government vis-a-vis Ho." It would, in short, "seem a poor investment to send an American." One alternative would be for the CIA to send a Chinese agent. "The value of information by a Chinese would depend on his keenness of observation," the officer wrote, "but he certainly would be in a position to add considerably to our sum total of knowledge of Ho's regime, particularly its ability to continue to offer military resistance to the French."[40]

The question of sending a CIA agent to Ho's Vietnam came up again four months later at a June 1948 conference American diplomats held in Bangkok. The department's representative at the meeting explained the problem: In the first place, we just couldn't do it because of our white skin. A white man would be very conspicuous in Indo-China. In order to have an effective intelligence officer, he would have to have a little brown blood. Then, we wouldn't be able to trust him.[41]

After Tito split with Stalin in the summer of 1948 (the Yugoslav leader left the Cominform on 28 June), the department did not revise its estimate of Ho and the Viet Minh. Indeed, SEA was slow to grasp the significance of the Tito phenomenon. As an approach to countering Soviet propaganda in the region, it recommended in mid-August 1948 that American propaganda emphasize "that a communist state is but a satellite of Moscow and with no scope for uncontrolled action or thought. We have plenty of ammunition for this attack in the examples of Yugoslavia, Czechslovakia, Poland, Rumania."[42]

In the first half of 1949 the department's fixed view of Ho and growing attachment to Bao Dai withstood the challenge of the Vietnam leader's persistent assertion that he was not a Russian puppet. In a radio interview with *Newsweek* Magazine reporter Harold Isaacs, Ho was asked if his government was Communist. "Pure French propaganda," he replied, and noted that his government was composed of many elements. Did he fear that his country would become a satellite? "No, I have no fear," he answered. The magazine's editors suggested that Ho might be "more of a Vietnamese nationalist right now than a Communist stooge."[43] Ho attempted to reinforce this image in an interview granted the United Press in late May. In one question, which was submitted to him in writing, he was asked if he was or ever had been a Communist. "When I was young," he replied cryptically, "I studied Buddhism, Confucianism, Christianism [*sic*] as well as Marxism. There's something good in each doctrine. The

Viet Nam Communist Party was dissolved in 1945. I have been in England, France, Russia, China and other countries."[44]

Along with Ho's direct testimony, the foremost French expert on Indochina offered the department a disquieting view of both Ho Chi Minh and Bao Dai. Paul Mus, director of the School of Overseas France in Paris, visited Washington in late April and paid a courtesy call on the department. Speaking to lower-level officials involved in research, Mus pointed out that the Bao Dai experiment had little chance for success. Ho Chi Minh, the professor was reported as saying, had "the complete support of the Vietnamese, except for a few hundred in Cochinchina presently backing Bao Dai." Even conservative and wealthy landowners who "know that Ho would kill them if he had complete power support Ho because of their desire for national independence." Describing Ho as "30% trustworthy," Mus considered him a nationalist above politics who "would become anything the situation made necessary." After independence Mus speculated that Ho's influence might decline and that Western diplomats would then "be in a position to exert a favorable influence on the development of democracy in the country."[45]

Such talk about Ho's ambiguity agitated American officials in Washington and posts in France and Vietnam. Reacting to the Harold Isaacs interview, the American consul in Hanoi reported on 11 May that members of Bao Dai's entourage were being led to think that the United States looked "almost favorably on Ho and considered him as much National[ist] as Communist."[46] The department offered reassurance nine days later in a cable, drafted by Ogburn, containing a remarkably vivid exposition of SEA's views about Ho becoming a Titoist.

> In light Ho's known background, no other assumption possible but that he outright Commie so long as (1) he fails unequivocally repudiate Moscow connections and Commie doctrine and (2) remains personally singled-out for praise by internatl Commie press and receives its support.... Question whether Ho as much nationalist as Commie is irrelevant. All Stalinists in colonial areas are nationalists. With achievement natl aims (i.e., independence) their objective necessarily becomes subordination state to Commie purposes and ruthless extermination not only opposition groups but all elements suspected even slightest deviation. On basis examples eastern Eur it must be assumed such wld be goal Ho and men his stamp if included Bao Dai Govt.... It must of course be conceded theoretical possibility exists estab National Communist state or pattern Yugoslavia in any area beyond reach Soviet army. However, US attitude cld take acct such possibility only if every other possible avenue closed to preservation area from Kremlin control. Moreover, while Vietnam out of reach Soviet army it will doubtless be by no means out of reach Chi Commie hatchet men and armed forces.[47]

When Harold Isaacs returned to the United States in late June, he called on Charles Reed, giving him the same story that Mus conveyed in the spring. "[The] only possible present action," said Isaac, "would be to contact Ho Chi Minh, find out what he wanted, and then accept his terms." The discussion became heated and Isaac left, leaving Reed unconvinced.[48]

While Ho, Mus, and Isaacs did not change the State Department's operating assumption about Ho Chi Minh, his ambiguity did trouble SEA. In April 1949 the division briefly considered promoting a French-Bao Dai accommodation with the Viet Minh. John Davies and Reed drafted a brief paper describing a "possible method of solving the Indochina problem" that would "once and for all 'smoke out' Ho Chi Minh and determine whether he is primarily a nationalist or a communist." Their plan called for consultation between France, Britain, India, the Philippines and the United States. Following establishment of a common position, either India or the Philippines would call a conference on Indochina. France would be induced to grant Vietnam full independence and the foreign powers would establish an international mission in the country to monitor developments in the new states. The mission would remain for "some years" and function as the internationally supervised customs office had once functioned in China.

In the course of erecting this new system, the international mission would consult both Bao Dai and Ho Chi Minh. The group visiting Ho, "preferably composed of Asiatics," would point out that he "claimed to be a nationalist first and foremost," remind him of his appeal for international support to achieve Vietnamese independence, and assure him that France was willing to grant the country freedom. The mission would then "suggest to Ho that if he is the real nationalist he professes to be" he would "accept loyally the decisions and mandates of the government and the subsequent constituent assembly, et cetera, and bind himself unequivocally not to ... subvert the true nationalism of his people" or a government that might emerge from the multilateral effort. The mission might even "suggest" that he leave Vietnam and "take up once more the philosophical studies to which he has devoted a great deal of his previous life, and it might even be suggested that there would be a pension adequate to support him in those studies."

Davies and Reed conceded that Ho might agree to such a plan and then try to subvert it. If he refused to cooperate at the outset, then the United States might be better off knowing "once and for all what we may expect from him and for what we should plan." Then it might be desirable to give France and the "nationalist Vietnamese" military help. One positive line of defense they suggested ran from Siam "down along the Mekong and cutting across Indochina to include Cambodia and Cochinchina."[49]

Reed sent the scheme to Butterworth, but the idea apparently never went much further. There is no evidence revealing what WE and EUR may have thought of the plan, if they saw it; if they did, the reaction was probably frosty. As the department's Europeanists demonstrated with their scuttling of the June demarché to France, they were not enthusiastic about leaning on the French government to do much of anything in Indochina.

By mid-summer 1949, SEA appears to have dropped all thought of seeking an accommodation with Ho Chi Minh. Ogburn dismissed the possibility of bringing the Viet Minh into Bao Dai's government in his June option paper. Even if the French would allow it and Ho were willing, the probability was, he wrote, that the Communists would quickly take over and "enlist Vietnam in the support of Communist China and the USSR. Such an outcome would...mean a failure of our policy and would reflect upon the Department's judgement." The consequences of Indochina falling to Communism might also cause a "chain reaction" in the rest of the subcontinent.[50]

The United States had three basic choices for Indochina policy in 1949: one was to do nothing; a second was to back the French; a third was to promote a compromise with Ho. The policy it pursued in the spring was a compromise between the first and second. The State Department ruled out the third as being too hazardous. There lay in it a serious domestic political risk in that a compromise with Ho might have invited an attack from the friends of China and other politicians willing to attack FE on the loyalty issue. Beyond that, the department did not want the Western position in Southeast Asia replaced by a revolutionary force directed by the Soviet Union. Given the subcontinent's strategic location, natural wealth, and relation to the economics of Western Europe and friendly Asian nations, such a takeover was potentially catastrophic.

POSTSCRIPT

After the short life of the "international mission" idea and the stillbirth of the demarché to France, PPS-51 persisted in its fragile life. When the secretary returned from Paris, he gave it his approval and on 1 July 1949, the department dispatched the document to the NSC for its information. However, the paper's problems continued even after that. The Policy Planning Staff wanted it sent to the field as a general policy statement, but Charles Bohlen requested that the recommendations be deleted. On 11 July, Acheson sent it to the field with covering instructions advising that no action be taken on its recommendations. Thus, five months after its drafting, PPS-51 went to posts in Europe and Asia only "as a source of information and not the basis for any action."[51] It had become, in effect, a non-policy paper.

The fate of the Southeast Asia paper reflected, among other things, the triumph of both FE and EUR over the Policy Planning Staff. The two offices and their subunits preferred negotiating policy between themselves; they tolerated the planning staff, apparently, only when it supported their own policy line. The paper's fate also reflected the reality that Southeast Asia policy remained in the doldrums in spite of the growing concern that something needed to be done to prevent the region from falling under communist control. The policy remained adrift until the department, stimulated by fortuitous events in Congress, reviewed it again in the winter.

NOTES

1. U.S., Congress, Senate, Committee on Foreign Relations, *Hearings on the Causes, Origins, and Lessons of the Vietnam War*, 92d Cong., 2d sess., p. 163.

2. On aid to the Philippines, see William Adams Brown, Jr., and Redvers Opie, *American Foreign Assistance*, (Washington: Brookings, 1950), p. 408.

3. U.S., Congress, Senate, Committee on Foreign Relations, *Hearings on Reviews of the World Situation*, 81st Cong., 1st and 2d sess. ("Historical Series" of hearings held in executive session) (Washington, D.C.: GPO, 1974), pp. 182–83.

4. For the aid cutoff, see Brown and Opie, *American Foreign Assistance*, p. 190. For congressional disapproval of Dutch action in Indonesia, see *Congressional Record*, 80th Cong., 2d sess., pp. 3383–94.

5. The best general source on development in Indochina in this period remains Ellen J. Hammer, *The Struggle for Indochina* (Stanford: Stanford University Press, 1954).

6. Memo, Reed to Butterworth, 29 March 1949, "Indochina 1946–1949, Military Forces Operation" folder, Records of the Office of Philippine and Southeast Asia Affairs, Lot 54D190, RG 59, NA.

7. Memo, Butterworth to Hickerson, 20 April 1948, folder unknown (document copied from loose collection temporarily unboxed and out of its folder), Lot 54D190, RG 59, NA.

8. For the text of the 8 March accord, see Allan W. Cameron, ed., *Vietnam Crisis: A Documentary History, Vol. I: 1940–1956* (Ithaca: Cornell University Press, 1970), pp. 122–128.

9. *Current Biography*, 1949, Mimeographed.

10. PPS-23, Review of Current Trends, 24 February 1948, *FR*, 1948, I, pt. 3 (Washington, D.C.: GPO, 1976) pp. 523–25.

11. For a recent interpretation of American strategy in the early postwar years, see Thomas H. Etzold, "The Far East in American Strategy, 1948–1951," *Aspects of Sino-American Relations Since 1784*, ed. Thomas H. Etzold (New York: New Viewpoints, 1978), pp. 102–26.

12. Memo, Reed to Butterworth, 13 August 1948, *FR*, 1948, I. pt. 3, p. 607.

13. Circular Instruction, acting secretary to certain diplomatic posts, 13 October 1948, ibid., pp. 638–44; see also the CIA's OIR Report No. 4778, "Appraisal of Communist Efforts in Southeast Asia: 1948," reproduced by Carrolton Press, Westport, Conn.

14. "Review of the World Situation," 16 December 1948, CIA 12–48, National Security Files, Truman Papers.

15. Charles B. McLane, *Soviet Strategies in Southeast Asia: An Explanation of Eastern Policy under Lenin and Stalin* (Princeton: Princeton University Press, 1966), pp. 352–54; Ruth T. McVey, *The Calcutta Conference and the Southeast Asia Uprisings* (Ithaca: Cornell University, 1958), p. 7; Andre Fontaine, *History of the Cold War From the October Revolution to the Korean War, 1917–1950* (New York: Vintage Books, 1968), pp. 334–35.

16. McLane, *Secret Strategies*, pp. 355–60: McVey, *The Calcutta Conference, passim*: CIA, "Appraisal of Communist Efforts, " pp. 13–16.

17. Memo, Reed to Butterworth, 13 August 1948, *FR*, 1949, I (Washington, D.C.: GPO, 1976), pp. 607–09.

18. "Transcript of Mr. Butterworth's speech at the National Conference on American Foreign Policy," 17 March 1949, pp. 12, 15, Butterworth Papers, George C. Marshall Research Foundation, Lexington, Va.

19. For Butterworth's views on a Marshall Plan for Asia, see memo, Butterworth to Labouisee, 2 March 1949, 893.50 Recovery/2-749, RG 59, NA; on a Pacific Pact, see telegram, secretary to Locket, 23 March 1949, and memo of conversation, Butterworth, Chang, Bond, 8 April 1949, *FR*, 1949, VII, pt. 2, pp. 1126, 1141–42.

20. For the position of Ambassador Bruce on supporting Bao Dai, see telegram, Bruce to secretary, 2 June 1949, *FR*, 1949, VII, pt. 1 (Washington, D.C.: GPO, 1976), pp. 36–38.

21. Memo of conversation, 17 May 1949, ibid., p. 27.

22. Telegram, secretary to Abbott, 10 May 1949, ibid., pp. 23–25.

23. PPS-51, "U. S. Policy Toward Southeast Asia," 29 March 1949, "Reports and Recommendations to the Secretary and Under Secretary of State, Vol. 3, 1949" (bound book), Records of the Policy Planning Staff, Lot 64D563, RG 59, NA. The date on this document is misleading as it was circulated within the department in a slightly different form in April; after revision it apparently retained its original date. For a summary of its contents, see UMD-26 (Summary), 4 April 1949, Under Secretary's Meetings file, Records of the Executive Secretariat, Lot 53D250, RG 59, NA.

24. Ibid.

25. Memo, Reed to Allison, 31 March 1949, "Southeast Asia, 1949 — U.S. Policy" folder, Lot 54D190, RG 59, NA.

26. UM S-25, 6 April 1949, and memo for files, 6 April 1949, Lot 53D250, RG 59, NA; memo, Butterworth to Reed, 6 April 1949, 890.00/4-649, RG 59, NA.

27. Secretary's Daily Meeting, 29 June 1949: memo, Kennan to secretary, 19 May 1949, "Reports and Recommendations to the Secretary of State and the Under Secretary of State, Vol. 3, 1949," Lot 64D563, RG 59, NA.

28. Ibid.

29. Memo, Reed to Butterworth, 14 April 1949, 851g.00/4-1449, RG 59, NA.

30. Memo, Reed to Butterworth, 17 May 1949. "Southeast Asia 1949 — U.S. Policy" folder, RG 59, NA.

31. Reed's deputy, William S. B. Lacy, states his view in an attachment to ibid., memo, Lacy to Reed, 13 May 1949.

32. Dispatch, Butterworth (for the acting secretary) to Bruce, 6 June 1949 (with enclosure), *FR*, 1949, VII, pt. 1, pp. 38–45.

33. Memo, Ogburn to Reed, O'Sullivan, 28 June 1949, "Indochina: French-Indochina Relations" folder, Lot 54D190, RG 59, NA.

34. Letter, Walner to MacArthur, 14 June 1949; memo, Bruce to secretary, 10 June 1949; memo, Bohlen to secretary, 13 June 1949, 851g.01/6-649; memo, Battle to Bohlen, 11 June 1949, 851g/6-1449, RG 59, NA.

35. Telegram, Bruce to the secretary, 13 June 1949, *FR*, 1949, VII, pt. 1, pp. 45–46.

36. Memo, Ogburn to Reed and O'Sullivan, 28 June 1949, "Indochina: French-Indochinese Relations", and memo by Ogburn, "Courses Open to United States in Indochina Situation" (n.d.), "Indochina 1947–1949—Policy and Information Papers" folder, Lot 54D190, RG 59, NA; U.S. Department of State, *Bulletin*, 18 July 1949, p. 75.

37. Memo, Ogburn to Reed and O'Sullivan, 28 June 1949, "Indochina: French-Indochinese Relations" folder, RG 59, NA.

38. Ibid.: memo by Ogburn, "Courses Open to United States in Indochina Situation" (n.d.), "Indochina 1947–1949—Policy Information Papers" folder, RG 59, NA.

39. For primary documents relating to Ho's wartime and early postwar activity, see Foreign Relations Committee, *Causes:* U.S., Department of Defense, *U.S.-Vietnam Relations*, I.C. (bk. 1) (Washington, D.C.: GPO, 1971), pp. C-66–C-104; and Papers of General Gallagher, Office of the Chief of Military History, Department of the Army, Washington, D.C. The author reviews this subject in U.S., Congress, Senate, Committee on Foreign Relations, "The United States and Vietnam, 1944–1947," 92d Cong., 2d sess. (Committee Print, Staff Study).

40. Memo, Landon to Penfield, 17 February 1948, folder and box unknown, Lot 54D190, RG 59, NA.

41. "SEA Conference—Communist Activities in Southeast Asia" (21–26 June 1948), "SEA Conference, 1948" folder, Lot 54D190, RG 59, NA.

42. Memo, Reed to Butterworth, 13 August 1948, *FR*, 1948. I, pp. 607–609.

43. *Newsweek*, 25 April 1949, p. 44.

44. *New York Times*, 22 May 1949, p. 2.

45. Memo of conversation, Mus, et al., 26 April 1949, 851g.01/4-2649, RG 59, NA.

46. Telegram, Gibson to secretary, 11 May 1949, *FR*, 1949, VII, pt. 1, pp. 25–27.

47. Telegram, secretary to Gibson, 20 May 1949, 851g.01/5-1149, RG, NA.

48. Memo of conversation, Isaacs and Reed, 29 June 1949, 851g.01/6-2949, RG 59, NA.

49. Blind memo attached to memo, Reed to Butterworth, 16 May 1949, Lot 54D190, RG 59, NA.

50. Memo by Ogburn, "Courses Open to United States in Indochina" (n.d.), "Indochina 1947–1949—Policy Information Papers" folder, RG 59, NA.

51. Secretary's Daily Meeting, 11 July 1949; draft letter (Rusk) to Bruce, n.d., "Southeast Asia 1949—U.S. Policy" folder, RG 59, NA; letter, Rusk to Lockett, 26 July 1949, *FR*, VII, pt. 2, pp. 1175–76.

3
An Encounter with Ho Chi Minh

ARCHIMEDES L. A. PATTI

Indoors I found Le Xuan impatiently awaiting me. He had said he would be in touch, but here he was with an invitation from Ho to luncheon and a car and driver to take me. I took a fast look at the incoming radio messages from Kunming, hoping to find something on surrender negotiations, but there was nothing on that, only more messages from Helliwell to the recalcitrant Captains Conein and Spaulding leading two separate units toward the Indochinese border, again advising them to return to Kunming for airlift to Hanoi sans the French. Le Xuan and I were soon in the back seat of a very old Citroen and on our way. It was almost one and Xuan was beside himself because he had been told I was expected for noon. I was amused but reassured him that I would explain the unavoidable delay and, anyhow, President Ho knew what was happening. Xuan was somewhat mollified but still wished we had started earlier.

Our Vietnamese driver maneuvered his ancient chariot expertly, avoiding the Sunday strollers and streams of bicyclists three and four abreast, talking to each other, oblivious of the vehicular traffic. We dodged down one street, through an alley, up another street, and so on in what seemed to me a very circuitous route. We had been riding almost ten minutes and at a fast clip, but we did not appear to have traveled far. I supposed the driver had been instructed to be sure he was not followed. Finally we stopped in front of a modest two-story house in what I judged to be the old Vietnamese section of the city. Neither Europeans nor Japanese were in sight. A young man standing at the door waiting for us exchanged a word or two with Xuan and led us into the house and up a flight of stairs.

As I entered the upper rooms, a wisp of a man came forward, both hands extended in a warm greeting. I was pleased to see him again but thoroughly shocked. Ho was only a shadow of the man I had met at Chiu Chou Chieh four months to the day earlier. I reached for his hands, and he seemed very unsteady on his sandaled feet. The thin, bony legs supporting his frail frame made a startling contrast with the large head and the radiant smile on his face. His clothes, a high-collared brown tunic and trousers, hung loosely, accentuating his wasted condition.

I started to apologize for being late, but Ho would have none of it, saying he knew it was not my fault, looking straight at Giap with a mischievous smile, and I was inwardly amused to find Giap there, since he had been mum to me about this luncheon. Drawing me toward the other men who stood discreetly apart, Ho introduced me as "our American friend from Washington." Somewhat embarrassed and not wanting a false impression regarding my official status, I corrected, "From Kunming, please!" Everyone laughed, and Ho repeated, "From Kunming." I have tried to recall with exactitude who was present but my only memory is of Ho, Giap, Truong Chinh, and possibly Nguyen Khang.

I inquired into the state of his health, and Ho readily admitted to a bout with malaria and intestinal ailments, but with a wide gesture dismissed the subject by asking me of news from Kunming and Washington. Before I could answer, the young man who had admitted us downstairs came in with a tray of six small glasses and a bottle of Vermouth. The young man poured, and Ho offered me the first. I was anticipating with displeasure a political toast but Ho did not embarrass me and only offered "*à votre santé*," and I had only to return "*à la votre.*" I noticed without surprise that he barely touched his lips to the glass, as I had heard he was abstemious.

Ho suggested we move into the next room where an attractive table had been laid for six. The meal was simple but delicious: an excellent fish soup followed by bowls of steamed rice and bite-sized pieces of braised chicken and pork, then rice cakes and fruit. My place at the table had been set to Ho's right and was the only one equipped with a European place setting of china and silver. A thoughtful gesture but, having acquired a degree of dexterity in the use of chopsticks and bowl in China, I asked if I, too, could not have them. They were all delighted, the oriental utensils were promptly provided, and it served to break the ice. Everyone relaxed.

Conservation was in French, with occasional English words for clarity. I gathered that only Ho spoke English, and he did most of the talking, keeping the conservation both bland and general. He reminisced somewhat on how his people had worked with AGAS, GBT, OWI, and, of course, the OSS and referred at one point to the American attempts in 1944–45 to recruit him for service with the OWI in San Francisco. He had hoped at the time, he said, that the American project would materialize so that he could meet and talk directly with the UN delegates about his country's aspirations for national independence. In retrospect, he said, he might have been no more successful than he had been in Versailles in 1919.

Lunch over, we moved to the balcony overlooking a courtyard for coffee; the other four excused themselves, and Ho and I were alone. He opened the conversation by saying that he was deeply grateful that I had been able to accept his invitation; he hoped we could review the current situation. I thought it would be useful but noted that my position was extremely limited by my directive and that I had no authority to become involved in French-Vietnamese politics. Ho nodded several times, raised his hands, palms out, and smilingly said, "I understand. I ask for nothing at this time, perhaps later. But today we will talk as friends, not diplomats." I replied with a smile: "Good. Then you don't mind if I report the substance of our conversation to Kunming?" "No," Ho said, "so long as neither the French nor the Chinese know of my whereabouts."

In the next two hours we covered a number of events and issues from the meeting of the "Deer" team to the "uprisings" in Saigon and Hanoi. Ho was eager to bring me up to date and I was glad to learn all I could of the situation.

Recalling with mild amusement the Montfort incident, Ho asked me why the French had ignored his invitations to meet with him in July. At that particular moment he had been interested not only in a clarification of the ambiguous 24 March declaration but also in opening talks with French officials in China. I professed ignorance of French intent except that OSS had passed the messages to AGAS and they had been delivered. Ho had been disappointed and offended with French haughtiness, which he blamed for the French anti-Vietnamese campaign in China. He was particularly irritated with Sainteny. Pointedly he said it was no secret that "Sainteny, the chief of M.5, is de Gaulle's representative." He saw Sainteny's mission as hostile to the Vietnamese and therefore bound to create problems for the Provisional Government.

As for the *"équipe"* at the Palace, he asked, "What did they hope to accomplish? Did they think for a moment they could stop the course of events at that juncture in Viet Nam's history?" I could not speak for the French but only explained that we had brought them to assist us in administering to the large contingent of French POW's and that we had purposefully limited their number to five. Ho was highly skeptical. "That may be your purpose but certainly it is not theirs."

Hoping to alleviate his concern, I suggested that perhaps Sainteny's group could be useful in establishing early contacts with the French, even to induce them to tentatively accept the fact that the Viet Minh was in power. Ho thought not. For the time being he was not disposed to make any further overtures. Later perhaps, when the French perceived their untenable position as pretenders, the situation might change. In the meantime they would be at the Palace where they could be watched. I suggested once more a dialogue with Sainteny, but Ho remained unconvinced that it would produce any constructive results. However, in deference to me, he said I could use my best judgment in the matter.

His concern was not about the French alone; he was uneasy about British and Chinese intentions. He spoke knowledgeably of Franco-British cooperation in Laos, Cambodia, and Cochinchina. Obviously, British interest coincided with French objectives in those areas and with their own long-range goal of reestablishing their prewar colonial sphere in Southeast Asia. As for the Chinese, Ho characterized their interest as "political blackmail." Word from Chungking was that the Kuomintang was already negotiating with the Paris government on several matters of special rights in Indochina and he was convinced the Franco-British-Chinese power play would jeopardize the integrity of the independence movement.

The conversation was depressing and I searched for a change of subject. I inquired into the relationship between the Japanese and the Provisional Government. Ho readily admitted that he had assurances of noninterference from the Japanese; they had been most cooperative. Since the Hanoi "uprising," a silent understanding existed without formal contact or agreement. The Japanese would simply withdraw in an orderly fashion as the Viet Minh authorities took over each government function. But Ho did not know what to expect from the Allies after the Japanese left nor was he certain who would replace them. I said it would be the Chinese, as agreed at Potsdam. Ho was not surprised, he had understood that would be the case, but he had not been sure until that moment. I wondered silently if he had hoped for an American occupation.

Ho was uneasy about the reception the Chinese troops would receive from the Vietnamese and speculated that a large influx of Chinese, added to the Japanese army, would put a terrible strain on the resources of the country. He also alluded, very delicately, to troubles Chinese occupation forces might create if they looted extensively or abused the populace. He asked me to alert the Allied authorities to this possibility and I assured him I would.

These were some of the problems besetting Ho for which there were no ready solutions and over which he could exert little influence.

Except to a handful of close associates and some Chinese, Ho Chi Minh, the man and the name, was still little known to the Vietnamese and even less so to the world leaders molding the shape of Asia. His earlier efforts to achieve American recognition had come to nothing. Ho felt it imperative to find a way to bring his government to the attention of the Allies before the arrival of their occupation forces. He had read Bao Dai's appeal for recognition of Viet Nam's independence sent a few days earlier to the heads of the Allied powers. It disturbed him because the appeal reinforced the Emperor's legal status as head of state but was silent on the existence of the Provisional Government. He was moving swiftly to correct that misapprehension.

According to Ho, Bao Dai was no longer in power; the only legitimate government at the moment was his Provisional Government. I did not dispute his claim with regard to Hanoi or even Tonkin but noted that countrywide. Bao Dai was still the head of state. With a knowing smile, Ho informed me that at that very moment a delegation of his government was en route to Hué to accept the Emperor's abdication. Once the abdication was received, he planned to issue a declaration of independence, establish a cabinet, set up a full-fledged government, and attempt to secure international recognition. In a casual tone he asked, "What will the United States do?" I could not speak for our government but gave my opinion that it would have to consider the situation in the light of events. Ho showed his disappointment but did not press me.

It was important to Ho that the United States continue its anticolonial policy regarding Indochina. He was searching for a way to dispel the "misconception" that he was "an agent of the Comintern" or that he was a communist. My willing attention provided him with the only channel to Washington available, and he took full advantage of it. He admitted quite candidly that he was a socialist, that he had associated and worked with French, Chinese, and Vietnamese communists, but added, "Who else was there to work with?" He labeled himself a "progressive-socialist-nationalist" with an ardent desire to rid his country of foreign domination. He spoke eloquently, not making a speech, but with sincerity, determination, and optimism.

As the clock inside struck the half-hour for 3:30, someone came to the door of the balcony and spoke briefly to Ho. Joyfully clasping his hands before his face, Ho turned to me with a beaming smile and announced, "The Khâm-sai of Cochinchina has just cabled his resignation to the Court. He has officially placed the rule of South Viet Nam into the hands of the Executive Committee for Nam Bo." I did not grasp the import of this news. We had heard the day before that the Viet Minh under the direction of Tran Van Giau had already assumed control there. Ho explained that Bao Dai had until now only announced his "intention" to abdicate. But with the last of the three Viceroys out of office there remained no legal obstacle to his actual abdication. It was obviously a matter for jubilation to Ho, and I could hear excited voices within.

I thought his friends were probably waiting to see him and decided to take my leave. Ho walked me to the door and happily said he would long remember our pleasant afternoon and that he would be pleased if I allowed him to stay in close touch. I said I would be seeing him again and very soon. The driver was waiting and within a few minutes I was back at Maison Gautier.

The United States delegation at the beginning of the Geneva Conference of 1954. The U.S. was unhappy with the settlement that temporarily partitioned Vietnam at the 17th parallel and promised only that they would not disturb the agreement by force. At center foreground is General Walter Bedell Smith, head of the U.S. delegation. UPI/BETTMANN NEWSPHOTOS

CHAPTER 2

Fighting Shy, 1950–1961

In May 1950, just before the Korean War broke out, President Truman authorized a modest program of economic and military aid for the French-backed government of Vietnam. It was a commitment from which the United States could not easily extricate itself. The readings in this section suggest why. President Dwight D. Eisenhower was unwilling to commit American power and prestige to salvage the dismal French military position in Vietnam in 1954, as George Herring and Richard Immerman demonstrate, but Eisenhower's refusal to rescue Dienbienphu did not mean the president was unconcerned with the fate of Vietnam. The Americans were dismayed when the French, in the aftermath of the defeat at Dienbienphu, agreed to partition Vietnam. Ellen Hammer places this American reaction in the context of the Geneva conference and the interests of the other nations represented there. Colonel Edward Lansdale picks up the story in 1955, when he was formally assigned to the U.S. Military Assistance Advisory Group (MAAG) in Saigon. Lansdale, who was reputed to have elevated counterinsurgency warfare to an art form in the Philippines, now worked to help the South Vietnamese leader Ngo Dinh Diem gain control of the southern part of Vietnam. Through Lansdale, the Eisenhower administration endeavored to build a nation out of a temporary ceasefire zone, subverting the intent of the Geneva accord. Although Eisenhower kept the United States for the most part out of a shooting war in Vietnam, one may legitimately ask whether the administration's attitude toward Geneva set the stage for deeper U.S. involvement in the future.

4
Eisenhower, Dulles, and Dienbienphu: "The Day We Didn't Go to War" Revisited

GEORGE C. HERRING AND RICHARD IMMERMAN

America's role in the Dienbienphu crisis of 1954 has been a source of persisting confusion and controversy. In a *Washington Post* story of June 7, 1954, subsequently expanded into a *Reporter* article provocatively entitled "The Day We Didn't Go to War," journalist Chalmers M. Roberts divulged that the Dwight D. Eisenhower administration had committed itself to a massive air strike to relieve the Vietminh siege of the French fortress at Dienbienphu. The United States would have intervened in the Indochina War, Roberts went on, had not the congressional leadership, after a secret meeting on April 3, made intervention conditional on British participation and had not the British refused. In their memoirs British and American officials confirmed some of Roberts's account. French memoirists went further, charging that Secretary of State John Foster Dulles and Admiral Arthur W. Radford, chairman of the Joint Chiefs of Staff (JCS), had proposed an air strike to save Dienbienphu, had even proposed the loan of atomic weapons, and then had callously reneged, sealing France's defeat in the war. On the other hand, administration officials at the time and Eisenhower later insisted that they had never seriously contemplated military intervention in Indochina. Eisenhower conceded only that he had attempted to put together an allied coalition to resist Communist encroachments in Southeast Asia but had been thwarted by the British.[1]

Despite lingering uncertainty about what actually happened, scholars have advanced numerous interpretations of the administration's handling of the crisis. Early writers typically used it to show how a reckless Dulles nearly pushed the passive Eisenhower into war. In the aftermath of Lyndon B. Johnson's massive intervention in Vietnam, however, scholars increasingly praised Eisenhower for his caution and for his involvement of Congress in policy formation. Some writers speculated that he had cleverly used Congress to restrain his more impulsive advisers. Others argued that the open process established by Eisenhower promoted a high level of "multiple advocacy," thereby producing sound policy. Whatever

Herring, George C. and Immerman, Richard H., "Eisenhower, Dulles, and Dienbienphu: 'The Day We Didn't Go to War' Revisited," *Journal of American History*, 71 (Sept. 1984), 343–63. Reprinted by permission.

the perspective, scholars viewed Eisenhower's decision not to intervene as exceptional in the long history or United States escalation in Vietnam.[2]

Recent declassification of an abundance of United States documents permits a new look at one of the most significant episodes of the Eisenhower years. Those documents make clear that the memoirs of the participants are often inaccurate and misleading and that Roberts's standard account, on which most scholars have relied, contains important errors and suffers from the bias of its own sources. The documents compel modification at a number of important points of recent favorable interpretations of Eisenhower's diplomacy.[3]

The Dienbienphu crisis stemmed at least indirectly from Franco-American adoption of the Navarre Plan in September 1953. To prevent the fall of Indochina to the Communist-led Vietminh insurgents, the United States since 1950 had supported France with steadily growing volumes of military and economic assistance. United States officials deplored the cautious, defensive military strategy pursued by France, however, and they feared that as long as France was fighting for essentially colonial goals, it could not win the war. Certain that the Harry S Truman administration had not effectively applied the leverage available to it, Dulles and Eisenhower conditioned further aid on French agreement to fight the war more agressively and to make firm promises of independence for the states of Indochina.[4]

Uneager to expand the war but unwilling to abandon it, the French bent to American pressure. The government of Joseph Laniel vaguely promised to "perfect" Vietnamese independence. The newly appointed commander of French forces in Indochina, General Henri Navarre, drew up a military strategy tailored to United States specifications, proposing to combine his scattered forces and to launch a major offensive in the Red River delta. Although Navarre himself was skeptical that the plan could produce victory, the French government adopted it to gain additional United States aid. Dubious of French intentitions and capabilities, the Eisenhower adminstration nonetheless felt compelled to go along, fearing that otherwise Laniel's government might be replaced by one committed to negotiations.[5]

Navarre abandoned his ill-fated plan before he had even begun to implement it. To parry a Vietminh invasion of Laos, he had to scatter the forces he had just started to combine. As part of a hastily improvised alternative strategy, he established in late 1953 a position at the remote village of Dienbienphu in northwestern Vietnam, where he hoped to lure the Vietminh into a set-piece battle. In a broad valley surrounded by hills as high as one thousand feet, he constructed a garrison ringed with barbed wire and bunkers and dispatched twelve battalions or regulars supported by aircraft and artillery. Vietminh commander Vo Nguyen Giap soon laid siege to the French fortress. By early 1954 twelve thousand of Navarre's elite forces were isolated in a far corner of Vietnam. Although uncertain that his troops could defend themselves against superior Vietminh numbers, Navarre decided to remain.[6]

Shortly after, the contingency Americans had so feared became reality. Facing growing political opposition at home, an uncertain military situation in Vietnam, and a depleted treasury, the Laniel government decided that it must negotiate a settlement. Over Dulles's vigorous protests, it agreed to place the Indochina question on the agenda of an East-West conference scheduled to meet in Geneva, Switzerland, in late April 1954.[7]

These developments generated great concern in Washington. An American military observer reported from Dienbienphu as late as February that the French fortress could "withstand any kind of attack the Vietminh are capable of launching," but United States officials could not ignore the possibility that the garrison might fall, causing a total French collapse. Reports of increased Chinese aid to the Vietminh raised additional fears that, as in Korea, China might intervene directly in the war. In any event, Americans suspected that French war-weariness might lead to a sellout in Geneva. "If the French were completely honest they would get out of Indochina," Dulles remarked, "and we certainly didn't want that." Accordingly, the adminstration searched desperately for means to deter Chinese intervention and to bolster French resistance. Eisenhower sent the French forty bombers and two hundred United States Air Force mechanics to service them. Conceding the risk of expanded involvment, he insisted, "My god, we must not lose Asia—we've got to look the thing right in the face."[8]

The adminstration concurrently began to face the prospect that United States forces might have to be used. Notwithstanding his determination to "keep out men out of these jungles," Eisenhower reminded the National Security Council (NSC) that "we could nevertheless not forget our vital interest in Indochina." He appointed a special committee to examine the circumstances under which directa United States involvment might be required and the means by which it could be made most effective. The study had not been completed by mid-March 1954, but the siege of Dienbienphu and the danger of a French cave-in at Geneva added a sense of urgency. The committee, headed by Under Secretary of State Walter Bedell Smith, had gone so far as to ask the JCS to develop a "concept of operations" for Indochina.[9]

In mid-March the siege tightened. French and American military experts had predicted that the Vietminh would not be able to transport artillery up the hills surrounding the fortress, but by sheer human exertion they did. In a series of attacks beginning on March 13, the Vietminh seized two major hill outposts established by the French to protect the fortress and the airfield below. Heavy Vietminh guns quickly knocked out the airfield, making resupply possible only by parachute drop. The Central Intelligence Agency (CIA) estimated no better than an even chance that the vulnerable French garrison could hold out.[10] It seemed increasingly clear that the United States might have to take drastic steps to save France or, in the event of a French collapse, to continue the struggle for Indochina on its own.

The vist of General Paul Ely to Washington in late March brought these pressing issues to the forefront. The Smith committee had invited the French chief of staff to discuss additional military assistance. It suspected, nevertheless, that he might request intervention. During his initial meetings with Radford and Dulles, Ely estimated a fifty-fifty chance that Dienbienphu might still hold and asked for the loan of twenty-five additional B-26 bombers and American volunteers to fly them. At that point he seems to have been concerned primarily with the threat of Chinese air intervention, and he inquired in writing what the United States would do if China sent aircraft into the war.[11]

Ely's visit took the form of a game of international cat and mouse, graphically revealing the accumulated frustrations of four years of Franco-American collaboration in Indochina. The United States approved Ely's request for the additional bombers (without the pilots), although Radford expressed grave doubts about France's ability to maintain them and use them in combat. When Radford pressed for a larger United States role in training indigenous forces and in determining strategy, Ely complained of the "invading nature" of the Americans and their apparent determination "to control ... everything of importance."[12]

Dulles and Radford responded noncommittally to Ely's query about Chinese intervention. They agreed that they would make no commitments until they "got a lot of answers" from the French on issues that divided the two nations. Dulles informed Ely point-blank that the United States would not invest its prestige except under conditions where military success was likely, which would require France to extend to the United States a "greater degree of partnership" than had prevailed in the past. The result was a tightly qualified "agreed minute" that directed "military authorities [to] push their planning work as far as possible so that there would be not time wasted when and if our governments decided to oppose enemy air intervention over Indochina if it took place."[13]

At Radford's request Ely remained in Washington for one more day, at which time the two men discussed the possibility of an air strike to relieve the siege of Dienbienphu. The idea apparently originated from American and French officers in Saigon. Code-named VULTURE, the plan called for massive night bombing attacks on Vietminh positions by as many as 300 United States aircraft launched from carriers in the region and perhaps from air bases in the Philippines. Who first raised the issue and what commitments resulted are impossible to determine.[14] Ely later declared that Radford had enthusiastically endorsed the plan and had intimated that he had Eisenhower's support. Radford admits telling Ely that within two days of a formal French request as many as 350 United States aircraft could be deployed, but he insists that he made clear that intervention would require a decision at the highest level of government and congressional approval. It is possible, of course, that the two men misunderstood each other. They spoke without an interpreter, Ely's English was not good, and he may have missed or minimized the qualifications Radford says he included. Or the French general may have understood the qualifications quite well and only later professed to have been misled. More likely, Radford was less circumspect than he allows. An Asia-firster in the mold of Douglas MacArthur and a firm believer in air power, he often advocated intervention in Indochina and at times even urged the use of atomic weapons against China. Before his last meeting with Ely, he warned Eisenhower that the United States "must be prepared to act promptly and in force possibly to a frantic and belated request by the French for U.S. intervention." Even if he had included the qualifications, as he late maintained, his obvious zeal for intervention might have left the impression that formal authority could be readily obtained, an impression, given certain of Eisenhower's comments, Radford probably believed.[15]

In the week after Ely left Washington, however, Radford was unable to generate support for VULTURE even among the JCS. Acting on his own initiative, he called a special meeting of the JCS on March 31 to consider the "necessity or desirability" of recommending to the president that the United States offer France naval and air units for use in Indochina. Army Chief of Staff Matthew B. Ridgway objected, arguing that the formulation of policy was "outside the proper scope of authority of the JCS." Undaunted, Radford came back two days later with a formal request from the secretary of defense for the JCS view on what the United States should do if the French asked for naval and air intervention. Only Air Force Chief of Staff Nathan F. Twining responded positively, and he insisted on conditions the French were unlikely to accept, including agreement to American training of indigenous forces and a grant of "true sovereignty" to the Indochinese states. With varying degrees of intensity, reflecting to some extent the interests of their respective services, the other chiefs warned that air intervention at Dienbienphu would not decisively affect the outcome of the war and questioned whether the limited tactical gains would be worth the risks of direct involvement.[16]

Among top civilian leaders there was no enthusiasm for air intervention at Dienbienphu. Vice-President Richard M. Nixon had been frequently cited as an advocate of intervention—and he was—but he did not play a consequential role in shaping policy. Dulles, often portrayed as a "hawk" in this crisis as in others, was in fact quite cautious. Deeply concerned that the Chinese might intervene or that France might hand Indochina over to the Communists at Geneva, the secretary was prepared to take risks in Indochina. He seems not to have been persuaded that VULTURE was either feasible or necessary, however. He stated that if the Chinese intervened he would prefer such things as "harassing tactics from Formosa and along the Chinese seacoast," measures, he added, that "would be more readily within our natural facilities than actually fighting in Indochina."[17]

Eisenhower's position is equally interesting, if characteristically elusive. He is typically depicted as at least a closet dove in this crisis, and he later dismissed VULTURE as military folly. Indeed, as early as 1951 he had entered in his diary, "I am convinced that no military victory is possible in that kind of theater [Indochina]." On March 24, nevertheless, he told Dulles that he would not "wholly exclude the possibility of a single strike, if it were almost certain this would produce decisive results." A week later he alluded to the idea again, adding that such an operation would have to be covert and that "we would have to deny it forever." The president was probably thinking out loud. Like Dulles, he seems never to have been persuaded that the plan would work, and he was equally opposed to intervention in any form in the absence of satisfactory military and political agreements with France. In the week after Ely's departure, VULTURE was not discussed seriously at the top levels, and the administration never made a commitment to it.[18]

Still, Eisenhower and Dulles recognized that something must be done, and between March 24 and April 1 they began to formulate an appropriate response. They proceeded with extreme caution, keeping numerous options open and covering their tracks so well that they baffled contemporaries and future scholars. Dulles labeled their plan "United Action." Based on a regional security program he had proposed under Truman when negotiating the peace treaty (Treaty of San Francisco, 1951) with Japan, United Action was designed to meet the many uncertainties and dilemmas of the Indochina crisis. It reflected the perceived lessons of the Koran War as well as the administration's concept of strategic deterrence and its New Look defense policy. The keystone of the plan was the creation of a coalition composed of the United States, Great Britain, France, Australia, New Zealand, Thailand, the Philippines, and the Associated States of Indochina and committed to the defense of Indochina and of the rest of Southeast Asia against the Communist menace. The mere establishment of such a coalition accompanied by stern warnings to the Communists might be sufficient to bolster the French will to resist and to deter Chinese intervention, thus making outside intervention unnecessary. It is even plausible, as one of Dulles's top aids later suggested, that United Action was merely a grand charade of deterrence and that Eisenhower and Dulles never seriously considered United States military involvement.[19]

It is more plausible that United Action was designed to ensure that if the United States intervened it would do so under favorable circumstances. The evidence indicates that although the administration never committed itself to intervention during the Dienbienphu crisis, that option was left open to meet the contingencies of Chinese intervention, a French military collapse, or, preferably, a breakdown of the Geneva negotiations and a continuation of the war. Eisenhower and Dulles agreed that the United States should go in only as part of a genuinely collective effort and that United States ground forces must not become bogged down in Asia. United Action would provide a legal basis for collective action. A multilateral effort would remove the taint of a war for colonialism and would provide additional leverage to force the French to share political and military decision making. If, on the other hand, France pulled out, United Action would ensure that the United States did not have to fight alone. In keeping with the New Look doctrine, local and regional forces would bear the brunt of the ground fighting while the Americans did those things Dulles proclaimed "we can do better," providing air and naval support, furnishing money and supplies, and training indigenous troops.[20]

The major problem was time. The Geneva conference was only a month away. Ely's query about a United States response to Chinese intervention needed to be answered promptly if it was to have the proper political effect in France. And on March 30 the Vietminh initiated the second stage of the battle for Dienbienphu, launching withering artillery barrages and a series of humanwave assaults against the hill outposts that constituted the outer defenses of the fortress. The French held the lines and even managed successful counterattacks at some points, but the decisive battle seemed to be underway. The fate of the fortress and the outcome of the war might be settled in a matter of weeks.[21]

Eisenhower and Dulles hence moved rapidly to lay the groundwork for United Action. In a March 29 speech designed to "puncture the sentiment for appeasement before Geneva," Dulles publicly unveiled the concept in deliberately vague terms. He warned that the Chinese now supported the Vietminh "by all means short of open invasion" and that Communist success in Indochina would lead to further aggression in Southeast Asia, the loss of which could have disastrous consequences for the entire free world. Using words that his aide Robert Bowie described as "deliberately picked" to sound "menacing without committing anybody to anything," the secretary declared that the possibility of a Communist conquest of Southeast Asia "should not be passively accepted but should be met by united action."[22]

Having raised the possibility of intervention, Eisenhower and Dulles next consulted with the congressional leadership. The president has been rightly praised for involving Congress at that stage, but his move was based as much on political exigency as on abstract respect for the Constitution. The administration carefully monitored public opinion, which overwhelmingly opposed United States military involvement. Further, Eisenhower had only the barest majorities in both houses (48-47-1 in the Senate; 221-212-1 in the House). The Republican right wing had been notoriously unreliable, and the Army-McCarthy hearings were soon to begin. Although the Democrats had supported the president faithfully on foreign policy through much of 1953, bipartisanship had begun to erode. Some Democrats were in a vengeful mood. Recalling the vicious attacks on Truman and Dean Acheson, Hubert H. Humphrey warned Dulles, "As ye [sow], so shall ye reap, and, believe me, you have so sown and so you reap." By the time of the Dienbienphu crisis, even moderate Democrats had begun to challenge the administration's Indochina policy. Congressional restlessness had been made abundantly clear in February when Democrats and Republicans attacked the administration for failing to consult before sending United States Air Force mechanics to Vietnam. To calm the legislators, the president had publicly pledged that the United States would not become involved in war "unless it is a result of the constitutional process . . . placed upon Congress to declare it."[23]

Eisenhower and Dulles perceived that whichever way they went they faced problems with Congress. Should they do nothing and Indochina fall, right-wing Republicans might join Democrats in condemning them for losing additional territory to Communism. If United States intervention were required, however, there would be little time for consultation and deliberation, and the experience of Korea left no doubt that intervention without some kind of congressional authorization would leave the administration politically vulnerable. Eisenhower thus had to implicate Congress at an early stage. "It might be necessary to move into the battle of Dien Bien Phu in order to keep it from going against us," he said in late March, "and in that case I will be calling in the Democrats as well as our Republican leaders to inform them."[24] Remaining cautiously in the background, the president had Dulles and Radford arrange an unusual Saturday morning meeting with the legislative leadership on April 3.

Recently declassified documents make clear that notwithstanding Eisenhower's remark he did not seek authority for an immediate air strike to relieve the siege of Dienbienphu, as Roberts and others have long argued. At a top-level White House meeting on April 2, an obviously isolated Radford conceded that the outcome at Dienbienphu would be "determined within a matter of hours, and the situation was not one which called for any U.S. participation." The administration sought, rather, congressional endorsement of a broad, blank-check resolution, not unlike the Formosa Resolution of 1955, that would give the chief executive discretionary authority to use United States air and sea power to prevent the "extension and expansion" of Communist aggression in Southeast Asia. The draft resolution that Dulles brought to the White House and that Eisenhower approved stipulated that the authority would terminate on June 30, 1955, and would in no way "derogate from the authority of Congress to declare war."[25]

Eisenhower and Dulles sought the resolution primarily to meet the immediate needs of United Action. Dulles indicated that he wanted the resolution mainly as a "deterrent" and to strengthen his hand in upcoming discussions with representatives of allied nations. The administration was also notably discreet in handling its presentation. Eisenhower insisted that the "tactical procedure should be to develop first the thinking of Congressional leaders without actually submitting in the first instance a resolution drafted by ourselves."[26]

Dulles followed the script, but the drama took a direction the administration had not intended. Radford briefed the legislators on Dienbienphu, perhaps mistakenly convincing them that the White House wanted to intervene immediately. Dulles then portrayed the threat to Indochina in the gravest terms and urged that the president be given "Congressional backing so that he could use air and sea power in the area if he felt it necessary in the interest of national security." No one challenged the assessment of the crisis, but the legislators, particularly Democratic senators Richard B. Russell and Johnson, insisted that there must be "no more

Koreas with the United States furnishing 90 percent of the manpower" and that there must be firm commitments of support from allies, specifically Great Britain. Dulles persisted, affirming that he had no intention of sending ground forces to Indochina and indicating that he could more easily gain commitments from other nations if he could specify what the United States would do. The congressmen were not swayed. "Once the flag is committed," they warned, "the use of land forces would surely follow." Sharing fully the administration's distrust of France, they also insisted that the United States must not go to war for colonialism. They would only agaree that if "satisfactory commitments" could be obtained from Britain and other allies to intervene collectively and from France to "internationalize" the war and to grant the Indochinese independence, a resolution authorizing the president to employ United States forces "could be obtained."[27]

Although less dramatic than often assumed, the outcome of the meeting was significant. Neither Eisenhower nor Dulles differed fundamentally with the congressmen on the form intervention ought to take, but the conditions did tie their hands by virtually eliminating any possibility of unilateral intervention, an option that they had not entirely ruled out. The conditions weakened Dulles's position with allied leaders by requiring the allies' commitment prior to action by Congress, an order the administration would have preferred to reverse. Most important, they made collective intervention dependent on British support and French concessions, each of which would be difficult to obtain. Eisenhower and Dulles admitted that the meeting raised some "serious problems."[28]

Ironically, at the very time the congressmen were setting guidelines for United States intervention, the French were concluding that Dienbienphu could be saved only by a United States air strike. Navarre had originally opposed United States involvement, fearing that it might provoke direct Chinese intervention. In the aftermath of the Vietminh offensive of early April, however, he revised his estimate, cabling the French government on April 4 that an air strike might spare the garrison if executed within the following week. After an emergency meeting that night, Foreign Minister Georges Bidault requested VULTURE, emphasizing that the extensive presence of Chinese matériel and advisers met the conditions under which United States involvement had been discussed by Radford and Ely.[29]

It seems unlikely that Eisenhower and Dulles would have approved the request under any circumstances, but the conditions imposed by the congressmen clinched the decision and probably provided a convenient excuse. Manifesting no sense of disappointment, they agreed that approving the request without "some kind of arrangement getting support of Congress, would be completely unconstitutional and indefensible." Expressing some annoyance with Radford for leading the French to believe that the United States would respond positively, Eisenhower instructed Dulles to see "if anything else can be done" to help the French. But, he concluded firmly, "we cannot become engaged in war."[30]

While the president and the secretary of state were setting policy, the NSC machinery was finally wrapping up the studies launched months earlier. The Smith committee report, dated April 5, recommended that the United States oppose any political settlement at Geneva and seek nothing less than a "military victory" in Indochina, using its own forces if necessary. An NSC planning board study, although hastily revised to incorporate the requirements of April 3, recommended that formal decisions about intervention ought to be reached at once and included a detailed annex itemizing the number and types of forces that might be employed in Indochina should intervention be required.[31]

Not surprisingly, the NSC refused to go as far as either study recommended. Ridgway vigorously objected to the planning board proposals, arguing that, if naval and air forces were used, ground troops would inevitably be required and insisting that the number of troops specified in the annex would represent only the beginning of what might become a huge commitment.[32] Although Ridgway later claimed a decisive influence on policy making, his opposition only reinforced prior decisions. At a meeting on April 6, the NSC postponed a recommendation on military intervention. "There was no possibility whatever of U.S. unilateral intervention in Indochina," Eisenhower declared "with great emphasis" at the outset, "and we had best face that fact." The NSC thus agreed that every effort ought to be made to create a "regional grouping" to defend Southeast Asia and that France ought to be pressed to grant full independence to the Associated States of Indochina. If those conditions could be met, the White House would seek congressional authorization for intervention. In the meantime, "military and mobilization planning" for possible later intervention "should be promptly initiated."[33]

During the following week the administration prepared the way for United Action. Dulles conferred with the British and the French ambassadors, and Eisenhower wrote a personal letter to Prime Minister Winston Churchill urging British support for a coalition that would be "willing to fight" to defend Southeast Asia. At a news conference on April 7, the president outlined what came to be known as the "domino theory," explaining that if Indochina fell the rest of Southeast Asia would "go over very quickly," with "incalculable" losses to the free world. A carrier strike force already on station in the South China Sea was moved to within one hundred miles of Hainan island and began air reconnaissance of Chinese airfields and staging areas.[34]

On April 10 Dulles traveled to Europe for the first round of three weeks of frantic shuttle diplomacy. Stopping first in London, he encountered immediate opposition. The British did not share the American view that the loss of Indochina would threaten all of Southeast Asia. Convinced that France retained sufficient influence to salvage a reasonable settlement at Geneva, they feared that outside intervention would destroy any hope of a negotiated settlement and perhaps would even provoke war with China. Most important, they had no inclination to entangle Britain in a war that could not be won. The persistent Dulles could get nothing more than Foreign Secretary Anthony Eden's grudging assent to participate in immediate multilateral talks to establish a common bargaining position at Geneva, with a coalition to be included on the agenda.[35]

Dulles met further obstacles in Paris. He held out the prospect of United States intervention but only on condition that France resist a negotiated settlement at Geneva, agree to fight in Indochina indefinitely, concede to the United States a greater role in planning strategy and in training indigenous troops, and accept Vietnamese demands for complete independence. Like Eden, French Foreign Minister Bidault insisted that nothing should be done to jeopardize the success of the Geneva negotiations. He also indicated that French public opinion would not support continuation of the war if the ties between the Associated States of Indochina and France were severed, and he made plain French opposition to internationalizing the war. As from the British, Dulles could obtain from the French an agreement only to join preliminary talks to be held in Washington on April 20.[36]

By the time Dulles returned to the United States, the administration's delicate strategy faced rising opposition at home. The possibility of some kind of intervention in Indochina elicited from members of Congress increasing protest about the danger of joining a war for French colonialism. In an April 6 speech that won praise from both sides of the aisle, Democratic Senator John F. Kennedy warned that victory could not be won so long as the French remained. Echoing Kennedy's sentiments, Senators Estes Kefauver, Wayne Morse, and Michael J. ("Mike") Mansfield demanded that France clarify its intentions regarding independence for Indochina. On April 7 Senator Henry Jackson hit closer to the point bothering many in Congress when he demanded that the administration reveal its own intentions in Indochina.[37]

The day after Dulles's return, a high administration source, subsequently identified as Vice-President Nixon, set the pot boiling again. Speaking before the American society of Newspaper Editors, Nixon, answering a "hypothetical" question about how the United States would respond to a French collapse in Indochina, affirmed that "we must take the risk by putting our boys in." Regarded at the time and since as a trial balloon, Nixon's remarks had not been authorized, and press secretary James Hagerty deemed them "foolish." Some administration officials rationalized that at least they might keep the Communists guessing, but the State Department, acting on instructions from Eisenhower, hurriedly put out an ambiguous statement to "clarify" United States policy without "cutting the ground from under Nixon."[38]

Nixon's indiscretion immensely complicated Dulles's task. Receiving extensive publicity in Europe, Nixon's remarks conveyed an impression of American belligerency at the very time Dulles was trying to curry British and French support. Congress reacted so adversely that the secretary feared that on the eve of the Geneva conference Congress might attempt to foreclose his options, weakening his hand in dealing with allies and adversaries.[39]

Worse, two days before the scheduled meeting with representatives of the proposed coalition, the British indicated that they would not attend. Dulles speculated that Eden had been swayed by India's neutralist prime minister, Jawaharlal Nehru; but the British may also have been alarmed by the implications of the Nixon statement, and they may have recognized belatedly that attendance at the meeting would trap them into endorsing Dulles's policy. Whatever the cause, the decision struck a body blow at United Action. An outraged Dulles reluctantly agreed to a hastily drawn compromise by which the British would attend the meeting provided that it dealt only with Korea. The meeting had been designed at least in part to signal the Communists of the threat of allied intervention in Indochina, however, and the change deprived it of its significance.[40]

The administration's strategy threatened from several directions, Dulles hastened back to Europe for a North Atlantic Treaty Organization (NATO) council session. The issue of United States air intervention at Dienbienphu immediately emerged. The situation of the French fortress had become perilous. Efforts to retake the inner hill positions had failed, costing France all its reserves. The beleaguered garrison had been reduced to about three thousand able-bodied fighting men, and resupply was virtually impossible. On April 22 Bidault, whom Dulles described as "totally exhausted mentally," hinted at French willingness to internationalize the war and warned that nothing short of "massive air intervention by the U.S." could save Dienbienphu. The following day the foreign minister showed Dulles an "urgent" cable from Navarre indicating that in the absence of an air strike Navarre would have no choice but to order a cease-fire.[41]

Bidault's later claim that at that point Dulles offered him the loan of two atomic weapons seems highly implausible. No other evidence of the alleged offer exists in available French or American sources. Dulles did not have the authority to take such a step, and for him to have so exceeded his prerogatives would have been inconsistent with his usual conduct and with the caution he displayed throughout the Dienbienphu crisis. Dulles had shown little interest in JCS contingency plans that called for atomic bombs should the United States intervene. Eisenhower did discuss the possibility of lending France "new weapons" but not until April 30, while Dulles was in Europe. Shocked when he learned of the charges, the secretary could only surmise that as a result of Bidault's highly agitated state of mind or of problems of translation, Bidault had interpreted as an offer a random statement that United States policy now treated nuclear weapons as conventional. Dulles may have been correct. Bidault attempted to blame the Dienbienphu debacle on his American counterpart, and he may have used the alleged offer to damage the reputation of a man he came to despise thoroughly.[42]

Whatever the case, Bidault's second request favor United States air intervention sparked a week of the most intense and nimble diplomatic maneuvering in recent history. Hoping to save Dienbienphu and to strengthen their bargaining position at Geneva, the French sought an American air strike without incurring commitments that would restrict their freedom of action. Dulles could not, of course, commit the United States without first extracting agreements from both Britain and France. In any event, he was less concerned with the immediate situation at Dienbienphu than with the long-term defense of Southeast Asia,and he sought to keep France in the war and to use the opening provided by Bidault's overture to revive the flagging prospects of United Action. Unwilling to enter the war under any circumstances, Britain attempted to restrain the United States and to keep France committed to a negotiated settlement without provoking an irreparable split in the alliance.

From Dulles's standpoint, Britain was the key, and on April 23 and April 24 he relentlessly pressured Eden. He warned that the French would not continue the war without assurance of British and American support and insisted that the mere knowledge that a "common defense system was in prospect" would deter the Communists and would strengthen the allied hand at the Geneva conference. If Britain agreed, he added, the president would seek immediate congressional authorization for United States intervention. When Eden expressed doubt that an air strike would accomplish anything, Radford, who had joined Dulles in Paris, declared that at least it would "stablize the situation." If the United States intervened, he went on, Navarre might be relieved of his command, and Americans from "behind the scenes" could exercise a "considerable voice" in the conduct of the war. To calm Eden's expressed fears of World War III, Radford minimized the risks of Soviet or Chinese intervention. The Americans also played down the anticipated cost of British participation, indicating that nothing more would be asked than the use of several air squadrons from Malaya and Hong Kong. Making clear his continued personal opposition, Eden agreed to return to London to consult with Churchill.[43]

Even with the fate of Dienbienphu in the balance, the United States and France could not bridge the vast gap that had long separated them. France had finally agreed to Vietnamese independence, but the question of internationalization of the war remained unsettled. Moreover, the two nations differed sharply in their approaches to the short-term issues. Bidault warned Dulles that making intervention conditional on British participation would merely cause delays when speed was of the essence and added that the British contribution would not "amount to much of anything." To secure an immediate air strike, he cleverly played on established American fears. If Dienbienphu fell, he warned, the French people would insist on getting out of the war and would have no use for a coalition, which they would view as a sinister means of keeping them fighting indefinitely.[44]

Not ruling out intervention while scrupulously avoiding anything that could be interpreted as a commitment, Eisenhower and Dulles urged Bidault to stand firm. In a carefully worded letter of April 24, Dulles informed the French foreign minister that an air strike would constitute "active United States belligerency" and would therefore require congressional authorization. That could not be obtained within a matter of hours, he added, and probably not at all except within the framework of United Action. He went on to insist that the fall of Dienbienphu need not cause a total French collapse—indeed, the Vietminh had incurred such heavy losses during the siege that the overall military balance would favor France. Dulles held out the prospect of future support through "collective action." Concurrently Eisenhower wrote Laniel, reminding him that France had "suffered temporary defeats" in the past and had still prevailed.[45]

Anticipating a negative British response, the French pressed for unilateral United States action. Bidault informed Dulles that French military experts had concluded that a massive air strike could deliver a "decisive blow" because the Vietminh had so many men and so much matériel concentrated around Dienbienphu. The French pleaded for "armed intervention" through "executive action" or some other "constitutional way to help," warning of ominous consequences to the war in Indochina and to Franco-American relations if nothing were done.[46]

Eisenhower and Dulles peremptorily rejected the French proposal. Dulles advised the administration that because the security of the United States was not directly threatened, the political risk could in no way be justified. Air intervention might not save Dienbienphu, he continued, and the United States could not be certain that France would continue the fight. Intervention without Britain would "gravely strain" relations with Australia and New Zealand as well as with Britain. There would not be time to "arrange proper political understandings" with the French, and "once our prestige is committed in battle, our negotiating position in these matters would be almost negligible." If necessary, it would be better to let Dienbienphu fall than to intervene "under the present circumstances." Eisenhower agreed. Years later, he contemptuously recalled Bidault's last-minute proposals to "solve . . . our 'constitutional problems' and launch a unilateral air strike—on their terms."[47]

Eden settled the issue on April 25, when he delivered the unwelcome, but not unexpected, news. Not even the "diplomatic" language of a memorandum of conversation can conceal the tension that followed. Eden insisted that an air strike might not be decisive and added that it would be a "great mistake" in terms of world opinion. He assured Dulles that Britain would give France "all possible diplomatic support" toward reaching a satisfactory political settlement at the Geneva conference. If such a settlement could be obtained, he would join the United States in guaranteeing it and would agree to immediate discussions about a collective effort to defend the rest of Southeast Asia. If not, Britain would cooperate with the United States in exploring the possibilities of United Action. Dulles protested vigorously that the British position might lead to total French capitulation. To write off Indochina and to believe the rest of

Southeast Asia could be held would be foolish, he argued. Eden retorted that "none of us in London believe that intervention in Indochina can do anything."[48]

Nor did direct appeals sway Churchill. The prime minister told Radford on April 26 that since the British people had let India go they could not be expected to give their lives to hold Indochina for France. At a formal dinner that evening, the old warrior went into a long and emotional discourse, asserting that the Indochina War could be won only by using "that horrible thing"—the atomic bomb—and noting Britain's vulnerability in the event of a nuclear war. "I have known many reverses myself," he concluded. "I have not given in. I have suffered Singapore, Hong-Kong, Tobruk; the French will have Dien Bien Phu." The British would not be drawn into what they feared would be "Radford's war against China."[49]

The British and French responses to the crisis infuriated American leaders. Privately, Eisenhower vented his rage with his allies. The British had shown a "woeful unawareness" of the risks "we run in that region," he confided to his diary. The French had used "weasel words" in promising independence to the Vietnamese, he wrote an old friend, and "through this one reason as much as anything else have suffered reverses that have been really inexcusable." They wanted the Americans "to come in as junior partners and provide materials, etc., while they themselves retain authority in that region," and he would not go along with them "on any such notion."[50]

For several days French and American officials toyed with various expedients. Dulles studied the possibility of proceeding without Britain and working for United Action with France, the ANZUS (Australia, New Zealand, United States) Pact, and the Associated States of Indochina. He also pondered the feasibility of having French forces withdrawn to defensible enclaves, where they could be supported by United States air and sea power, with the United States assuming responsibility for training indigenous forces. The French government warned Dulles that something must be done to compensate for the anticipated blow to French morale, imploring Dulles to create ad hoc machinery for allied consultation on measures to defend Southeast Asia or, as a last resort, to sponsor a public announcement that nations with vital interests in the area were consulting. French and American military officials explored the possibility of using United States C-119s, with American crews, to fly supplies and ammunition into the war zones to support a last-ditch effort to relieve Dienbienphu.[51]

None of those options produced anything of substance, however, and after Eisenhower told the American public that the United States must steer a course between the "unattainable" and the "unacceptable," the decision against immediate intervention was formalized at a long and heated NSC meeting on April 29. The possibility of an air strike was reconsidered, and several of the conferees, led by Harold Stassen, administrator of the Foreign Operations Administration, proposed that the United States intervene unilaterally and with ground troops if necessary to retrieve the situation. Vice-President Nixon suggested the establishment of a "Pacific Coalition" without Britain and the dispatch of a United States Air Force contingent to make plain American determination to resist further encroachments. The Communists must be put on notice that "this is as far as you go, and no further."[52]

As with the April 6 meeting, the result was both inconclusive and anticlimactic. Eisenhower firmly reiterated that unilateral military intervention would be impossible. "Without allies ... the leader is just an adventurer like Genghis Khan," he asserted. Moreover, "if our allies were going to fall away in any case, it might be better for the United States to leap over the smaller obstacles and hit the biggest one [the Soviet Union] with all the power we had." After extended discussion the NSC decided to "hold up for a time being any military action on Indo-China" pending developments at Geneva. In the meantime, the United States ought to explore the possibilities of establishing a coalition without Britain while urging France to hold on in the hope that "some formula may be found which would permit additional aid of some sort." In brief, there would be "no intervention based on executive action."[53]

The American decision sealed Dienbienphu's doom. The hopelessly outnumbered defenders finally surrendered on May 7 after fifty-five days of heroic, but futile, resistance. The attention of the belligerents and of interested outside parties immediately shifted to Geneva, where the following day the Indochina phase of the conference was to begin.

The fall of Dienbienphu did not end discussion of United States intervention in Indochina. Throughout the first weeks of the Geneva conference, Dulles continued to promote United Action, hoping that Communist recalcitrance would force the French to accept American support on American terms. This time the plan was contingent merely on British acquiescence. The State Department drafted another joint congressional resolution authorizing the president to employ air and naval forces in Asia to assist friendly governments "to maintain their authority ... against subversive and revolutionary efforts fomented by Communist regimes." Administration officials even drew up a detailed working paper outlining the day-to-day measures that would be taken and calling for a presidential request on June 2 for congressional backing. French and American military officials discussed possible military collaboration, and the JCS developed detailed plans of operation.[54]

The United States and France still could not agree on the terms of United States intervention. The Eisenhower administration insisted on an unqualified French commitment to internationalize the war. Although Eisenhower privately conceded a willingness to use marines under certain contingencies, he would formally agree only to use naval and air forces in Indochina. Consenting merely to "discuss" the conditions proposed by the United States, France added unacceptable conditions of its own, including an advance commitment from the United States to use ground forces and a promise of full-fledged intervention if China entered the war. The talks ended in mid-June when the Laniel government fell and was replaced by a government headed by Pierre Mendés-France and committed to a negotiated settlement. From that point, the Eisenhower administration devoted its efforts to attaining the best possible settlement at Geneva and to salvaging what it could in Southeast Asia.[55]

The evidence presented here permits firm conclusions about the role of the United States in the Dienbienphu crisis. Contrary to Robert's view, the Eisenhower administration clearly was at no point committed to an air strike at Dienbienphu. Even when faced with a total French collapse in the frantic days of late April, the administration did not deviate from the position it had staked out before Dulles and Radford met with congressional leaders. At the same time, Eisenhower and Dulles seem to have been much more willing to intervene militarily than the president later indicated in his memoirs. United Action was certainly part bluff, but it also involved a willingness to commit United States military power if conditions warranted it and if the proper arrangements could be made.

The praise accorded Eisenhower for consulting with Congress seems overstated. The political situation left him little choice but to consult, and in any event his intent was to manipulate Congress into giving him a broad grant of authority not unlike that which President Johnson secured in 1964. Implicating Congress in the Dienbienphu decisions protected the administration's domestic flank, but it represented at best a hollow victory. Instead of a blank check, the administration got a tightly drawn contract, and Dulles later conceded that Congress had "hamstrung" his policy.

Because of congressional restrictions, British rejection was decisive in the defeat of United Action, but Franco-American differences played a larger role than scholars have recognized. Long divided on Indochina, the two nations never came close to agreeing on the form United States intervention ought to take, on their respective roles in the proposed coalition, or even on the purposes of the war. It seems likely, therefore, that had other conditions been met, Franco-American divisions might still have prevented United States intervention.

Recent praise for the decision-making process may also be misplaced. The NSC structure encouraged a full review of policy and a high level of multiple advocacy and team building, but what is striking about the Dienbienphu crisis is the extent to which the formal machinery was peripheral to the actual decision making. The NSC role was restricted to planning, but even in that realm it consistently lagged behind the unfolding of events in Indochina.[56]

Regarding the quality of the decision, there seems little reason to quarrel with the view that the administration acted wisely in staying out of war in 1954. It may deserve credit only for making a virtue of necessity, however, and after the Geneva conference it made political commitments to South Vietnam fraught with fateful long-range consequences. The "day we didn't go to war" merely postponed for a decade large-scale United States military involvement in Vietnam, and the decision not to intervene militarily may well loom as less important than the political commitments made after the fall of Dienbienphu.

NOTES

1. *Washington Post*, June 7, 1954, pp. 1,4; Chalmers M. Roberts, "The Day We Didn't Go to War," *Reporter*, 11 (Sept. 14, 1954), 31–35; Anthony Eden, *Full Circle: The Memoirs of Anthony Eden* (Boston, 1960), 100–119; Matthew B. Ridgway, *Soldier: The Memoirs of Matthew B. Ridgway* (New York, 1956), 275–78; Richard M. Nixon, *RN: The Memoirs of Richard Nixon* (New York, 1978), 150–55; Arthur W. Radford, *From Pearl Harbor to Vietnam: The Memoirs of Admiral Arthur W. Radford*, ed. Stephen Jurika, Jr. (Stanford, 1980), 398–406; Henry Navarre, *Agonie de L'Indochina (1953–1954)* (Paris, 1956), 242–46; Joseph Laniel, *Le drame Indochinois: De Dien-Bien-Phu au pari de Genéve* (Paris, 1957), 82–89; Paul Ely, *Mémoires: L'Indochine dans la tourmente* (Paris, 1964), 76–98; Georges Bidault, *Resistance: The Political Autobiography of Georges Bidault*, trans. Marianne Sinclair (London, 1967), 192–200; "Did U.S. Almost Get into War?" *U.S. News and World Report*, June 18, 1954, pp. 35–38; Dwight D. Eisenhower, *Mandate for Change 1953–1956* (Garden City, N.Y., 1963) 332–75. For evidence that the *U.S. News and World Report* story was planted by the administration and represented an official response to Chalmers M. Roberts's story, see John Foster Dulles, telephone conversation with Carl McCardle, July 23, 1954, Telephone Conversations series, "July 1–August 31, 1954 (3)," John Foster Dulles Papers (Dwight D. Eisenhower Library, Abilene, Kans.).

2. Bernard B. Fall, *Hell in a Very Small Place: The Siege of Dien Bien Phu* (Philadelphia, 1967), 297; David Halberstam, *The Best and the Brightest* (New York, 1972), 141; Leslie H. Gelb and Richard K. Betts, *The Irony of Vietnam: The System Worked* (Washington, 1979), 57; Alexamder L. George, *Presidential Decisionmaking in Foreign Policy: The Effective Use of Information and Advice* (Boulder, 1980), 152–54, 191–208, 236; Charles R. Scribner, "The Eisenhower and Johnson Administrations' Decisionmaking on Vietnamese Intervention: A Study of Contrasts" (Ph.D. diss., University of California, Santa Barbara, 1980), 17–20; Melvin Gurtov, *The First Vietnam Crisis: Chinese Communist Strategy and United States Involvement, 1953–1954* (New York, 1967), 144–45; Robert A. Divine, *Eisenhower and the Cold War* (New York, 1981), 39–51; Melanie Sue Billings-Yun, "Decision against War: Eisenhower and Dien Bien Phu, 1954" (Ph. D. diss., Harvard University, 1982).

3. Roberts has since divulged that he got much of his information from congressional Democrats, especially Rep. John W. McCormack of Massachusetts. Chalmers M. Roberts, *First Rough Draft: A Journalist's Journal of Our Times* (New York, 1973), 114–15.

4. George C. Herring, *America's Longest War: The United States and Vietnam, 1950–1975* (New York, 1979), 15–25.

5. For an extended discussion of Franco-American collaboration in Indochina and the orgins of the Navarre Plan, see *ibid.*, 9–23. Robert R. Bowie, an aide to Dwight D. Eisenhower, admitted that the adminstration viewed the plan as a "last long shot." Robert R. Bowie interviewed by Richard H. Immerman, Oct. 29, 1981 (in Immerman's possession).

6. Fall, *Hell in a Very Small Place*. 1–52.

7. Herring, *America's Longest War*, 27–28.

8. Report of Special U.S. Mission to Indochina, Feb. 5, 1954, "Project 'Clean Up,' Indochina," Records of the White House Office of the Special Assistant for National Security Affairs (Gordon Gray, Robert Cutler, Henry R. McPhee, and Andrew J. Goodpaster), 1953–61 (Dwight D. Eisenhower Librart); *Foreign Relations of the United States, 1952–1954* (5 vols., Washington, 1979-), XIII, pt. 1, p. 519; Eisenhower, *Mandate for Change*, 341; Gurtov, *First Vietnam Crisis*, 69; James C. Hagerty Diary, Feb. 7, 1954, James C. Hagerty Papers (Dwight D. Eisenhower Library).

9. *Foreign Relations of the United States, 1952–1954*, XIII, pt. 1, p. 952; Radford, *From Pearl Harbor to Vietnam*, 389–90; *The Pentagon Papers: The Defense Department History of United States Decisionmaking on Vietnam, Senator Gravel Edition* (4 vols., Boston, 1971), I, 89–90. An appendage of the National Security Council (NSC), the special committee established a working group under retired Gen. Graves B. Erskine of the Department of Defense. *Ibid.*, 90.

10. Herring, *America's Longest War*, 29; John Forster Dulles, telephone conversation with Allen Dulles, March 16, 1954, Telephone Conversations series, "March 1–April 30, 1954 (3)," Dulles Papers.

11. Radford, *From Pearl Harbor to Vietnam*, 390–91; Ely, *Mémoires*, 59–62; *Foreign Relations of the United States, 1952–1954*, XIII, pt. 1, pp. 1133–34; memorandum of conversation, Radford, Ely, and Dulles, March 23, 1954, file 751G.00/3-2354, Records of the Department of State, RG 59 (National Archives); *Pentagon Papers*, I, 458–59.

12. *Pentagon Papers*, I 458–59.

13. *Ibid.*, 460; John Foster Dulles, telephone conversation with Arthur W. Radford, March 25, 1954, Telephone Conversations series, "March 1–April 30, 1954 (3)," Dulles Papers; memorandum of conversation, Radford, Ely, and Dulles, March 23, 1954, file 751G.00/3-2354, Records of the Department of State; John Foster Dulles, memorandum of conversation with Dwight D. Eisenhower, March 24, 1954, box 222, Lot 64D199, *ibid.*, Radford, *From Pearl Harbor to Vietnam*, 394.

14. Laniel, *Le drame Indochinois*, 82–88. Paul Ely states that Arthur W. Radford raised the offer unsolicited, but Radford insists that Ely raised the issue, indicating that the French did not seek an American air strike at that time. Further, the summary of his discussions with Ely dated March 29 that Radford forwarded to Walter Bedell Smith's special committee omits any mention of that March 26 meeting when they signed the minute, which underwent several drafts. Ely, *Mémoires*, 83–84; Radford, *From Pearl Harbor to Vietnam*, 392–95; *Pentagon Papers*, I, 455–58. For previous drafts of the minute, see 091 "Indochina" file, Records of the Joint Chiefs of Staff, RG 218 (National Archives).

15. Ely, *Mémoires*, 66–68; Radford, *From Pearl Harbor to Vietnam*, 392–94, 435–36; *Pentagon Papers*, I, 460; Herbert S. Parmet, *Eisenhower and the American Crusades* (New York, 1972), 296; George W. Anderson, Jr., interview by Immerman, April 17, 1981 (in Immerman's possession); *Foreign Relations of the United States, 1952–1954*, XIII, pt. 1, pp. 947–53. The day before Radford met with Ely to discuss VULTURE, Eisenhower suggested that "this might be the moment to begin to explore with the Congress what support could be anticipated in the event that it seemed desirable to intervene in Indochina." *Ibid.*, 1165–66.

16. Radford, memorandum for Secretary of Defense, March 31, 1954, box 30, Matthew B. Ridgway Papers (U.S. Army Military History Institute, Carlisle, Pa.); Matthew B. Ridgway, memorandum for the Joint Chiefs of Staff, April 2, 1954, *ibid.*; Nathan F. Twining, memorandum for Chairman of the Joint Chiefs of Staff, April 2, 1954, *ibid.*, Chief of Naval Operations Robert B. Carney equivocated. Marine Commandant Lemuel C. Shepherd, Jr., dismissed VULTURE as an "unprofitable adventure" that might damage United States prestige in a way that could only be recouped by intervention with ground forces. Matthew B. Ridgway answered Radford's query with an "emphatic and immediate 'No.'" Radford omits mention of these meetings in his memoir, perhaps to obscure the extent to which he took the initiative in pressing for VULTURE. The Joint Chiefs of Staff (JCS) later endorsed military intervention in Indochina provided that it included authorization to attack China if necessary. What they apparently wanted to avoid was a limited war, one fought under tight restrictions as in Korea. Robert B. Carney, memorandum for the Joint Chiefs of Staff, April 2, 1954, *ibid.*; Lemuel C. Shepherd, Jr., memorandum for the Joint Chiefs of Staff, April 2, 1954, *ibid.*; Ridgway, memorandum for the Joint Chiefs of Staff, April 2, 1954, *ibid.*; John Foster Dulles, memorandum of conversation with Eisenhower, May 25, 1954, White House Memoranda series, "Meetings with the President 1954 (3)," Dulles Papers.

17. Roberts, "Day We Didn't Go to War," 31–35; Hagerty Diary, March 26, 1954; John Foster Dulles, memorandum of conversation with Eisenhower, March 24, 1954, box 222, Lot 64D199, Records of the Department of State.

18. Halberstam, *Best and the Brightest*, 141–44; Robert H. Ferrell, ed., *The Eisenhower Diaries* (New York, 1981), 190; Dwight D. Eisenhower interview by Philip A. Crowl, July 28, 1964, transcript, p. 26, John Foster Dulles Oral History Collection (Seely G. Mudd Manuscript Library, Princeton University, Princeton, N.J.); Chester L. Cooper, *The Lost Crusade: America in Vietnam* (New York, 1970), 73; John Foster Dulles, memorandum of conversation with Eisenhower, March 24, 1954, box 222, Lot 64D199, Records of the Department of State; Hagerty Diary, April 1, 1954. When Radford raised the issue at the NSC on April 1, Eisenhower, evidently aware of the special meetings at the Pentagon, announced that all the service chiefs except Radford "were opposed to an airstrike using U.S. planes and pilots." *Foreign Relations of the United States, 1952–1954*, XIII, pt. 1, p. 1201.

19. *Executive Sessions of the Senate Foreign Relations Committee (Historical Series)* (12 vols., Washington, 1976–), VI, 263–64; Bowie interview.

20. John Foster Dulles, telephone conversation with H. Alexander Smith, April 19, 1954, Telephone Conversations series, "March 1–April 30, 1954 (1)," Dulles Papers. Although Eisenhower and John Foster Dulles never spelled out their intentions or perhaps even formulated them in detail, their willingness to intervene and the form intervention would have taken can be pieced together from various sources. On April 7, 1954, Dulles told Sen. Alexander Wiley that his objective was to create a "solid front" of nations that could "hold the Communists at Geneva," but he added, "we may have to take a share if... the fighting continues." On March 12 he testified to the Senate Foreign Relations Committee that it ought not be necessary for the United States to make an "appreciable contribution of land forces." The most effective contribution the United States could make would be with naval and air power and training

indigenous forces. Dulles told Australia's Minister for External Affairs Richard Casey on April 25 that if the United States intervened, "we would of course expect to rely upon Vietnamese troops which could probably be wielded into an effective fighting force under training by a man like General Van Fleet." The plans actually developed by the JCS for United Action called for the commitment of a carrier attack force and supporting elements and of United States Air Force units operating from bases outside Indochina. The diversion of additional forces to an area "devoid of decisive military objectives," the JCS feared, would leave the United States incapable of responding to Chinese probes elsewhere. John Foster Dulles, telephone conversation with Alexander Wiley, April, 7, 1954, Telephone Conversations series, "March 1–April 30, 1954 (1)," Dulles Papers; *Executive Sessions of the Senate Foreign Relations Committee*, VI, 263–64; *Foreign Relations of the United States, 1952–1954*, XVI, 558; Radford, *From Pearl Harbor to Vietnam*, 425–27.

21. Fall, *Hell in a Very Small Place*, 191–213.

22. John Foster Dulles, telephone conversation with William Knowland, March 30, 1954, Telephone Conversations series, "March 1–April 30, 1954 (2)," Dulles Papers; Bowie interview; "The Threat of a Red Asia: Address by Secretary Dulles," *Department of State Bulletin*, April 12, 1954, p. 540. At his March 31 press conference, Eisenhower artfully dodged questions concerning the implications of Dulles's speech. *Public Papers of the Presidents of the United States: Dwight d. Eisenhower, 1954*, (Washington, 1960), 366–67.

23. Halberstam, *Best and the Brightest*, 144; *Foreign Relations of the United States, 1952–1954*, XIII, pt. 1, pp. 944–45; George H. Gallup, *The Gallup Poll: Public Opinion, 1935–1971* (3 vols., New York, 1972), II, 1170–71, 1235–36, 1243; Hagerty Diary, April 19, April 20, 1954; Gary W. Reichard, "Divisions and Dissent: Democrats and Foreign Policy, 1952–1956," *Political Science Quarterly*, 93 (Spring 1978), 51–60; *Executive Sessions of the Senate Foreign Relations Committee*, VI, 181; *Public Papers of the Presidents of the United States*, 306.

24. Nixon, *RN*, 151.

25. John Foster Dulles, memorandum of conference with Eisenhower, April 2, 1954, White House Memoranda series, "Meetings with the President 1954 (4)," Dulles Papers; "Joint Resolution, Draft Taken to WH by JFD, 4/2/54," attached to *ibid.*

26. John Foster Dulles, memorandum of conference with Eisenhower, April 2, 1954, White House Memoranda series, "Meetings with the President 1954 (4)," Dulles Papers.

27. John Foster Dulles, memorandum of conference with congressional leaders, April 5, 1954, Chronological series, "April 1954," *ibid.* See also the cryptic but useful notes taken by Richard B. Russell. "Red-Line File," Richard B. Russell Papers (Richard B. Russell Library, University of Georgia, Athens, Ga.).

28. John Foster Dulles, telephone conversation with Eisenhower, April 3, 1954, Telephone Conversations series (White House), "January 1–June 30, 1954 (2)," Dulles Papers.

29. U.S. Congress, House, Committee on Armed Services, *United States–Vietnam Relations, 1945–1967; Study Prepared by the Department of Defense* (12 vols., Washington, 1971), IX, 296–97.

30. Eisenhower, telephone conversation with John Foster Dulles, April 5, 1954, Diary series, "Phone Calls—January–May 1954," Ann Whitman File, Dwight D. Eisenhower Papers as President of the United States, 1953–1961 (Dwight D. Eisenhower Library). The Ann Whitman File, maintained by the president's personal secretary, includes among other things his personal diary, drafts of his speeches, transcriptions of his telephone conversations, and a huge volume of correspondence and memoranda.

31. *Pentagon Papers*, I, 462–71, 474.

32. *Ibid.*, 471–72. In a memorandum dated April 6 and submitted to the Secretary of Defense on decisive objectives," a statement with the definite ring of Gen. Omar N. Bradley's criticism of expanding the Korean War. Ridgway further indicated that if the United States went to war in Asia, it ought to strike at the heart of the problem—China. Ridgway, memorandum for the joint Chiefs of Staff, April 6, 1954, box 30, Ridgway Papers; Radford, memorandum for Secretary of Defense, April 22, 1954, *ibid.*

33. Ridgway, *Soldier*, 276–77; *Foreign Relations of the United States, 1952–1954*, XIII, pt. 1, p. 1253; "Record of Actions by the National Security Council at Its One Hundred and Ninety Second Meeting, April 6, 1954," reel 5, "Documents of the National Security Council, 1947–1977" (University Publications of America microfilm, 1980).

34. *Pentagon Papers*, I, 460–61; John Foster Dulles to Amembassy, London, April 4, 1954, Subject series, "Indochina 1954 (3)," Dulles Papers; "Chronology of Actions on the Subject of Indochina," Jan. 27, 1956, *ibid.; Public Papers of the Presidents of the United States*, 382–84; Edwin Bickford Hooper, Dean C. Allard, and Oscar P. Fitzgerald, *The United States Navy and the Vietnam Conflict* (2 vols. Washington, 1976–), I, 252–55.

36. "Chronology of Actions on the Subject of Indochina," Jan 27, 1956, Subject series, "Indochina 1954 (3)," Dulles Papers; John Foster Dulles, memorandum of conversation with Georges Bidault, April 14, 1954, 'Dulles—April 1954 (2)," Dulles-Herter series, Whitman File.

37. *Congressional Record*, 83 Cong., 2 sess., April 6, 1954, pp. 4672–81; *New York Times*, April 7, 1954, pp. 1, 2; *ibid.*, April 8, 1954, p. 26; *ibid.*, April 11, 1954, sec. 1, pp. 3, 9, sec. 4, p. 1; *ibid.*, April 15, 1954, p. 3.

38. Hagerty Diary, April 16, April 17, 1954; John Foster Dulles, telephone conversation with Richard M. Nixon, April 19, 1954, Telephone Conversations series, "March 1–April 30, 1954 (1)," Dulles Papers; *New York Times*, April 18, 1954, p. 2

39. John Foster Dulles, telephone conversation with H. Alexander Smith, April 19, 1954, Telephone Conversations series, "March 1–April 30, 1954 (1)," Dulles Papers.

40. *Foreign Relations of the United States, 1952–1954*, XVI, 532–34, 535–38.

41. *Ibid.*, 544n; John Foster Dulles to State Department, April 22, April 23, 1954, "Dulles—April 1954 (2)," Dulles-Herter series, Whitman File.

42. Bidault, *Resistance*, 94–96, 170, 191, 196–97, 198; Richard H. Immerman, "Eisenhower and Dulles; Who Made the Decisions?" *Political Psychology*, 1 (Autumn 1979), 21–38; Committee on Armed Services, *United States—Vietnam Relations*, X, 705–06; *Foreign Relations of the United States, 1952–1954*, XIII,

pt. 1, pp. 1270–72, pt. 2, pp. 1446–48. Some top army and air force officers had grave doubts about the military value and expressed concern about the possible political consequences of using atomic weapons around Dienbienphu. Ronald H. Spector, *The United States Army in Vietnam: Advice and Support: The Early Years, 1941–1960.* (Washington, 1983), 200–201. See also John Foster Dulles, memorandum of conversation with Eisenhower, May 19, 1954, White House Memoranda series, "Meetings with the President 1954 (3)," Dulles Papers.

43. John Foster Dulles to State Department, April 23, 1954, "Dulles—April 1954 (2)," Dulles-Herter series, Whitman File; memorandum of conversation, John Foster Dulles, Radford, and Anthony Eden, April 26, 1954, Subject series, "Mr. Merchant Top Secret (Indochina) (2)," Dulles Papers.

44. John Foster Dulles to State Department, April 23, 1954, "Dulles—April 1954 (2)," Dulles-Herter series, Whitman File.

45. John Foster Dulles to Bidault, April 24, 1954, Subject series, "Indochina 1954 (3)," Dulles Papers; Eisenhower to Joseph Laniel, April 24, 1954, *ibid.*. Dulles designed the letter to "establish the record clearly since the French might attempt to pin on us the responsibility for their withdrawal from Indochina." John Foster Dulles to State Department, April 24, 1954, "Dulles—April 1954 (1)," Dulles-Herter series, Whitman File.

46. Bidault to John Foster Dulles, April 24, 1954, summarized in "Chronology of Actions on the Subject of Indochina," Jan. 27, 1956, Subject series, "Indochina 1954 (3)," Dulles Papers; John Foster Dulles to State Department, April 25, 1954, "Dulles—April 1954 (1)," Dulles-Herter series, Whitman File.

47. John Foster Dulles to State Department, April 25, 1954, "Dulles—April 1954 (1)," Dulles-Herter series, Whitman File; Eisenhower, *Mandate for Change*, 354.

48. *Foreign Relations of the United States, 1952–1954*, XVI, 553–57; John Foster Dulles to State Department, April 25, 1954, "Dulles—April 1954 (1)," Dulles-Herter series, Whitman File.

49. Radford, *From Pearl Harbor to Vietnam*, 408–09; Winthrop Aldrich to State Department, April 26, 1954, "Dulles—April 1954 (1)," Dulles-Herter series, Whitman File; Anderson interview; Fall, *Hell in a Very Small Place*, 310; *Foreign Relations of the United States, 1952–1954*, XVI, 629.

50. Dwight D. Eisenhower Diary, April 27, 1954, Diary series, "April 1954," Whitman File; Eisenhower to Everett "Swede" Hazlett, April 27, 1954, *ibid.*.

51. John Foster Dulles to State Department, April 29, 1954, "Dulles—April 1954 (1)," Dulles-Herter series, *ibid.*; Douglas Dillon to State Department, April 26, 1954, *ibid.*; Eisenhower, telephone conversation with Walter Bedell Smith, April 27, 1954, Diary series, "Phone calls—January–May 1954," *ibid.*; *Foreign Relations of the United States, 1952–1954*, XVI, 581–82; Committee on Armed Services, *United States–Vietnam Relations*, IX, 393–94.

52. *Public Papers of the Presidents of the United States*, 427–28; *Foreign Relations of the United States, 1952–1954*, XIII, pt. 2, pp. 1431–43; Nixon, *RN*, 153–54.

53. *Foreign Relations of the United States, 1952–1954*, XIII, pt. 2, pp. 1440–41, 1446; Hagerty Diary, April 29, 1954.

54. *Foreign Relations of the United States, 1952–1954*, XIII, pt. 2 pp. 1534–36, 1590–92; John Foster Dulles, telephone conversation with Radford, May 10, 1954,

Telephone Conversations series, "May 1–June 30, 1954 (3)," Dulles Papers; draft joint resolution, May 17, 1954, Subject series, "Indochina, May 1953–May 1954 (4)," *ibid.*; "Procedural Steps for Intervention in Indochina," n.d., *ibid.*; Radford, *From Pearl Harbor to Vietnam*, 417–31; *Pentagon Papers*, I, 122-32.

55.   John Foster Dulles, memorandum of conversation with the president, May 19, 1954, White House Memoranda series, "Meetings with the President 1954 (3)," Dulles Papers; *Pentagon Papers*, I, 122–30, 135–36.

56.   Richard H. Immerman, "The Anatomy of the Decision Not to Fight: Multiple Advocacy or Presidential Choice?" 1982 (in Immerman's possession).

5
Geneva, 1954: The Precarious Peace
ELLEN J. HAMMER

In 1954 a precarious peace came to Indochina. It came because Frenchmen had lost any desire to continue a fight which they could not possibly win against the Viet Minh; because the United States was not prepared to take over the war alone; because for the Soviet Union an Indochinese cease-fire seemed consistent with Communist international strategy; because the Chinese, finally, courting public opinion in neutral Asia and the free world, urged concessions on the Viet Minh. Even so, peace came only with difficulty.

Making peace was such a complex task because it had been so long neglected. More than ten years before, Franklin D. Roosevelt, who was concerned about the future of Indochina, had expressed the belief that the Vietnamese people merited a regime under which they could achieve their freedom, and that it was the responsibility of the United States and its allies to establish such a regime. In the years that followed, the American people and the leaders of both parties, Democrats and Republicans alike, often forgot the meaning of these objectives even though they sometimes paid lip service to them. It was only in 1954 that an American delegation arrived in Geneva to consider how to stop a war which should never have been allowed to start; and then the bargaining power of the United States' friends in Indochina was so slight that American officials were not at all sure that the timing or the circumstances were right for negotiations.

This was an awkward time for American policy-makers; they were forced to recognize the unpalatable fact that practically all of the assumptions underlying United States policy in Indochina were simply not true.

First, there was the assumption that the American Government had been helping the French and the peoples of Indochina not only to fight Communism but also to win freedom for Viet Nam, Laos, and Cambodia. In Viet Nam, this would have made sense if the people knew something of the nature of political freedom and understood the oppressive nature of international Communism; some American officials seemed to have confused the Vietnamese peasant masses with the sophisticated German workers who rose in open revolt against Communism in East Berlin. The

Reprinted from *The Struggle for Indochina, 1940–1955* by Ellen J. Hammer with the permission of the publishers, Stanford University Press. © 1954 and 1955 by the Institute of Pacific Relations.

only freedom that most Vietnamese wanted was not from Communism, about which they knew little and understood less, but from France; and Communist-dominated though it was, the Viet Minh was the only force in the country fighting for an independence which the French were persistently unwilling to grant. This was the reason why so many Vietnamese supported the Viet Minh and why the neutralist nations of Asia, with their aversion for colonialism, no matter how anti-Communist their own internal policies, would not take an open stand against the Viet Minh. Only in Laos and Cambodia was the independence issue fairly clear-cut; and the people of both those countries, although determined to oppose any Viet Minh encroachments on their territory, were primarily interested in achieving their independence from France—which they did by means of diplomacy, exploiting in their own interests French difficulties with the Viet Minh.

Second, there was the assumption that the Bao Dai regime, put into power by the French and recognized by the United States, had substantial popular support. This corrupt, ineffectual government had been instituted by French officials in 1949 not to oppose Communism, for the Vietnamese were not alone in making the Communism of the Viet Minh a secondary issue (the French have never felt so intensely as the United States about the Communist menace in Asia), but to enable France to divide and win control over the Vietnamese independence movement. There was never any secret that this was French strategy and the Vietnamese did not have to be particularly intelligent to realize it. It is true that there were honest Nationalists anxious to set up a truly independent and representative regime which could compete effectively with the Viet Minh for popular support but they received little help from the United States and, not unnaturally, none at all from France. As a result, most Vietnamese withheld their active support from Bao Dai, with grave political and military consequences for American policy.

It is not surprising that American officials did not wish to probe too deeply into the validity of their assumptions; it was naturally painful to have to recognize that by choosing to oppose Vietnamese Communism almost entirely by military means, the United States had failed to win the friendship of the Vietnamese people. This does not mean that the Vietnamese wanted to be Communists and that the Americans tried in vain to stop them. What it does mean is that they wanted to be independent under their own leaders, with American aid, and that the United States refused them. Even when the American Government started pouring money into the military effort against the Viet Minh, the United States refused to give meaning to that military effort by helping the men around Bao Dai to stand on their own feet and make an honest bid for popular support.

American policy was based on still a third and equally erroneous assumption. This was that the French military position in Indochina was strong and growing stronger. For seven and a half years France and the United States had been fed on illusions and half-truths about the Vietnamese situation; they regarded Indochina through a thick fog of unreality. The American Government continued to give the French Union forces substantial aid but failed to give the Vietnamese who supported the Viet Minh, or were asked to go to war against it, a reason for fighting alongside the French; and by 1954 the most important single fact in Indochina was the grave deterioration of the French military position in the north. If French officials were reluctant to admit this fact before French public opinion, they were even more reluctant to admit it before their American allies. The result was a widening gap between the two countries. As the French spoke of the need for negotiations, the Americans called for a war to the end; when the French talked of necessary concessions to the Communists, the Americans warned against appeasement and capitulation.

Foreign Minister Georges Bidault carried home a diplomatic success from the four-power conference in Berlin, in February 1954, when Secretary of State John Foster Dulles and Soviet Foreign Minister Molotov, as well as British Foreign Secretary Anthony Eden, agreed to the holding of a conference in Geneva not only to discuss Korean problems but also to try to reach a peace settlement in Indochina. But that was not to meet until April 26 and in the meantime the war went on, on the political front as well as the military one.

The problem for the West was that it had little with which to bargain at Geneva. The obvious method of trying to moderate the demands of the Communist powers by promising American recognition of Communist China or its admission to the United Nations would have been rejected by the American Senate under the leadership of Senator Knowland; the Senate would not accept at any price even the appearance of conciliation of the Chinese, nor would most of the American public at that time. There remained the bargaining strength of military force, but this, it was soon clear, would have to be American force; the French were hardly in a position to bargain. The first official intimation that the United States received of French military weakness came when General Paul Ely arrived in Washington in March and described the difficult situation of the French forces in the strong terms which French generals had used privately for years. French sources, in fact, reported General Ely's mission to be a request by the French Government, hitherto firmly opposed to more open American intervention in the war, for such intervention, although it does not appear to have been treated as such by the United States.

Highlighting General Ely's gloomy report was the military situation itself. General Vo Nguyen Giap had opened an all-out offensive after the announcement of the forthcoming Geneva Conference, and on March 13 he launched an attack on Dien Bien Phu. This was no guerrilla maneuver, as so many previous Viet Minh actions had been; backed by substantially increased Chinese aid, it was a major action that speedily developed into a nutcracker movement as the Viet Minh slowly and mercilessly closed in on the highly vulnerable French positions.

Under other circumstances this could have been just one battle among many, with a Viet Minh victory or defeat at Dien Bien Phu of no determining importance for the outcome of the war; although some attempt was made by Frenchmen to explain the action as defending Laos, it had no overriding strategic importance. But it rapidly assumed enormous political meaning as the imminence of the Geneva Conference turned a high-powered lens upon each event of these March and April weeks.

For the Viet Minh, Dien Bien Phu had a crucial significance. This was the last opportunity before the Geneva Conference for the Viet Minh to show its military strength, its determination to fight until victory. And there were those who thought that General Giap was resolved on victory, no matter the cost, not only to impress the enemy but also to convince his Communist allies that the Viet Minh by its own efforts had earned a seat at the conference table and the right to a voice in its own future.

For the French people, who watched the siege of Dien Bien Phu with a strained attention they had not shown any previous event of the war, it became a symbol of their will to fight. Upon the outcome of the battle depended much of the spirit in which they would send their representatives to Geneva.

Dien Bien Phu was a poorly chosen place in which to make a stand, a valley exposed on all sides to the enemy artillery in the hills and impossible to supply except by air. And having chosen it, General Navarre was later accused by well-informed critics of failing to give the embattled garrison the total support it needed. Certainly French Intelligence underestimated the effectiveness of the heavy artillery supplied by the Chinese which the Viet Minh was able to bring against Dien Bien Phu.

For fifty-six days Viet Minh troops pounded at the beleaguered fortress. In desperation, the Laniel-Bidault government, taking literally Washington's frequent affirmations of the importance of the American stake in Indochina, appealed for American air intervention. They made one appeal early in April and another more urgent one later that month.

At one point in these tense days high American military authorities considered seriously dropping some atomic bombs on the Viet Minh but decided against it. The United States did not only decide against using atomic bombs; it also announced that it was not prepared to undertake any military intervention of its own in Indochina. An astonishing attempt was made at one point by State Department spokesmen to place the responsibility on the refusal of the British to join in any military action on the eve of Geneva, but in fact the decision not to intervene was an American one. Put to the test, the American Government, with Congress lacking support from a public disillusioned over the Korean war, was not prepared to give the all-out help that the belligerent declarations of American officials had led the French Government to expect.

Secretary Dulles tried to create a position of strength through diplomacy. Even before the April 3rd request of the French for aid, he had issued a call for "united action" against the Communists in Southeast Asia, and he hurried off to London and Paris in an effort to bring his allies into a formal Southeast Asian alliance of ten anti-Communist nations which would have had the effect of including Viet Nam, Laos, and Cambodia in a Southeast Asian defense system guaranteed by the Western powers. But this maneuver did not work. Even when Mr. Dulles said that the Chinese were "awful close" to intervention, he could not persuade the British and the French to join him in a move which seemed to them inevitably to give the impression that the United States had no intention of taking the Geneva Conference seriously. Eventually the British and the French were prepared to consider a Southeast Asian alliance but, having committed themselves to the principle of negotiation, they were determined first to give that a fair trial, and they pointedly noted that the Americans had done the same in Korea after a much shorter war.

The weeks leading up to the Geneva Conference were thus a record of failure for the West. The American diplomatic barrage of threats and warnings directed against increasing Chinese aid to the Viet Minh proved to signify nothing more than Washington's quite understandable dissatisfaction with the state of affairs in Southeast Asia, and contrasted sharply with its evident reluctance to undertake any concrete action. From the viewpoint of Western solidarity and American prestige, it was unfortunate that the French Government had been allowed to get to the point of asking for an intervention which the United States had no intention of undertaking, and that "united action" had been proclaimed only to spotlight disunity and inaction in the West.

From some of the neutralist Asian governments came proposals for a cease-fire in Indochina. Prime Minister Nehru took the lead in this peace drive and India was followed by its fellow members of the Colombo bloc, Indonesia, Burma, Pakistan, and Ceylon. The importance of these well-intentioned gestures was underscored by the course of the military struggle. On May 8, the anniversary of the end of the Second World War in Europe, France mourned the fall of Dien Bien Phu. It was a poor omen for the outcome of the conference already in session in Geneva. Frenchmen saw it as a symbol of the tragedy and mismanagement of the eight-year struggle and in France there was despair and final disillusionment.

In Geneva, the fall of Dien Bien Phu came as a body blow to the West.

Few international conferences have begun in an atmosphere of greater uncertainty than the Far Eastern Conference which opened in Geneva on April 26, 1954. Its discussions on Korea will not be dealt with here; it is enough to state that, to no one's surprise, they proved fruitless. The Korean situation remained unchanged. For a while it seemed that the Indochinese conversations might also be deadlocked, there was so little initial agreement among the great powers. But as the weeks passed it became evident that the Geneva Conference was going to be a tremendous victory for China, Russia, and the Viet Minh.

The conference marked wide international acceptance, outside the United States, of Communist China as one of the five great powers, although American officials made a great point of avoiding even the most casual contacts with the Chinese during the time they spent at Geneva.

The Chinese and Russians insisted on the presence of the Viet Minh at the conference table, and out of the jungles and mountains of northern Viet Nam came the delegation of the Viet Minh or, more accurately, "the Democratic Republic of Viet Nam." [1] Three of the four delegates were no strangers to negotiations with France; in 1946, when they found that they were getting nowhere with their demands, they had broken off their talks with the French at Fontainebleau. Now they came to Geneva determined to force far more drastic terms on France and this time with the strength to back them up. Heading the delegation, as he had formerly headed the delegation at Fontainebleau, was Pham Van Dong, Vice President and Acting Foreign Minister, and with him were two other Fontainebleau veterans, Phan Anh, Minister of Economy, and Ta Quang Buu, Vice Minister of National Defense. The fourth delegate was the Viet Minh ambassador to Peking, Hoang Van Hoan.

The French Government had not demonstrated much interest in consulting the Associated States but at the last moment delegations from Laos, Cambodia, and Viet Nam also arrived in Switzerland. It was part of the tragic irony of the Vietnamese war that the key figures in the Vietnamese Nationalist delegation, Nguyen Quoc Dinh and Nguyen Dac Khe, had last seen members of the Viet Minh delegation when acting as legal advisors to them during the Fontainebleau Conference.

Behind the scenes were certain prominent figures on the Nationalist side, like former Prime Minister Tran Van Huu, who also came to Geneva to investigate the intentions of the Viet Minh and to advocate a united Viet Nam, neutralized politically and strategically, and independent of China. Even the Cao Dai pope, Pham Cong Tac, went there to try to evaluate Viet Minh intentions.

Foreign Minister Bidault, who attacked the problem from a different angle, had long been counting on opening negotiations with Communist China to strike a bargain under which the Chinese would have ended their considerable aid to the Viet Minh, leaving it an easy prey to the French Union forces. Bidault had never sought or even believed in the usefulness of direct negotiations with the Viet Minh, but his exaggerated expectations of American military aid backfired and for the first time he had to try to reach a compromise with the enemy.

In this effort he found himself quite alone. The American delegates, divided among themselves and highly sensitive to domestic political pressures against any concessions to the Communists, having nothing to offer either to their allies or to their enemies in the direction of conciliating their opposing positions, could hardly take over leadership at Geneva. It was left to Foreign Secretary Anthony Eden, who attempted to link the Colombo Powers to the Geneva Conference, to act as mediator between the Communists and the French. The Indian Government, which was well intentioned if not always well informed on Indochina, although not officially a member of the conference, also played a certain role, directly through Krishna Menon, Nehru's personal representative in Geneva, and indirectly by means of the influence which India as a key member of the Commonwealth exerted on the British.

Unlike the United States, the British came to Geneva with a plan for peaceful settlement; and their plan, which called for a partition of Viet Nam, was in the end accepted by the conference. But what kind of partition? A division of the country by which at least a part of Viet Nam could be saved from the Communists? Or just a face-saving device for giving the entire country to the Viet Minh?

The Russians had come to Geneva because they were ready to negotiate on Indochina. And if Chou En-lai was there, it was obviously because he was prepared to make some concessions, or at least to make the Viet Minh consent to them. This was particularly the case after Chou, during a recess in the conference, made flying visits to Nehru in New Delhi and U Nu in Rangoon, and then conferred with Ho Chi Minh in northern Viet Nam, reportedly to convince him of the opposition of non-Communist Asia to Viet Minh insistence on French capitulation.

The French, for their part, were in Geneva because they had to negotiate; they had no other choice since they now knew finally that the United States was not willing to intervene in the war. Evidently the French would have to give up something, and it was soon clear that this would be northern Viet Nam, where the Communists were most firmly entrenched.

None of the Western governments liked this. The "State of Viet Nam" (the Nationalist government), which was most directly affected, was very unhappy about it, but did not help the situation when it insisted at all costs on unifying Viet Nam under Bao Dai. This was a preposterous demand at a time when the intrinsic failure of his regime was more obvious than ever. And the insistence on a unified Viet Nam was a dangerous one. If military and political necessity dictated partition, an intelligent diplomacy should have recognized this, however unpleasant it was, and fought to safeguard whatever region was granted to the Nationalists. Above all, it was essential to construct a juridical wall at the northern limits of the Nationalist zone which the Communists could not penetrate under any pretext; but that would have required a political realism which was absent from Geneva. Instead, the Nationalist delegates, supported by the United States, insisted righteously and unrealistically on unity, which led inevitably to their acceptance of the principle of national elections to determine the future even of their own zone. And any elections, in view of the political chaos in the non-Communist areas of Viet Nam, threatened to open the entire country to the highly organized Communists.

Cambodia, though a small state, demonstrated that it was possible to make an independent policy even at a great power conference like Geneva. With Laos, it received Western help in successfully opposing Viet Minh claims on behalf of the Laotian and Cambodian dissident movements and in rejecting Viet Minh demands on the territories of the two states. But at the eleventh hour, with all the powers against it, Cambodia stood alone. It declared that it would not be neutralized and insisted on its right to self-defense. And the great powers gave way.

The Cambodian delegates followed the spirited precedent laid down by their King Norodom Sihanouk, standing up for their own rights when these were challenged. But the Vietnamese Nationalists had only Bao Dai, who had long since given up any hope of independent action, relying on foreigners to save himself.

Bidault, struggling to salvage something for France, tried to separate the arrangements for a cease-fire in Viet Nam from those for a political settlement, reasoning soundly enough that he could get better terms once the fighting had ceased. He tried to avoid even a temporary partition, which would come about if the opposing military forces were regrouped in separate zones, suggesting instead that the cease-fire be imposed on pockets of French and Viet Minh troops scattered throughout the country. But the obvious advantages to France of such proposals made them naturally unacceptable to the Communists.

To all the weaknesses of the French position was now added the instability of the French Government itself. Within the period of a month the Cabinet of Premier Laniel had twice had to ask the French Assembly for votes of confidence on its Indochina policy. It had won them but not easily, and by June? Bidault was under bitter attack in the Assembly. Having continually to fight on two fronts, in Paris as well as Geneva, while the military situation deteriorated daily in Viet Nam, he was badly placed to carry on effective negotiations.

The Laniel government finally fell after a smashing attack on the Indochina issue led by Pierre Mendès-France, who on June 17 succeeded Laniel as Premier. He carried the Assembly by an impressive majority when he promised that in thirty days (by July 20) he would either achieve peace terms ending the Indochina war or resign.

As his own Foreign Minister, Mendès-France hurried off to Geneva to take up where Bidault had left off. The bitter personal enmity between the two men and the widespread personal antagonisms which afflicted French internal politics had the effect of obscuring many of the realities of the Indochinese situation. It is little wonder that foreign governments and the French public experienced such difficulty in arriving at a correct estimate of the French position. If his predecessors had painted the French military position in too rosy a light, Mendès-France now had his own reasons for darkening it.

Whereas Bidault had long since been identified with a "tough" policy toward the Viet Minh grounded on internationalizing the peace and the war, Mendès-France had consistently favored a negotiated peace, achieved by direct talks with the Viet Minh; and soon after he assumed office he proceeded to initiate conversations with Pham Van Dong. American suspicions of this policy were highlighted rather overdramatically when Mr. Dulles decided to withdraw the official American representation at

Geneva, thereby undercutting the Western position by underlining the general impression that the United States had washed its hands of the conference.

Bowing to urgent French and British requests, however, Dulles dashed over to Paris and, after consultations with Mendès-France and Eden, announced that he did after all have confidence in the intentions of the French Premier to conclude an honorable peace. Under Secretary of State Walter Bedell Smith, who for a time had replaced Dulles at the conference, was sent back to Geneva.

But this byplay did not really alter the situation. The United States had in fact washed its hands of the conference, thereby facilitating the task of the Communists at Geneva. It would seem that the Communists, suspecting premeditated organization against them even when it did not exist, had placed an unwarranted faith in the unity of the Western powers and had believed, at first, that they might be called upon to make substantial concessions. There is some evidence that at a time when they were insisting publicly on Vietnamese unity, they would actually have been prepared to accept a Korean-type settlement, namely, partition of the country for an indefinite period.[2] However, as the conference proceeded, they saw that the unified Western front which they dreaded did not exist; and so the negotiations revolved around, not the maximum concessions which the Communists would make, but their maximum demands which, with some modifications, were finally accepted. By failing to take a leading role in the discussions once it became clear that the West had no choice but to surrender at least a part of Viet Nam to the Communists, the American delegation withheld from Mendès-France the only real bargaining strength he had left, that of diplomacy, making it impossible for him to salvage intact even southern Viet Nam from the Geneva debacle. Instead, he had to agree that national elections be held in Viet Nam in the near future, even though there was good reason to fear that such elections would give the entire country to the Communists.

If the conference moved faster after Mendès-France replaced Bidault, it was partly because of the thirty-day limit he had set for himself, which, given the willingness of the Communists to make peace terms, undoubtedly speeded up the proceedings considerably. Also the Communists were aware that Mendès-France would give them the best terms they could expect from France; if he failed it was fairly certain that the conference would break down and that he would be replaced by a government determined to continue the war, doubtless with increased American military backing.

To these political advantages, Mendès-France tried to add a third when he announced that if the conference failed, French conscripts would be sent for the first time to Indochina to reinforce the expeditionary corps. This was a move so unpopular among the French public that hitherto no French politician had dared to advocate it. But even this announcement did not counteract the devastating news of the sudden withdrawal of

French Union forces from the southern part of the Tonkinese Delta, where they were under strong Viet Minh pressure, in order to strengthen what remained of the French military position in the rest of the country. The evacuation left the French in control of a small area around Hanoi (which almost certainly would fall to the Communists anyway in a partition agreement), but abandoned to the Viet Minh important non-Communist areas, notably the Catholic bishoprics of Phat Diem and Bui Chu.

On the diplomatic front, once Mendès-France had accepted the basic Communist demands—not only that the Viet Minh be given immediate control over northern Viet Nam, but also that national elections be held fairly soon—final agreement could hardly be in doubt. It was then only a question of deciding where the partition line would be drawn (the Communists had asked for the thirteenth parallel but finally agreed on the seventeenth[3]); when the Vietnamese elections were to be held to re-establish national unity (the Viet Minh had asked for six months but finally accepted two years); and what international controls were to be set up.

In the meantime, discussions between the military authorities of both sides on a cease-fire agreement began in Geneva, then were transferred to Trung Gia in Viet Minh territory in North Viet Nam. In Geneva, the nine delegations, making no genuine attempt to negotiate real political problems, worked out a series of face-saving devices, avoiding the basic issues involved. The result was the Geneva accord (finished just in time to meet the deadline set by Mendès-France) which divided Viet Nam at the seventeenth parallel.[4] All of north Viet Nam and part of central Viet Nam—from the Chinese frontier almost down to the old imperial capital of Huè, and including the important cities of Hanoi and Haiphong—were recognized as under the control, no longer of "rebels," as they had been described for years by the French, but of the Democratic Republic of Viet Nam. The south was left under the control of the State of Viet Nam.

Other provisions of the agreement called for the grouping of the military forces of one side which remained in the territory of the other into specified areas, which were to be evacuated in stages over a period of three hundred days; a broad political amnesty throughout the country and a ban on reprisals against citizens for their wartime activities; the safeguarding of democratic liberties; and a free option for all Vietnamese to choose in which zone they wished to live.

Neither zone was permitted to receive reinforcements of foreign troops, arms, or military supplies, or to establish new military bases. Nor could either government have foreign bases in its territory nor enter military alliances. The French Union forces in southern Viet Nam were the exception to this rule; they were to remain, to be withdrawn only at the request of the southern Vietnamese government.

Responsibility for the carrying out of these terms was, in the first instance, recognized as that of the French and the Viet Minh. They in turn were made subject to the surveillance of an international commission (composed of Canadian, Indian, and Polish representatives, under Indian chairmanship) which was generally to vote by majority although on certain important questions unanimity was required.

The independence of Viet Nam, as of Laos and Cambodia, and also the principle of Vietnamese unity, were formally recognized by the conference.[5] In July 1956 the future of Viet Nam was to be decided by free and secret elections under the control of the international commission constituted by Canada, India, and Poland. And consultations between the Democratic Republic of Viet Nam and the State of Viet Nam about the elections were scheduled to begin a year in advance, on July 20, 1955.

For Laos and Cambodia, the peace arrangements, although on paper not unlike the Vietnamese settlement, were in practice very different. They also were to have national elections—the Cambodians in 1955, the Laotians in September 1956—and the carrying out of the accords was to be under the surveillance of the same three nations as in Viet Nam. But while elections in Viet Nam looked like a convenient way of giving the entire country to the Communists, in Cambodia and Laos they seemed certain to constitute popular endorsement of the royal governments which were recognized by the Communist powers as well as by the West as the only legitimate authorities in both countries.

The agreement on Laos, which recognized the right of the Laotians to keep two French military bases and French military instructors, as the Laotians had requested, offered a general amnesty to the Viet Minh-controlled Laotian dissidents known as Pathet Lao. However, this did not finally settle the Communist problem in Laos. Alien military troops were to be evacuated within four months, but the Laotian rebels who did not choose to be reintegrated into the Laotian community were given two northern provinces of Laos, Phang Saly and Sam Neua, where they were to have special representation under the royal administration. This arrangement was supposed to last only until the elections.

The agreement on Cambodia made no provision for setting up regrouping areas. Within three months all French and other foreign troops were to have evacuated Cambodia. Although until the last hours of the conference it had been accepted that Laos and Cambodia would be neutralized, thanks to Tep Phan, Cambodian Foreign Minister, both countries won recognition of their right to ask for foreign aid in men and matériel if it became necessary to do so to defend themselves, to allow foreign military bases on their territory if their security was menaced, and to enter into alliances which were not contrary to the United Nations Charter.

On July 21 the official documents were signed, which brought peace to Indochina. The United States maintained its strong reservations on the accord and, like the State of Viet Nam, which protested hopelessly against the agreement, did not join the other seven countries in accepting the final declaration of the conference. General Bedell Smith, who thanked Eden and Molotov, the two presidents of the conference, for their good will and tireless efforts in reaching an agreement, issued a separate American declaration. It declared that the United States would abstain from any threat to modify the accords, and that it would regard any resumption of aggression in violation of the accords with grave concern and as a serious menace to international peace and security.

The Viet Minh may not have won all that it wanted at Geneva but it had every reason to be pleased. Its Communist dictatorship was reinforced by international recognition. And not only was its control recognized over the northern and more populous half of Viet Nam, but excellent opportunities were opened to the Viet Minh to take over the south as well, by infiltration. In large part at least, this was the inevitable result of the disastrous political and military policy pursued over the years by the French Government in Indochina, supported by the United States.

In any case, peace, however controversial its form and dubious its content, had come to Viet Nam. On August 11, after nearly eight years of war, the cease-fire was operating throughout all Indochina.

NOTES

1. In deference to popular usage, the less accurate term, "the Viet Minh," has been and will continue to be used here to designate the Ho Chi Minh regime, even though, technically, the Viet Minh as a national front movement has been absorbed into the Lien Viet.

2. According to a report of Colonel (now General) de Brébisson, who negotiated military questions with the Viet Minh at Geneva, the Viet Minh took the initiative to propose a private discussion at which, on June 10, the French were told that "for the Viet Minh, Tonkin was the essential and vital region, and that it was necessary to concentrate on two large regroupment zones, one in the north, for the Viet Minh, the other in the south, where the forces of the French Union would be regrouped. The dividing line between the two zones should be established somewhere near Hué." *Journal Officiel*, Assemblée Nationale, December 17, 1954, p. 6517.

3. M. Mendés-France reported to the National Assembly that the Viet Minh had first asked for the thirteenth parallel. (*Journal Official*, Assemblée Nationale, July 23, 1954, p. 3580.) Yet the line mentioned above, in the previous footnote, proposed by the Viet Minh some six weeks before the conclusion of the conference, was actually the seventeenth, the one finally agreed upon. It can be seen that the Viet Minh altered its strategy between June 10, when it offered concessions, and the following period when it found it more profitable to make demands.

4. For British and French texts of these accords, see British White Paper, Cmd. 9239, *Further Documents Relating to the Discussion of Indochina at the Geneva Conference June 16–July 21, 1954*. And *Notes et Etudes Documentaires* No. 1901, *Documents relatifs á la Conference de Genéve sur l'Indochina (21 juillet 1954)*; and *ibid.*, No. 1909, *Accords sur la cessation des hostilits en Indochina (Genéve, 20 juillet 1954)*.

5. The independence of Viet Nam had been formally recognized by France on June 4.... And in December 1954 the three Associated States signed agree-

ments with France giving them full financial and economic independence. (See Notes et Etudes Documentaires No. 1973, *Accords et Conventions signs lors de la conférence quadripartite entre le Cambodge, La France, le Laos, et le Viet-Nam, Paris 29 et 30 décembre 1954.*

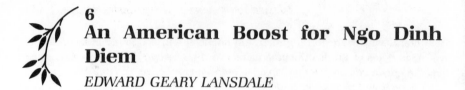

6
An American Boost for Ngo Dinh Diem

EDWARD GEARY LANSDALE

After months of doing business out of my hip pocket in Vietnam, I was delighted to be assigned a formal office of my own in January 1955. Perhaps "formal" is too elegant a term. It actually was a little shed in the yard of MAAG headquarters in Cholon. Duckboards covered the dirt floor. Two bare lightbulbs, dangling from their cords, lit the interior. Folding chairs and field tables, and some open crates to hold files, completed the furnishings. The shed was one of several clustered around the main building of the headquarters, which was an old French colonial schoolhouse of cement and stucco noted principally in the neighborhood for having once been a whorehouse set up by the Japanese for the convenience of their troops. The French had assigned this place to the Americans as one of their many "in" jokes. I never did find out the genesis of my own particular shed.

My move to a daily stint in this shed at MAAG came after I volunteered for the Franco-American organization that had been agreed upon in December as the instrument for training the Vietnamese Army. While details of just how the French and the Americans were to work together were being thrashed out, General O'Daniel gathered together the Americans selected to staff the new organization and put us in the only available space at his headquarters, the sheds in the yard, to do some advance planning for the work ahead. There were four staff divisions: army, navy, air force, and pacification. I headed pacification, which was to guide the Vietnamese Army in its moves to reoccupy former Vietminh zones as well as to oversee any security operations in areas where querrillas were still terrorizing the population.

The next couple of weeks saw most of our basic planning done, including suggested directives for the Vietnamese whenever they were ready to start the program. Although my own planning drew heavily upon the lessons I had learned in the Philippines and from my travels around the Vietnamese countryside, it also was tailored and shaped by the Vietnamese. I discussed each step with the prime minister, the minister of national defense, and the leaders of the Vietnamese Army, whom I was continuing to see almost daily. This Vietnamese input was the most important element in the planning. We Americans and French would be guiding the Vietnamese into taking control of their own affairs. If they were to succeed, the proposed operations would have to be wholly understood and accepted by the Vietnamese.

The first change they made was in the name of our program. They objected to the word *pacification,* saying that it denoted a French colonial practice devised by General Lyautey in North Africa and applied to Vietnam by GAMOs (Mobile Administrative Groups) which had set up local governments and home guards in areas cleared by French Union forces. (I had seen the work of the GAMOs and thought that much of it was excellent.) The Vietnamese leaders did agree with the concept of using the Vietnamese Army to help and to protect the people, so I insisted that if they didn't like *pacification,* they pick a name themselves. After much head-scratching, the leaders chose a Vietnamese term for the work, which translated into English as *national security action.* We adopted this name promptly. Amusingly enough, the Vietnamese themselves (along with the French and Americans) continued to speak of the work as *pacification.* Years later, despite other official changes of name, it still is spoken of as *pacification.* Habit dies hard.

Toward the end of January, the new Franco-American training organization, TRIM, became a reality. The French command made the Cité Lorgeril, a walled compound in Cholon, consisting of a collection of pleasant villas around a courtyard, available as headquarters. Its organization was balanced, with scientific precision, between the Americans and the French. General O'Daniel was the chief of TRIM but acted under the authority of the top French commander, General Ely. TRIM's chief of staff (and my immediate boss) was [the] French briefing officer, Colonel Jean Carbonel.... His deputy was an American, Lieutenant Colonel Bill Rosson. Under them were the chiefs of the four staff divisions (army, navy, air, and national security), two of whom were French and two American, each with a deputy of the other nationality. I was chief of the national security division. My deputy was a French paratrooper, Lieutenant Colonel Jacques Romain-Defosses. Our staff division had equal numbers of French and American officers.

There was too little amity in TRIM for me. The French chief of staff who was my immediate boss seemed perpetually piqued at me and showed his feelings by refusing to speak to me directly. Instead, he would position his adjutant, a French officer, next to him and, while looking at me, would ask the adjutant to relay such and such a message to me. When the adjutant had finished, I would reply directly to the chief of staff, who promptly would ask the adjutant, "What did he say?" My reply would be repeated. It was lugubrious, since we all were being stiffly correct in military fashion and were speaking English face-to-face. He carried this practice into our official social life. At receptions he would stamp his feet and turn his back when I approached. I hardly endeared myself to him by my own behavior. I would put an arm across his shoulders familiarly and announce to those standing nearby in a grating American manner, "This guy is my buddy. You treat him right, you hear?" This made him explode, angrily shaking my arm off his shoulders.

Most of the French officers in my staff division let me know openly that they were from various intelligence services. Once in a while, they would have the grace to blush when I came upon them as they were busy writing reports of my daily activities, presumably for a parent service. On the other hand, all of them had served in Vietnam for periods of six years or more and were exceptionally well-informed about Vietnamese life and geography. Thus my problem was to divert them from an unduly psychotic suspicion of everything I did and toward genuine help in the Vietnamese preparation for the serious and complex national security operations then underway. I was only partially successful.

For example, one of the French officers was from a clandestine service. He sat at a desk facing me, busied himself with paper work for a time, and then just sat there, staring. I noticed that his stare became more and more fixed on a telephone near me which was designated for English-language use. Even the telephones at TRIM were evenly divided between the two nationalities, although the execrable service was impartial. Both the French- and English-speaking phones were subject to sound effects apparently from outer space, additional voices picked up in midsentence or in shouts of "Allo, allo!" and dead silences. Nearly every incoming call would begin with blasphemous complaints about the long delays and frustrations involved in getting the call through to us. Then the caller would hurriedly shout his message before he was cut off. Knowing the performance record of the telephone, I assumed that the French officer staring at it was simply giving it a silent hate treatment.

But one morning, this English-language telephone rang. The French officer, who had been scribbling on a piece of paper and referring frequently to his French-English dictionary, jumped to his feet, snatched up the piece of paper, and rushed over to the ringing telephone before an American could reach it. Holding up the paper and reading from it, he spoke carefully into the mouthpiece, "I do not speak English, goodbye." Then he hung up. He looked at me to see if I had noticed his zany prank. I laughed aloud. He looked a bit surprised at my reaction and then grinned himself.

I went back to his desk with him. The French officer at the next desk was fluent in English and I asked if he would mind interpreting for the two of us. It was time that we all became better acquainted. We embarked upon a session of mutual talk. The prankster admitted that he had only three months longer to stay in Vietnam and frankly was sitting out the time until departure. I confessed that I didn't have all the answers on how to help the Vietnamese at the present moment. Since he had served many years among them, surely there must be at least one thing that he had long wanted to do for the Vietnamese that the war had prevented him from doing? If he named it, and if it could be fitted into our work, he could spend all of his remaining time at such a self-chosen task and have all the support I could muster.

He replied thoughtfully that he had long waited to assist Vietnamese children and would like to draft an explicit proposal for a youth program to fit in with the national security concept. This sounded good, I said, worthy of backing, and his eyes lighted up. With such work to do, he told me that he would put in for further service in Vietnam, although he did want some brief home leave first because he had been away from his family for years. We parted on this agreeable note. The next day, at TRIM, he stood at attention before my desk, saluted, and informed me in formal tones that he had been ordered rotated back to France. His departure was set for the next day. Did he ask for an extension of duty in Vietnam, as we had discussed? He answered brusquely, "Yes, sir," his eyes showing a silent inner hurt. He told me that he would have to go. We said farewell.

Other French officers in my division also had deep feelings about ways in which they would really like to help the Vietnamese. I dug patiently for their ideas and put them to work on self-projects whenever I could. Abrupt departures continued. The staff division gradually settled into an atmosphere of surface civility, marred occasionally by outbursts pinned up on the bulletin board anonymously by both nationalities. We tackled a heavy workload of operational and logistical planning with the Vietnamese. Two large-scale national security campaigns and scores of other activities were enough to keep us all busy for a time.

The preoccupation of the French establishment in Vietnam with my presence led to a confrontation in this period. Apparently the various stories about my doings had been collected by the French clandestine service, whose officers made complaints about me to the CIA, their normal liaison. They claimed they had a long list of charges against my conduct. I learned of this from the ambassador, who said that the French wanted to confront me, make the charges one by one, and record my answers. Although he warned me that he objected to such a confrontation, because of the star-chamber aspect of the proceeding, I was eager to accept. I had had my fill of attempts at character assassination by so many of the French, and it was time to meet them head-on.

When this was being discussed in the ambassador's office, the CIA chief, a smug smile on his face, offered to host the meeting with the French at a luncheon at his home, saying that this would be acceptable to the French. He seemed to be relishing the meeting, apparently expecting me to get a severe verbal mauling or worse from his French associates. The French, he added, would let him sit in as an observer of the interrogation, and he promised to give the ambassador a complete report for forwarding to Washington. I said quickly that I would submit a report also, which could be forwarded concurrently. I felt like Daniel about to enter the lion's den.

So, one noon soon afterward, I met with the French at the home of the CIA chief in Saigon. The local director of the French clandestine service, a colonel with whom I had had a most friendly association in my work with the O'Daniel mission to Indochina in 1953, sat at a card table, papers spread out before him, face stern, back rigidly erect, and started the meeting by formally requesting that I respond as I wished to any of the charges which were listed in the papers before him. Since the list was very long, it was doubtful that all the items could be taken up before luncheon. We could break the meeting long enough to dine and then return to the inquisition. There were several of his officers present who were thoroughly knowledgeable about the incidents on his list, and did I mind their presence, since they would be advising him on the correctness of any answers I gave? I assured him that I was pleased to have them present.

The first item charged me with supplying arms to Ba Cut, the Hoa Hao rebel, by an airdrop on a specific date. I could hardly believe my ears. I broke out laughing. The French officers glared. My laughter offended them. When I caught my breath again, I explained to them that on the specific date they had named, an airdrop indeed had been made to Ba Cut (who had been made a colonel in the Vietnamese Army by General Hinh just before his departure for Paris, although Ba Cut remained antagonistic toward the Saigon government). However, the operation demonstrably wasn't mine.

The Vietnamese Army, I informed them, had observed this airdrop and had investigated it. The Vietnamese Army had recovered three of the parachutes and traced them by their markings to a French military unit. French officers had been present with Ba Cut when he received the airdrop. The tail markings of the delivery aircraft had been noted, and a check with flight operations records and personnel at Tan Son Nhut airport had revealed the names of the French pilots and crew who had been aboard the aircraft at the time the delivery was made to Ba Cut. The Diem government had lodged a formal complaint to the French command about this incident, thoroughly documented. Whatever made them feel that, by some magic, I had had a hand in this purely French operation?

My inquisitors were shaken. The colonel turned aside and whispered urgently to the panel of "informed experts" who were sitting in. Then he gamely read off the second item. I was charged with supplying arms to Trinh minh Thé, thus assisting him in his fight against the French who, after all, were allies of the Americans. I answered this assertion in as quiet a tone as I could. Trinh minh Thé and his Lien-Minh troops were on their way to Saigon to be integrated into the regular Vietnamese Army and were certainly not about to fight the French unless the French tried to stop this move and thus interfere with the best interests of the Vietnamese Army — which they had asserted formally that they would aid. The fighting had ended *after* I had visited Trinh minh Thé in Tay Nihn, and I trusted that the significance of this fact, along with the safe return of three French prisoners whom the Lien-Minh had held, wasn't lost on them.

However, I continued, speaking of weapons, I had noticed several U.S. machine guns which the Lien-Minh had captured from French forces sent against them, and I had copied down the serial numbers of these guns to have them checked against U.S. lists in Saigon. They had been supplied originally by the U.S. to the French in Hanoi in 1951, to support French actions against the Communists. I had some sharp questions in my mind about how these weapons had been switched from use against the Communists to use by French forces against a Vietnamese officer who was known to be fighting the Communists, since he had captured the weapons in question from the French.

At this point in the proceedings, luncheon was announced. The French officers told our host that they couldn't stay for lunch. As a matter of fact, they couldn't continue the meeting any longer because they had urgent business to attend to elsewhere. They rose, gathered up their papers, and prepared to depart. Their faces were flushed with embarrassment. The first two items had blown up against them like exploding cigars, and they didn't want to sit there and be exposed to further humiliation. I insisted that they stay and finish the inquisition, whether they ate lunch or not, since the whole business was their idea, not mine. Reluctantly, they sat down again and we worked our way through the whole list. It was clear that the French officers thoroughly regretted having to go through with the farce they had begun.

All but one of the charges were patently inventions, easily destroyed fictions. The exception was the charge that my team in Haiphong was planning "to blow up the harbor of Haiphong." I admitted that they had talked about this subject and then explained the background. The French admiral commanding in Haiphong was an older man who lived next door to the house where my team and other Americans lived. The Americans had noticed that the French admiral's water closet was only a few feet from their house and that he spent an unusually long time seated on the toilet every morning; and whimsy had seized them. How could they give the old gentleman a thrill while he sat there of a morning? Should they throw firecrackers through the window? No, his heart might not stand the strain. They had hit instead upon the idea of talking loudly about blowing up the whole harbor, water and all, before it had to be turned over to the Vietminh. The admiral, overhearing this, bolted out of the bathroom to send an urgent message to General Ely. I had been informed of the incident promptly and had told these American officers to stop scaring French admirals. They had promised to behave. However, if the French Navy officers were still frightened, I would take further measures. The French officers told me curtly that that wouldn't be necessary.

The meeting ended. Presumably, the French command received a report of these proceedings. I gave my own summary report to our ambassador, to forward to Washington with whatever information the local CIA chief was reporting. The whole business should have ended there. Of course it didn't, the perversity of human nature being what it is. French attempts at character assassination continued, reaching their peak some weeks later in the spring of 1955. The fictions invented by French circles in Saigon found their way into the French press and eventually into the lurid journalism of weekend supplements in newspapers of other European countries. Well-meaning people would clip these stories and send them to me. They added a Mad Hatter touch to the events I was living through.

The whistle could have been blown on me for other activities in early 1955, though. For example, I passed along some psywar ideas to a group of Vietnamese nationalists who were getting ready to leave North Vietnam for the South. They described the long barrage of Communist propaganda which they had suffered for years. They were burning to strike a final blow in return before they departed from their northern homes. Did I have any suggestions? Indeed I did. I gave them two, which they promptly adopted.

The first idea was used just before the French quit the city of Hanoi and turned over control to the Vietminh. At the time, the Communist apparatus inside the city was busy with secret plans to ready the population to welcome the entry of Vietminh troops. I suggested that my nationalist friends issue a fake Communist manifesto, ordering everyone in the city except essential hospital employees to be out on the streets not just for a few hours of welcome but for a week-long celebration. In actuality this would mean a seven-day work stoppage. Transportation, electric power, and communication services would be suspended. This simple enlargement of plans already afoot should give the Communists an unexpectedly vexing problem as they started their rule.

An authentic-looking manifesto was printed and distributed during the hours of darkness on the second night before the scheduled entry of the Vietminh. The nationalists had assured me that they could distribute it safely because the chief of police in Hanoi was a close friend of theirs and would rescue any of them who might be caught and arrested. The next day the inhabitants of Hanoi read the fake manifesto and arranged to be away from homes and jobs for a one-week spree in the streets. The manifesto looked so authentic that the Communist cadre within the city bossily made sure, block by block, that the turnout would be 100 percent. A last-minute radio message from the Communists outside the city, ordering the Communists inside to disregard this manifesto, was taken to be a French attempt at counterpropaganda and was patriotically ignored. When the Vietminh forces finally arrived in Hanoi, their leaders began the touchy business of ordering people back to work. It took them three days to restore public services. A three-day work stoppage was a substantial achievement for a piece of paper.

When the nationalists saw me later in Saigon, however, they were woebegone. One arrest had been made when the manifesto was distributed. Their friend, the chief of police, became so imbued with the spirit of the affair that he had taken a stack of the manifestoes out in his car to help directly in the distribution. The French caught him in the act and, with the evidence of the copies of the manifesto in his possession, were convinced that he was a Communist agent. They had arrested him and put him in his own prison. He begged to be taken south as a prisoner. The French had done so and had turned him over to the Vietnamese government in Saigon. Nobody believed his story that the manifesto was a fake. He was being held in jail. Would I help? I explained what had happened to Prime Minister Diem. It took me until January to overcome his skepticism and obtain the release.

The second idea utilized Vietnamese superstitions in an American form. I had noted that there were many soothsayers in Vietnam doing a thriving business, but I had never seen any of their predictions published. Why not print an almanac for 1955 containing the predictions of the most famous astrologers and other arcane notables, especially those who foresaw a dark future for the Communists? Modestly priced—gratis copies would smack too much of propaganda—it could be sold in the North before the last areas there were evacuated. If it were well done, copies would probably pass from hand to hand and be spread all over the Communist-controlled regions.

The result was a hastily printed almanac filled with predictions about forthcoming events in 1955, including troubled times for the people in Communist areas and fights among the Communist leadership. To my own amazement, it foretold some things that actually happened (such as the bloody suppression of farmers who opposed the poorly-executed land reforms and the splits in the Politburo). The almanac became a best seller in Haiphong, the major refugee port. Even a large reprint order was sold out as soon as it hit the stands. My nationalist friends told me that it was the first such almanac seen in Vietnam in modern times. They were embarrassed to discover that a handsome profit had been made from what they had intended as a patriotic contribution to the nationalist cause. Unobtrusively, they donated this money to the funds helping the refugees from the North.

South Vietnam. Marines maneuvering a 105mm howitzer, a weapon that was especially effective for striking at a target in a trench or behind cover.
OFFICIAL U.S. MARINE CORPS PHOTO

CHAPTER 3

Digging In, 1961–1968

The American presence in Vietnam escalated steadily during the administrations of two Democrats, John F. Kennedy and Lyndon B. Johnson. Historians and political scientists have been most curious about the recklessness of policies undertaken by these apparently bright and sensitive men. Kennedy's most momentous decision was to send thousands of Special Forces to support the Army of the Republic of Vietnam (ARVN). The selection from Herbert Parmet's book on the Kennedy presidency offers a possible explanation for this step. In 1965, President Johnson raised the stakes in Vietnam when he authorized the bombing of targets in North Vietnam and sent Marines into South Vietnam. George C. Herring, one of the leading historians of the U.S. war in Vietnam, discusses the steps by which LBJ reached these decisions. Political scientist Larry Berman analyzes events leading up to and including Lyndon Johnson's Waterloo: the Communist Tet offensive in eary 1968. Finally, George Ball, Undersecretary of state in the Johnson administration, offers the perspective of an in-house dissenter from July 1965 (where the Herring piece leaves off) to early 1968. In light of what happened in Vietnam, Ball's views seem almost startling in their prescience.

7
No "Non-Essential Areas": JFK and Vietnam

HERBERT S. PARMET

The presidential summer retreat that year was not at Hyannis Port but at the nearby Squaw Island cottage that [Kennedy] rented from his father's friend Morton Downey, the tenor. There, just a few miles to the west of the family compound, was the possibility of more seclusion for himself, Jackie, and the children.

While Jackie was there, she had to be rushed to the nearby Otis Air Force Base Hospital for an emergency cesarean operation. The President heard the news while meeting with his Citizens Committee for a Nuclear Test Ban. By the time his plane landed at Otis at 1:30 that afternoon, their baby had already arrived. Five weeks premature and weighing just four pounds, ten and a half ounces, he had to struggle against a burden not uncommon among infants born so early, hyaline membrane disease. A coating of the air sacs was making breathing so difficult that although he seemed to be doing well at first, emergency assistance soon became necessary. He was rushed from Otis to the Children's Hospital Medical Center in Boston and placed in a chamber where oxygen was administered under pressure. But the infant, who was baptized as Patrick Bouvier Kennedy before leaving Otis, still couldn't overcome the condition. At 4:04 A.M. on August 9, just thirty-nine hours after his birth, his heart gave out under the strain.

The President was with his wife almost constantly during those hours. After the death he stayed at Squaw Island with Caroline and little John until their mother returned from the hospital. Patrick was originally buried near the President's birthplace, at Holyhood Cemetery in Brookline. O'Donnell and Powers have written that "The loss of Patrick affected the President and Jackie more deeply than anybody except their closest friends realized."[1]

By the late afternoon of Monday, August 12, the President was back in the Oval Office for a meeting on the situation in the Far East. With the ratification of the test ban treaty at the center of his attention, and with Cuba remaining as a potentially vulnerable spot politically, there were new

---

dangers to his position emanating from deteriorating conditions in South Vietnam. After a long period of relative stability, one in which Kennedy had been able to maneuver between those advocating stronger American commitments to the government in Saigon and others, such as Averell Harriman and Chester Bowles, who had opposed any major involvement, the "limited partnership" with Diem was becoming less tenable. North Vietnamese support for the Vietcong had been stepping up. By the end of 1962 there was a tenfold increase in the number of Americans killed and wounded over the previous year. In December, Mike Mansfield had gone there at the President's request and in effect confirmed what such American correspondents as David Halberstam and Neil Sheehan were filing from the war zone. Just as had the French, Mansfield warned, the United States was in danger of being sucked into a futile conflict. "It wasn't a pleasant picture I depicted for him," said the senator afterward.[2] Diem had resisted having American combat troops. He did not want the U.S. to take over his war and his country. Moreover, he continued to defy the Kennedy administration's insistence that he make internal reforms.

Kennedy's "limited partnership," as General Taylor called the enterprise, was characteristic of his approach. He increased the level of American "advisers," and the numbers of helicopters and other equipment. The CIA, under Station Chief John Richardson, worked actively to provide intelligence support. Diem meanwhile adopted the strategic-hamlet program of Sir Robert Thompson. Thompson, a British counterinsurgency expert, had experimented with the plan in Malaya and the Philippines. In South Vietnam, it was hoped, the guerrillas could in effect be starved out by preventing peasant villages from becoming sanctuaries, and that meant regrouping the villages into hamlets under the protection of the army with such barriers as moats and stake fences. At the same time, the number of Americans there under the Military Assistance and Advisory Group headed by General Paul Harkins escalated to some eleven thousand by the end of 1962.[3]

Later on it would become almost inconceivable to realize that the Vietnamese situation did not capture major attention from the American press until after the start of 1963. Only then did stories from that part of Southeast Asia command steady front-page coverage. Nor was it at the center of the President's own interest. Such matters as the Congo, Berlin, and Cuba had taken far more of his time.

In December, in addition to the Mansfield trip and the gloomy dispatches about the Diem government's inability to make much progress, further discouragement came from a State Department intelligence report. There was, in short, little room for optimism. Instead of giving more emphasis to nonmilitary means of counterinsurgency, reorganizing his government, and sharing some of his authority, Diem was moving too slowly in that direction and relying too much on the strategic-hamlet program and military measures. The adjustments he had been tentatively making in response to Washington's pressures had slowed down the Vietcong somewhat, but neither had their forces weakened nor the "national liberation war" abated. The guerrilla force was estimated at about twenty-three thousand elite fighting personnel, in addition to another 100,000 irregulars and sympathizers. The enemy still controlled about one fifth of the villages, had varying degrees of influence among an additional forty-seven percent, and was thought to be dominant over some nine percent of the population. Furthermore, "Viet Cong influence has almost certainly improved in urban areas not only through subversion and terrorism but also because of its propaganda appeal to the increasingly frustrated non-Communist anti-Diem elements," reported Roger Hilsman in an intelligence memorandum to Dean Rusk.[4]

There was increasing internal discontent among important military and civilian officials, who were participating in plots to overthrow Diem. If the fight against the Communists should deteriorate much further, Hilsman also warned, a "coup could come at any time."[5] Diem himself had been responding by turning inward and relying more on his brother, Nhu. "The two men," George Herring has written, "personally controlled military operations in the field and directed the strategic hamlet program, and they brooked no interference from their American advisers."[6] Nhu's wife had become the government's chief spokesman. Her insensitivity to the Buddhist critics of the Catholic family oligarchy ruling the government gradually brought increasing unpopularity to the regime.

Kennedy meanwhile feared the consequences of negotiating an American way out. His position had not altered from the off-the-record press briefing he gave on August 30, 1961, in which he said, "It is probably true in hindsight that it was not wise to become involved in Laos, but how do we withdraw from South Korea, from Viet-Nam. I don't know where the non-essential areas are. I can't see how we can withdraw from South Korea, Turkey, Iran, Pakistan. Over-extended commitments is a phrase with a lot of appeal, including to some at Harvard."[7] Holding fast in each area had long since become a test of American credibility. To yield in one would mean signaling susceptibility to withdrawal everywhere. As late as September 9, 1963, he was asked by David Brinkley on an NBC television program whether he subscribed to the domino theory. "I believe it," he replied. "I think that the struggle is close enough. China is so large, looms so high just beyond the frontiers, that if South Viet-Nam went, it would not only give them an improved geographic position for a guerrilla assault on Malaya, but would also give the impression that the wave of the future in southeast Asia was China and the Communists. So I believe it."[8]

At the start of the year Roger Hilsman and Michael Forrestal went to Saigon for the President. Kennedy wanted still another view. This time he knew it would come from two critics of Diem. Considering their outlook, a glowing report would have relaxed him.

Forrestal and Hilsman had separate sessions with Diem and his brother. From Diem, Forrestal heard about the importance of strength rather than reforms for maintaining loyalty from the peasants. The long conversation left the American visitor convinced that the South Vietnamese president was not only immovable but had rationalized the rule exerted by his own family as one that was consistent with the family structure of the society itself. Forrestal left without many doubts that Diem was a serious obstruction to any kind of settlement. Hilsman himself was an experienced guerrilla fighter. During World War II he had served with the famed Merrill's Marauders in Asia and with the Office of Strategic Services. When he met with Diem's brother, he thought that Nhu had been on drugs. He seemed devious, unattractive, harsh, and very explicit about his own ambitions. He also boasted about his connections with the northerners and some of their leaders. His attitude toward the problem of relocating the peasants in the delta was far more brutal than Diem's. Nhu also supported the use of chemical warfare and defoliants. Both Americans, Hilsman explained afterward, discovered that the war was "a fraud, a sham. The American military are still chasing Viet Cong and advising the Vietnamese to chase Viet Cong. They're not adopting the program the President has recommended, our own military are not. Diem has turned the strategic-hamlet program over to Nhu, who's taken the title, the name of it, and nothing else. And in fact, what Diem signed, what we persuaded him to, had not been adopted."[9]

Their report was less critical than Mansfield's, but still disturbing. Conceding that some progress had been made over the past year, it pointed out that the negatives were still "awesome." Even the officially supplied figures were disturbing. Despite U.S. urgings, it said, "there is still no single country-wide plan worthy of the name but only a variety of regional and provincial plans," and they seemed to be "both inconsistent and competitive." The strategic-hamlet program was mostly a sham, "inadequately equipped and defended," or "built prematurely in exposed areas." But the real question Forrestal and Hilsman raised was "whether the concentration of power in the hands of Diem and his family, especially Brother Nhu and his wife, and Diem's reluctance to delegate is alienating the middle and higher level officials on whom the government must depend to carry out its policies." The government had to be pushed harder for an overall plan.[10]

Meanwhile the Joint Chiefs of Staff came up with a plan for the possible withdrawal of American advisers starting in late 1963 and ending in 1965.[11] It was, however, one plan among many, and Kennedy's own reevaluation of the situation offered little evidence for believing that he was ready to negotiate and begin pulling out. He knew that falling back would leave him wide open to American conservatives. "If I tried to pull out completely now from Vietnam," he explained to Mansfield, "we would have another Joe McCarthy red scare on our hands, but I can do it after I'm reelected. So we had better make damned sure that I *am* reelected."[12]

Then came a sharp setback, an entirely new phase, and the upgrading of the war on the President's list of priorities. On May 8 a crowd gathered in Hué to celebrate the anniversary of Buddha's birth was fired into by government troops. Protesting against religious persecution and demanding a reversal of such policies, Buddhist priests went on hunger strikes. Far more startling to the world was the subsequent photograph of a monk seated in the middle of a downtown Saigon street totally enveloped in flames. That picture of his self-immolation in protest against the government became the most graphic evidence of the dissension. It was only the first in a series of such suicides and helped raise new questions about the entire American commitment.[13]

The division within Kennedy's administration was centered around whether or not support for Diem should be withdrawn. Those who argued against undermining the regime held that there was no adequate replacement in sight. Meanwhile Kennedy had sent several emissaries to Saigon to try to get Diem and the Buddhists together, but each side was immovable. When Ambassador Frederick Nolting's tour of duty expired that summer, the President replaced him by sending Henry Cabot Lodge, Jr., to Saigon.

Why Lodge? He spoke French, he had had experience in international affairs as Eisenhower's representative to the United Nations, but most of all, as Dean Rusk's biographer explains, Kennedy was persuaded by his secretary of state that "Lodge was to the Republican Party of 1963 what Dulles had been in 1950: the personification of its liberal internationalist wing.... Rusk sought to coopt part of the Republican Party, to outmaneuver ...Goldwater..."[14]

Actually the Lodge appointment was entirely consistent with Kennedy's placement of people like John McCloy and John McCone in positions of potential partisan conflict. In his 1964 interview Bob Kennedy explained that "Lodge was interested in going someplace where there was a difficult problem, they needed somebody who would work with the military, spoke French, had some diplomatic experiences. So he fitted into it."[15]

The most intriguing possibility eventually raised is that Lodge was sent to effectuate the overthrow of Diem by working with the generals who hoped to bring about a coup.[16] Lodge has explained that Kennedy was very much disturbed by the picture of the monk on fire. He talked about the overall reportage of what was going on in Saigon and said that the Diem government was entering a terminal phase. The American embassy had also had poor press relations. "I suppose that there are worse press relations to be found in the world today," Lodge remembered that the President told him, "and I wish you would take charge of press relations." As far as helping to overthrow Diem, Kennedy said that the "Vietnamese are doing that for themselves and don't need any outside help."[17]

Almost immediately after that, Diem helped to speed his own downfall. Just before Lodge's arrival, in complete contradiction of a promise made to Ambassador Nolting, Nhu's American-trained Special Forces went on a rampage against Buddhist pagodas in Hué, Saigon, and other cities. More than fourteen hundred Buddhists were arrested. Right after that

American intelligence also reported that Diem was actively engaged in trying to work out a deal with the Hanoi regime of North Vietnam.[18]

If Lodge had been sent with an understanding that he might have to support the generals wanting to get rid of Diem, his actions appeared to confirm that purpose. He showed as little outward support toward the South Vietnamese president as possible, disassociating himself almost completely.[19] On August 24, with Kennedy at Hyannis Port and, "by a strange coincidence, most of the other senior members of the administration" out of town for the weekend, word arrived that South Vietnamese generals knew that Ngo Dinh Nhu was negotiating with the Communists. The information was relayed to Washington via long-distance telephone by Admiral Harry Felt.[20]

Quickly on that Saturday, after a series of consultations and telephone calls—including to the President, Forrestal, and Hilsman—Harriman sent a cable to Lodge in the name of the State Department. Its message was clear: The U.S. could no longer tolerate a situation where power remained in Nhu's hands. "We wish to give Diem reasonable opportunity to remove Nhus, but if he remains obdurate, then we are prepared to accept the obvious implication that we can no longer support Diem. You may also tell appropriate military commanders we will give them direct support in any interim period of breakdown central government mechanism." Lodge cabled back that it was most unlikely that Diem would get rid of both his brother and sister-in-law and that Nhu was in control of the combat forces in Saigon. "Therefore," he replied, "propose we go straight to Generals with our demands, without informing Diem. Would tell them we prepared to have Diem without Nhus but it is in effect up to them whether to keep him."[21]

For a time it almost seemed that it was the American State Department, in the absence of Dean Rusk, Robert McNamara, John McCone, or McGeorge Bundy, that had undertaken its own coup against those who continued to believe that there was little choice but to back Diem. General Maxwell Taylor first heard about the cable when Ros Gilpatric called him that evening at Fort Myer with the information that clearance from the President had already been obtained and that, in Rusk's absence, George Ball had consented while playing golf. Gilpatric has since observed that "I frankly thought it was an end run. I didn't see why it had to be done Saturday night with the President away, with Rusk away, with McNamara away, Bundy away. I was suspicious of the circumstances in which it was being done. . . . In other words the Defense and military were brought in sort of after the fact."[22] To General Taylor it seemed somewhat of a *fait accompli.* Even if Diem wanted to comply, the telegram to Lodge was obviously an open encouragement "to plotters to move against him at any time."[23]

Mike Forrestal agrees that the circumstances indeed were suspicious. Harriman had originated the cable. The senior diplomat, by then undersecretary of state for political affairs, wanted to take advantage of the weekend conditions because he knew how much trouble he would have getting support if everybody were present.[24] Still, the most important—and often the least noticed element—was the endorsement that came from the President himself, not at the center of action in the Oval Office, but at the other end of a wire in Hyannis Port.

But there was no immediate result. The cable had advised the Voice of America radio people to publicize only that part of the message that would prevent the Vietnamese army from being associated with any plot. Hilsman tried to work that out by briefing a news correspondent so the information could be fed to the Voice, thereby maintaining the usual procedure according to which the propaganda network operated. But the people who actually made the broadcast failed to check their instructions with a telegram sent to guide them. The entire story then went out on the airwaves, "not only," as Hilsman wrote, "that the United States had proof that the Vietnamese Army was innocent of the assault on the pagodas and that Nhu's secret police and Special Forces were to blame," but about the threatened sharp American reduction of aid to Diem.[25]

At a meeting in the embassy in Saigon, Lodge was furious. "Jack Kennedy would never approve of doing things this way," he shouted. "This certainly isn't his way of running a government."[26]

When the President returned from the Cape and met with his staff that Monday, he found more opposition to the Harriman cable than he had evidently expected. "And so the government split in two," the attorney general later said. "It was the only time really, in three years, the government was broken in two in a very disturbing way."[27] In Saigon the generals were unable to get the backing of key army units and remained uncertain, despite CIA assurances, of what American intelligence would do, and withheld any actions.[28]

When the coup came, it resulted from the appropriate opening, which was a combination of the muffled hand from Washington and changed circumstances in Saigon. In the interim Kennedy's customary indecision made the entire process seem more diabolical than it was. First of all the failed move of August provided an opportunity to reassess the situation. At the end of the month Lodge cabled that there was "no turning back" from the overthrow. American prestige was already too committed.[29] Kennedy sent him a personal and private message that pledged his full support to enable his ambassador to "conclude this operation successfully," and, with the clear memory of what happened at the Bay of Pigs, added, "I know from experience that failure is more destructive than an appearance of indecision."[30] On September 2, after De Gaulle had criticized the American involvement in Vietnam, Kennedy was interviewed by Walter Cronkite on a CBS television news program. At that point, in response to a question about Diem changing his pattern, the President answered in a matter that has too often been quoted incompletely. What he said at that point was: "We hope that he comes to see that, but in the final analysis it is the people and the government itself who have to win or lose this struggle. All we can do is help, and we are making it very clear, but I don't agree with those who say we should withdraw. That would be a great mistake."[31] It was not immediately evident that, in reality, he was talking just as much about the Vietnamese choice of a leader as about the American commitment. On the same day that he talked to Cronkite, Kennedy called Hilsman and asked whether his undersecretary of state had done any thinking about "selective cuts in aid that would not hurt the war effort but still make Diem and Nhu understand that we mean business."[32] Encouragement was also given to Senator Church's threat to introduce a resolution calling for the suspension of aid to South Vietnam unless it ended its repressive policies.[33] During this period, however, the President had no way of knowing that things in Saigon would be better without Diem. But his hand was being pushed. An Alsop story in *The Washington Post* on September 18, evidently based on interviews with Diem and Nhu, gave further information about their dealings with Hanoi.[34] Reacting to such stories, Kennedy sent McNamara and General Taylor to Saigon. Once again Diem was immovable, contending that the war was going well, pointing with pride to favorable results from just completed rigged elections, and, as McNamara wrote, offering "absolutely no assurances that he would take any steps in response to the representations made to American visitors.... His manner was one of at least outward serenity and of a man who had patiently explained a great deal and who hoped he had thus corrected a number of misapprehensions." The McNamara-Taylor report, however, cautioned that it was not the time to take the initiative in trying to change the government. "Our policy should be to seek urgently to identify and build contacts with an alternative leadership if and when it appears." Mainly the suggestion of the mission was to apply selective pressures on the regime.[35]

On October 2 the White House announced that a thousand men would be withdrawn by the end of the year. Gilpatric later stated that McNamara did indicate to him that the withdrawal was part of the President's plan to wind down the war, but, that was too far in the future. They were still, at that moment, deeply divided about what to do about the internal situation in Saigon.[36] At just that point the recall of John Richardson, the CIA station chief who was close to the regime, seemed to be another signal, although it may not have been intended for that purpose.[37] Still, it is hard to believe that the move, along with the talk about reductions of American aid to the government, lacked the purpose of giving further encouragement to the anti-Diem generals.

During a series of meetings that were held from August 23 through October 23 between Lodge, General Harkins, and the anti-Diem plotters, including Duong Van Minh (Big Minh), there was agreement on what had to be done: The U.S. agreed that Nhu had to go and that the disposition of Diem ought to be left to the generals. There could be no American help to initiate the action, but support would come during the interim period in case of a breakdown of the central government's mechanism. What was also clear was that if they did not get rid of the Nhus and the Buddhist situation were not redressed, the United States would end economic and military support.[38]

Lodge later reported that he had advised the President "not to thwart" a coup. That act, rather than initiating one, would have constituted interference.[39] Yet even at that point Kennedy wavered, suffering a recurrence of earlier doubts. He told Bundy that the U.S. should be in a position to blow the whistle if it looked as though the coup was failing.[40] Bundy cabled Lodge that there should be no American action that would reveal any knowledge that a coup was even possible. The "burden of proof" must be on the plotters "to show a substantial possibility of quick success; otherwise we should discourage them from proceeding since a miscalculation could result in jeopardizing U.S. position in Southeast Asia."[41] Indeed, the Americans in Saigon behaved as though things were normal.

On the morning of November 1 Admiral Felt paid a courtesy call on Diem at the presidential palace. In the afternoon Diem called Lodge to ask about the American attitude toward the coup. Lodge was evasive, but admitted he was worried about Diem's personal safety. That night, the president and Nhu escaped from the palace to a hideout in the Chinese quarter of Saigon. From there Diem contacted the generals and asked for safe conduct back so he could make a graceful exit from power. On his return, however, according to a prearranged plan, he and his brother were shot and killed by Big Minh's personal bodyguard.[42]

The news of Diem's death outraged Kennedy. General Taylor wrote that he "leaped to his feet and rushed from the room with a look of shock and dismay on his face which I had never seen before."[43] George Smathers remembered that Jack Kennedy blamed the CIA, saying "I've got to do something about those bastards"; they should be stripped of their exorbitant power.[44] Mike Forrestal called Kennedy's reaction "both personal and religious," and especially troubled by the implication that a Catholic President had participated in a plot to assassinate a coreligionist.[45] Every account of Kennedy's response is in complete agreement. Until the very end he had hoped Diem's life could be spared.

It has now become clear that however futile his efforts Kennedy tried to prevent the murder. He told Francis Cardinal Spellman that he had known in advance that the Vietnamese leader would probably be killed, but in the end he could not control the situation.[46] At least one attempt, and possibly three, came from a direct attempt to communicate with Diem by using a personal emissary, someone completely loyal to Jack Kennedy, someone totally without any other obligation, his intimate friend, Torby Macdonald, the Massachusetts congressman.

As far as is known, there are no written records. It was completely secret. Mike Forrestal remembers briefing Macdonald for the trip.[47] Torbert Macdonald, Jr., recalls that his father told him about it.[48] The congressman's widow is certain that he made at least three trips to Saigon for the

President.[49] Torby's closest friend during his final years, who desires to remain anonymous, has a photograph of him posing before the ancient temple at Angkor-Wat in Cambodia, indicating that he went through that country while traveling to South Vietnam as a private citizen.[50]

Macdonald himself explained why Kennedy sent him. The President had begun to develop personal sources of information from FBI men who were bypassing J. Edgar Hoover and going directly to him. Some CIA people were following a similar route and avoiding the Agency. By that time the President was learning. When he first came into office, he had been intimidated by the Pentagon and the CIA, but he had begun to find out how to get around them. When he heard that Big Minh and his group were planning to assassinate Diem, he wanted to make a direct contact. He was hesitant about using the embassy in Saigon because he could not trust his own people there. Nor did he have enough confidence in Lodge, who had maintained a distant relationship with Diem. Finally, there was no South Vietnamese he could trust. So he called on Torby, who then carried the President's personal plea, which was to get rid of his brother and take refuge in the American embassy. As Macdonald later explained it, he told Diem: "They're going to kill you. You've got to get out of there temporarily to seek sanctuary in the American embassy and you must get rid of your sister-in-law and your brother." But Diem refused. "He just won't do it," Macdonald reported to the President. "He's too stubborn; just refuses to."[51]

Diem's death preceded Jack Kennedy's by just three weeks. What JFK would have done about American involvement in South Vietnam can never be known for certain. It is probable that not even he was sure.

Ken O'Donnell has been the most vigorous advocate of the argument that the President was planning to liquidate the American stake right after the completion of the 1964 elections would have made it politically possible. The withdrawal of those thousand advisers, he said, was but a first step in that process.[52] At the time the Joint Chiefs asked for an increase of American strength to seventeen thousand, Kennedy told his military aide, Ted Clifton, that he would go along with the request but had warned that he would approve no more.[53]

At that moment Kennedy could not have anticipated the shape of either the domestic political climate or the situation in Southeast Asia. Still, for him to have withdrawn at any point short of a clear-cut settlement would have been most unlikely. As Sorensen has said in an oral-history interview, Kennedy "did feel strongly that for better or worse, enthusiastic or unenthusiastic, we had to stay there until we left on terms other than a retreat or abandonment of our commitment."[54] The remarks he had planned to deliver at the Trade Mart in Dallas on the afternoon of November 22 contained the following statement of purpose: "Our assistance to these nations can be painful, risky and costly, as is true in Southeast Asia today. But we dare not weary of the test."[55] "I talked with him hundreds of times about Vietnam," said Dean Rusk, "and on no single occasion did he ever whisper any such thing to his own secretary of state." In addition, and what was more important, Rusk pointed out, was that a decision in 1963 to take troops out in 1965 following the election of 1964 "would have been a decision to have Americans in uniform in combat for domestic political reasons. No President can do that and live with it."[56] When Ken O'Donnell was pressed about whether the President's decision to withdraw meant that he would [not] have undertaken the escalation that followed in 1965, the position became qualified. Kennedy, said O'Donnell, had not faced the same level of North Vietnamese infiltration as did President Johnson, thereby implying that he, too, would have responded in a similar way under those conditions.[57] As Bobby Kennedy later said, his brother had reached the point where he felt that South Vietnam was worth keeping for psychological and political reasons "more than anything else."[58]

NOTES

1. O'Donnell and Powers, "*Johnny,*" p. 378; cf. Travell, *Office Hours*, p. 421; Lincoln, *Twelve Years*, pp. 349–354; Gallagher, *My Life*, pp. 283–289.

2. Herring, *America's Longest War,* p. 92.

3. Walt W. Rostow, JFK Symposium Remarks, Los Angeles, California, November 14, 1980.

4. Gravel, *Pentagon Papers*, v. 2, pp. 690–691.

5. Ibid., p. 691.

6. Herring, *America's Longest War,* p. 90.

7. Memorandum, Chalmers Roberts, August 30, 1961, Roberts Personal Papers.

8. Kennedy, *Public Papers . . . 1963*, p. 659.

9. Michael Forrestal, interview, February 17, 1981; Roger Hilsman, JFKL-OH (Dennis J. O'Brien interview).

10. Gravel, *Pentagon Papers*, v. 2, pp. 717–725.

11. Herring, *America's Longest War,* p. 94.

12. O'Donnell and Powers, "*Johnny,*" p. 16.

13. Herring, *America's Longest War,* p. 96.

14. Cohen, *Rusk,* p. 189.

15. Robert F. Kennedy, JFKL-OH (John Bartlow Martin interview).

16. Geoffrey Warner, "The United States and the Fall of Diem," *Australian Outlook*, 28 (December 1974), p. 247.

17. Henry Cabot Lodge, Jr., JFKL-OH (Charles Bartlett interview).

18. Herring, *America's Longest War,* p. 97.

19. Ibid., p. 103; Robert F. Kennedy, JFKL-OH (John Bartlow Martin interview).

20. Warner, "Fall of Diem," pp. 249–250.

21. Gravel, *Pentagon Papers*, v. 2, pp. 734–735.

22. Roswell Gilpatric, JFKL-OH (Dennis J. O'Brien interview).

23. Taylor, *Swords*, p. 293.

24. Michael Forrestal, interview, February 17, 1981.

25. Hilsman, *To Move a Nation*, p. 489.

26. Warner, "Fall of Diem," p. 252.

27. Robert F. Kennedy, JFKL-OH (John Bartlow Martin interview).

28. Taylor, *Swords*, p. 293.

29. David Halberstam, *The Best and the Brightest* (New York: Random House, 1972), p. 264; Gravel, *Pentagon Papers*, v. 2, pp. 728–739.

30. Warner, "Fall of Diem," p. 255.

31. Kennedy, *Public Papers...1963*, p. 652.

32. Hilsman, *To Move a Nation*, p. 500.

33. Gravel, *Pentagon Papers*, v. 2, pp. 245–246.

34. *Washington Post*, September 18, 1963.

35. Gravel, *Pentagon Papers*, v. 2, pp. 750–751, 752–753.

36. Roswell Gilpatric, JFKL-OH (Dennis J. O'Brien interview); Sorensen, *Kennedy*, p. 659.

37. Geoffrey Warner, "The Death of Diem," *Australian Outlook* (April 1975), pp. 12–13; Roger Hilsman, JFKL-OH (Dennis J. O'Brien interview).

38. CIA Chronological Report, October 23, 1963, DDRS (78) 142A.

39. Henry Cabot Lodge, Jr., JFKL-OH (Charles Bartlett interview).

40. Warner, "Death of Diem," p. 14.

41. Gravel, *Pentagon Papers*, v. 2, p. 789.

42. Warner, "Death of Diem," pp. 15–16.

43. Taylor, *Swords*, p. 301.

44. George Smathers, JFKL-OH (Don Wilson interview).

45. Michael Forrestal, interview, February 17, 1981.

46. Blair Clark, interview, July 20, 1977.

47. Michael Forrestal, interview, February 15, 1981.

48. Torbert Macdonald, Jr., interview, August 6, 1979.

49. Phyllis Macdonald, interview, August 9, 1979.

50. Confidential interview, July 25, 1977

51. Ibid.

52. O'Donnell and Powers, "*Johnny*," p. 382.

53. Chester V. Clifton, interview, October 1, 1981.

54. Theodore C. Sorensen, JFKL-OH (Carl Kaysen interview).

55. Kennedy, *Public Papers...*1963, p. 892.

56. Dean Rusk, interview, April 27, 1981.

57. Kenneth P. O'Donnell, interview, December 4, 1976.

58. Robert F. Kennedy, JFKL-OH (John Bartlow Martin interview).

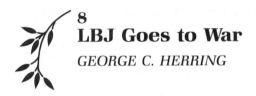

8
LBJ Goes to War
GEORGE C. HERRING

Between November 1963 and July 1965, Lyndon Baines Johnson transformed a limited commitment to assist the South Vietnamese government into an open-ended commitment to preserve an independent, non-
Communist South Vietnam. Johnson inherited from Kennedy a rapidly
deteriorating situation in South Vietnam. Fearing that large-scale American involvement might jeopardize his chances of election in 1964 and
threaten his beloved Great Society domestic programs, he temporized for
over a year, expanding American assistance and increasing the number
of advisers in hopes that a beefed-up version of his predecessor's policy
might somehow stave off disaster. South Vietnam's survival appeared more
in doubt than ever in early 1965, however, and over the next six months
Johnson made his fateful decisions, authorizing a sustained air offensive
against North Vietnam and dispatching American ground forces to stem
the tide in the south. By July 1965, the United States was engaged in a
major war on the Asian mainland.

In late 1963, North Vietnam significantly escalated the war. The overthrow of Diem had been at best a mixed blessing for Hanoi. It eliminated
a potentially dangerous anti-Communist leader, but it also removed the
rallying point of the opposition in South Vietnam, and for a time the revolutionary spirit ebbed in the south. Desertions from the NLF increased
and recruitment stalled, and even where the government lost ground the
Vietcong did not always gain. North Vietnam attempted to negotiate with
the junta the sort of deal discussed with Diem, but it seems to have gotten
nowhere and it saw no weakening of U.S. resolve. Determined to attain the
goal that had eluded them in 1954, the North Vietnamese leaders increasingly recognized that they could not succeed without a major commitment of their own resources. At the Central Committee's Ninth Plenum
in December 1963, the party leadership decided to instruct the Vietcong
to step up its political agitation and military operations against the South
Vietnamese government. More important, Hanoi decided to expand infiltration into the south and even to send its own regular units into the war.
The North Vietnamese at this point seem to have been unsure of Soviet
support and they recognized the possibility of war with the United States.

From *America's Longest War*, 2e by George C. Herring, copyright © 1986 by McGraw-
Hill Publishing Company. Reproduced with permission.

In what turned out to be a colossal miscalculation, they gambled that rapid escalation might force the disintegration of South Vietnam, leaving the United States no choice but to disengage.

For Johnson and the United States, the road to war was longer and more torturous. After listening to Ambassador Lodge's gloomy assessment of the post-coup prospects of the Saigon government on November 24, 1963, Johnson claimed to feel like a catfish that had just "grabbed a big juicy worm with a right sharp hook in the middle of it." The new President expressed his determination to meet the Communist challenge, however, and he vowed not to let Vietnam go the way of China. He instructed Lodge to "go back and tell those generals in Saigon that Lyndon Johnson intends to stand by our word...." Two days later, National Security Council Action Memorandum (NSAM) 273 incorporated his pledge into policy, affirming that it was "the central objective of the United States" to assist the "people and Government" of South Vietnam "to win their contest against the externally directed and supported communist conspiracy."[1]

During the first three months of Johnson's presidency, the situation in South Vietnam got steadily worse. Some Americans had assumed that the removal of Diem and Nhu would restore domestic harmony and promote political unity, but the effect was quite the opposite. Diem had systematically destroyed the opposition, and his death left a gaping political vacuum. Buddhists and Catholics comprised the most coherent groups in the cities, but their hatred of each other was implacable and neither represented a viable political force. The Buddhists were splintered into a bewildering array of factions. Although tightly disciplined, the Catholics had no political program or mass appeal. The coup released long pent-up forces, and in the months that followed new groups proliferated, but they were leaderless and hopelessly fragmented. In the countryside, decay was also the norm. The removal of Diemist controls over information made clear that the statistics compiled by the government to demonstrate progress had been grossly in error. U.S. officials were alarmed to discover that the insurgents controlled more people and territory than had been assumed. The strategic hamlet program was in shambles, many of the key hamlets in the critical Mekong Delta having been torn down either by the Vietcong or their own occupants. The situation was "very disturbing," McNamara warned Johnson in late December, and unless the trend could be reversed within the next few months, South Vietnam might be lost....[2]

Under these circumstances, Americans increasingly looked north for a solution they could not find in the south. Alarmed by the persistent lack of progress in South Vietnam, annoyed by Hanoi's defiant response, and fearful that the North Vietnamese might seek to exploit the administration's presumed immobility in an election year, some of Johnson's advisers by the midsummer of 1964 had developed a full "scenario" of graduated overt pressures against the north, according to which the President, after securing a Congressional resolution, would authorize air strikes against selected North Vietnamese targets. Secretaries Rusk and McNamara finally

rejected the program for fear that it would "raise a whole series of dis-
agreeable questions" which might jeopardize passage of the administration's civil rights legislation, but the proposals clearly indicate the drift of
official attitudes during this period.[3]

The administration implemented much of the proposed "scenario"
in response to a series of incidents in the Gulf of Tonkin in early August.
While engaged in electronic espionage off the coast of North Vietnam
on the morning of August 1, the destroyer *Maddox* encountered a group
of North Vietnamese torpedo boats. South Vietnamese gunboats involved
in OPLAN 34A operations had bombarded the nearby island of Hon Me
the preceding evening, and the North Vietnamese, apparently assuming
that the *Maddox* had been supporting the covert attacks, closed in on the
destroyer. In a brief and frenzied engagement, the *Maddox* opened fire, the
patrol boats launched torpedoes, and aircraft from the *USS Ticonderoga*
joined the fighting. The torpedo boats were driven away, and one was
badly damaged.

Johnson was reportedly enraged when he learned of the encounter,
but no retaliation was ordered. "The other side got a sting out of this,"
Secretary of State Rusk remarked. "If they do it again, they'll get another
sting."[4] To avoid any appearance of weakness and to assert traditional
claims to freedom of the seas, the Navy ordered the *Maddox* to resume
operations in the Gulf of Tonkin and sent the destroyer *C. Turner Joy* to
support it. The United States was not seeking to provoke another attack, but
it did not go out of its way to avoid one either. The administration kept the
destroyers close to North Vietnamese shores, where they were vulnerable
to attack. Eager for "open season" on the North Vietnamese, responsible
military officials in the area were choosing targets for retaliatory raids
before reports of a second attack began to come in.

On the night of August 4, while operating in heavy seas some sixty
miles off the North Vietnamese coast, the *Maddox* and *Turner Joy* suddenly
reported that they were under attack. The initial reports were based on
sonar and radar contacts, both of which were admittedly unreliable under
the adverse weather conditions, and on visual sightings of torpedoes and
enemy searchlights on a night which one seaman described as "darker
than the hubs of Hell." The captain of the *Maddox* later conceded that
evidence of an attack was less than conclusive. North Vietnamese gunboats were probably operating in the area, but no evidence has ever been
produced to demonstrate that they committed hostile acts.

This time, Washington was poised to strike back. Reports of an impending attack began to arrive in the capital early on the morning of
August 4, and the Joint Chiefs immediately insisted that the United States
must "clobber" the attackers. Throughout the morning, while the destroyers reported being under continuous attack, the Joint Chiefs worked out a
series of retaliatory options ranging from limited air strikes against North
Vietnamese naval installations to mining of parts of the coastline. When
the President met with his advisers in the early afternoon, there was no

doubt that an attack had taken place. The CIA pointed out quite logically that the North Vietnamese might be responding defensively to the commando raids on their territory, but the administration concluded that Hanoi was trying to make the United States appear a "paper tiger." Johnson and his advisers agreed, as McNamara put it, that "we cannot sit still as a nation and let them attack us on the high seas and get away with it." They quickly decided on a "firm, swift retaliatory [air] strike" against North Vietnamese torpedo boat bases.[5]

Although serious questions were subsequently raised about the nature and even existence of the alleged attacks, the administration stuck by its decision. "FLASH" messages from the *Maddox* arriving in Washington early in the afternoon indicated that "freak weather effects" on the radar and sonar, as well as "overeager" sonarmen, may have accounted for many of the reported torpedo attacks and enemy contacts. Contradicting earlier messages, the commander of the *Maddox* also reported that there had been no "visual sightings" and that a "complete evaluation" of all the evidence should be made before retaliation was ordered. McNamara postponed implementation of the air strikes temporarily to make "damned sure that the attacks had taken place." By late afternoon, however, he was convinced, on the basis of evidence which appears suspect. Ignoring the belated uncertainty of the men on the scene, the Secretary of Defense accepted at face value the judgment of the Commander-in-Chief, Pacific Fleet, Admiral U.S. Grant Sharp, in Honolulu, whose certainty was based on the first reports from the *Maddox* and intercepts of North Vietnamese messages indicating that two patrol boats had been "sacrificed." McNamara and his military advisers did not knowingly lie about the alleged attacks, but they were obviously in a mood to retaliate and they seem to have selected from the evidence available to them those parts that confirmed what they wanted to believe. Accepting McNamara's conclusions without question, Johnson in the late afternoon authorized retaliatory air strikes against North Vietnamese torpedo boat bases and nearby oil storage dumps. Described by the Joint Chiefs as a "pretty good effort," the strikes destroyed or damaged twenty-five patrol boats and 90 percent of the oil storage facilities at Vinh.[6]

The President also seized the opportunity to secure passage of a Congressional resolution authorizing him to take "all necessary measures to repel any armed attacks against the forces of the United States and to prevent further aggression." Johnson did not seek the resolution as a blank check for a later expansion of the war to which he was already committed. At this point, he still hoped that American objectives in Vietnam could be achieved by limited means. His main purpose rather was to indicate to North Vietnam that the nation was united in its determination to stand firm in Vietnam. The resolution also served immediate domestic political needs. The show of force and the appeal for national support permitted him to disarm his Republican challenger, Senator Barry Goldwater, who had vigorously urged escalation of the war, and to demonstrate that he could be firm in defending American interests without recklessly expanding the war. In presenting its case, however, the administration deliberately misled Congress and the American people. Nothing was said about the covert raids. Official reports indicated that the *Maddox* was engaged in routine patrols in international waters. The incidents were portrayed as "deliberate attacks" and "open aggression on the high seas."

Congress responded quickly and pliantly. Senator Wayne Morse of Oregon raised some embarrassing questions about the covert raids and the mission of the American destroyers. Senator Ernest Gruening of Alaska attacked the resolution as a "predated declaration of war," and Senator Gaylord Nelson of Wisconsin attempted to limit the grant of authority to the executive. During a period when America's national interests seemed constantly in peril, however, Congress had grown accustomed to approving executive initiatives without serious question, and the crisis atmosphere seemed to leave no time for debate. "The American flag has been fired upon," Representative Ross Adair of Indiana exclaimed. "We will not and cannot tolerate such things."[7] The Senate debated the resolution less than ten hours, during much of which time the chamber was less than one-third full. By his own admission more concerned with the challenge posed by Goldwater than with giving a blank check to Johnson, Senator J. William Fulbright carefully shepherded the resolution through, choking off debate and amendments. The vote in the Senate was an overwhelming 88 to 2, with only Morse and Gruening dissenting. Consideration in the House was even more perfunctory, passage taking a mere forty minutes and the vote unanimous.

From a domestic political standpoint, Johnson's handling of the Tonkin Gulf incident was masterly. His firm but restrained response to the alleged North Vietnamese attacks won broad popular support, his rating in the Louis Harris poll skyrocketing from 42 to 72 percent overnight. He effectively neutralized Goldwater on Vietnam, a fact which contributed to his overwhelming electoral victory in November. Moreover, this first formal Congressional debate on Vietnam brought a near-unanimous endorsement of the President's policies and provided him an apparently solid foundation on which to construct future policy.

In time, Johnson would pay a heavy price for his easy victory. U.S. prestige was now publicly and more firmly committed not merely to defending South Vietnam but also to responding to North Vietnamese provocations. By attacking North Vietnamese targets, the President temporarily silenced his hawkish critics inside and outside of government, but in doing so he had broken a long-standing barrier against taking the war to the north. The first steps having been taken, the next ones would be easier. Johnson's victory in Congress probably encouraged him to take the legislators lightly in making future policy decisions on Vietnam. And when the administration's case for reprisals later turned out to be less than overwhelming, many members of Congress correctly concluded that they had been deceived. The President's resounding triumph in the Tonkin Gulf affair brought with it enormous, if still unforeseen, costs....

By the end of January, most of Johnson's advisers agreed that persisting instability in the south required the United States to bomb the north. The bombing might not have a decisive impact on the war, William Bundy advised, but it offered "at least a faint hope of really improving the Vietnamese situation." More important, the impending collapse in South Vietnam made clear that a continuation of existing policies could "only lead to a disastrous defeat." Even if the United States could not hold South Vietnam, Assistant Secretary of Defense John McNaughton argued, it would appear stronger to allies and adversaries alike if it "kept slugging away" rather than meekly accepting defeat. No formal policy decision was made, but by the end of January most administration officials agreed that the United States should seize the first opportunity to launch air strikes and should then "feel its way" into a sustained bombing campaign against North Vietnam.[8]

The opportunity was not long in coming. On February 6, Vietcong units attacked a U.S. Army barracks in Pleiku and a nearby helicopter base, killing nine Americans and destroying five aircraft. That evening, after a meeting of less than two hours, the administration decided to strike back. Only Senator Mansfield dissented, arguing that the United States might provoke Chinese intervention, but Johnson brusquely dismissed Mansfield's argument. "We have kept our guns over the mantel and our shells in the cupboard for a long time now," he exclaimed with obvious impatience. "I can't ask our American soldiers out there to continue to fight with one hand behind their backs."[9] The President ordered the immediate implementation of FLAMING DART, a plan of reprisal strikes already drawn up by the Joint Chiefs of Staff. Later that day and again the following day American aircraft struck North Vietnamese military installations just across the seventeenth parallel. When the Vietcong on February 10 attacked an American enlisted men's quarters at Qui Nhon, the President ordered another, even heavier series of air strikes.

Within less than forty-eight hours, the administration had moved from reprisals to a continuing, graduated program of air attacks against North Vietnam. McGeorge Bundy returned from a visit to South Vietnam the day after the Pleiku raids and warned that "without new U.S. action defeat appears inevitable—probably not in a matter of weeks or perhaps even months, but within the next year or so." Bundy and McNaughton, who had accompanied him to Vietnam, urged the immediate implementation of a policy of "sustained reprisal" against the north. McNaughton conceded the risks but argued that "measured against the cost of defeat" the program would be "cheap," and even if it failed to turn the tide "the value of the effort" would "exceed the costs."[10] The next day, apparently without extended debate, the administration initiated ROLLING THUNDER, the policy of gradually intensified air attacks which Bundy and McNaughton had advocated.

The administration was considerably less than candid in explaining to the American public the reasons for and significance of its decision to bomb North Vietnam. Spokesmen from the President down justified the air strikes as a response to the Pleiku attack and emphatically denied implementing any basic change of policy. It is abundantly clear, however, that Pleiku was the pretext rather than the cause of the February decision. The possibility of a South Vietnamese collapse appeared to make essential the adoption of a policy American officials had been advocating for more than two months. It was, therefore, simply a matter of finding the right opportunity to justify measures to which the administration was already committed. Pleiku provided such an opportunity, although it could as easily have been something else. "Pleikus are like streetcars," McGeorge Bundy later remarked.[11] And despite the administration's disclaimers, the February decisions marked an important watershed in the war. The initiation of regular bombing attacks advanced well beyond the limited "tit-for-tat" reprisal strikes of Tonkin Gulf and provided a built-in argument for further escalation should that become necessary.

Indeed, almost as soon as ROLLING THUNDER got underway, there were pressures to expand it. The initial attacks achieved meager results, provoking Taylor to complain that ROLLING THUNDER had constituted but a "few isolated thunder claps" and to call for a "mounting crescendo" of air strikes against North Vietnam.[12] Intelligence reports ominously warned that the military situation in South Vietnam was steadily deteriorating and that at the present rate the government within six months might be reduced to a series of islands surrounding the provincial capitals. From the outset, Johnson had insisted on maintaining tight personal control over the air war; "they can't even bomb an outhouse without my approval," he is said to have boasted.[13] But in response to these urgent warnings, the President permitted a gradual expansion of the bombing and a relaxation of the restrictions under which it was carried out. The use of napalm was authorized to ensure greater destructiveness, and pilots were given the authority to strike alternative targets without prior authorization if the original targets were inaccessible. In April, American and South Vietnamese pilots flew a total of 3,600 sorties against North Vietnamese targets. The air war quickly grew from a sporadic, halting effort into a regular, determined program.

The expanded air war also provided the pretext for the introduction of the first U.S. ground forces into Vietnam. Anticipating Vietcong attacks against U.S. air bases in retaliation for ROLLING THUNDER, General Westmoreland in late February urgently requested two Marine landing teams to protect the air base at Danang. Although he conceded the importance of protecting the base, Taylor expressed grave concern about the long-range implications of Westmoreland's request. He questioned whether American combat forces were adequately trained for guerrilla warfare in the Asian jungles, and he warned that the introduction of such forces would encourage the ARVN to pass military responsibility to the United States. Most important, the introduction of even small numbers of combat troops with a specific and limited mission would violate a ground rule the United States had rigorously adhered to since the beginning of the Indochina wars, and once the first step had been taken it would be "very difficult to hold [the] line."[14]

Taylor's objections were in many ways prophetic, but they were ignored. The need appears to have been so pressing and immediate, the commitment so small, that the decision was made routinely, with little discussion of its long-range consequences. After less than a week of apparently perfunctory debate, the President approved Westmoreland's request, and on March 8, two battalions of Marines, fitted out in full battle regalia, with tanks and 8-inch howitzers, splashed ashore near Danang where they were welcomed by South Vietnamese officials and by pretty Vietnamese girls passing out leis of flowers. It was an ironically happy beginning for what would be a wrenching experience for the two nations.

As Taylor had predicted, once the first step had been taken it was very difficult to hold the line. Alarmed by the slow pace of the ARVN buildup and fearful of a major Vietcong offensive in the Central highlands, Westmoreland concluded by mid-March that if the United States was to avert disaster in Vietnam there was "no solution . . . other than to put our own finger in the dike."[15] He therefore advocated the immediate commitment of two U.S. Army divisions, one to the highlands and the other to the Saigon area. The Joint Chiefs forcefully endorsed Westmoreland's request. Long impatient with the administration's caution and eager to assume full responsibility for the war, they even went beyond Westmoreland, pressing for the deployment of as many as three divisions to be used in offensive operations against the enemy.

The administration now found itself on what McNaughton called "the horns of a trilemma." The options of withdrawal and a massive air war against North Vietnam had been firmly rejected. It was apparent by mid-March, however, that the limited bombing campaign undertaken in February would not produce immediate results, and Westmoreland's urgent warnings raised fears that further inaction might lead to a South Vietnamese collapse. Many administration officials therefore reluctantly concluded that there was no alternative but to introduce American ground forces into Vietnam. They fully appreciated, on the other hand, the possible domestic political consequences of the sort of commitment Westmoreland proposed. And Taylor ominously warned that to place major increments of American forces in the highlands would invite heavy losses, even the possibility of an American Dienbienphu.

The administration resolved its "trilemma" with a compromise, rejecting the proposals of Westmoreland and the Joint Chiefs but still approving a significant commitment of ground forces and an enlargement of their mission. At a conference in Honolulu in late April, McNamara, Taylor, and the Joint Chiefs put aside their differences and agreed upon a hastily improvised strategy, the object of which was to "break the will of the DRV/VC by depriving them of victory." The bombing would be maintained at its "present tempo" for six months to a year. But the conferees agreed, as McNamara put it, that bombing "would not do the job alone."[16] They therefore decided that some 40,000 additional U.S. ground combat forces should be sent to Vietnam. These forces were not to be used in the highlands or given an unrestricted mission, as Westmoreland and the Joint Chiefs had advocated, but would be used in the more cautious "enclave strategy" devised by Taylor. Deployed in enclaves around the major U.S. bases, their backs to the sea, they would be authorized to undertake operations within fifty miles of their base areas. The administration hoped that this limited commitment of forces would be adequate to deny the enemy a knockout blow, thus allowing time for the South Vietnamese buildup and for the bombing to take its toll on Hanoi. Although the April decisions stopped short of the commitment urged by the military, they advanced well beyond the original objective of base security and marked a major step toward a large-scale involvement in the ground war. The new strategy shifted emphasis from the air war against North Vietnam to the war in the south, and by adopting it, the administration at least tacitly committed itself to expand its forces as the military situation required.

By this time Johnson recognized that achievement of American objectives in Vietnam would require a sustained and costly commitment, but he refused to submit his policies to public or Congressional debate. Many administration officials shared a view widely accepted at the height of the Cold War that foreign policy issues were too complex and too important to be left to an indifferent and ignorant public and a divided and unwieldly Congress. Johnson seems to have feared that a declaration of war might trigger a Chinese or Soviet response or increase domestic pressures for an unlimited conflict in Vietnam. He particularly feared, as he later put it, that a Congressional debate on "that bitch of a war" would destroy "the woman I really loved—the Great Society."[17] The President's unparalleled knowledge of Congress and his confidence in his renowned powers of persuasion encouraged him to believe that he could expand the war without provoking a backlash, and the repeated deference of the Congress to executive initiatives gave him no reason to anticipate a major challenge.

Johnson thus took the nation into war in Vietnam by indirection and dissimulation. The bombing was publicly justified as a response to the Pleiku attack and the broader pattern of North Vietnamese "aggression," rather than as a desperate attempt to halt the military and political deterioration in South Vietnam. The administration never publicly acknowledged the shift from reprisals to "sustained pressures." The dispatch of ground troops was explained solely in terms of the need to protect U.S. military installations, and not until June, when it crept out by accident in a press release, did administration spokesmen concede that American troops were authorized to undertake offensive operations....

At the same time, Westmoreland and the Joint Chiefs advocated a drastic expansion of American ground forces and the adoption of an offensive strategy in the south. More certain than ever that South Vietnam lacked sufficient manpower to hold the line on its own, Westmoreland, with the support of the Joint Chiefs, requested and additional 150,000 U.S. troops in early June. Traditionalists in their attitude toward the use of military power, Westmoreland and the Joint Chiefs had opposed the enclave strategy from the start and now insisted that it be abandoned in favor of an aggressive, offensive strategy. "You must take the fight to the enemy," General Earle Wheeler, the Chairman of the Joint Chiefs affirmed. "No one ever won a battle sitting on his ass." [18] Indeed, by the summer of 1965, even Ambassador Taylor conceded, as he later put it, that "the strength of the enemy offensive had completely overcome my former reluctance to use American ground troops in general combat."[19]

Only George Ball and Washington attorney Clark Clifford, a frequent personal adviser to Johnson, vigorously opposed a major commitment of American ground forces. Ball expressed profound doubt that the United States could defeat the Vietcong "or even force them to the conference table on our terms, no matter how many hundred thousand *white, foreign* (U.S.) troops we deploy." He expressed grave concern that approval of Westmoreland's proposals would lead to a "protracted war involving an open-ended commitment of U.S. forces, mounting U.S. casualties, no assurances of a satisfactory solution, and a serious danger of escalation at the end of the road." Once committed, he warned, there could be no turning back. "Our involvement will be so great that we cannot—without national humiliation—stop short of achieving our complete objectives." Clifford concurred, urging the President to keep U.S. forces to a minimum and to probe "every serious avenue leading to a possible settlement." "It won't be what we want," he concluded, "but we can learn to live with it."[20]

The clinching argument was provided by McNamara after another of his whirlwind visits to Saigon in early July. The Secretary of Defense underscored the pessimistic reports from Westmoreland and Taylor, and warned that to continue "holding on and playing for the breaks" would only defer the choice between escalation and withdrawal, perhaps until it was "too late to do any good." McNamara conceded that the expansion of American involvement would make a later decision to withdraw "even more difficult and costly than would be the case today." On the other hand, it might "stave off defeat in the short run and offer a good chance of producing a favorable settlement in the longer run." The Secretary recommended the gradual deployment of an additional 100,000 American combat forces.[21]

In late July, Johnson made his fateful decisions, setting the United States on a course from which it would not deviate for nearly three years and opening the way for seven years of bloody warfare in Vietnam. The President did not approve the all-out bombing campaign urged by Westmoreland and the Joint Chiefs. He and his civilian advisers continued to fear that a direct, full scale attack on North Vietnam might provoke Chinese intervention. They also felt that the industrial base around Hanoi was a major trump card held by the United States and that the threat of its destruction might be more useful than destruction itself. The administration approved Westmoreland's request to use B-52s for saturation bombing in South Vietnam and permitted a gradual intensification of the bombing of North Vietnam; sorties increased from 3,600 in April to 4,800 in June and would continue to increase thereafter. Johnson kept tight control over the bombing, personally approving the targets in advance of each strike and restricting air attacks to the area south of the twentieth parallel.

At the same time, the President approved a major new commitment of ground forces and a new strategy to govern their deployment. Determined to prevail in Vietnam and increasingly alarmed by the reports of steady military and political decline, in July he approved the immediate deployment of 50,000 troops to South Vietnam. Recognizing that this would not be enough, however, he privately agreed to commit another 50,000 before the end of the year, and implicitly, at least, he committed himself to furnish whatever additional forces might be needed later. Johnson also authorized Westmoreland to "commit U.S. troops to combat independent of or in conjunction with GVN forces in any situation . . . when . . . their use is necessary to strengthen the relative position of GVN forces."[22] These decisions rank among the most important in the history of American involvement in Vietnam. In July 1965, Johnson made an open-ended commitment to employ American military forces as the situation demanded. And by giving Westmoreland a free hand, he cleared the way for the United States to assume the burden of fighting in South Vietnam.

Some of Johnson's advisers strongly recommended that he place the July decisions squarely before the nation. The Joint Chiefs pressed for mobilization of the reserves and calling up the National Guard to make clear, as Wheeler later put it, that the United States was not becoming engaged in "some two-penny military adventure."[23] McNamara was sufficiently concerned with the domestic political implications of the decisions to urge Johnson to declare a state of national emergency and to ask Congress for an increase in taxes—in short, without seeking a declaration of war, to put the nation on a war footing. The President himself apparently toyed with the idea of securing another Congressional resolution explicitly endorsing his policies.

After extensive deliberation, Johnson decided against any such steps. He continued to fear that anything resembling a declaration of war might provoke the Soviet Union and China. His attorney general assured him that he had the power to commit large-scale forces without going to Congress.[24] Perhaps most important, the civil rights and Medicare bills were then at crucial stages in the legislative process, and Congressional approval was pending on numerous other administration proposals. The President was determined to establish his place in history through the achievement of sweeping domestic reforms, and he feared that going to

Congress for authority to wage war in Vietnam would destroy his dream of creating the Great Society at home. Johnson thus rejected the advice of the Joint Chiefs and McNamara, informing his staff that he wished the decisions implemented in a "low-keyed manner in order (a) to avoid an abrupt challenge to the Communists, and (b) to avoid undue concern and excitement in the Congress and in domestic public opinion."[25]

To avoid "undue excitement," the President continued to mislead Congress and the public as to the significance of the steps he was taking. To make his decisions more palatable to potential waverers, he and his aides issued dire warnings that a failure to act decisively would play into the hands of those who wanted to take drastic measures, the "Goldwater crowd," who were "more numerous, more powerful and more dangerous than the fleabite professors."[26] To appease skeptics such as Senate Majority Leader Mike Mansfield, Johnson implied that he would give equal priority to seeking a diplomatic settlement of the conflict, without divulging his certainty that such efforts were doomed to failure. In meetings with Congressional leaders and in a televised speech on July 28, he indicated that he was sending 50,000 troops to Vietnam and that more would be required later. But he emphatically denied that he had authorized any change in policy and he did not give a clear indication—even in the sense that he understood it at the time—of what lay ahead. His tactics reflected his continuing determination to achieve his goals in Vietnam without sacrificing the Great Society and his certainty that he could accomplish both things at once.

The July decisions—the closest thing to a formal decision for war in Vietnam—represented the culmination of a year and a half of agonizing on America's Vietnam policy and stemmed logically from the administration's refusal to accept the consequences of withdrawal. Johnson and Rusk had been at the center of the political upheaval that had followed the fall of China in 1949, and they were certain that the "loss" of Vietnam would produce an even more explosive debate, "a mean and destructive debate," Johnson once commented, "that would shatter my Presidency, kill my administration, and damage our democracy."[27] They also deeply feared the international consequences of withdrawal. The decision-makers of 1965 felt that they were upholding policies the United States had pursued since the late 1940s, policies that still had validity despite the enormous changes that had taken place in the world. They were frequently vague as to what they were containing; sometimes they stressed China, other times Communism, and still other times wars of liberation in general. In any case, they believed that to withdraw from Vietnam would encourage disorder throughout the world and drastically weaken American influence. Men of action and achievement, leaders of a nation with an unbroken record of success, they were unwilling to face the prospect of failure. If the United States pulled out of Vietnam, Johnson warned on one occasion, "it might as well give up everywhere else—pull out of Berlin, Japan, South America."[28]

In making the July commitments, the administration saw itself moving cautiously between the two extremes of withdrawal and total war; it sought, in Johnson's words, to do "what will be enough, but not too much." The President and his advisers did not seek the defeat of North Vietnam. They did not "speak of conquest on the battlefield ... as men from time immemorial had talked of victory," the historian Henry Graff recorded. Their objective rather was to inflict sufficient pain on the North Vietnamese and Vietcong to force them to negotiate on terms acceptable to the United States—in Johnson's Texas metaphor, to apply sufficient force until the enemy "sobers up and unloads his pistol."[29]

Displaying the consummate political skill that had become his trademark, Johnson in the last week of July shaped a consensus for his Vietnam policy in his administration, in Congress, and in the country. He appears to have been committed from the outset to a policy that would give the United States "the maximum protection at the least cost."[30] During the week of July 21–28, however, he gave the Joint Chiefs and George Ball their days in court, listening carefully to their arguments and raising numerous probing questions before rejecting their proposals for large-scale escalation and withdrawal.[31] In meetings with the Congressional leadership, he emphasized to conservatives his determination to hold the line in Vietnam, while reassuring liberals that he would not permit the war to get out of hand. "I'm going up old Ho Chi Minh's leg an inch at a time," he told Senator George McGovern.[32] Johnson's middle course probably reflected the aspirations of the American public and Congress, and the President went to war with support that appeared to be solid.

Getting into war would turn out to be much easier for Johnson than getting out. The administration's decisions of July 1965 proved to be based on two crucial miscalculations. In seeking to do what would be "enough, but not too much," the President and his advisers never explored with any real precision how much would be enough. They had no illusions that success could be achieved painlessly, but they grossly underestimated the determination of the enemy to resist and they did not foresee the cost the war would bring the United States. When Ball warned that it might take as many as a half million troops, McNamara dismissed the argument as "dirty pool" and called the figure "outrageous." [33] Leaders of the most powerful nation in the history of the world, U.S. officials simply could not conceive that a small, backward country could stand up against them. It would be like a filibuster, Johnson speculated, "enormous resistance at first, then a steady whittling away, then Ho hurrying to get it over with."[34]

Miscalculating the costs that the United States would incur in Vietnam, the administration could not help but overestimate the willingness of the nation to pay. On July 27, 1965, Senator Mike Mansfield penned a long, eloquent, and prophetic warning to his old friend and political mentor. He advised Johnson that Congress and the nation supported him because he was President, not because they understood or were deeply committed to his policy in Vietnam, and that there lingered beneath the surface a confusion and uncertainty that could in time explode into out-right opposition.[35] Mansfield correctly perceived the flimsiness of John-son's backing. As long as U.S. objectives could be obtained at minimal cost, Americans were willing to stay in Vietnam. When the war turned out to last much longer and cost much more than had been anticipated, how-ever, the President's support began to wither away and the advocates of escalation and withdrawal whom he had parried so skillfully in July 1965 became less manageable.

Johnson disregarded Mansfield's admonitions. After months of un-certainty, he had finally set his course, and in July 1965, quietly and with-out fanfare, he launched the United States on what would become its longest, most frustrating, and most divisive war.

NOTES

1. Bill Moyers, "Flashbacks," *Newsweek* (February 10, 1975), 76; U.S. Congress, Senate, Subcommittee on Public Buildings and Grounds, *The Pentagon Papers* (*The Senator Gravel Edition*) (4 vols.; Boston, 1971), III, 17–20. Hereafter cited as *Pentagon Papers (Gravel)*.

2. McNamara to Johnson, December 21, 1963, Declassified Documents Reference System (R)88E. Hereafter cited as DDRS.

3. McNamara-Rusk memorandum, June 11, 1964, Johnson Papers, National Se-curity File, Country File: Vietnam, Box 4.

4. Quoted in John Galloway, *The Gulf of Tonkin Resolution* (Rutherford, N.J., 1970), p. 52. For a good short account, see "The 'Phantom Battle' That Led to War," *U.S. News & World Report* (July 23, 1984), pp. 56–67.

5. "Chronology of Events, Tuesday, August 4 and Wednesday, August 5, 1964, Tonking Gulf Strike," Johnson Papers, National Security File, Country File: Vietnam, Box 18; summary notes of 538th NSC meeting, August 4, 1964, John-son Papers, National Security File, NSC Meetings File, Box 1; Rusk to Taylor, August 8, 1964, DDRS(75)845-H.

6. "Chronology of Events," Johnson Papers, National Security File, Country File: Vietnam, Box 18; "Transcripts of Telephone Conversations, 4–5 August, " John-son Papers, National Security File, Country File: Vietnam, Box 228.

7. Quoted in Anthony Austin, *The President's War* (Philadelphia, 1971), p. 98.

8. Bundy to Rusk, January 6, 1965, *Pentagon Papers (Gravel)*, III, 685.

9. Johnson, *The Vantage Point*, (New York, 1971), p. 125.

10. *Ibid.*, pp. 127–128.

11. Quoted in Anthony Lake, ed., *The Vietnam Legacy* (New York, 1976), p. 183.

12. *Pentagon Papers (Gravel)*, III, 335.

13. William Westmoreland, *A Soldier Reports* (Garden City; N.Y., 1976), p. 119.

14. *Pentagon Papers (Gravel)*, III, 418.

15. Westmoreland, *Soldier Reports*, p. 126.

16. McNamara to Johnson, April 21, 1965, Johnson Papers, National Security File, Country File: Vietnam, Box 13.

17. Quoted in Doris Kearns, *Lyndon Johnson and the American Dream* (New York, 1976), p. 251.

18. Graff, *The Tuesday Cabinet*, (Englewood Cliffs, N.J., 1970) p. 138.

19. Maxwell Taylor, *Swords and Ploughshares*, (New York, 1972) p. 347.

20. Ball to Johnson, July 1, 1965, in Sheehan, *Pentagon Papers (NYT)*, pp. 449-454; Clifford to Johnson, May 17, 1965, Johnson Papers, National Security File, Country File: Vietnam, Box 16.

21. Johnson, *Vantage Point*, pp. 145–146.

22. Sheehan, *Pentagon Papers (NYT)*, p. 412.

23. Earle Wheeler oral history interview, Johnson Papers.

24. Nicholas Katzenbach to Johnson, June 10, 1965, Johnson Papers, National Security File, Country File: Vietnam, Box 17.

25. Benjamin Read memorandum, July 23, 1965, Johnson Papers, National Security File, Country File: Vietnam, Box 16.

26. McGeorge Bundy to Johnson, July 14, 1965, Johnson Papers, Diary Backup File, Box 19.

27. Kearns, *Johnson*, p. 252.

28. John D. Pomfret memorandum of conversation with Johnson, June 24, 1965, Krock Papers, Box 59.

29. Graff, *Tuesday Cabinet*, pp. 54, 59.

30. Summary notes of National Security Council meeting, June 11, 1965, Johnson Papers, National Security File, NSC Meetings, Box 1.

31. Larry Berman, *Planning a Tragedy: The Americanization of the War in Vietnam* (New York, 1982).

32. George McGovern, *Grassroots* (New York, 1977), pp. 104-105.

33. Benjamin Read oral history interview, Johnson Papers.

34 Kearns, *Johnson*, p. 266.

35. Mansfield to Johnson, July 27, 1965, Johnson Papers National Security File, National Security Council Histories: Deployment of Major U.S. Forces to Vietnam, July 1965, Box 40.

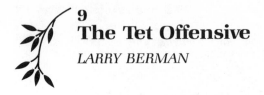

9
The Tet Offensive

LARRY BERMAN

*War is an ugly thing, but not the ugliest: the decayed and
degraded state of moral and patriotic feeling which thinks
nothing worth a war is worse....A man who has nothing
which he cares about more than his personal safety is a
miserable creature who has no chance of being free, unless
made and kept so by the exertions of better men than himself.*

On February 8, 1968 President Johnson sent this quotation from John
Stuart Mill to Dean Rusk, Robert McNamara, Clark Clifford, and the Joint
Chiefs.

*I just don't understand it. Am I that far off? Am I wrong? Has
something happened to me? My wife said, I think so. But she
said you don't know what year you are living in. This is '68.*

Remarks by President Lyndon Johnson to a Congressional delegation
in the White House, January 30, 1968.

KHE SANH

On January 11, 1968, U.S. intelligence detected a buildup of forces in the
Laotian panhandle west of the demilitarized zone, threatening the Marine
base at Khe Sanh in western Quang Tri province of South Vietnam. Khe
Sanh was located eight miles east of Laos and eighteen miles south of
the DMZ. The base occupied a strategically important location for the
purposes of hindering enemy infiltration down the Ho Chi Minh Trail as
well as providing a staging post for possible operations into Laos.

The enemy force buildup of two additional North Vietnamese divisions was incontrovertible; but Hanoi's motives were wildly disputed.
Prisoner reports and captured documents revealed that a massive winter-
spring offensive was being planned. Truck traffic down the Ho Chi Minh
Trail had reached massive proportions and major North Vietnamese troop
reinforcements were in the border areas. Was Hanoi merely setting the

Reprinted from *Lyndon Johnson's War, The Road to Stalemate in Vietnam,* by Larry
Berman, by permission of W. W. Norton & Company, Inc. Copyright © 1989 by Larry
Berman.

stage for negotiations or was the offensive intended to topple the government of South Vietnam? What was the enemy up to? General Westmoreland believed a maximum military effort was underway, possibly to improve chances of achieving an end to the war through negotiations that would lead to a coalition government involving the NLF. A major offensive by Hanoi might also be aimed at achieving one major psychological victory in the United States prior to the start of the presidential campaign.

The enemy was finally coming to Westmoreland for battle. This would not be search and destroy in the jungle. Years of waiting for the enemy were almost over, and even though U.S. forces were significantly out-numbered, Westmoreland cabled Wheeler on January 12 that a withdrawal from Khe Sanh was unthinkable. "I consider this area critical to us from a tactical standpoint as a launch base for Special Operations Group teams and as flank security for the strong point obstacle system; it is even more critical from a psychological viewpoint. To relinquish this area would be a major propaganda victory for the enemy. Its loss would seriously affect Vietnamese and US morale. In short, withdrawal would be a tremendous step backwards."

With 15–20,000 North Vietnamese reinforcements circling Khe Sanh, Westmoreland bit the lure by ordering the 6000 Marine troops to defend the garrison. General Westmoreland also set in motion plans for implementing Operation Niagara (evoking an image of cascading bombs and shells), which became the most intense and successful application of aerial firepower yet seen in the war.

During the predawn hours of January 21, 1968, Khe Sanh came under constant rocket and mortar fire from the North Vietnamese. The battle was on, and it appeared to President Johnson and his principal advisors that the North Vietnamese envisioned Khe Sanh as a potential Dien Bien Phu. During a January 14 White House meeting with members of the Democratic leadership, the president reported that "intelligence reports show a great similarity between what is happening at Khe Sanh and what happened at Dien Bien Phu." Johnson became preoccupied with the analogy and had a table model made of sand of the Khe Sanh plateau constructed in the bunker-like Situation Room of the White House. He feared that Khe Sanh would be his "Dinbinphoo," as LBJ was prone to pronounce it.

PROMETHEUS BOUND

The enemy build up at Khe Sanh was followed on January 23, 1968, by North Korea's capture of the U.S. Navy Intelligence ship *Pueblo* on grounds of espionage. Seized in international waters some 26 miles off the coast of Japan, the 906-ton USS *Pueblo* was on its first electronic surveillance mission. The crew of 83, captained by Lloyd Bucher, was forced into the North Korean port at Wonsan, the first U.S. naval vessel captured since the USS *Chesepeake* in 1807—during the Napoleonic wars.

Had the seizure been a pre-planned effort to provoke a U.S. response and to exert pressure on the United States in Vietnam? Were the North Koreans supporting their Communist allies in North Vietnam and trying to create fear in South Korea? "Prometheus Bound," proclaimed a *Newsweek* article in describing how "a tenth-rate country" had "abruptly confronted Lyndon B. Johnson with one of the most delicate and intractable emergencies of his crisis-wracked Administration." Secretary of State Dean Rusk declared publicly, "I would not object to designating this an act of war in terms of the category of actions to be so construed. My strong advice to North Korea is to cool it." But North Korea had no intention of cooling it; instead, it released a confession signed by the *Pueblo's* skipper, Commander Bucher, obviously obtained under duress, which contained alleged admissions of CIA contacts and proposed aggression against Korea.

Ironically, the seizure allowed Johnson to mobilize 15,000 Air Force and Navy Reservists as well as 370 inactive aircraft. Johnson also convened a "crisis" meeting of an informal planning committee which included all of the principal advisors to the president, somewhat like President Kennedy's Executive Committee (ExComm) during the Cuban Missile Crisis of 1962. The president was determined not to act hastily and to do everything possible diplomatically to get the crew returned safely. (Which succeeded only after a protracted period of eleven months.)

The seizure raised difficult problems for Johnson's political leadership. The president could hardly afford a second war front in Asia, yet he was being pressured at home to retaliate against what Massachusetts congressman William Bates, senior Republican on the House Armed Services Committee, called, "a dastardly act of piracy." Hawks were not the only ones pressuring Johnson. Democratic senator Frank Church of Idaho, one of the Senate's most outspoken doves on Vietnam, derided the *Pueblo's* seizure as "an act of war," in which the honor of the United States was at stake.

TET: MOVE FORWARD TO ACHIEVE FINAL VICTORY

During the early morning hours of January 31 (the Vietnamese New Year, Tet) approximately 80,000 North Vietnamese regulars and guerrillas attacked over 100 cities throughout South Vietnam. Tet involved enemy attacks on 35 of 44 province capitals, 36 district towns and many villages and hamlets. For weeks prior to the offensive, enemy forces had been infiltrating into Saigon in civilian clothes in preparation for a well-planned campaign of terror. The goal was to achieve a popular uprising against the GVN and to show the American public that the very notion of security in the South was null and void.

Communist forces had been given the general order "Move forward to achieve final victory." Combat orders had urged the assaulters to do everything possible to completely liberate the people of South Vietnam.

The orders found on captured guerrillas described the Tet strategy as one that would be "the greatest battle ever fought throughout the history of our country." The infiltrators were exhorted to "move forward aggressively to carry out decisive and repeated attacks in order to annihilate as many American, Satellite and Puppet troops as possible in conjunction with political struggles and military proselyting activities.... Display to the utmost your revolutionary heroism by surmounting all hardships and difficulties and making sacrifices as to be able to fight continually and aggressively. Be prepared to smash all enemy counter attacks and maintain your revolutionary standpoint under all circumstances. Be resolute in achieving continuous victories and secure the final victory at all costs."

While the attack itself did not surprise the principals, its timing during the Tet holiday phase-down did. In Washington, Walt Rostow was called away from a foreign-affairs advisors' luncheon to receive news of the offensive. Rostow quickly returned to report, "We have just been informed we are being heavily mortared in Saigon. The Presidential palace,... the Embassy and the city itself have been hit." General Wheeler did not seem very alarmed: "It was the same type of thing before. You will remember that during the inauguration that the MACV headquarters was hit. In a city like Saigon people can infiltrate easily. They carry in rounds of ammunition and mortars. They fire and run. It is impossible to stop this in its entirety. This is about as tough to stop as it is to protect against an individual mugging in Washington, D.C. We have got to pacify all of this area and get rid of the Viet Cong infrastructure. They are making a major effort to mount a series of these actions to make a big splurge at TET."

But General Westmoreland quickly cabled Admiral Sharp that the enemy attacks constituted more than a D.C. mugging. The enemy "appears to be [using] desperation tactics, using NVA troops to terrorize populated areas. He attempted to achieve surprise by attacking during the truce period. The reaction of Vietnamese, US and Free World Forces to the situation has been generally good. Since the enemy has exposed himself, he has suffered many casualties. As of now, they add up to almost 700. When the dust settles, there will probably be more. All my subordinate commanders report the situation well in hand."

From a military assessment, the VC suffered a major defeat at Tet. Over half of their committed force was lost and perhaps a quarter of their whole regular force. Moreover, the Communists failed to bring about the diversion of U.S. forces from Khe Sanh or elsewhere. Nevertheless, the psychological impact of Tet was demoralizing to the American public. The enemy had demonstrated a capability to enter and attack cities and towns and had employed terrorism for doing vast damage. Bunker cabled Johnson on February 8, "Hanoi may well have reasoned that in the event that the TET attacks did not bring the outright victory they hoped for, they could still hope for political and psychological gains of such dimensions that they could come to the negotiating table with a greatly strengthened hand. They may have very well estimated that the impact of the TET attacks would at the very least greatly discourage the United States and cause other countries to put more pressure on us to negotiate on Hanoi's terms."

The impact on the American public was indeed great. A front-page photograph on the *New York Times* February 1 edition showed three military policemen, rifles in hand, seeking protection behind a wall outside the consular section of the U.S. Embassy in Saigon. The bodies of two American soldiers slain by guerrillas who had raided the compound lay nearby. All 19 guerrillas had been killed, but not until they had blasted their way into the embassy and had held part of the grounds for six hours. Four MPs, a Marine Guard, and a South Vietnamese employee were killed in the attack. President Thieu declared a state of martial law, yet during a news conference from the Cabinet room, President Johnson likened Tet to the Detroit riots, asserting "a few bandits can do that in any city."

Meeting with key congressional leaders in the evening of January 31, LBJ reviewed the events preceding Tet as well as Khe Sanh. "The Joint Chiefs, and all the Joint Chiefs, met with me the day before yesterday and assured me that they had reviewed the plans and they thought they were adequate. I told them I thought I almost had to have them sign up in blood because if my poll goes where it has gone, with all the victories, I imagine what it would do if we had a good major defeat. So General Westmoreland and the Joint Chiefs of Staff are sure that we are not anticipating some major activity there that we have not heard about."

General Wheeler then explained that Hanoi's military purpose in the Tet offensive had been to draw forces away from the Khe Sanh area. The second objective seemed to have been more political, to demonstrate to the South Vietnamese people and the world, that the Communists still possessed a considerable strength in the country and thereby shake the confidence of the Vietnamese people in the ability of their government to provide them security, even when they were within areas held by government and U.S. troops. "A significant thing about this attack," Wheeler said, "is that in many areas, particularly in Saigon, and at Bien Hoa, the attackers were dressed in one of three types of clothing: Civilian clothes, military, ARVN military police uniforms, or national police uniforms. Apparently, they gave no attention at all to whether or not they killed civilians. This is a sort of an unusual action for them because they have posed as the protectors of the civilian populace. Apparently this is the effort to reestablish by terror a degree of control over the population."

The meeting of congressional leaders was followed by a Cabinet meeting which Johnson opened by acknowledging, "There is a lot of stress and plenty of overtime for us all." President Johnson then engaged in a series of free-flowing remarks in which he came close to blaming the pope for Tet:

I think I admired President Kennedy most during the Bay of Pigs when he said "no one is to blame but me." I know that wasn't true.... We went into Rome at night and we could have been faced with two million Red demonstrators. The Pope appealed to me. We had no differences, no quarrels. He said "I want to do something, anything for peace—can't you give us one extra day of the holiday truce?" General Westmoreland told me how many American lives it would cost, but we did give the Pope his extra day. Now it's hard not to regret the number of boys who were killed. It is now so much worse after the Tet truce. Westmoreland cancelled the Tet truce because the house was on fire. So you look at *Pueblo*, Khe Sanh, Saigon and you see them all as part of the Communist effort to defeat us out there. We can dodge it by being weak-kneed if we want to. I said at San Antonio that we have gone as far as we could—farther, I might add, than the military wanted. We made it clear how much we want to talk and not bomb, just so long as there is some prompt and productive response. But if you sneak in the night and hit us, we can't stop bombing. Now we have their answer with this new offensive. It just should satisfy every dove who loves peace as much as any mother does.

The president then read excerpts from a memorandum received from Ambassador Bunker, calling particular attention to a passage recalling Thomas Paine's remark, "These are the times that try men's souls.... What we attain too cheaply, we esteem too lightly."

Attending the annual presidential prayer breakfast at the Shoreham Hotel, the president sounded weary and burdened by events. "The nights are very long. The winds are very chill. Our spirits grow weary and restive as the springtime of man seems farther and farther away. I can, and I do, tell you that in these long nights your President prays." Indeed, as these personal pressures grew, LBJ sought private solace in late-night prayer at St. Dominic's Church, in southwest Washington. Accompanied only by the secret service, the president and his "little monks" would read scriptures, psalms, and sing hymns.

On February 1, Wheeler cabled Sharp and Westmoreland raising the possibility of "whether tactical nuclear weapons should be used if the situation in Khe Sanh should become that desperate." While Wheeler considered that eventuality unlikely, he requested a list of susceptible targets in the areas "which lend themselves to nuclear strikes, whether some contingency nuclear planning would be in order, and what you would consider to be some of the more significant pros and cons of using tac [tactical] nukes in such a contingency."

Westmoreland responded, "The use of tactical nuclear weapons should not be required in the present situation." However, should the situation change, "I visualize that either tactical nuclear weapons or chemical agents would be active candidates for employment." During an emotional February 16 news conference, Johnson vehemently denied that nuclear weapons had ever been considered, adding even more fuel to the credibility gap fire. LBJ stated that it was "against the national interest to carry on discussions about the employment of nuclear weapons with respect to Khesanh."

While Wheeler and Westmoreland privately discussed tactical nukes, Walt Rostow privately drew charts for his wife Elspeth. "Responding to a question from Elspeth last night, " Rostow wrote Johnson, "I explained events in Vietnam as follows. The war had been proceeding in 1967 on an attritional basis with our side gradually improving its position, the Communists gradually running down..."

But administration critics weren't convinced. Satirist Art Buchwald likened administration optimism to another historical event: " 'We have the enemy on the run,' says General Custer at Big Horn. 'It's a desperation move on the part of Sitting Bull and his last death rattle.' " Senator George Aiken wryly remarked, "If this is a failure, I hope the Viet Cong never have a major success." Yet Rostow again wrote Johnson that the degree of Communist terrorism during the Tet period would actually strengthen the South Vietnamese resolve to get even with these terrorists. "There is a chance that South Viet Nam will emerge in the weeks and months ahead with stronger political institutions and a greater sense of nationhood and common destiny than before."

MORE TROOPS

General Wheeler understood the severity of Westmoreland's military position. Allied forces were stretched to their maximum extent and effectiveness. On February 3, Wheeler cabled Westmoreland, "The President asks me if there is any reinforcement or help that we can give you?" Receiving no answer, Wheeler tried again on February 8: "Query: Do you need reinforcements? Our capabilities are limited.... However, if you consider reinforcements imperative, you should not be bound by earlier agreements. ...United States government is not prepared to accept defeat in Vietnam. In summary, if you need more troops, ask for them."

Westmoreland now cabled Wheeler that there was cause for alarm. "From a realistic point of view we must accept the fact that the enemy has dealt the GVN a severe blow. He has brought the war to the towns and the cities and has inflicted damage and casualties on the population. Homes have been destroyed, distribution of the necessities of life has been interrupted. Damage has been inflicted to the LOC's [Lines of communication] and the economy has been decimated. Martial law has been invoked, with stringent curfews in the cities. The people have felt directly the impact of the war."

While U.S. forces had repelled the Communist onslaught and inflicted major losses on the enemy manpower pool, Tet revealed the enemy's great skill in planning, coordination, and courage. The enemy had infiltrated previously secure population centers and exploited the GVN claim of security from attack. But there had been no general uprising, and the enemy did not hold a single city, although enemy units had waged a fierce three-week battle at the ancient city of Hué where they had occupied the Citadel—a nineteenth-century fortress which shielded the nation's historic imperial palace. Hué, a city of 100,000, was also the traditional center of religious and intellectual life in Vietnam. After weeks of fighting, U. S. and ARVN forces secured Hué, but not until some of the worst carnage of the war had been unleashed on its civilian inhabitants.

Westmoreland cabled Wheeler that enemy activity at Hué and elsewhere had helped Hanoi to score "a psychological blow, possibly greater in Washington than in South Vietnam, since there are tentative signs that the populace is turning against the Viet Cong as a result of these attacks." The enemy had also succeeded in temporarily disrupting South Vietnam's economy, and Westmoreland believed the enemy would continue to strain the will of the people by maintaining pressure on the populated areas with his forces already committed. The general also expected another major offensive in the Saigon area, commencing in mid-February.

Meeting with the democratic congressional leadership at breakfast on February 6, 1968, the president once again faced tough questions from Senator Robert Byrd. "I am concerned about: 1. That we had poor intelligence; 2. That we were not prepared for these attacks; 3. We underestimated the morale and vitality of the Viet Cong; 4. We over-estimated the support of the South Vietnamese government and its people." Johnson shot back at Byrd: "I don't agree with any of that. We knew that they planned a general uprising around TET. Our intelligence showed there was a winter-spring offensive planned. We did not know the precise places that were going to be hit. General Abrams said the Vietnamese are doing their best. There was no military victory for the Communists. Just look at the casualties and the killed in action."

The discussion then moved to a more general level of political analysis:

SENATOR BYRD: I have never caused you any trouble in this matter on the Hill. But I do have very serious concerns about Vietnam. I think this is the place to raise these questions, here in the family.

CONGRESSMAN HALE BOGGS: What about Bob Byrd's charge that we are under-estimating the strength of the VC? I personally do not agree with that.

THE PRESIDENT: I have never under-estimated the Viet Cong. They are not push-overs. I do not think we have bad intelligence or have under-estimated the Viet Cong morale.

SENATOR BYRD: Something is wrong over there.

THE PRESIDENT: The intelligence wasn't bad.

SENATOR BYRD: That does not mean the Viet Cong did not succeed in their efforts. Their objective was to show that they could attack all over the country and they did.

THE PRESIDENT: That was not their objective at all.

SENATOR BYRD: You have been saying the situation with the Viet Cong was one of diminishing morale. When I say you, I mean the Administration.

THE PRESIDENT: I personally never said anything of the sort. I am not aware that anyone else has been saying that. What do you think the American people would have done if we had sent in troops and had lost 21,000 of them as the enemy has?

SENATOR RUSSELL LONG: If we had planned to have an up-rising in Cuba and you had caused 21,000 men to be lost as the Viet Cong did, I am sure you would have been impeached.

THE PRESIDENT: I am of the opinion that criticism is not worth much. I look at all these speeches that are in the [congressional] Record. I look at all the people who are going around the country saying our policy is wrong. Where do they get us? Nowhere. The popular thing now is to stress the mis-management to Vietnam. I think there has been very little. I wish Mike (Senator Mansfield) would make a speech on Ho Chi Minh. Nothing is as dirty as to violate a truce during the holidays. But nobody says anything bad about Ho. They call me a murderer. But Ho has a great image.

SENATOR BYRD: I don't want the President to think that I oppose you. I am just raising these matters.

THE PRESIDENT: I don't agree with what you say.

SENATOR LONG: I am happy you raised the point, Bob.

THE PRESIDENT: Everybody should say and do what they want to. But we have put our very best men that we have out there. I believe that our military and diplomatic men in the field know more than many of our Congressmen and Senators back here. Anybody can kick a barn down. It takes a good carpenter to build one. I just wish all of you would expose the Viet Cong and Ho. We have got some very crucial decisions coming up. Personally, I think they suffered a severe defeat. But we knew there would be a general uprising, and they did not win any victory. It seems to be an American trait to ask why. I just hope that we don't divert our energies and our talents by criticizing unnecessarily. We've got all we can of this "What's wrong with our country?" Fulbright, Young and Gruening haven't helped one bit.

SENATOR BYRD: I do not want to argue with the President. But I am going to stick by my convictions.

The Tuesday luncheon following Tet revealed frustration amongst the advisors. For the departing Secretary of Defense Robert McNamara, the Tet offensive demonstrated that Hanoi had "more power than we credit them with. I do not think it was a 'last-gasp' action. I do think that it represents a maximum effort in the sense that they poured on all of their assets and my guess is that we will inflict a very heavy loss both in terms of personnel and material and this will set them back some but that after they absorb the losses they will remain a substantial force. I do not anticipate that we will hit them so hard that they will be knocked out for an extended period or forced to drop way back in level of effort against us. I do think that it is such a well-coordinated, such an obviously advanced planned operation, that it probably relates to negotiations in some way. I would expect that were they successful here they would then move forward more forcibly on the negotiation front and they are thinking they have a stronger position from which to bargain."

Johnson wanted to know what should be done militarily to punish the enemy. McNamara argued that the Joint Chiefs had no answer. "I have talked to the Chiefs about some kind of a reciprocal action—retaliation for their attack on our Embassy or in retaliation for their attack across the country. There just isn't anything the Chiefs have come up with that is worth trying. They talk about an area-bombing attack over Hanoi but the weather is terrible. You can't get in there with pinpoint targeting. The only way you could bomb it at all at the present time is area bombing and I would not recommend that to you under any circumstances. They have just not been able to think of retaliation that means anything. My own feeling is that we ought to be able to depend upon our ability to inflict very heavy casualties on them as our proper response and as the message we give to our people."

But the chiefs did have an answer. In a meeting with the president on February 5, they proposed removing the restrictions around Hanoi and Haiphong, reducing the circles to three miles around Hanoi and one-and-one-half miles around Haiphong. Secretary of State Rusk feared that the proposed action "opens up the possibility of large civilian casualties and leads to extensive devastation of the area. From what we have seen in other areas this leads to almost total devastation. What to hit is up to the pilot." Wheeler responded, "We do not advocate attacking the population centers. We never have before, and we don't ask for that now. I admit there will be more civilian destruction, but we will be going after trucks and water craft. They are secure now, but represent genuine military targets."

Secretary McNamara challenged Wheeler's logic. "Any attack of this type is very expensive both in the number of U.S. aircraft lost and in civilian destruction. I do not recommend this. The military effect is small and our night time attack capability is small. Civilian casualties will be high. In my judgment, the price is high and the gain is low. The military commanders will dispute all the points I have made except aircraft loss."

Wheeler directly contradicted Secretary McNamara: "I do not think the effects on the civilian population will be that high. As you know, they have an excellent warning system and most of them go to shelters and tunnels. From that standpoint, civilian loss could be lower than it is in other areas. We have had nothing like the civilian destruction that took place in World War II and Korea. But the targets which are there are military targets of military value. Frankly, this (civilian casualties which might result) does not bother me when I compare it with the organized death and butchery by the North Vietnamese and the Viet Cong during the last two weeks in South Vietnam. All of this relates to the matter of pressure."

Choices had to be made. The president told the chiefs, "I believe somebody in government should say something. I do not share the view that many people have that we took a great defeat. our version is not being put to the American people properly....What are we going to do now on these bombing targets?" It was the incoming secretary of defense, Clark Clifford, who recommended accepting the Chiefs' proposal. Clifford believed that the Tet offensive was Hanoi's answer to the San Antonio formula. "I am inclined to resume the bombing in North Vietnam and go ahead with the suggested three-mile and one-and-a-half mile limits. As long as the enemy has demonstrated that they are not going to respond positively we should go ahead with this."

When Rusk and McNamara warned about the need to distinguish restricted from authorized targets, Wheeler showed his discontent: "I am fed up to the teeth with the activities of the North Vietnamese and the Viet Cong. We apply rigid restrictions to ourselves and try to operate in a humanitarian manner with concern for civilians at all times. They apply a double standard, Look at what they did in South Vietnam last week. In addition, they place their munitions inside of populated areas because they think they are safe there."

The discussion between the principles in the February 7 National Security Council meeting reveals their continuing uncertainty concerning enemy capabilities and U.S. military strategy:

SECRETARY RUSK: What about the possibility of the MIGs attacking a carrier?

GENERAL WHEELER: No, I do not think this is likely. The carriers do have air caps and are distant from the MIG bases.

THE PRESIDENT: Go in and get those MIGs at Phuc Yen.

GENERAL WHEELER: We will as soon as the weather permits.

SECRETARY MCNAMARA: The MIGs would have negligible military effects but they would have spectacular psychological impact. We do get the feeling that something big is ahead. We do not exactly know what it is, but our commanders are on alert.

THE PRESIDENT: I want all of you to make whatever preparations are necessary. Let's know where we can get more people if we need to move additional ones in.

GENERAL WHEELER: I have a preliminary list on my desk. I am not satisfied with it.

SECRETARY MCNAMARA: This would include Army, Navy, Air Force and Marine units.

THE PRESIDENT: What about the allies?

GENERAL WHEELER: The Australians are incapable of providing more troops. The problems in Korea are such that it will be hard to get the South Koreans to even send the light division they had promised. The Thai troops are in training and to move them in now would be more detrimental than helpful.

THE PRESIDENT: So it would be only Americans? Well, I want you to know exactly where you could get them, where they are located now and what we need to do. Get whatever emergency actions ready that will be necessary.

SECRETARY MCNAMARA: All we should recommend at this time are the three items we had discussed earlier. There may be some increase in draft calls but this would have no immediate effect.

THE PRESIDENT: Do we have adequate hospitals and medical personnel?

GENERAL WHEELER: We have ample space, ample supplies, and enough doctors for the present.

SECRETARY MCNAMARA: There are 6,400 military beds. Of that, 2900 are occupied by U.S. troops and 1100 by Vietnamese civilians. So we have an additional capacity of about 2400.

THE PRESIDENT: Look at this situation carefully. If we have another week like this one, you may need more.

SECRETARY RUSK: How do you interpret their use of tanks?

GENERAL WHEELER: They had to bring them all the way from Hanoi. This shows that this plan has been in staging since September. It represents a real logistic feat. They want to create maximum disruption.

USIA DIRECTOR LEONARD MARKS: Could they do anything at Cam Ranh Bay?

GENERAL WHEELER: They could. On this attack, we caught frogmen in there. They could put rockets in the hills and fire on to the base.

THE PRESIDENT: How many of the 25,000 killed were North Vietnamese Regulars?

GENERAL WHEELER: Approximately 18,000 were of a mixed variety of South Vietnamese enemy. Approximately 6,000 to 7,000 were North Vietnamese.

THE PRESIDENT: How do things look at Khesanh? Would you expect to have to move out of Lang Vie?

GENERAL WHEELER: It was not planned that we would hole some of these outposts. We may have to move back that company on Hill 861.

THE PRESIDENT: Bob, are you worried?

SECRETARY MCNAMARA: I am not worried about a true military defeat.

GENERAL WHEELER: Mr. President, this is not a situation to take lightly. This is of great military concern to us. I do think that Khesanh is an important position which can and should be defended. It is important to us tactically and it is very important to us psychologically. But the fighting will be very heavy, and the losses may be high. General Westmoreland will set up the forward field headquarters as quickly as possible. He told me this morning that he has his cables and his communications gear in. He is sending a list of his needs, including light aircraft. We are responding to this request.

THE PRESIDENT: Let's get everybody involved on this as quickly as possible. Everything he wants, let's get it to him.

10
A Dissenter in the Government
GEORGE W. BALL

THE CRITICAL DECISION

...[T]he war continued to go badly. When my colleagues and I assembled at the White House on the morning of July 21,1965, we were given a memorandum from the Joint Chiefs of Staff. Only the prompt deployment of large bodies of American troops could, it argued, save the situation. That meant committing thousands of our young men not merely to passive defense missions but to aggressive combat roles. The war would then become unequivocally our own. There would be no turning back for months, perhaps years—not until we had suffered horrible casualties, killed thousands of Vietnamese, and raised the level of national anxiety and frustration above the threshold of hysteria.

Because of the importance of the July 21 meeting it may be useful to outline the colloquy which suggests the substance and flavor of our many long discussions. It also provides some sense of the President's agonizing reluctance to go forward, his desire to explore every possible alternative, and, finally, his inability to reconcile his vaunted Texas "can-do" spirit with the shocking reality that America had painted itself into a corner with no way out except at substantial costs in terms of pride and prestige.

The President began with searching questions. Could we get more soldiers from our allies? What had altered the situation to the present point of urgency? McNamara produced a map. The Viet Cong, it showed, controlled about 25 percent of the South. United States forces would not be committed in those areas; they would be deployed "with their backs to the sea, for protection." They would conduct search and destroy operations against large-scale units.

"Why," I asked, "does anyone think that the Viet Cong will be so considerate as to confront us directly? They certainly didn't do that for the French." General Wheeler, the chairman of the Joint Chiefs of Staff, replied, "We can force them to fight by harassment."

After the others had expressed support for the proposed new escalation, the President asked whether any of us opposed it, looking directly at me. I made my usual speech, pointing out that we would be embarking on "a perilous voyage" and could not win. But, he asked, what other courses were available? We must, I replied, stop deceiving ourselves, face reality, and cut our losses. "If we get bogged down, the costs will be far greater than a planned withdrawal, while the pressures to create a larger war could become irresistible. We must stop propping up that absurd travesty of a government in Saigon. Let's let it fall apart and negotiate a withdrawal, recognizing that the country will face a probable take-over by the Communists."

The President replied, "You've pointed out the dangers but you've not really proposed an alternative."

After others had expressed similar sentiments, the President once more turned to me. "George," he asked, "do you think we have another course?" I answered, "I certainly don't agree with the course Bob McNamara's recommending." "All right," said the President, "we'll hear you out; then I can determine if any of your suggestions are sound and can be followed. I'm prepared to do that if convinced."

I could, I said, present to him only "the least bad of two courses." The course I could recommend was costly, but we could a least limit the cost to the short-term. At that point—just as I was beginning to speak–the President interrupted. "We'll have another meeting this afternoon where you can express your views in detail." Meanwhile, he wanted a further justification for the introduction of one-hundred-thousand more troops. In response to the President's concern about increased losses, General Taylor directly contradicted a view expressed earlier by Secretary McNamara that our losses in Vietnam would be proportional to the number of our men in that country. "The more men we have," the General now declared, "the greater the likelihood of smaller losses."

When we reconvened at 2:30 that afternoon, the President asked me to explain my position. I outlined why, in my view, we could not win. Even after a protracted conflict the most we could hope to achieve was "a messy conclusion" with a serious danger of intervention by the Chinese. In a long war, I said, the President would lose the support of the country. I showed him a chart I had prepared showing the correlation between Korean casualties and public opinion. As our casualties during the Korean War had increased from 11,000 to 40,000, the percentage of those Americans who thought that we had been right to intervene had diminished from 56 percent in 1950 to a little more than 30 percent in 1952. Moreover, as our losses mounted, many frustrated Americans would demand that we strike at the "very jugular of North Vietnam" with all the dangers that entailed. Were it possible for us to win decisively in a year's time, friendly nations might continue to support us. But that was not in the cards.

"No great captain in history ever hesitated to make a tactical withdrawal if conditions were unfavorable to him," I argued. "We can't even find the enemy in Vietnam. We can't see him and we can't find him. He's

BALL: A DISSENTER IN THE GOVERNMENT **167**

indigenous to the country, and he always has access to much better intelligence. He knows what we're going to do but we haven't the vaguest clue as to his intentions. I have grave doubts that any Western army can successfully fight Orientals in an Asian jungle."

"That's the key question," the President remarked. "Can Westerners, deprived of accurate intelligence, successfully fight Asians in the jungles and rice paddies?"

We had, I continued, underestimated the critical conditions in South Vietnam. "What we are doing is giving cobalt treatment to a terminal cancer case. A long, protracted war will disclose our weakness, not our strength."

Since our main concern was to avoid undermining our credibility, we should shift the burden to the South Vietnamese government. We should insist on reforms that it would never undertake, which would impel it to move toward a neutralist position and ask us to leave. "I have no illusions," I said, "that after we were asked to leave South Vietnam, that country would soon come under Hanoi's control. That's implicit in our predicament." I then discussed the effect on other nations in the area.

The President then asked the question most troubling him, "Wouldn't we lose all credibility by breaking the word of three Presidents?" I replied, "We'll suffer the worst blow to our credibility when it is shown that the mightiest power on earth can't defeat a handful of miserable guerrillas."

Then, asked the President, "aren't you basically troubled by what the world would say about our pulling out?"

"If we were helping a country with a stable, viable government, it would be a vastly different story. But we're dealing with a revolving junta. How much support," I asked rhetorically, "do we really have in South Vietnam?"

The President then mentioned two of my points that particularly troubled him. One was that Westerners could never win a war in Asia; the other was that we could not successfully support a people whose government changed every month. He then asked, "What about the reaction of the Europeans? Wouldn't they be shaken in their reliance on us if we pulled out of Vietnam?"

"That idea's based on a complete misunderstanding of the way the Europeans are thinking," I said. "They don't regard what we are doing in Vietnam as in any way comparable to our involvement in Europe. Since the French pulled out of Vietnam, they can hardly blame us for doing the same thing; they cut their losses, and de Gaulle is urging us to follow suit. Having retired from their empire, the British recognize an established fact when they see one. They're not going to blame us for doing the same thing, although they might get a little mischievous pleasure from it—what the Germans call *schadenfreude*. But basically they only care about one thing. They're concerned about their own security. Troops in Berlin have real meaning; troops in Vietnam have none."

I then summarized the alternatives. "We can continue a dragged out, bitterly costly, and increasingly dangerous war, with the North Vietnamese digging in for a long term since that's their life and driving force." Or "we can face the short-term losses of pulling out. It's distasteful either way; but life's full of hard choices."

McGeorge Bundy then intervened to suggest that, while I had raised truly important questions, the course I recommended would be a "radical switch in policy without visible evidence that it should be done." "George's analysis," he said, "gives no weight to losses suffered by the other side. The world, the country, and the Vietnamese people would have alarming reactions if we got out." Dean Rusk then stated that, if the Communist world found out that we would not pursue our commitment to the end, there was no telling where they would stop their expansionism. He rejected my assessment of the situation. The Viet Cong had not established much of a position among the Vietnamese people, and he did not foresee large casualties unless the Chinese should come in. Ambassador Lodge agreed. There would, he said, be a greater threat of starting World War III if we did not go in with our forces. There were great seaports in Vietnam, and we did not have to fight on the roads.

After more talk along the same lines the meeting was adjourned.

SUPPORT FROM AN UNEXPECTED QUARTER

The next day we met once more to hear the President's report of what the generals had told him. That meeting stands out in my memory not for anything I said—I had, after all, exhausted my persuasive arsenal—but rather because, for the first time, I found support from an unexpected quarter.

The President had asked his old friend Clark Clifford to attend and called on him to express his views. Presenting his argument with elegant precision and structure as though arguing a case before the Supreme Court, Clifford voiced strong opposition to the commitment of combat forces. He put forward the same arguments I had made the day before; in addition, he gave the President a more authoritative assessment of the probable domestic consequences. Whether or not President Johnson knew in advance of the position Clifford would take I cannot say; sometimes I suspected that he staged meetings for the benefit of the rest of us. But, whatever the answer to that question, Clifford emerged as a formidable comrade on my side of the barricades.

When the meeting was over, I asked Clifford to join me in the Fish Room. I told him that ever since the fall of 1961 I had been making the same arguments he now made so eloquently, and I gave him copies of the memoranda I had submitted to the President. The next day Clifford told me that he had spent the previous evening until two in the morning carefully studying my memoranda. They were, he said, "impressive and persuasive." Throughout the last year he had come more and more to my opinion as he continued to receive reports of our deteriorating situation.

I told Clark that judging from the meeting we had just had that day with the President, his intervention had had a salutary effect. Clifford replied that he had been told through "another source" that there would have to be a great effort made if we were to block this critical escalatory step that would change the character of the war. Though he hoped that through our combined exertions we could make progress, he was not optimistic. Unfortunately, "individuals sometimes become so bound up in a certain course it is difficult to know where objectivity stops and personal involvement begins." In any event, he had tried to impress on the President that we should down-play the talk that "this was the Armageddon between Communism and the Free World."

Clark Clifford had been close to the President for many years. Perhaps his opposition might turn the balance. We had one other powerful supporter, Senate Majority Leader Mike Mansfield, who, at the President's meeting with the Congressional leadership, had weighed in along the same line we were taking. There was, he had argued, no legitimate government in South Vietnam and we owed nothing to the current cabal. We were being pushed progressively deeper into the war, and even total victory would be enormously costly. Our best hope was for a quick stalemate and negotiation; the American people would never support a war that might last three to five years. We were about to get into an anti-Communist crusade. "Remember," he had concluded prophetically, "escalation begets escalation." Finally, there was my friend Senator J. William Fulbright, who had arrived at a position similar to mine, but the President had already written him off and rejected his view of the war.

As the whole world now knows, we did not carry the day—neither Mansfield, Clifford, Fulbright, nor I—and the balloon went up farther and farther.

As the war became progressively larger and bloodier, some of my colleagues talked with increasing wistfulness of a negotiated solution, which, in their vocabulary, meant Hanoi's capitulation. That was, I thought, quite unrealistic; the North Vietnamese would never stop fighting until they had obtained terms that would assure their takeover of the entire country. I had, therefore, only a marginal interest in efforts to open channels: they were not the answer. I did not see us achieving peace by the two techniques then being strongly urged: bombing pauses and the establishment of a multiplicity of diplomatic contacts. The battle-hardened leaders in Hanoi had no interest in mechanisms that would facilitate their crying "Uncle" in a low voice and with minimal loss of face: their interest was in forcing us to go home.

BOMBING PAUSES

A bombing pause, unaccompanied by significant concessions was merely pulling up a plant to see how well its roots were growing. From the middle of 1964 until the end of September 1966, when I left the State Department, there were two pauses. I supported both, not because I expected anything to come of them, but because I hoped they would break the rhythm of escalation. The first pause, which began on May 13, 1965, and lasted only until May 18, was, as I pointed out to my staff, not so much a pause as a hiccup. We told the Soviets in advance and tried to pass word to Hanoi (which rejected the receipt of our message) but we neglected to tell the American people or even the American military. The foreign minister of Hanoi denounced the pause as a "deceitful maneuver to pave the way for American escalation"—which I thought a perceptive appraisal. Peking called it a "fraud."

In spite of the failure of the first pause, Secretary McNamara continued to advocate "low-key diplomacy" to lay the groundwork for a settlement, stating that "We could, as part of a diplomatic initiative, consider introducing a 6–8 week pause in the program of bombing the North." He repeated that recommendation in a memorandum to the President on November 3. On November 30, 1965, he sought to justify it as primarily a ritual gesture "before we either greatly increase our troop deployments to Vietnam or intensify our strikes against the North." It would, he argued, "lay a foundation in the mind of the American public and in world opinion for such an enlarged phase of the war, and" — he added, I thought, with no conviction— "it should give North Vietnam a face-saving chance to stop the aggression." Secretary Rusk was not convinced; a pause was a serious diplomatic instrument; it could be used only once, and this was not the time to use it. President Johnson had a different concern; a pause that evoked no response would, he feared, provoke a demand for much stronger action from the American right wing—and they, he warned me, were "the Great Beast to be feared."

For several weeks the debate continued. On December 23, I left to spend Christmas at our family house in Florida. On the evening of Monday, December 28, the President telephoned me to say, "George, you wanted a pause and I'm giving you one. Now I need you to get it going. I'm sending a plane for you in the morning."

The President called me home to help plan a diplomatic extravaganza. He would send Administration personalities flying all over the world; they would tell heads of state and chiefs of government about the pause and enlist their help to bring Hanoi to the negotiating table. Averall Harriman would visit Poland and Yugoslavia, McGeorge Bundy Canada, Ambassador Foy Kohler would speak with Soviet officials, while Arthur Goldberg would call on General de Gaulle, Prime Minister Wilson, the Pope, and the Italian government. My own travel assignments were modest. I was to fly to Puerto Rico to meet Senator Fulbright fresh off the eighteenth green and then to Florida to see Senators Dirksen and Mansfield.

Although President Johnson obviously enjoyed this frenetic to-ing and fro-ing (he delighted in his ability to send well-known people flying all over the world), I thought the spectacle futile and unbecoming. Still, as I was to reflect later, better a Christmas peace extravaganza than the Christmas bombing Nixon ordered in 1974 [1972]. If that was part of the price we paid for a bombing pause, so be it; we at least broke the momentum of escalation, even though we would be under grave pressure to increase the pace of the war once the pause was completed.

NEGOTIATING GESTURES

The Administration constantly scanned the sky for smoke signals from Hanoi. It used disavowable envoys to try to provoke indications of willingness to talk and carried on probing operations with Iron Curtain diplomats. Meanwhile, more and more of our young men were being sent to South Vietnam and casualties were rising. To borrow a phrase I had once heard Walter Lippmann use to describe his own frustrations, I felt I was "trying to swim up Niagara Falls." Not that I was idle; the President constantly pressed me for new negotiating ideas—though he really meant merely new channels and procedures. We were, as I told my colleagues, "following the traditional pattern for negotiating with a mule: just keep hitting him on the head with a two-by-four until he does what you want him to do." But that was useless with Hanoi; the mule's head was harder than the two-by-four.

On January 5, 1966, I sent the President two memoranda. One called for him to approach the heads of governments of the United Kingdom, Soviet Union, China, North Vietnam, and South Vietnam to request a secret meeting of the foreign ministers of those five countries with the United States to be held in Vienna beginning January 17, for preliminary discussions of the problem of Vietnam. The timing seemed propitious since a key member of the Soviet politburo, Alexander Shelepin, would shortly be visiting Hanoi, and we might thus arm him with specific proposals to press on the North Vietnamese. The second memorandum discussed possible ways and means of involving the United Nations in a peace effort, using either the Security Council or a special session of the General Assembly. Though I had little faith the United Nations could be useful, I still included a draft Security Council resolution.

As expected, the bombing pause evoked no response: by January, pressures were mounting to resume bombing and escalate the war. On January 20, I sent a memorandum to the President arguing that "the resumption of bombing may well frustrate the very political objectives we have in mind. There is no evidence that bombing has so far had any appreciable effect in weakening the determination of Ho Chi Minh and his colleagues. Whatever evidence there is points in the opposite direction." I recalled my experience on the Strategic Bombing Survey, pointing out that in both Europe and Japan the Survey found that "one does not break the will of the population of a police state by heavy bombing."

I followed my memorandum against bombing with a long analytical memorandum to the President. Prepared with the advice of recognized China experts Professors Allen Whiting and Fred Green, it pointed out why and how our bombing posed grave dangers of war with China. Today—with the wisdom of hindsight—it is clear that I overestimated the prospect of Chinese intervention. But President Johnson was deeply preoccupied with the China menace and the more I emphasized it, the stronger was my case for cutting our losses.

MCNAMARA'S VIEWS

I had a distaste for ex parte Presidential approaches and whenever I wrote a memorandum to the President calling for our extrication, I showed it first to Rusk, McNamara, and Mac Bundy. Secretary McNamara and John McNaughton almost always responded by a prompt and courteous visit. Two or three times they showed me memoranda prepared by McNaughton commenting on what I had written, sometimes expressing views along the same general line while avoiding my hard conclusions. Though momentarily exhilarated by this prospect of support, I found McNamara unwilling to express those same realistic, if discouraging, views in meetings called by the President to discuss my various memoranda. Whether he privately discussed them with the President I do not know.

By May 1967, seven months after I had left the government, a draft memorandum by John McNaughton finally accepted the analysis I had been urging for the three previous years: "it now appears that no combination of actions against the North short of destruction of the regime or occupation of North Vietnamese territory will physically reduce the flow of men and materiel below the relatively small amount needed by enemy forces to continue the war in the South."

FIRST MEETING OF "THE USUAL SUSPECTS"

Even after my resignation in September 1966, I could not free myself from the oppressive burden of the war. It was a blight on all America—the continued killing, the dark apprehensions as we ventured more and more onto bottomless quicksand, and the hysteria in the universities that was taking an increasingly nasty turn. On November 1, 1967, at President Johnson's request, I attended a meeting at the State Department as a member of the so-called Senior Advisory Group—or, as the press called us, "the wise old men," the "elder statesmen" or, more derisively, "the usual suspects." We had dinner with Secretary Rusk and then met the following morning with the President. I made my usual plea for extrication to the usual deaf ears; the war, said the other members of the group, must be vigorously pursued. The major problem, they superciliously asserted, was how to educate American opinion. As I came out of the Cabinet Room, I said to Dean Acheson, John J. McCloy, and—if I recall properly—John

Cowles of Minneapolis, "I've been watching across the table. You're like a flock of old buzzards sitting on a fence, sending the young men off to be killed. You ought to be ashamed of yourselves." I was as surprised as they—and a little embarrassed—by the intensity of my outburst.

The year 1968 caught Washington off guard with the shattering Tet offensive, which lasted for twenty-five days, from dawn on January 31 until February 24. In February, the President commissioned Dean Acheson to make an independent study of the war. Much to the President's dismay, Acheson concluded that we could not win without an unlimited commitment of forces—and that even then it might take five years. The country, Acheson told Johnson, was no longer behind the Administration, nor did Americans any longer believe what the President was telling them. Then, during the next few months, Clark Clifford, the newly appointed Secretary of Defense, accumulated mounting evidence that the war could not be won. Outnumbered eight to one within the circle of advisers closest to the President, and now faced with a request from General Westmoreland for the deployment of 206,000 additional men, Clifford looked about, as I had done earlier, for outside help. The President should, he proposed, meet once again with members of the Senior Advisory Group, who would be briefed on the war and asked to express their views.

SECOND "SENIOR ADVISORY GROUP" MEETING

At 7:30 P.M. on Monday, March 25, 1968, five months after our earlier meeting, we met in the office of Secretary of State Dean Rusk: Dean Acheson, Omar Bradley, McGeorge Bundy, Arthur Dean, Douglas Dillon, Abe Fortas, Robert Murphy, General Matthew Ridgway, Cyrus Vance, and I. After dinner we heard briefings from three government officials: Deputy Assistant Secretary of State Philip Habib, who reviewed the political situation, Major General William DePuy, who spoke of our military posture, and George Carver of the CIA, who talked about pacification and the condition of the enemy. If the North Vietnamese were to be expelled from the South and the country pacified, it would—so our briefers estimated—take at least five to ten more years. The following morning, we talked with the senior officials of the government: Dean Rusk, Clark Clifford, and others. Secretary Clifford spoke bluntly about the choices our country faced. We could either expand the war and muddle along or pursue a "reduced strategy"— cutting back on the bombing and using American troops only to defend certain populated areas.

Dean Acheson was the first of our group to acknowledge that he had changed his mind; we could not, he said, achieve our objective through military means. Views were expressed around the table, and I thought to myself, "there's been a mistake in the invitation list; these can't be the same men I saw here last November." Toward noon, we went to the White House to lunch with the President in the family dining room. During lunch, General Creighton Abrams, just back from Vietnam, told us how he was training the South Vietnamese army with the object of "Vietnamizing" the war.

The President then dismissed all members of the government so as to meet alone with our group of outsiders. When we had gathered in the Cabinet Room, he asked McGeorge Bundy to summarize our collective views. Bundy mentioned particularly Dean Acheson's current opinion that we could not achieve our objectives within the limits of time and resources available. We would therefore have to change our policy drastically. Though that reflected the general view of the group he noted that Abe Fortas and Bob Murphy had dissented. Bundy then made a remark that deeply impressed me not merely for its import but its generosity: "I must tell you what I thought I would never say—that I now agree with George Ball." Bombing in the North, which Bundy had earlier favored as the way of raising the price of insurgencies around the world, staving off defeat in the South, and providing an ultimate bargaining chip was, he had now decided, doing more to erode the support of the war on the homefront than harming the North Vietnamese.

Dean Acheson announced his position in his clear, lawyerlike way. We could not stop the "belligerency" in Vietnam by any acceptable means within the time allowed to us. In view of our other problems and interests, including the dollar crisis, we should seek to disengage by midsummer. There was little support for the war in South Vietnam or in the United States. Acheson did not think the American people would permit the war to go on for more than another year. Douglas Dillon spoke against sending additional troops and advocated stopping the bombing in an effort to move toward a negotiated settlement. He had been deeply impressed by the comments he had heard the night before that it would take five to ten years to conclude the war. General Ridgway, who had, from the first, opposed our intervention, also recommended the withdrawal of American forces, while Cyrus Vance, who, when Deputy Secretary of Defense, had always appeared to support our Vietnamese efforts, now insisted that since the war was bitterly dividing the country, it was time to seek a negotiated settlement.

I made my usual speech against the war. We could not hope to negotiate a sensible withdrawal until we stopped bombing North Vietnam. I emphasized, as I had done many times before, that the war was demoralizing our country and creating grave political divisions and that we had to get out.

There is no doubt that the unexpected negative conclusions of the "elder statesmen" profoundly shook the President. Later he grumbled to me, "Your whole group must have been brainwashed and I'm going to find out what Habib and the others told you."

No one will ever know the extent to which our advice contributed to President Johnson's decision—announced to the American people in a television speech six days after our meeting—that he would not run for President in 1968. He had, he announced, "unilaterally" ordered a halt to the air and naval bombardment of most of North Vietnam. Even that "very limited bombing of the North could come to an early end if our restraint is matched by restraint in Hanoi." Only at the end of his address did he announce his decision to withdraw from the Presidential race.

Though I knew President Johnson desperately wanted to get us out of Vietnam, he was incapable of it. His Administration had accumulated too much baggage of past statements and actions, too many fixed ideas, and too many positions it could not easily reverse. But by taking himself out of the Presidential race, Lyndon Johnson had paved the way for America's extrication, and I hoped our Vietnamese nightmare might soon be over. In spite of Hubert Humhrey's loyal and excessively exuberant support for President Johnson, I knew that he was personally revolted by the war. Once a Humphrey Administration were in place, we might then move promptly toward extrication....

Richard M. Nixon with Henry Kissinger, who was National Security Advisor from 1969 through 1973 and Secretary of State from 1973 to 1977. CAMERA PRESS/GLOBE PHOTOS

CHAPTER 4

Getting Out,
1968–1975

In the aftermath of the Tet offensive, many Americans had grown tired of the war and responded well to candidates who promised a way out of Vietnam. During the 1968 presidential campaign the Democratic candidate, Vice President Hubert Humphrey, was unwilling to challenge publicly the policies of President Johnson, whereas Republican Richard Nixon was elected in good part because he made himself credible as a man of peace. How to extricate the United States from the conflict was the real challenge for Nixon and his national security adviser (later secretary of state), Henry Kissinger. Stanley Karnow, a reporter who is knowledgeable about both Washington and East Asia, depicts the Nixon policy of 1969 and 1970, as the president groped for a way to wind down the war. Historian Gareth Porter looks closely at the 1972 Christmas bombings and the period following the signing of the Paris peace agreement in January 1973 and concludes with a critical assessment of American policy. The last two readings are excerpts from books by British scholar William Shawcross and Kissinger, offering two versions of the Nixon administration's secret decision to bomb North Vietnamese sanctuaries inside Cambodia in 1969. The Shawcross-Kissinger debate remains one of the most bitter from the period and raises a host of troubling questions. Did Vietnamization work, or did it needlessly prolong the war? Were the bombings of Cambodia a risk worth taking, or did they contribute to the disaster that followed in that unhappy country? Was the secrecy of the bombing justified? Finally, do the excerpts in this chapter indicate that Nixon and Kissinger were ultimately successful, or was their stewardship of the Vietnam War no less tortured than that of their predecessors?

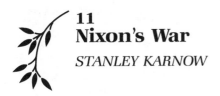

11
Nixon's War
STANLEY KARNOW

Some thirty thousand Americans had been killed in Vietnam by the time Nixon entered office—and nearly ten thousand were to perish there during his first year as president. The Communists greeted him with a series of attacks that stretched through the spring of 1969, causing heavy U.S. casualties. In May, continuing their massive search-and-destroy drives into the hinterlands, American forces fought one of the fiercest battles of the war to capture Apbia mountain, located in the Ashau valley a mile from the Laotian border. The peak, gruesomely nicknamed "Hamburger Hill" because the clash ground up so many GIs, was reoccupied by the North Vietnamese a month later, and the human cost of the futile engagement further roused criticism of the war at home. Soon afterward, as a grim reminder that the war was far from finished, *Life* published photographs of the two hundred and forty-two young Americans slain in a single week. Official spokesmen tried to justify the value of dynamic actions, but General Abrams was quietly instructed to scale down the military effort. For different motives, the Hanoi hierarchy sent similar orders to its field commanders.

By early 1970, about two thirds of the estimated one hundred and twenty-five thousand Communist regulars in the south were North Vietnamese, deployed to replace the main-force Vietcong troops devastated during the Tet offensive two years earlier. For all their skill in battle, the northerners were handicapped politically by their unfamiliarity with the region. The Vietcong political structure was also suffering, largely as a consequence of the Phoenix program, one of the more controversial American operations of the war. Conceived by the CIA three years before, Phoenix was basically another American solution grafted onto a South Vietnamese problem. The Saigon government intelligence services, responsible for uprooting Vietcong agents, were typically a tangle of rival groups competing with each other for power and graft. By centralizing these factions under sound management, the American theory went, the rural apparatus on which the Vietcong relied for recruits, food, money, and asylum could be crushed. So Phoenix was created as a cooperative enterprise— its title a rough translation of *phung hoang*, a mythical Vietnamese bird

From *Vietnam: A History* by Stanley Karnow. Copyright © 1983 by WGBH Educational Foundation and Stanley Karnow. Reprinted by permission of Viking Penguin, a division of Penguin Books USA Inc.

endowed with omnipotent attributes. Saigon government military, police, and civilian officials, trained by U.S. army advisers, were supposed to penetrate the peasant population to gather information and to arrest or slay Communist cadres. In 1969, according to the wondrously precise statistics released by the American mission in Saigon, 19,534 Vietcong organizers, propagandists, tax collectors, and the like were listed as having been "neutralized"—6,187 of them killed.

The Phoenix operation aroused an outcry from American antiwar activists, who labeled it "mass murder." But several Americans involved in Phoenix described it instead as a program riddled with inefficiency, corruption, and abuse. South Vietnamese officials, interested only in promoting themselves, balked at working together, robbed much of the U.S. aid appropriated for the exercise, and were so receptive to bribes that 70 percent of the Vietcong suspects captured bought back their freedom. Worse yet, Phoenix required village authorities to fulfill monthly quotas, which they did by classifying anyone killed in a skirmish as a member of the Vietcong—thereby distorting the figures of "enemy" dead. They also rounded up innocent peasants in order to inflate police blotters, then spared those who could pay them off, and they frequently tortured villagers on no more evidence than the accusation of jealous neighbors. Looking back on his experience in one district, Lieutenant Colonel Stuart Herrington recalled that "no single endeavor caused more grief and frustration" for an American adviser like himself.

Thus I was inclined to discount the claim advanced during the war by William Colby, the CIA executive who ran Phoenix, that the endeavor as a whole, despite its flaws and excesses, eliminated some sixty thousand authentic Vietcong agents. My perspective changed after the war, however, when top Communist figures in Vietnam confirmed Colby's assessment. Madame Nguyen Thi Dinh, a veteran Vietcong leader, told me that Phoenix had been "very dangerous," adding: "We never feared a division of troops, but the infiltration of a couple of guys into our ranks created tremendous difficulties for us." To Colonel Bui Tin, a senior officer, it had been a "devious and cruel" operation that cost "the loss of thousands of our cadres," and the deputy Communist commander in the south at the time, General Tran Do, called it "extremely destructive." Nguyen Co Thach, Vietnam's foreign minister after 1975, admitted that the Phoenix effort "wiped out many of our bases" in South Vietnam, compelling numbers of North Vietnamese and Vietcong troops to retreat to sanctuaries in Cambodia.

Early in 1970, aware that the battlefield was deadlocked, the Communists began to revamp their strategy. With Nixon under pressure at home to remove the GIs from Vietnam, time seemed to be on their side. Nevertheless, they faced grave uncertainties. The unpredictable Nixon might halt U.S. troop withdrawals. Nor could they be sure of defeating the South Vietnamese army, which in any case would continue to be stiffened by American advisers, equipment, and the formidable fleet of B-52 bombers. One possible option was to drop their demand that Thieu's regime be dissolved and agree to some kind of political compromise with him. But they rejected that alternative because, as Foreign Minister Thach confided to me in 1981, they felt too weak to make such a concession. Instead, they retrenched by switching back to small operations, promising that the "protracted" struggle would eventually regain momentum.

Morale was a problem, especially among the southern Vietcong insurgents who had borne the brunt of the fighting, only to be told that victory was still a distant dream. Thousands surrendered to the Saigon regime, or simply returned to their native villages. The Vietcong's rural machinery had been badly damaged, either as a result of the Phoenix program or because peasant sympathizers fled to urban refugee camps to escape the horrendous American bombing of the countryside. The South Vietnamese government, realizing that U.S. troops would not remain in Vietnam forever, was also beginning to improve its "pacification" performance by promoting land reform and arming local militia. General Giap adapted to these developments as he planned ahead. He foresaw the war becoming, ultimately, a conventional conflict, with big divisions clashing in showdown battles. "Great strides" would be made, he wrote in January 1970, "only through *regular war* in which the main forces fight in a concentrated manner" (his italics).

While Nixon could not plausibly point to dramatic progress after a year in office, he was nevertheless moving in a fresh direction in Vietnam. The Communists had lost much of their steam, the South Vietnamese were showing signs of assuming responsibility for themselves, and he had repatriated more than a hundred thousand young Americans and promised to bring home another hundred and fifty thousand over the next year. But in the spring of 1970, determined to demonstrate his power, he plunged into a crazy sequence of events in Cambodia.

Prince Sihanouk's charisma was fading. The Cambodian economy was in shambles, drained partly by his extravagances and the cupidity of his court, and also because his attempts to raise revenues by building hotels and a gambling casino had gone awry. Though the peasants still revered him as a *devaraja*, a god-king descended from the sacred serpent of the Mekong, he had alienated the middle classes of Phnompenh, his capital. Envious of Saigon and Bangkok, flourishing on American dollars, they yearned to share in the wealth lavished by the United States on its southeast Asian clients. The ragtag Cambodian army was particularly disaffected. Senior Cambodian officers were nostalgic for the days before Sihanouk's mercurial neutralism deprived them of American military aid. Along with the prime minister, General Lon Nol, many of them had privately profited from shipping weapons and other supplies from the port of Sihanoukville to the North Vietnamese and Vietcong bases near the Vietnam border. But the lure of renewed U.S. assistance was more attractive, and they dreamed of shifting squarely into the American camp. Besides, their relations with the Vietnamese Communists had deteriorated.

Early in 1969, after Sihanouk acquiesced to the American bombing of their sanctuaries, the North Vietnamese had expected him to swing against them completely. They had been arming and training guerrillas of the Khmer Rouge—the Cambodian Communist movement—in North Vietnam. To exert pressure on Sihanouk, they infiltrated a Khmer Rouge force of some twelve thousand back into Cambodia, spurring an incipient civil war. As the tension mounted, so did Sihanouk's denunciations of the Vietnamese Communists. But he and his top soldiers differed in their prescription for the dilemma. They believed, naively, that they could count on the United States to help them evict their hated neighbors. He believed, naively, that he could get them to quit his territory through diplomatic maneuvers.

But no crisis could deter Sihanouk from his annual "cure" for obesity at a clinic on the Côte d'Azur. He departed for France in January 1970, complacently entrusting Cambodia to Lon Nol and the deputy prime minister, Prince Sisowath Sirik Matak, a cousin belonging to a rival royal clan. The two men, neither very brainy, blundered from the start by assuming that they could effectively crack down on the Vietnamese Communist presence in Sihanouk's absence. Beginning in March, they exhorted Cambodian youths to sack the North Vietnamese and Vietcong legations in Phnompenh, and followed the riots with an ultimatum to the Vietnamese Communists to leave their remote Cambodian bases. Soon Cambodian mobs were running amok, slaughtering innocent Vietnamese civilian residents in an explosion of primeval ethnic passion that portended horrors yet to come. Lon Nol and especially Sirik Matak, hoping to benefit from the chaos, now contemplated Sihanouk's ouster. Allegations to the contrary, there is no firm evidence to substantiate the speculation that CIA agents encouraged them—though contacts with American operatives may have inspired their wishful thinking that the United States favored a *coup d'état*.

In Paris at this juncture, Sihanouk erred. As he acknowledged later, he should have rushed home, where he could have deployed his immense prestige and skill to reimpose his authority. But his mother warned him that danger awaited his return, and he chose instead to go to Moscow to enlist Soviet support to eject the North Vietnamese and Vietcong from Cambodia. Accomplishing nothing there, he decided to fly to Beijing for the same purpose. On March 18, as they drove to the Moscow airport, Soviet Prime Minister Aleksei Kosygin informed him that he had been deposed by his opponents that morning. Sihanouk had once observed Emperor Bao Dai on the Côte d'Azur, and the memory of the deposed ruler wasting in luxurious exile haunted him. Rather than seek a safe haven in France, he proceeded to China.

The French had set up the eighteen-year-old Sihanouk as their puppet ruler in 1941, when they controlled Cambodia as a colonial protectorate, and they felt a special responsibility for him. Now, after his overthrow, they began to ponder the possibility of an international initiative to reinstall him in Phnompenh. There was a precedent for the idea. In 1964, the major powers had acted in concert to reinstate Prince Souvanna Phouma, prime minister of Laos, who had been toppled by an army colonel. The French now suggested the Cambodian problem be considered at a new version of the Geneva Conference of 1954, which had confirmed Cambodia's independence. Some French officials even envisioned the expansion of such a meeting to discuss peace for Vietnam.

Both the North and South Vietnamese regimes, reluctant to allow other nations to dictate their fate, promptly rejected the proposal. By contrast, the idea struck a chord in Britain, which with the Soviet Union had served as cochairman of the earlier Geneva conclave. Negative noises emanated from the Kremlin, but a positive response was advanced by the Polish foreign minister, Stefan Jedrychowski, an oblique signal that the Soviets were not totally averse to the notion. The Chinese ambassador had stayed on in Phnompenh, also a hint that the Chinese might be receptive to an accommodation.

In Washington, meanwhile, senior State Department figures urged flexibility. Marshall Green, assistant secretary of state for Far Eastern affairs, recommended that the French proposal be explored—or, in any case, that military moves that would impede American troop withdrawals from Vietnam be avoided. Secretary of State William Rogers was equally prudent. On March 23, he assured reporters of America's respect for "the neutrality, sovereignty, and independence" of Cambodia, adding that events there "will not cause the war to be widened in any way." Melvin Laird, as usual sensitive to American public opinion, also favored restraint.

Sihanouk, by now in Beijing, characteristically zigzagged. One of his first gestures was to see an old acquaintance, Ambassador Etienne Manac'h of France, in an effort to keep his lines open to the West. But shortly afterward, his regal pride affronted by the Lon Nol regime's vulgar attacks against himself and his family, he publicly announced the creation of a coalition with his former Communist foes to "liberate our motherland." Years later, after the Khmer Rouge had killed several of his children, he still justified his impetuous political decision as having been a personal necessity. His soprano voice rising emotionally, he told me: "I had to avenge myself against Lon Nol. He was my minister, my officer, and he betrayed me."

Cambodia was being convulsed by anarchy in late March 1970. Rival Cambodian gangs were hacking each other to pieces, in some instances celebrating their prowess by eating the hearts and livers of their victims. Cambodian vigilantes organized by police and other officials were murdering local Vietnamese, including women and infants. North Vietnamese and Vietcong troops and their Khmer Rouge confederates were pushing the Cambodian army back into the interior as South Vietnamese units covertly penetrated the border areas accompanied by their U.S. advisers—despite a Pentagon directive prohibiting Americans from crossing the boundary. The hapless Lon Nol, realizing that he had unleashed the furies, decried all foreign intrusion and asserted Cambodia's "strict neutrality." Then, reversing himself on April 14, he broadcast a desperate appeal for outside help. American officials in Phnompenh had prompted the plea as a device to lend legitimacy to a forthcoming U.S. step. For Nixon had secretly decided to aid Lon Nol a month earlier—indeed, even before Sihanouk had been overthrown.

The complicated and often confused machinations that went on inside the Nixon administration during that period have not been—and may never be—fully clarified. Kissinger has noted, however, that "historians rarely do justice to the psychological stress on a policy-maker," and Nixon's mood at the time was certainly a factor. He was more than usually tense, defiant, isolated. The Senate had just enraged him by rejecting in succession two of his candidates for a vacant Supreme Court seat. He was infuriated by press revelations of a covert American bombing campaign against the Communists in Laos, whose "neutrality" the United States theoretically honored. His testiness was also aggravated when Kissinger returned from a first futile round of secret talks in Paris with Le Duc Tho, the new high-ranking North Vietnamese negotiator. And, among other challenges to his authority, there was Cambodia. Much has been made of his infatuation then with the film *Patton*, starring George C. Scott as the lonely, stubborn, aggressive general whose daring risks had won decisive battles in World War II. Nixon watched the movie again and again, and made his aides watch it with him, pointing out to them with admiration Patton's disregard for his critics.

But more tangible motives also propelled Nixon toward Cambodia. With the Communists swiftly closing in on Phnompenh, he feared that the whole country would "go down the drain" unless he acted. General Abrams and other senior officers were warning him as well that another large U.S. troop withdrawal, imperative for domestic political reasons, would jeopardize the American forces remaining in South Vietnam unless the enemy sanctuaries in Cambodia could be eliminated. Nor had Nixon abandoned his original belief that a spectacular manifestation of American power would, by showing the North Vietnamese leaders that "we were still serious about our commitment in Vietnam," drive them to an acceptable compromise at the conference table. Nevertheless, he edged toward direct American intervention gradually—and deceptively.

"We don't anticipate that any request will be made," replied Secretary of State Rogers on March 23, when a reporter asked him whether the United States might grant military assistance to Lon Nol. But Rogers was excluded from the decisions being made at the White House. Six days earlier, on the eve of Sihanouk's ouster, Kissinger had told Nixon that Lon Nol intended to enlarge the Cambodian army by ten thousand men. Two days later, with Sihanouk gone, Nixon instructed Kissinger to "get a plan to aid the new government." Secret orders went out to the American mission in Saigon to furnish Lon Nol's force with weapons captured from the Communists. Dissident Cambodian soldiers, trained by the Americans in Vietnam for clandestine operations in Cambodia, were flown to Phnompenh. To cut the State Department out of the picture further, Nixon directed the CIA to beef up its staff in the Cambodian capital.

By late April, different aides were giving Nixon different advice. General Abrams and his military colleagues in Saigon and Washington were predictably pressing for vigorous measures. Laird, by contrast, was worried. And Rogers, again thinking that he could speak for the administration, told a congressional subcommittee that the administration had "no incentive to escalate" the war into Cambodia because that would jeopardize the Vietnamization program. Kissinger, at first ambivalent, shifted to adjust to Nixon's hardening attitude. CIA analysts, whose only function was to forecast, estimated that American and South Vietnamese infantry would be required to rescue Lon Nol, but however much an allied drive into Cambodia harmed the Communists, "it probably would not prevent them from continuing the struggle."

Anxiety pervaded Capitol Hill, where Senators Frank Church and John Sherman Cooper began to draft legislation to forbid American fighting men from entering Cambodia. On April 20, 1970, Nixon announced the withdrawal of another hundred and fifty thousand U.S. troops from Vietnam within a year—adding that "we finally have in sight the just peace we are seeking." Two days later, at five o'clock in the morning, he dictated a memorandum to Kissinger declaring that "we need a bold move in Cambodia to show that we stand with Lon Nol." Though Lon Nol might collapse anyway, "we must do something symbolic" for the Cambodian regime in twenty-five years with "the guts to take a pro-Western and pro-American stand."

The question was how to proceed. Laird, reconciled to Nixon's determination to "do something," tried to minimize the action. He favored a foray against Communist bases in the "Parrot's Beak," a narrow Cambodian frontier area, to be conducted by only South Vietnamese forces and their American advisers. The recommendation, as Nixon later described it, was "the most pusillanimous little nitpicker I ever saw." He wanted to stage "the big play"—going for "all the marbles," since he expected "a hell of an uproar at home" whatever he did. He indirectly encouraged General Abrams to propose intervention by American combat units as well. Abrams broadened the targets to include sanctuaries in the "Fish Hook" border region, farther north, where he also claimed to have located the legendary Communist headquarters, COSVN. On Sunday night, April 26, Nixon decided to "go for broke" with the entire "package."

Despite Nixon's solicitude for Lon Nol, the Cambodian leader was neither consulted nor even informed in advance of the American project to invade his country. To his dismay, he learned of the operation only after it had started from Lloyd Rives, head of the U.S. mission in Phnompenh— who himself had learned of it only from Nixon's speech broadcast by the "Voice of America." But the deeper issue revolved around Nixon's constitutional prerogatives, a matter that in different guise was to spell his ultimate downfall. Lon Nol's approval notwithstanding, it was doubtful if Nixon had the authority to broaden the war without congressional authority—just as it was doubtful that he had the power to begin, in secrecy, the bombing of Cambodia the year before. Almost as an afterthought, he assigned the task of preparing a legal justification to William Rehnquist, an assistant attorney general, who came up with the argument that the law mandated presidents to deploy troops "in conflict with foreign powers at their own initiative."

Nor did Nixon seem to be conforming to the "doctrine" he had enunciated in Guam, which was to spare GIs from battles on alien soil. One of Nixon's speech writers, William Safire, raised this point during a briefing session with Kissinger, who exploded: "We wrote the goddam doctrine, we can change it!"

Kissinger was under tremendous pressure. Several members of his staff, hostile to the Cambodian venture, were about to quit. He was concerned about his connections with Harvard, where antiwar fever ran high. At the same time, he had to appear belligerent to retain his place in Nixon's inner circle. According to William Watts, one of his aides, Kissinger received a telephone call one evening during this period from Nixon, who at critical moments frequently sought the company of his crony, Charles "Bebe" Rebozo. Nixon, sounding drunk, passed the telephone to Rebozo, who said: "The president wants you to know if this doesn't work, Henry, it's your ass." Watts, who was monitoring the conversation for Kissinger, heard Nixon add in a slurred voice: "Ain't that right, Bebe?"

Nixon unveiled the Cambodian "incursion" on the evening of April 30, 1970, in a televised address that was, as Kissinger derisively put it later, "vintage Nixon." He could have depicted the operation as a minor tactic, designed merely to crush the Communist bases in order to bring the boys home faster. But, consonant with his pugnacious paranoia, he chose instead to be pious and strident, to respond defiantly to his critics, and to defend an overblown reaction to what he perceived as a challenge to America's global credibility. Resorting to coarse jingoism, he had spurned "all political considerations," he said, preferring to follow his conscience rather than "be a two-term president at the cost of seeing America become a second-rate power." International equilibrium hinged on the Cambodian venture: "If, when the chips are down, the world's most powerful nation, the United States of America, acts like a pitiful helpless giant, the forces of totalitarianism and anarchy will threaten free nations and free institutions throughout the world."

An allied force of twenty thousand men, supported by American aircraft, were attacking the two main North Vietnamese and Vietcong bases in Cambodia as Nixon spoke. The South Vietnamese had initially crossed the border two days before. The drive against COSVN, the Communist headquarters supposedly situated in the "Fish Hook," turned out to be quixotic. Instead of the miniature Pentagon imagined by official U.S. spokesmen, American troops found a scattering of empty huts, their occupants having fled weeks before in anticipation of the assault. Meanwhile, Nixon's claims of success for the campaign as a whole were debatable. As usual, the computers compiled impressive statistics of the enemy arms, ammunition, food, and other supplies destroyed; and indeed the damage inflicted on the Communist logistical apparatus was a benefit, for it relieved the military pressure on the heavily populated region around Saigon, thereby giving the South Vietnamese a bit of additional time to prepare replacements for the withdrawing American troops.

But the triumph was temporary and, in long-range terms, illusory. The Communists were soon able to supplant their lost equipment from the vast stocks furnished by the Soviet Union and China. They also shifted their strategic focus to the northern provinces of South Vietnam, where they were to move toward the conventional conflict forecast by General Giap. More critically for the future, the United States was now going to be responsible for the flimsy Lon Nol regime in addition to propping up the shaky Saigon government. Nixon had promised only a couple of weeks earlier that "the just peace we are seeking" was in sight, yet he had expanded the war. The antiwar movement at home, which he had skillfully subdued, suddenly erupted again in the biggest protests to date.

A large proportion of the American people, traditionally loyal to the president in crucial moments, supported the Cambodian incursions. Once again, however, the opinion leaders set the pace. Press commentators lashed out at Nixon, with *The New York Times* calling the action a "virtual renunciation" of his pledge to end the war and the *Wall Street Journal* warning against "deeper entrapment" in Southeast Asia. Educators, clergymen, lawyers, businessmen, and others protested. Nixon's secretary of the interior, Walter Hickel, publicly objected and was later fired, and more than two hundred State Department employees registered their dissatisfaction in a public petition. In many instances, top administration figures were stunned by the anguish of their children. A poignant scene occurred at the home of one senior official who had strenuously worked against the Cambodian offensive from behind the scenes. His two sons, unaware of their father's exertions, denounced him over dinner—and walked out of the house.

Nixon went into a rampage even before the full storm of domestic opposition had burst, almost as if he relished the coming onslaught. At the Pentagon on the morning after the invasion, he interrupted a briefing and embarrassed the officers present by exhorting them in foul language to "blow the hell out" of the Communist sanctuaries in Cambodia. Out in the corridor, he also uncorked a diatribe against antiwar students, whose fresh round of demonstrations had not yet even occurred. Not knowing that his remarks were being taped, he branded the youths as "bums blowing up campuses." He later advised his staff on how to deal with congressional critics: "Don't worry about divisiveness. Having drawn the sword, don't take it out—stick it in hard.... Hit 'em in the gut. No defensiveness."

Universities and colleges across the country were then seething over one issue or another, but Cambodia suddenly crystallized the unrest, and disaster struck at Kent State University in Ohio. There, as elsewhere, antiwar students had attacked the reserve officers training building. Echoing Nixon's inflammatory rhetoric, Governor James Rhodes assailed the rioters as "worse than the brownshirts" and vowed to "eradicate" them. He ordered national guardsmen onto the campus to impose order. On May 4, 1970, nettled by the demonstrators, they shot a volley of rifle fire into the crowd, killing four youths. The administration initially reacted to this event with wanton insensitivity. Nixon's press secretary, Ron Ziegler, whose statements were carefully programmed, referred to the deaths as a reminder that "when dissent turns to violence, it invites tragedy."

Kissinger was torn. On the one hand, he was chagrined by the resignation of four of his aides, who urged him to quit as well. A group of Harvard colleagues also came to Washington to tell him personally of their revulsion, and he felt that the angry meeting marked his final rupture with the academic community. In an interview with me years later, he blamed Nixon for failing to find "the language of respect and compassion that might have created a bridge at least to the more reasonable elements of the antiwar movement." But according to Nixon's recollections, Kissinger "took a particularly hard line" at the time, stressing that "we had to make it clear that our foreign policy was not made by street protests." Roger Morris, one of the assistants who left his staff, recalled that Kissinger was chronically alarmed by demonstrations, which summoned up the Nazi mobs of Germany during his childhood.

The Kent State killings sparked protests across the country. More than four hundred universities and colleges shut down as students and professors staged strikes, and nearly a hundred thousand demonstrators marched on Washington, encircling the White House and other government buildings. The spectacle briefly sobered Nixon. One night, accompanied only by his valet, he drove to the Lincoln Memorial, where young dissidents were conducting a nocturnal vigil. He treated them to a clumsy and condescending monologue, which he made public in an awkward attempt to display his benevolence. But not long afterward, when several senators nearly succeeded in restricting his military activities in Cambodia, he decided to stop "screwing around" with his congressional adversaries and other foes. He ordered the formation of a covert team headed by Tom Huston, a former army intelligence specialist, to improve the surveillance of domestic critics. During later investigation into Nixon's alleged violations of the law, Senator Sam Ervin of North Carolina called the Huston project evidence of a "Gestapo mentality," and Huston himself warned Nixon that the internal espionage was illicit. Nixon afterward contended, however, that "when the president does it, that means it is not illegal."

Nixon had campaigned for election on a pledge to "end the war and win the peace." But after nearly a year and a half in office, he seemed to have gone in the opposite direction. He had extended the war beyond Vietnam into Cambodia, and he had brought the war home with greater intensity. And despite his pretension of toughness, he was not going to extricate himself without offering significant concessions to the Communists.

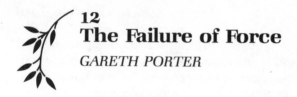

12
The Failure of Force

GARETH PORTER

THE BATTLE OF HANOI

Since the beginning of 1969 Richard Nixon had used the threat of unprecedented devastation of North Vietnam for a variety of diplomatic purposes:
to prod the DRV into moving toward terms acceptable to the United States,
to deter any move to upset his Vietnamization policy, to warn Hanoi to call
off its offensive and finally to accept American terms for a revised settlement. The December bombing was the logical culmination of his heavy
reliance on this ultimate sanction to gain leverage over the Vietnamese
revolutionaries.

The retribution which Nixon and Kissinger had so often threatened
was to be swift, sudden, and brutal, unlike the Johnson administration's
cautious and gradual escalation. Nixon was hoping that intensive attacks
on the only two remaining urban agglomerations in North Vietnam would
force Hanoi to accept his terms for an agreement. And if the suddenness
and indiscriminateness of the bombing of those cities frightened the rest
of the world, Nixon told columnist Richard Wilson on December 18, so
much the better. "The Russians and Chinese might think they were dealing
with a madman and so had better force North Vietnam into a settlement
before the world was consumed by a larger war.[1]

All 200 B-52s in Southeast Asia—one-half of the entire B-52 fleet—
were involved in the effort.[2] And three-fourths of all the Strategic Air Command's combat crews were mobilized to participate in the campaign.[3]
There were also F-111s and F-4s carrying out strikes in the area, but
Linebacker II was an operation planned around the B-52.

American officials acknowledged that the attacks were "aimed at crip-
pling the daily life of Hanoi and Haiphong and destroying North Vietnam's
ability to support forces in South Vietnam."[4] The target list was not limited
to military objectives but included political, social, and economic targets
as well, including the water infiltration plant for Hanoi and factories manufacturing textiles and noodles.[5] It was accepted by the planners that
populated areas of Hanoi and Haiphong located next to the targets would
simply be wiped out. The B-52 was, of course, a weapon for destroying a

large area, not for hitting a specific building or other target. The *Baltimore Sun* pointed out that the usual three-plane mission would drop 276 500- or 750-pound bombs in a rectangular area a mile and a half long and a half mile wide. The result was that little remained within the target area except rubble.[6]

Nixon clamped an unprecedented complete blackout on the targets and the actual destruction done by the B-52s in Hanoi and Haiphong.[7] But foreign journalists saw the remains of an entire residential neighborhood in Hanoi razed by B-52s on the night of December 26–27. Kham Thien district in the heart of Hanoi had been home for 28,198 people. Most of them had fortunately been evacuated to the countryside already. What remained was a swath of destruction about a mile and a half long and a half mile wide, within which only a few houses without roofs or windows remained standing.[8] The main train station, which was located in Kham Thien, had already been demolished one week earlier, along with the bus station.[9]

Although Kham Thien was apparently the most heavily destroyed residential area, it was not the only one. Telford Taylor, chief prosecutor at the Nuremberg war crimes trials, who saw the ruins of a housing project in the An Duong district, wrote, "Some 30 multiple dwelling units covering several acres had suffered 20 or more hits leaving fresh bomb craters 50 feet in diameter and virtually total destruction of the homes."[10]

The most famous target of Linebacker II, however, was the Bach Mai hospital on the southwest edge of Hanoi. The 900-bed hospital, composed of many buildings spread over five acres, was the country's most complete, modern health facility, with 250 doctors and 800 medical students.[11] According to Telford Taylor the hospital was "completely destroyed."[12] A French doctor who was visiting instructor in genetics at the hospital had photographs of the damage showing the destruction of many buildings. According to hospital officials, Bach Mai was hit by three bombs on December 19 and more than 100 bombs at 4:00 A.M., December 22.*

After nine days of heavy bombing, French correspondents reported seeing "craters and uprooted trees" in the main streets of Hanoi, which were delaying the movement of ambulances and rescue teams. More and more of the remaining families were moving into the diplomatic section of the city in the hope that they would be safer from B-52 attacks.[13] The pattern of bombing in and around Hanoi suggested to the North Viet-

---

* Pentagon spokesman Jerry Friedheim, asked about the reports of the destruction of Bach Mai, replied on December 28 that the Department had "no information" that indicated any attack on "any large 1,000 bed civilian hospital." On January 2, he admitted that there had been limited damage to the hospital. Only ten months later, after considerable prodding by the Senate Subcommittee on Refugees, did the Pentagon admit that the hospital was indeed virtually destroyed in the December bombing. (*Boston Globe*, December 28, 1972 and September 2, 1973.)

namese that the purpose was to paralyze the city and isolate it from the rest of the world (Gia Lam, North Vietnam's only international airport, was destroyed by the bombing, but planes continued to take off and land). The bombing appeared to be aimed at leaving Hanoi, in the words of one DRV official, "without any electricity, traffic or relations abroad, and its voice shut—a complete blockade by air.[14]

If that was the strategy of Linebacker II, it was a failure. Despite the fact that the Radio Hanoi transmitters were struck four times in three days, the station was only off the air for nine minutes before resuming with a standby transmitter. Similarly, although 80 percent of the city's electrical power was wiped out, Hanoi had many small power generators with which it could replace power facilities destroyed by the bombing in order to carry out essential services.[15] DRV authorities claimed that, because of previous evacuation of the city and Hanoi's effective system of air raid shelters, only 2,200 people were killed in the capital—far fewer than the 5,000 to 10,000 deaths estimated by US intelligence.[16]

In fact, the idea of coercing the DRV by destroying or paralyzing its urban centers was illusory. For it failed to take account of either the psychology of the North Vietnamese or their capacity to adapt successfully to an all-out war of destruction.

The North Vietnamese had from the beginning of the war expected that their cities would be destroyed, and had made plans to deal with that contingency. In 1966 Jacques Decornoy told of being startled to hear the Vietnamese sitting with him in a Hanoi hotel lobby say, "This lobby in which you are now sitting—we already consider it destroyed. We are ready. We are accepting it all beforehand.[17] And in 1972, at the height of the offensive in the South, DRV officials were certain that the United States would still destroy Hanoi and Haiphong in a last spasm of violence before the end of the war. American visitors were reminded that Ho Chi Minh wrote before he died that the two cities would be destroyed just when they were closest to victory.[18] Factories, schools, universities—everything but the skeleton of the urban centers—had already been moved to the countryside. In fact, the government itself had moved its decision-making headquarters out of the city into areas which were safe from American bombs, and high officials traveled back to the city only to receive foreign dignitaries.[19]

More important than the failure of the bombing to disrupt the functioning of government in North Vietnam, however, was the damage which the North Vietnamese were able to inflict on the US air armada, which had only lost one B-52 in the war before Linebacker II. During 1972 the DRV had been secretly making radical improvements in the capability of its radar system for tracking US planes, increasing its coverage from an extremely low percentage of the incoming planes to a very high percentage. North Vietnamese scientists had made the improvements without the help—or the knowledge—of the Soviet Union, according to DRV officials.

Armed with this new capability for foiling the electronic counter-measures used by US bombers to evade the antiaircraft missiles around Hanoi, the North Vietnamese prepared their defense of the capital metic-ulously. The respite between October 25 and December 18 was used to build up the supply of antiaircraft missiles, and by the time the bombing began the capital was ringed by an estimated 850 SAM missile launchers.[20]

The result of Hanoi's strategic surprise was a toll of B-52s which shocked US strategists. In the twelve days of bombing, the DRV claimed to have brought down thirty-four B-52s.[21] The US claimed only fifteen were lost and that this was less than had been expected.[22] But it was unofficially leaked to the press by Pentagon officials who were obviously unsympathetic to the use of the strategic bomber fleet over Hanoi and Haiphong that this figure did not include planes which had gone down at sea or planes which managed to get back to their bases but were actually put out of action. A high administration source was quoted as saying that the actual number of B-52s damaged seriously was "nearer to what Hanoi says than what we have been saying."[23]

Pentagon officials, who had expected to lose few if any B-52s, con-ceded privately that they could not accept losses at this rate much longer.[24] Although Admiral Moorer would later call Linebacker II "the greatest devastation of the war" to North Vietnam,[25] it was actually the US Air Force which suffered the most serious loss, since the B-52s were no longer in production and could not be replaced.* Within a few days, the mounting air losses were bringing strong pressure on Nixon from the military to end the bombing soon.[26]

Meanwhile, the bombing brought opposition of unprecedented in-tensity in countries normally friendly to the United States. Not only the government of Sweden, which had long been openly critical of US pol-icy in Vietnam, but the governments of Denmark, Finland, Belgium, Italy, Canada, Australia, New Zealand, and Japan openly expressed varying de-grees of hostility or dismay toward the bombing, and the governments of Britain and West Germany were under strong pressure to express their opposition as well.[27] Even Pope Paul, who had been previously reluctant

---

* The feelings of shock and bewilderment at the heavy losses which the DRV inflicted on the US strategic bomber fleet were apparent in the statement of Con-gressman Daniel Flood of the House Defense Appropriations Committee in a hear-ing with Admiral Moorer just ten days after the bombing was halted: "My, my, my . . . that the . . . Department of Defense, the Pentagon, that they were going to be hand-cuffed by some little country called North Vietnam and completely knocked off balance, good gravy . . . here this little backward, these gooks . . . are knocking down your B-52s like clay pigeons, with all the sophisticated hardware which was be-yond our own ken, being run by 'gooks.' This is some kind of lesson." (*Department of Defense Appropriations*, Hearings before a Subcommittee of the Committee on Appropriations, House of Representatives, 93rd Congress, 1st Session, 1973, p. 30.)

to criticize the United States in Vietnam, deplored the "sudden resumption of harsh and massive war actions" in Vietnam.[28]

Perhaps even more important, there was evidence that the bombing was threatening Nixon's détente with the Soviet Union and China. Immediately after the battle of Hanoi began, the United States was in contact with both governments, seeking their help in bringing Hanoi back to the negotiating table in a more cooperative mood.[29]

But in contrast to their reactions to the events of April, both the Soviet Union and China now not only strongly reaffirmed their support for the Vietnamese negotiating position but also suggested that they would put opposition to American policy in Vietnam ahead of their desire for improvement in relations with the United States. On December 21, with Truong Chinh in the audience, Brezhnev devoted a substantial portion of a three and a half hour speech to the Vietnam issue, in which he "emphatically stressed" that the future of Soviet-American relations depended on "the question of ending the war in Vietnam."[30] In early January *Pravda* revealed that the Soviets had stepped up deliveries of antiaircraft sales and jet fighter planes to the DRV during the December bombing, thus confirming US intelligence of such an increase in military assistance.[31]

Peking was even more disturbed by the US *volte-face* of October and November. The Chinese made it clear, both in public and in private communications, that they were not interested in any further negotiations with the United States as long as the bombing continued.[32] The state of Sino-American relations was described by one US official in January as "frozen as hard as before the President went to China."[33]

On December 29 the first anti-United States mass rally in more than a year was held in China to condemn the bombing.[34] Hanoi thus achieved a diplomatic united front with its socialist allies at a time when the United States faced the open opposition of many countries that were friendly or militarily allied with it.

The December bombing further seriously eroded the Nixon administration's already shrinking political support at home for continuing the war. There was a wide consensus among political figures, editorialists, and other opinion-makers that the bombing was an outrage. Typical of the reaction was a *Los Angeles Times* editorial which said that "of all the willful uses of arbitrary power, this is one of the most shocking because the means used are so grossly disproportionate to the ends sought."[35]

There were clear signs that Congress did not support the resumption of the bombing north of the 20th parallel and would move quickly to end the war through legislation. Senators' polls by *Congressional Quarterly* on December 21 opposed the renewed bombing by 45 to 19, with 9 expressing no opinion, and favored legislation to end US involvement in the war by a similar 45 to 25 margin.[36] Republican Senators Charles Mathias and Clifford Case issued statements condemning the bombing and warning that they would urge the Senate to end the war through legislation.[37]

Chairman of the House Ways and Means Committee Wilbur Mills predicted that in 1973 Congress would approve legislation forcing the United States to withdraw its forces from Indochina.[38]

Nixon thus found himself under pressure not only from foreign allies and adversaries, but from Congress and even his own military leaders, to end the bombing and go back to negotiations once more. He had insisted when the bombing began that it would go on "until a settlement is arrived at," apparently assuming that the North Vietnamese could be forced to negotiate while their capital was being bombed.[39] But after five days of bombing he altered that position to insist on some indication from Hanoi that it would negotiate "in a spirit of good will and in a constructive attitude."[40] This was formula which would permit Nixon to end the bombing at any time without loss of face, should he decide that it was necessary.

On December 30, after domestic and foreign pressures had continued to build for several more days, Nixon gave in. The White House press spokesman avoided any mention of the bombing when he said on December 30: "The President has asked me to announce this morning that negotiations between presidential adviser Dr. Kissinger and special adviser Le Duc Tho and Minister Xuan Thuy will be resumed in Paris on January 8. Technical talks will be resumed on January 2. That is the extent of the announcement."[41]

It was only under questioning that the spokesman said, "The President has ordered that all bombing will be discontinued above the 20th parallel as long as serious negotiations are under way." Despite the implied threat of a renewal of bombing if the North Vietnamese did not agree to the US demands, it would have been difficult for Nixon to repeat the December bombing.

The White House was silent on the reason for the reversal of Nixon's earlier threat to continue the bombing "until a settlement is arrived at." But the White House plan for forcing the acceptance of its demands for a revised agreement had clearly been foiled by the unexpected military reverses over Hanoi and the surprisingly strong political reaction at home and abroad. According to Lao Dong Party Central Committee spokesman Hoang Tung, the crucial factor in defeating Nixon's effort to rewrite the agreement was the strategic surprise which Hanoi's antiaircraft units had in store for the US bomber fleet. "If we had not been able to bring down the B-52's," he said, "the situation might have been different. Their side would have made other steps forward to impose their conditions."[42]

As Kissinger and Le Duc Tho prepared to return to the negotiating table in Paris, Nixon's bargaining hand had been greatly weakened. His last major bargaining chip had been used to no avail, and now his administration was under even more intense pressure than before to reach agreement without much delay. Far more than in the October or November-December rounds, the DRV was in a position to reject American demands.

Later the administration would do its best to persuade the US public that the bombing had made the North Vietnamese more cooperative at the peace table.* A Gallup poll taken some weeks later showed that 57 percent of those polled believed that the Christmas bombing had contributed to the peace settlement.[43] In an ironic way, it was true: by its political and military failure, the bombing of Hanoi and Haiphong made the Paris Agreement possible. For it forced Nixon and Kissinger to accept the very terms which they had rejected in October, November, and December. While the threat of massive bombing had seemed to give Nixon leverage over the North Vietnamese, the battle of Hanoi showed how that apparent strength could be transformed into diplomatic weakness. . . .

Only a few weeks after this manuscript was originally completed in February [1975], the end of the Vietnam war came with stunning swiftness and finality. Both sides had been prepared for a struggle which would continue for many more months. But military pressure by the PLAF against a military and administrative structure which was far more fragile than American officials had ever acknowledged publicly produced a process of unraveling so rapid that the Communist forces could scarcely keep pace.

This process of disintegration, which took place over a period of six weeks, overtook the formula for a political solution which had been outlined in the Paris Agreement and offered by the PRG. Although the shifting balance of military and political forces made it clearer than ever that a tripartite National Council of National Reconciliation and Concord would be dominated by the PRG, this body still offered a way of ending the war by a peaceful transition rather than a military victory for the Communists. But the United States made no diplomatic effort to achieve a political settlement by replacing Thieu until the very last minute, and then only to gain time to evacuate the Vietnamese it had already promised to get out of the country.

By the time a leader was finally brought in who *could have* negotiated a settlement earlier, there was nothing left to negotiate, and the higher echelons of the Saigon administration and army were already in the process of fleeing. Thus Washington chose, in effect, to have the end

---

* In an interview with CBS News, Kissinger was asked whether he wasn't leaving the public with the "assumption . . . that without that kind of heavy bombing the North Vietnamese would not have become serious—your term—and that therefore one could conclude that it was the bombing that brought the North Vietnamese into a serious frame of mind?" Kissinger replied carefully that the bombing "came at the end of a long process in which they too had suffered a great deal." He added that, on the eve of his own trip to Hanoi, it would "not serve any useful purpose for me . . . to speculate about what caused them to make this decision." (Transcript of "A Conversation with Henry Kissinger," CBS News Special Report, February 1, 1973, p. 7.)

come through a military victory for the Communist forces rather than a face-saving arrangement such as it had vainly sought in Cambodia. It appeared, in fact, that Kissinger wished to be able to argue that the Communists had never really been interested in a nonmilitary solution, and that the United States had no alternative but to support Saigon's war effort to the end.

The Communist's 1975 dry season campaign, as originally envisioned by PLAF military planners, was aimed at creating stronger pressures for Thieu's removal by further eroding Saigon's control and destroying part of his army. Although it was to include the capture of several objectives with great psychological impact, it was not expected to end the war immediately but rather to lay the groundwork for a war-ending offensive the following year.[44] Nevertheless, it set in motion a dynamic which went far beyond that. For it turned an army which had appeared to be a formidable fighting force into a mob of frightened and demoralized men who made the unspoken decision that the war was over for them.

Despite its massive size and modern armaments, the Saigon army's morale had long since declined to a point where disintegration was an ever-present danger. ARVN was not held together by any commonly held aspirations or cause, nor by any personal bonds of respect and affection between officers and men. It had been able to survive until the Paris Agreement under the umbrella of American power, on which ARVN troops had come to depend. The absence of US air support after the agreement and the growing military potential of the PLAF had created profound doubts that the ARVN could resist a determined offensive effort by the Communists, while PRG propaganda on the Paris Agreement and reconciliation policy had further reduced the willingness of ARVN soldiers to continue fighting. An American consular official in Quang Ngai province, Paul Daley, told a journalist in early March 1975 that he had visited an ARVN unit on the front line and had seen some soldiers taking off on Hondas. When he asked the battalion commander why he let them go, Daley said, the reply was, "What can you do?" The problem was, Daley continued, "These guys think that peace should have come twenty-four hours after the agreement was signed."[45]

Finally, due to soaring inflation, ARVN troops had been reduced more and more to robbery and pillage for their daily economic survival. By mid-1974, 92 percent of the soldiers surveyed by the US Defense Attaché's Office said their pay and allowances were not adequate to provide food, clothing, and shelter for their families. The DAO concluded that the economic crisis had caused a "deterioration of performance, which cannot be permitted to continue, if [the ARVN is] to be considered a viable military force."[46]

Accommodation and outright desertion or defection to the PLAF were rampant in 1974. One ARVN outpost, originally carrying 129 men on its rolls, lost all but twenty-three of them in desertions and defections before it was finally abandoned. When ARVN tried in 1974 to assign local militiamen to the regional forces, which were expected to fight farther away from home within the same province, the result was mass desertion. In one newly formed battalion of six hundred men drawn from the local forces, only three soldiers were left after a few weeks away from their home villages.[47]

The dry season campaign began with a move calculated to have a particularly devastating effect on Saigon's morale: an attack on Ban Me Thuot by troops of the Montagnard autonomy movement, FULRO, which had pledged its allegiance to the government in January 1969 but had drawn closer to the PRG because of Saigon's exploitative policies toward the tribal minorities. On March 10, FULRO troops fought their way into the central highlands capital and on the following day, they gained un-contested control of the city.[48]

Suddenly realizing that the central highlands were indefensible, Thieu ordered an unexpected strategic withdrawal from the remaining highlands provinces, Pleiku and Kontum. But the withdrawal quickly turned into a rout, as the 23rd Division was outflanked and essentially destroyed before it reached the coast. At the same time, Thieu decided to give up the provinces of Quang Tri and Thua Thien in order to estab-lish a new defense line at Danang. He later changed his mind, fearing the political impact of the withdrawal from Hue, and ordered his troops once more to stand and fight for Hue. Although the Marines turned back toward Hue, the 1st Division troops refused the orders and ARVN began to fall apart as they streamed into Danang in complete disorder. Meanwhile, resistance to the PLAF melted away all along the central coast, as Quang Nam, Quang Tin, and Quang Ngai quickly fell without a fight, having been abandoned by their defenders.[49]

The demoralized Saigon soldiers who fled to Danang from other provinces brought social chaos and panic in their wake, just as they had in Hue in 1972. Their despair signaled to the population of Danang that the city was already lost, and the exodus began almost immediately. Within two days after the fall of Hue to the Communists, most government offi-cials, including nearly all the policemen, had already disappeared from their posts in Danang, and order inevitably broke down.[50] Danang was ruled by horror for three days, as hysterical troops began to shoot civil-ians indiscriminately in the streets. The worst disorders occurred when Americans attempted to evacuate refugees from the airport and then from the port of Danang. Soldiers shot and killed hundreds of civilians in order to get themselves and their families on to evacuation aircraft. On board an American refugee ship, they beat and raped refugees and killed those who protested.[51] On March 30, Liberation Army troops moved into Danang without resistance and established order within less than an hour, accord-ing to eyewitness reports.[52]

The rout continued southward down the coast. In only three days Qui Nhon, Tuy Hoa, Nha Trang, Cam Ranh, and Dalat went through the same sequence of developments: officers and civilian officials pulled out, soldiers began looting, and finally Liberation Army forces arrived to restore order.[53]

By April 2, the PRG found itself master of two-thirds of the country, with its foes in a state of shock. Saigon appeared for the first time to be virtually indefensible with its dwindling and demoralized forces. Six Saigon divisions had been eliminated from the battlefield, including the most reliable combat units, and half of its air force was gone. The PLAF, which had overwhelmingly superior forces around Saigon, was now in a position to force a quick end to the war.

Assessing the new situation, the Party leadership quickly revised its strategy to take advantage of the Saigon government's collapse, in two-thirds of the country. On April 4, the PLAF sent out orders to its units to prepare for an attack on Saigon itself.[54] While making plans for a military take-over, however, PRG officials did not rule out a return to the Paris formula, provided that the United States would replace Thieu with a government which would renounce the violently anti-Communist policies of the past. On April 1, and again on April 2, the PRG offered to negotiate with such a government on the basis of the Paris Agreement.[55] In the latter statement PRG Foreign Minister Nguyen Thi Binh suggested for the first time that General Duong Van Minh would be a logical replacement for Thieu: "We understand that General Minh is ready to negotiate peace, and we are ready to talk with him," she said. On April 9, in a press conference, she again demanded a government which would "insure strict application of the Paris Agreement," offering once again to arrive at a political settlement with such a regime.[56]

But the offer to return to the Paris Agreement's political formula was ignored by Washington and the US Embassy in Saigon. State Department officials had gone out of their way in late March to make it clear to the press that the Peace Agreement was, in their view, "inoperable," and that there was no possibility of a negotiated settlement.[57] In mid-April, Ambassador Graham Martin said in an interview, "There has been no advice from Washington for Thieu to step down."[58] At the same time, Martin was actively discouraging a military coup against Thieu, assuring former Vice-President Ky that Thieu would soon step down.[59] This attitude of determined disinterest in a political solution was consistent with earlier reports from State Department Sources familiar with Kissinger's thinking emphasizing that a North Vietnamese military victory was already considered inevitable and that Kissinger's only concern was to appear to be a "good ally" to the very end.

Instead of trying to end the killing as soon as possible by pressing for a change of regime in Saigon, therefore, the Ford administration went through the motions of asking for an additional $722 million in military aid on April 11. Kissinger, in a background briefing for the press, suggested that the administration understood that the war was already lost, and hinted that the posture of all-out support for the Thieu regime was necessary in order to have its cooperation in the evacuation of Americans from Saigon. Kissinger spoke of trying to establish a perimeter around Saigon in the hope of negotiating a cease-fire and evacuating large numbers of Vietnamese from the city. But he did not indicate any intention to work for a political solution by replacing Thieu.[60]

On April 19, with the Liberation Army poised to begin its final drive on the capital, the PRG spokesman at Tansonnhut, Colonel Vo Dong Giang, publicly warned that there would be a military takeover if negotiations were not begun soon by a new government without the "Thieu clique."[61] At the same time, according to US sources, an ultimatum was passed on to the United States through the Hungarian and Polish ICCS delegations demanding that Thieu resign within forty-eight hours and that a new government be established within a few days with which the PRG could negotiate a political settlement. The note gave assurances that during those few days, there would be no military interference with the American evacuation of its personnel.[62]

The ultimatum finally mobilized the Embassy to action. It needed more than forty-eight hours to evacuate the Americans and South Vietnamese who had been promised evacuation. The Embassy immediately put intense pressure on Thieu to step down. As a high Embassy official put it, "The old man had to lean on him substantially."[63] On the evening of April 21, Thieu announced his resignation and was soon on a US military plane bound for Taiwan. The PLAF, which was conceded to be in a position to attack the city at will, then reduced its military activities to a minimum.

For the next six days, as the military lull and the stepped-up US evacuation continued, Thieu's successor, the ailing, seventy-one-year-old Tran Van Huong, who had been closely identified with Thieu's rule for many years, seemed unable or unwilling to turn the government over to General Duong Van Minh, who could have negotiated peace. Not until April 27 did the National Assembly finally vote unanimously to turn the Presidency over to Minh. But by that time the lull had ended and with it any chance for a negotiated settlement.[64] As the PRG began its "Ho Chi Minh" campaign to take the city, the PRG delegation in Paris raised the new demand that the Saigon army and administration be dissolved.[65] And even as Minh was being inaugurated, virtually the entire military and civilian leadership of the Saigon government was fleeing the country in the US airlift.[66]

After futile attempts to get the PRG representatives at Tansonnhut to negotiate with him, Minh ordered his troops to surrender on April 29. Liberation Army troops entered Saigon shortly thereafter to find that the Saigon Army in and around the city had vanished into history, leaving tens of thousands of boots, helmets, and uniforms lying in the streets and sidewalks.[67] Within hours of the departure of the last American, the military and administrative apparatus which the United States had spent more than twenty years and billions of dollars building up and protecting had ceased to exist. The quarter-century effort by the United States to prevent the completion of the Vietnamese revolution was ending in complete victory for the revolutionaries. When the revolutionary troops entered the presidential palace, General Minh told them that he was ready to meet with them to "hand over the administration." But the PLAF officer responded, "One cannot hand over what one does not control."[68]

Now that the whole experience of the Vietnam intervention is behind us, it should be possible to view the policies of the parties to the struggle with greater detachment and to discern certain historical realities which were more or less obscure at the time. Inevitably, the relentless researching of the history of this war will show that the claims of successive administrations about their own policies and those of their adversaries were false or misleading. For it was the kind of war in which dishonorable and ultimately futile deeds were always clothed in the rhetoric of peace.

This study was intended as a contribution to the process of clarifying the record of the Vietnam war, so that the right lessons might be learned from a tragic and ignoble chapter in American history. Some of the major conclusions which emerged from the foregoing narrative and analysis are worth repeating for emphasis:

1. *The US executive's definition of America's interests in Vietnam required that it deny peace to that country from the beginning of its involvement to the very end.* American geopolitical interests were invariably held to be absolute ones which took priority over any consideration of the interests and aspirations of the Vietnamese people themselves. Permitting a political solution at any time which would have given up the right of American intervention would have meant jeopardizing the client regime's chances for survival. Despite many opportunities to resolve the conflict by diplomatic formulas which, in other contexts, would have been regarded as fair and acceptable, the United States invariably chose to rely on force to try to consolidate the power of the anti-Communist regime.

2. *The Christmas bombing of 1972 was probably the most important defeat suffered by the US executive in the entire war.* Although there was no single decisive battle in the fifteen years of war in Vietnam, there were campaigns which opened up a new phase of the conflict, representing a strategic setback for the United States and a gain for the revolutionaries. The bombing of Hanoi and Haiphong in December 1972 appears to have been the most important such campaign. Intended to facilitate a more favorable agreement and to suggest that the United States could reintervene if necessary, it made such reintervention far less likely. It aroused strong public opposition and provoked Congressional moves to cut off funds for any further bombing. It not only failed to force North Vietnam to rewrite the Paris Agreement in order to make it easier for Saigon accuse its foes of violations; it also prepared the way for the mid-1973 legislative prohibition against

any further military action in Indochina without prior Congressional approval.

3. *The Paris Agreement could not end the war, because Thieu had been assured by the Nixon Administration that he would get full US backing for a policy of avoiding political accommodation and continuing the military offensive.* Thieu had a strong incentive, moreover, to provoke a military confrontation with the Communists while he still had the strong support of the White House. The Nixon administration's backing for Thieu—and especially its pledge to resume bombing in the event of any "violation"—thus had the effect of nullifying the terms of the accord, which depended upon Thieu's having an incentive to make political compromises which he had been adamantly resisting for years. The United States thus rejected an opportunity to bring about a cease-fire and political settlement, to which the Communist leaders were willing to agree for their own reasons in 1973.

4. *The conflict ended in complete military victory for the PRG rather than in a negotiated political solution, because the United States refused to adjust its policy to the new balance of forces reflecting the fact that the United States clearly would not again intervene with air power in Vietnam.* Kissinger and Nixon refused to use their power to force a political change because they found it more compatible with both domestic political needs and foreign policy objectives to lose militarily while playing the "good ally" than to actively seek a political solution to bring an end to the war. The Paris Agreement's formula depended on a US interest in finding a way to end the war short of total defeat; in the absence of such an interest, a Saigon regime whose *raison dètre* had been to repress the revolutionaries had to be replaced by a regime established by those very revolutionaries.

NOTES

1.   Quoted in Thomas L. Hughes, "Foreign Policy: Men or Measures?" *Atlantic,* October 1974, p. 56.

2.   *Washington Star-News,* December 20, 1972.

3.   *Los Angeles Times,* July 22, 1973.

4.   Associated Press dispatch, *Baltimore Sun,* December 30, 1972.

5.   "Bach Mai Witness: Dr. Yvonne Capdeville," Paris Chapter, Committee of Concerned Asian Scholars, Information Packet No. 9 (January 1973), p. 2; *Washington Post,* December 30, 1972.

6.   *Baltimore Sun,* December 28, 1972.

7.   *New York Times,* December 22, 1972.

8.   Agence France-Presse dispatch, *Le Monde,* December 30, 1972.

9.   Marder, *Washington Post,* February 4, 1973.

10.   *New York Times,* December 31, 1972.

11.   "Bach Mai Witness," p. 1.

12. *Baltimore Sun,* December 28, 1972.

13. *Washington Post,* December 30, 1972.

14. Marder, *Washington Post,* February 4, 1973.

15. Ibid.

16. *U.S. News and World Report,* February 5, 1973, p. 18.

17. *Le Monde,* November 25, 1966.

18. Interview with Marge Tabankin, former president of the US National Student Association, on a visit to the DRV in June 1972, in *Off Our Backs,* September 1972, p. 26.

19. Marder, *Washington Post,* February 4, 1973.

20. Hanson Baldwin, *Boston Globe,* January 22, 1974.

21. Marder, *Washington Post,* February 4, 1973.

22. *Department of Defense Appropriations,* Hearings before Subcommittee of the Committee on Appropriations, House of Representatives, 93rd Congress, 1st Session, 1973, p. 18.

23. *Manchester Guardian Weekly,* January 6, 1973, p. 10; also Jack Anderson, *Washington Post,* January 3, 1973.

24. *U.S. News and World Report,* January 8, 1973, p. 17; ABC Evening News, December 22, 1972.

25. *Department of Defense Appropriations,* p. 14.

26. *Manchester Guardian Weekly,* January 6, 1973, p. 10.

27. *Washington Post,* December 21, 30, 1972; *New York Times,* December 21, 24, 1972; on Japan's reaction, see *Christian Science Monitor,* December 26, 1972. Reactions from foreign governments were reported to be far worse than anticipated. See Jack Anderson, *Syracuse Post-Standard,* January 9, 1973.

28. *Washington Post,* December 21, 1972.

29. *New York Times,* December 19, 1972.

30. *Washington Post,* December 22, 1972; also see *Baltimore Sun,* December 30, 1972.

31. *Baltimore Sun,* January 29, 1973.

32. *Baltimore Sun,* December 21, 1972; *U.S. News and World Report,* January 22, 1973, p. 8.

33. *U.S. News and World Report,* January 22, 1973, p. 8.

34. *Baltimore Sun,* December 30, 1972.

35. Quoted in *Time,* January 8, 1973, p. 14.

36. "The Vietnam Bombing: Senate Opposition Grows," *Congressional Quarterly Weekly Reports,* December 23, 1972, p. 3171.

37. *Baltimore Sun,* December 30, 1972.

38. *Washington Post,* December 30, 1972.

39. White House press secretary Ron Ziegler, quoted in *New York Times,* December 19, 1972.

40. *New York Times,* December 23, 1972.

41. *Boston Globe,* December 31, 1972.

42. Interview with Hoang Tung, Hanoi, January 7, 1975.

43. Richard Dudman, "The Lesson of Vietnam," *Congressional Record*, February 26, 1973, p. S3275.

44. *Time*, March 24, 1975, p. 20.

45. William Goodfellow, Pacific News Service dispatch from Quang Ngai, March 3, 1975.

46. *Christian Science Monitor*, April 1, 1975.

47. Don Oberdorfer, *Washington Post*, April 7, 1975.

48. The report of FULRO troops leading the operation on Ban Me Thuot was reported by Agence France-Presse correspondent Paul Leandri in *Le Monde*, March 14, 1975. Leandri was summoned to the National Police station for questioning about his dispatch and was shot by police as he tried to leave his compound in his car. *New York Times*, March 16, 1975. Leandri's story was confirmed by Catholic leader Father Tran Huu Thanh on the basis of conversations with refugees and priests from Ban Me Thuot. *Le Figaro*, March 19, 1975.

49. Oberdorfer, *Washington Post*, April 7, 1975.

50. Ibid.

51. Agence France-Presse dispatch by George Herbouze, *Los Angeles Times*, March 31, 1975 (Herbouze interviewed a French schoolteacher who was in Danang when the PRG took over); Associated Press dispatch from aboard the freighter *Pioneer Contender*, *Washington Star*, March 31, 1975.

52. Agence France-Presse dispatch, *New York Times*, April 24, 1975.

53. *Christian Science Monitor*, April 3, 1975.

54. In his news conference of April 19, PRG spokesman Vo Dong Giang announced that the general order for the assault on Saigon had gone out on April 4. *Washington Post*, April 20, 1975.

55. *New York Times*, April 2 and 3, 1975.

56. *Washington Post*, April 10, 1975. In an interview with a group of Americans, including the author, on April 7, 1975, the PRG ambassador to the Political Talks in Paris, Dinh Ba Thi, went considerably further in indicating his government's willingness to return to the political formula of the Paris Agreement. "We aimed at a higher goal during the negotiations," he said, "but Kissinger wouldn't accept it, so the power of the National Council was very limited. But since the agreement talked about the National Council we must implement that." He further confirmed that the PRG was still prepared to accept the existence of two administrations through the electoral process outlined in the agreement, and that they were ready to reconstitute the Joint Military Commission by negotiations with a new Saigon government.

57. *Los Angeles Times*, March 22, 1975.

58. *Time*, April 21, 1975, p. 19.

59. See the interview with Ky's personal assistant, Deputy Nguyen Van Cu, *Chicago Tribune*, April 24, 1975.

60. Kissinger's background briefing, including substantial quotations, is covered, without naming Kissinger, in the *Los Angeles Times*, April 12, 1975.

61. *Washington Post,* April 20, 1975.

62. *Washington Post,* April 26, 1975 and May 5, 1975.

63. *Time,* May 5, 1975.

64. A Liberation Radio broadcast on April 30 said the final drive on the city began at 5 P.M. April 26. The highways leading out of Saigon were immediately cut and the airport was rocketed by the following night. *Washington Post,* April 26, 1975.

65. *Washington Post,* April 18, 1975.

66. *Time,* May 12, 1975; *Washington Star,* April 29, 1975; *Chicago Tribune,* April 29, 1975.

67. For an eyewitness account of the Saigon army's surrender, see James Fenton, "How War's End Came to Saigon," *Washington Post,* May 11, 1975.

68. Interview with Hoang Tung by an American delegation in Hanoi, May 6, 1975 (*Indochina Peace Campaign Newsletter,* May 18, 1975).

13
The Secret Bombing of Cambodia
WILLIAM SHAWCROSS

The first request was unpretentious. On February 9, 1969, less than a month after the inauguration of Richard Nixon, General Creighton Abrams, commander of United States forces in South Vietnam, cabled General Earle G. Wheeler, Chairman of the Joint Chiefs of Staff, to inform him that "recent information, developed from photo reconnaissance and a rallier gives us hard intelligence on COSVN HQ facilities in Base Area 353."

COSVN HQ was the acronym for the elusive headquarters—"Central Office for South Vietnam"—from which, according to the United States military, the North Vietnamese and Viet Cong were directing their war effort in South Vietnam. Until then, Abrams remarked, the military had placed COSVN in Laos. Now he was certain the headquarters was much farther south, in one of neutral Cambodia's border states which were being used by the Communists as bases and sanctuaries from the fighting in Vietnam. Abrams wanted to attack it.

> The area is covered by thick canopy jungle. Source reports there are no concrete structures in this area. Usually reliable sources report that COSVN and COSVN-associated elements consistently remain in the same general area along the border. All our information, generally confirmed by imagery interpretation, provides us with a firm basis for targeting COSVN HQs.

Already Abrams had been instructed by the new administration to discuss United States troop withdrawals with the South Vietnamese. Now he reminded Wheeler that he had predicted a large-scale enemy offensive around Saigon in the near future. An attack on COSVN, he argued, "will have an immediate effect on the offensive and will also have its effect on future military offensives which COSVN may desire to undertake." An appropriate form of assault would be "a short-duration, concentrated B-52 attack of up to 60 sorties, compressing the time interval between strikes to the minimum. This is more than we would normally use to cover a target this size, but in this case it would be wise to insure complete destruction."

Abrams seems to have understood some of the implications of this request. Prince Norodom Sihanouk, Cambodia's ruler, had long been trying to keep his country out of the war in Vietnam. Abrams assured Wheeler that "there is little likelihood of involving Cambodian nationals if the target boxes are placed carefully. Total bomber exposure over Cambodian territory would be less than one minute per sortie." (put another way, sixty sorties would take about one hour.) The general also thought it necessary to point out that "the successful destruction of COSVN HQs in a single blow would, I believe, have a very significant impact on enemy operations throughout South Vietnam." He asked for authority for the attack.

The Joint Chiefs sent Abrams' memo up to Melvin R. Laird, a former Wisconsin Republican Congressman, who was the new Secretary of Defense. Laird passed it to the White House, where it received the immediate attention of the new President and his National Security Affairs adviser, Dr. Henry Kissinger.

Two days later General John P. McConnell, the acting chairman in Wheeler's absence, sent a reply that must have cheered Abrams; it indicated that Washington was taking the idea even more seriously than Abrams himself. His request to Wheeler had not been highly classified, but simply headed "Personal for Addressees." McConnell's answer, however, was routed so that almost no one but he and Abrams could see it and was plastered with classifications: "Top Secret"—"Sensitive"—"Eyes Only"—"Delivery During Waking Hours"—"Personal for Addressee's Eyes Only."

McConnell told Abrams that his request had been presented to "the highest authority." In the conventions of cable language, this meant that President Nixon himself had seen it. The President had not rejected the idea; Abrams was told that "this matter will be further considered." The cable went on:

2. The highest authority desires that this matter be held as closely as possible in all channels and in all agencies which have had access to it.
3. The highest authority also wants your estimate on the number of Cambodian civilians who might become casualties of such an attack.
4. It will not, repeat not, be necessary for you to send a briefing team to Washington. However, it will be important for you to keep me informed on any further developments from your viewpoint. Warm regards.

Despite McConnell's advice, Abrams did send a briefing team to Washington. Two colonels arrived at the Pentagon, and a special breakfast meeting was arranged at which they could explain Abram's proposals to a number of senior officials. These included Melvin Laird, General Wheeler, Colonel Robert Pursley, Laird's military assistant, and Lieutenant General John Vogt, then the Air Force's Assistant Deputy Chief of Staff for Plans and Operations. The meeting was also attended by a representative from Dr. Kissinger's National Security Council staff, Colonel Alexander Haig.

The colonels outlined their argument with conviction. This time, they claimed, it really was true: Viet Cong and North Vietnamese headquarters had been located. Base Area 353 was in the so-called Fish Hook, a corner of Cambodia that jutted into South Vietnam, northwest of Saigon. Even without COSVN, it was considered one of the most important Communist sanctuaries in Cambodia. Several regiments were based there and it also contained military hospitals and large caches of food and arms.

Over the next five weeks Abrams' request was frequently discussed by the National Security Council staff and Presidential meetings in the Oval Office of the White House. Understandably perhaps, the Joint Chiefs were enthusiastic in support of the proposal. Melvin Laird was more skeptical. But he acknowledged that if COSVN had really been discovered it should be destroyed and argued that it could be publicly justified as an essential precondition to troop withdrawal. Nixon and Kissinger, however, were adamant that if it were done, it had to be done in total secrecy. Normal "Top Secret" reporting channels were not enough. Later General Wheeler recalled that the President said—"not just once, but either to me or in my presence at least half a dozen times"—that nothing whatsoever about the proposal must ever be disclosed.

Before a final decision was made, the Chiefs cabled Abrams to tell him that he could make tentative plans for launching the strike on the early morning of March 18. He was told of the demands for secrecy and was given a code name for the operation—"Breakfast," after the Pentagon briefing.

The cable set out in detail the way in which the raids were to be concealed. The planes would be prepared for a normal mission against targets in Vietnam. If the Joint Chiefs sent the signal "Execute repeat Execute Operation Breakfast," they would then be diverted to attack the Cambodian base area. No announcement would be made. "Due to sensitivity of this operation addressees insure that personnel are informed only on a strict need-to-know basis and at the latest feasible time which permits the operation to be conducted effectively."

Abrams made the necessary dispositions, and on March 17 Wheeler cabled him: "Strike on COSVN headquarters is approved. Forty-eight sorties will be flown against COSVN headquarters. Twelve strikes will be flown against *legitimate* targets of your choice in SVN not repeat not near the Cambodian border" (Emphasis added).

The strikes were to take place almost at once, between three o'clock and seven o'clock on the morning of March 18, unless Abrams received a priority "Red Rocket" message "Cancel repeat Cancel Operation Breakfast."

The cable described how the press was to be handled. When the command in Saigon published its daily bombing summary, it should state that, "B-52 missions in six strikes early this morning bombed these targets: QUOTE Enemy activity, base camps, and bunker and tunnel complexes 45 kilometers northeast of Tay Ninh City. UNQUOTE. Following the above, list two or more other B-52 targets struck (12 sorties)."

Wheeler continued:

In the event press inquiries are received following the execution of the Breakfast Plan as to whether or not U.S. B-52s have struck in Cambodia, U.S.
spokesman will confirm that B-52s did strike on routine missions adjacent
to the Cambodian border but state that he has no details and will look into
this question. Should the press persist in its inquiries or in the event of a
Cambodian protest concerning U.S. strikes in Cambodia, U.S. spokesman will
neither confirm nor deny reports of attacks on Cambodia but state it will be
investigated. After delivering a reply to any Cambodian protest, Washington
will inform the press that we have apologized and offered compensation.

Finally, Wheeler reminded Abrams and the B-52 commanders, "Due
to the sensitivity of this operation all persons who know of it, who participate in its planning, preparation or execution should be warned not
repeat not to discuss it with unauthorized individuals."

Many of the B-52s used in Indochina were based at Anderson Air
Force Base in Guam. The planes had been built in the 1950s as an integral
part of the United States' nuclear deterrent, but since 1965 more than a
hundred of them had been adapted to carry dozens of conventional 750-
lb. bombs in their bellies and under their wings. They were still controlled
by Strategic Air Command but were at the disposition of the commander
of U.S. Forces in South Vietnam. Abrams could call upon sixty planes a
day. Each plane could carry a load of approximately thirty tons of bombs.

Before takeoff, the crews of the B-52s were always briefed on the
location of their targets in South Vietnam. After Wheeler's March 17 "Execute Operation Breakfast" order was received, the pilots and navigators of
the planes to be diverted were taken aside by their commanding officer
and told to expect the ground controllers in Vietnam to give them the
coordinates of new targets—they would be bombing Cambodia.

That evening the heavily laden planes rumbled off the long run-
way, rose slowly over the Russian trawlers, which almost always seemed
to be on station just off the island, and climbed to 30,000 feet for the
monotonous five-hour cruise to Indochina. There was little for the six-
man crew to do—except watch for storm clouds over the Philippines and
refuel in mid-air—until they were above the South China Sea approaching
the dark line of the Vietnamese coast.

At this point they entered the war zone and came under control of
the ground radar sites in South Vietnam. But even now there was little
reason for concern. There were no enemy fighter planes to harass and
chivvy them, no antiaircraft fire, no ground-to-air missiles. A ground radar
controller gave the navigator the coordinates of the final bomb run. Then
the controller watched on his radar screen as the planes, in cells of three,
approached the target; as they did so he counted down the bombardiers
with the words "Five—four—three—two—one—*hack*."

Twenty times that night the ground controllers, sitting in their air-
conditioned "hootches" in South Vietnam, cans of Coke or 7-Up by their
elbows, called out *hack*. Sixty long strings of bombs spread through the
dark and fell to the earth faster than the speed of sound. Each plane load

dropped into an area, or "box," about half a mile wide by two miles long, and as each bomb fell, it threw up a fountain of earth, trees and bodies, until the air above the targets was thick with dust and debris, and the ground itself flashed with explosions and fire. For the first time in the war, so far as is known, forty-eight of such boxes were stamped upon neutral Cambodia by the express order of the President.

One group of men was especially delighted by the event. Since May 1967, when the U.S. Military Command in Saigon became concerned at the way the North Vietnamese and Viet Cong were evading American "search and destroy" and air attacks in Vietnam by making more use of bases in Laos and Cambodia, the U.S. Special Forces had been running special, highly classified missions into the two countries. Their code name was Daniel Boone.

The Daniel Boone teams entered Cambodia all along its 500-mile frontier with South Vietnam from the lonely, craggy, impenetrable mountain forests in the north, down to the well-populated and thickly reeded waterways along the Mekong river. There was a quality of fantasy about the missions. They usually contained two or three Americans and up to ten local mercenaries, often recruited from the hill tribes of the area. All the Americans were volunteers, and they were enjoined to the strictest secrecy: the release they had to sign subjected them to a $10,000 fine and up to ten years' imprisonment for disclosing details of the forays. Because the missions were supposed to be what the Army called "sterile," the Americans either wore uniforms that could not be traced to any American unit or were disguised in the black pajamas of the Viet Cong. They carried what had become by the middle '60s the universal symbol of revolution, the Soviet-designed AK-47 automatic rifle made in China. Deaths were reported to relatives as having occurred "along the border."

These and other precautions helped conceal the work from the American press and the Congress. But black pajamas do not really hide well-fed Caucasians prowling around Southeast Asian jungles. Teams often found that, within two hours of being "inserted" by helicopter (parachutes were not used, because the Americans fell so much faster than the Vietnamese), their opponents had put trackers onto them. Their reconnaissance mission abandoned, they had to flee through the jungle or crawl through the thick fifteen-foot grass, evading their stalkers until they could find a suitable clearing to call helicopter support for rescue.

Randolph Harrison, who saw himself then as a "gung-ho lieutenant," arrived at the Special Forces headquarters in Ban Me Thuot, in the Central Highlands, in August 1968. He was given command of one of the reconnaissance companies, and he made his first mission into Cambodia on November 17, 1968, just after the American people, in the hope of peace, narrowly elected Nixon. At this time there was no consensus within the United States' intelligence establishment on the extent to which the North Vietnamese and Viet Cong were using Cambodia as a sanctuary or as a supply route, but Harrison was shocked by the evidence he saw of the enemy's insouciance just across the border from his own camp.

"There were hard-surface roads, those concrete reinforced bunkers. I personally found some abandoned base camps that were acres in size" he said later. "When you get an opportunity to see that blatant an example of their presence there, you scream and beg and do everything you can to get somebody to come in there and blast them." What he and his friends wanted most of all, he said, were B-52 "Arclight" strikes—"We had been told, as had everybody...that those carpet bombing attacks by B-52s [were] totally devastating, that nothing could survive, and if they had a troop concentration there it would be annihilated." They were enthusiastic when, on the morning of March 18, Major Michael Eiland, the Daniel Boone Operations officer, came up from Saigon to tell them of Operation Breakfast. He ordered a reconnaissance team into Area 353 by helicopter to pick up any possible Communist survivors. "We were told that...if there was anybody still alive out there they would be so stunned that all [we would] have to do [was] walk over and lead him by the arm to the helicopter."

Captain Bill Orthman was chosen to lead this team; he was given a radio operator named Barry Murphy and eleven Vietnamese. All were confident and rather excited. They were flown over the border and landed in rubble and craters. After the helicopters had taken off, the Daniel Boone men moved toward the tree line in search of their dead or dazed enemy. But within moments they were, in Harrison's words, "slaughtered."

The B-52 raid had not wiped out all the Communists as the Special Forces men had been promised. Instead, its effect, as Harrison said, had been "the same as taking a beehive the size of a basketball and poking it with a stick. They were mad."

The Communists fired at them from behind the trees on three sides. Three of the Vietnamese soldiers were immediately hit and Orthman himself was shot both in the leg and in the stomach. The group split apart and Orthman stumbled toward a bomb crater. Then a C.S. gas grenade in his rucksack burst into flames, searing the flesh off his back and his left arm. Barry Murphy threw himself into another crater and radioed frantically for the helicopters to return. Back at base they heard his call, "This is Bullet. We've got four wounded and are taking fire from all directions. We don't...Oh God! I'm hit!, hit! I'm hit! My leg! Ow! I'm...again! My back ahh can't move!" His last scream was indecipherable.

Eventually one helicopter managed to come back down through the automatic-weapons fire to pick up the survivors. Orthman was saved because a friend jumped out and rushed across the ground to carry him aboard. Three of the Vietnamese made it to the helicopter; Barry Murphy's body was not recovered.

Despite the setback, another reconnaissance team was immediately ordered to take off for Cambodia to gather "dazed" Viet Cong. Their earlier enthusiasm for the mission was now gone and in a rare breach of discipline the Daniel Boone men refused. Three of them were arrested. "You can't be court-martialled for refusing to violate the neutrality of Cambodia," Randolph Harrison reassured them. They were not.

> As that night fell over Indochina, day was beginning in Washington. In his basement office in the White House, Henry Kissinger was discussing a point of policy with Morton Halperin, a young political scientist who had worked in the Pentagon during the previous administration and was now Kissinger's assistant for planning.
>
> As the two men were talking, Colonel Alexander Haig came into the room and handed Kissinger a paper. As he read it, Halperin noticed, Kissinger smiled. He turned to Halperin and said that the United States had bombed a base in Cambodia and the first bomb-damage assessment showed that the attack had set off many secondary explosions. What did Halperin think of that? Halperin, who knew nothing of Breakfast, made a noncommittal answer. Kissinger told him that he was placing great trust in him and he must respect the confidence; almost no one else knew about the attack and no one else must know.

In his February 9 cable, Abrams had asked for a single attack to destroy COSVN headquarters. But once the decision had been made in principle that communist violations of Cambodia's neutrality justified aggressive reciprocal action, it was not difficult to repeat the performance. The first mission had not been discovered by the press, nor had Cambodia protested. Indeed, it would now have been hard for the White House to insist on only one attack: Base Area 353 was, according to Abrams' headquarters, the Military Assistance Command, Vietnam (MACV), only one of fifteen Communist sanctuaries.

Over the next fourteen months 3,630 B-52 raids were flown against suspected Communist bases along different areas of Cambodia's border. Breakfast was followed by "Lunch," Lunch by "Snack," Snack by "Dinner," Dinner by "Dessert," Dessert by "Supper," as the program expanded to cover one "sanctuary" after another. Collectively, the operation was known as "Menu."

In 1973, after the bombing was finally discovered, both Nixon and Kissinger maintained, and still maintain, that the secrecy was necessary to protect Sihanouk, who was variously described as "acquiescing in," "approving," "allowing" or even "encouraging" the raids, so long as they were covert. They maintained that the areas were unpopulated and that only Vietnamese Communist troops, legitimate targets, were there. When he was confirmed as Secretary of State in 1973, for example, Kissinger declared that "It was not a bombing of Cambodia, but it was a bombing of North Vietnamese in Cambodia," and "the Prince as a minimum acquiesced in the bombing of unpopulated border areas." In 1976 he stated that "the government concerned [Sihanouk's] never once protested, and indeed told us that if we bombed unpopulated areas they would not notice." In fact, the evidence of Sihanouk's "acquiescence" is at least questionable, and the assertion that no Cambodians lived in these areas not only was untrue, but was known to be untrue at the time. The Joint Chiefs themselves informed the administration as early as April 1969 that many of the sanctuary areas were populated by Cambodians who might be endangered by bombing raids. The White House was to ignore this reservation.

The Chief's description of the bases is contained in a memorandum of April 9, 1969, written for the Secretary of Defense, in which they advocated invasion as well as bombing of Cambodia. Its conclusions were based on "Giant Dragon" high-altitude overflights, "Dorsal Fin" low-level serial surveys and the Daniel Boone ground forays, among other evidence. It described the military purpose as well as the nature of each of the fifteen bases they had identified, and went on to estimate the number of Cambodians they contained. The figures are worth considering.

Base Area 353, Breakfast, covered 25 square kilometers and had a total population of approximately 1,640 Cambodians, of whom the Joint Chiefs reckoned 1,000 to peasants. There were, according to the Chiefs, thirteen Cambodian towns in the area. (Villages would be a more accurate description.)

Base Area 609, Lunch, was north, near the Laotian border, in wild country without any towns. The Chiefs asserted that there were an estimated 198 Cambodians there, all of them peasants.

Base Area 351, Snack, covered 101 square kilometers and had an estimated 383 Cambodians, of whom 303 were considered peasants. There was one town in the area.

Base Area 352, Dinner, had an estimated Cambodian population of 770, of whom 700 were peasants. It contained one town.

Base Area 350, Dessert, had an estimated Cambodian population of 120, all peasants.

The Chiefs believed that all these "sanctuaries" should be attacked. They attempted to estimate how many Cambodians would be killed; they maintained that, as the Cambodians lived apart from the Vietnamese troops, their casualties would be "minimal." But they conceded that such calculations depended on many variables and were "tenuous at best." There was no pretense that the raids could occur without danger to the Cambodians—"some Cambodian casualties would be sustained in the operation." And they agreed that "the surprise effect of attacks could tend to increase casualties, as could the probable lack of protective shelters around Cambodian homes to the extent that exists in South Vietnam." Cambodian peasants, unlike the Vietnamese, had little experience of being bombed.

Some scruples, however, were brought to bear. Three of the fifteen sanctuaries—base areas 704, 354 and 707, which had "sizeable concentrations of Cambodian civilian or military population" in or around them—were not recommended for attack at all. (The definition of "sizeable" is not known; presumably it was higher than the 1,640 Cambodians living in the Breakfast site, which they had approved.) The Chief's warning seems to have made no difference. Base Area 704 appeared on the White House's Menu as Supper. In the course of events, 247 B-52 missions were flown against it.

Because of Nixon's repeated insistence on total secrecy, few senior officials were told about Menu. The Secretary of the Air Force, Dr. Robert Seamans, was kept in ignorance; since he is not in the chain of command, this was not illegal, but General Wheeler later said that, if necessary, he would have lied to him and denied that the raids were taking place. The Chief of Staff of the Air Force, General John Ryan, was not informed; nor were the Cambodian desk officers on Abrams' intelligence arm in Saigon, the Office of Strategic Research and Analysis. None of the Congressional committees, whose duty it is to recommend appropriations and thus enable the Congress to fulfill its constitutional function of authorizing and funding war, was notified that the President had decided to carry war into a third country, whose neutrality the United States professed to respect. Instead, only a few sympathetic members of Congress, who had no constitutional authority to approve this extension of war, were quietly informed.

But if Congress and the public were easily kept in ignorance, the official record-keeping system required more sophisticated treatment. The Pentagon's computers demanded, for purposes of logistics, a complete record of hours flown, fuel expended, ordnance dropped, spare parts procured. In response to Nixon's demands for total and unassailable secrecy, the military devised an ingenious system that the Joint Chiefs liked to describe as "dual reporting."

Whether they flew from Guam, from Okinawa, or from Thailand, most B-52 missions over South Vietnam were guided to their targets by the "Skyspot" ground radar controllers at one of four radar sites in the country. The controllers received details—known as the "frag"—of the proposed strike after it had been approved in Washington. From the "frag," they calculated the range and bearing of the target from the radar site and the altitude, airspeed and ballistics of the bomb load. They then guided the planes down a narrow radar beam to target.

After missions were completed, B-52 crews reported what primary or secondary explosions they had seen to their debriefing officer at base, and the ground controllers sent their own poststrike reports to Saigon. Both reports entered the Pentagon computers and the official history of the war.

The procedures for Menu were modeled on Operation Breakfast. After a normal briefing on targets in Vietnam, the pilots and navigators of the planes that were to be diverted that night were told privately to expect the ground controllers to direct them to drop their bombs on a set of coordinates that were different from those they had just received. It was not a wide diversion; the South Vietnamese cover targets were usually selected so that the planes could simply fly another few kilometers beyond, until they were over the Cambodian target.

Major Hal Knight of Memphis was, for much of 1969, supervisor of the radar crews for the region of Vietnam that lay between Saigon and the Cambodian border. Every afternoon before a Menu mission, a special Strategic Air Command courier flight came to Bien Hoa airbase, where he worked, and he was handed a plain manila envelope containing an ordinary poststrike report form on which target coordinates had already been filled in. He locked it in his desk until evening and then, when the shift had assembled, gave the coordinates to his radar crew. They fed them through their Olivetti 101 computers to produce the details of the final bombing run for the new Cambodian target. These were called to the navigators when the B-52s arrived on station overhead in the early-morning dark.

After the bombs were released, the plane's radio operator—who was not supposed to know of the diversion—called his base by high-frequency radio to say that the mission had been accomplished. At base, the intelligence division, which also knew nothing of the change, entered the original South Vietnamese coordinates on the poststrike report. When the crews landed and were debriefed they were asked routine questions about malfunction, bomb damage and weather. The pilots and navigators were to make no mention of the new target—they had, after all, been forewarned, so it did not really count as a diversion.

At Bien Hoa itself Knight was under instructions to gather up every scrap of paper and tape with which the bombing had been plotted and lock them in his desk until daybreak. Only then (his superiors were afraid that pieces of paper might be dropped in the dark) was he to take the documents to an incinerator behind the hut and very carefully burn them. He was then to call a Saigon number he had been given—it was at Strategic Air Command Advanced Echelon—in order to tell the unidentified man who answered the telephone that "the ball game is over." The normal poststrike reports from the radar site were filled out with the coordinates of the original South Vietnamese cover target and sent, in the ordinary way, to Saigon by security mail. The night's mission over Cambodia entered the records as having taken place in Vietnam. The bombing was not merely concealed; the official, *secret* records showed that it had never happened.

The system worked well by the book, but it took no account of the attitudes of the men who were expected to implement it. Hal Knight, for example, accepted the military logic of bombing Cambodia but intensely disliked this procedure. Strategic Air Command is responsible for the nation's nuclear defense, and falsification of its reporting process was, for him, alarming; Knight had been trained to believe that accurate reporting was "pretty near sacred." He was especially concerned that he was violating Article 107 of the Military Code of Justice, which provides that any one "who, with intent to deceive, signs any false record, return, regulation, order or other official document, knowing the same to be false...shall be punished as a court martial may direct."

Red tape protects as well as restricts, and Knight feared that the institutional safeguards and controls that are integral to the maintenance of discipline and of a loyal, law-abiding army were being discarded. He did not know at what level the bombing had been authorized or whom these unprecedented procedures were supposed to deceive; but he did appreciate, to his dismay, that the practice gave him horrifying license.

A normal target was known to many people at the radar site, to the entire B-52 crew, to the intelligence unit at the plane's base and to dozens of Pentagon officials; a Menu mission was known only to him and a very few others. There was nothing to stop him from choosing the coordinates of a town in South Vietnam or Cambodia and having it bombed. Indeed, "if someone could have punched the right number into the right spot they could have had us bombing China," he observed later.

Knight discussed the falsification with other radar operators on other sites; they too found it hard to explain. If confidentiality were so important, why not simply raise the classification from "Secret" to "Top Secret"? He asked his commanding officer, Lieutenant Colonel David Patterson, about it; he was told not to do so.

"So I said, well, what is the purpose of it?"

Patterson replied "Well, the purpose is to hide these raids."

"Who from?" asked Knight.

He was apparently told, "Well, I guess the Foreign Relations Committee."

The Foreign Relations Committee did not find out about the unauthorized and illegal extension of the war into a neutral country until 1973, when Knight himself wrote to Congress to complain. But even under the restrictions imposed, the campaign was, to paraphrase Dean Rusk, known to the President, two members of the NSC, a couple of State Department officials and three hundred colonels in the Pentagon.

One evening soon after the raids began, the pilot of a Forward Air control plane (FAC), which guided fighter bombers to their targets in South Vietnam, was sitting outside his hootch at An Loc, a few miles from the Cambodian border. "We saw beacons going overhead to the West," said Captain Gerald Greven later. "We saw the flames in the distance and the trembling of the ground from what appeared to be B-52 strikes." He was surprised, because he knew of no targets in that area. The next morning he flew to find the craters, and "to my astonishment they were on the West side of the river separating the borders of South Vietnam and Cambodia."

Greven was impressed by the amount of destruction the raids had caused, but puzzled. "I went back to my commander and he said he had no knowledge of the strike and why it had taken place." He spoke to the regional commander for the Forward Air Controllers—"he also declared to have no knowledge." He then went on to Air Support headquarters at Bien Hoa and spoke to the commanding officer. "I was told, with a slight smile, that obviously my 'maps were in error.'" Greven correctly took that to mean that he "did not have a need to know." He asked no more questions. But eventually he, too, contacted Congress.

William Beecher was *The New York Times* Pentagon correspondent, a diligent reporter. After Nixon's victory in November 1968, Beecher asked his contacts in the Defense Department how they would advise the new President to extricate American troops from Vietnam. He was told that one possible way of "buying time" would be to bomb the sanctuaries. Beecher noted this hypothesis and by April 1969 began to suspect that it was being carried out. The Pentagon was reporting its bombing strikes in South Vietnam near the Cambodian border, but he knew that no targets were there. And, despite the special "security precautions," information began to leak almost at once. On March 26, one week after the Breakfast mission, *The New York Times* reported briefly but accurately that Abrams had requested B-52 strikes against the sanctuaries. Ronald Ziegler, the White House Press Secretary, was quoted as giving a "qualified denial" to the reports. "He said that to his knowledge no request had reached the President's desk." This story was followed by comments—in *U.S. News & World Report* and by columnist C. L. Sulzberger in *The New York Times*—urging that Nixon do what he had in fact already begun. But only Beecher took the trouble to follow the obvious lead that any "qualified denial" offers. He revisited those to whom he had talked at the end of 1968, and on May 9 he revealed in the *Times* that "American B-52 bombers have raided several Viet Cong and North Vietnamese supply dumps and base camps in Cambodia for the first time, according to Nixon Administration sources, but Cambodia has not made any protest."

Beecher wrote that the bombing had started because of the increase in supplies reaching South Vietnam by sea and through Cambodia, supplies that "never have to run any sort of bombing gauntlet before they enter South Vietnam." He claimed that Prince Sihanouk had dropped hints that he would not oppose American pursuit of Communist forces which he was himself unable to dislodge. Perhaps most important, Beecher stated that the bombing was intended "to signal" Hanoi that the Nixon administration, "while pressing for peace in Paris, is willing to take some military risks avoided by the previous Administration... to demonstrate that the Nixon Administration is different and 'tougher.'"

The revelation aroused no public interest. Four years later, this same account was to cause at least a short-lived uproar and spark demands for impeachment, but at the time it had little obvious effect. There was no press follow-up, and no members of the Senate Foreign Relations Committee, the Senate Armed Services Committee or the Appropriations committees voiced concern. In Key Biscayne, however, where Nixon and Kissinger and their staffs were working on the first of Nixon's major Vietnam speeches, the article provoked reactions that verged on hysteria.

After reading the story with Nixon, Kissinger spent much of his morning on the telephone with FBI Director J. Edgar Hoover. According to Hoover's detailed memoranda of the conversations, Kissinger asked him, in his first call at 10:35 A.M., to make "a major effort to find out where [the story] came from." A half hour later Kissinger telephoned again to say that while the FBI was about it they should try to find the sources of previous Beecher stories as well. Hoover replied that he would call back the next day with any information they had managed to gather. But within two hours Kissinger was on the line again, this time to ask Hoover to be sure he was discreet "so no stories will get out." Just how the Director liked being told how to protect his beloved FBI is not recorded, but Hoover assured Kissinger that discretion would be maintained; he had decided, he said, not to contact Beecher directly but to try to divine the source of the story from other reporters.

That afternoon, relaxing by the swimming pool with other members of the National Security Council staff, Kissinger invited his aide Morton Halperin to walk with him down the beach. Strolling along the sand, Kissinger told him of the great concern he felt over the Beecher leak. Halperin knew Kissinger well; they had been together at Harvard. He recalls that Kissinger assured him of his personal trust in him but reminded him that there were others in the Nixon administration who were suspicious of Halperin's New York and Harvard background and the fact that he had worked in McNamara's Pentagon. It was he who was suspected of leaking to Beecher. Halperin replied that he could not have been the source; after all, it was only by chance (and Kissinger's indiscretion) that he knew anything about the bombing. Kissinger apparently agreed that this was so, but said that he was under great pressure from other members of the administration and the White House.

Kissinger now proposed an ingenious way of justifying his confidence in Halperin to the others. So that he could not possibly be held responsible for any future leaks, Kissinger suggested that he be taken off the distribution list for highly classified material. Then, when a leak next occurred, he would be above suspicion and also retroactively cleared.

Halperin did not find the arrangement amusing; he had been dealing with classified materials for years and had never been asked to prove his loyalty. But Kissinger was such an old friend and presented his case with such charm and solicitousness, Halperin recalls, that he agreed to the proposal.

Kissinger and Hoover talked once more that day. At 5:05 P.M., the FBI director telephoned to report his progress. To judge by Hoover's memo, it was a bizarre conversation.

Hoover told Kissinger that Beecher "frequented" the Pentagon press office (hardly a surprising piece of information, in view of the fact that he was a Pentagon correspondent). There were still many pro-Kennedy people in the Pentagon, Hoover remarked, and they all fed Beecher with information. But on this occasion he was convinced that Morton Halperin was the culprit. According to FBI files, Halperin believed the United States had "erred in the Vietnam commitment"; moreover, the Canadian Mounted Police had discovered that he was on the mailing list of a Communist publication, "Problems of Peace and Socialism." Both Halperin and Beecher were members of the "Harvard clique" (as, of course, was Kissinger), and it was clear where the blame must lie. At the end of his memo Hoover noted, in words which resonate down the years, "Dr. Kissinger said he appreciated this very much and he hoped I would follow it up as far as we can take it, and they will destroy whoever did this if we can find him, no matter where he is."

That same afternoon the FBI placed a wiretap on Halperin's home in Bethesda, a bedroom suburb of Washington. This tap was immediately followed by others. In important, specific detail, these taps infringed the limits of the law. They marked the first of the domestic abuses of power now known as Watergate.

Night after night through the summer, fall and winter of 1969 and into the early months of 1970 the eight-engined planes passed west over South Vietnam and on to Cambodia. Peasants were killed—no one knows how many—and Communist logistics were somewhat disrupted. To avoid the attacks, the North Vietnamese and Viet Cong pushed their sanctuaries and supply bases deeper into the country, and the area that the B-52s bombarded expanded as the year passed. The war spread.

14
In Defense of the Nixon Policy
HENRY KISSINGER

The 1968 understanding with the North Vietnamese that led to the bombing halt included the "expectation" that there would be no attacks on major cities or across the DMZ. When we took office, however, enemy infiltration was mounting, which strongly indicated that a new offensive was in the offing.

The only plan we found for such a contingency was for renewal of bombing of the North. On November 24, 1968, Secretary of Defense Clark Clifford had declared on ABC-TV's "Issues and Answers": "If they, at some time, show us that they are not serious and that they are not proceeding with good faith, I have no doubt whatsoever that the President will have to return to our former concept and that is to keep the pressure on the enemy and that would include bombing if necessary." Averell Harriman made the same point in a White House briefing on December 4, 1968. General Earle Wheeler, Chairman of the Joint Chiefs, was only following inherited doctrine when he told Nixon at the NSC meeting of January 25, 1969, that everything possible was being done in Vietnam "except the bombing of the North."

No one in the new Administration, however, could anticipate a resumption of the bombing of the North with anything but distaste. We were savoring the honeymoon that follows the Inauguration of a new President; Nixon had never previously enjoyed the approval of the media. None of us had the stomach for the domestic outburst we knew renewed bombing would provoke—even if it were the direct result of North Vietnamese betrayal of the understandings that had led to the bombing halt. Above all, we had not yet given up hope, in the first month of the new Presidency, of uniting the nation on an honorable program for settlement of the war.

Unfortunately, alternatives to bombing the North were hard to come by. On January 30, I met in the Pentagon with Defense Secretary Melvin Laird and Wheeler to explore how we might respond should there be an enemy offensive in South Vietnam. Wheeler reiterated that American forces within South Vietnam were already fully committed; the only effective riposte would be operations in the DMZ or renewed bombing of the North. Laird demurred at the latter suggestion, emphasizing that the bombing halt had encouraged public expectations that the war was being wound down. Nor did I favor it, because I was eager to give negotiations a chance. On February 1, Nixon sent me a note: "I do not like the suggestions that I see in virtually every news report that 'we anticipate a Communist initiative in South Vietnam.' I believe that if any initiative occurs it should be on our part and not theirs." But my request to the Joint Chiefs for suggestions elicited the now familiar response outlining various levels of air or naval attacks on North Vietnamese targets and Mel Laird's (and my) equally standard reluctance to accept the recommendation.

Thought then turned to bombing of the North Vietnamese sanctuary areas in Cambodia, for reasons exactly the opposite of what has been assumed; it was not from a desire to expand the war, but to avoid bombing North Vietnam and yet to blunt an unprovoked offensive which was costing 400 American lives a week.

Revisionists have sometimes focused on the Nixon Administration's alleged assault on the "neutral" status of a "peaceful" country. These charges overlook that the issue concerned territory which was no longer Cambodian in any practical sense. For four years as many as four North Vietnamese divisions had been operating on Cambodian soil from a string of base areas along the South Vietnamese border. In 1978 the Communist victors in Cambodia put the uninvited North Vietnamese presence in northeastern Cambodia in 1969–1970 at 300,000, which far exceeded our estimates. Cambodian officials had been excluded from their soil; they contained next to no Cambodian population.* They were entirely controlled by the North Vietnamese. From these territories North Vietnamese forces would launch attacks into South Vietnam, inflict casualties, disrupt government, and then withdraw to the protection of a formally neutral country. It requires calculated advocacy, not judgment, to argue that the United States was violating the neutrality of a peaceful country when with Cambodian encouragement we, in self-defense, sporadically bombed territories in which for years no Cambodian writ had run, which were either minimally populated or totally unpopulated by civilians, and which were occupied in violation of Cambodian neutrality by an enemy killing hundreds of Americans and South Vietnamese a week from these sanctuaries.

The first suggestion came from General Wheeler. When Laird on January 30 had expressed doubt that a renewed bombing of the North was politically supportable, Wheeler proposed, as an alternative, attacks on

---

* The Communist deserter who helped pinpoint the location of the North Vietnamese headquarters reported that no Cambodians were permitted in the headquarters area. General Abrams reported this to the President in February along with an assurance that the target was at least a kilometer distant from any known Cambodian hamlets.

the complex of bases that the North Vietnamese had established illegally across the border in Cambodia. On February 9, General Creighton Abrams cabled General Wheeler from Saigon that recent intelligence from a deserter, as well as photo reconnaissance, showed that the Communist headquarters for all of South Vietnam was located just across the Cambodian border. (As a novice I was more impressed by such seemingly definitive evidence than I would be later on. As it turned out, the Communist leaders in Phnom Penh eight years later also confirmed that the deserter's information had been accurate on that score.) Abrams requested authority to attack the headquarters from the air with B-52s. Ambassador Ellsworth Bunker endorsed the idea in a separate cable through State Department channels.

These recommendations fell on fertile ground. In the transition period on January 8, 1969, the President-elect had sent me a note: "In making your study of Vietnam I want a precise report on what the enemy has in Cambodia and what, if anything, we are doing to destroy the buildup there. I think a very definite change of policy toward Cambodia probably should be one of the first orders of business when we get in." General Andrew Goodpaster had drafted a reply for my signature with detailed information about the North Vietnamese base areas along the Cambodian border. He reported that "our field command in South Vietnam is convinced that the vast bulk of supplies entering Cambodia come in through Sihanoukville. ...What we are doing about this is very limited.... The command in the field has made several requests for authority to enter Cambodia to conduct pre-emptive operations and in pursuit of withdrawing forces that have attacked us. All such requests have been denied or are still pending without action."

The importance of Sihanoukville was one of the contested issues in the NSSM I study. The US military command in Saigon was convinced that between October 1967 and September 1968 some ten thousand tons of arms had come in through Sihanoukville. But CIA and State disputed this. According to them the flow of supplies down the Ho Chi Minh Trail through Laos was more than adequate to take care of the external requirements of *all* Communist forces in South Vietnam. At stake in this analysts' debate, of course, was whether the Cambodian sanctuaries were so crucial a target that they should be attacked; as happens all too frequently, intelligence estimates followed, rather than inspired, agency policy views. Those who favored attacks on the sanctuaries emphasized the importance of Sihanoukville; those who were opposed depreciated it. (When US and South Vietnamese forces moved into these sanctuaries in April 1970, documents in Communist storage dumps indicated that shipments through Cambodia far exceeded even the military's highest estimates.)

But whatever the dispute about whether the matériel traveled through Sihanoukville or down the Ho Chi Minh Trail, there was no dispute about the menace of the North Vietnamese bases in Cambodia to American and South Vietnamese forces. On February 18, I received a briefing by a two-man team from Saigon, together with Laird, Deputy Secretary Packard, General Wheeler, and Laird's military assistant, Colonel Robert E. Pursley. I reported to the President the conviction of General Abrams that no Cambodian civilians lived in the target area. Nevertheless, I advised against an unprovoked bombing of sanctuaries. We should give negotiations a chance, I argued, and seek to maintain public support for our policy. We could review the situation again at the end of March—the classic bureaucratic stalling device to ease the pain of those being overruled. Nixon approved that recommendation on February 22, the day before he was to leave on his trip to Europe.

On the very day of Nixon's decision to defer action against the sanctuaries, the North Vietnamese transformed vague contingency planning into a need to deal with a crisis. After weeks of preparation antedating the new Administration, Hanoi launched a countrywide offensive. Americans killed in action during the first week of the offensive numbered 453, 336 in the second week, and 351 in the third; South Vietnamese casualties were far heavier, averaging over 500 a week. It was an act of extraordinary cynicism. No substantive negotiating sessions had been held in Paris with our new delegation, headed by Henry Cabot Lodge; the Administration could hardly have formed its policy. Whether by accident or design, the offensive began the day before a scheduled Presidential trip overseas, thus both paralyzing our response and humiliating the new President. It occurred despite the fact that Nixon had communicated with the North Vietnamese in the transition period (as we shall see below), emphasizing his commitment to settle the war on the basis of the self-respect and honor of all parties involved. Without even testing these professions of intent, the first major move of Hanoi was to step up the killing of Americans. I noted in a report to the President that the North Vietnamese had been "able to achieve a relatively high casualty rate among US and South Vietnamese forces while not exposing their own main units."

Nixon received a military briefing on the enemy offensive in the Oval Office surrounded by piles of loose-leaf briefing books compiled by my staff and the State Department for each country he was about to visit. (Nixon later came to use the Oval Office mostly for ceremonial occasions; he usually preferred to work in his informal office in the Executive Office Building.) Nixon was going through the books, committing them to memory, grumbling about the effort he had to make to do so. He was also seething. All his instincts were to respond violently to Hanoi's cynical maneuver. For years he had charged his predecessors with weakness in reacting to Communist moves. But he was eager also that his first foreign trip as President be a success. American retaliation might spark riots in Europe; passivity might embolden our adversary. He did not resolve this dilemma immediately. The only White House reaction on the day the offensive started was a phone call by me to Soviet Ambassador Dobrynin. The President wanted Moscow to understand, I said, that if the North Vietnamese offensive continued we would retaliate.

But the next day, on February 23, while in the air en route from Washington to Brussels, Nixon made up his mind; he suddenly ordered the bombing of the Cambodian sanctuaries. It seemed to me that a decision of this magnitude could not be simply communicated to Washington and to Saigon by cable from *Air Force One* without consulting relevant officials or in the absence of a detailed plan for dealing with the consequences. I therefore recommended to Nixon to postpone the final "execute" order for forty-eight hours and sent a flash message to Colonel Alexander Haig, then my military assistant in Washington, to meet me in Brussels, together with a Pentagon expert. I wanted to go over the military operations once again and to work out a diplomatic plan.

Haig, presidential aide H.R. Haldeman (representing Nixon, who could not attend without attracting attention), the Pentagon planning officer, and I met on board *Air Force One* at the Brussels airport on the morning of February 24, just before the President spoke at NATO headquarters. The plane that Nixon used had been built to Johnson's specifications. Directly behind a stateroom for the President was a conference area with an oversized chair fitting into a kidney-shaped table; both the chair and the table were equipped with buttons that enabled them to develop a life of their own. The chair could assume various positions; the table could move hydraulically up and down. If one pressed the wrong button the table would slowly sink, pinning one helplessly in the chair; the situation could turn critical if the chair was rising at the same time. In this awesome setting we worked out guidelines for the bombing of the enemy's sanctuaries: The bombing would be limited to within five miles of the frontier; we would not announce the attacks but acknowledge them if Cambodia protested, and offer to pay compensation for any damage to civilians. In the short time available, we developed both a military and a diplomatic schedule as well as guidance for briefing the press. Haig and the Pentagon expert left immediately for Washington to brief Laird. Nixon later in London gave Secretary of State William Rogers a cryptic account of his thinking but no details.

Before the day was out, Laird cabled his reservations from Washington. He thought that it would be impossible to keep the bombing secret, the press would be difficult to handle, and public support could not be guaranteed. He urged delay to a moment when the provocation would be clearer. It was symptomatic of the prevalent mood of hesitation, the fear to wake the dormant beast of public protest. In retrospect, it is astonishing to what extent all of us focused on the legal question of whether the understanding had been violated, and not on the four hundred American deaths a week by which Hanoi sought to break our will before we could develop any course of action. Even more astonishing now is that during this entire period no serious consideration was given to resuming the bombing of North Vietnam; the bombing halt, entered to speed a settlement, was turning into an end in itself.

I agreed with Laird's conclusions about the Cambodian bombing, if not with his reasoning. I thought that a failure to react to so cynical a move by Hanoi could doom our hopes for negotiations; it could only be read by Hanoi as a sign of Nixon's helplessness in the face of domestic pressures; it was likely to encourage further military challenges, as North Vietnam undertook to whipsaw Nixon as it had succeeded with Johnson. But the timing bothered me. I did not think it wise to launch a new military operation while the President was traveling in Europe, subject to possible hostile demonstrations and unable to meet with and rally his own government. I also did not relish the prospect of having Vietnam the subject of all our European press briefings or of privately trying to offer explanations to allied governments not always eager to reconcile their private support of our Vietnam efforts with their public stance of dissociation. I said as much to the President. The following day, while we were in Bonn, Nixon canceled the plan.

The so-called mini-Tet exposed the precariousness of our domestic position. The enemy offensive surely must have been planned over many months. It occurred when we were barely four weeks in office and before the enemy could possible know what we intended—since we did not know ourselves. Yet the *New York Times* on March 9 blamed the new Administration for having provoked Hanoi by presuming to spend a month in studying the options in a war involving an expeditionary force of over 500,000 men: "The sad fact is that the Paris talks have been left on dead center while Ambassador Lodge awaits a White House go-ahead for making new peace proposals or for engaging in private talks out of which the only real progress is likely to come. Everything has been stalled while the Nixon Administration completes its military and diplomatic review." This theme soon was repeated in the Congress.

The President adopted a restrained posture in public while champing at the bit in private. At a news conference on March 4 he declared:

> We have not moved in a precipitate fashion, but the fact that we have shown patience and forbearance should not be considered as a sign of weakness. We will not tolerate a continuation of a violation of an understanding. But more than that, we will not tolerate attacks which result in heavier casualties to our men at a time that we are honestly trying to seek peace at the conference table in Paris. An appropriate response to these attacks will be made if they continue.

On March 4 I passed on to the President without comment a Laird memo recommending against proposals by the Joint Chiefs to attack North Vietnam. Laird was far from a "dove"; in normal circumstances his instincts were rather on the bellicose side. He would have preferred to aim for victory. But he was also a careful student of the public and Congressional mood. He was a finely tuned politician and as such he had learned that those who mount the barricades may well forgo a future in politics; he was not about to make this sacrifice. He therefore navigated with great care between his convictions, which counseled some military reaction, and his political instinct, which called for restraint. He opposed bombing North

Vietnam; he became a strong supporter of the attack on the Cambodian sanctuaries. (His only disagreement had to do with public relations policy; he did not think it possible to keep the bombing secret, on practical, not on moral, grounds.) The President, following a similar logic, ordered a strike against the Cambodian sanctuaries for March 9. On March 7 Rogers objected because of prospects for private talks in Paris.

Nixon retracted his order a second time. With each time he marched up the hill and down again, Nixon's resentments and impatience increased. Like Laird he kept saying that he did not want to hit the North, but he wanted to do "something." On March 14, Nixon was asked at a news conference whether his patience was wearing thin. He replied:

> I took no comfort out of the stories that I saw in the papers this morning to the effect that our casualties for the immediate past week went from 400 down to 300. That is still much too high. What our response should be must be measured in terms of the effect on the negotiations in Paris. I will only respond as I did earlier....We have issued a warning. I will not warn again. And if we conclude that the level of casualties is higher than we should tolerate, action will take place.

Next day the North Vietnamese fired five rockets into Saigon—a further escalation and violation of the understanding. There were thirty-two enemy attacks against major South Vietnamese cities in the first two weeks of March. At 3:35 P.M. the day the rockets hit Saigon I received a phone call from the President. He was ordering an immediate B-52 attack on the Cambodian sanctuaries. Capping a month of frustration, the President was emphatic: "State is to be notified only after the point of no return.... The order is not appealable." ("Not appealable" was a favorite Nixon phrase, which to those who knew him grew to mean considerable uncertainty; this of course tended to accelerate rather than slow down appeals.)

I told the President that such a decision should not be taken without giving his senior advisers an opportunity to express their views—if only to protect himself if it led to a public uproar. No time would be lost. A detailed scenario would have to be worked out in any event, and to prepare instructions would require at least twenty-four-hours. A meeting was therefore scheduled for the following day in the Oval Office. I consulted Laird, who strongly supported the President's decision. To prepare for the meeting, I wrote a memo for the President listing the pros and cons. The risks ranged from a pro forma Cambodian protest to a strong Soviet reaction; from serious Cambodian opposition to explicit North Vietnamese retaliation—though it was hard to imagine what escalation Hanoi could undertake beyond what it was already doing. Finally, there was the risk of an upsurge of domestic criticism and new antiwar demonstrations. I recommended that our Paris delegation ask for a private meeting on the day of the bombing so as to emphasize our preference for a negotiated solution. I urged the President to stress to his associates that the proposed bombing was *not* to be a precedent. What my checklist did not foresee (what none of our deliberations foresaw) is what in fact happened: no reaction of any kind—from Hanoi, Phnom Penh, Moscow, or Peking.

The meeting on Sunday afternoon, March 16, in the Oval Office was attended by Rogers, Laird, Wheeler, and myself. It was the first time that Nixon confronted a concrete decision in an international crisis since becoming President; it was also the first time that he would face opposition from associates to a course of action to which he was already committed. He approached it with tactics that were to become vintage Nixon. On the one hand, he had made his decision and was not about to change; indeed, he had instructed me to advise the Defense Department to that effect twenty-four hours before the meeting. On the other hand, he felt it necessary to pretend that the decision was still open. This led to hours of the very discussion that he found so distasteful and that reinforced his tendency to exclude the recalcitrants from further deliberations.

The Oval Office meeting followed predictable lines. Laird and Wheeler strongly advocated the attacks. Rogers objected not on foreign policy but on domestic grounds. He did not raise the neutral status of Cambodia; it was taken for granted (correctly) that we had the right to counter North Vietnam's blatant violation of Cambodia's neutrality, since Cambodia was unwilling or unable to defend its neutral status. Rogers feared that we would run into a buzz saw in Congress just when things were calming down. There were several hours of discussion during which Nixon permitted himself to be persuaded by Laird and Wheeler to do what he had already ordered. Having previously submitted my thoughts in a memorandum, I did not speak. Rogers finally agreed to a B-52 strike on the base area containing the presumed Communist headquarters. These deliberations are instructive: A month of an unprovoked North Vietnamese offensive, over a thousand American dead, elicited after weeks of anguished discussion exactly *one* American retaliatory raid within three miles of the Cambodian border in an area occupied by the North Vietnamese for over four years. And this would enter the folklore as an example of wanton "illegality."

After the meeting, the Joint Chiefs sought to include additional attacks on North Vietnamese troop concentrations violating the Demilitarized Zone. Laird and I agreed that it was more important to keep Rogers with us and the proposal was not approved.

The B-52 attack took place on March 18 against North Vietnamese Base Area 353, within three miles of the Cambodian border....For this strike the Pentagon dug into its bottomless bag of code names and came up with "Breakfast"—as meaningless as it was tasteless. When an air attack hits an ammunition or fuel depot, there are always secondary explosions that provide nearly conclusive evidence of a successful raid. The initial assessment by the crew of the March 18 Breakfast strike reported "a total of 73 secondary explosions in the target area ranging up to five times the normal intensity of a typical secondary."

Originally the attack on Base Area 353 was conceived as a single raid. Nixon ordered another strike in April 1969 partly because there had been no reaction from either Hanoi or Phnom Penh to the first, partly because the results exceeded our expectations, but above all because of an event far away in North Korea. Nixon had wanted to react to the shooting down of an unarmed American reconnaissance plane by bombing North Korea. (He had severely criticized Johnson for his failure to take forceful measures in response to the capture by North Korea of the electronic ship *Pueblo*.) Nixon had refrained, primarily because of the strong opposition of Rogers and Laird. But as always when suppressing his instinct for a jugular response, Nixon looked for some other place to demonstrate his mettle. There was nothing he feared more than to be thought weak; he had good foreign policy reasons as well for not letting Hanoi believe that he was paralyzed.

In May Nixon ordered attacks on a string of other Cambodian base areas, all unpopulated and within five miles of the border. The strike on Base Area 350 was given the code name of "Dessert"; Base Area 351 was "Snack," Base Area 704 was "Supper," Base Area 609 was "Lunch," and Base Area 352 was "Dinner." On the theory that anything worth doing is worth overdoing the whole series was given the code name of "Menu." From April through early August 1969 attacks were intermittent; each was approved specifically by the White House. Afterward, general authority was given; raids were conducted regularly. The map, defining the narrow strip of base areas within a few miles of the border, refutes the charges of "massive bombing of neutral Cambodia" that impelled twelve members of the House Judiciary Committee in 1974 to propose an article of impeachment on the theory that Nixon had concealed from Congress this "presidential conduct more shocking and more unbelievable than the conduct of any president in any war in all of American history," as Representative Robert Drinan imagined it. Neither Cambodia nor North Vietnam ever claimed that there were Cambodian or civilian casualties. The statistics of tonnage dropped during these raids, so often invoked as an example of Administration barbarity, conveniently omit this salient fact or that it was confined to a strip only a few miles wide along the border. The series continued until May 1970, when strikes began openly in support of US and South Vietnamese ground operations against the North Vietnamese bases.

Periodic reports on the Menu strikes were sent to the President. In November 1969, he wrote on one, "continue them." In December 1969 and February 1970, he asked for an evaluation of their usefulness. Each time, Laird reported that General Abrams and Ambassador Bunker were convinced (as he reported on one occasion) that "Menu has been one of the most telling operations in the entire war." General Abrams credited the Menu operations with disrupting enemy logistics, aborting several enemy offensives, and reducing the enemy threat to the whole Saigon region. Laird endorsed the Joint Chiefs' and General Abrams's view that the Menu strikes "have been effective and can continue to be so with acceptable risks."

The original intention had been to acknowledge the Breakfast strike in response to a Cambodian or North Vietnamese reaction, which we firmly anticipated. For example, the CIA predicted in memoranda of February 20 and March 6 that Hanoi would "certainly" or "almost certainly" seek to derive propaganda advantages from charging an American expansion of the conflict. The Defense Department doubted that the attacks could be kept secret; my own view on that subject was agnostic. In a conversation with Nixon on March 8, I said: "Packard and I both think that if we do it, and if silence about it doesn't help, we have to step up and say what we did." The President agreed. A formal acknowledgment was prepared for the contingency of a Cambodian protest. It offered to pay damages and asked for international inspection.

Our initial reticence was to avoid *forcing* the North Vietnamese, Prince Sihanouk of Cambodia, and the Soviets and Chinese into public reactions they might not be eager to make. A volunteered American statement would have obliged Hanoi to make a public response, perhaps military retaliation or interruption of the peace talks. It would have required Sihanouk to take a public stand, tilting toward Hanoi as he tried to walk a tightrope of neutrality. It could have prompted reactions from the Soviet Union and China in the midst of our serious pursuit of triangular diplomacy.

But Hanoi did *not* protest. In fact, its delegation in Paris accepted Lodge's proposal for private talks on March 22 within seventy-two hours of our request. And Sihanouk not only did not object; he treated the bombing as something that did not concern him since it occurred in areas totally occupied by North Vietnamese troops and affected no Cambodians; hence it was outside his control and even knowledge.

In fact, our relations with Cambodia improved dramatically throughout the period of the bombing. Sihanouk's subtle and skillful balancing act between domestic and foreign pressures had been a cause of wonderment for a decade. An hereditary prince, Norodom Sihanouk had managed to obtain a mass support among the population that appeared to make him unassailable. He had established his country's independence and acquired the aura of indispensability. He had maneuvered to keep his country neutral. After the Laos settlement of 1962, he had concluded that the communists, whom he hated, would probably prevail in Indochina. He adjusted to that reality by acquiescing in the North Vietnamese establishment of base areas in his country. In 1965 he found a pretext to break diplomatic relations with us. Yet his collaboration with the Communists was reluctant; Hanoi was encouraging the Khmer Rouge (Cambodian Communists), who began guerrilla activity long before there was any American action in Cambodia; Sihanouk sentenced the Communist leaders to death in absentia. For all these reasons I strongly supported a Rogers recommendation to the President in February 1969 that we approach Sihanouk with a view to improving relations.* These overtures were eagerly received. Our Embassy in Phnom Penh reopened, headed by a chargé d'affaires.

Sihanouk's acquiescence in the bombing should have come as no surprise. As early as January 10, 1968, during the previous Administration, he had told Presidential emissary Chester Bowles:

> We don't want any Vietnamese in Cambodia.... We will be very glad if you solve our problem. We are not opposed to hot pursuit in uninhabited areas. You would be liberating us from the Viet Cong. For me only Cambodia counts. I want you to force the Viet Cong to leave Cambodia. In unpopulated areas, where there are not Cambodians—such precise cases I would shut my eyes.

On May 13, 1969, nearly two months after the bombing had begun, Sihanouk gave a press conference which all but confirmed the bombings, emphatically denied any loss of civilian life, and to all practical purposes invited us to continue:

> I have not protested the bombings of Viet Cong camps because I have not heard of the bombings. I was not in the know, because in certain areas of Cambodia there are no Cambodians.
>
> Cambodia only protests against the destruction of the property and lives of Cambodians. All I can say is that I cannot make a protest as long as I am not informed. But I will protest if there is any destruction of Khmer [Cambodian] life and property.
> Here it is—the first report about several B-52 bombings. Yet I have not been informed about that at all, because I have not lost any houses, any countrymen, nothing, nothing. Nobody was caught in those barrages—nobody, no Cambodians.
>
> That is what I want to tell you, gentlemen. If there is a buffalo or any Cambodian killed, I will be informed immediately. But this is an affair between the Americans and the Viet Cong–Viet Minh without any Khmer witnesses. There have been no Khmer witnesses, so how can I protest? But this does not mean—and I emphasize this—that I will permit the violation by either side. Please note that.

---

* Interestingly enough, these diplomatic overtures to Cambodia were opposed by the Department of Defense and the Joint Chiefs of Staff, who feared that they might interfere with possibilities of bombing the Cambodian sanctuaries. I received a memorandum from Defense warning against such "diplomatic action which implies a restraint or inhibition in any expansion of current operating authorities designed to protect our forces in South Vietnam." This was signed by Paul Warnke, then still Assistant Secretary of Defense for International Security Affairs.

On August 22, 1969, Sihanouk said the same to Senator Mansfield*
(according to the reporting cable):

> there were no Cambodian protests of bombings in his country when these
> hit only VC's and not Cambodian villages or population. He declared that
> much of his information regarding US bombings of uninhabited regions of
> Cambodia came from US press and magazine statements. He strongly re-
> quested the avoidance of incidents involving Cambodian lives.

And on July 31, 1969, after four and a half months of bombing
of North Vietnamese sanctuaries inside Cambodia, Sihanouk warmly invited President Nixon to visit Cambodia to mark the improvement of US-
Cambodian relations. Relations continued to improve until Sihanouk was
unexpectedly overthrown.

No one doubted the legality of attacking base areas being used to
kill American and friendly forces, from which all Cambodian authority
had been expelled and in which, according to Sihanouk himself, not even
a Cambodian buffalo had been killed. We saw no sense in announcing
what Cambodia encouraged and North Vietnam accepted. The reason for
secrecy was to prevent the issue from becoming an international crisis,
which would almost certainly have complicated our diplomacy or war effort. The war had been expanded into Cambodia four years earlier by the
North Vietnamese, who occupied its territory. The war had been escalated
within Vietnam from February 22 on, with North Vietnamese attacks on
cities in violation of the 1968 understandings. To bomb base areas from
which North Vietnamese soldiers had expelled all Cambodians so that
they could more effectively kill Americans—at the rate of four hundred a
week—was a minimum defensive reaction fully compatible with international law. It would surely have been supported by the American public. It
was kept secret because a public announcement was a gratuitous blow to
the Cambodian government, which might have forced it to demand that
we stop; it might have encouraged a North Vietnamese retaliation (since
how could they fail to react if we had announced we were doing it?). The
North Vietnamese kept silent because they were not eager to advertise
their illegal presence on Cambodian soil. Our bombing saved American
and South Vietnamese lives.

This is why the press leaks that came from American sources struck
Nixon and me as so outrageous. Accounts of B-52 or other air strikes
against sanctuaries in Cambodia appeared in the *New York Times* (March
26, April 27) and *Washington Post* (April 27); a detailed story by William
Beecher appeared in the *New York Times* on May 9; there was another

---

* Senator Mansfield did not know of the Menu program and undoubtedly assumed
Sihanouk was speaking of accidental bombings.

in the *Wall Street Journal* on May 16; a widely disseminated UPI story appeared in the *Washington Post* on May 18; *Newsweek* reported it on June 2.

The conviction that press leaks of military operations were needlessly jeopardizing American lives, which I shared, caused the President to consult the Attorney General and the Director of the FBI about remedial measures. J. Edgar Hoover recommended wiretaps, which he pointed out had been widely used for these (and other much less justified) purposes by preceding administrations. The Attorney General affirmed their legality. Nixon ordered them carried out, in three categories of cases: officials who had adverse information in their security files; officials who had access to the classified information that had been leaked; and individuals whose names came up as possibilities in the course of the investigation according to the first two criteria. On the basis of these criteria, seventeen wiretaps were established by the FBI on thirteen officials and also four newsmen, lasting in some cases only a few weeks and in other cases several months. (My office was not aware of all of them.) Contrary to malicious lore, senior officials did not spend time pruriently reading over lengthy transcripts of personal conversations. What was received were brief summaries (usually about a page in length) of what the FBI considered discussions of sensitive military or foreign policy matters. The FBI's threshold of suspicion tended to be much lower than the White House's. In May 1971 Nixon cut off the reports sent to my office; thereafter, they went only to Haldeman, who had been receiving them all along....

I...wish to record that I went along with what I had no reason to doubt was legal and established practice in these circumstances, pursued, so we were told, with greater energy and fewer safeguards in previous administrations. The motive, which I strongly shared, was to prevent the jeopardizing of American and South Vietnamese lives by individuals (never discovered) who disclosed military information entrusted to them in order to undermine policies decided upon after prayerful consideration and in our view justified both in law and in the national interest. I believe now that the more stringent safeguards applied to national security wiretapping since that time reflect an even more fundamental national interest—but this in no way alters my view of the immorality of those who, in their contempt for their trust, attempted to sabotage national policies and risked American lives.

At the same time, we were wrong, I now believe, not to be more frank with Congressional leaders. To be sure President Nixon and I gave a full briefing in the Oval Office on June 11, 1969, to Senators John Stennis and Richard Russell, Chairmen of the Senate Armed Services and Appropriations committees. Senate Minority Leader Everett Dirksen was also informed. In the House, Representatives Mendel Rivers and Leslie Arends, the Chairman and a ranking minority member of the House Armed Services Committee, as well as Minority Leader Gerald Ford, were briefed. Laird briefed key members of the Armed Services and Appropriations committees of both houses. Not one raised the issue that the full Congress should be consulted. This was at that time the accepted practice for briefing the Congress of classified military operations. Standards for Congressional consultation, too, have since changed, and this is undoubtedly for the better.*

Nor is it true that the bombing drove the North Vietnamese out of the sanctuaries and thus spread the war deep into Cambodia. To the extent that North Vietnamese forces left the sanctuaries it was to move back into Vietnam, not deeper into Cambodia—until after Sihanouk was unexpectedly overthrown a year later. Then, North Vietnamese forces deliberately started to overrun Cambodian towns and military positions in order to isolate Phnom Penh and topple Sihanouk's successors.... * And the widened war caused by that new act of North Vietnamese aggression, while searing and tragic, was not secret. It was fully known by our public, debated in the Congress, and widely reported in the press. Our air operations then were conducted under strict rules of engagement, supervised by our Ambassador in Phnom Penh and aided by aerial photography, designed to avoid areas populated by Cambodian civilians to the maximum extent possible. The "secret" bombing concerned small, largely uninhabited territories totally occupied by the North Vietnamese. The picture of a warlike, bloodthirsty government scheming to deceive is a caricature of the reality of harassed individuals, afraid alike of capitulation on the battlefield and more violent escalation, choosing what they considered a middle course between bombing North Vietnam and meekly accepting the outrage of a dishonorable and bloody offensive. The attacks on the enemy sanctuaries in Cambodia were undertaken reluctantly, as a last resort, as a minimum response, when we were faced with an unprovoked offensive killing four hundred Americans a week. We attacked military bases unpopulated by civilians and at most only five miles from the border. We would have been willing to acknowledge the bombing and defend it had there been a diplomatic protest. There was no protest; Cambodia did not object, nor did the North Vietnamese, nor the Soviets or the Chinese. Pro-

---

* The Pentagon's double-bookkeeping had a motivation much less sinister than that described in revisionist folklore. To preserve the secrecy of the initial (originally intended as the only) raid, Pentagon instructions were kept out of normal channels. The purpose was not to deceive Congress (where key leaders were informed) but to keep the attack from being routinely briefed to the Saigon press. The procedure was continued by rote when bombing became more frequent two months later. When Congressional committees asked for data four years later, new Pentagon officials, unaware of the two reporting channels, unwittingly furnished data from the regular files. This was a bureaucratic blunder, not deliberate design.

* Sihanouk in a conversation with me on April 25, 1979, in front of witnesses denied that our bombing had had any effect in pushing the North Vietnamese to move westward. Our bombing "did not impress them," he said jovially.

ceeding secretly became, therefore, a means of maintaining pressure on the enemy without complicating Cambodia's delicate position, without increasing international tensions in general, and without precipitating the abandonment of all limits.

TWO

IN COUNTRY

July 29, 1966. Marines look on as a South Vietnamese officer interrogates a suspected Viet Cong guerilla. OFFICIAL U.S. MARINE CORPS PHOTO

CHAPTER 5

The American Enemy

Through one of his characters, the cartoonist Walt Kelly once made the memorable comment: "We have met the enemy, and it is us." Although this was true to some extent of United States intervention in Vietnam, the war there was finally won by Vietnamese, who fought with patience, skill, and ferocity. The readings in this chapter concern some of the principles and methods of the Communists and their allies as they struggled against the Americans, whom they regarded as the latest in a long line of imperialists. Like many revolutionary Vietnamese, Truong Nhu Tang received a political education in Paris, where he had gone to study pharmacy in 1946. He returned to southern Vietnam and helped found the National Liberation Front (NLF), called the Viet Cong by the South Vietnamese government. (In a split foreshadowed in this section, Tang later left the NLF when it became, in his judgment, a tool of rigid ideologues from the north.) Douglas Pike, who spent many years studying the Vietnamese revolution, looks at the organizational dynamics within the National Liberation Front and its political core, the Communist People's Revolutionary Party (PRP). At the height of the war in 1966 and 1967, analyst Konrad Kellen interviewed captured and deserting NLF and North Vietnamese fighters. The evidence presented here suggests that the Communists and their allies were able to persuade people in the countryside that their battle against the Americans was both necessary and virtuous. The last selection, by Tom Mangold and John Penycate, is an imaginative and highly compelling story of an NLF fighter who battles against the Americans within the vast system of tunnels his comrades made in the south. This passage vividly contrasts the stealthy confidence of the NLF and the technocratic blunderings of the American troops. Partly on the basis of readings like these four, many scholars have argued that the United States could not have won the war. The NLF drew on a long tradition of struggle against foreign invaders, knew how to draw strength from the people and the land, and understood that it had to mobilize the people politically before it could expect their military assistance—something three American presidents proved unable to do.

15
The Making of a Revolutionary
TRUONG NHU TANG

Even as I began getting down to my pharmaceutical studies, [in Paris], I was thinking feverishly about my country in a way that was altogether novel to me. Everything that I knew and that I had seen in Vietnam— the French administrators, the privileged position of French families, the poverty of the countryside, the racial bigotry—all began to appear in a new light. It suddenly dawned on me that these things were *not* part of the natural order on the universe. On the contrary, there was a single cause, a comprehensible pattern that was amenable to analysis. The subordination of the Vietnamese nation to France could be understood as a historical and social phenomenon, and it could be fought—if one had the right tools. Before long I was spending the better part of my days in the library of the National School of Political Science (soon to be renamed the Institute of Political Studies), devouring everything I could get my hands on about political philosophy in general and colonialism in particular.

As my eyes opened to Vietnam's political situation, I also began to see France in a new light. For a young man brought up to the strict order and stagnant oppressiveness of colonial rule, Paris in 1946 was a bracing north wind. I was living right in the middle of the wild political ferment of the Fourth Republic. With my understanding of politics expanding each day, the ideals of the French Revolution seemed to be taking life before my eyes. At the very moment I had become addicted to reading political theory, the French, possessed by their own political demons, were thrashing out a new constitution. Socialists, Communists, Republicans, and a variety of lesser enthusiasts were embroiled with each other in a display of political contentiousness amazing to anyone not born to it. The entire apparatus of democratic politics was laid bare, as government succeeded government and one unlikely coalition dissolved before another even more wondrous. Already in love with French culture, I was now utterly fascinated by the spirit and vitality of French political life. I wished ardently that a fraternal cooperation between my country and France would grow out of the modus vivendi that Ho and Colonial Minister Marius Moutet had just signed. Meanwhile, I decided to join the movement for Vietnamese independence that was beginning to percolate in the Paris streets and debating halls.

In the midst of this excited awakening to my new life, I received a letter straight out of my old one. It was from my father. In courteous tones of paternal affection, he announced his decision: My conjugal happiness was not to be indefinitely delayed. My fiancée would arrive in Paris, along with her father, the following summer. All that remained (he wrote) was for me to finish my pharmaceutical studies. Then, with diploma in hand, I could step immediately into the golden future that awaited me.

His announcement filled me with confusion. I was hardly ready to jettison all the expectations I had grown up with, and filial obedience had laid very deep claims on my soul. But neither was I prepared to abandon the changes I had undergone since my arrival in France. Whatever my father's thoughts on the subject, marriage was not foremost in *my* mind, and this marriage threatened to bring with it overwhelming pressures to live a quiet and civilized life—the kind of life I was just now learning to live without. It seemed to me an almost Shakespearean quandary: to be or not to be. And I was not sure which life I really wanted.

I still hadn't resolved the confusion when I took my first steps into politics. I started to attend meetings of the Association of Vietnamese in France, then to participate in its activities. I took part in the demonstrations, conferences, and debates that were beginning to mobilize opposition to the breakdown of peace in Vietnam. Against what I knew to be my father's deepest wishes—not to mention his explicit orders—I was now on my way to becoming a rebel. To compound matters, as the semester advanced, I abandoned my pharmaceutical studies and enrolled at the École Nationale des Sciences Politiques, where I avidly attended lectures and seminars that complemented the reading I was more and more immersed in. In my mind's eye, I began to envision a radical westernization of Vietnam along the lines of Japan's miraculous industrialization of the late nineteenth and early twentieth centuries. There seemed to me no reason that Vietnam, newborn to independence but full of hard-working, intelligent citizens, could not adopt the best from the world's political and economic cultures: the American approach to economics, the German scientific spirit, the French fervor for democracy.

But as I groped passionately, if awkwardly, toward a concept of Vietnam's future, actual conditions inside the country were deteriorating quickly. The cease-fire between French and Vietminh forces that Ho and Moutet had agreed to fell apart on November 20, 1946, when a bloody street battle was fought in Haiphong. A few days later the French renewed their assault with tanks, air attacks, and a naval bombardment from their ships anchored in Haiphong harbor, causing many civilian casualties and a flood of refugees out of the city. By December there seemed little hope for conciliation. Even when the Socialist Leon Blum (an old friend of Ho's) came to power, there was no stopping the inexorable march toward war. Ho's last appeals for negotiation were received in silence. (It is likely that these messages to the government in Paris were purposely delayed by the French high command in Saigon.) On December 19, pushed to the brink, Ho issued an appeal to the people:

Compatriots throughout the country!

Out of love for peace we have made concessions. But the more concessions we made, the further the French colonialists went because they are resolved to invade our country once again. No! We would rather sacrifice everything than lose our country, than return to slavery.

Compatriots! Rise Up!

Men and women, old and young, regardless of creeds, political parties, or nationalities, all the Vietnamese must stand up to fight the French colonialists to save the Fatherland. Those who have rifles will use their rifles. Those who have swords will use their swords. Those who have no swords will use their spades, hoes, and sticks. Everyone must endeavor to oppose the colonialists and save his country.

Soldiers, self-defense guards, militiamen!

The hour of national liberation has struck! We must sacrifice to our last drop of blood to save our country. Whatever hardships we must endure, we are ready to endure them. With the determination to sacrifice, victory will be ours!

Long live an independent and unified Vietnam!

Long live the victorious resistance!

In Paris I became more and more involved in the agitation against the war. At the same time my reading began to focus on military and diplomatic subjects and especially on what was for me the great theme: colonialism. I raced through Machiavelli's *Discourses*, Talleyrand's *Mémoires*, Clausewitz, histories of the First and Second World Wars. The vogue for Marxism then current among French intellectuals led me to Lenin and to Stalin's *Book of Contradictions*. Lenin's *Imperialism, the Highest Stage of Capitalism* impressed me as an excellent justification for Vietnamese nationalism. I was beginning to understand in my own right the economic background to French intransigence and why the British, fearful for their own colonial empire, had been so eager to reestablish French colonial claims after the war. I began for the first time to explore the contradictions between France's democratic ideals and her imperialistic motives. And I was struck by the complete absence of support among the democracies for the colonized and oppressed peoples.

My father, already deeply upset by my political activities and my desertion from the pharmacy school, began to threaten a cutoff of funds. In an attempt to induce me to return to the path of filial duty, my fiancée (accompanied by her father) was dispatched to Paris to formalize our marriage—the idea being that mature responsibilities, combined with her gentle suasions, would rekindle my sense of propriety. Indeed, by this time I had not the least opposition to these arrangements. I had already begun to feel secure in my understanding of events and in my politics, but separation from home and family had not been easy for me, and memories of my fiancée often vied with thoughts about the national struggle. My parents' attempt to use this marriage to steer me away from what I considered was the right path no longer troubled me greatly, while the prospect of sharing my fiancée's love and companionship exerted a powerful attraction.

When they arrived, the three of us left for a tour of France, Italy, and Switzerland, returning to celebrate the wedding in the office of the mayor of Paris' Fifteenth Arrondissement (at the same time the ritual ceremonies were performed by the two families in front of the ancestral altars in Saigon). To my father's way of thinking, of course, the peace and sweetness of conjugal life and obvious prospects for a family and established career could hardly fail to snap his son out of the spell that had strangely transformed him into a political sorcerer's apprentice. But nothing in my father's experience or training had prepared him for the earthquake that was now swallowing up the old familial and colonial order of things. As for me, my heart had embraced the patriotic fire, and my soul was winging its way toward the empyrean of national liberation. I was already well on the far bank of my personal Rubicon. Nor did he recognize the fiery spirit that lived beneath my new wife's outwardly respectful demeanor. The happiness we were now discovering together was unmarred by political discord. Instead of bringing with her the irresistible attractions of a quiet and traditional life, once in Paris she responded as willingly as I had to the call of Vietnamese independence.

As the war intensified in Vietnam, so did the antiwar movement in Paris. I was now a regular in the fight against what was now becoming known as *la sale guerre* ("the dirty war"), throwing myself into the drive to mobilize the overseas Vietnamese community as well as French public opinion. In this work, my militant friends and I found our chief allies among progressive intellectuals and especially in the French Communist Party. Though the FCP had an undeniably schizophrenic outlook on Vietnamese independence (Maurice Thorez, the secretary general, had once announced, "If we can't reach an agreement with them [the Vietnamese nationalists], we'll talk to them with cannons"), they provided almost the only organized French opposition to the war, and we did everything we could to assist them.

At one particularly large and well-publicized meeting held by the Party to rally French opinion, the Vietnamese Association chose my wife to present a bouquet of flowers to Madame Jeannette Versmersch, Thorez's wife and a member of the FCP Central Committee. My parents heard about this affair, and the news that I had now succeeded in involving my wife with the French Communists spurred them to take action. Both her father and mine, speaking with their combined authority and utilizing every imprecation at their disposal, now issued a direct and explicit order for us to return to Saigon immediately.

My wife did not want to go. She was ready to defy the immense authority wielded by her father. I had broken the chains of my own obedience well before this. But she was now six months pregnant, and our parents had promised to cut off every penny of the allowances we were living on. We agonized for days over what to do. How would we live? If it were just myself, I was sure I could find a way to get along. But how could I possibly support my wife and a baby as well? We desperately wanted to stay together. But my wife too was afraid for our child. Had she not been pregnant, we would have both stayed. As it was, we finally decided that she should go back by herself. We hoped that our parents' feelings would be softened by the arrival of a grandchild and that eventually they would accommodate themselves to my disobedience and forgive it. This reasoning, though, did not give us great comfort, and it was with the deepest foreboding that we embraced each other for what we secretly feared might be the last time.

So my wife went back alone. When my father realized the irrevocable nature of my disobedience, he flew into a rage that dwarfed his previous displays of anger. I quickly found myself not only completely cut off from the parental love that had enveloped me for my entire life, but also without a sou for food or rent. I longed for my wife and found myself in anguish over the estrangement from my parents (though I hoped both would be temporary). Money was a different story. Within a few days I had a job as a *plongeur*, dishwasher and assistant potato peeler, at the university restaurant. It was the first manual labor I had ever done. But before long I felt I had been at this kind of work forever.

Perhaps my parents had thought that destitution, in addition to the separation from my wife, would eventually work the desired reform. But when they heard that I was now supporting myself as well as persisting in my incomprehensible political agitation, they had had enough. My father and my wife's father now ordered my wife to stop communicating with me altogether. Then they moved to break up our marriage. In her last letter, my wife wrote that she would always love me. But she was unable to stand up alone against both sets of parents. She was just twenty. We had been married two and a half years.

When I received her letter, I went into a state of mental shock. I locked myself up in my room. I had never believed that our darkest forebodings would really come true. It just wasn't possible that my parents would go so far, that they might really consider me a lost son and cast me out of their lives for good. That they and my parents-in-law would decide that my wife should remake her life with someone who better conformed to their ideas of propriety—no, I could not accept such an idea. But they had done exactly that. I lived like an automaton in a dark fog, my soul hovering between going home and trying to remake my life, on the one hand, and continuing my resistance activities in Paris on the other. After several months of violent inner turmoil, I decided that I had to stay....

By the time 1957 merged into 1958, Ngo Dinh Diem had exhausted the patient hopefulness that had initially greeted his presidency. From the first he had moved ruthlessly to consolidate his personal power, crushing the private army of the Binh Xuyen,* then subduing the armed religious

---

* A tightly run organized crime syndicate that controlled underworld activities in Saigon and Cholon and was not averse to injecting itself into politics.

sects. From there he attacked those suspected of communist sympathies in what was called the To Cong ("Denounce the Communists") campaign, jailing and executing thousands who had fought against the French. Each of these moves was carried out with surprising energy, and in their own terms they succeeded. As he surveyed the political landscape three years after assuming power, Diem could see no well-organized centers of opposition to his rule. The National Assembly was wholly dominated by his brother's National Revolutionary Movement, the troublesome private armies had been severely handled, the Communist-dominated resistance veterans were cowed and in disarray.

But Diem's successes had all been of a negative sort. Though he had asserted his authority and gained time, he had done nothing about establishing positive programs to meet the nation's economic and social needs. He had not used the time he had gained. After three years it was apparent that the new president was a powermonger, not a builder. For those who could see, the fatal narrowness of his political understanding was already evident.

In the first place, Diem's armed enemies had for the most part only been mauled, not destroyed. Elements of the defeated sect armies went underground, licking their wounds and looking for allies. Gradually they began to link up with groups of former Vietminh fighters fleeing from the To Cong suppression. The core of a guerrilla army was already in the making.

Even as old enemies regrouped, Diem was busy adding new ones. In the countryside he destroyed at a blow the dignity and livelihood of several hundred thousand peasants by canceling the land-redistribution arrangements instituted by the Vietminh in areas they had controlled prior to 1954. He might have attempted to use American aid to compensate owners and capitalize on peasant goodwill; instead he courted the large landholders. Farmers who had been working land they considered theirs, often for years, now faced demands for back rent and exorbitant new rates. It was an economic disaster for them.

In 1957 Diem promulgated his own version of land reform, ostensibly making acreage available, though only to peasants who could pay for it. But even this reform was carried out primarily on paper. In the provinces it was sabotaged everywhere by landowners acting with official connivance. The result of all this was a frustrated and indignant peasantry, fertile ground for anti-Diem agitation.

Meanwhile, the city poor were tasting their own ration of misery. In Saigon the government pursued "urban redevelopment" with a vengeance, dispossessing whole neighborhoods in favor of modern commercial buildings and expensive apartments, which could only be utilized by Americans and the native upper classes. Not a few times, poorer quarters were completely razed by uncontrollable fires (Khanh Hoi and Phu Nuan were particularly calamitous examples). Few thought these fires were accidental; they were too closely followed by massive new construction. The displaced moved onto sampans on the river or to poorer, even more distant districts. In the slums and shanty villages resentment against the Americans mixed with a simmering anger toward the regime.

In the highland regions of the Montagnards too, Diem's policies were cold-blooded and destructive. Attempting to make the tribes-people more accessible to government control, troops and cadres forced village populations down out of the mountains and into the valleys—separating them from their ancestral lands and graves. In Ban Me Thuot and other areas, the ingrained routines of social life were profoundly disrupted by these forced relocations, which seemed to the tribespeople nothing more than inexplicable cruelty.

By the end of 1958, Diem had succeeded brilliantly in routing his enemies and arrogating power. But he had also alienated large segments of the South Vietnamese population, creating a swell of animosity throughout the country. Almost unknown at first, in a few short years he had made himself widely detested, a dictator who could look for support only to the Northern Catholic refugees and to those who made money from his schemes. Most damning of all, he had murdered many patriots who had fought in the struggle against France and had tied his existence to the patronage of the United States, France's successor. To many nationalist-minded Vietnamese, whose emotions were those of people just emerging from a hundred years of subjection to foreigners, Diem had forfeited all claims to loyalty.

In light of Diem's conduct of the presidency, two facts were clear: First, the country had settled into an all too familiar pattern of oligarchic rule and utter disregard for the welfare of the people. Second, subservience to foreigners was still the order of the day. We had a ruler whose overriding interest was power and who would use the Americans to prop himself up—even while the Americans were using him for their own strategic purposes.

As far as I was concerned, this situation was intolerable. Replacing the French despots with a Vietnamese one was not a significant advance. It would never lead to either the broad economic progress or the national dignity which I (along with many others) had been brooding about for years. Among my circle of friends there was anger and profound disappointment over this turn of events. We were living, we felt, in historic times. A shameful, century-long era had just been violently closed out, and a new nation was taking shape before our eyes. Many of us agreed that we could not acquiesce in the shape it was taking. If we were not to be allowed a say about it from within the government, we would have to speak from without.

By the end of 1958, those of us who felt this way decided to form an extralegal political organization, complete with a program and plan of action. We had not moved toward this decision quickly; it was an undertaking of immense magnitude, which would require years of effort before giving us the strength to challenge Diem's monopoly on power. To some, that prospect seemed quixotic at best. But most of us felt we had little choice.

From casual discussions, we began to meet in slightly more formal groups, sometimes only a few of us, sometimes eight or ten together. Two doctors, Duong Quynh Hoa and Phung Van Cung, took active roles, as did Nguyen Huu Khuong, a factory owner, Trinh Dinh Thao, a lawyer, and the architect Huynh Tran Phat. We were joined by Nguyen Van Hieu and Ung Ngoc Ky, who were lycée teachers, and other friends such as Nguyen Long and Tran Buu Kiem. Our first order of business was to identify and make contact with potential allies for what we knew would be a long and bitter struggle.

To do this we formed what we called the mobilization committee, whose members were myself, Hieu, Kiem, Ky, Long, Cung, and architect Phat. Through friends, relatives, business and political contacts we began to establish a network of people who felt as we did about Diem and his policies. Phat and a few of the others were old resisters and had kept their ties with fellow veterans of the French war, many of whom were hiding with friends and family from the To Cong hunters. They too were beginning to organize, and they had colleagues and sympathizers in every social stratum throughout the country. They were natural allies.

Among us we also had people with close ties to the sects, the legal political parties, the Buddhists. In each group we made overtures, and everywhere we discovered sympathy and backing. Sometimes individuals would indicate their desire to participate actively. More often we would receive assurances of quiet solidarity. At the same time, we sent Nguyen Van Hieu to Hanoi to begin working out a channel of support from our Northern compatriots.

At each stage we discussed carefully the ongoing search for allies, wary about how to gather support and still retain our own direction and freedom of action. It was a delicate and crucial problem, of the utmost complexity. The overwhelming strength of our enemy urged us to acquire whatever assistance we could, from whatever source. In addition, the anti-colonial war had not simply ended in 1954; a residual Vietminh infrastructure was still in place and was beginning to come alive again. For better or worse, our endeavor was meshed into an ongoing historical movement for independence that had already developed its own philosophy and means of action. Of this movement, Ho Chi Minh was the spiritual father, in the South as well as the North, and we looked naturally to him and to his government for guidance and aid.... And yet, this struggle was also our own. Had Ngo Dinh Diem proved a man of breadth and vision, the core of people who filled the NLF and its sister organizations would have rallied to him. As it was, the South Vietnamese nationalists were driven to action by his contempt for the principles of independence and social progress in which they believed. In this sense, the Southern revolution was generated of itself, out of the emotions, conscience, and aspirations of the Southern people.

The complexity of the struggle was mirrored in the makeup of our group. Most were not Lao Dong ("Workers' Party"—the official name of the Vietnamese Communist Party) members; many scarcely thought of themselves as political, at least in any ideological way. Our allies among the resistance veterans were also largely nationalist rather than political (though they had certainly been led and monitored by the Party). But we also had Party activists among us, some open, some surreptitious. Tran Buu Kiem, the architect Phat, and the teachers Hieu and Ky I knew as politically-minded individuals, who had been leaders of the New Democratic Party during their student years at Hanoi University in the early forties. This militant student union had been absorbed by the Lao Dong in 1951, some of its members enrolling in the Party, some defecting altogether, some simply accepting the change in leadership without themselves becoming Communists. What I didn't know was that Phat had been a secret Party member since 1940 while Hieu, Ky, and Kiem had rallied to the Party in 1951.

But I was not overly concerned at the point about potential conflicts between the Southern nationalists and the ideologues. We were allies in this fight, or so I believed. We needed each other, and the closest ties of background, family, and patriotism united us in respect for each other's purposes. This was my reading of the situation in 1959 as the yet-to-be-named National Liberation Front gathered momentum. I was not alone in drawing this conclusion. And I was not the only one whom time would disabuse....

Now we divided up our more numerous membership into many small working groups of three, four, or five people, no single group knowing who belonged to the other groups. This cell structure is sometimes thought of as a communist innovation, but for the Vietnamese, with their long history of secret societies, it is practically second nature. Each cell included people from different classes and backgrounds to insure a wide range of thinking. I found myself working with three others: Sau Cang, a small businessman; Le Van Phong, a resistance veteran; and Truong Cao Phuoc, a schoolfellow of mine who had also fought with the Vietminh and whose family owned a large rubber plantation.

The mobilization committee also appointed a leadership group made up of Phat, Hieu, and Kiem—responsible for overseeing the details of organization and bringing together input from the different working groups. After two months or so of intense activity throughout the organization, the leadership was ready to circulate a consensus of the ideas that had been generated. General agreement had been reached on the following objectives:

1. Bring a sense of unity to the different classes of people in the South, regardless of their position in society or their political or religious views.
2. Overthrow the Diem regime.
3. Achieve the withdrawal of American advisers and an end to American interference in the self-determination of the South Vietnamese people.

4. Defend and protect the rights of Vietnamese citizens, including demo-
    cratic freedoms and respect for private property rights.
5. Carry out a "land to the tiller" policy.
6. Build an independent economy.
7. Establish an educational system that will protect Vietnamese tradi-
    tions and culture.
8. Establish a pluralistic national government, nonaligned and neutral.
9. Unify the North and the South on the basis of mutual interest through
    negotiations, without war.

As we finished shaping our broad objectives and began grappling
with their ramifications, we also set a tentative date for the first general
meeting: December 19 and 20 of the following year. We decided too on a
name for our movement: the National Liberation Front of South Vietnam.
We devised a flag (later to become famous as the flag of the Vietcong)
and an anthem, "Liberate the South." At the same time, Hieu was sent
North again, this time for guidance from Uncle Ho on the platform we
had enunciated. By the end of 1959, work was complete on transforming
these general principles into a manifesto and a formal political program.
. . .

Reading through the finished documents, I was impressed by the
analysis they presented of the South's political situation and the balance of
forces within the country as well as in Southeast Asia and throughout the
world. It was clear that these works had been finely crafted to appeal to the
broadest spectrum of people in the South and to marshal the anticolonial
emotions that animated almost everyone. At the same time, the manifesto
and program responded forcefully and specifically to the interests of the
various elements of South Vietnamese society—the intellectuals, students,
middle class, peasants, and workers.

As I read, I had the distinct sense that these historical documents
could not have been the work of just the leadership group. They had too
much depth, they showed too expert a grasp of politics, psychology, and
language. I suspected I was seeing in them the delicate fingerprints of Ho
Chi Minh. There seemed nothing strange about this. Ho's experience with
revolutionary struggle was not something alien, to arouse suspicion and
anxiety. It was part and parcel of our own background.

We were now, in the winter of 1959–1960, ready to move into the next
phase of the struggle. In early March as internal tension grew, the Resistance Veterans' Association suddenly launched an appeal to the people of
the South. Spread through leaflets and posters, broadcast by Hanoi Radio,
it called for an armed struggle to begin. It was a signal that the political action, which had been our focus for the past two years, would now
acquire a coordinated military dimension. With this step, the Northern
government had reinforced the Front's credibility and had flashed its own
readiness for a wider conflict.

I felt a hint of trepidation at this. For several years there had been
violence in the countryside; indeed, violent conflict had been a fact of

life since Diem's suppression of the sects and the former Vietminh fighters. But the struggle we were now embarked on would involve military confrontation on a different scale altogether. My colleagues and I had known from the start that moving Diem into any serious negotiations regarding political participation would require the sustained use of force. Regardless of our personal predilections, there was no choice in this. But our priorities had always been distinctly political. We envisioned as our goal a political settlement that could be brought about largely by political means. Military victory was seen neither by us nor by anyone else as a serious possibility. Diem's own army was vastly superior to any forces we might deploy—and behind Diem were the Americans. A high level of warfare would bring with it the grave danger of direct American intervention, which we wished at all costs to avoid. What all this meant was that violence was called for, but a carefully controlled violence that would serve political ends. In addition, I believed that the core group of the NLF, men who felt much as I did, would act as an effective brake against those who might be tempted to look for a military solution. Nevertheless, now that the engagement was opened, there was occasion for a surge of doubt.

But events quickly pushed trepidation aside. The signal given by the Resistance Veterans' Association was loudly confirmed by the Third National Congress of the Workers' Party, which met in Hanoi during the second week of September. Proclaiming the liberation of the South as a major priority, the Northern government was formally announcing its readiness in the most unambiguous fashion. The stage was now fully set....

Early on the morning of December 17, 1960, I left my house for the Saigon bus station, where Le Van Phong, one of my work-group colleagues, was waiting for me. After a few minutes we were approached by a woman whom Phong introduced as Ba Xuyen ("Woman Number Three"). "Ba Xuyen," he told me, "will take you where you have to go." My guide and I bought tickets for Tay Ninh, about seventy miles from Saigon and the home province of the Cao Dai sect, a place I knew intimately from my childhood visits to the sect's "Vatican." On the bus, Ba Xuyen gave me explicit instructions. "If any security people stop us," she said "let me do the talking. If you have to answer, say that we are going to Can Dang to visit our Uncle Kiem."

The trip was uneventful though, and at Tay Ninh we switched to a Lambretta three-wheel carrier headed for Can Dang, a government outpost village about ten miles from the Cambodian border. At the outpost we stopped for a minute while Ba Xuyen passed a few words with the soldier on duty, slipping something into his breast pocket as she talked. Back on the Lambretta, she directed the driver to follow a dirt path into the jungle. About a mile and a half along this track we arrived at a tiny hamlet, the home, it turned out, of the "uncle" we were visiting. Here we got off, and my guide led me into one of the houses, where old Kiem himself was waiting. As Ba Xuyen slipped out the front door, Kiem showed me to a little outbuilding behind the house, where I would wait my escort for the next stage of the journey.

Here we had lunch, and I dozed off on a cot next to the wall. Sometime later I was awakened to find Kiem gently shaking me, a set of black pajamas in his hand, which he indicated I was to change into. Darkness had fallen. As I put on the pajamas, I became aware that someone was standing in the doorway, a young man also dressed in black. He had come on a bicycle to chauffeur me to the next rendezvous. Sitting on a makeshift seat attached over the rear wheel of his bike, I rode with him through fields of sugarcane and manioc that were barely visible in the last of the twilight. About an hour later we arrived at a small cottage deep in the jungle. Inside, sitting around a table dimly lit by a smoking oil lamp, sat three local guerrillas, drinking tea.

They offered me a cup, and I sat down with them for a few minutes, happy for the rest. Before long, however, another bicycle driver appeared for the next leg. This was turning out to be quite an adventure—and, I realized, quite a meticulously organized one. My new driver pedaled into the heart of the blackened jungle, the invisible trail sloping upward as we came into the foothills of the border region. We drove until well past midnight, stopping every hour or so at a guerrilla cottage for a cup of tea and a brief rest. Sometime in the early hours of the morning we found ourselves among a cluster of small buildings—we had arrived at the meeting site.* I was sore and exhausted from sitting on the back seat for so long, and I marveled at the endurance of my driver. In a minute though, I had been escorted to one of the cottages, and whatever thoughts I was having about this remarkable journey were blotted out in a dreamless sleep.

I awoke refreshed on the morning of the eighteenth, alone in the cottage. As I got up to look around, however, a black-pajamaed guerrilla appeared in the doorway, introducing himself as my escort for the next two days. He told me that, like the other secret delegates, I would be staying alone, and that he would take care of my needs. He also described the security precautions. I would be shielded from contact with others and was to use only the code name "Ba Cham" when I talked with anybody. Soon Huynh Tan Phat came by with another man whom he introduced as Hai Xe Ngua ("Brother Two Horse Car"). Brother Two Horse Car was about fifty years old and especially large for a Vietnamese, though trim and muscular. He was, Phat said, in charge of finances for the Front. (I later found out that this personage was Nguyen Van So, a Central Committee member of the Workers' Party.) We exchanged pleasantries, and Brother Two Horse gave me a sheaf of papers. If I had any suggestions or comments, I was to write them out, and they would be taken into account at the meeting.

---

* When I returned to the jungle in 1968, I learned that this original meeting had been held at Xom Giua ("Middle Hamlet"), along the Vam Co River near the Cambodian border.

I spent the day poring over these documents, breaking for a light lunch and dinner prepared by my helpful attendant. That evening, I was given a large checkered scarf to muffle my face, and shepherded to a hall with a low stage on one end and a row of curtained boxes along the left side—into one of which I was ushered. Slowly the benches in the middle of the hall filled, and I heard the shuffle of people being shown to the boxes alongside mine. When everybody had arrived, a troupe of entertainers took the stage, a unit of resistance veterans there to put on a rousing variety show. Singers, mimes, and comic acts followed each other, with a heavy emphasis on political satire, which the audience enjoyed hugely. When it was over, my escort led me back to the cottage, taking pains to avoid other members of the audience, some of whom were, like me, carefully attended.

The next morning, December 19, I was again taken to the hall, which now had acquired a different set of trappings. Over the entrance hung a red-and-white banner proclaiming "Welcome General Congress for the Foundation of the National Liberation Front for South Vietnam." Flanking this banner were two flags, red and blue with a yellow star in the center, the flag we had devised during our working meetings the previous year. Inside, last night's stage had become a dais, above which the same banner was draped. On the dais sat Phat, Hieu, and Kiem, our leadership group, together with Ung Ngoc Ky, Dr. Cung, and several others I didn't recognize. These others turned out to be representatives of various groups, youth, peasants, workers, and women—Pham Xuan Thai, Nguyen Huu The, Nguyen Co Tam, and Nguyen Thi Dinh respectively. Again I was shown into one of the curtained boxes along the side, hidden from the public delegates, who were seating themselves on the middle benches and from the other secret members occupying the adjoining boxes.* There were perhaps sixty participants in all, including twenty or so behind the curtains. Over all of us a sense of expectancy began to build, as a spokesman got up to announce the agenda.

After the agenda was read, a security force representative described the safety measures that had been taken and gave instructions about what to do should there be an alarm or an attack by air or land forces. Then Dr. Cung arose for a short inaugural statement, declaring the congress in session and wishing us success in our great undertaking. He was followed by Kiem, who read a report on the political situation in South Vietnam, and Hieu, who presented the manifesto and political program.

The hortatory language of these documents seemed to heighten the drama of what was happening; each individual in the hall was aware that

---

* The "public" delegates were people who were living in the jungle as full-time revolutionaries. "Secret" delegates were those who, like me, led open lives in government controlled areas and whose Front identities had to be closely guarded.

he was participating in a historic event. Sensing the excitement, Hieu went on to explain that the name "National Liberation Front for South Vietnam" symbolized the unity of the Southern people in their struggle to free the country from *My Diem* ("America/Diem"). The flag, he said, red and blue, signified the two halves of the nation, united under the star—in a single purpose. The anthem, "Liberate the South," echoed the appeal with simple clarity.

At midday when the meeting broke for lunch, the delegates were visibly moved by feelings of brotherhood and resolution. For me,though, these feelings were to remain private as, muffled in my scarf, I was led back to the cottage to eat in solitude.

After lunch, the meeting reconvened to hear statements from representatives of various social elements—the sects, the intellectuals, students, peasants—each speaking of the aspirations of his group. When these had been given, we recessed for a dinner of soup, vegetables, and rice, returning to hear statements and suggestions from those who had submitted them in writing the previous day. Near midnight we voted to accept the manifesto, program, flag, everything that was before us. There were no dissenters.

Finally, Huynh Tan Phat moved that we adopt a suggested list of names as a Provisional Committee to carry the movement forward until the next general congress could be held. Specifically, the Provisional Committee would proclaim the creation of the NLF and publicize its manifesto and program not only throughout Vietnam but internationally as well. (The diplomatic front was to open immediately.) The committee would also intensify our proselytizing efforts and make preparations for the next congress, at which a regular Central Committee and organizational hierarchy would be established. It would, in addition, continue to develop our infrastructure throughout the South, with special attention to the Saigon/Cholon/Giadinh zone.

Phat's proposal was passed, again unanimously, and Dr. Cung was elected chairman of the Provisional Committee, with Hieu to serve as secretary general. In the early hours of December 20, we adjourned.

Once finished with our business, the delegates dispersed as quickly as they could, knowing that each moment the danger of discovery increased. I left immediately by bicycle, retracing the arduous trail back to old Kiem's house, where I arrived dead with fatigue but spiritually exalted. In the little outbuilding I changed out of the pajamas into my own clothes and boarded the Lambretta for Tay Ninh. There a bus was waiting to take me back to Saigon. This time I had no need of a guide.

By the following morning I had fully recovered from the lost night's sleep, though my body still ached. From Hanoi that morning a special broadcast reached every corner of the South, announcing the formation of the NLF and offering congratulations from the Worker's Party and the Northern government. It was a time for nourishing the most sublime hopes.

16
The Communists' Road to Power
DOUGLAS PIKE

The struggle movement was the route to power. Declared an early PRP [People's Revolutionary Party] document:

> By applying creative reasoning of Marxism-Leninism to conditions in Vietnam, the Party, with reality and capability, has set forth the line and direction of the Revolution in South Vietnam, which is the political struggle combined with the armed struggle marching forward toward the General Uprising.

Vo Nguyen Giap wrote that if an uprising was an art, the chief characteristic of its leadership was the ability to change the struggle form in accordance with changed events. At the beginning, he said, the political struggle dominated and the armed struggle was secondary. Gradually the two assumed equal roles. Then the armed struggle dominated. In the end came the return to the political struggle. Struggle was *the word*. Its goal, toward which the cadres pledged themselves, toward which each Vietnamese was expected daily to contribute a little, was the General Uprising, the nationwide, simultaneous grand struggle movement.

An early NLF document spelled out the scenario in specific terms:

> The government of South Vietnam is brutal, reactionary, imperialist, feudal, dictatorial.... The people have no means short of revolution to liberate themselves from slavery. That is why we march forward in a Revolution to seize power by means of the General Uprising. Our immediate goal is preparation of the people for the General Uprising.... We must utilize the strength of the people as our great force.... This is the struggle movement.... The enemy relies on its armed forces. We rely on the people...., the people strongly bound together in the struggle movement.

As one PRP indoctrination booklet indicated when it asked "what must we do each day to move toward the General Uprising?" the answer was:

> We must make a continuous effort to strengthen and develop the Party. ...and promote Party-mass relations to ensure continued Party leadership. ...We must build up the worker-farmer alliance as the basic force of the Revolution.... We must press forward with the struggle movement, develop unity among the masses and win support among the enemy's military and administrative workers.... We must press the *binh van* movement.... We must do agit-prop work among the masses....

From the struggle toward the General Uprising came the creation of the myth of the heroic struggle out of which was fashioned the hero-martyr, described in an early Radio Liberation broadcast:

> A woman plugged a gun muzzle with her own body, an old woman burned her own house and the enemy with it to resist the strategic-hamlet program. Groups of people stood facing enemy guns to shield the retreat of the people's forces. Such martyrs will go down as heroes in the history of the nation. How I wish talented moviemakers the world over would come and record these heroic deeds on the part of the people of South Vietnam.... Thousands of women and old people advance in orderly ranks toward an enemy post. They brave the enemy planes overhead. They ignore enemy warning shots and give no notice when the guns fire into them. Bringing their wounded along with them, they advance until they come to the U.S.-Diem administrative buildings. They demand an end to arson, looting, murder, cannibalism, and raids against the people. Blows rain upon them while these mothers, sisters, and wives tearfully tell their tales of woe to the evildoers....

In order to understand fully the NLF's use of the struggle movement as its chief offensive device, we should take a brief look at the NLF's perception of the GVN's over-all counterinsurgency strategy. The GVN had no national policy or even official attitude toward the NLF's struggle movement, nor was there any systematic effort at the district and village operational levels to develop techniques designed either to head off a struggle movement as it was being launched or to blunt it once under way. The posture of the Diem government was to pretend it did not exist or, if forced to take notice, to characterize it as an insignificant and ineffectual Communist effort to create disorder. District and village officials were left to their own resources when confronted by a struggle movement, and their responses depended largely on their personalities. Some officials attempted to ameliorate the situation if in their power to do so; others simply ordered their police and troops to disperse the crowds. Occasionally an official was politically astute enough to regard the struggle movement as an opportunity to seize the initiative from the NLF and would alleviate a genuine grievance and turn the crowd's attitude from hostility to amity; this was a difficult manipulation, for it involved both acquiescing to a demand without appearing to surrender in the face of force and structuring the solution so as to maneuver the NLF out of credit for the change.

An early NLF document (1961) assessed the GVN's response to a struggle movement as follows:

> In the face of the struggle movement the enemy usually becomes puzzled, panic-stricken, and troubled from the highest to the lowest rank. In many villages the enemy government's machine has deteriorated; even in some districts this has happened. The arrogant attitude of the enemy has abated. This proves two things.... that the foundation of the enemy government is not solid.... and, if we lead the struggle movement properly, it will paralyze the enemy's administrative machine and destroy their schemes and policies.

Another document of the same period outlined some of the uses of confusion:

> After a serious political struggle [at the village level] the enemy is thrown into confusion. Administrative officials, security agents go into hiding or they surrender themselves to the people. Cadres must make use of this state of confusion to further increase enemy dislocation. Officials or soldiers who are confused and frightened because they are in trouble with the government must be guided into supporting the National Liberation Front.... Say to them that since they do not want to serve as cannon fodder they must resign their jobs or desert the army. Point out the errors they have made, welcome them for choosing the right path, and praise their progressive spirit.

Nhan Dan, on August 28, 1961, evaluated the over-all potency of the struggle movement as follows:

> Starting with struggles against oppression, restrictions, preventing persons from earning a livelihood by wicked village notables, puppet administrative organs, secret agents, and against exploitation, the merging of villages, evicting people from their villages, and the establishment of agrovilles, the movement went forward with such slogans as "Overthrow the U.S.-Diem regime," "Establish a national-democratic coalition government."... From small-group complaints, petitions, and small demonstrations, the movement has advanced toward big demonstrations, including thousands of persons...uprising that exterminated 'wicked agents' ...and smashed agrovilles.... University students protest against examinations in which many fail.... Merchants, proprietors, and tradesmen protest against high taxes.... During the last few months the struggle movement has defeated many major U.S.-Diem schemes...such as mopping-up operations and ranger and antiguerrilla tactics....

... The NLF's extended and vitriolic attack on U.S. economic aid programs indicated a sensitive nerve. However, civic action programs as such did not necessarily counter the thrust of the struggle movement; their contribution was in direct proportion to their responsiveness to the issues involved in a particular struggle movement or to the degree that the programs indicated serious governmental concern for village problems. In any case they would have no lasting effect unless coupled to village social organization work, thereby enhancing both the public and the private non-NFL infrastructure in the village. The struggle movement was an organizational effort, and any counter effort also had to be essentially organizational.

As employed by the NLF the technique of the political struggle movement is neither as strange nor as alien to Americans as might be supposed on first encounter. The efforts by American Negroes and their supporters in the 1960's to achieve racial equality introduced Americans to a similar type of activity. The type of struggle that the rural Vietnamese felt was justified and just, the "peaceful struggle movement," was akin to what Arthur

Waskow has called "creative disorder."[1] In the American context, Waskow distinguished the politics of order, that is, the courts, the legislature, the public forum such as the mass media (which were closed to all dissidents in Vietnam until the end of the Diem regime), and the sporadic bombings and clashes of mobs with police or troops (which would correspond to the NLF's violence program) from a third type of activity—"creative disorder," which lies between the two. It is exemplified by the civil rights march, the school boycott, the sit-in, the pray-in, the wade-in, the rent strike and economic boycott, highway blocking, telephone jamming, and other nonviolent action, which most Americans regard, if not with full approval, at least as legitimate activities that deserve legal protection as much as labor's right to strike. Vietnamese, even strongly anti-Communist Vietnamese, saw nothing improper in the struggle movement; they objected to Communist manipulation of such movements just as Americans fighting for racial equality object to communism's efforts to insinuate itself into the civil rights struggle.

The struggle movement had a long and honorable history in Vietnam. During the Yen Bay mutiny of 1930 long lines of unarmed and impressively silent Vietnamese marched past the French governor-general's residence.[2] In earlier days the struggle movement was little more than a technique for riot manufacture or instigating mob violence. But in the hands of the NLF it developed far beyond such crude usage. Combined with the organizational weapon and employing various communication techniques, the struggle movement became a vast effort to organize and direct rural Vietnamese opposition to the GVN to such a degree that the GVN would be unable to withstand the pressure and would collapse, and in such depth that the United States would find its support of repressive GVN measures so costly that it would choose to withdraw.

The NLF initially approached the entire Revolution not as a small-scale war but as a political struggle with guns, a difference real and not semantic. It maintained that its contest with the GVN and the United States should be fought out at the political level and that the use of massed military might was in itself illegitimate. Thus one of the NLF's unspoken, and largely unsuccessful purposes was to use the struggle movement before the onlooking world to force the GVN and the United States to play the game according to its rules: The battle was to be organizational or quasi-political, and battleground was to be the minds and loyalties of the rural Vietnamese, the weapons were to be ideas; therefore military assaults, as opposed to the NLF's self-defense efforts, were beyond permissible limits of the game, and all force was automatically condemned as terror or repression. In such perspective the struggle movement obviously became a powerful weapon.

If the General Uprising was the great NLF social myth, the struggle movement was its great social fantasy. For here, with a backdrop of high drama, every man could fling himself into the hero's role. The young crusader could embark on a great quest and look the dragon Authority in the face with courage. To the timid old man, for all his life the Persevering Tortoise, came the moment of destiny when he could say to himself and all the world: "This one thing I do." Cinderella and all the other fools could still believe there was magic in the mature world if one mumbled the secret incantation: solidarity...union...concord. The meek, at last, were to inherit the earth; riches would be theirs and all in the name of justice and virtue. So out of their thatch-roofed houses they came, pouring through their villages and onto the highways of Vietnam, gullible, misled people, pawns of a vast and abstract power struggle, turning the countryside into a bedlam, toppling one Saigon government after another, confounding the Americans, a sad and awesome spectacle, a mighty force of people, a river the Communists hoped to use and then dam. This was the struggle movement.

POLITICAL STRUGGLE

The political struggle movement operated on two levels. First, it sought intermediate goals. An early NLF document stated: "The struggle movement in rural areas should lessen enemy pressure, oppose military operations and terrorism, oppose the strategic hamlet and extortion, and halt the seizure of land, the corvée labor system, and the army draft." Another document of the same period declared: "The struggle movement in the ...[people's] terms has four goals: economic betterment, democratic freedom, opposition to the U.S. Diem warmongering, and unification.... Every struggle should attempt to attain these four goals."

The second level was an effort to engage, activate, and immerse the persons involved in the movement in the Revolution. Said the document just cited: "In all struggle movements bear in mind...the need to preserve and expand the various revolutionary organizations, train the people, give them struggle experience, draw lessons and learn from each struggle." A widely used cadre handbook entitled *Needs of the Revolution*,[3] dated July 1962, added: "Our [struggle movement] actions should be designed to influence the people in all walks of life in Vietnam and also abroad, thus gaining the support of the world population. All classes of people must be enlisted to take part in the struggle movement..., thus building a large resistance movement that includes the entire population and simultaneously indoctrinating the masses in the Front's policies." Still another directive, dated 1963, declared: "The political struggle...is the mobilization of the masses and the assertion of the strength of the revolutionary climate...with the masses moving deeply into the enemy's rear to struggle directly with enemy officials...The forms and goals are firm, the masses bare-handed opposing the enemy's military force."

Originally the NLF assumed that the weak, chaotic government of Vietnam, already tottering, could be brought down solely by means of the struggle movement, a series of small-scale, deliberately created local anarchies throughout the rural areas. The theoretical base, and the indoctrinational cement that held this belief together, was the myth of the General Uprising. Engaging a rural Vietnamese in a specific struggle movement such as a demonstration or recruiting him into a guerrilla band imposed self-control on him. Commitment led to adherence, public acts developed self-discipline. The violence program played a vital but limited part in this effort. The guerrilla was important (the NLF employed the slogan "Be a guerrilla or support a guerrilla"), but the bulk of the NLF's day-to-day activity was in the political struggle, in the "people's war."

From a functional standpoint the NLF considered their struggle activities in the villages they controlled to be of two types: the coacting group, or what the NLF called the "meeting for propaganda in width," in which individual members were subjected to outside stimulus, and the face-to-face group, or what was called "the meeting for propaganda in depth," in which the members reacted to each other. The coacting group in turn was divided into various types of meetings for specific purposes:

1. The struggle meeting. This could be a village demonstration that began and ended in the village and was known as the "far from the enemy meeting"; or it could be a meeting that culminated in a struggle movement at a GVN administrative office or military post. Ideally it was a means to seize political control of the village, as outlined in this rather simplistic view:

    The meeting is the chief device for motivating the people in the villages to throw out enemy control. Cadres and guerrillas go into a village, capture enemy spies, and hold a meeting of thousands of people to denounce the enemy. The people, supporting the move, destroy the enemy's control. At these meetings the cadres may speak only five or ten sentences, which satisfies the desires of the people. The people rise up. The cadres should not stop them or speak further.

    However, there is little indication that such meeting results were common if indeed they occurred at all. In practice the struggle meeting did not differ greatly from the demonstration.[4]

2. The denunciation meeting or, as it was often called, the misery-telling meeting. This could be similar to the Chinese denunciation meeting or, as was more common in Vietnam, a meeting at which individuals arose and described their plight in life. A memorandum dated mid-1962 outlined two incidents from a typical denunciation meeting of the first type:

    A Cao Dai priest from Tay Ninh lived in the area, and we had a grudge against him from the Resistance period. He was denounced as an enemy of the Revolution and driven out. In another village recently liberated, women stood up and denounced local men who had violated them; they were motivated by hate and wrath and did not feel shame to denounce them in public.

More commonly these consisted of villagers airing personal complaints or "denouncing" the life they led.

3. The ceremonial meeting. This was designed to commemorate an event or celebrate an NLF victory. In January 1962, at the time of the formation of the PRP, a directive went to all district cadres outlining in detail the staging of the village ceremony to commemorate the establishment of the PRP[5]. Its purpose, it said, was "to cause all people to appreciate the establishment of the PRP... and to create in all classes of people a strong image of the PRP...."

4. The people's convention. The exact nature and purpose of this type of meeting is not clear. One document referred to it as "the highest form of democratic life of the people." Another warned cadres not to organize a struggle meeting and call it a people's convention "because a people's convention should include only people of the same social class." It listed the "four revolutionary classes of people: the workers, the peasant-farmers, the petite bourgeoisie [*tieu tu san*], and the national bourgeoisie [*tu san dan toc*]," stating that the people's convention should include either the first or second group but should not mix the two.

The face-to-face meeting actually was a combined indoctrination session and mutual-aid society gathering. Frequently cadres were criticized for making use of only coacting groups and underestimating the face-to-face group, defined as "meetings that assemble a small number of people usually from three to five families but not more than 30 people, ... at which there are long and deep political discussions aimed at promoting the struggle movement, ... which seek to supply the masses with information about the success of the political and armed struggle throughout Vietnam ... or which promote hate and resentment.[6] Instructions to cadres on the use of the social movement were extremely detailed, and no aspect, however small, was overlooked. For example, one directive even dealt with the matter of dress at a meeting:

People should be asked to wear clothes proper for the meeting, good clothes for a ceremonial meeting, solemn clothes at a struggle meeting, and old torn clothes at a misery-telling or denunciation meeting.... In one district women met to discuss the WIDF [Women's International Democratic Federation] resolution regarding colonialist oppression of women. Some women wore their best clothes and some wore poor clothes because they did not understand the purpose of the meeting.

One way of grasping the substance of a struggle demonstration is to inspect specific instructions to NLF cadres on its use. *Needs of the Revolution* directed that the cadres

1. Begin by investigating and studying the enemy situation, as well as our own. Evaluate the power balance between ourselves and the enemy. Bear

in mind that the enemy will flatter the people and employ demagogic appeals. Search for contradictions in the enemy camp that may be exploited. Consider the various issues most likely to arouse public interest and cause the people to become militant. At all times evaluate realistically the capacity of the Revolution and the political strength of the people.

2. In preparing for the struggle: Seek to know the target (Who are they? What position do they hold? Whom are they in conflict with? Whom must we isolate?). Set clear purposes and realistic goals that reflect the people's demands. Choose the form of struggle most suitable to the degree of enlightenment of the people. Use the correct forces from among the people, that is, those most directly involved. Choose individuals carefully, picking those who have the courage to deal with the enemy or who have the ability to win the sympathy of enemy officials and troops. Build up determination for the struggle. Use hard-core Party members to support the struggle (do not send them [to participate in the actual demonstration]), such as comforting the families of those engaged in the struggle or supplying food to those elements who are actually struggling. Set up a lead group that will be in the midst of the actual struggle (if absolutely necessary, include a covert Party member) to lead the struggle. Set up a guide group, which should be stationed a few hundred meters away from the struggle scene (this may include a Party member), to act as an adviser and to send messages to the lead group leader. Set up a third unit, the front group, made up of local sympathizers with high fighting morale, to meet and negotiate with the enemy.... Make plans to have other social groups support the struggle; one class supports the struggle of another class; strong areas support weak areas; cities support rural struggles; etc. This may be manifested by sympathy struggles, spreading rumors, sending gifts or letters, or even making visits.... Try to foresee the enemy's response and plan to counter the repressive measures taken by him. In large-scale and protracted struggles make plans to supply food to those who are struggling.

3. Agit-prop work preparing for the struggle.... Educate the people to understand the struggle; teach struggle techniques, how to reason with the enemy; also stress discipline, the importance of following the leaders and avoiding imprudent violence or actions that may provoke the enemy. Make clear-cut assignments of responsibilities (who subverts whom, who does what, who is on the three committees, etc.).

4. When an incident or issue arises, cell leaders and cadres should meet and make plans, which include (a) arousing the people so they realize the necessity of a struggle; (b) gathering all social groups whose interests and aspirations are involved; (c) deciding the date and time of the struggle; (d) coining slogans and determining the forms of struggle (mass meeting, demonstration, petition, etc.); and (e) determining the struggle target (whether village officials, district, provincial, or central government authorities, army camps, etc.). In preparing for a struggle keep in mind that it will be successful when it brings material benefits to the people and at the same time (a) achieves for the Party a deeper influence of the Party with the people; (b) increases faith by the people in the struggle method by demonstrating their strength and making them confident in

the struggle methods; (c) causes the enemy difficulties; (d) exposes the true face of the country-selling U.S.-Diemists; and (e) generally promotes the struggle movement, especially in the villages.

The above deals with the struggle where there is time and when conditions are proper for a relatively large-scale struggle. Daily there are opportunities for smaller struggles that may be staged without complete preparations. Party members should be prepared to take advantage of all opportunities to conduct struggles, large and small....

The struggle movement, not the battle, was the payoff, the culmination of carefully nurtured efforts, the fruit of the labor. "Enthusiasm for revolution is not enough," warned one document, "we must know how to get the masses to struggle, for this is the way we conduct the Revolution."

THE VIOLENCE PROGRAM

To the onlooking world Vietnam's agony of the 1960's appeared to result chiefly from guerrilla warfare.... Guerrilla warfare, or in NLF terminology the "armed struggle," or what in the author's terms is the "violence program," was only that part of the revolutionary iceberg above water. It has been well and frequently described by American news media, and its pattern certainly is now familiar to those who followed events in Vietnam even casually during 1960–1965. Therefore we are not reviewing here guerrilla warfare in Vietnam but only those aspects that concern the general struggle movement and were part of a broader category, the violence program.

The rural Vietnamese climate of opinion, the availability of supplies and manpower, the inherent dangers involved in the use of force, as well as such abstractions as theoretical considerations, historical lessons, and grand strategy—all helped shape the character and dictate the scope of the NLF's violence program. Never treated as a separate entity, never conceived of in exclusively military terms, and at no time the chief prop of the Revolution, the armed struggle or violence program served to reinforce or make possible the other struggle activities—the *dich van, dan van,* and *binh van.* It was the hardener in the formula, the steel in the superstructure. The two hundred to five hundred "guerrilla incidents" per week that went on in Vietnam week after week and month after month for five years had no purpose in themselves—and indeed when viewed in themselves often made no sense—except to serve the political struggle movement. Thus the primary purpose of the violence program was to make possible the political struggle movement. One NLF document, dated October 1961, assessed the previous three months' work by declaring:

The best feature of the period is that we boldly coordinated the military activities with the political struggle. Because of our perseverance and because we used the correct antiterror measures, in many places the masses had the opportunity to stand up and struggle against the enemy. Reality proves that our policy of "pushing forward the political struggle closely and properly coordinated with the military activities" is the correct one.

At the same time the political struggle, especially in the early days, laid the groundwork for the later increased emphasis on the armed struggle movement. Said an early document:

> These continual and strong struggles illlustrate the indomitability and strong will of our compatriots in South Vietnam, . . . for they have helped mobilize, organize, and educate the masses so that the latter might be trained to increase their combat strength. . . .

The public rationale for the use of force was that the enemy had given the NLF no alternative. Said an early indoctrination booklet:

> During the first years following the re-establishment of peace [post-1954] the people of South Vietnam engaged in a peaceful political struggle. But the warlike and terrorist policies of the enemy forced them to take up rifles and begin an armed struggle. . . . The U.S.-Diem clique uses collaborators, villains, spies, Self-Defense Corps members, and secret police agents to carry out fascist policies and to terrorize and suppress the people's political struggle. Thus it is necessary to have an armed force to counterattack the enemy's military units, destroy collaborators, villains, secret police agents, and spies, and efficiently support, preserve, and develop the political struggle. . . . Armed struggle is required (1) because the enemy's political weaknesses have forced him to resort to the force of arms to impose his will, and this must be countered; . . . (2) because armed struggle will enhance the political struggle; . . . and (3) because it prevents the enemy from mingling freely among the village masses, . . . helps isolate him and thins out his ranks. . . .

A later document outlined the three GVN "policies of force" that, it said, caused the NLF to use counterforce:

> Since 1954 the U.S. imperialists and their lackeys have adopted the following principal measures with which we must cope. . . . : (1) terrorism, including both the Denunciation of Communism [campaign] and anticommunism; (2) mopping-up operations and pacification efforts; (3) the national policy of strategic hamlets. . . .

Later, and chiefly for the benefit of cadres, justification for the use of violence added doctrinal correctness to necessity. Justification was never an easy matter for the NLF. The natural abhorrence by rural Vietnamese of systematic slaughter formed a major and continuing problem that the leadership constantly sought to overcome. Among NLF cadres, especially those recruited locally, unsophisticated and with great faith in the myth of the General Uprising, the use of force seemed both repugnant and unnecessary; even among more sophisticated cadres the belief was widespread that perhaps there was something to the General Uprising notion after all, that perhaps the NLF could win by the political struggle alone.

The response of the leadership to these reactions was to mix thoroughly the armed and political struggles and insist that the result was essentially political: and to administer, especially to cadres, massive doses of indoctrination 'proving" that victory could be achieved only by measured use of force and violence. "We have learned," said a 1962 indoctrination booklet,

> that the only correct way to organize revolutionary forces and make preparations in all areas to smash the enemy's machinery of violence is to use the appropriate form of armed struggle.... In the beginning the people pursued the legal and illegal political struggle but soon discovered they were not strong enough or effective enough to prevent enemy mopping-up operations and the killing and imprisoning of people. Therefore from the masses' struggle movement there emerged a new struggle form, the armed struggle, and a new organization, the Liberation Army. Emergence of this new struggle form not only met an urgent demand but was an inevitable result of the revolutionary movement. It did not contradict the political struggle but supplemented it and paved the way for the political struggle to develop.

Increasingly and perhaps inevitably after mid-1963, the armed struggle moved to the forefront, tending to dominate the scene and push the political struggle into the background. An internal document of that period declared:

> We should urgently intensify the armed struggle to keep up with the political movement...and also intensify the guerrilla movement...and intensify combined operations of the three forces and attack the enemy continuously and everywhere....The three forces should be built up proportionately. Only by building up the concentrated forces [NLF army] can we intensify the destruction of the enemy forces. But be careful not to build up the concentrated forces and neglect the guerrilla movement,...which means building combat hamlets and training self-defense forces.... In leading armed activities, be fully aware of the neccessity of combining the military and political struggles to loosen enemy pressure, oppose military operations, oppose the strategic-hamlet program.... Organize attacks against the enemy in his rear areas to upset him....Especially communication centers, warehouses, airports, and U.S. offices should be attacked by specialized forces and clandestine units.... Public utilities such as electricity producing plants are not to be sabotaged at this stage....

There appeared to be several reasons for this shift. In the first place, armed combat was a GVN-imposed requirement; the NLF was obliged to use counterforce to survive. This resulted in the creation of guerrilla units with an ever-increasing military cast and a correspondingly improved military capability. As the units' military effectiveness increased and they began to deal serious blows to the ARVN, the argument was pressed that larger and more numerous guerrilla bands would mean more victories over the ARVN as well as a quicker ultimate victory. In short, a militarization cycle began. Second, reinterpretation of doctrine—especially by the Northern cadres, veterans of the more militarized Viet Minh war—placed greater stress on the armed struggle than before 1963. This was also a reflection of the increased DRV influence or intervention in the management of the Southern struggle. Reliable GVN intelligence reports indicate that in August and September 1963 at least two generals from Hanoi arrived in the highlands of the South to act as advisers, or possibly commanders, in the NLF's armed struggle movement. They were professional military, and their advice or orders had the effect of militarizing the looser, more self-contained guerrilla units and restructuring them into more traditional armed forces with more orthodox military assignments. The third reason was a general increase in the use of violence throughout the rural areas by the NLF. The bloom of revolution began to fade for the rural Vietnamese at the end of the Diem regime, and sympathy for the NLF diminished. This called for stricter and more forceful control measures by the NLF in its administration of the liberated area. Finally, in revolutionary guerrilla warfare a sort of Gresham's Law appears to be at work, under which violent acts tend to drive out political acts.

At any rate there is no doubt that the historical development of the NLF from 1960 to 1965 was characterized by a growing use of the armed struggle and by increased efforts to make its use more palatable in and out of the NLF ranks. Whereas to the NLF the Revolution during Diem's time had been essentially a political struggle, the Revolution against the post-Diem governments was basically an armed struggle.

NOTES

1. In a conversation with the author.

2. An account of a March 19, 1959, incident in Saigon was written later, and broadcast by Radio Liberation on March 19, 1964, to provide a struggle movement heritage:

   On that date [March 19] in 1950 a heroic example of the struggle movement was raised in Saigon....A half million people went into the streets to shout "Down with the U.S. interventionists who seek an extension of the war."...."Down with the puppet traitors."..."U.S. imperialist go home." ...Downtown Saigon was crowded with unsubmissive people. Students, schoolchildren, workers, teachers, writers, artists, doctors, lawyers, merchants, industialists, civil servants, in other words all the beloved children of Saigon, regardless of political tendency, religion, or social class, closely united in the struggle to defend the Fatherland. Many soldiers and policemen of the colonialist and puppet regime sided with the people. Obeying the U.S. imperialists' orders, the warring French colonialists and their faithful lackeys pitilessly repressed and terrorized the compatriots....but despite their violence...these vanguard troops of the Fatherland moved forward and overwhelmed the cruel enemies....U.S. cars were burned, U.S. French colonialist and puppet flags were torn to pieces and trampled underfoot.... Roadblocks were set up.

3. This printed booklet, which was in effect a handbook on the struggle movement, was frequently captured in NLF-controlled areas.

4. The technique of the meeting of this type was outlined in *Needs of the Revolution:*

The demonstration [or struggle meeting] must aim at strongly promoting hatred, and this requires an assembly of several hundred people. The person who delivers the main speech must be well prepared and must [so arrange it] that at the end of his speech the masses will shout slogans expressing their determination to struggle.... Then leaders of various groups and organizations will come to the platform one by one and call on each of their groups to shout slogans. The atmosphere must be heated. Slogans should concentrate on one subject. Do not drag things on too long. Don't include an entertainment show, as is often done now, because this dilutes the significance of the struggle demonstration. A well-organized demonstration requires meticulous preparation, with objectives kept well in mind. The order of appearance on the platform must be carefully thought out. Also, have a plan to stir up the masses by first holding small group [face-to-face] meetings in hamlets and then staging a larger joint meeting.... In areas newly liberated it is necessary to hold continuous meetings to boost the revolutionary spirit. But in areas that have been liberated for a longer period they should be used sparingly. When held, they should be larger, including people from several villages. End these with a parade, which helps express the spirit of the Revolution.

5. First, Party members were to meet privately, coin slogans to be used, and plan the day's events:

The ceremony should be observed solemnly in a manner worthy of the PRP.... Each hamlet will erect a triumphal arch bearing the main slogan.... Other banners and slogans will be hung throughout the hamlet.... A grandstand will be constructed and various committees set up, such as the organization committee, order and security committee protocol committee, first-aid committee, etc.,... but do not display Front flags.... One comrade will act as master of ceremonies and read the speech, which will be supplied to you later.... When he has finished, representatives of the liberation associations and other groups are to come forward and express their appreciation for the PRP.... [Their remarks] should be written in advance, should be short and clear and should stress faith in Party leadership and determination to pursue the Revolution.... After the ceremony a theatrical event or dragon dance may be performed.... Warning: At the ceremony keep the initiative and do not allow the people to ask too many questions. For instance, they may ask, "With the formation of the PRP does this mean the Lao Dong [Party] no longer exists?" or "What is the policy of the PRP?" or "What is the flag of the Party?" or "What is its relationship to the Front?" Since no directive on these matters has yet been issued, we are not qualified to answer such questions.

6. *Needs of the Revolution* also said the face-to-face meeting should

discuss the personal problems of members and convince members they can rely on the group for help.... For instance, provide economic help for the member who is ill or hard up; or, if a member has been arrested, organize a struggle to secure his release.... Discussions should also deal with the defense of the members' daily interests in class-consciousness terms.... Indulge in criticism and self-criticism to improve members' work.... Reward outstanding members and discipline those who neglect their duties.... Raise funds and recruit new members.

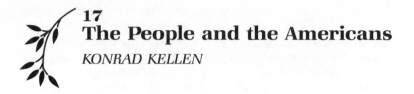

17
The People and the Americans
KONRAD KELLEN

THE FISH AND ITS WATER RESERVES

Even though Mao's famous quotation about the fish and the water may no longer fully apply to the situation in Vietnam,* his comparison continues to reflect the vital needs of the "fish": For the VC, their relationship with the people in the countryside is of great importance, both physically and psychologically. To some extent, their food, shelter, security, intelligence, mobility, and sense of mission depend on that relationship.

In the early days of the insurgency, the villagers were apparently much attracted to the VC. "When they first came to the village," reports a hamlet guerrilla who defected in mid-1966, "they made propaganda. They said beautiful things. They told the villagers of the liberation of the South and the unification of the country. What they told us appealed to us. Later," said the guerrilla, "some villagers became 'distrustful' of the VC, when 'nothing the VC had promised actually materialized.'" Still, according to the respondent, "the villagers mostly [continued to] like the Front cadres because the latter knew how to appeal to the people's emotions. They talked about beautiful things, and what they said was so pleasant to hear." This deposition, it should be noted, was made at a time when people in the hamlets might have had ample opportunity to become sufficiently disillusioned no longer to "like the Front cadres." Yet, at least according to this source, they continued to do so, which may indicate, among other things, that even a certain amount of "distrust" or disappointment does not automatically produce dislike or actual hostility.

A captured Main Force lieutenant, a regroupee from the North, put his claim to the people's devotion in sterner terms: "We are the people's sons. We and the people are one. We and the people are like body and

---

* Mao speaks of guerrillas existing in the enemy's rear who "cannot alienate the people as long as they are disciplined." (*On Guerrilla Warfare*, translated by S. Griffith, New York, 1956). Mao did not foresee—at least not in this passage—that in a protracted war guerrilla forces may be forced, whether they are disciplined or not, to resort to measures such as heavy taxation, forced draft and so on that strain their relationship with the people.

shadow. Therefore we get cover and protection from the people. They do not drive us away when we come to them. Instead, they give us food and shelter. Our relationship with the people is very close, now as in the Resistance days."

To attain and maintain satisfactory working relations with the village population, the VC not only resort to propaganda, but exhort their men to treat the people well. An NVA corporal, when asked what he had been told his behavior toward the people must be, couched his reply in Mao's dictum: "Towards the people: no stealing, not even a needle or a piece of thread." As a result, according to some of the interviews, harmony reigns between the VC and the people, despite the pressures the war is exerting on both.* To the question as to whether the villagers were happy to "have you camp in their homes," one captive, a corporal, replied: "The people in Nhan Thinh [Binh Dinh Province] were very happy to have us stay in their homes; some even lent us their cooking implements, others cooked for us. The people liked the soldiers very much and treated them like their relatives." Or another prisoner, a platoon leader: "In my area of operations [the Highlands] the villagers were friendly toward us. We were given food. From time to time, the villagers gave us money, too." And a Local Force private had this to say: "My company never had to buy rice. All the rice we ate was the people's contribution to the Front.... Some people refused us salt, but they were very few."

One guerrilla speaks of a different experience: "Once we were short of rice when our supplies were delayed, and so we went to several villagers to ask for a few cans of rice, but each of them refused." However, perhaps significantly, the soldier had no hard feelings: "I think the villagers were right. They were poor themselves. How could we expect to receive help from them?" The answer seems to indicate that the VC—if they so elect—can be as forbearing with the villagers as the villagers can be with them, a forbearance likely to bring flexibility into the relationship.

A guerrilla platoon leader made this estimate: "About one-third of the people liked us because they were VC sympathizers. The rest of the people didn't." In terms of percentages, a third may not be very much. But, considering the fact that in revolutionary situations the activists, though

---

* It is this analyst's impression that rejection of VC troops by villagers, where it occurs, is of a different nature from rejection of GVN soldiers. Negative villagers' feeling to the VC seems to be the result of actual damage incurred by bombings in response to VC presence, taxation, draft, and, occasionally, disappointment with a lack of VC victory, whereas negative villager feeling toward the GVN seems to be a more basic hostility resulting from GVN aims and behavior.... In fact, it is one of [our] tentative findings...that negative feelings toward the VC, where they occur, differ substantially from those toward the GVN. Villagers apparently reject the VC "in sorrow rather than in anger," but reject the GVN, where they reject it, "in anger rather than in sorrow." It is clear that, should this hypothesis stand up to further analysis, it would have some bearing on any struggle "for the hearts and minds" of the villagers.

generally in the minority, are the ones that count, even this figure—if accurate—would be quite impressive. As to "the rest" the VC continued the struggle for their "hearts and minds," VC-style: "The people had to put up with us. They were told to help the Revolution. They had no choice. If they had shown dissatisfaction, they would have been sent to reeducation sessions. They had to please us in order to avoid trouble." One repondent stated that the villagers supported the VC not just with food and shelter, but also with care of the disabled: "The sick and severely wounded were entrusted to the care of the villagers' families. The amputees, too, were sent to the various villagers where families belonging to various Front organizations took care of them."

Were the villagers not worried about the VC presence? According to a captured platoon leader, "The villagers seemed to be afraid that our presence might cause the village to be bombarded by GVN artillery or aircraft, but they never asked us to leave." The same topic received the following treatment in a captured VC document: "People's attitudes: no longer afraid of troops in the area. The people also stopped reporting our arrival to the enemy. Instead, when our troops come to the village, the people buy rice for them, cook for them and protect them." One captured fighter, when asked how the villagers had reacted to his unit being stationed in their village, presented this idyllic picture: "The people were very happy about it, because life in the village became much gayer. At night we gathered all the children and sang. It was fun and the villagers liked it a lot." But were they not scared their village might be bombed? "A number of villagers were afraid of this, but these people were in the minority. Most villagers said the Americans bombed anywhere and any way, and didn't bomb troops only. So, they said, if the Americans wanted to bomb the village they would do so whether the troops were there or not."

Still, the soldiers's unit eventually moved into the forest. Why did they move? "Because we would have more security living in the forest than in the village. If we were detected and bombed, the people would be caught in the bombing." This response suggests that the VC were in some instances not merely concerned with their own security, but also with the lives of the villagers. Whether this was due to their chivalrous concern, or whether the statement was merely propagandistic embroidery around a military necessity, the cadre reported it as part of the VC's motivation to take the additional hardships of jungle life upon themselves in order to save the population unnecessary exposure to bombs. The people might well have been grateful for such consideration.

Some villagers, in turn, apparently responded on occasion in ways that would reflect true sympathy and encouragement for the VC: "I myself have seen dead revolutionaries receive honors from the people. I participated in the attack on Tanh Binh Thay Post, near My Tho. It wasn't a successful attack, and four bodies of my comrades were left behind. The local people around there took up a collection, bought four nice coffins and then asked the authorities in the post for permission to let them bury the four bodies. I saw the four graves side by side in the cemetery. This was done by people who were not related to the dead fighters. The people mourned their deaths." The respondent in this case is an assistant company commander.

In a rallier's account of a dramatic moment of high excitement, the villagers seemed to have actively and spontaneously sided with the VC: "At Son Chau I witnessed a would-be deserter get caught...he was one of four soldiers coming into the village. Suddenly he began running toward the GVN military post at Hui Tron....The three other soldiers opened fire, and the people started running after the man with machetes and sticks. they caught up with him, and he had to surrender....Another soldier, a captured fighter, reports a general reaction—shared by himself—that attests to the hold of VC propaganda on villagers in certain instances of stress and confusion: "Once every two months the ARVN came [to a village formerly under GVN control] and all the village youth would run away."— "Why were the villagers so afraid of the GVN?"—"I don't understand why, but after listening to VC propaganda I got frightened too. I had lived happily under the GVN; I had been able to go to school there, and never heard my mother complain about high taxes there. Yet, the VC had a way of scaring the wits out of us."

Few, if any, of the villagers are reported in the interviews as having behaved in an actively hostile fashion to the VC soldiers, let alone voiced hostility to the VC cause. This finding concerning the villagers' attitudes and actions is thrown into clearer relief if viewed in the light of the striking absence, in the interviews, of evidence that the villagers liked the GVN or favored their victory, or actually helped them. While some allegiance for the GVN in GVN areas is reported by some respondents, none report hidden sympathies for the GVN in VC-controlled hamlets. Thus, as suggested by the foregoing, what began as a romance between the villagers and the VC may have lost some of its luster; but there is some evidence that instead of evanescing, the romance has rather turned into a workable marriage of convenience, and there is nothing to indicate that the two hard-pressed partners are considering an early divorce. The analogy, of course, limps, as the VC would not seek a divorce from the people in any event. But—from the interviews examined here—the people do not give any evidence of seeking it either, least of all because of blandishment from the Saigon suitor. This is of crucial importance for the VC who, in the words of one prisoner, "couldn't exist for a month without the people's help." Thus, continued and apparently often voluntary support by the villagers emerges as one of the elements of support which the VC need to maintain cohesion and give battle.

THE EVIL AMERICANS

If strong hostility to the enemy and all he stands for is one token of an army's cohesion and resolve, the VC leadership can be pleased with the attitudes prevailing in its forces on this score. Even though a captive or rallier who is careful and pragmatic—and many Vietnamese apparently are—might think twice before telling his interrogator that he hated Americans, the underlying materials collected during 1966–1967 contain so many examples of strong VC hostility to Americans on so many different grounds that it is hard to select the most telling examples.

Some respondents, of course, attribute imperialist designs to the Americans. One captured Main Force corporal, when asked what his cadres had said about the Americans, reported: "The cadres explained that the Americans do not think the GVN capable of defeating the Front.... The Americans, they said, had come to help the GVN, but in reality they had come to take over South Vietnam. The cadres also said that...after having taken over the South, the Americans would take over North Vietnam, and then attack Red China." Did the men in his unit believe what they were told? "Yes, everyone of us did." The corporal added: "Thus to liberate the South would also serve the purpose of defending the North." It must be conceded to the VC that this is a rather clever—and in this instance apparently effective—line to take with an NVA soldier (as this man was); should the NVA soldiers become weary of "liberating the South," they are to remember that they are not fighting in the South for altruistic reasons only, but to protect their homeland which the Americans would otherwise take.*

The same corporal was even willing to give American soldiers the benefit of the doubt: "If asked, any American G.I. would say in all sincerity that he believes the Americans have indeed come to help the GVN." But the respondent said he knew better: "I personally think this war has cost the United States a lot, and if the United States should win, South Vietnam would have nothing to pay them back. When that time comes, whether anybody wants it or not, the United States will have to rule over South Vietnam. The Americans are good people, but they will be forced to do this to compensate themselves for what they have put into Vietnam. In short, South Vietnam would take over sooner or later."

The same doctrinal view, to the effect that there is a split between the Americans and their leaders, recurred in this sergeant's statement: "The cadre said that only the American imperialists were bad men, and that the American people were very nice. Some Americans told their sons not to go to Vietnam to shoot at the Vietnamese people. They said some elements in the United States had staged antiwar demonstrations." This interviewee added a note which appears frequently also in other interviews: "The cadres said the war could only end if the Americans withdrew...." On the

---

* Of course, NVA soldiers tend to insist on the "one country" view with regard to South and North Vietnam, so that by definition they cannot consider themselves aggressors while fighting in the South. Thus, their minds may be regarded as free of the corroding thought that their mission is not legitimate.

subject of imperialist intent, a captured Main Force private presented this rather original version: "The cadres said the American imperialists were kind to the GVN now...so that when the South was pacified, they could start exploiting the people in the South just as in the old times when the emperors forced the people to dive for pearls, or hunt for elephant tusks in the forests...." The respondent gave no indication whether he believed this.

In most instances the response to the Americans is less abstract. One Labor Youth Group member made this entry in his diary: "...in my first engagement I recieved two wounds on my body that left, I think, permanent marks. Every time I looked at them, my hatred against the imperialists and capitalists, particularly the Americans, welled up." Almost equally personal and direct is an account by a captured corporal: "The cadre said to us "...as you can see, the Americans never let our people live in peace. They are bombing the North.... Peace loving people, children and students are killed in the North. Market places are attacked. What do you think, comrades? Should we let them do all that?" And the corporal who reported this speech by his cadre, added in conclusion: "Frankly, we hated the Americans."

A rallier presented a racial version, which he seemed to have accepted: "I was told the Americans hired the GVN to wage war on their behalf. This would kill many Vietnamese young people and leave the Americans free to take all the Vietnamese girls. I was told it was our duty to help the Front save our race." A captured regroupee lieutenant, when asked what he had been told about the American forces while in the Front, simply stated: "I heard that the Americans had come to kill the Vietnamese people"—an explanation he apparently believed. Similarly negative was this reported response of the villagers: "They said that [because of the spraying] they could not live with the invaders." When asked what the villagers would have meant by the "invaders," the respondent (a captured fighter) replied: "By the invaders they meant the Americans." A hamlet guerrilla reported the negative attitude of the population in the following interchange: "Did the people in your village want the Americans to leave the South?"—"Will any harm come to me if I tell you the truth?"—"No."—"Well, I can tell you this: the majority of the people in the village would prefer the Americans to leave the South."

A more drastic response by villagers to the Americans was reported by this assistant company commander in the Local Forces, who added that he shared that response: "They [the people] hated the Americans. This is the truth. Take me, for example. I consider the Americans my enemy. The people blamed the Americans for the attacks [on the villages] ...The Vietnamese couldn't have done that. People of the same race, the same country, wouldn't kill each other. Only the Americans would kill so senselessly..." The speaker, a Party member in addition to his rank in the Local Forces, was here expressing a view contrary to demonstrable reality:

after all, Vietnamese have found it quite easy in this war to kill each other. But he sounds convinced and, to his men, probably quite convincing.

Some respondents give evasive answers when asked, "What do you think about the Americans?": "I only see that the people are suffering hardships. Now, I only want to know what can be done to make the Americans go back to their country so that both (Vietnamese) governments can come to an agreement to relieve the people's suffering." Others express perplexity as to the American presence and purpose; such as this fighter, a captive: "Certainly, to come here like this, they (the Americans) must want something, but what it is I cannot understand." Or: "From the newspapers I know that America is a rich country. It helps the GVN fight the Communist government. I don't know what America wants in Vietnam." A more definite view of the American presence was expressed by a Local Force platoon leader: "It is my opinion that if the Americans hadn't come to South Vietnam, the differences between North and South Vietnam could have been settled by different and more peaceful means." And the same captive, also a Party member and guerrilla instructor, added: "The Nationalist government claims that the North wanted to take over the South, and that it therefore needed assistance from the Americans. This was the cause of all the fighting."

Some men—in this case a fighter—have no opinions of their own about the American presence: "I have no particular thoughts about the Americans. We were told the Americans were aggressors, and we just took them as such." A captured senior lieutenant, on the other hand, regarded Americans as inherently evil: "Why do you think the Americans are bombing North Vietnam?"—"You should know that better than I do."—"I want your opinion."—"The Americans are a warlike people. They bomb North Vietnam because they like to."

But, perhaps surprisingly, some VC respondents who showed strong hostility to the Americans and deplored their presence in Vietnam—aside from seeing in that presence the "cause for all the fighting" and *the* obstacle to peace—did not seem to consider the American presence a reason to expect a quick defeat for their cause. As one private put it: "You see, when you look at the facts, and when you see that today American troops in Vietnam exceed 300,000, and that more and more Americans directly participate in the war, how can peace come, how can anyone hope for the end of the war to come?" In other words, this respondent did not conclude that such a large American force could terminate the war quickly in its favor. Similarly, a corporal, when asked whether the influx of American troops had had any effect on his men's morale replied: "Yes. They thought it would be harder for them to end the war and liberate the South, because the more ARVN soldiers they killed, the more Americans would arrive to take their place." Harder—not hopeless. Another corporal, on the same subject: "In my view the war will last longer because we now have to fight the Americans, too. As to the effects of the American presence on the outcome of the war, I don't know."

Hand in hand with the conviction, held by some VC soldiers, that American assistance to the GVN will not lead to a VC defeat (although, on the whole they do not hold positive expectations of victory either... is the feeling encountered in some interviews that with some effort, the Americans can be coped with on the field of battle. At least on NVA squad leader gave evidence that such efforts to put Americans in their place had worked, as shown by this cool appraisal: "I have had contact with American soldiers. Generally speaking, they have their strong points: They are very brave and their marksmanship is good. Their weak points are, they are too much used to modern battlefields, and to apply the same tactics to this battlefield is not advisable. Take this example: When they move toward a certain position, they all move forward at once. Meanwhile, the other side uses guerrilla tactics—a few fighters hide here, fire a few rounds, and run to another place. When the Americans move in where the shots have come from, they find nothing. Meanwhile the same few fighters fire a few more shots from their new hideouts. These shots cause the Americans casualties, dead or wounded." The man sounds rather confident.

As to American aims, do individual VC captives or ralliers ever say anything positive, or do they ever report anything positive about such aims being said by their comrades?* Not according to the available data. Thus, if being "soft on Americans" could be regarded as a factor gnawing away at cohesion, that factor seems absent. True, some VC prisoners and ralliers occasionally make positive statements about American aims and behavior, but they invariably add that they came to hold such positive views only after capture or surrender, and not while they still served in the VC. There is, then, much reason to assume that the VC machine derives considerable strength and cohesion from a genuinely felt rather than merely propagandistically spread or superficially accepted hostility to Americans. This may be regarded as reinforced by their vague, yet presumably quite sustaining, feelings that the Americans can be coped with in one way or another.

---

* As, for example, many *Wehrmacht* soldiers did among themselves prior to capture in World War II.

18

The National Liberation Front and the Land

TOM MANGOLD AND JOHN PENYCATE

He heard the tracks of the armored personnel carriers long before the malignant clouds of dust came into view. Nam Thuan lay very still, trying to count the number, but in his eyes and ears was only the fusion of squeaky steel belts and the approaching halo of dirt as the American armor moved busily out of the early morning sun and straight toward him.

As Communist party secretary of Phu My Hung village with its six small hamlets, Nam Thuan was automatically political commissar of the village defense force, a small unit already much depleted by action and promotions to the regional fighting forces. His small platoon that morning comprised a good deputy commander and a couple of village farm boys. His orders had been simple enough: He was to delay any American thrust on Phu My Hung by luring the enemy into engagement. He would destroy them if possible; if not, his diversionary battle would allow ample time for the village to be evacuated and the arms and guerrillas to be hidden.

It was August 1968; the war against the Americans was three years old. The great Tet offensive seemed to have taken many lives, yet South Vietnam had still not been reunited with the North. If anything, Thuan thought, the Americans seemed more confident and more powerful than ever. But at least they were predictable—it was a necessary consolation as the small armored column rattled nearer; the Americans always came when expected, came noisily, and came in strength.

He counted thirteen M-113 carriers. It was a larger force than he had expected. Thuan needed to move quickly if he was to draw the column toward him and toward the tunnels. To fight with he had just two remote-controlled mines which he would detonate, and a boxful of captured American M-26 grenades. In the confusion, he would retreat and escape down the tunnel, but not so quickly that the Americans would not see him.

Things went wrong from the beginning. He detonated the first DH-10 mine prematurely and it exploded harmlessly just ahead of the lead

American APC. The second mine failed to go off. The column was still too far away for Thuan to hurl the grenades. He stood up, deliberately breaking cover, and began to run awkwardly toward the tunnel entrance— its position marked by the open trapdoor—hugging the box of grenades. The lead APC spotted him and changed course to follow. Thuan wondered whether the Americans would now fire the turret-mounted machine gun; even if they did, it was improbable that a bumping gun would hit a small running target. Hands reached out of the open tunnel trapdoor to take the box of grenades. Thuan vaulted into a shaft and closed the door above his head. Blinded by the sudden change from sunlight to darkness, Thuan remained still for a few moments, crouching in the three-foot-deep shaft, gathering breath, waiting for images to return to his retinas. At the bottom of the shaft in which he stood and almost at a right angle to it began a sixty-foot communication tunnel. Thuan wriggled easily into its secure embrace. He realized he could no longer hear the noisy tracks of the APCs. Control of the battle had now passed from his hands to those of an American above ground. If the carriers passed overhead it would be impossible to rechallenge them before they reached Phu My Hung. He had been ordered not to allow that to happen.

For a few moments Thuan considered his environment. He had just entered the shaft that connected with the communication tunnel. At the end of the communication tunnel was a second shaft going down another three feet and at the end of that was a second communication tunnel. If he crawled along that, he would eventually reach a similar shaft and tunnel system leading up and out. However, the exit point for *this* system was some 120 feet away from the place where the Americans had seen him. It was crucial to his plan that they never discover the second exit. It was only sparsely camouflaged, but he had his own man hidden there who could tell him with minimum delay what the Americans were doing above ground while Thuan was below.

The tunnel was still cool from the evening air of the night before. Thuan crawled carefully into a small alcove dug some four feet into the first communication tunnel. As he hunched inside, he heard a muffled explosion followed by a blast, and a sudden beam of dust-filled sunlight pierced the shaft. The Americans had hit the tunnel trapdoor, blowing it clean away. It was what he had prayed for. The column was bound to stop while the tunnel system was fully explored and then destroyed by the Americans. As the dust and debris stung his eyes, Thuan squinted through the gloom and picked up his AK-47 automatic rifle, hugged it to his chest, and waited quietly in the alcove.

He waited over an hour. When he heard the first American helicopter he knew there would be no attempt to explode the tunnel without exploration. As the machine clapped and whirred its noisy way to the ground, Thuan assumed that the Americans had flown in their special tunnel soldiers, trained to fight in the honeycomb of underground tunnels and caverns that spread beneath the protective clay of the district of Cu Chi.

Thuan's observer, secreted above ground in the second hidden tunnel exit, had sent a messenger through the tunnels to Thuan in the alcove. The message was wholly predictable. The Americans had indeed brought more men by helicopter. They were small. They were tunnel soldiers.

The first GI did not even approach the open tunnel entrance for another hour. Earlier, Thuan had heard some conversation above his hiding hole, but nothing for about thirty minutes. Whatever happened, only one American could come in at a time. Both the first entrance shaft and the second long communication tunnel were only just wide enough for one thin man. The tunnel soldiers were thin; they fought well, but unlike Nam Thuan and his small village platoon of Communist guerrillas, they had not spent years inside the tunnels of Cu Chi; they had not fought many battles in their dank blackness.

Thuan could not conceive of failure. He had already been awarded one Victory Medal third class and one Victory Medal second class. He was about to earn another. Small even by Vietnamese standards, naturally slender, Thuan had never known peace in his land. His father had fought the French from similar tunnel complexes in Cu Chi when Thuan was still a child. Thuan had been allowed occasional tunnel sorties, playing soldiers with his friends. The enemy had been other village boys, ludicrously made up to look like the French soldiers, with charcoal mustaches and charcoaled arms, in an attempt to ape the perpetual wonder of hirsute Westerners.

As he grew up, it was the Americans who took the place of the French, and their hairy arms and large frames were no joke to the handful of village children who had been selected by the Communist party to receive a full education. He soon hated the Americans. A friend from Hanoi had told him the Americans called the village fighters Viet Cong, to him an insulting and derogatory term. Now, at thirty-three and still unmarried, Thuan was waiting for the call to join the regular soldiers, but the party had deliberately kept him as a village commander of the part-time self-defense force. He had fought a brave war. He was cunning and ruthless and, above all, he was one of the few cadres who knew the geography of all the eight miles of underground tunnels that the villagers had built in the area. Sometimes he was the only man who could guide the soldiers from Hanoi along the tunnels on their secret journeys through Cu Chi; the men from the North marveled at being able to travel safely under the Americans' noses.

A small earth-fall from the exposed tunnel entrance warned Thuan that the first American tunnel soldier was descending. He had purposely ordered that the first shaft be dug just over three feet deep; it meant the American would have to descend feet first and then wriggle awkwardly into the long communication tunnel where Thuan waited, hidden in an alcove. In the past, as a GI's feet had touched the bottom, Thuan had stabbed the soldier in the groin with his bayonet. This time, as the green-and-black jungle boots descended, Thuan leaned out of his alcove and, using the light from the tunnel entrance, shot the soldier twice in the lower body.

Above ground, the Americans were now in trouble. They could not drop grenades down the shaft because their mortally wounded comrade jammed the hole—anyway, he might still be alive. Slumped in the narrow shaft, he prevented other soldiers from making their way down to chase Thuan. He guessed it would take the Americans at least thirty minutes to get the ropes slipped under the dying man's arms and then haul him out. The Americans' concern for their dead and wounded remained a source of bewilderment and relief to the Communist soldiers. Anything that delayed the battle inevitably favored the weaker side and allowed reloading, regrouping and rethinking.

Once the American's body had been removed from the shaft, Thuan anticipated that his comrades would probably drop a grenade or two down the hole, wait for the smoke to clear, then climb into the shaft and crawl quickly into the first communication tunnel, firing ahead with their pistols. They would be smarter this time and they would be angrier. He would not wait where he was.

His next fighting position was the second shaft, some four feet deep, which connected the first communication tunnel with the second lower one. There was a trapdoor at the top of the second shaft, but Thuan had to remove it for his next operation to succeed. He prayed the Americans would not be using gas at this early stage to flush him out. If they did not, and he was very lucky, the Americans would follow him, using flashlights. Thuan hid in the second shaft, its trapdoor off. He crouched low enough to be invisible to the Americans as they groped their way along the communication tunnel toward him. And yes, they were using flashlights. They might as well have been using loudspeakers to announce their intentions.

The tunnel soldiers had not thrown grenades but they had fired their pistols in volleys to clear the tunnel ahead. From his crouching position in the shaft at the end of this tunnel, Thuan could look up and feel sharp splinters of clay falling on his face as the bullets struck the end of the tunnel above the open shaft. The noise of the firing was deafening. Now the tunnel soldiers were slowly advancing. As soon as their flashlights saw an open shaft entrance ahead, they would roll a grenade down it and Thuan would be blown to pieces. The timing was now critical. He waited for a pause in the pistol volleys and then popped his head and shoulders out of the shaft. He saw at least two flashlights, they blinded him. As a foreign voice shouted, he fired the first clip from his AK-47, loaded the second by touch, and fired that, too. The tunnel exploded in a roar of noise, orange light, and screams of the wounded. He ducked back into the shaft, picking up the trapdoor from the bottom and replacing it above his head. He wriggled down the shaft and slipped along the second communication tunnel far enough for safety should the Americans be able to remove the trapdoor and throw grenades down after him. He lay breathless and sweating on the earth.

From his hiding place above ground at the top of the secret shaft, about 120 feet away from the American position, Thuan's observer watched as the Americans slowly brought out their dead and wounded from Thuan's attack. Three helicopters arrived for the victims. Thuan carefully noted all the information the messenger brought him from above ground. It gave him the basic material to make this next plan for below ground. Thuan's deputy was convinced that now, surely, the Americans would dynamite the tunnel. Thuan was not so sure. It was four in the afternoon, and the Americans would want to leave, spend the night in Dong Zu base, next to Cu Chi town, and return by helicopter at first light. They still had not discovered the second secret tunnel entrance; they had lost surprise; they had lost men. They might hope there was a tunnel complex large enough to be worth exploring for documents or Communist military equipment. Thuan still had his box of grenades and a perfect escape route behind him. He gambled on another battle.

That night Thuan developed a mild fever and went to a small sleeping hole inside the tunnel. Just large enough for one man but with the luxury of a specially dug air ventilation hole leading in from the surface three feet above, the hole was also used for the wounded before they could be taken by tunnel on the longer trip to the underground tunnel hospital at Phu My Hung. Indeed, there were still bloodstained bandages in the hole. The guerrillas had been unable to burn them or bury them since the last battle. The incessant heavily armored sweeps mounted by the 25th Division from their huge fortress next to Cu Chi town had kept the Communist defense forces pinned inside their tunnels for weeks on end. Sometimes there had been surprise raids by the tunnel soldiers; sometimes there had been many deaths. As Thuan sweated his way through the night, he assumed the new tunnel soldiers would be more careful and cautious than the last squad. Success would depend on the Americans' not knowing the layout of the system, and anticipating that the Communists had now fled.

This time, he would allow the Americans to crawl forward without any impedance and let them travel much farther than they had gone before. Their journey would take them down the first shaft and along the first communication tunnel, then down the second shaft (scene of the previous day's attack) and along the second, or bottom, communication tunnel. They would then reach a third shaft, one that led *up*. The tunnel soldiers would know what Nam Thuan knew, that this was the most dangerous and critical moment of any tunnel exploration. Thuan would be waiting for them.

He called one of the village boys and ordered him to fill a bag with earth. Then he checked and rechecked his grenades. The American ones were infinitely superior to the homemade ones or even the grenades the Chinese had sent, but tunnels had a way of destroying sensitive mechanisms. In the kind of war that Nam Thuan fought in the tunnels, there were only first chances—never seconds.

The Americans came, as they always seemed to, shortly after eight in the morning. A team crawled with exaggerated care through the tunnel system that had seen such havoc the day before. They moved by inches, looking for tunnel booby traps, but Thuan had dismantled everything— he wanted the soldiers dead, not saved through their own vigilance. He waited until the first dim hint of light announced they were now on their way along the second, the lower, communication tunnel. The leader would find himself facing the shaft at the end of the tunnel. He would shine his flashlight up. He might even have time to see the grenade that would fall to end his life.

In the five seconds before the grenade exploded in the middle of the Americans—Thuan never knew how many there were—he had time to slam the trapdoor shut and heave the heavy bag of earth on top and himself on top of the bag. The explosion just managed to lift the trapdoor with its extra weight. Afterward there was complete silence.

Before American soldiers later destroyed the tunnel with Bangalore torpedoes—chains of explosives linked by detonating cord—Thuan's men had time to retrieve four working pistols, all .38s, and two broken flashlights left by the Americans. His platoon escaped from the secret exit. In fact, the explosions destroyed only some seventy feet of the tunnel complex, and the system was usable again within a few weeks.

Fourteen months later, Nam Thuan was invited to join the regular forces as an officer. He became fully responsible for the defense of the six hamlets of Phu An village. Three years later, in November 1973, the Americans were gone and the war was being fought only by the South Vietnamese army; Thuan was a member of the district party committee when the guerrilla forces of Cu Chi, strengthened by regular troops from North Vietnam, went on the offensive for the first time in five years. They wiped out forty-seven South Vietnamese military posts in one month alone. Two years later, on 28 March 1975, Thuan was with the forces who raised the flag of the Communist National Liberation Front over the town of Cu Chi. He is now a major in the People's Army of Vietnam.

OFFICIAL U.S. MARINE CORPS PHOTO

CHAPTER 6

The Battlefield

Most Americans who went to Vietnam, to join the battle or report on it, described it as a lushly beautiful land in which it was impossible to fight a civilized war. The heat was incredible. Soldiers who slogged through rice paddies were almost never dry or clean, and suffered a variety of ailments, from trench foot to dysentery to fevers that would not break. They were bitten by insects and snakes and sucked by leeches. The human enemy, often unseen for days, could turn up suddenly, firing from a village only recently "pacified" by the Americans. Women and children frequently helped the Viet Cong, or were the Viet Cong. Trails were booby-trapped with horrific devices, the thought of which jangled the nerves of the toughest GI.

The most powerful American writing about the Vietnam War was done by those who experienced or witnessed it firsthand. Michael Herr's piece, from his book *Dispatches*, is a kinetic soliloquy that seems to have been produced by someone who has been awake too long. Philip Caputo was a gung-ho Marine from Chicago who came enthusiastically to Vietnam with the first Marine units in March 1965. By the time he led his patrol down Purple Heart Trail, Caputo had changed his thinking, as the excerpt here indicates. Tim O'Brien also fought in the war. This passage is from his novel *Going After Cacciato*, in which the title character decides to run away from the war and head for Paris. The final reading is the story of First Lieutenant Archie "Joe" Biggers, as told by himself to Wallace Terry. Biggers was a black Marine platoon leader from Texas. His style here is straightforward, but the implications are at least as harrowing as those of the previous readings.

19
At the Edge of Sanity
MICHAEL HERR

There were times during the night when all the jungle sounds would stop at once. There was no dwindling down or fading away, it was all gone in a single instant as though some signal had been transmitted out to the life: bats, birds, snakes, monkeys, insects, picking up on a frequency that a thousand years in the jungle might condition you to receive, but leaving you as it was to wonder what you weren't hearing now, straining for any sound, one piece of information. I had heard it before in other jungles, the Amazon and the Philippines, but those jungles were "secure," there wasn't much chance that hundreds of Viet Cong were coming and going, moving and waiting, living out there just to do you harm. The thought of that one could turn any sudden silence into a space that you'd fill with everything you thought was quiet in you, it could even put you on the approach to clairaudience. You thought you heard impossible things: damp roots breathing, fruit sweating, fervid bug action, the heartbeat of tiny animals.

You could sustain that sensitivity for a long time, either until the babbling and chittering and shrieking of the jungle had started up again, or until something familiar brought you out of it, a helicopter flying around above your canopy or the strangely reassuring sound next to you of one going into the chamber. Once we heard a really frightening thing blaring down from a Psyops soundship broadcasting the sound of a baby crying. You wouldn't have wanted to hear that during daylight, let alone at night when the volume and distortion came down through two or three layers of cover and froze us all in place for a moment. And there wasn't much release in the pitched hysteria of the message that followed, hyperVietnamese like an icepick in the ear, something like, "Friendly Baby, GVN Baby, Don't Let This Happen to *Your* Baby, Resist the Viet Cong Today!"

Sometimes you'd get so tired that you'd forget where you were and sleep the way you hadn't slept since you were a child. I know that a lot of people there never got up from that kind of sleep; some called them lucky (Never knew what hit him), some called them fucked (If he'd been on the stick...), but that was worse than academic, everyone's death got talked about, it was a way of constantly touching and turning the odds, and real sleep was at a premium. (I met a ranger-recondo who could go to sleep just like that, say, "Guess I'll get some," close his eyes and be there, day or night, sitting or lying down, sleeping through some things but not others; a loud radio or a 105 firing outside the tent wouldn't wake him, but a rustle in the bushes fifty feet away would, or a stopped generator.) Mostly what you had was on the agitated side of half-sleep, you thought you were sleeping but you were really just waiting. Night sweats, harsh functionings of consciousness, drifting in and out of your head, pinned to a canvas cot somewhere, looking up at a strange ceiling or out through a tent flap at the glimmering night sky of a combat zone. Or dozing and waking under mosquito netting in a mess of slick sweat, gagging for air that wasn't 99 percent moisture, one clean breath to dry-sluice your anxiety and the backwater smell of your own body. But all you got and all there was were misty clots of air that corroded your appetite and burned your eyes and made your cigarettes taste like swollen insects rolled up and smoked alive, crackling and wet. There were spots in the jungle where you had to have a cigarette going all the time, whether you smoked or not, just to keep the mosquitoes from swarming into your mouth. War under water, swamp fever and instant involuntary weight control, malarias that could burn you out and cave you in, put you into twenty-three hours of sleep a day without giving you a minute of rest, leaving you there to listen to the trance music that they said came in with terminal brain funk. ("Take your pills, baby," a medic in Can Tho told me. "Big orange ones every week, little white ones every day, and don't miss a day whatever you do. They got strains over here that could waste a heavyset fella like you in a week.") Sometimes you couldn't live with the terms any longer and headed for air-conditioners in Danang and Saigon. And sometimes the only reason you didn't panic was that you didn't have the energy.

Every day people were dying there because of some small detail that they couldn't be bothered to observe. Imagine being too tired to snap a flak jacket closed, too tired to clean your rifle, too tired to guard a light, too tired to deal with the half-inch margins of safety that moving through the war often demanded, just too tired to give a fuck and then dying behind that exhaustion. There were times when the whole war itself seemed tapped of its vitality: epic enervation, the machine running half-assed and depressed, fueled on the watery residue of last year's war-making energy. Entire divisions would function in a bad dream state, acting out a weird set of moves without any connection to their source. Once I talked for maybe five minutes with a sergeant who had just brought his squad in from a long patrol before I realized that the dopey-dummy film over his eyes and the fly abstraction of his words were coming from deep sleep. He was standing there at the bar of the NCO club with his eyes open and a beer in his hand, responding to some dream conversation far inside his head. It really gave me the creeps—this was the second day of the Tet Offensive, our installation was more or less surrounded, the only secure road out of there was littered with dead Vietnamese, information was scarce and I was pretty touchy and tired myself—and for a second I imagined that I was talking to a dead man. When I told him about it later he just laughed and said, "Shit, that's nothing. I do that all the time."

One night I woke up and heard the sounds of a firefight going on kilometers away, a "skirmish" outside our perimeter, muffled by distance to sound like the noises we made playing guns as children, KSSSHH KSSSHH; we knew it was more authentic than BANG BANG, it enriched the game and this game was the same, only way out of hand at last, too rich for all but a few serious players. The rules now were tight and absolute, no arguing over who missed who and who was really dead; *No fair* was no good, *Why me?* the saddest question in the world.

Well, good luck, the Vietnam verbal tic, even Ocean Eyes, the third-tour Lurp, had remembered to at least say it to me that night before he went on the job. It came out dry and distant, I knew he didn't care one way or the other, maybe I admired his detachment. It was as though people couldn't stop themselves from saying it, even when they actually meant to express the opposite wish, like, "Die, motherfucker." Usually it was only an uninhabited passage of dead language, sometimes it came out five times in a sentence, like punctuation, often it was spoken flat side up to telegraph the belief that there wasn't any way out; tough shit, *sin loi*, smack it, good luck. Sometimes, though, it was said with such feeling and tenderness that it could crack your mask, that much love where there was so much war. Me too, every day, compulsively, good luck: to friends in the press corps going out on operations, to grunts I'd meet at firebases and airstrips, to the wounded, the dead and all the Vietnamese I ever saw getting fucked over by us and each other, less often but most passionately to myself, and though I meant it every time I said it, it was meaningless. It was like telling someone going out in a storm not to get any on him, it was the same as saying, "Gee, I hope you don't get killed or wounded or see anything that drives you insane." You could make all the ritual moves, carry your lucky piece, wear you magic jungle hat, kiss your thumb knuckle smooth as stones under running water, the Inscrutable Immutable was still out there, and you kept on or not at its pitiless discretion. All you could say that wasn't fundamentally lame was something like, "He who bites it this day is safe from the next," and that was exactly what nobody wanted to hear.

After enough time passed and memory receded and settled, the name itself became a prayer, coded like all prayer to go past the extremes of petition and gratitude: Vietnam Vietnam Vietnam, say again, until the word lost all its old loads of pain, pleasure, horror, guilt, nostalgia. Then and there, everyone was just trying to get through it, existential crunch, no atheists in foxholes like you wouldn't believe. Even bitter refracted faith was better than none at all, like the black Marine I'd heard about during heavy shelling at Con Thien who said, "Don't worry, baby, God'll think of something."

Flip religion, it was so far out, you couldn't blame anybody for believing anything. Guys dressed up in Batman fetishes, I saw a whole squad like that, it gave them a kind of dumb esprit. Guys stuck the ace of spades in their helmet bands, they picked relics off an enemy they'd killed, a little transfer of power; they carried around five-pound Bibles from home, crosses, St. Christophers, mezuzahs, locks of hair, girlfriends' underwear, snaps of their families, their wives, their dogs, their cows, their cars, pictures of John Kennedy, Lyndon Johnson, Martin Luther King, Huey Newton, the Pope, Che Guevara, the Beatles, Jimi Hendrix, wiggier than cargo cultists. One man was carrying an oatmeal cookie through his tour, wrapped up in foil and plastic and three pair of socks. He took a lot of shit about it ("When you go to sleep we're gonna eat your fucking cookie"), but his wife had baked it and mailed it to him, he wasn't kidding.

On operations you'd see men clustering around the charmed grunt that many outfits created who would take himself and whoever stayed close enough through a field of safety, at least until he rotated home or got blown away, and then the outfit would hand the charm to someone else. If a bullet creased your head or you'd stepped on a dud mine or a grenade rolled between your feet and just lay there, you were magic enough. If you had any kind of extra-sense capacity, if you could smell VC or their danger the way hunting guides smelled the coming weather, if you had special night vision, or great ears, you were magic too; anything bad that happened to you could leave the men in your outfit pretty depressed. I met a man in the Cav who'd been "fucking the duck" one afternoon, sound asleep in a huge tent with thirty cots inside, all empty but his, when some mortar rounds came in, tore the tent down to canvas slaw and put frags through every single cot but his, he was still high out of his mind from it, speedy, sure and lucky. The Soldier's Prayer came in two versions: Standard, printed on a plastic-coated card by the Defense Department, and Standard Revised, impossible to convey because it got translated outside of language, into chaos—screams, begging, promises, threats, sobs, repetitions of holy names until their throats were cracked and dry, until some men had bitten through their collar points and rifle straps and even their dog-tag chains.

Varieties of religious experience, good news and bad news; a lot of men found their compassion in the war, some found it and couldn't live with it, war-washed shutdown of feeling, like who gives a fuck. People retreated into positions of hard irony, cynicism, despair; some saw the action and declared for it, only heavy killing could make them feel so alive. And some just went insane, followed the black-light arrow around the bend and took possession of the madness that had been waiting there in trust for them for eighteen or twenty-five or fifty years. Every time there was combat you had a license to go maniac, everyone snapped over the line at least once there and nobody noticed, they hardly noticed if you forgot to snap back again.

One afternoon at Khe Sanh a Marine opened the door of a latrine and was killed by a grenade that had been rigged on the door. The Command tried to blame it on a North Vietnamese infiltrator, but the grunts knew what had happened: "Like a gook is really gonna tunnel all the way in here to booby-trap a shithouse, right? Some guy just flipped out is all." And it became another one of those stories that moved across the DMZ, making people laugh and shake their heads and look knowingly at each other, but shocking no one. They'd talk about physical wounds in one way and psychic wounds in another, each man in a squad would tell you how crazy everyone else in the squad was, everyone knew grunts who'd gone crazy in the middle of a firefight, gone crazy on patrol, gone crazy back at camp, gone crazy on R&R, gone crazy during their first month home. Going crazy was built into the tour, the best you could hope for was that it didn't happen around you, the kind of crazy that made men empty clips into strangers or fix grenades on latrine doors. That was *really* crazy; anything less was almost standard, as standard as the vague prolonged stares and involuntary smiles, common as ponchos or 16's or any other piece of war issue. If you wanted someone to know you'd gone insane you really had to sound off like you had a pair, "Scream a lot, and all the time."

Some people just wanted to blow it all to hell, animal, vegetable and mineral. They wanted a Vietnam they could fit into their car ashtrays; the joke went, "What you do is, you load all the Friendlies onto ships and take them out to the South China Sea. Then you bomb the country flat. Then you sink the ships." A lot of people knew that the country could never be won, only destroyed, and they locked into that with breathtaking concentration, no quarter, laying down the seeds of the disease, roundeye fever, until it reached plague proportions, taking one from every family, a family from every hamlet, a hamlet from every province, until a million had died from it and millions more were left uncentered and lost in their flight from it.

Up on the roof of the Rex BOQ in Saigon I walked into a scene more bellicose than a firefight, at least 500 officers nailed to the bar in a hail of chits, shiny irradiant faces talking war, men drinking like they were going to the front, and maybe a few of them really were. The rest were already there, Saigon duty; coming through a year of that without becoming totally blown out indicated as much heart as you'd need to take a machine-gun position with your hands, you sure couldn't take one with your mouth. We'd watched a movie (*Nevada Smith*, Steve McQueen working through a hard-revenge scenario, riding away at the end burned clean but somehow empty and old too, like he'd lost his margin for regeneration through violence); now there was a live act, Tito and His Playgirls, "Up up and awayeeyay in my beaudifoo balloooon," one of those Filipino combos that even the USO wouldn't touch, hollow beat, morbid rock and roll like steamed grease in the muggy air.

Roof of the Rex, ground zero, men who looked like they'd been suckled by wolves, they could die right there and their jaws would work for another half-hour. This is where they asked you, "Are you a Dove or a Hawk?" and "Would you rather fight them here or in Pasadena?" *Maybe we could beat them in Pasadena*, I'd think, but I wouldn't say it, especially not here where they knew that I knew that they really weren't fighting anybody anywhere anyway, it made them pretty touchy. That night I listened while a colonel explained the war in terms of protein. We were a nation of high-protein, meat-eating hunters, while the other guy just ate rice and a few grungy fish heads. We were going to club him to death with our meat; what could you say except, "Colonel, you're insane."? It was like turning up in the middle of some black looneytune where the Duck had all the lines. I only jumped in once, spontaneous as shock, during Tet when I heard a doctor bragging that he'd refused to allow wounded Vietnamese into his ward. "But Jesus Christ," I said, "didn't you take the Hippocratic Oath?" but he was ready for me. "Yeah," he said, "I took it in America." Doomsday celebs, technomaniac projectionists; chemicals, gases, lasers, sonic-electric ballbreakers that were still on the boards; and for back-up, deep in all their hearts, there were always the Nukes, they loved to remind you that we had some, "right here in-country." Once I met a colonel who had a plan to shorten the war by dropping piranha into the paddies of the North. He was talking fish but his dreamy eyes were full of mega-death.

"Come on," the captain said, "we'll take you out to play Cowboys and Indians." We walked out from Song Be in a long line, maybe a hundred men; rifles, heavy automatics, mortars, portable one-shot rocket-launchers, radios, medics; breaking into some kind of sweep formation, five files with small teams of specialists in each file. A gunship flew close hover-cover until we came to some low hills, then two more ships came along and peppered the hills until we'd passed safely through them. It was a beautiful operation. We played all morning until someone on the point got something—a "scout," they thought, and then they didn't know. They couldn't even tell for sure whether he was from a friendly tribe or not, no markings on his arrows because his quiver was empty, like his pockets and his hands. The captain thought about it during the walk back, but when we got to camp he put it in his report, "One VC killed"; good for the unit, he said, not bad for the captain either.

Search and Destroy, more a gestalt than a tactic, brought up alive and steaming from the Command psyche. Not just a walk and a firefight, in action it should have been named the other way around, pick through the pieces and see if you could work together a count, the sponsor wasn't buying any dead civilians. The VC had an ostensibly similar tactic called Find and Kill. Either way, it was us looking for him looking for us looking for him, war on a Cracker Jack box, repeated to diminishing returns.

A lot of people used to say that it got fucked up when they made it as easy for us to shoot as not to shoot. In I and II Corps its was "loose policy" for gunships to fire if the subjects froze down there, in the Delta it was to shoot if they ran or "evaded," either way a heavy dilemma, which would you do? "Air sports," one gunship pilot called it, and went on to describe it with fervor, "Nothing finer, you're up there at two thousand, you're God, just open up the flexies and watch it pee, nail those slime to the paddy wall, nothing finer, double back and get the caribou."

"Back home I used to fill my own cartridges for hunting," a platoon leader told me. "Me and my father and my brothers used to make a hundred a year between us maybe. I swear to God, I never saw anything like this."

Who had? Nothing like it ever when we caught a bunch of them out in the open and close together, we really ripped it then, volatile piss-off, crazed expenditure, Godzilla never drew that kind of fire. We even had a small language for our fire: "discreet burst," "probe," "prime selection," "constructive load," but I never saw it as various, just compulsive eruption, the Mad Minute for an hour. Charles really wrote the book on fire control, putting one round into the heart of things where fifty of ours might go and still not hit anything. Sometimes we put out so much fire you couldn't tell whether any of it was coming back or not. When it was, it filled your ears and your head until you thought you were hearing it with your stomach. An English correspondent I knew made a cassette of one of the heavy ones, he said he used it to seduce American girls.

Sometimes you felt too thin and didn't want to get into anything at all and it would land on you like your next-to-last breath. Sometimes your chops for action and your terror would reach a different balance and you'd go looking for it everywhere, and nothing would happen, except a fire ant would fly up your nose or you'd grow a crotch rot or you'd lie awake all night waiting for morning so you could get up and wait on your feet. Whichever way it went, you were covering the war, your choice of story told it all and in Vietnam an infatuation like that with violence wouldn't go unrequited for very long, it would come and put its wild mouth all over you.

"Quakin' and Shakin'," they called it, great balls of fire, Contact. Then it was you and the ground: kiss it, eat it, fuck it, plow it with your whole body, get as close to it as you can without being in it yet or of it, guess who's flying around about an inch above your head? Pucker and submit, it's the ground. Under Fire would take you out of your head and your body too, the space you'd seen a second ago between subject and object wasn't there anymore, it banged shut in a fast wash of adrenaline. Amazing, unbelievable, guys who'd played a lot of hard sports said they'd never felt anything like it, the sudden drop and rocket rush of the hit, the reserves of adrenaline you could make available to yourself, pumping it up and putting it out until you were lost floating in it, not afraid, almost open to clear orgasmic death-by-drowning in it, actually relaxed. Unless of course you'd shit your pants or were screaming or praying or giving anything at all to the hundred-channel panic that blew word salad all around you and sometimes clean through you. Maybe you couldn't love the war and hate it inside the same instant, but sometimes those feelings alternated so rapidly that they spun together in a strobic wheel rolling all the way up until you were literally High On War, like it said on all the helmet covers. Coming off a jag like that could really make a mess out of you.

In early December I came back from my first operation with the Marines. I'd lain scrunched up for hours in a flimsy bunker that was falling apart even faster than I was, listening to it going on, the moaning and whining and the dull repetitions of whump whump whump and dit dit dit, listening to a boy who'd somehow broken his thumb sobbing gagging, thinking, "Oh my *God*, this fucking thing is on a *loop!*" until the heavy shooting stopped but not the thing: at the lz waiting for choppers to Phu Bai one last shell came in, landing in the middle of a pile of full body bags, making a mess that no one wanted to clean up, "a real shit detail." It was after midnight when I finally got back to Saigon, riding in from Tan Son Nhut in an open jeep with some sniper-obsessed MP's, and there was a small package of mail waiting for me at the hotel. I put my fatigues out in the hall room and closed the door on them, I may have even locked it. I had the I Corps DT's , livers, spleens, brains, a blue-black swollen thumb moved around and flashed to me, they were playing over the walls of the shower where I spent a half-hour, they were on the bedsheets, but I wasn't afraid of them, I was laughing at them, what could they do to me? I filled a water glass with Armagnac and rolled a joint, and then I started to read my mail. In one of the letters there was news that a friend of mine had killed himself in New York. When I turned off the lights and got into bed I lay there trying to remember what he had looked like. He had done it with pills, but no matter what I tried to imagine, all I saw was blood and bone fragment, not my dead friend. After a while I broke through for a second and saw him, but by that time all I could do with it was file him in with the rest and go to sleep.

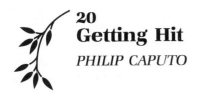

20
Getting Hit

PHILIP CAPUTO

The platoon reached Hill 92 in the midafternoon. The men were worn out by that time, their shoulders aching from the weight of rifles, packs, and flak jackets. They had been under one kind of fire or another for twenty-four hours and were dazed with fatigue. Rigging shelters against the drumming rain, they lay down to rest. Some did not bother to build shelters. They had ceased to care even for themselves. I walked around, checking their feet. A few had serious cases of immersion foot, their shriveled skin covered with red pustules and blisters. It amazed me that they could walk at all. We ate lunch. Our rations were the same as the Viet Cong's: cooked rice rolled into a ball and stuffed with raisins. The rice-balls were easier to carry than the heavy C-ration tins and alleviated the diarrhea from which we all suffered. Eating the rice on that desolate hill, it occurred to me that we were becoming more and more like our enemy. We ate what they ate. We could now move through the jungle as stealthily as they. We endured common miseries. In fact, we had more in common with the Viet Cong than we did with that army of clerks and staff officers in the rear.

I was putting on dry socks when Captain Neal called on the radio. A Christmas cease-fire had gone into effect. The operation had been secured. My platoon was to return to friendly lines as quickly as possible. Why not lift us out with helicopters? I asked. No, Neal said, that was out of the question. I passed the word and the troops cheered. "Hey-hey. We're gonna get some slack. Merry fuckin' Christmas."

"No, no. I want to stay out here," said PFC Baum. "I just love it out here in the mud and the rain and the shit."

Shouldering our packs, we tramped down to Purple Heart Trail, the quickest route back. The trail forked near Dieu Phoung, a hamlet several hundred yards west of Charley Hill. The right fork led along the river; the left over the foothills toward the outpost. We took the latter because it was shorter and less likely to be mined or ambushed.

Outside the hamlet was a flooded rice paddy with a steep embankment at its far end. A barbed wire fence, anchored at one end to a dead tree, ran along the length of the embankment. The trail climbed through a hole in the fence near the tree. The lead squad, Sergeant Pryor's, Jones, and I crossed the rice paddy. The water was cold and chestdeep in places, and the rain dimpled the water in a way that reminded me of an evening rise on a trout stream. That was how the Ontonogan River looked in the evenings, in the place where it made a slow, wide bend around a wooded bluff upstream from the rocky, white-water narrows at the Burned Dam. There, the river had been deep and smooth where it curved, and the big trout rising made rings in the copper-colored water. Bill, my fishing buddy, and I used to cast for browns in the deep pool at sunset. We never caught many, but we had a fine time, casting and talking about the things we were going to do when we left school, about all that awaited us in the great outside world, which seemed so full of promise. We were boys and thought everything was possible. The memory sent a momentary pang through me: not so much a feeling of homesickness as one of separation—a distancing from the hopeful boy I had been, a longing to be like that again.

Pryor's squad climbed the embankment, the men slipping on the muddy trail, slipping and falling into each other until they were bunched in a knot. The rest of the platoon waded through the rice paddy behind us, holding their rifles in the air. A snake made a series of S's in the black water as it slithered between two men in the column. On dry ground again, Pryor's marines picked up their interval and hiked up the ridgeline that rose above the embankment. The Cordillera loomed in the distance, high and indomitable. The last two squads started to struggle up the bank, bunching up as one man after another slipped and slid into the man behind him.

Standing by the dead tree, I helped pull a few marines up the trail. "Pass it back not to bunch up," I said. To my left, a stream whispered through a brushy ravine. "Don't bunch up," a marine said. "Pass it back." On the other side of the paddy, the rear of the column was filing past a hut at the edge of the hamlet. Smoke started to roll from the hut and a woman ran out yelling.

"Bittner," I called to the platoon sergeant, who was bringing up the rear; "what the hell's going on?"

"Can't hear you, sir."

"The hut. Who the hell set fire to the hut?"

"Somebody said you passed the word to burn the hut, sir."

"What?"

"The word came back to burn the hut, sir."

"Jesus Christ. I said, 'Don't bunch up.' DON'T BUNCH UP. Put that fire out."

"Yes, sir."

I stood by the leafless tree, watching the marines douse the fire with helmets full of water. Fortunately, the thatch had been wet to begin with and did not burn quickly. Turning to walk back toward the point squad, I saw Allen stumbling on the trail.

"Allen, how're you doing?" I asked, extending my arm. Taking hold of it, he hauled himself over the lip of the embankment.

"Hackin' it, lieutenant. I'm hackin' it okay," Allen said, walking beside me. Ahead, I could see Pryor's squad trudging up the ridge and the point man briefly silhouetted on the ridgeline before he went down the other side. "But this here cease-fire's come along at the right time," Allen was saying. "Could use a little slack. This here cease-fire's the first slack..."

There was a roaring and a hot, hard slap of wind and a needle prick-ing my thigh and something clubbed me in the small of the back. I fell face down into the mud, my ears ringing. Lying on my belly, I heard an automatic carbine rattle for a few seconds, then someone calling "Corps-man! Corpsman!" Because of the ringing in my ears, the shots and voice sounded far away. "Corpsman! Corpsman!" Someone else yelled "Incom-ing!" I got to my hands and knees, wondering what fool had yelled "in-coming." That had not been a shell, but a mine, a big mine. Who the hell had yelled "incoming"? You did, you idiot. It was your voice. Why did you say that? The fence. The barbed wire fence was the last thing you saw as you fell. You had fallen toward the fence, and it was like that time when you were six and walking in the woods with your friend Stanley. Stanley was nine, and he had been frightening you with stories about bears in the woods. Then you had heard a roaring, growling sound in the distance and, thinking it was a bear, you had run to the highway, tried to climb the barbed wire fence at the roadside, and caught your trousers on the barbs. Hanging there, you had cried, "Stanley, it's a bear! A bear, Stanley!" And Stan had come up laughing because the growling noise you had heard was a roadgrader coming up the highway. It had not been a bear, but a machine. And this roaring had not been a shell, but a mine.

I stood, trying to clear my head. I was a little wobbly, but unmarked except for a sliver of shrapnel stuck in one of my trouser legs. I pulled it out. It was still hot, but it had not even broken my skin. Allen was next to me on all fours, mumbling. "What happened? I don't believe it. My God, oh my God." Some thirty to forty feet behind us, there was a patch of scorched, cratered earth, a drifting pall of smoke, and the dead tree, its trunk charred and cracked. Sergeant Wehr was lying near the crater. He rose to his feet, then fell when one leg collapsed beneath him. Wehr stood up again and the leg crumpled again, and, squatting on his good leg, holding the wounded one straight out in front of him, he spun around like a man doing a cossack dance, then fell onto his back, waving one arm back and forth across his chest. "Boom. Boom," he said, the arm flopping back and forth. "Mah fust patrol, an' boom."

Allen got to his feet, his eyes glassy and a dazed grin on his face. He staggered toward me. "What happened, sir?" he asked, toppling against me and sliding down my chest, his hands clutching at my shirt. Before I could get a grip on him, he fell again to all fours, then collapsed onto his stomach. "My God what happened?" he said. "I don't believe it. My head hurts." Then I saw the blood oozing from the wound in the back of his head and neck. "Dear God my head hurts. Oh it hurts. I don't believe it."

Still slightly stunned, I had only a vague idea of what had happened. A mine, yes. It must have been an ambushdetonated mine. All of Pryor's squad had passed by that spot before the mine exploded. I had been standing on that very spot, near the tree, not ten seconds before the blast. If it had been a booby trap or a pressure mine, it would have gone off then. And then the carbine fire. Yes, an electrically detonated mine set off from ambush, a routine occurrence for the rear-echelon boys who looked at the "overall picture," a personal cataclysm for those who experienced it.

Kneeling beside Allen, I reached behind for my first-aid kit and went numb when I felt the big, shredded hole in the back of my flak jacket. I pulled out a couple of pieces of shrapnel. They were cylindrical and about the size of double-O buckshot. A Claymore, probably homemade, judging from the black smoke. They had used black powder. The rotten-egg stink of it was in the air. Well, that shrapnel would have done a fine job on my spine if it had not been for the flak jacket. *My spine.* Oh God—if I had remained on that spot another ten seconds, they would have been picking pieces of me out of the trees. Chance. Pure chance. Allen, right beside me, had been wounded in the head. I had not been hurt. Chance. The one true god of modern war is blind chance.

Taking out a compress, I tried to staunch Allen's bleeding. "My God, it hurts," he said. "My head hurts."

"Listen, Allen. You'll be okay. I don't think it broke any bones. You'll be all right." My hands reeked from his blood. "You're going to get plenty of slack now. Lotsa slack in division med. We'll have you evacked in no time."

"My God it hurts. I don't believe it. It hurts."

"I know, Bill. It hurts. It's good that you can feel it," I said, remembering the sharp sting of that tiny sliver in my thigh. And it had done nothing more than raise a bump the size of a beesting. Oh yes, I'll bet your wounds hurt, Lance Corporal Bill Allen.

My head had cleared, and the ringing in my ears quieted to a faint buzz. I told Pryor and Aiker to form their squads into a perimeter around the paddy field. Casualty parties started to carry the wounded out of the paddy and up to the level stretch of ground between the embankment and the base of the ridgeline. It was a small space, but it would have to do as a landing zone.

A rifleman and I picked up Sergeant Wehr, each of us taking one of the big man's arms. "Boom. Boom," he said, hobbling with his arms around our necks. "Mah fust patrol, lieutenant, an' boom, ah got hit. Gawd-damn." A corpsman cut Wehr's trouser leg open with a knife and started to dress his wounds. There was a lot of blood. Two marines dragged Sanchez up from the paddy. His face had been so peppered with shrapnel that I hardly recognized him. Except for his eyes. The fragments had somehow missed his eyes. He was unconscious and his eyes were half closed; two white slits in a mass of raspberry red. Sanchez looked as if he had been clawed by some invisible beast. The marines fanned him with their hands.

"He keeps going out, sir," said one of the riflemen. "If he don't get evacked pretty quick, we're afraid he'll go out for good."

"Okay, okay, as soon as we get the others up."

"Rodella, sir. Get Rodella up. Think he's got a sucking chest wound."

I slid down the embankment and splashed over to where the corpsman, Doc Kaiser, was working to save Corporal Rodella. There were gauze and compresses all over his chest and abdomen. One dressing, covering the hole the shrapnel had torn in one of his lungs, was soaked in blood. With each breath he took, pink bubbles of blood formed and burst around the hole. He made a wheezing sound. I tried talking to him, but he could not say anything because his windpipe would fill with blood. Rodella, who had been twice wounded before, was now in danger of drowning in his own blood. It was his eyes that troubled me most. They were the hurt, dumb eyes of a child who has been severely beaten and does not know why. It was his eyes and his silence and the foamy blood and the gurgling, wheezing sound in his chest that aroused in me a sorrow so deep and a rage so strong that I could not distinguish the one emotion from the other.

I helped the corpsman carry Rodella to the landing zone. His comrades were around him, but he was alone. We could see the look of separation in his eyes. He was alone in the world of the badly wounded, isolated by a pain none could share with him and by the terror of the darkness that was threatening to envelop him.

Then we got the last one, Corporal Greeley, a machinegunner whose left arm was hanging by a few strands of muscle; all the rest was a scarlet mush. Greeley was conscious and angry. "Fuck it," he said over and over. "Fuck it. Fuck it. Fuck the cease-fire. Ain't no fuckin' cease-fire, but they can't kill me. Ain't no fuckin' booby trap gonna kill me." Carrying him, I felt my own anger, a very cold, very deep anger that had no specific object. It was just an icy, abiding fury; a hatred for everything in existence except those men. Yes, except those men of mine, any one of whom was better than all the men who had sent them to war.

I radioed for a medevac. The usual complications followed. How many wounded were there? Nine; four walking wounded, five needing evacuation. *Nine?* Nine casualties from a single mine? What kind of mine was it? Electrically detonated, black-powder, a homemade Claymore probably. But what happened? Goddamnit, I'll tell you later. Get me a medevac. I've got at least one, maybe two who'll be DOW if we don't get them out of here. How big was the mine? Four to five pounds of explosive, plenty of shrapnel. It was placed on an embankment and the platoon was down in a rice paddy below it. Most of the shrapnel went over their heads. Otherwise, I'd have several KIAs. Okay? Now get me those birds. "Boom. Boom," said Sergeant Wehr. "Mah fust patrol an' boom, ah get hit." Charley Two,

I need the first letter of the last names and the serial numbers of the WIAs needing evac. Now? Yes, now. Rodella and Sanchez had lapsed into unconsciousness. The corpsmen and some marines were fanning them. Doc Kaiser looked at me pleadingly.

"Hang loose, doc," I said. "The birds'll be here, but the assholes in the puzzle-palace have to do their paperwork first. Bittner! Sergeant Bittner, get me the dog tags of the evacs, and hustle."

"Yes, sir," said Bittner, who was one of the walking wounded. A green battle dressing was wrapped around his forehead. One of the walking wounded. We were all walking wounded.

Bittner gave me the dog tags. I tore off the green masking tape that kept the tags from rattling and gave Captain Neal the required information. Then the radio broke down. Jones changed batteries and started giving long test-counts: "Ten-niner-eight-seven..." I heard Neal's voice again. Did I have any serious casualties? For Christ's sake, yes, why do you think I'm asking for a medevac?

"Charley Two," said Neal, "you must have not been supervising your men properly. They must have been awfully bunched up to take nine casualties from one mine."

"Charley Six," I said, my voice cracking with rage. "You get me those birds now. If one of these kids dies because of this petty bullshit I'm going to raise somekinda hell. I want those birds."

There was a long pause. At last the word came: "Birds on the way."

The helicopters swooped in out of the somber sky, landing in the green smoke billowing from the smoke grenade I had thrown to mark the LZ. The crew chiefs pushed stretchers out of the hatches. We laid the casualties on the stretchers and lifted them into the Hueys, the rain falling on us all the time. The aircraft took off, and watching the wounded soaring out of that miserable patch of jungle, we almost envied them.

Just before the platoon resumed its march, someone found a length of electrical detonating cord lying in the grass near the village. The village would have been as likely an ambush site as any: the VC only had to press the detonator and then blend in with the civilians, if indeed there were any true civilians in the village. Or they could have hidden in one of the tunnels under the houses. All right, I thought, tit for tat. No cease-fire for us, none for you, either. I ordered both rocket launcher teams to fire white-phosphorus shells into the hamlet. They fired four altogether. The shells, flashing orange, burst into pure white clouds, the chunks of flaming phosphorus arcing over the trees. About half the village went up in flames. I could hear people yelling, and I saw several figures running through the white smoke. I did not feel a sense of vengeance, any more than I felt remorse or regret. I did not even feel angry. Listening to the shouts and watching the people running out of their burning homes, I did not feel anything at all.

21
"They Did Not Know Good from Evil"
TIM O'BRIEN

"*LUI LAI, LUI LAI!*" Stink would scream, pushing them back. "*Lui lai*, you dummies....Back up, move!" Teasing ribs with his rifle muzzle, he would force them back against a hootch wall or fence. "*Coi Chung!*" he'd holler. Blinking, face white and teeth clicking, he would kick the stragglers, pivot, shove, thumb flicking the rifle's safety catch. "Move! *Lui lai*....Move it, go, go!" Herding them together, he would watch to be sure their hands were kept in the open, empty. Then he would open his dictionary. He would read slowly, retracing the words several times, then finally look up. "*Nam xuong dat,*" he'd say. Separating each word, trying for good diction, he would say it in a loud, level voice. "Everybody...*nam xuong dat.*" The kids would just stare. The women might rock and moan, or begin chattering among themselves like caged squirrels, glancing up at Stink with frazzled eyes. "Now!" he'd shout. "*Nam xuong dat....*Do it!" Sometimes he would fire off a single shot, but this only made the villagers fidget and squirm. Puzzled, some of them would start to giggle. Others would cover their ears and yap with the stiff, short barking sounds of small dogs. It drove Stink wild. "*Nam xuong* the fuck down!" he'd snarl, his thin lips curling in a manner he practiced while shaving. "Lie down! *Man len*, mama-san! Now, goddamn it!" His eyes would bounce from his rifle to the dictionary to the cringing villagers. Behind him, Doc Peret and Oscar Johnson and Buff would be grinning at the show. They'd given the English-Vietnamese dictionary to Stink as a birthday present, and they loved watching him use it, the way he mixed languages in a kind of stew, ignoring pronunciation and grammar, turning angry when words failed to produce results. "*Nam thi xuong dat!*" he'd bellow, sweating now, his tongue sputtering over the impossible middle syllables. "*Man len*, pronto, you sons of bitches! Haul ass!" But the villagers would only shake their heads and cackle and mill uncertainly. This was too much for Stink Harris. Enraged, he'd throw away the dictionary and rattle off a whole magazine of ammunition. The women would moan. Kids would clutch their mothers, dogs would howl, chickens would scramble in their coops. "*Dong* fuckin *lat thit!*" Stink would be screaming, his eyes dusty and slit like a snake's. "*Nam xuong dat!* Do it, you ignorant bastards!" Reloading, he would keep firing and screaming, and

---

the villagers would sprawl in the dust, arms wrapped helplessly around their heads. And when they were all down, Stink would stop firing. He would smile. He would glance at Doc Peret and nod. "See there? They understand me fine. *Nam xuong dat*....Lie down. I'm gettin' the hang of it. You just got to punctuate your sentences."

Not knowing the language, they did not know the people. They did not know what the people loved or respected or feared or hated. They did not recognize hostility unless it was patent, unless it came in a form other than language; the complexities of tone and tongue were beyond them. Dinkese, Stink Harris called it: monkey chatter, bird talk. Not knowing the language, the men did not know whom to trust. Trust was lethal. They did not know false smiles from true smiles, or if in Quang Ngai a smile had the same meaning it had in the States. "Maybe the dinks got things mixed up," Eddie once said, after the time a friendly-looking farmer bowed and smiled and pointed them into a minefield. "Know what I mean? Maybe...well, maybe the gooks cry when they're happy and smile when they're sad. Who the hell knows? Maybe when you smile over here it means you're ready to cut the other guy's throat. I mean, hey...didn't they tell us way back in AIT that this here's a different culture?" Not knowing the people, they did not know friends from enemies. They did not know if it was a popular war, or, if popular, in what sense. They did not know if the people of Quang Ngai viewed the war stoically, as it sometimes seemed, or with grief, as it seemed other times, or with bewilderment or greed or partisan fury. It was impossible to know. They did not know religions or philosophies or theories of justice. More than that, they did not know how emotions worked in Quang Ngai. Twenty years of war had rotted away the ordinary reactions to death and disfigurement. Astonishment, the first response, was never there in the faces of Quang Ngai. Disguised, maybe. But who knew? Who ever knew? Emotions and beliefs and attitudes, motives and aims, hopes—these were unknown to the men in Alpha Company, and Quang Ngai told nothing. "Fuckin beasties," Stink would croak, mimicking the frenzied village speech. "No shit, I seen hamsters with more feelings."

But for Paul Berlin it was always a nagging question: Who were these skinny, blank-eyed people? What did they want? The kids especially— watching them, learning their names and faces, Paul Berlin couldn't help wondering. It was a ridiculous, impossible puzzle, but even so he wondered. Did the kids *like* him? A little girl with gold hoops in her ears and ugly scabs on her brow—did she feel, as he did, goodness and warmth and poignancy when he helped Doc dab iodine on her sores? Beyond that, though, did the girl *like* him? Lord knows, he had no villainy in his heart, no motive but kindness. He wanted health for her, and happiness. Did she know this? Did she sense his compassion? When she smiled, was it more than a token? And...and what *did* she want? Any of them, what did they long for? Did they have secret hopes? His hopes? Could this little girl—her eyes squinting as Doc brushed the scabs with iodine, her lips sucked in, her nose puckering at the smell—could she somehow separate him from the war? Even for an instant? Could she see him as just a scared-silly boy from Iowa? Could she feel sympathy? In it together, trapped, you and me, all of us: Did she feel that? Could she understand his own fear, matching it with hers? Wondering, he put mercy in his eyes like lighted candles; he gazed at the girl, full-hearted, draining out suspicion, opening himself to whatever she might answer with. Did the girl see the love? Could she understand it, return it? But he didn't know. He did not know if love or its analogue even existed in the vocabulary of Quang Ngai, or if friendship could be translated. He simply did not know. He wanted to be liked. He wanted them to understand, all of them, that he felt no hate. It was all a sad accident, he would have told them—chance, high-level politics, confusion. He had no stake in the war beyond simple survival; he was there, in Quang Ngai, for the same reasons they were: the luck of the draw, bad fortune, forces beyond reckoning. His intentions were benign. By God, yes! He was snared in a web as powerful and tangled as any that victimized the people of My Khe or Pinkville. Sure, they were trapped. Sure, they suffered, sure. But, by God, he was just as trapped, just as injured. He would have told them that. He was no tyrant, no pig, no Yankee killer. He was innocent. Yes, he was, He was innocent. He would have told them that, the villagers, if he'd known the language, if there had been time to talk. He would have told them he wanted to harm no one. Not even the enemy. The enemy! A word, a crummy word. He *had* no enemies. He had wronged no one. If he'd known the language, he would have told them how he hated to see the villages burned. Hated to see the paddies trampled. How it made him angry and sad when...a million things, when women were frisked with free hands, when old men were made to drop their pants to be searched, when, in a ville called Thin Mau, Oscar and Rudy Chassler shot down ten dogs for the sport of it. Sad and stupid. Crazy. Mean-spirited and self-defeating and wrong. Wrong! He would have told them this, the kids especially. But not me, he would have told them. The others, maybe, but not me. Guilty perhaps of hanging on, of letting myself be dragged along, of falling victim to gravity and obligation and events, but not—not!—guilty of wrong intentions.

After the war, perhaps, he might return to Quang Ngai. Years and years afterward. Return to track down the girl with gold hoops through her ears. Bring along an interpreter. And then, with the war ended, history decided, he would explain to her why he had let himself go to war. Not because of strong convictions, but because he didn't know. He didn't know who was right, or what was right; he didn't know if it was a war of self-determination or self-destruction, outright aggression or national liberation; he didn't know which speeches to believe, which books, which politicians; he didn't know if nations would topple like dominoes or stand separate like trees; he didn't know who really started the war, or why, or when, or with what motives; he didn't know if it mattered; he saw sense in both sides of the debate, but he did not know where truth lay; he didn't know if Communist tyranny would prove worse in the long run than the tyrannies of Ky or Thieu or Khanh—he simply didn't know. And who did? Who really did? He couldn't make up his mind. Oh, he had read the newspapers and magazines. He wasn't stupid. He wasn't uninformed. He just didn't know if the war was right or wrong. And who did? Who really *knew*? So he went to the war for reasons beyond knowledge. Because he believed in law, and law told him to go. Because it was a democracy, after all, and because LBJ and the others had rightful claim to their offices. He went to the war because it was expected. Because not to go was to risk censure, and to bring embarrassment on his father and his town. Because, not knowing, he saw no reason to distrust those with more experience. Because he loved his country and, more than that, because he trusted it. Yes, he did. Oh, he would rather have fought with his father in France, knowing certain things certainly, but he couldn't choose his war, nobody could. Was this so banal? Was this so unprofound and stupid? He would look the little girl with gold earrings straight in the eye. He would tell her these things. He would ask her to see the matter his way. What would *she* have done? What would *anyone* have done, not knowing? And then he would ask the girl questions. What did she want? How did she see the war? What were her aims—peace, any peace, peace with dignity? Did she refuse to run for the same reasons he refused—obligation, family, the land, friends, home? And now? Now, war ended, what did she want? Peace and quiet? Peace and pride? Peace with mashed potatoes and Swiss steak and vegetables, a full-tabled peace, indoor plumbing, a peace with Oldsmobiles and Hondas and skyscrapers climbing from the fields, a peace of order and harmony and murals on public buildings? Were her dreams the dreams of ordinary men and women? Quality-of-life dreams? Material dreams? Did she want a long life? Did she want medicine when she was sick, food on the table and reserves in the pantry? Religious dreams? What? What did she *aim* for? If a wish were to be granted by the war's winning army—any wish—what would she choose? Yes! If LBJ and Ho were to rub their magic lanterns at war's end, saying, "Here is what it was good for, here is the fruit," what would Quang Ngai demand? Justice? What sort? Reparations? What kind? Answers? What were the questions: What did Quang Ngai want to know?

In September, Paul Berlin was called before the battalion promotion board.

"You'll be asked some questions," the first sergeant said. "Answer them honestly. Don't for Chrissake make it complicated—just good, honest answers. And get a fuckin haircut."

It was a three-officer panel. They sat like squires behind a tin-topped table, two in sunglasses, the third in skintight tiger fatigues.

Saluting, reporting with his name and rank, Paul Berlin stood at attention until he was told to be seated.

"Berlin," said one of the officers in sunglasses. "That's a pretty fucked-up name, isn't it?"

Paul Berlin smiled and waited.

The officer licked his teeth. He was a plump, puffy-faced major with spotted skin. "No bull, that's got to be the weirdest name I ever run across. Don't sound American. You an American, soldier?"

"Yes, sir."

"Yeah? Then where'd you get such a screwy name?"

"I don't know, sir."

"Sheeet." The major looked at the captain in tiger fatigues. "You hear that? This trooper don't know where he got his own name. You ever promoted somebody who don't know how he got his own fuckin name?"

"Maybe he forgot," said the captain in tiger fatigues.

"Amnesia?"

"Could be. Or maybe shell shock or something. Better ask again."

The major sucked his dentures halfway out of his mouth, frowned, then let the teeth slide back into place. "Can't hurt nothin'. Okay, soldier, one more time—where'd you find that name of yours?"

"Inherited it, sir. From my father."

"You crappin' me?"

"No, sir."

"And just where the hell'd he come up with it...your ol' man?"

"I guess from his father, sir. It came down the line sort of." Paul Berlin hesitated. It was hard to tell if the man was serious.

"You a Jewboy, soldier?"

"No, sir."

"A Kraut! Berlin...by jiminy, that's a Jerry name if I ever heard one!"

"I'm mostly Dutch."

"The hell, you say."

"Yes, sir."

"Balls!"

"Sir, it's not—"

"Where's Berlin?"

"Sir?"

The major leaned forward, planting his elbows carefully on the table. He looked deadly serious. "I asked where Berlin is. You heard of fuckin Berlin, didn't you? Like in East Berlin, West Berlin?"

"Sure, sir. It's in Germany."

"Which one?"

"Which what, sir?"

The major moaned and leaned back. Beside him, indifferent to it all, the captain in tiger fatigues unwrapped a thin cigar and lit it with a kitchen match. Red acne covered his face like the measles. He winked quickly—maybe it wasn't even a wink—then gazed hard at a sheaf of papers. The third officer sat silently. He hadn't moved since the interview began.

"Look here," the major said. "I don't know if you're dumb or just stupid, but by God I aim to find out." He removed his sunglasses. Surprisingly, his eyes were almost jolly. "You're up for Spec Four, that right?"

"Yes, sir."

"You want it? The promotion?"

"Yes, sir, I do."

"Lots of responsibility."

Paul Berlin smiled. He couldn't help it.

"So we can't have shitheads leadin' men, can we? Takes some brains. You got brains, Berlin?"

"Yes, *sir*."

"You know what a condom is?"

Paul Berlin nodded.

"A condom," the major intoned solemnly, "is a skullcap for us swingin' dicks. Am I right?"

"Yes, sir.""

"And to lead men you got to be a swingin' fuckin dick."

"Right, sir."

"And is that you? You a swingin' dick, Berlin?"

"Yes, sir!"

"You got guts?"

"Yes, sir. I—"

"You 'fraid of gettin' zapped?"

"No, sir."

"Sheeet." The major grinned as if having scored an important victory. He used the tip of his pencil to pick a speck of food from between his teeth. "Dumb! Anybody not scared of gettin' his ass zapped is a dummy. You know what a dummy is?"

"Yes, sir."

"Spell it."

Paul Berlin spelled it.

The major rapped his pencil against the table, then glanced at his wristwatch. The captain in tiger fatigues was smoking with his eyes closed; the third officer, still silent, stared blankly ahead, arms folded tight against his chest.

"Okay," said the major, "we got a few standard-type questions for you. Just answer 'em truthfully, no bullshit. You don't know the answers, say so. One thing I can't stand is wishy-washy crap. Ready?"

"Yes, sir."

Pulling out a piece of yellow paper, the major put his pencil down and read slowly.

"How many stars we got in the flag?"

"Fifty," said Paul Berlin.

"How many stripes?"

"Thirteen."

"What's the muzzle velocity of a standard AR-15?"

"Two thousand feet a second."

"Who's Secretary of the Army?"

"Stanley Resor."

"Why we fightin' this war?"

"Sir?"

"I say, why we fightin' this fuckin-ass war?"

"I don't—"

"To win it," said the third, silent officer. He did not move. His arms remained flat across his chest, his eyes blank. "We fight this war to win it, that's why."

"Yes, sir."

"Again," the major said. "Why we fightin' this war?"

"To win it, sir."

"You sure of that?"

"Positive, sir." His arms were hot. He tried to hold his chin level.

"Tell it loud, trooper: Why we fightin' this war?"

"To win it."

"Yeah, but I mean *why?*"

"Just to win it," Paul Berlin said softly. "That's all. To win it."

"You know that for a fact?"

"Yes, sir. A fact."

The third officer made a soft, humming sound of satisfaction. The major grinned at the captain in tiger fatigues.

"All right," said the major. His eyes twinkled. "Maybe you aren't so dumb as you let on. *Maybe.* We got one last question. This here's a cultural-type matter...listen up close. What effect would the death of Ho Chi Minh have on the population of North Vietnam?"

"Sir?"

Reading slowly from his paper, the major repeated it. "What effect would the death of Ho Chi Minh have on the population of North Vietnam?"

Paul Berlin let his chin fall. He smiled.

"Reduce it by one, sir."

In Quang Ngai, they did not speak of politics. It wasn't taboo, or bad luck, it just wasn't talked about. Even when the Peace Talks bogged down in endless bickering over the shape and size of the bargaining table, the men in Alpha Company took it as another bad joke—silly and said—and there was no serious discussion about it, no sustained outrage. Diplomacy and morality were beyond them. Hardly anyone cared. Not even Doc Peret, who loved a good debate. Not even Jim Pederson, who believed in virtue. This dim-sighted attitude enraged Frenchie Tucker. "My God," he'd sometimes moan in exasperation, speaking to Paul Berlin but aiming at everyone, "it's your *ass* they're negotiating. Your ass, my ass....Do we live or die? That's the issue, by God, and you blockheads don't even talk about it. Not even a lousy *opinion*! Good Lord, doesn't it piss you off, all this Peace Talk crap? Round tables, square tables! Idiotic diplomatic etiquette, power plays, maneuvering! And here we sit, suckin' air while those mealy-mouthed sons of bitches can't even figure out what kind of table they're gonna sit at.

Jesus!" But Frenchie's rage never caught on. Sometimes there were jokes, cynical and weary, but there was no serious discussion. No beliefs. They fought the war, but no one took sides.

They did not know even the simple things: a sense of victory, or satisfaction, or necessary sacrifice. They did not know the feeling of taking a place and keeping it, securing a village and then raising the flag and calling it a victory. No sense of order or momentum. No front, no rear, no trenches laid out in neat parallels. No Patton rushing for the Rhine, no beachheads to storm and win and hold for the duration. They did not have targets. They did not have a cause. They did not know if it was a war of ideology or economics or hegemony or spite. On a given day, they did not know where they were in Quang Ngai, or how being there might influence larger outcomes. They did not know the names of most villages. They did not know which villages were critical. They did not know strategies. They did not know the terms of the war, its architecture, the rules of fair play. When they took prisoners, which was rare, they did not know the questions to ask, whether to release a suspect or beat on him. They did not know how to feel. Whether, when seeing a dead Vietnamese, to be happy or sad or relieved; whether, in times of quiet, to be apprehensive or content; whether to engage the enemy or elude him. They did not know how to feel when they saw villages burning. Revenge? Loss? Peace of mind or anguish? They did not know. They knew the old myths about Quang Ngai—tales passed down from old-timer to newcomer–but they did not know which stories to believe. Magic, mystery, ghosts and incense, whispers in the dark, strange tongues and strange smells, uncertainties never articulated in war stories, emotion squandered on ignorance. They did not know good from evil.

22
A Black Man in Vietnam
WALLACE TERRY

The first one I killed really got to me. I guess it was his size. Big guy. Big, broad chest. Stocky legs. He was so big I thought he was Chinese. I still think he was Chinese.

We were on this trail near the Ashau Valley. I saw him and hit the ground and came up swinging like Starsky and Hutch. I shot him with a .45, and I got him pretty good.

He has an AK-47. He was still holding it. He kicked. He kicked a lot. When you get shot, that stuff you see on Hoot Gibson doesn't work. When you're hit, you're hit. You kick. You feel that stuff burning through your flesh. I know how it feels. I've been hit three times.

That's what really got to me—he was so big. I didn't expect that.

They were hard core, too. The enemy would do anything to win. You had to respect that. They believed in a cause. They had the support of the people. That's the key that we Americans don't understand yet. We can't do anything in the military ourselves unless we have the support of the people.

Sometimes we would find the enemy tied to trees. They knew they were going to die. I remember one guy tied up with rope and bamboo. We didn't even see him until he shouted at us and started firing. I don't know whether we killed him or some artillery got him.

One time they had a squad of sappers that hit us. It was like suicide. They ran at us so high on marijuana they didn't know what they were doing. You could smell the marijuana on their clothes. Some of the stuff they did was so crazy that they had to be high on something. In the first place, you don't run through concertina wire like that. Nobody in his right mind does. You get too many cuts. Any time you got a cut over there, it was going to turn to gangrene if it didn't get treated. And they knew we had the place covered.

Another time this guy tried to get our attention. I figured he wanted to give up, because otherwise, I figured he undoubtedly wanted to die. We thought he had started to *chu hoi* [defect]. And we prepared for him to come in. But before he threw his weapon down, he started firing and we had to shoot him.

And, you know, they would walk through our minefields, blow up, and never even bat their heads. Weird shit.

But I really thought they stunk.

Like the time we were heli-lifted from Vandergrift and had to come down in Dong Ha. There was this kid, maybe two or three years old. He hadn't learned to walk too well yet, but he was running down the street. And a Marine walked over to talk to the kid, touched him, and they both blew up. They didn't move. It was not as if they stepped on something. The kid had to have the explosive around him. It was a known tactic that they wrapped stuff around kids. That Marine was part of the security force around Dong Ha, a lance corporal. He was trying to be friendly.

I think it stinks. If those guys were low enough to use kids to bait Americans or anybody to this kind of violent end, well, I think they should be eliminated. And they would have been if we had fought the war in such a manner that we could have won the war. I mean total all-out war. Not nuclear war. We could have done it with land forces. I would have invaded Hanoi so many times, they would have thought we were walking on water.

The people in Washington setting policy didn't know what transpired over there. They were listening to certain people who didn't really know what we were dealing with. That's why we had all those stupid restrictions. Don't fight across this side of the DMZ, don't fire at women unless they fire at you, don't fire across this area unless you smile first or unless somebody shoots at you. If they attack you and run across this area, you could not go back over there and take them out. If only we could have fought it in a way that we had been taught to fight.

But personally speaking, to me, we made a dent, even though the South did fall. Maybe we did not stop the Communist takeover, but at least I know that I did something to say hey, you bastards, you shouldn't do that. And personally I feel good about it. People like Jane Fonda won't buy that, because they went over there and actually spent time with the people that were killing Americans. That's why I feel that I shouldn't spend $4 to see her at the box office. She's a sexy girl and all that other kind of stuff, but she's not the kind of girl that I'd like to admire. She was a psychological setdown, and she definitely should not have been allowed to go to Hanoi.

I learned a lot about people in my platoon. I learned you have to take a person for what he feels, then try to mold the individual into the person you would like to be with. Now my platoon had a lot of Southerners, as well as some Midwesterners. Southerners at the first sign of a black officer being in charge of them were somewhat reluctant. But then, when they found that you know what's going on and you're trying to keep them alive, then they tried to be the best damn soldiers you've got. Some of the black soldiers were the worse I had because they felt that they had to jive on me. They wanted to let me know, Hey, man. Take care of me, buddy. You know I'm your buddy. That's bull.

As long as a black troop knows he's going to take a few knocks like everybody else, he can go as far as anybody in the Corps. Our biggest problem as a race is a tendency to say that the only reason something didn't go the way it was programmed to go is because we are black. It may be that you tipped on somebody's toes. We as blacks have gotten to the place now where we want to depend on somebody else doing something for us. And when we don't measure up to what the expectations are—the first thing we want to holler is racial discrimination. My philosophy is, if you can't do the job—move.

Let's face it. We are part of America. Even though there have been some injustices made, there is no reason for us not to be a part of the American system. I don't feel that because my grandfather or grandmother was a slave that I should not lift arms up to support those things that are stated in the Constitution of the United States. Before I went to Vietnam, I saw the "burn, baby, burn" thing because of Martin Luther King. Why should they burn up Washington, D.C., for something that happened in Memphis? They didn't hurt the white man that was doing business down there on 7th Street. They hurt the black man. They should have let their voices be known that there was injustice. That's the American way.

I still dream about Vietnam.

In one dream, everybody has nine lives. I've walked in front of machine guns that didn't go off. When they pulled the trigger, the trigger jammed. I've seen situations where I got shot at, and the round curved and hit the corner. I'd see that if I had not made that one step, I would not be here. I think about the time where a rocket-propelled grenade hit me in the back, and it didn't go off. We were in a clear area and got hit by an enemy force. The RPG hit me. Didn't go off. Didn't explode. We kept walking, and five of us got hit. I got frags in the lower back and right part of the buttocks. I didn't want to go back to the hospital ship, so I just created the impression that I could handle it. But the stuff wouldn't stop bleeding, and they had to pull the frags out. There was this doctor at Quang Tri, Dr. Mitchell, who was from Boston, a super guy. He painted a smile on my rear end. He cut a straight wound into a curve with stitches across so it looks as if I'm smiling. When I drop my trousers, there's a big smile.

I dream about how the kids in my platoon would come to talk to you and say things about their families. Their families would be upset when they heard I was black. But then some guy would give me a picture of his sister. He would say, "She's white, but you'd still like her. Look her up when you get back to the States." And there would be the ones who did not get a letter that day. Or never got a letter their whole tour. In those cases, I would turn around and write them letters and send them back to Vandergrift.

And you dream about those that you lost. You wonder if there was something you could have done to save them. I only lost two kids. Really.

Cripes was a white guy. I think he was from St. Louis. He was a radio operator. You could tell him. "Tell the battalion commander that everything is doing fine." He would say, "Hey, Big Six. Everything is A-okay. We are ready, Freddie." You know, he had to add something to whatever you said. Otherwise, he was a very quiet guy. But one big problem he had was that he wanted to get into everything. He was trying to prove something to himself. If he saw somebody move, he was going to follow him. No matter what you could do to tell him not to fire, he'd fire. One night, after we got out to Fire Support Base Erskine, we got hit. It was about eleven. Cripes got shot. We don't know if he got hit by our fire or their fire. I just know he crawled out there. He must have seen something. Cripes just had a bad habit of being in the wrong place at the wrong time.

Lance Corporal Oliver was a black kid from Memphis. He carried an automatic rifle. He had been with us maybe three months. He was a very scary kid. He was trying to prove a lot of things to himself and to his family, too. So he was always volunteering to be point. It was very difficult to appoint someone as a point man. A lot of times when you had a feeling you were going to be hit, you asked for volunteers. Oliver always volunteered.

We were on Operation Dewey Canyon. In February of 1969. We had been told the NVA was in there that night. One platoon had went out and got hit. And we got the message to go in next. I got the whole platoon together and said, "Listen. I'm going to walk point for you." My troops said, "No, sir, you don't need to walk. We will arrange for someone to walk point." So the next day the whole platoon got together and said, "Who wants to walk point today?" Oliver stuck up his hand. I said, "I'll be the second man."

Now we had this dog to sniff out VC. Normally he would walk the point with the dog handler. His handler, Corporal Rome from Baltimore, swore Hobo could smell the Vietnamese a mile away. If he smelled one, his hair went straight. You knew something was out there.

One time, when we were walking a trail near Con Thien, this guy was in this tree. At first we thought he was one of the local indigenous personnel, like the ARVN. He turned out to be something else. He had his pajamas on and his army trousers. He wasn't firing. He was just sitting there. Hobo just ran up in that tree, reached back, and tore off his uniform. He was armed with an AK-47. Hobo took that away from him, threw him up in the air, and grabbed him by the neck and started dragging him. We learned a lot from that guy. You put a dog on a guy, and he'll tell you anything you want to know.

Another time at Vandergrift, Hobo started barking in the officers' hootch. We had sandbags between us. And Hobo just barked and barked at the bags. Nobody could figure out what was wrong. Finally I told Hobo to shut up, and I walked over to the sandbags. There was this viper, and I took a shotgun and blew its head off.

We used to dress Hobo up with a straw hat on his head and shades on. All of us had shades. And we used to take pictures of Hobo. And sit him on the chopper. And he'd be in the back of the chopper with his shades on and his hat, and he would smile at us.

We got to the place where we could feed him, and put our hands in his mouth. We would give him Gravy Train or Gainsburgers. If we ran out on patrol, we would give him our C-rations. He really liked beef with spice sauce.

Hobo was so gullible and so lovable that when you had a problem, you ended up talking to him. You could say, "Hobo, what the hell am I doing here?" Or, "Hey, man. We didn't find nothin' today. We walked three miles and couldn't find nothin'. What the hell are you doing walking this way?" And he'd look at you and smile, you know, in his own little manner. And he'd let you know that he should really be here to understand all this shit we're putting down. Or he would do things like growl to let you know he really didn't approve of all this bullshit you're talking. It's hard to explain. But after eight months, Hobo was like one of the guys.

Hobo signaled the ambush, but nobody paid any attention. We walked into the ambush. A machine gun hit them. Oliver got shot dead three times in the head, three times in the chest, and six times in the leg. Rome got hit in the leg. Hobo got shot in the side, but even though he was hit, he got on top of Rome. The only person that Hobo allowed to go over there and touch Rome was me.

It never got better. It seemed like everyday somebody got hurt. Sometimes I would walk point. Everybody was carrying the wounded. We had 15 wounded in my platoon alone. And the water was gone.

Then on the twelfth day, while we were following this trail through the jungle, the point man came running back. He was all heated up. He said, "I think we got a tank up there." I told him, "I don't have time for no games." The enemy had no tanks in the South.

Then the trail started converging into a really well-camouflaged road, about 12 feet wide and better made than anything I had ever seen in Vietnam. Then I saw the muzzle of this gun. It was as big as anything we had. And all hell broke open. It was like the sun was screaming.

I thought, my God, if I stay here, I'm going to get us all wiped out.

In front of us was a reinforced platoon and two artillery pieces all dug into about 30 real serious bunkers. And we were in trouble in the rear, because a squad of snipers had slipped in between us and the rest of Charlie Company. My flanks were open. All the NVA needed to finish us off was to set up mortars on either side.

Someone told me the snipers had just got Joe. He was my platoon sergeant.

That did it. I passed the word to call in napalm at Danger Close, 50 meters off our position. Then I turned to go after the snipers. And I heard this loud crash. I was thrown to the ground. This grenade had exploded, and the shrapnel had torn into my left arm.

The Phantoms were doing a number. It felt like an earthquake was coming. The ground was just a-rumbling. Smoke was everywhere, and then the grass caught fire. The napalm explosions had knocked two of my men down who were at the point, but the NVA were running everywhere. The flames were up around my waist. That's when I yelled, "Charge. Kill the gooks. Kill the motherfuckers."

We kept shooting until everything was empty. Then we picked up the guns they dropped and fired them. I brought three down with my .45. In a matter of minutes, the ridge was ours. We had the bunkers, an earth mover, bunches of documents, tons of food supplies. We counted 70 dead NVA. And those big guns, two of them. Russian-made. Like our 122, they had a range of 12 to 15 miles. They were the first ones captured in South Vietnam.

Well, I ordered a perimeter drawn. And since I never ask my men to do something I don't do, I joined the perimeter. Then this sniper got me. Another RPG. I got it in the back. I could barely raise myself up on one elbow. I felt like shit, but I was trying to give a command. The guys just circled around me like they were waiting for me to tell them something. I got to my knees. And it was funny. They had their guns pointed at the sky.

I yelled out, "I can walk. I can walk."

Somebody said, "No, sir. You will *not* walk."

I slumped back. And two guys got on my right side. Two guys got on my left side. One held me under the head. One more lifted my feet. Then they held me high above their shoulders, like I was a Viking or some kind of hero. They formed a perimeter around *me*. They told me feet would never touch ground there again. And they held me high up in the air until the chopper came.

I really don't know what I was put in for. I was told maybe the Navy Cross. Maybe the Medal of Honor. It came down to the Silver Star. One of those guns is at Quantico in the Marine Aviation Museum. And the other is at Fort Sill in Oklahoma. And they look just as horrible today as they did when we attacked them.

Rome lost his leg. From what I'm told, they gave him a puppy sired by Hobo. So Hobo survived Dewey Canyon. They wanted to destroy him at first, but he got back to the kennel. If anybody would've destroyed that dog, it would have been me.

But Hobo didn't get back to the States. Those dogs that were used in Vietnam were not brought back. The Air Force destroyed all those dogs. They were afraid of what they might do here.

If I had Hobo right now, he wouldn't have to worry about nothing the rest of his life. He was a hell of a dog. He could sense right and wrong. I would have trusted Hobo with my own children. If somebody got wrong or was an enemy of my family, Hobo would have brought his ass to me. There ain't no doubt about it. Yet he was a nice dog. He would give me a kiss on the jaw. I loved that dog.

One day I wore my uniform over to Howard University in Washington to help recruit officer candidates. Howard is a black school, like the one I went to in Texas, Jarvis Christian College. I thought I would feel at home. The guys poked fun at me, calling me Uncle Sam's flunky. They would say the Marine Corps sucks. The Army sucks. They would say their brother or uncle got killed, so why was I still in. They would see the Purple Heart and ask me what was I trying to prove. The women wouldn't talk to you either.

I felt bad. I felt cold. I felt like I was completely out of it.

June 9, 1970. Major General Glenn D. Walker, commanding general of the 4th Infantry Division, is briefed at a fire base. OFFICIAL U.S. ARMY PHOTO

CHAPTER 7

The Military

Above the battlefield, off the line, or back in the Pentagon, the war looked very different. There is an old cliché that generals are always fighting the last war, and in Vietnam there was something to this. Suffusing the writings of military leaders during the 1960s and 1970s is a quiet confidence that, with enough manpower and firepower, the Americans could defeat the Asian enemy (like the Japanese in 1945) or at least halt the Asian enemy's aggression (as in Korea, 1950–1953). At the same time, the military establishment was quick to embrace new and sophisticated weaponry that made the Vietnam War unlike any other in history. The U.S. frequently used napalm, chemical defoliants, laser-guided "smart" bombs, and electronic troop detection devices disguised as pieces of mud. Although these weapons took a tremendous toll on the NLF and North Vietnamese, they were not enough to win the war.

Commentators vary in their assessments of the military's performance. General Bruce Palmer, Jr., was intimately involved in military decision making during the 1960s, both in Washington and Vietnam. He is not uncritical of command's practices, but, as he writes in the preface to the book from which this piece is excerpted, mistakes made in Vietnam were "honest mistakes, and many were mistakes only in hindsight." Loren Baritz, a historian, offers a more penetrating indictment of military practice. Unlike Palmer, Baritz places the performance of the military in the larger context of American culture and draws a sharp distinction between the behavior of the grunts on the ground and the officers living in relative safety some distance from the front. The third reading, taken from an article by political scientist Guenter Lewy, focuses on atrocities committed or allegedly committed by American troops in Vietnam. Using "after-action" reports of military operations written by the military itself, Lewy concludes that American soldiers on the whole conducted themselves with admirable restraint, and that there was in any case no plan by command to perpetrate immoral acts.

23
Assessing the Army's Performance
BRUCE PALMER, JR.

American direction and conduct of the war and the operational performance of our armed forces, particularly during the 1962–69 period, generally were professional and commendable. Performance continued to be of a high quality until the 1969–70 period, when dissent at home began to be reflected in troop attitudes and conduct in Vietnam. From 1969 until the last U.S. combat troops left in August 1972, a decline in performance set in; the discovery of widespread drug use in Vietnam in the spring of 1970 signalled that more morale and disciplinary troubles lay ahead. The so-called "fraggings" of leaders that began in 1969–70 were literally murderous indicators of poor morale and became a matter of deep concern.

Extremely adverse environmental conditions and very trying circumstances contributed to this decline in performance. Particularly galling to our forces in the field were the widely publicized statements of highly placed U.S. officials, including senators, against American involvement. Such statements were perceived to support the enemy and badly damaged the morale of our troops. The deteriorating climate at home also affected the conduct of American prisoners of war (mostly airmen) held in North Vietnamese POW camps; this was reflected in the increasing number of men who were accused of collaborating with the enemy in the 1969–71 period, as compared to the very few during the earlier years of the war.

For the ground combat troops, Vietnam was a light infantry war of small units, mostly rifle platoons and companies, rarely of formations larger than a battalion. The Army tailored its basic fighting units of infantry and direct support artillery to the terrain and the peculiar nature of combat in Vietnam. Rifle companies, for example, were reduced in strength and lightened up by eliminating some of the heavier supporting weapons and equipment found in the normal organization. As a result, American infantry could move more swiftly and easily over the ground, and the tactical airmobility of the modern assault helicopter could be fully exploited.

Before Vietnam, the Army was primarily geared to fighting a highly sophisticated, mechanized war in Europe. Although a few relatively light

Reprinted from Bruce Palmer, Jr. *The 25-year War: America's Military Role in Vietnam.* © 1984 by the University Press of Kentucky. Used by permission of the publishers.

divisions existed, most of the Army divisions were heavy armor or mechanized divisions either already deployed in Germany or earmarked for service in Europe. Thus the Army's problem of adjusting to a much different kind of warfare in Vietnam on terrain far different from the European scene was a complex one. The Army had to maintain a ready capability to fight in Europe even while conducting a major war in Vietnam. The questions of priorities between the two theaters were never answered satisfactorily.

The military helicopter truly came of age in Vietnam, where the Army, at times opposed by its sister services, never lost its faith in this remarkable instrument. Clearly the single most outstanding military innovation in the Vietnam War was the development and introduction into combat of the "chopper" in various forms—the troop-carrying assault helicopter, the helicopter gunship for escort and close fire support missions, the attack helicopter with a tank-killing capability, and the scout helicopter for performing classic but still essential cavalry missions.

The contribution of the Army's organic aviation arm, rotary and fixed wing, cannot be overstated. These aircraft were involved in practically every military function—command and control, reconnaissance, firepower, mobility, medical evacuation, and supply, as well as utility missions of every conceivable description. But it was the airmobile divisions (1st Cavalry and 101st Airborne) and air cavalry squadrons that brought the airmobile concept to the pinnacle of its potential. In these units the helicopter literally substituted for ground vehicles of every kind and totally freed the fighting elements from the tyranny of surface obstacles to movement. "Owning" their own helicopters and possessing a field maintenance capability that could accompany the forward assault forces, these units gave the theater commander a "Sunday punch" of unequalled flexibility and versatility.

Army aviators were committed in combat in the early 1960s, providing aviation support to South Vietnamese troops and developing battle-tested airmobility tactics and techniques long before the first Army ground combat forces arrived on the scene. In Vietnam these pioneer flying men earned a permanent place among the Army's elite—the combat arms. These men and their wondrous flying machines are here to stay in the Army—they will more than pay their way on future battlefields.

Although it was essentially a light infantry war, armor played a valuable role and did it well. The 11th Armored Cavalry Regiment was the largest armor unit in Vietnam and performed a variety of important reconnaissance, security, and offensive combat missions. The regiment was often employed on independent missions with decisive results. Each Army division had its own organic armored cavalry squadron, and at least one of its infantry battalions was mechanized; that is, its infantry was normally transported in armored personnel carriers. Armored units fought numerous key battles in every corps tactical zone: their heavy firepower and high ground mobility were well known to and respected by the enemy. In the dry monsoon they could operate almost anywhere, penetrating some of the most rugged and densely covered enemy war zones and base areas in Vietnam and Cambodia.

Army field artillery performed extremely well in Vietnam. In the American artillery system the ubiquitous forward observer, accompanying his supported infantry rifle company wherever it moves, is the key to the optimum functioning of the entire system. Despite the unusual terrain encountered—thick jungle foliage, rugged mountains, and land like the Mekong Delta, so flat and unvarying that determining troop positions was especially difficult—our forward observers performed effectively. Quick response was often a problem when operating near populated areas because of the necessity to make checks and even double checks to insure safety and accuracy. On the other hand, in a situation such as the defense of Khe Sanh, rounds were on the way in forty seconds after fire was requested.

Vietnam also brought out the need for fire support coordinators in modern battle, even in counterinsurgency situations, because of the proliferation of weapons systems available to support ground troops. The high density of aircraft in the battle area—Air Force, Marine, and Army—further complicated fire coordination. Overlapping control of airspace brought on by the legitimate claims of each service to control the use of airspace, required by its forces, was often a potential problem. Nevertheless overall fire support coordinators in Vietnam performed generally in an outstanding manner.

At Khe Sanh, the Air Force (that is, MACV's component air command, the 7th Air Force) was designated as the overall manager of airspace, and although the Marine Corps objected vehemently to the arrangement, it worked well. Indeed, the close and skillful coordination of Marine light artillery fires, Army long-range (175 mm) artillery fires, Air Force B-52 strikes, and Air Force and Marine tactical air strikes resulted in devastating casualties among attacking enemy troops.

The most common military term, and certainly one of the major tactical innovations, to come out of the Vietnam War was the "fire support base," or simply "fire base." The fire base was not just a defensive position but also the firepower element integral to any offensive effort. The concept developed partly because of the vulnerability of artillery firing batteries in unsecured areas to close-in mass enemy assault and hence the need to protect them with infantry. Thus a position jointly occupied by supporting artillery and defending infantry became known as a fire base. Normally the fire base was also the location of the forward command post of the infantry battalion conducting operations in the area and providing for the defense of the base. This arrangement insured that the artillery firing units would always be effective, day or night, when called upon to support offensive operations with indirect fire. Infantry and artillery units located on a fire base came in close, intimate contact with each other, and when the fire base was attacked infantrymen and artillerymen soon learned to value highly the mutual support they could give each other. There were many variations of fire bases according to their location, the ground available for defense, the units and weapons involved, and the like. In short, the organization of a fire base reflected the flexibility and ingenuity of the American soldier and his leaders.

Battalion, brigade, and division commanders generally showed considerable professional skill in maneuvering their units and employing their combined arms. The 4th Infantry Division, for example, operating in the vast Kontum-Pleiku plateau region of the Highlands, time and again outwitted, outmaneuvered, and outfought its NVA foes despite the latter's inherent advantages—the enemy's ability to decide when to leave the sanctuary of Cambodia, where to cross the border, and what objectives to attack in South Vietnam.

Having addressed the performance of U.S. troops in action, I would be very remiss if I did not include at least a brief word about the selfless service of our advisers. Their performance—Army, Navy, Air Force, and Marine—generally was outstanding throughout the war, from the earliest days in the 1950s to the end. The great majority were U. S. Army officers and NCOs who served from the palace level to the ARVN battalion and the district/subdistrict level in the field. As ARVN advisers, they shared the hardships and dangers of infantry combat; as CORDS advisers, the equally risky and austere environment of a South Vietnamese district chief in a Viet Cong-infested area; and as Special Forces advisers, the lonely, perilous life in a CIDG camp on the border. In the vast majority of cases they never complained, asked for very little, and literally gave their all for their South Vietnamese counterparts. The American people should be very proud of them.

These comments on the performance of our ground forces have been made basically with the U.S. Army in mind. Marine and Army ground combat elements, because of the commonality of their primary task—combat on the ground—have many similar interests, characteristics, organizational patterns, and operational modes. Recognizing that comparisons can be odious, and usually are, I hesitate to make any. Nevertheless, having had some close experience with U.S. Marines in various operational theaters in the past, I will venture one major observation, a difference between the Marine Corps and the Army that I have found striking. Marines traditionally place far more responsibility and authority on their noncommissioned officer corps. Inherently this is a sound principle, and I fault the Army for the converse—not giving NCOs sufficient authority and responsibility, and instead putting too great a load on company grade officers. But as a result of this Marine emphasis on NCOs, I have repeatedly noted two general shortcomings—inadequate supervision of NCOs by the Marine officer corps, and marine officers, especially the more senior ones, not always knowing what is going on at the troop level and consequently not taking adequate care of their men.

The offensive air war, controlled by CINCPAC more or less independently of the war in South Vietnam conducted by COMUSMACV, was con-

ducted by and large in a very commendable manner. These air operations consisted of two different but concurrent campaigns—the offensive
against North Vietnam itself, and the interdiction campaign along inland
and coastal routes in North Vietnam and inland routes through the panhandle of Laos.

The two air campaigns, frequently overlapping in a geographical
sense, were conducted primarily by the land-based aircraft of the 7th
U.S. Air Force located in South Vietnam and Thailand, and by U.S. Navy
carrier-based aircraft located in the South China Sea. CINCPAC assigned
to MACV the responsibility for air operations in Laos, basically an interdiction mission; MACV in turn delegated control of these operations to
MACV's air component, 7th Air Force. But for air strikes against North Vietnam, CINCPAC decentralized operations to the Pacific Air Forces and the
Pacific Fleet, coordinating their operations principally by geographic assignment of targets, the Navy taking targets generally more accessible by
attack from the sea, and the Air Force taking targets further inland. But
true unity of air operations against North Vietnam was never fully achieved;
B-52 operations in the region, for example, remained under the control of
SAC throughout the war.

CINCPAC's geographic assignment of targets nevertheless worked
well primarily because it avoided the inherently far more difficult task
of coordinating the operations of aircraft from two different services. Such
coordination would have been quite difficult because the Navy and the
Air Force have different doctrine and operating procedures, their communications systems and equipment are different, and they do not normally
train and operate together. These are basic facts of life which are all too
often overlooked by ardent proponents of joint operations.

Combat aircraft pilots and crews performed exceptionally well under
very tough conditions. As I have already observed, enemy air defenses were
the heaviest and most formidable ever encountered by our air and naval
forces in history. The advent of the "smart bomb" in later stages of the war
was a great boon, but the losses of U.S. aircraft and crews continued to
be heavy. Adverse weather and rugged terrain were also major handicaps.
Finally, our incredibly complicated rules of engagement, which varied from
country to country and even from area to area, were often too much for
pilots to handle. These rules, imposed by the U.S. government, were simply
unreasonable for men flying at 500 knots, trying to stay alive and yet close
on their targets. Near the end of American involvement, when Chinese
territory was unintentionally violated by our aircraft, the Chinese seemed
to understand the problem better than our own statesmen.

One lesson that seems rather apparent has emerged from these operations. Sustained air operations during a long, difficult war are more
readily conducted by land-based aircraft with their land-based support, a
system designed for the long haul. Carrier-based aircraft and their carriers,
on the other hand, are not designed to remain on station for prolonged
periods. As a result, our carrier task groups took a terrific beating and fell

far behind in their ship overhaul schedules. The impact of this extraordinary strain is felt even today [early 1970s] in the Navy.

In terms of tactical air support in South Vietnam, Army-Air Force relations were close, cordial, and mutually satisfying, and the Air Force's performance was generally outstanding. Emergency tactical air support was available on short notice, day or night, in almost any kind of weather. B-52 support was more than impressive—when a B-52 saturation attack occurred, the ground nearby literally shook and our own troops well understood why the enemy was terrified. Aerial resupply reached new levels of reliability, accuracy, and volume in Vietnam. Various parachute drop techniques, including low-level parachute extraction, were extensively used and successfully demonstrated. Medical air evacuation was also well executed.

Organic Marine aviation support of their own Marine forces on the ground was likewise outstanding. The Marine system, whereby the Marine division commander has full control of the Marine Air Wing associated with his division, works well for their purposes. The only area where the Marines seemed to come up short lay in airmobility, that is, the exploitation of the helicopter's unique capabilities. Because of the relatively larger size of their assault helicopters (compared to the Army's squad-carrying-sized "Huey") and their centralized control of helicopters under the Air Wing commander, the Marines, in my opinion, did not fully achieve the tactical advantages of integrated airmobility.

The overall control of air operations involving more than one service caused a major problem only once in South Vietnam—during the siege of Khe Sanh in western I CTZ in the winter of 1968. General William Momyer, commanding the 7th Air Force, insisted that his headquarters, under the overall command of General Westmoreland, be assigned the responsibility, with commensurate authority, for controlling all air operations, regardless of the services involved, in support of the besieged Marines at Khe Sanh. The Marines strongly objected and carried their case through Marine channels all the way to the JCS. Westmoreland agreed with and supported Momyer's position, which the JCS carefully considered and finally approved. But the matter left some bitterness in the Marines, who understandably resist any attempt to interpose external control between their ground and supporting air elements.

Very few joint Army-Air Force operations, other than normal tactical air support missions, were undertaken in Vietnam. Only one sizable airborne (parachute assault) operation was conducted, but it was not of major consequence. Nevertheless, countless American paratroopers served with distinction in practically every combat unit in Vietnam, although the nature of the war was not conducive to airborne operations.

But there was one major joint operation, the Son Tay POW camp raid of November 1970. The main effort of this raid was made by a joint Army-Air Force task force, with the Air Force providing large troop-carrying helicopters, air cover, and air support, and the Army providing the assault ground force. The Navy and Marines flew major air attacks in other areas of North Vietnam as diversionary efforts designed to deceive the enemy as to the true location, direction, and nature of the main attack. The plan worked well, the enemy was confused, and surprise was achieved. Unfortunately, our POWs had been removed from the camp before the operation was launched and the mission was unsuccessful—an intelligence failure but an operational success.

This raid also raised the morale of the families of our prisoners of war and of our men missing in action. These gallant relatives never gave up hope and very properly kept the pressure on the State and Defense departments to do everything humanly possible to determine the status of their men. Fortunately, too, the raid resulted in noticeably improved treatment of our POWs in North Vietnam. Unfortunately, the situation of many of our men lost, missing, or captured in Laos, Cambodia, and South Vietnam has never been satisfactorily established, and the agony of uncertainty about the fate of their loved ones continues in some American families to this day.

But even sustained, outstanding operational performance can go for naught if the intelligence that guides operations and generates the thrust of operational efforts is lacking in quality. Accordingly, let us turn to a brief examination of the performance of American intelligence at the national level as well as in the theater of operations.

For the president and other U.S. policymakers in Washington, there was a plethora of intelligence studies and estimates about the Vietnam War originating from a wide variety of official organizations, ranging from the U.S. Embassy, the CIA station chief, and HQ MACV in Saigon, as well as HQ CINCPAC in Honolulu, to the proliferation of intelligence agencies in Washington. Most of the Washington-level wartime studies were produced by a single agency, some by two agencies working together, and only relatively few by the whole intelligence community.

The Washington players making up the community were: (1) The director of Central Intelligence (DCI), his Central Intelligence Agency, and the now-defunct Board of National Estimates, reporting through the DCI to the president and the National Security Council. (2) From the Pentagon, the Defense Intelligence Agency (DIA), responsible to the secretary of defense and the JCS; and the intelligence organizations of the services, each reporting to its own service chief. (3) From the Department of State, the Bureau of Intelligence and Research (INR), responsible to the secretary of state. And (4) The cryptological community, consisting of the National Security Agency (NSA), responsible to the secretary of defense; and the service security agencies each reporting to its service chief.

The DCI presided over this basically loose confederation and chaired the U. S. Intelligence Board, now known as the National Foreign Intelligence Board, whose principal members are the heads of the CIA, DIA, INR, and NSA. Obviously, the DCI's authority over this board is somewhat attenuated, inasmuch as three of the four other principals are responsible to a cabinet member.

In wartime the theater commander, usually a unified commander, normally assumes control of all intelligence assets, including the CIA's, in his area of responsibility. The Vietnam War was a unique case, however, and this wartime takeover was not invoked. So the CIA station chief in Saigon continued his regular peacetime function as the senior intelligence adviser to the U.S. ambassador. As a consequence, unity of U.S. intelligence effort was not achieved in Vietnam and, despite coordination and cooperation between the CIA and the MACV J-2, undesirable duplication and competition did take place. Unfortunately, this jurisdictional problem spilled over into combined U.S.-South Vietnamese intelligence activities, resulting in such unhelpful consequences as having separate CIA-South Vietnamese and MACV J-2-South Vietnamese interrogation centers operating in the same provincial and district capitals.

While the CIA station chief in Saigon, MACV, and CINCPAC naturally concentrated on the more immediate aspects of the conflict, the national-level intelligence organs focused on the longer-term strategic aspects. The latter included such matters as the assessment of opposing U.S./allied and North Vietnamese strategies; North Vietnamese perceptions of the U.S. war effort; the effectiveness of the U.S. air war against North Vietnam; North Vietnamese capacity to wage a prolonged war and their dependence on the Soviet Union and China; and the prospects for survival over the longer term of a free and independent South Vietnam.

During the earlier years of the direct American military involvement in Vietnam, up until the time of the enemy's Tet offensive of 1968, the military held the center of the intelligence stage. MAVC, CINCPAC, and DIA were the dominant voices and had the ear of the president and his NSC staff. But beginning a few months after the start of the sustained American air offensive in March 1965, the CIA, at the request of Defense Secretary McNamara, played an active intelligence role, initially evaluating the effectiveness of U.S. air attacks against North Vietnam and later judging the progress of the war and the prospects of allied success. After Tet 1968 and the turn-about in the Johnson administration's attitude toward the war, the intelligence clout in Washington shifted more in favor of the CIA.

On balance, the Agency did a good job in assessing the situation in Southeast Asia during the 1965–74 period. Its overall intelligence judgments were generally sound and its estimates were mostly on the mark. Several facts illustrate the truth of this statement. First, the Agency, in evaluating the effectiveness of U.S. air attacks, consistently concluded that the attacks did not reduce North Vietnamese logistic capabilities to sustain the war; that North Vietnam could afford to take the punishment, that Hanoi's will was not shaken, and that the material cost of the resulting damage to North Vietnam was simply passed on to the USSR and China, while Hanoi's constantly improving air defense system (provided by the USSR and China) inflicted rising air losses on the United States.

Second, with respect to North Vietnam's ability to wage a prolonged war, the Agency consistently estimated that Hanoi would continue to base its strategy on a war of attrition, since North Vietnam had the manpower base as well as an assured source of adequate arms and supplies to continue such a grinding war indefinitely, and that Hanoi's leaders believed they possessed more staying power than the United States and South Vietnam, and would ultimately prevail. Because of redundant land routes linking North Vietnam to China and the Soviet Union, the Agency did not judge North Vietnam to be vulnerable to a U.S. naval blockade.

Finally, as South Vietnam's fortunes waned and U.S. support faltered in late 1973 and in 1974, the Agency consistently warned that the South Vietnamese situation was becoming parlous and that the North Vietnamese would exploit their military advantage to gain their long-sought final victory. The Agency did not, however, anticipate that this victory would come as early as the spring of 1975. As South Vietnam's security posture deteriorated in 1975, especially after Hanoi's final offensive was launched early that year, the military situation on the ground became the preeminent factor in deciding the country's fate. Thereafter, overall strategic-political assessments of South Vietnam's longer-term viability were simply not possible.

One particularly complex and contentious problem plagued the intelligence community throughout the war—estimating enemy troop strength and determining the composition of his major units, the so-called order of battle. These are among the most difficult military intelligence judgments of all to make in wartime, especially in a people's war like Vietnam in which regular troops (so-called main force and local force units), their administrative and logistic support forces, part-time guerrillas and militia, and political cadres are often intermingled. Enemy ground combat casualties are particularly difficult to estimate as a result of battles involving civilians, regular soldiers, and local guerrillas and militiamen.

The CIA's estimates were probably more accurate overall than MACV's. As time went by, CIA and MACV estimates moved much closer together in the category of regular combat units but were never fully reconciled with respect to guerrilla strengths. In this latter category, the differences were partly conceptual, partly philosophical, and partly methodological. Basically, MACV held to a conservative approach in recognizing military capabilities that resulted in an underestimation of guerrilla forces. Likewise, MACV's conservative approach to estimates of enemy units and personnel infiltrating from the North led to a time lag in MACV's acceptance of new infiltrators, and hence higher total infiltration figures.

Estimating enemy casualties—the "body count" syndrome—is not a new problem; it has been a complicating factor in past wars. More than one example of highly exaggerated body counts resulting in inflated enemy loss estimates can be found in the American campaign records of World War II and the Korean War. In both Korea and Vietnam, the United States was faced with the very different and complex problems of fighting a major war but in a limited manner—limited in terms of objectives, geography, means employed, and resources committed. In both wars there was no territorial objective other than to defend the status quo ante; thus it was not possible to demonstrate or assess progress in terms of territory gained and held. Leaders quite naturally turned to other indicators of how the war was going, among them the number of enemy battle casualties. At one point in the Korean War, the explicit, if crudely stated, military objective was to kill as many Chinese ("Chinks") as possible. In Vietnam a similar objective of attriting enemy forces was present. Moreover, the difficulty of distinguishing regular and irregular forces from noncombatants tended to break down normal inhibitions against causing civilian casualties. Such incentives were invitations for fighting units to exaggerate claims of "enemy" killed. Unfortunately, a few small-unit commanders condoned or even encouraged padded reports, further exacerbating the "body count" syndrome.

Higher headquarters, nonetheless, have ways to judge the validity of unit claims; for example, by weighing the intensity of the fighting by comparing friendly and enemy casualties and by noting the number of weapons captured in comparison with the number of enemy reported killed. Comparatively low friendly casualties and few enemy weapons captured should arouse the suspicions of the higher headquarters and call for a check on the intensity of fighting when a high "body count" is reported.

In Vietnam, especially in the Delta, some units were inclined to exaggerate claims of enemy killed and were careless about avoiding civilian casualties. But by and large the great majority of American units tried to submit factual reports based on actual evidence rather than estimations, and conscientiously sought to limit casualties among noncombatants. In addition, field force headquarters and HQ MACV, whenever feasible, checked the overall circumstances of the battle reported before accepting the enemy casualty figures submitted.

Even when heavy enemy battle losses are substantiated, one must be careful not to judge their psychological effect on the enemy on the basis of occidental values. Indeed, American military professionals who fought in the Pacific in World War II or in Korea became acutely aware of differing oriental values with respect to human life, and knew the pitfalls of putting too much store in the impact of heavy casualties on the morale of a determined foe or on the will of a ruthless totalitarian government.

In Vietnam, the factual evidence concerning the enemy's manpower capacity seemed pretty clear to our leaders in the field. We realized that the enemy decided where and when he would do battle and could therefore control his casualty rate. We repeatedly saw specific, identified enemy fighting units decimated in combat only to return a few months later from their base sanctuaries at full strength, ready to fight again. These facts, coupled with what theater intelligence told us about the rate of infiltration of enemy troop units and replacements down the Ho Chi Minh Trail, timed with planned enemy "high points" (offensives), constituted positive indications that the enemy could fight this kind of war indefinitely. Raw manpower did not seem to be a limitation. Moreover, frightful enemy casualties, which, had they been American would have had major repercussions in our society, seemed to have no effect on the leadership in Hanoi or on the North Vietnamese people. Thus one might conclude with some reason that U.S. officials should not have been misled by faulty estimates of enemy losses and of the enemy's effective troop strength.

One might well ask why senior U.S. policymakers in Washington, with the exception of Defense Secretary McNamara, did not pay more attention to CIA views and to the disagreements within the intelligence community. There is no simple answer to this complex question. As already indicated, given the nature of the intelligence community it would be unreasonable to expect unanimous views, especially when matters of great import are involved. Moreover, the exposure of differing views, particularly on major issues, can be considered a strength rather than a weakness, because to paper over or submerge them runs the risk of badly misleading policymakers. International relations are difficult to judge even in normal times, but when examining them through the fog of war, policymakers are entitled to know what honest differences of opinion may exist before making judgments. With respect to Vietnam, the head of the CIA was up against a formidable array of senior policymakers, including the president, the secretary of state, the secretary of defense, the chairman of the JCS, and the national security adviser to the president—all strong personalities who knew how to exercise the clout of their respective offices. It is not surprising then that the director of Central Intelligence, Richard Helms (from 30 June 1966 to 2 February 1973), who served under both Presidents Johnson and Nixon, was reportedly content to let the responsible policy officials make up their own minds. No doubt Helms was also determined to protect and preserve the traditional objectivity of intelligence vis-a-vis policy. But, as alluded to above, McNamara was not entirely satisfied with his intelligence from the Defense Department and beginning in late 1965 relied more and more on the CIA for what he believed were more objective and accurate intelligence judgments.

At this point, several comments in the realm of tactics and techniques should be underscored. First, let us look at the matter of surprise. Whether the North Vietnamese achieved truly strategic surprise in an overall political-military sense during the Vietnam War is arguable. But unquestionably they achieved surprise in a tactical sense in two notable cases before the January 1973 cease-fire. These were their Tet offensive of 1968 and their March 1972 "Easter" offensive across the eastern part of the DMZ. The NVA also achieved major tactical surprise after the cease-fire when it attacked Ban Me Thuot in II CTZ in March 1975 at the beginning of the final offensive against South Vietnam.

Examining the question of why this came about, one must conclude that a major factor was our overreliance on signal intelligence, from which we derived most of our strategic and tactical information pertaining to Southeast Asia. This kind of intelligence can be very misleading and is also subject to manipulation by the enemy. It is more suitable for judgments of a longer-term strategic nature, and is not always reliable or appropriate for short-term tactical purposes. Identifying and, by direction-finding techniques, locating a radio transmitter belonging to a specific NVA regiment, for example, does not necessarily mean that the regiment is there too, although it is a good indication that elements of the regiment are in the vicinity. But in actuality, a small forward communications detachment might be the only element of the regiment present. One obvious conclusion is that we did not put enough emphasis on direct human sources of intelligence, as opposed to those of the electronic variety.

We were also weak in counterintelligence, that is, an organized, disciplined effort to deny information about our own plans, operations, and other military matters to the enemy. U.S. communications security, for example, was not satisfactory in Southeast Asia; we never achieved even a reasonably good posture. Because of our careless habits, talking in clear (uncoded) text over insecure phone or voice radio, and our frequent failure to use truly secure codes, the enemy all too often knew our planned moves well in advance, even strikes by the Strategic Air Command, and took action to alert their units and people. As a consequence we deprived ourselves of numerous opportunities to surprise the enemy, a prized advantage.

At times we used more military force than was called for by the situation, especially when fighting near or in populated areas. Since heavy firepower and area-type weapons, such as tactical air support, artillery, and mortars, are not discriminating enough, their use risks civilian casualties and material damage which can be self-defeating in pacification efforts. Unobserved "H& I" (harassing and interdiction) artillery fire and air strikes, often based on dubious intelligence reports, were at times directed into areas (sometimes designated by South Vietnamese officials as "free fire zones") believed to be occupied only by enemy forces. This practice was not really effective militarily and was generally a waste of ammunition. Moreover, it ran the unnecessary risk of inflicting casualties on civilians and being counterproductive politically and psychologically, whether the people concerned were helping the enemy or not.

Related to the foregoing, American and South Vietnamese troops during the period when U.S. troops were still present in strength (1966–71) often became too accustomed to an abundance of externally provided heavy firepower and neglected their own organic capabilities that were more discriminating. This habit can also result in less capable infantry troops who come to rely on massive externally provided firepower rather than on the skillful use of fire and maneuver on their own.

In later years (1971–75), however, after most U.S. ground forces had been withdrawn, massive U.S. airpower was needed to make up for South Vietnam's principal shortcomings: the lack of enough forces overall (in particular armor and artillery), an inadequate strategic reserve, and an inability to shift forces from one region to another. After the cease-fire in January 1973, when U.S. airpower was no longer available, a new situation existed wherein the South Vietnamese simply lacked enough airpower, armor, and larger caliber artillery of their own to handle the numerous large, modern NVA formations arrayed against them.

The helicopter can be both an asset and liability. This is a costly resource requiring considerable logistic and maintenance support that must be used wisely. Airmobile operations require tactical skill and intensive training by both aviation and infantry elements; a poorly conducted operation can be disastrous. U.S. and allied forces at times became too heavily dependent on helicopter support. The "chopper" is a versatile machine which accords great advantages of mobility, logistic support, fire support, and medical evacuation. But there is still no substitute for lean, tough troops who can march long distances on foot and can survive with minimum support. The availability of the helicopter makes it too easy to overfly trouble on the ground or to withdraw troops from difficult positions. The latter action in particular can undermine the tenacity and willingness of troops to fight to the finish that must characterize first-class infantry.

The helicopter also allows senior officials to visit their people operating on the ground more readily, but this is a double-edged sword. It can lead to oversupervision of junior officials and can make senior leaders believe they know more about the situation on the ground than they actually do.

As I indicated in a previous chapter, logistic support of American forces was generally outstanding. Americans tend to be profligate, however, and our armed forces are no exception. Amassing huge quantities of all kinds of supplies in Vietnam on the grounds that supply lines might be interrupted was an example of overly cautious logistic planning. Similarly, administrative support and base facilities were too comfortable for some American headquarters and personnel in Vietnam. This had bad psychological effects, set a poor example for our own fighting soldiers as well as those of our allies, and lent an air of unreality at times to the American military presence. A more spartan existence would have been better for all.

Overall, our troops had little, if anything, to complain about. Communications support, logistic support of all kinds, medical care which made miracles seem commonplace, and engineer support—all without exception were outstanding. Even the military police earned the respect if not affection of the "GI" in Vietnam. Nevertheless, a more efficient logistic system could have conserved precious resources without hurting overall troop performance.

The Army's most serious problems were in the manpower and personnel area. Basically they stemmed from the failure to mobilize and the decision to hold to a one-year tour in Vietnam. Without at least a partial mobilization the Army was denied the use of the trained, experienced units and personnel present in the National Guard and organized reserves. This meant that, as the Army expanded from roughly 950,000 in

1964 to about 1,550,000 in 1968 to meet the requirements of Vietnam, the additional men and women entering the service were mostly very young, untrained, and inexperienced, resulting in the dilution of overall experience in the Army, particularly in the leadership ranks, the officers and noncommissioned officers. The failure to mobilize or to declare an emergency also meant that personnel would flow in and out of the armed forces on a peacetime basis rather than being held in the service for the duration of the emergency. Thus draftees conscripted for two years could serve at the most about sixteen months overseas. This factor, coupled with a judgment that all personnel (career and noncareer) serving in Vietnam would perform better if on a known, fixed tour, led to the one-year rotation policy, a very bad mistake in my view. Finally, as its troop strength built up in Vietnam, the Army reached the point at which almost as many soldiers (about 725,000) were serving overseas as in the continental United States (about 825,000). Of those overseas, more than half were serving in Vietnam and Korea and had to be replaced every year. The number of replacements required in Vietnam steadily grew, of course, as the fighting intensified and battle losses and noncombat casualties rose. Moreover about 250,000 soldiers in the United States (almost one-third of the total on duty there) were undergoing basic training and were not available for assignment to units.

For the Army the overall simple arithmetic was that its so-called sustaining rotation base in the continental United States was not large enough to furnish the large number of trained replacements required each year for Vietnam and Korea, to maintain the forces in Europe on a three-year tour, and to give career soldiers much of a breathing spell between repetitive tours in Vietnam. The length of the tour in Europe had to be progressively shortened and in the end the proud, combat-ready Seventh Army ceased to be a field army and became a large training and replacement depot for Vietnam. For political reasons ("guns and butter" and the demands of "The Great Society"), Defense Secretary McNamara would not recognize the legitimate manpower shortfalls of the Army and disapproved Army requests for increases in its authorized strength to meet worldwide demands. The principal cumulative effects of these misguided policies on the Army's posture in Vietnam are discussed below.

Although new units, with very few exceptions, arrived in Vietnam with a reasonably high level of unit proficiency, and incoming replacement personnel likewise generally possessed the required individual skills, the problem was to maintain unit efficiency and cohesion, and develop teamwork in the face of a high personnel turnover rate. Because of battle casualties, injuries, sickness, and other personnel losses, and the steady loss of soldiers returning home at the end of their one-year tour, the average rifle company, for example, became an entirely different outfit in terms of individual men every nine or ten months.

Maintaining a high standard of leadership in Vietnam was another major problem. The Army simply was unable to provide an adequate replacement flow of leaders, officers, and NCOs with experience commensurate with their responsibilities. The one-year tour, as well as the failure to mobilize, stretched the experienced leadership available from career personnel very thin throughout the Army worldwide. Moreover, many career and noncommissioned officers, after completing two or three tours in Vietnam and coming under increasing pressure from their families, decided to retire, thus further increasing the loss of experience. The end result was a slow, steady deterioration of experienced leadership in Vietnam that hurt the continuity of our effort and eroded our dedication to assigned missions.

Without mobilization, the one-year rotation policy was logical for our two-year draftees. But the tour for the career officer and NCO should have been two to three years. Proponents of the one-year tour for careerists argued that the high tempo of combat operations and the severe, constant strain on leaders dictated the shorter tour in the combat zone. They pointed out that helicopter operations could keep troops in almost constant contact with the enemy and that combat units could be shifted suddenly from the relatively safe environment of a base camp into a hot fire fight in a matter of minutes. This is a telling point, but such a problem could have been alleviated by in-country rotation between combat jobs and more secure noncombat positions.

Vietnam uncovered a major deficiency in the training of American military personnel, both officer and enlisted. This weakness lay in the area of the Geneva Conventions and their applicability to unconventional, guerrilla warfare. Our armed forces did not do an effective job—either in the United States or in Southeast Asia—of orienting their uniformed personnel, particularly ground combat troops, to what they would face in this kind of war. As a result, our troops were not prepared for this ambiguous, complex type of warfare and did not fully understand how the internationally accepted rules of warfare applied to Vietnam. One can make the case that the tragic My Lai aberration largely stemmed from inadequate orientation and training on the Geneva Conventions, further aggravated by the scarcity of mature, experienced leadership among lower ranking American officers and noncommissioned officers. As a result of My Lai, while American soldiers were still in combat in Vietnam, the Army inaugurated a massive orientation program to correct this deficiency.

Having examined the performance of American forces, U.S. intelligence, some of our tactical and logistic shortcomings, and the serious weaknesses of our manpower system, we might well ask whether any significant improvements in U.S. performance would have made any difference in the outcome. The answer is probably "no." The war was lost primarily at strategic, diplomatic, and domestic political levels, although the final defeat of South Vietnamese forces on the ground was more tactical and military in nature. Nevertheless, we American military professionals have much to learn from the tragic experience of Vietnam, because heeding those lessons could mean the difference between winning and losing in a future conflict.

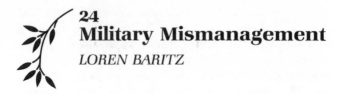

24
Military Mismanagement
LOREN BARITZ

The moral decay and increasing incompetence of the army's senior officers in Vietnam was minimally caused by personal failures of individuals. ... The corruption in Vietnam was systemic and was caused by procedures within the army that had been borrowed from other American bureaucratic institutions, primarily industry.

When the army adopted the "up or out" model of personnel management soon after World War II, it assumed that if an employee is not promotable, he is not employable. That meant that individuals with long and useful experience, who had found their right rung on the bureaucratic ladder, could not be retained. Up or out always devalues experience and always demands change at the price of stability. Americans seem unable to imagine an individual being satisfied by doing a job for which he is suited. We insist that job advancement must be perpetual. This constant upward swimming produced the bends, maybe not for the individuals concerned, but for the army as an institution.

Although the industrial bureaucratization of the army began in the 1940s, the extent of its corrosive damage was first made undeniable in Vietnam. What had happened was that a system of rewards was imposed on the military that changed the senior officer from a military leader into a bureaucratic manager. Many senior officers in other times and places led their men into battle, shared their risks, and were respected if not loved. Vietnam proved that men cannot be "managed" into battle.

Why should a bureaucrat risk his life to manage his men? When the code of the military was replaced with that of the bureaucracy, personal risk became not only meaningless, but stupid. If the point was promotion, not victory, risk was, as they say, counterproductive. The details of the army's definition of career management assaulted military logic, morale, and honor. The My Lai slaughter was a consequence of this deformation.

The bureaucratization of the army led to a definition of officers as personnel managers and troops as workers. It was not clear why the "workers" should have risked their lives to follow the orders of the "boss" who was not at risk himself. This sort of corruption invariably starts at the top, with the big boss. In 1966, General Westmoreland reported in unashamed industrial language and with apparent pride, "[My troops] work, and they work hard. It has been my policy that they're on the job seven days a week, working as many hours as required to get the job done."[1] Perhaps his bureaucratic instincts, as deep as any man's could be, had been reinforced by his stint at the Harvard Business School. Vice Admiral James B. Stockdale wrote that "our business school-oriented elite tried to manipulate rather than fight the Vietnam War."[2]

General Westmoreland was America's senior personnel manager in-country, and that is how he thought of himself. He reported to the National Press Club that by 1967 the armed forces of South Vietnam had made progress. The first reason for this good news was: "Career management for officers, particularly infantry officers, has been instituted." The second reason was: "Sound promotion procedures have been put into effect." As a consequence of these and other "improvements," he concluded, "the enemy's hopes are bankrupt."[3]

The peculiar swagger of Americans, as John Wayne personified it, had been changed from confidence born of competence and courage to confidence wrung from ignorance. Bureaucrats are planners, and they must always believe, or pretend very hard to believe, or at least insist they believe, in the effectiveness and wisdom of their plans. The result is the sort of arrogance that drains the oxygen from a room, that makes the bureaucrat-in-chief light-headed. For example, General Westmoreland had not one doubt: "We're going to out-guerrilla the guerrilla and out-ambush the ambush...because we're smarter, we have greater mobility and firepower, we have endurance and more to fight for.... And we've got more guts."[4]

It is written that one should know one's enemy, that pride precedes failure. The general had insulated himself from reality, was unable to hear criticism, and seemed quite pleased with himself. He was America's perfect manager of a war. As a result he was more interested in procedures and public relations than content. He wanted to engineer appearances, not substance. Every reporter who listened to his Saigon briefings understood that it was a shell game. Evidently, he himself had no idea that this was so.

Under the leadership of General Westmoreland and the rotating Chiefs of Staff, the military bureaucracy became so top-heavy that it lost its balance. There was a higher percentage of officers in the field during the Vietnam War than in other American wars, and higher than in the armies of other nations. At its peak the percentage of officers in Vietnam was almost double what it had been in World War II. In 1968, there were 110 generals in the field in Vietnam. In absolute terms there were about as many generals, admirals, colonels, and navy captains in Vietnam as there were at the height of World War II. There was a lower ratio of officer deaths than was true earlier and elsewhere. Of the seven generals who died, five lost their lives in their helicopters. There was a higher ratio of medals distributed to officers, especially as the combat began to wind down, than ever before.

Colonel John Donaldson's Vietnam career is illustrative. In 1968, he was given command of the Americal Division's 11th Brigade, which a few months earlier had sent Lieutenant Calley's platoon into My Lai. The colonel replaced Colonel Oran Henderson, who would be acquitted of the charge of a My Lai cover-up. In his first six months of command, Colonel Donaldson "earned" an "average of about one medal a week: two Distinguished Flying Crosses, two Silver Stars, a Bronze Star Medal for Valor, twenty Air Medals, a Soldier's Medal, and a Combat Infantryman Badge." He was soon promoted to brigadier general and won nine additional Air Medals and two Legions of Merit, and was transferred to the Pentagon as a strategist.[5] During the My Lai investigation it was thought that to protect his predecessors he had destroyed key documents needed by the investigators. He denied this. In 1971, he was the first American general charged with a war crime since about 1900. He was accused of "gook hunting," shooting Vietnamese from his helicopter. He was acquitted.

In 1962, military promotion decisions had been centralized under the Chiefs of Staff. Thereafter, the military became a bureaucratic promotion machine. Meanwhile, the grunts continued to slog through the paddies and jungles. Many of them knew that something was rotten. By 1967, combat troops made up 14 percent of the troops in Vietnam; in World War II it was 39 percent; 34 percent at the end of the Korean War; and, 29 percent in 1963.[6] Approximately 86 percent of the military in Vietnam was not assigned to combat. At the height of the buildup in 1968, when there were about 540,000 military personnel in Vietnam, 80,000 were assigned to combat. The rest, the other 460,000, constituted the grunts' enormous category of REMFs [rear echelon mother fuckers].

It is probably true that never before, in the military or anywhere, had bureaucratic officials so enthusiastically served their own interests to the detriment of the objective they were supposed to accomplish. The managerial corps finally lost to dedicated troops in black pajamas.

As the officers blamed the politicians, many grunts blamed the officers. Bruce Lawlor, a CIA case officer, knew what was happening: "The only thing the officers wanted to do was get their six months in command and then split back to the States and be promoted and go on to bigger and better things. It doesn't take long for the average guy out in the field to say, 'Fuck it!' "[7] Or, as another example, a colonel sent troops into action without telling them (to make sure they would not evade a fight) that they would encounter an enemy base camp. Herb Mock, an infantryman who walked point on that mission, later went to find the colonel: "You made us walk right into the ambush. That's a sorry goddamn thing to do. You ain't worth shit as an officer."[8] Herb Mock's best friend was killed in the ambush.

The army itself recognized that something was wrong. In 1970, General Westmoreland ordered the Army War College to conduct an analysis of the officer corps. The study was so damaging that he at first had it classified. What had happened, in the language of the Army War College study, was that, "careerism" in the officer corps had replaced the ethic of the officer. Careerism means that personal advancement replaces the desire to get the job done. In fact, the "job" *is* personal advancement. (This helps to explain the cheating scandals at the service academies.) Bureaucratic employees get paid to get promoted.

In April General Westmoreland ordered the commandant of the Army War College to study the moral and professional climate of the army. Although he did not believe that the army was suffering a "moral crisis," he directed the study to focus "on the state of discipline, integrity, morality, ethics, and professionalism in the Army."[9]

In the study's preface, Major General G. S. Eckhardt, Commandant, simply stated, "This study deals with the heart and soul of the Officer Corps of the Army."[10] The study involved interviewing about 420 above-average officers, an extensive questionnaire, and many group discussions. As a result, the study concluded that "prevailing institutional pressures" had created a divergence between the ideals and the current practices of the officers corps. "These pressures seem to stem from a combination of self-oriented, success-motivated actions, and a lack of professional skills on the part of middle and senior grade officers."[11] The officers participating in the study described the typical Vietnam commander: "an ambitious, transitory commander—marginally skilled in the complexities of his duties—engulfed in producing statistical results, fearful of personal failure, too busy to talk with or listen to his subordinates, and determined to submit acceptably optimistic reports which reflect faultless completion of a variety of tasks at the expense of the sweat and frustration of his subordinates."[12]

Many of the officers involved in the study agreed that the cause of this breakdown was that the army itself had "generated an environment"[13] that rewarded trivial and short-run accomplishments to the neglect of significant achievement and the longer-term health of the army. The cause was not the "permissive society"[14] at home, or the antiwar and antimilitary protests, but the army itself.

The study reported that junior officers were better officers than their own commanders, and that the younger men "were frustrated by the pressures of the system, disheartened by those seniors who sacrificed integrity on the altar of personal success, and impatient with what they perceived as preoccupation with insignificant statistics." A captain was quoted: "Many times a good soldier is treated unfairly by his superiors for maintaining high standards of professional military competence." A colonel said, "Across the board the Officer Corps is lacking in their responsibilities of looking out for the welfare of subordinates."[15]

An important conclusion of the study was that moral failure and technical incompetence was closely connected. Incompetence seemed to come first and the need to cover it up created the thousand techniques for lying, passing the buck, and avoiding responsibility. The study acknowledged that such behavior was army-wide: "signing of false certificates; falsification of flight records; condoning of the unit thief or scrounger; acceptance by middle and upper grade officers of obviously distorted reports; falsification of...trips for self gain and the attendant travel pay; hiding of costs under various programs; hiding AWOLs by placing them on leave to satisfy commander's desire for 'Zero Defect' statistics."[16]

The army's emphasis on quantification (a disease it caught when Secretary McNamara sneezed) meant that success was defined only by what could be measured. This was partly caused by the computer craze and resulted in the application to the army of "the commercial ethic."[17] This contributed to two unfortunate consequences: ignoring characteristics that could not easily be expressed in numbers, such as leadership, and emphasizing activities that could be measured, such as "savings bond scores and the reenlistment rate."[18] Officers were promoted for doing well in these "programs," while they were not reprimanded for failures in areas that the computers could not be programmed to measure, such as duty, honor, country. One captain complained: "The fact that my leadership ability is judged by how many people in my company sign up for bonds or give to the United Fund or Red Cross disturbs me."[19] (One noncom told me that his superior in Vietnam always forced him to buy bonds, but encouraged him to cancel as soon as the good report went out.)

This definition of what mattered to the army as an institution suited the careerist officers who were in "the business" to make a good living. One captain described his battalion commander as a man who "had always his mission in mind and he went about performing that mission with the utmost proficiency. His mission was getting promoted."[20] A major exploded: "The only current decorations I admire are the DSC and the Medal of Honor, all others are tainted by too often being awarded to people who do not deserve them.... Duty, Honor, Country is becoming—me, my rater, my endorser, make do, to hell with it."[21] Another major was a little more relaxed: "My superior was a competent, professional, knowledgeable military officer that led by fear, would double-cross anyone to obtain a star, drank too much and lived openly by no moral code."[22] This "superior" was soon promoted and got his first star.

The Army War College study revealed how the officers derived bureaucratic lessons even from My Lai. Officers got into trouble at My Lai because they found no AK47s, Soviet-made rifles carried by both the guerrillas and by the North's army; that made it difficult to claim that all the villagers were combatants. "This exposure to My Lai...it has driven some of the units to carry AK47s around with them so that if they did kill someone they've got a weapon to produce with the body."[23]

When General Westmoreland read the study he proclaimed it a "masterpiece," and restricted its distribution to generals only. As a group they had quite substantial reservations about its conclusions. General Westmoreland did, however, write a number of letters to inform the officer corps that integrity was important. That was the most significant result of this remarkable study. Young Pentagon officers formed a group called GROWN: Get Rid of Westmoreland Now.

Vietnam was the only available war for upwardly mobile officers, and if they failed to get an assignment in Vietnam, called getting their ticket punched, their careers would be thwarted. This infected the officer corps from top to bottom, beginning even before the West Point cadets graduated. For example, James Lucian Truscott IV arrived at West Point in 1965, where he hoped to follow his family's tradition of soldiering:

> When I was 22 years old I was pretty well convinced from having officer after officer after officer—major, lieutenant colonel, full colonel—come and tell me, personally or in front of a class, "You've got to go to Vietnam and get your fucking ticket punched. The war sucks. It's full of it. It's a suck-ass war. We're not going to win it. We're not fighting it right, but go and do it." You know, "Duty, Honor, Country" had suddenly become "Self-Duty, Honor, Country."[24]

A year after he graduated from West Point, Mr. Truscott resigned his commission rather than go to Vietnam.

For the office warriors, Vietnam was a marvelous opportunity to get ahead in the world. According to marine General David Shoup, some of the generals and admirals hoped to deepen America's involvement in Vietnam to speed promotions.[25] But such motivation was not a sufficient reason to risk getting hurt or killed, or even to suffer through the war in more discomfort than was absolutely necessary.

Among the Vietnam generals he surveyed, Brigadier General Kinnard found that 87 percent believed that careerism was "somewhat of a problem" or "a serious problem."[26] Careerist officers would not take risks in combat or in their relations with their superiors. Risk could lead to error, and a single mistake noted on an officer's efficiency report could ruin his career. This produced an equivalence of error, from incorrect table manners at "the Club" to a failure of judgment in combat. An instructor at the Command and General Staff College, said this of the rating procedure: "The system demands perfection at every level—from potatoes to strategy. It whittles away at one's ethics."[27]

When every glitch, however petty, might end up as a black mark on the rating sheet, officers of course trained themselves to be passive, to keep quiet, and to worry more about pleasing those above them than those below. Carried to an extreme in Vietnam, the rating system produced an even conformity of thought, a religion of pleasing superiors, a very high price on dissent, and a comfortable tour for the three- and four-star generals who were not rated. Careerism inevitably forced officers to think of their subordinates as their most important resource for making them look good, to protect their "image" on paper.

Career management and sound promotion procedures, as General Westmoreland described them, motivated the bureaucratic colonels and generals who observed the war, if they observed it all, safe in their helicopter offices fifteen hundred feet above the danger. They claimed they needed to be in the air to see the bigger picture, so as not to lose perspective by the more limited horizons of the earthbound warriors. Sometimes this was true, but the grunts hated it. Whether it was necessary or not, the chopper always gave the officers an opportunity to have the desired combat experience without the risks of combat. The availability of helicopters meshed perfectly with the imperatives of ticket-punching. Field commanders, especially lieutenants and captains, resented it also, but for obvious reasons they were less outspoken. For the grunts, the appearance of the colonel's chopper was a reminder that they and not he might get blown away. He would not be late for the happy hour at the Club, while they would remain in the field with another meal of C-rats. It reinforced a class hatred that was, in its pervasiveness, probably unique to the Vietnam War. Mike Beamon, a navy antiguerrilla scout—he called himself a terrorist—said it all: "I was more at war with the officers there than I was with the Viet Cong."[28]

The length of time an officer in Vietnam served in a combat assignment was not a matter of established military doctrine. It was a rule of thumb of the commanders in the field. Although there were exceptions, and although some officers served more than one tour, the expectation of a twelve-month tour, even for officers, set the outer limit of a combat assignment. In 1968, the systems analysts in the Office of the Secretary of Defense studied the length of time officers served in combat. They found that the typical combat command of a maneuver battalion or a rifle company was "surprisingly short."[29] More than half the battalion commanders, usually lieutenant colonels, were rotated out of combat command in less than six months. More than half the company commanders, usually captains, were relieved before they completed four months. One of the reasons for so short a command tour was reported in a secret document prepared in the Office of the Deputy Chief of Staff for Personnel in 1970: "Career personnel have greater opportunity for career development and progression...."[30] With short assignments more officers could get their tickets punched.

After 1970, 2,500 lieutenant colonels each hoped to command one of the 100 battalions, 6,000 colonels wanted a command of one of the 75 brigades, and 200 major generals wanted to get one of the 13 divisions.[31] The competition for one of these assignments was fierce, and the office politicking was everywhere. As they got the right punches, the right assignments, the officers' careers flourished. Of the men who were considered for promotion to major, 93 percent succeeded, as did 77 percent to lieutenant colonel, and 50 percent to colonel. Colonel David Hackworth understood what was happening:

We had all the assets to win this war. We had half a million troops, unlimited amounts of money and the backing of the administration. No doubt we could have won if we'd had commanders who knew how to use these assets, instead of these amateurs, these ticket punchers, who run in for six months, a year, and don't even know what the hell it's all about.[32]

There were two important consequences of these short command assignments: Officers did get the "experience" required for their promotions; and the men under their command were killed in higher numbers because of their commanders' inexperience. The systems analysts discovered that a maneuver battalion under a commander with more than six months experience suffered only two thirds the battle deaths of battalions commanded by officers with less than six months of experience. The average command lasted 5.6 months. The analysts discovered that a battalion commander with less than six months experience lost an average of 2.5 men a month; those with more experience lost 1.6 men a month. In their technocratic, economistic, dehydrated view of the world, the analysts explained that "the rate of battle deaths is a measure of the cost of success." They wanted a "cheaper price."[33]

The analysts also found that the length of experience of a company commander reduced the battle deaths of his troops. The average command was just under four months. These officers were themselves killed at a higher rate than more experienced officers, a rate that rose in each of the first four months, and that dramatically dropped by two thirds in the fifth month, from which point it remained low and stable. In the first four months, about 4 percent of these officers were killed; afterward, 2.5 percent were killed. "This implies," the systems analysts concluded, "that a company commander could be left in office 6 more months, for a total of 10, without incurring an additional risk as great as that to which he was exposed during his first 4 months in command."[34] Nonetheless, they were "relieved" (perhaps in several senses of that word) in four months so that another green commander could step onto the promotion escalator, and two thirds of them were sent out of combat to staff positions. The typical captain in Vietnam had three different "jobs" during his twelve-month tour in Vietnam. The companies commanded by officers with less than five-months experience had an average of .8 killed in action each month; those with more than four months lost .6 KIA, a drop of 25 percent.

As usual, the military was not delighted by the work of the Whiz Kids. As usual, the military argued that the systems analysts did not understand war. The deputy chief of staff for operations concluded, "Our commanders in the field can best judge the length of time an officer should remain in command of a unit in combat."[35] The brass on the spot had not "arbitrarily" set the average command assignments at six months and four months. These periods of time were selected because "we know from experience that a commander begins to 'burn out' after a period in this hazardous and exacting environment." After the typical time in command, and after burnout, "the commander is not fighting his unit as hard as he did during the first few months of command when he was full of snap, zest and aggressiveness and eager to destroy the enemy."[36]

The analysts were unimpressed by the Pentagon's argument. They claimed there was "no data" to prove that commanders burn out. Their conclusion was ominous: "We cannot prove its existence and we suspect that the present rotation policy may be based more on considerations of providing a wide base of combat experience than on the 'burn out' factor."[37]

The military headquarters in Saigon obviously had to join this argument, to "rebut" the analysts. MACV acknowledged that there was a "learning curve" for battle commanders, contested the statistical reliability of the figures used, and insisted that the analysts had failed to understand that battles vary in intensity. The analysts agreed about varying intensity, but added that "regrettably, data are not available," presumably unavailable in Saigon as well as Washington. They did not believe this was a serious point because their study covered so many areas of combat that differences would cancel each other out. They agreed that more information would always be helpful and might have produced different results. "But we doubt it. It was our view (and MACV confirms this) that more experienced battalion commanders are more effective: on the average fewer of their men get killed in combat."[38]

The American military establishment took pride in its effective adoption of "sound business practices." But, on the question of the duration of command, the military borrowed from no one. There is no other institution that transfers its leaders before they can learn their jobs. There is also no other institution in which the price of ignorance is the death of other people. One scholar compared the time in office between military officers and business executives and found that military officers with less than one year's experience was 46 percent of all officers; the comparable figure for executives was 2 percent. Military officers with five or more years of experience were 6 percent of the total; 88 percent of business executives had that much experience.[39] There were reasons why the military moved its people so quickly, but the development of competence and the safety of the troops were not among them.

General Westmoreland uncharacteristically said, "It may be that I erred in Vietnam in insisting on a one-year tour of duty...." But, as he reconsidered the possibility of an error, he concluded that longer tours would have been "discrimination against officers" and would have added to his difficulties in getting enough junior officers from OCS and ROTC. Perhaps, he said, an eighteen-month tour would have been "a workable compromise,"[40] He did not mention the fate of the GIs.

Yet, every sane observer of the rotation system agreed that it interfered with conducting the war. The Army War College study of the careerism of officers cited the short tour as a major factor in the deformation of the code of officers. Careerism, it said, can be diminished "by building mutual trust and confidence, and loyalty that comes from being in one assignment long enough to be able to recover from mistakes; and to have genuine concern—as a practical matter—about the impact which expedient methods will have on the unit next year."[41] After questioning and interviewing hundreds of officers, this study pointed out that the army had not questioned its promotion policy "for some time," and had simply continued to make the assumption that moving officers through the wide variety of jobs required for promotion was a sound policy. "The implications of this assumption," the study said, "are so far-reaching that possibly no single personnel management concept—save that of the uninhibited quest for the unblemished record—has more impact on the future competence of the Officer Corps."[42]

Before a company commander learned his job he was sent elsewhere. Before an intelligence officer could establish all his contacts he was sent elsewhere. There was no way the military could learn from its experience. That is what John Paul Vann, a distinguished officer who had resigned in disgust from the military, meant when he said that America did not fight a ten-year war, but rather ten one-year wars. For the officers the spin was even faster. Experience obviously could not accumulate. Lessons could not be learned. It was not only a teenage war, but a war in which no one had time to become seasoned or wise. There was no institutional memory, and with every year's rotation, the war began anew, with staff trying to hold up "the old man" who always had the power of command.

It was thus a teenage war led by amateurs. The GIs did not complain, of course, about serving "only" one year, but some of them knew, as Thomas Bird, a grunt with the 1st Cavalry, admitted:

> Toward the end of my tour, when I started knowing what I was doing in the jungle and started knowing what to do under fire, it was just about time to go home. I'm going to be replaced by a guy who is as green as I was when I got here, and by the time he gets good at it he's going to be replaced by a guy who is green. It's no wonder we never got a foothold in the place.[43]

Keeping the war's score by counting bodies, an index imposed by Washington, was made to order for careerist officers. They could and did distinguish themselves by reporting more bodies than their competitors. One general later concluded that the body count was "gruesome—a ticket punching item."[44] Another said, "Many commanders resorted to false reports to prevent their own relief," that is, to prevent someone else from replacing them and getting ahead by filing more acceptable reports. Another general said, "I shudder to think how many of our soldiers were killed on a body-counting mission—what a waste."[45]

When a career depends on the reported height of a pile of bodies, several sorts of decay result. Once, when the men of Charlie Company engaged the enemy, their lieutenant called for a helicopter to evacuate the wounded. "To hell with the wounded, *get those gooks*,"[46] the lieutenant colonel radioed back from his helicopter above the action. The lieutenant turned to see his machine gunner firing at the commander's chopper.

Having instituted a process that rewarded cheating, the bureaucratic bosses simply denied that it could have happened. Most (61 percent) of the generals in Vietnam knew that the statistics were snake oil,[47] but none complained in public. They were wedded to the system. For example, in 1973, some of the majors at the army's Command and General Staff College at Leavenworth asked the commandant to permit a discussion of the ethics of officers in Vietnam. According to a reporter:

> One general was saying that he was right on top of things in his units, that no one would dare submit a falsified report there. A young major stood up and said, General, I was in your division, and I *routinely* submitted falsified reports. The General's response was, When you speak to a general officer, stand at attention.[48]

The most senior officers, "Old Bulls," then at Leavenworth rejected what they called this "moralistic streaking." It is an iron law of bureaucracy that the higher one is in the organization, the more optimistic one is. How could it be otherwise? If one is in charge, things must be working well. A corollary is that the more senior one is, the more one is subject to the disease of being hard-of-listening. This law and its corollary may also partly explain General Westmoreland's constant assurances that things were working out satisfactorily, and that a solution would come soon. It seems reasonably clear that he really believed his own crooning. It is extremely difficult for the chief administrative officer of an organization to think that someone else would have done a better job. The Old Bulls at Leavenworth were not different from senior supervisors in Saigon, Washington, or anywhere else where bureaucracy is a settled fact of life.

Some defenders of the bureaucratic army argue that the problem in Vietnam was caused by the disorganization of American society at the time. They say that the pool of men from which the military had to draw was inadequate for military purposes. The "permissive society," the availability and use of drugs, and, most of all, the collapse of respect for authority throughout American culture apparently produced some officers who were not up to the military's legitimate expectations of correct conduct. The conclusion to this argument is that something did go wrong in Vietnam, but it was the fault of American culture, not the military.

The most careful work on this subject was done by two former officers, Richard Gabriel and Paul Savage. They argue that it was the army itself, not permissive American society, that produced the Vietnam officers' conduct. They show that earlier armies had always enforced conduct separate from contemporary fashions. That is what the military must do, and formerly had done, because it is a unique institution. It cannot function if its style of command, leadership, and even management is responsive to changing social fashions. The necessary characteristics for an officer in combat has no useful civilian analogy. Combat is unique. The army must train soldiers to perform specific functions regardless of any set of social circumstances.

The Army War College study itself asserts that the failures were inside the military and not a result of any "defects" in American society. It also concluded that the antiwar movement had no discernible impact on the quality or motivation of "officer material." If the crisis was, and is, internal to the army, the solution must also be. Yet, those who rose to the most senior levels of military command were precisely the bureaucrats who benefited by the corruption. The army's own study, in stunning bureaucratic language, acknowledged that for this very reason, reform was unlikely: "The fact also that the leaders of the future are those who survived and excelled within the rules of the present system militates in part against any self-starting incremental return toward the practical application of ideal values."[49] That is to say, reform must and cannot be internal.

The grunts understood that they were endangered by the guerrillas, the regular army of North Vietnam, and their own temporary, rotating officers, in no particular order of threat. They knew that the home front did not support what they were doing. If no one cared about them, they could not care about the rules or established authority. Occasionally, around 1970, grunts would scribble UUUU on their helmets: the unwilling, led by the unqualified, doing the unnecessary, for the ungrateful. Other helmets proclaimed POWER TO THE PEOPLE, KILL A NONCOM FOR CHRIST, or NO GOOK EVER CALLED ME NIGGER. It was finally as if all that they could believe and remember were pain and death. One young man from the Bronx, for example, was cited for heroism:

> They gave me a Bronze Star and they put me up for a Silver Star. But I said you can shove it up your ass. I threw all of the others away. The only thing I kept was the Purple Heart, because I still think I was wounded.[50]

A wound is the most intimate souvenir.

It cannot be surprising that the grunts found ways to resist corrupt officers in a war that could not be understood. Desertions, excluding AWOLs, in the army alone rose from 27,000 in 1967 to 76,634 in 1970, a rate increase of 21 per thousand to 52 per thousand.[51] The marines were even worse with 60 desertions per thousand.[52] According to the Department of Defense, the rate of desertion in Vietnam was higher than in either Korea or World War II, and the rate increased as the intensity of the fighting declined and absurdity increased. As President Nixon began withdrawing troops, many of the grunts remaining on the ground lost even more conviction about why they should stay and fight. The desertion rate from 1965 to 1971 increased by 468 percent.[53]

Fragging, defined as an attempt to murder by using a grenade, reached astonishing levels in Vietnam. It was usually a result of the fear and hatred felt by the workers toward their bosses. For example, marine Private Reginald Smith testified in a court-martial that his lieutenant was so slow in setting up a listening post that by the time he sent three marines out, the NLF was waiting and killed two of them. The troops were discussing the incompetence of this lieutenant just before he was killed by a fragmentation grenade.[54] It was frequently said that combat squads raised a bounty to be awarded to anyone who would "waste" a particularly hated officer. The Criminal Investigating Department of the Third Marine Amphibious Force said there were more than 20 fraggings in eight months of 1969, according to the transcript of a court-martial. The Defense Department admits to 788 fraggings from 1969 to 1972.[55] This figure does not include attempts to kill officers with weapons other than "explosive devices," such as rifles. Richard Gabriel calculated that "as many of 1,016 officers and NCOs may have been killed by their own men,"[56] but he points out that this figure includes only men who were caught and tried. There is no precedent in American military history for violence against officers on anything like this scale.

Another response of the "workers" was to "strike," that is, to disobey a combat order, that is, to commit mutiny. The Pentagon kept no records of mutinies, but Senator Stennis of the Senate Armed Forces Committee said that there were 68 mutinies in 1968 alone.[57]

Yet another form of resistance by grunts was the pandemic use of hard drugs. In the spring of 1970, 96 percent pure white heroin appeared in Saigon; by the end of the year it was everywhere, sold in drugstores and by Vietnamese children on street corners. This junk was so pure and cheap that the troops smoked or sniffed, with only a minority reduced to injection. Its use was not remarkable in Vietnam because smoking was usually a group activity, accepted by almost everyone, and common for clean-cut Midwestern boys as well as for city kids. Nothing in all of military history even nearly resembled this plague. About 28 percent of the troops used hard drugs, with more than half a million becoming addicted.[58] This was approximately the same percentage of high school students in the States who were using drugs, but they were using softer stuff. In Vietnam, grass was smoked so much it is a wonder that a southerly wind did not levitate Hanoi's politburo.

The failure of senior officers is partly reflected in the fact that they knew what was going on and did nothing to stop it, and did not protest. Richard Gabriel and Paul Savage concluded that "the higher officer corps was so committed to expedience that the organized distribution of drugs was accepted as necessary to the support of the South Vietnamese government, which often purveyed the drugs that destroyed the Army that defended it."[59] The CIA and the diplomatic corps in Vietnam prevented other governmental agencies from getting at the truth, while individuals with the CIA, if not the Agency itself, helped to fly drugs into Vietnam from Laos.

Despite an occasional attempt to do something—usually punishing the troops—about the blizzard of skag, neither the U.S. government nor the military ever accomplished anything worth mentioning. The much advertised urine testing (to be conducted in what the GIs called The Pee House of the August Moon) was ineffective because the tests were unreliable, the troops who were not hooked could flush their bodies before the tests, and no one was prepared actually to help the soldiers who were addicts. One scholar concluded that "in not rooting out the sources of heroin in Laos and Thailand, the government had simply made a calculation that the continued political and military support of those groups profiting from the drug traffic was worth the risk of hooking U.S. soldiers."[60] General Westmoreland, as usual, blamed everyone but his own senior officers: "The misuse of drugs...had spread from civilian society into the Army and became a major problem.... A serious dilution over the war years in the caliber of junior leaders contributed to this...."[61]

Racial conflict was suffused throughout the war, from 1968 until the end. Every service, including the previously calm air force, had race riots of varying magnitude. As some of America's cities burned, or rather as the ghettos in some cities burned, the domestic rage found its counterpart in the military. Fraggings were sometimes racially motivated. One battalion commander said, "What defeats me is the attitude among the blacks that 'black is right' no matter who is right or wrong." One black soldier said, "I'd just as soon shoot whitey as the VC."[62] In one incident that is what actually happened: Two white majors were shot trying to get some black GIs to turn down their tape recorder.

White officers were sometimes offended by expressions of black solidarity, including ritual handshakes, the closed fist, swearing, black jargon, and, especially, blacks arguing that they were being forced to fight "a white man's war." (The North Vietnamese and the NLF often tried to exploit that theme through various forms of psychological warfare.) The weight of the military justice system was lowered on black GIs far out of proportion to their numbers. The congressional Black Caucus did a study in 1971 that showed that half of all soldiers in jail were black.[63] The next year, the Defense Department learned that blacks were treated more harshly than whites for identical offenses. The occasional race riots were invariably triggered by the increasing militance of American blacks in general, the peculiarly obtuse social attitudes of many older military officers, the frustrated hopes of the Great Society, the sense of an unfair draft, and an unfair shake in Vietnam.

NOTES

1. "General Westmoreland Reports on Vietnam War," *U.S. News & World Report*, Nov. 28, 1966, p. 48.

2. James B. Stockdale, Foreword in Richard A. Gabriel, *To Serve with Honor* (Westport, Conn.: Greenwood Press, 1982), p. xiv.

3. William C. Westmoreland, "Progress Report on the War in Viet-Nam," Nov. 21, 1967, *Department of State Bulletin*, Dec. 11, 1967, p. 788.

4. Cincinnatus, *Self-Destruction*, p. 112.

5. Maureen Mylander, *The Generals* (New York: Dial Press, 1974), p. 12.

6. Starr, *The Discarded Army*, p. 12.

7. Bruce Lawlor in Santoli, *Everything We Had*, p. 176.

8. Herb Mock in *Ibid.*, p. 183.

9. William C. Westmoreland, "Analysis of Moral and Professional Climate in the Army," April 18, 1970, in U.S. Army War College, "Study on Military Professionalism," Carlisle Barracks, Pa., June 30, 1970, p. 53.

10. *Ibid.*, p. i.

11. *Ibid.*, p. iv.

12. *Ibid.*, pp. 13–14.

13. *Ibid.*, p. v.

14. *Ibid.*, p. B44.

15. *Ibid.*, pp. 12, 15.

16. *Ibid.*, p. B29.

17. *Ibid.*, p. 20.

18. *Ibid.*, p. 21.

19. *Ibid.*, pp. B1, B5.

20. *Ibid.*, p. 25.

21. *Ibid.*, pp. B1–2.

22. *Ibid.*

23. *Ibid.*, pp. B1–14.

24. A. D. Horne, ed., *The Wounded Generation*, (Englewood Cliffs, N.J.: Prentice-Hall, 1981), pp. 143–44.

25. David Shoup, "The New American Militarism," *The Atlantic Monthly*, April 1969, pp. 51–56.

26. Douglas Kinnard, *The War Managers*, (Hanover, N.H.: University Press of New England, 1977) p. 174.

27. Cincinnatus, *Self-Destruction*, p. 144.

28. Santoli, *Everything We Had*, p. 219.

29. Office of Systems Analysis, Office of the Secretary of Defense, "Experience in Command and Battle Deaths," January 1968, p. 24; Center of Military History, Department of the Army.

30. Office of the Deputy Chief of Staff for Personnel, Department of the Army, "Study of the 12-Month Vietnam Tour," June 29, 1970, Appendix: "Advantages and Disadvantages of 12-Month Hostile Fire Area Tour," p. 1; Center of Military History, Department of the Army.

31. Mylander, *The Generals*, p. 74.

32. Haynes Johnson and George C. Wilson, *Army in Anguish* (New York: Pocket Books, 1972), p. 76.

33. Office of Systems Analysis, "Experience in Command," p. 25.

34. *Ibid.*, p. 27.

35. *Ibid.*, p. 29.

36. *Ibid.*

37. *Ibid.,* p. 30.

38. *Ibid.,* "MACV Rebuttal," p. 15.

39. Oscar Grutsky, "The Effects of Succession," in Morris Janowitz, ed., *The New Military* (New York: Russell Sage Foundation, 1964), p. 89.

40. Westmoreland, *A Soldier Reports,* p. 417.

41. Army War College, "Study on Military Professionalism," p. 23.

42. *Ibid.,* p. 26.

43. Santoli, *Everything We Had,* p. 43.

44. Kinnard, *The War Managers,* p. 75.

45. *Ibid.*

46. Peter Goldman and Tony Fuller, *Charlie Company* (New York: William Morrow, 1983), p. 98.

47. Kinnard, *The War Managers,* p. 172.

48. James Fallows, *National Defense* (New York: Random House, 1981), p. 121.

49. Army War College, "Study on Military Professionalism," p. 29.

50. Robert J. Lifton, *Home from the War,* (NY: Simon & Schuster, 1973), p. 178.

51. Richard A. Gabriel and Paul L. Savage, *Crisis in Command* (New York: Hill and Wang, 1978), p. 182.

52. William Hauser, *America's Army in Crisis,* (Baltimore: John Hopkins University Press, 1973), p. 94.

53. Gabriel and Savage, *Crisis in Command,* p. 42.

54. Charles J. Levy, *Spoils of War* (Boston: Houghton Mifflin Co., 1974), p. 46.

55. Gabriel and Savage, *Crisis in Command,* p. 183.

56. Gabriel, *To Serve with Honor,* p. 4.

57. Gabriel and Savage, *Crisis in Command,* p. 45.

58. Gabriel, *To Serve with Honor,* p. 3.

59. Gabriel and Savage, *Crisis in Command,* p. 48.

60. Starr, *The Discarded Army,* p. 114.

61. Westmoreland, *A Soldier Reports,* p. 371.

62. Baskir and Strauss, *Chance and Circumstance,* p. 137.

63. *Ibid.,* p. 138.

25
The Question of American War Guilt
GUENTER LEWY

To large numbers of Americans, the defeat of their country's arms in Vietnam not only represents a deserved national humiliation in an ill-advised foreign involvement, and not only proves the political and military ineptitude of those who waged the war, but also constitutes just retribution for what amounts to a moral outrage. This view of the American record in Vietnam is by now very widely accepted, especially among younger people, for whom the American role in Vietnam appears to stand as the epitome of evil in the modern world.

I have just spent five years studying the record, including classified documents not previously examined by any outside researchers. My conclusion is that while the charges of American political and military ineptitude in Vietnam can be sustained by all the available evidence, and while the question of the overall prudence or justice of the American involvement is not easily resolved, the charges of officially condoned crimes and grossly immoral conduct are without substance. It is to this last class of issues that I address myself here.

Every war has its share of atrocities, and Vietnam was no exception. Every war also causes large-scale death and suffering to the civilian population on whose territory it is fought. But the horrors and outrages inherent in war are often ignored when the fighting is crowned with success and when the conflict is seen as morally justified. Thus, despite the fact that the Allies in World War II engaged in terror bombing of the enemy's civilian population, and generally paid only minimal attention to the prevention of civilian casualties, scarcely anyone on the Allied side objected. The war against Nazism and fascism was regarded as a crusade in which the Allies could do no wrong, and the fact that it ended in victory further vindicated the use of means that were questionable on both legal and moral grounds.

The Vietnam war, on the other hand, dragged on for years without a real decision, and it was never perceived as a clear-cut struggle between good and evil—unless it was they who were good and we who

This article is based on the author's book *American in Vietnam* published by Oxford University Press in 1978 (Galaxy Paperback 1980). From *Commentary* February 1978 "Vietnam: New Light on the Question of American Guilt" by Guenter Lewy. Reprinted by permission.

were evil. And this indeed is how the conflict was seen by many: a heroic underdog fighting the world's strongest and best-equipped military power. Moreover, on the Allied side the war took place in a fish bowl (the Communists barred all observers except those known to be supportive of their cause). Every mistake, failure, or misdeed was sooner or later exposed to view, and was widely reported by journalists who were generally critical of the American and South Vietnamese effort. On the other hand, the numerous violations of the law of war and of standards of human decency on the part of the Vietcong (VC) received only sporadic attention and were often rationalized as the justified tactics of resistance fighters battling an oppressive regime and its foreign helpers.

Thus, a situation gradually developed in which the Americans and the South Vietnamese could do hardly anything right. The Communists made skillful use of their worldwide propaganda apparatus to disseminate charges of American war crimes, and they found many Western intellectuals only too willing to accept at face value every conceivable allegation of wrongdoing. Repeated unceasingly, these accusations—no matter how flimsy the evidence for them—eventually came to be widely believed. Among rational people, claimed Noam Chomsky, it was not in dispute that the "United States command is responsible for major crimes in the layman's sense of this term." "The fact is," declared the Committee of Concerned Asian Scholars, "that U.S. war crimes are an accepted and regularly used method of waging war in Indochina."

There soon emerged a veritable industry publicizing alleged war crimes. American servicemen stepped forward with articles and books based on their experience in Vietnam, and became star witnesses before self-appointed bodies like the International War Crimes Tribunal organized by Bertrand Russell. These proceedings condemned as criminal such American actions as the relocation of population and the creation of free-fire zones, the use of napalm and herbicides, and the treatment of prisoners; they also indicted and convicted the American military for committing atrocities, and for the indiscriminate killing of civilians through bombing and other tactics amounting ultimately to genocide.

Basing myself on a wider range of evidence than has been available till now, I will in the pages that follow deal with these charges one at a time in terms of the international law of war, which aims at mitigating the ravages and cruelties of armed conflict and seeks to impose minimum standards of humane and civilized behavior upon the savagery of combat.

POPULATION RELOCATIONS AND FREE-FIRE ZONES

Throughout the war, but especially during the years 1966–70, the U.S. and the government of South Vietnam (GVN) engaged in extensive relocations of population, clearing areas of civilians and making them free-fire zones (after December 1965 known as specified strike zones—SSZ).

"One of the most flagrant violations of civilian rights is the forcible relocation of large units of people, in specific violation of Article 49 of the [Geneva] Civilians Convention of 1949, an article framed to avert repetition of the forcible relocations that took place in World War II." This was the finding in 1967 of a group of well-known American theologians, including Martin Luther King, Jr., Harvey G. Cox, Robert F. Drinan, Abraham Joshua Heschel, Martin E. Marty, and others. It appears, however, that these religious figures were mistaken in their interpretation of the law. Strictly speaking, there is a serious question as to whether Article 49 even applies to the hostilities in Vietnam. But if we stipulate that it does, we have to conclude that it not only *allows* the evacuation of civilians from a combat zone, but can be read to impose a *duty* of carrying out such relocations.

Relevant parts of Article 49 read as follows:

> Individual or mass forcible transfers, as well as deportations of protected persons from occupied territory to the territory of the Occupying Power or to that of any other country occupied or not, are prohibited, regardless of their motive.
>
> Nevertheless, the Occupying Power may undertake total or partial evacuation of a given area if the security of the population or imperative military reasons so demand.... Persons thus evacuated shall be transferred back to their homes as soon as hostilities in the area in question have ceased.
>
> The Occupying Power undertaking such transfers or evacuations shall ensure, to the greatest practicable extent, that proper accommodation is provided to receive the protected persons, that the removals are effected in satisfactory conditions of hygiene, health, safety, and nutrition, and that members of the same family are not separated.

The references to "Occupying Power" show that one of the main intents of this article is to prevent the deportation of people for purposes of subjecting them to forced labor—as the Germans did in World War II. The U.S. in Vietnam was not an occupying power but a co-belligerent, there with the approval of the government of South Vietnam. But even if we were to regard the U.S. as an occupying power, Article 49 specifically recognizes that "the Occupying Power may undertake total or partial evacuation of a given area if the security of the population or imperative military reasons so demand." It is certainly reasonable to suggest that the relocations carried out in Vietnam qualified on both of these counts.

While it is true that the American command was not merely unselfishly concerned with the "security of the population"—in the sense of protecting people against harm—but also sought to enhance the efficacy of its firepower, nevertheless the relocation of civilians did in fact provide the population with greater security than if it had remained in the combat zone. Conditions in the refugee camps were generally dismal, but the state of hygiene, health, and nutrition was on the whole in line with the local standard of living and with what one could expect in a wartime situation. Efforts were made to return evacuees to their homes as soon as hostilities ceased. (Some of the relocations of Montagnards carried out by the South Vietnamese probably did not live up to the standards laid down in Article 49, but a country's authority to move its *own* inhabitants is surely not covered by the Geneva conventions.)

As for "imperative military reasons," the principle of military necessity allows a belligerent to take all measures not forbidden by international law that are necessary for the defeat of the opponent in the least possible time and at the least cost to himself. In the light of this principle, the relocation of Vietnamese civilians in order to deprive the VC of support does not seem an unreasonable act. An eminent British juridical authority, Hersh Lauterpacht, even grants an occupying power the right to "general devastation" in cases "when, after the defeat of his main forces and occupation of his territory, an enemy disperses his remaining forces into small bands which carry on guerrilla tactics and receive food and information, so that there is no hope of ending the war except by general devastation which cuts the supplies of every kind from the guerrilla bands."

It is clear that the American command, however mistaken its judgment, really believed that forcible relocation of the civilian population would hasten the end of the war and was the most effective way of depriving the VC of supplies and manpower—the water in which they swam. The question as to what in such a situation constitutes "imperative military reasons" must be answered not by hindsight but in terms of what the military commanders at the time believed to be militarily necessary. As the Nuremberg tribunal ruled in the *Hostages* case: "It is our considered opinion that the conditions, as they appeared to the defendant at the time, were sufficient upon which he could honestly conclude that urgent military necessity warranted the decision made. This being true, the defendant may have erred in the exercise of his judgment, but he was guilty of no criminal act."

There is other evidence pointing toward a duty to remove civilians from a combat zone. In 1956, the International Committee of the Red Cross proposed that belligerents be required "to protect the civilian population subject to their authority from the dangers to which they would be exposed in an attack—in particular by removing them from the vicinity of military objectives and from the threatened areas." In 1970, the Secretary General of the United Nations argued, similarly, that civilians would be best protected if they did not remain in areas of danger, and he urged that the General Assembly "consider the usefulness of an appropriate resolution—a call on all authorities involved in armed conflicts of all types to do their utmost to insure that civilians are removed from, or kept out of, areas where conditions would be likely to place them in jeopardy or expose them to the hazards of warfare."

Unhappy with life in the refugee camps, or out of sympathy with the Vietcong, many villagers drifted back into or remained in areas declared SSZ's. Hence, when allied troops carried out ground operations or air strikes in these zones, there were civilians in them who were killed or wounded. However terrible on humanitarian grounds, and however counterproductive from the political point of view, these civilian casualties do not appear to raise an issue of criminal liability so long as adequate notice was given that an area was being designated an SSZ. Applicable rules of engagement did require such notice—after February 1969, a minimum of 72 hours notification in advance. If individual offers occasionally violated these rules, as they undoubtedly did, this was not authorized practice but a transgression of military regulations. Nor can the American command be held responsible for those instances in which the VC forcibly prevented villagers from leaving areas under their control. Lastly, while the Americans for a short time counted the large number of refugees as a political bonus (they later realized that refugees were a heavy liability), there existed no directives by the American command specifically authorizing the generating of refugees.

BOMBARDMENT AND DESTRUCTION OF POPULATED AREAS

It is incontrovertible that the allied military effort in Vietnam was characterized by the lavish use of firepower and caused much destruction and death. From this, many critics of American policy in Vietnam have concluded that American combat practices violated the law of war and that the U.S. was therefore guilty of war crimes. U.S. battlefield tactics, charged Richard A. Falk of Princeton University in 1971, involved "the massive use of cruel tactics directed indiscriminately against the civilian population in flagrant violation of the minimum rules of war."

An analysis of the applicable law of war suggests a different conclusion. It should be recognized, first, that the VC's practice of "clutching the people to their breast" and of converting hamlets into fortified strongholds was one of the main reasons for the occurrence of combat in populated areas. The existing law of war was not written to encompass this kind of warfare; to the extent that it does apply to insurgency warfare, it prohibits such tactics, for it seeks to achieve maximum distinction between combatants and innocent civilians. According to the Geneva convention of 1949, resistance fighters must carry arms openly and have "a fixed, distinctive sign recognizable at a distance"; the civilian population may not be used as a shield—"the presence of a protected person may not be used to render certain points or areas immune from military operations." Whether the VC were justified in disregarding these internationally accepted legal norms, as some writers have maintained, is an arguable question. The fact remains that by carrying the war into the hamlets and by failing properly to identify their combatants, the VC exposed the civilian population to grave harm.

The Fourth Hague Convention (1907) prohibits "the attack or bombardment, by whatever means, of towns, villages, dwellings, or buildings which are undefended." "Firing on localities which are undefended and without military significance," stated a 1966 directive of the American command in Vietnam, "is a war crime." Yet according to the general practice of states, once a village or town is occupied by a military force, or is fortified, it becomes a defended place and is subject to attack. The same holds true for civilian homes used to store war materiel. Such places become legitimate military objectives, and injuries suffered by the civilian population are considered incidental and unavoidable. Indeed, as the Geneva convention acknowledges, even hospitals lose their immunity if "they are used to commit, outside their humanitarian duties, acts harmful to the enemy," and if due warning has been given to cease such use. One can question the wisdom of attacking the VC once they had holed up in a hamlet—such a response might well be counterproductive in a counterinsurgency setting—but the practice was surely not a violation of the law of war.

In attacking a defended place, did American forces observe the rule of proportionality? The U.S. Army's Law of Land Warfare (1956) lays down that "loss of life and damage to property must not be out of proportion to the military advantage to be gained." In the context of Vietnam, this meant, for example, that an American unit drawing a single sniper shot from a village did not justify obliterating the entire village with artillery and air strikes. But what if there were five snipers blocking an important bridge situated in a hamlet? How could a commander make a precise estimate of the size of the enemy unit that was firing upon his men? One sniper using an automatic weapon could sound like a platoon. These were the sorts of difficult situations faced by American officers in Vietnam who, as always in combat, had to act on incomplete information.

There is no question that some military men panicked and overreacted to provocation. But, as with the policy of relocation, the question of whether a certain action was justified by military necessity must be decided in terms of the way a commander judged the specific circumstances of the situation at the time. "If the facts were such," declared the Nuremberg tribunal in the *Hostages* case, "as would justify the action by the exercise of judgment, after giving consideration to all the factors and existing possibilities, even though the conclusion reached may have been faulty, it cannot be said to be criminal." If a commander in Vietnam employed artillery and air strikes against a village—whether because he overestimated the size of the enemy force or because he sought to avoid excessive casualties to his own men—and his action resulted in the loss of civilian life, he may have damaged the effort to win the political support of the people of the South, but his action was probably not illegal.

Another source of confusion in judging the issue of civilian casualties was the designation by many critics of all villagers as innocent civilians. Yet we know that on occasion in Vietnam, women and children set mines and booby traps in place, and that villagers of all ages and sexes, willingly or under duress, served as porters, built fortifications, or engaged in other acts helping the Communist armed forces. It is well established under the laws of war that once civilians act as support personnel, they cease to be noncombatants and are subject to attack. Of course, allied troops had no way of knowing how many dead persons found after battle in a defended hamlet were VC or VC helpers and how many were innocent civilians. Here again we see the terrible consequence of the fact that the VC chose to fight from within villages and hamlets which provided useful cover, avenues of escape, and a source of labor for the building of fortifications. Inevitably the civilian population was involved in the fighting.

The Geneva convention forbids the destruction of personal property "except where such destruction is rendered absolutely necessary by military operations." It does allow the destruction of fortifications. Since the VC often built their trenches, bunkers, and escape tunnels right in the middle of hamlets—if not in, around, and underneath huts and houses—the destruction of fortifications usually amounted to the destruction of homes or even entire hamlets. This is what happened in the widely publicized case of Cam Ne (4) in 1965 as well as in numerous other instances, and critics soon began accusing U.S. forces of conducting a scorched-earth policy. In response to one such complaint, involving the burning of two villages in Binh Dinh province, the Army's Assistant Judge Advocate General explained that "the two Vietnamese villages were not burned as a reprisal for the hostile fire that came from the houses in the village. They were destroyed because the houses and tunnel networks connecting them constituted enemy fortified positions." There undoubtedly were many cases where houses were destroyed without compelling justification: in practice it was often difficult to distinguish an enemy bunker, constructed right under a hut, from a shelter built by a villager for his protection. Once again, we are dealing here with incidents that were a consequence of the war-fighting methods of the VC and not of the Americans.

NAPALM

The Fourth Hague Convention forbids the employment of "arms, projectiles, or material calculated to cause unnecessary suffering," and the American Law of Land Warfare accepts this prohibition. The rule is an expression of the general principles of proportionality and humanity which reflect the intent of the law of war to avoid needless suffering. Yet in practice states have drawn the line between necessary and unnecessary suffering in a way hardly suggested by the humanitarian spirit of the Hague convention. The criterion has normally been whether a weapon inflicts suffering disproportionate to the military advantage to be gained by its use, and this has meant that no militarily decisive and effective weapon has ever been regarded as causing "unnecessary suffering." Suggestions that humanitarian factors such as the nature of the injury, long-term medical effects, the risk of death, etc., be given greater weight have so far not been accepted, and the test has remained that of actual practice. According to the U.S. Law of Land Warfare: "What weapons cause 'unnecessary injury' can only be determined in light of the practice of states in refraining from the use of a given weapon because it is believed to have that effect."

Fire as a weapon of war has a long history. In this century, petroleum fuels have been used in flamethrowers, bombs, shells, and mines, but it was the discovery of the thickener napalm in World War II that greatly increased the effectiveness of incendiary weapons, especially against equipment and fortified positions. It is estimated that during World War II, about 14,000 tons of napalm bombs were used, two-thirds of them in the Pacific area: in the Korean war, the U.S. Far East Air Force dropped a total of 32,557 tons of napalm. But the most extensive reliance on incendiary weapons took place in Indochina. Napalm bombs there constituted about 10 per cent of all fighter-bomber munitions, reaching an estimated total of close to 400,000 tons during the course of the war.

Incendiary munitions proved particularly important against enemy forces holed up in caves, bunkers, and tunnel complexes, and against targets in such close proximity to allied troops that high-explosive fragmentation bombs could not be employed. The American command's rules of engagement provided that in attacks on villages and hamlets, "the use of incendiary-type ammunition will be avoided unless absolutely necessary in the accomplishment of the commander's mission," but in practice this rule does not appear to have restricted the use of such weapons. A Marine captain told the House Armed Services Committee in September 1965 that napalm at first was denied in some instances, but "now we can have napalm whenever we want it." Air strikes with napalm bombs are indeed mentioned routinely in most after-action reports. Also, during Operation Cedar Falls in January 1967, flamethrowers were employed "to assist in the capture of VC located in bunkers and tunnels. The flamethrowers reduced the amount of oxygen in the tunnels, to say nothing of producing a significantly adverse psychological effect on the enemy."

Protests against incendiary weapons were heard early in the war. Critics charged that napalm was being used indiscriminately against civilian targets, and they argued that it was an illegal weapon because it maximized suffering by killing its victims slowly and maiming permanently. In January 1967, *Ramparts* magazine published an article which included large color photographs of burned children; the author stated that he personally had seen thousands of infants and small children burned by napalm in Vietnamese hospitals. The International Commission of Inquiry into U.S. Crimes in Indochina, meeting in Oslo in 1971, concluded that napalm and phosphorus bombs constituted a prohibited method of warfare because they were "designed to cause 'unnecessary suffering' as defined in Article 23 of the Fourth Hague Convention of 1907." During the fighting near An Loc in the spring of 1972, a little girl was hit by napalm; the picture of this naked child running in terror along a road shocked the world.

There is no question that incendiary munitions in Vietnam caused civilian casualties, including children. But there is also no question that the impression created by America's critics of many thousands of villagers and children being burned by napalm was false. In the spring of

1967, a team of physicians representing the Committee of Responsibility to Save War-Burned and War-Injured Vietnamese Children (COR) visited 35 of the 45 government hospitals in South Vietnam and reported 105 burn victims, 29 of whom were children. Thirty-eight of these 105 burns were war-caused; the rest were so-called household burns. The total number of war-burned children seen was 16.

Another medical team, organized by the Agency for International Development (AID), visited Vietnamese hospitals in the summer of 1967 at the suggestion of President Johnson, and found a similar situation: "Throughout our visit, individual teams paid particular attention to burns. The cases were relatively limited in number in relation to other injuries and illnesses, and we saw no justification for the undue emphasis which had been placed by the press upon civilian burns caused by napalm." In a separate account, Dr. John H. Knowles of the Massachusetts General Hospital, a member of the AID-sponsored team, wrote that, in all, "burns due to napalm are very few and far between...."

Both medical teams agreed that the majority of burns were due to the explosion of gasoline used in lanterns and for cooking as well as from the spillage of hot boiling water from rice pots. Other observers on the scene, including non-American physicians who worked as volunteers in Vietnamese hospitals, have confirmed this finding. An Australian doctor reported in 1968 that exploding petrol lanterns were "probably a more frequent cause of serious burns in Vietnam than napalm or white phosphorus," and the wife of an English doctor who served on a medical team at Saigon Children's Hospital wrote that they looked for positive evidence of napalm burns "without seeing a case about which we could be certain. Most of the burns had been caused by domestic accidents...." A radio campaign to alert the Vietnamese to the danger involved in using mixtures containing highly combustible jet fuel had had some success by 1973, though accidents continued to happen. Two fires in refugee camps, which resulted in loss of life, were traced to this source.

Another cause of burn wounds which received even less attention outside Vietnam was the use of napalm-fueled Russian-made flamethrowers by the Vietcong and the North Vietnamese. One incident that did receive publicity because of the scope and enormity of the atrocity was the attack in December 1967 on the Montagnard hamlet of Dak Son in Phuoc Long province, some 75 miles northeast of Saigon, which contained a large number of refugees. Seeking to drive home the point that the South Vietnamese government could not protect refugees, some 600 Vietcong, armed with an estimated 60 flamethrowers, attacked the hamlet at midnight. The ensuing massacre left 252 of the Montagnards dead and nearly 50 wounded, 33 of them with severe burns.

The fact that hospitals in Vietnam had relatively few civilian patients with napalm-caused burn wounds does not in and of itself prove that few civilians were hurt by napalm. Medical studies have shown that napalm burns are deep and that mortality from respiratory embarrassment, shock, fluid loss, and sepsis is high in proportion to the total body surface area involved, especially in the case of children. According to some observers, this meant that under wartime conditions relatively few napalm burn victims were able to reach a hospital alive or, if they did reach medical help, they died soon after admission. In conformity with Vietnamese custom, moreover, many moribund patients were taken by their relatives to die at home. Napalm, wrote the leader of an Australian surgical team which spent three months in 1967 in a Vietnamese hospital, is "an all-or-nothing weapon, and just as it was not usual to be called upon to treat bayonet wounds in World War I or II, . . . it is rare to see napalm burns; in 3 months we did not encounter a single instance." But the evidence for napalm's unusually high mortality rate is fragmentary and inconclusive.

There is general agreement that while many patients with third-degree burns will die without feeling much pain, those who survive or those with less severe burns will experience excruciating pain over a long period of time. But it is questionable whether the suffering caused by incendiary weapons is worse than that resulting from the crush and blast effects of high explosives, and even more doubtful is the claim that this suffering is disproportionate to the military advantage derived from the use of such weapons. Because these munitions are grimly effective against underground bunkers and fortified positions, and because their area of effectiveness is more limited than that of high explosives, they are not easily replaceable by other weapons. The consensus of legal opinion, therefore, is that as the law of war stands today, incendiary weapons employed against targets necessitating their use do not violate Article 23 of the Fourth Hague Convention. The actual practice of states in relying on flamethrowers and firebombs in most military conflicts since World War I further demonstrates that no customary rule of international law exists which forbids resort to these weapons.

DEFOLIATION AND CROP DESTRUCTION

In October 1962, the first large-scale defoliation mission was flown by American planes against some 8,000 acres of mangrove forest along rivers and canals in the Ca Mau peninsula, a longtime VC stronghold in the southern tip of South Vietnam. The first crop-destruction mission carried out by South Vietnamese personnel and helicopters was undertaken on November 21, 1962.

Once approved in principle, both defoliation and crop-destruction programs quickly escalated, reaching a high point in 1967. Between 1965 and 1971, 3.2 per cent of South Vietnam's cultivated land and 46.4 per cent of the total forest area were sprayed one or more times. Only about 3 per cent of the population lived in defoliated areas, and less than 1 per cent in areas where crops were destroyed. According to the guidelines laid down by the Department of Defense, crop destruction was limited to VC-controlled territory in I, II, and III Corps, "where food is scarce and where denial of food would create an operational burden on the enemy." Special care was to be taken to prevent damage to rubber and fruit trees. The entire herbicide program was formally directed by the South Vietnamese government; U.S. personnel assisted in the selection of targets, planning, and evaluation. A special Air Force unit flew light (C-123) planes with spraying equipment in what was known as Operation Ranch Hand. Aircraft participating in the crop-destruction program had to be flown under the so-called Farmgate rules which required Vietnamese markings and a Vietnamese observer aboard.

Approximately 90 percent of the total herbicide effort was devoted to defoliation. Carried out along roads and canals, with emphasis on ambush sites and tax-collection points, and in jungle terrain, defoliation was held to be effective in improving aerial observation and inhibiting enemy movement during daylight hours. It also improved the defense of base perimeters by opening fields of fire and facilitating observation from outposts. The crop-destruction program, on the other hand, drew a more mixed evaluation. Given the close relationship between the VC and the rural population, the major portion of the crops destroyed through aerial spraying was inevitably civilian-owned and cultivated. The chief sufferers when crops were destroyed were the local people, because the VC compensated for their own losses by confiscating more food.

The question whether the crops destroyed belonged to the civilian population or were grown solely for the enemy's armed forces is significant in assessing the legality of herbicide operations. There exists general agreement that enemy forces may be deprived of food and water in order to compel them to surrender. But when measures are taken to render stocks of food and water unusable, this intent should be evident to the enemy to avoid offending Article 23(a) of the Fourth Hague Convention which forbids employment of "poison or poisoned weapons" and which thus prohibits the deliberate contamination of food and water actually consumed by the enemy.

American belief in the legality of the chemical destruction of crops used by enemy forces was based on a memorandum prepared in March 1945 by Major General Myron C. Cramer, then Judge Advocate General, concerning the possible use of chemical anti-crop agents against pockets of Japanese on the Pacific islands. Cramer argued that the use of chemical agents to destroy cultivations or retard their growth would not violate international law, provided "that such chemicals do not produce poisonous effects upon enemy personnel, either from direct contact, or indirectly from ingestion of plants and vegetables which have been exposed thereto." Following this interpretation, the Army's manual of land warfare states that the general proscription of poison and poisoned weapons "does not prohibit measures being taken to dry up springs, to divert rivers and aqueducts from their courses, or to destroy, through chemical or bacterial agents harmless to man, crops intended solely for consumption by the armed forces (if that fact can be determined)." But in Vietnam it was impossible to establish with certainty that the crops to be destroyed were intended solely for the enemy's armed forces.

In such situations, crop destruction can still be lawful if it is demanded by the necessities of war and if the extent of destruction is not disproportionate to the military advantage gained. The property of noncombatants in a war zone does not enjoy complete immunity from attack, and the humanitarian principle that noncombatants should not be deprived of food is similarly not absolute. Thus, it is considered legal to prevent noncombatants from leaving a besieged place in order to worsen the logistical burden of the defenders and hasten their surrender. The 1949 Geneva Convention for the Protection of Civilian Persons in Time of War requires the passage of "essential foodstuffs ... intended for children under fifteen, expectant mothers, and maternity cases," subject to the condition that there exist no serious grounds for fearing "that the consignments may be diverted from their destination" or will cause a definite advantage to the enemy's military efforts or economy. While the application of some of these provisions to the hostilities in South Vietnam is problematic, they do show that civilians may in certain circumstances be deprived of food.

Then there is the question of whether herbicides used for defoliation and crop destruction had poisonous effects upon humans and therefore violated the Fourth Hague Convention. This was the charge made by Communist propaganda from the time herbicides were first employed in Vietnam in 1962.

In America itself, criticism of the use of herbicides was at first limited to concern for the ecology of South Vietnam, and did not endorse Communist charges of poisonous effects on humans. The first intimation of possible harm to man came when a study by the Bionetic Research Laboratories of selected pesticides and industrial chemicals used in the U.S. reported teratogenic effects (malformations) in test animals caused by 2,4,5-T, a component of Agent Orange (named for the color markings on its shipping container), the principal herbicide used in Vietnam. This study, undertaken during the period of 1965–68 and then filed and forgotten, was accidentally found in an office of the Food and Drug Administration in the summer of 1969, and when brought to the attention of the White House led to an announcement on October 29, 1969 that the use of 2,4,5-T was being partially curtailed. When other studies confirmed the teratogenic effects of 2,4,5-T, the Department of Defense began to reduce the scope of the herbicide program. On March 11, 1970, it was announced that all defoliation operations in Vietnam were being reduced by 25 percent, and on April 15, 1970, the use of Agent Orange was suspended pending a review. At the same time, the Department of Agriculture announced a ban on the domestic use of 2,4,5-T except along rights-of-way and in remote forest and range areas.

The suspension of Agent Orange resulted in a further decrease of herbicide operations. Because of a shortage of Agent Blue, the other commonly used herbicide in Vietnam, two brigades of the Americal Division in the summer of 1970 continued to use Agent Orange for crop destruction in violation of the suspension order. A subsequent investigation by the Inspector General revealed that brigade and division commanders had falsified reports to hide this practice. Disciplinary action was taken against the officers involved, and remaining stocks of Agent Orange were put under stringent control. Both defoliation and crop destruction were phased out completely by June 30, 1971.

Meanwhile, reports were coming out of Vietnam of an increase in the number of stillbirths and birth defects among Vietnamese exposed to herbicide operations. In 1969, the American Association for the Advancement of Science (AAAS) appointed a Herbicide Assessment Commission headed by Professor Matthew Meselson of Harvard University. The commission spent months in preparatory study and in the summer of 1970 went on an inspection tour of about six weeks in South Vietnam. In its report to the AAAS in December 1970, the commission stated that it found no evidence of sudden or new appearance of congenital abnormalities, but added that inadequate health statistics and wartime conditions made any firm conclusions impossible.

In October 1970, Congress ordered the Secretary of Defense to contract with the National Academy of Science (NAS) for a full study of herbicide operations in Vietnam. This assignment was undertaken by a committee headed by Dr. Anton Lang, director of the MSU/AEC Plant Research Laboratory, and a lengthy report was completed by January 1974. The committee had received reports of serious illness and death allegedly caused by herbicide operations, especially among children of the Montagnard people heavily affected by the crop-destruction program, but it could not visit the central highland and concluded that, in the absence of medical studies of the exposed populations, these reports could be neither confirmed nor refuted. With regard to congenital malformations, the committee studied the records of several hospitals but could find no conclusive evidence of an association between herbicides and birth defects. The committee recommended further studies of the effects of dioxin, an ingredient of Agent Orange known to have teratogenic effects in mice and rats, which could be found in the Vietnamese food chain.

As of now, therefore, we have no firm scientific evidence of any direct damage to human health caused by herbicides. The reported increase in the incidence of birth defects may simply be a result of the fact that in the late 1960's more people in Vietnam were receiving medical care, which would lead to greater reporting of such cases. The damage to the ecology of South Vietnam has no doubt been substantial, though the NAS study shows that the fertility of the soil has not suffered any permanent damage and the loss of timber stocks has also been somewhat less than was originally feared. The charge of "ecocide" has been a politically effective slogan, though its precise meaning is not clear and no evidence whatever of any lasting damage to the economic sustenance of South Vietnam has so far been produced. In any event, the issue of ecological damage is irrelevant to the question of whether herbicides violate the Hague convention, which is concerned only with the effect of weapons upon humans. In a situation where defoliation could prevent casualties, the preoccupation of the critics with environmental issues also demonstrates a certain callousness and indifference to the value of human life.

It is possible to argue that the military should have been more alert and sensitive to the possible biological consequences of herbicide operations, but it must be remembered that the herbicides in question had been used worldwide for the control of weeds and unwanted vegetation without causing serious hazards. The record of the military in this respect is probably no worse than that of civilian authorities with regard to various domestically used pesticides and herbicides. As mentioned above, soon after serious questions about the teratogenic effects of Agent Orange were raised, its use was suspended, and the entire herbicide effort was finally halted. The charge of a deliberate violation of article 23(a) of the Fourth Hague Convention, forbidding the employment of poison or poisoned weapons, would therefore appear to be baseless.

Another legal challenge to herbicides in war has been based on the Geneva Gas Protocol of 1925 which forbids, in addition to poisonous gases, "all analogous liquids, materials, or devices" and "bacteriological methods of warfare." Even though the U.S. at the time of the war in Vietnam was not a party to this treaty, it has been argued that the treaty had become declaratory of customary law and therefore was binding on all states irrespective of their adherence to the protocol. But there is some question whether the Geneva protocol really applies to herbicides, for both the text and the legislative history are ambiguous on this point. The State Department in 1969 took the position that the U.S., although not a party to the agreement, was "pledged to observe strictly the principles and objectives of the protocol," but that chemical anti-plant agents like those used domestically in many countries, unlike living organisms causing plant diseases, were not prohibited by the protocol. Moreover, even if the protocol is held to outlaw herbicides, it is not at all clear that the use of such weapons has been absorbed in customary law. The fact that little resort has so far been made to them is not in itself decisive. The international lawyers Ann van Wynen Thomas and A. J. Thomas, Jr., therefore conclude: "The split of authority among reputable international jurists makes evidence of the existence of a customary rule doubtful, and, if it is in existence, evidence of its extent equivocal."

On November 25, 1969, President Nixon renounced the first use of lethal or incapacitating chemical agents and of all methods of biological warfare. The renunciation did not include herbicides. A treaty prohibiting the development, production, and stockpiling of bacteriological (biological) weapons was signed on April 10, 1972, in Washington, Moscow, and

London, and was submitted to the Senate for approval in August of that year. But the Senate Foreign Relations Committee delayed action, because it sought first a resolution of the riot-control and herbicide questions involved in the Geneva protocol. By 1974, the Ford administration was prepared to yield on these two issues and agreed to renounce the first use of herbicides in war except for control of vegetation within U.S. bases and installations or around their immediate defensive perimeters. Any use of herbicides in war would have to be approved by the President. Executive Order 11850, issued April 8, 1975, made this renunciation of the first use of herbicides in war national policy. Thus, even though defoliation and crop destruction as practiced in Vietnam did not violate the laws of war, they have now been ruled out as acceptable military tactics by the United States.

COUNTERINSURGENCY: THE PHOENIX AND EMERGENCY-DETENTION PROGRAMS

Among the important measures introduced by the new pacification program that began in 1967 was a stepped-up attack on the Vietcong Infrastructure (VCI) in the villages. This was the apparatus—made up of Communist-party, National Liberation Front (NLF), and (after 1969) Provisional Revolutionary Government (PRG) cadres—which directed the insurgency against the government of South Vietnam. Its members engaged in acts of terrorism, extortion, sabotage, and abduction; they also contributed to the enemy's military operations by recruiting soldiers and collecting taxes and intelligence as well as by providing guides, food, clothing, weapons, medical supplies, and logistical support. As long as this clandestine organization maintained its strength amid the rural population, the victories scored by the allies in the war against Vietcong and North Vietnamese main-force units were in large part irrelevant. The belated realization of the importance of destroying this politico-military apparatus led to the establishment of the Phuong Hoang (Phoenix) program.

In a war not short on misconceptions, misinformation, and deception, the Phoenix program ranks high as a focus of misunderstanding. Despite repeated attempts by American officials to explain its purpose and mode of operation to both the Congress and the American public, the explanations somehow never managed to catch up with sensationalist media reports and the barrage of accusations made by the critics of American policy in Vietnam who called Phoenix an assassination program and an example of the moral depravity of the American involvement. In evaluating these charges, it should be borne in mind that since in the eyes of many of these critics the VC were revolutionaries and fighters for national liberation, the insurgents' use of terror was regarded as a necessary and legitimate tactic, while any concerted action *against* the VC apparatus became, almost by definition, illegitimate and immoral.

The aim of the Phoenix program was to improve the collection of information about the VCI, to identify its members, and to conduct operations leading to their apprehension. It was a Vietnamese program for which, as in the case of all war-related programs mounted by the government of South Vietnam, the U.S. provided advice and financial assistance. Its origin can be traced to the CIA-directed Intelligence Coordination and Exploitation (ICEX) advisory program of 1967, which sought to bring all military and civilian agencies concerned with intelligence into alignment. On July 1, 1968, the South Vietnamese accepted formal responsibility for this program, which was now named Phuong Hoang (translated Phoenix). After January 1, 1969, CIA responsibility was gradually phased out and on July 1, 1969, the program was put under the advisory function of CORDS (Civil Operations and Revolutionary Development Support), the agency within the American command coordinating the pacification effort. By 1971, Phoenix had about 600 American military and 40–50 civilian advisers. Most of them served in the District Intelligence and Operation Centers which supervised the collection of information on individual members of the VCI and planned operations against those identified as Vietcong operatives by using appropriate police, military, or paramilitary forces. Those arrested were subject to trial by military courts or to an administrative-detention procedure known as *an tri.*

In earlier years, the pressure on the VCI had been erratic at best. Intelligence was poor, and thanks to corruption those arrested were often released quickly. "There is reason to believe," concluded a CORDS study in December 1967, "that any individual possessing a sufficient amount of cash can purchase his freedom at any level of the penal system in Vietnam." The new procedures sought to improve the accuracy of information about the VCI and to achieve a more effective and consistent handling of Vietcong suspects. The word "neutralize" was applied to the overall goal of destroying the VCI—whether its members were captured or were killed or defected.

The charge that Phoenix was an assassination program arose because reports always included a considerable number listed as killed. When administration spokesmen explained that these were killed in the course of normal military operations, or police actions, or in fighting off arrest with the use of armed force, their explanations were met with considerable skepticism. The administration could have strengthened its position by introducing other available data on the Phoenix program which showed, for example, that during the 15 months from January 1970 to March 1971 less than 6 percent of those killed were killed as a result of special targeting. The vast majority of VCI killed (9,827 of 10,443) were killed in the course of operations, many of which were not even initiated by government forces, and were only later identified as VCI. The fact that so few of those killed were on the Phoenix target list certainly undermines the charge that Phoenix was a program of planned assassinations. But for the administration to introduce these data would also have demonstrated the weakness of the entire program: relatively few operations were targeted against known members of the VCI because despite a large, organized intelligence effort, the identity and/or whereabouts of most of these men were just not known. The full story, consequently, was withheld, and the result was a further widening of the "credibility gap."

Individuals found to belong or suspected of belonging to the VCI— seized by the police, territorial forces, or in allied military operations— were either tried by military courts or were subject to emergency detention (*an tri*). The need for such administrative procedure arose from the desire not to have to produce valuable intelligence agents in open court and from the difficulty of obtaining sufficient evidence or finding witnesses who would dare to testify against Vietcong cadres. These problems are encountered in many countries having to deal with terrorist organizations, and the establishment of an administrative emergency-detention program is not unique to Vietnam. Wartime emergencies, moreover, often require protective measures unprovided for in normal peacetime legal procedures; here, too, there are many historical precedents, including in the United States.

In view of the fact that emergency detention generally involves the treatment of civilian persons by their own government, such programs are not regulated by international law. The Geneva Convention for the Protection of Civilian Persons in Time of War applies to persons who "find themselves, in case of a conflict or occupation, in the hands of a Party to the conflict or Occupying Power of which they are not nationals." Hence South Vietnamese civilians detained by the government of South Vietnam were not "protected persons" within the meaning of this convention. The convention also does not apply to persons who are citizens of a co-belligerent state (as was South Vietnam in regard to the U.S.) if the state holding them has normal diplomatic relations with their own government. This means that South Vietnamese civilians, captured or detained by U.S. forces, were similarly not covered by the Geneva convention on civilians. (Captured members of the Vietcong main or local forces were considered prisoners of war and were not subject to the Phoenix or *an tri* programs.)

None of the specific provisions of the 1949 Geneva conventions is applicable to terrorists except that such persons, like all individuals not considered "protected persons," are to be treated humanely—ruling out, presumably, such punishments as shooting without trial. With regard to the VCI, both the Americans and the South Vietnamese accepted as binding Article 3, common to the four Geneva conventions, which prescribes minimum standards of humanitarian treatment to be extended to all individuals not considered "protected persons" within the terms of the conventions. Article 3 prohibits "the passing of sentences...without previous judgment by a regularly constituted court," but this provision is generally held to apply only to sentencing for crimes and does not prohibit emergency detention without formal trial as practiced since World War II in Malaya, Kenya, Northern Ireland, and Vietnam. Article 23(b) of the Fourth

Hague Convention makes it illegal "to kill or wound treacherously individuals belonging to the hostile nation or army," and this provision has been construed as ruling out assassinations or putting a price on the head of enemy individuals. But the Phoenix program neither involved "individuals belonging to the hostile nation or army" nor did it constitute a program of planned assassinations.

By 1972–73, the *an tri* procedure had become a favorite target of Hanoi's sympathizers. The United States was held at least indirectly responsible for it, and it was also cited as proof of the repressive character of the Thieu regime. But if emergency detention in and of itself is not necessarily an unacceptable violation of individual liberty, it is also necessary to reject the allegation that the South Vietnamese government imprisoned hundreds of thousands of political prisoners. This charge had its origin in Hanoi. On January 18, 1971, the *Vietnam Courier* in Hanoi asserted that South Vietnamese prisons held over 200,000 South Vietnamese patriots who were dying a slow death there. In the summer of 1973, a Paris-educated Redemptorist priest in Saigon, Father Chan Tin, charged in a mimeographed handout that as of June 1, 1973, the South Vietnamese government was detaining 202,000 prisoners. Chan Tin said that he headed an organization called the Committee to Investigate Mistreatment of Political Prisoners. Western newsmen and Americans visiting Vietnam reported him to be a man deeply concerned with human suffering. In September 1973, some of Hanoi's friends in Washington, operating the Indochina Resource Center, presented Chan Tin's charges and figures to a congressional committee, where they appeared to make an impression. After the fall of Saigon in 1975, it turned out that Chan Tin and several other Catholic priests had been part of the Vietcong underground in Saigon. "They presented themselves as exponents of the Third Force," writes a well-informed European journalist with left-wing political leanings, Tiziano Terzani, who stayed in Saigon after the Communist takeover, "but in reality they were part of an operation whose purpose was to back up the struggle of the National Liberation Front."

Chan Tin's figure of 202,000 political prisoners was checked in two exhaustive investigations by American embassy officials in Saigon and was found to exceed by far the total prison and detention population in South Vietnam, which in the July–August 1973 period was around 35,000. This figure included all common criminals as well as all *an tri* detainees. The American surveys were based on statistics supplied by the Saigon government to the approximately 200 CORDS public-safety advisers, who were in a good position to check their trustworthiness, as well as on South Vietnamese records meant for internal use, i.e., what the government in Saigon was telling itself on this subject. The broad accuracy of the embassy figures was confirmed after the fall of Saigon. For example, Terzani reports that 7,000 prisoners were freed from the Chi Hoa prison in Saigon; the embassy survey in 1973 had given the number of prisoners there as 7,911.

But the most serious flaw in Chan Tin's charges was his use of the term "political prisoner" applied indiscriminately to all *an tri* detainees. The *an tri* net at times caught innocents, seized to extort a bribe, or anti-Communist oppositionists to Thieu's autocratic rule, but to maintain that all detainees were political prisoners surely was to take unacceptable liberties with the meaning of this term. The friendly neighborhood Communist who planted bombs under civilian buses or assassinated teachers and hamlet chiefs was no more a "political prisoner" when apprehended than Lee Harvey Oswald or Sirhan Sirhan.

The naiveté with which many Americans approached the entire problem was exemplified by the support extended in this country to one of the best-known "political prisoners," Huynh Tan Mam. Supposedly a pacifist and neutralist, he repeatedly participated in and led demonstrations in Saigon protesting the government's war policy and U.S. involvement in Southeast Asia, for which actions he was arrested many times. The *Vietnam Courier* in Hanoi reported happily on February 13, 1971, for example, that at a demonstration held on February 9, a day after the incursion into Laos, "a military vehicle was burned in front of the U.S. embassy" and Huynh Tan Mam denounced the collusion of Thieu and Nixon who were "sending South Vietnamese youth to a senseless death in Laos in place of GI's to the only interests of the U.S. imperialists." It is possible to argue that on the whole the Saigon government could have been more tolerant of political dissent, but it is difficult to deny that leading street demonstrations accompanied by violence constitutes an overt act which a country at war fighting for its life may be legitimately unwilling to allow. On May 1, 1975, a day after the fall of Saigon, Huynh Tan Mam was honored and rewarded for his services to the Communist cause. At the beginning of the first TV broadcast from Saigon celebrating the "liberation" of the capital, the playing of the NLF anthem was followed by a speech by Huynh Tan Mam, with the screen showing a portrait of Ho Chi Minh.

Detention as a VC suspect under the *an tri* procedure, and life in South Vietnamese jails generally, were obviously no picnic. As is the case in most developing nations, the guards were poorly paid and were not paragons of enlightened correctional practice. American financial assistance and American advisers, in the face of heavy odds, gradually improved prison conditions somewhat. Housing, sanitation, medical care, and food were upgraded, and the death rate was reduced substantially. Given all this, it is unlikely that the termination of all public-safety programs in South Vietnam, mandated by Congress in 1973, contributed to the well-being of the inmates of the South Vietnamese correctional system. But Congress was impressed by the horror stories about political prisoners in South Vietnam and was anxious to liquidate all remnants of the American involvement.

Another dubious tale that influenced Congress was that of the prisoners allegedly paralyzed in the "tiger cages" of Con Son. This began with the charge that the South Vietnamese government at its Con Son island prison, a former French penal colony, kept inmates in underground cells which were fit only for caged animals. Congressmen William Anderson and Augustus Hawkins, accompanied by staff aide Thomas Harkin and Don Luce of the World Council of Churches, who came upon these cells during an inspection tour of the prison in July 1970, did not in fact report that they were below ground. But use of the term "pits" by Harkin and the publication of his photographs in *Life* magazine, taken looking down into the cells, created the impression of subterranean, tiny, dark dungeons. The imaginations of other writers soon enlarged upon this initial report. "The tiger cages," wrote Alfred Hassler, director of the Fellowship of Reconciliation, in 1970, "are too short for even the small Vietnamese to lie full-length in them, and the ceilings are so low that the inmates can barely stand." In 1973, Sylvan Fox described them in the New York *Times* as "small concrete trenches with bars on top, in which five to seven prisoners were cramped in a space about 5 feet wide, 6 feet long, and 6 feet deep."

In point of fact, the 48 cells were entirely above ground, they had ordinary doors in front, and they measured 6 feet 3 inches in width, 10 feet 6 inches in length, and 10 feet in height. Built by the French in 1941 as punishment cells for unruly prisoners, in 1970 they were still being used for this purpose, usually five prisoners to a cell. This gave each prisoner about 13 ⅛ square feet of floor space. The distance of 10 feet from the floor to the ceiling bars would have accommodated a standing human giant, and the length of 10 feet 6 inches would have enabled him to stretch out as well.

The prisoners in the tiger cages, reported the visiting Congressmen and Don Luce, were unable to stand up and claimed to be paralyzed. "Until a few days ago, they said they had been shackled to a bar that went across one end of the cage.... 'We will be shackled again in a few days,' one said as he crawled around the cage using his hands to move himself. One of the prisoners pointed to the scars on his useless legs and said, 'We were shackled here for months.' "

The facts again were somewhat different. The prisoners were shackled between the hours of 5 P.M. and 6 A.M. because the doors to the old cells were no longer strong enough to withstand pressure. As to the claimed paralysis, there is evidence to indicate that this condition was simulated as part of a propaganda scheme. Thus on December 22, 1970, and on January 5-6, 1971, three military neurologists examined 116 of the prisoners who complained of paralysis of the legs. They reported: "All patients had normal musculature without atrophy or fasciculation.... All patients had normal ankle and knee deep-tendon reflexes with no pathological reflexes.... In addition, patients who complained of total paralysis were observed to move the legs when asked to roll over, slide back on the examination table, or remove clothing." The three physicians concluded: "There is no objective evidence of organic neurological disease at this time." All of these prisoners were offered therapy for their condition; all refused.

ATROCITIES

The conflict in Vietnam was a guerrilla war without fronts—a setting especially conducive to atrocities. In such a setting, frustration and anxiety run
high, and these give rise in turn to aggressive behavior. This certainly was
the experience of American servicemen in Vietnam. Troops would tramp
for days in tropical heat through swamps and rice paddies, wade through
streams and canals, climb hills and fight dense jungle growth—all without
making contact with the evasive foe. Meanwhile, they suffered the deadly
depredations of enemy activity—ambushes, snipers, mines, and booby
traps. Buddies were killed and maimed, yet there was no enemy in sight
on whom to avenge these losses. People who seemed to be civilians were
actually combatants; women and children tossed grenades or planted
traps. Gradually the entire Vietnamese population became an object of
fear and hatred. As a Marine lieutenant told an American doctor: "You
walk through the fucking bush for three days and nights without sleep.
Watch your men, your buddies, your goddamn kids get booby trapped.
Blown apart. Get thrown six feet in the air by a trap laid by an old lady
and come down with no legs." Eventually, he said, a soldier concludes
that the only thing to do is to "kill them all."

The extent of atrocities committed by American soldiers cannot be
established with any precision. Between January 1965 and March 1973,
201 Army personnel in Vietnam were convicted by court-martial of serious offenses against Vietnamese; and during the period from March 1965
to August 1971, 77 Marines were convicted of serious crimes against Vietnamese. These figures encompass both civilian crimes, such as traffic incidents resulting in death or the killing of a bar-girl in Saigon, and offenses
connected with military operations—the kinds of crimes usually referred
to as atrocities or war crimes.

In 1967, a President's commission concluded that about twice as
many major crimes are committed in America as are known to the police; similar conclusions have been reached in other countries. There is
no reason to assume that the situation was very different with regard to
military personnel in Vietnam. Despite many directives requiring the reporting of war crimes and acts causing death, injury, or property damage
to noncombatants, it is likely that many such incidents remained unre-
ported.

This does not, however, mean that large-scale massacres of civilians
such as the one that occurred at My Lai were common. On the contrary,
in view of the openness of the fighting in South Vietnam and the encouragement which the My Lai affair gave to other servicemen to come forward
with reports of atrocities, it is highly unlikely that anything like the My
Lai massacre did escape detection. Villagers were regularly killed in combat assaults on defended hamlets, but the cold-blooded rounding up and
shooting of civilians was an unusual event. The "reported reaction of some
of the soldiers at Son My," writes Telford Taylor, formerly chief counsel

for the prosecution at the Nuremberg trials, "strongly indicates that they regarded it as out of the ordinary."* Even Daniel Ellsberg, not known for his reticence in criticizing American actions in Vietnam, rejects the idea that incidents like My Lai happened all the time. "My Lai was beyond the bounds of permissible behavior, and that is recognizable by virtually every soldier in Vietnam. They know it was wrong.... The men who were at My Lai knew there were aspects out of the ordinary. That is why they tried to hide the event, talked about it to no one, discussed it very little even among themselves."

Attempts to develop an accurate picture of the conduct of American troops in Vietnam have not been helped by the sensationalist accounts found in many segments of the media and the generally unsubstantiated charges spread by what I have called the war-crimes industry. The Russell tribunal acted as accuser, juror, and judge all at once; American guilt was assumed from the start. The tribunal, as Bertrand Russell put it, was convened "in order to expose...barbarous crimes...reported daily from Vietnam." At other proceedings staged in the U.S., standards of evidence, decorum, and impartiality were no higher.

In early 1970, for example, three young American anti-war activists, including a West Point graduate disillusioned after service in Vietnam, dubbed themselves the National Committee for a Citizens' Commission of Inquiry on U.S. War Crimes in Vietnam (CCI) and organized a series of hearings in various locations across the country at which veterans testified about their personal experiences. In December 1970, they convened a large hearing, lasting three days, in the nation's capital.

Some forty veterans testified in Washington from December 1–3, 1970. Among them, and making his first public appearance, was a former military intelligence officer, Kenneth Barton Osborn, an alleged CIA operative, whom one sympathetic reporter called the inquiry's uncontested superstar. Osborn testified to instances of torture, but he refused to give names of the individuals involved on the ground that he had signed an agreement with the CIA not to reveal the specifics of secret operations. Such agreements, he explained, "are an attempt on the organization's part to cover their ass," but he had decided to adhere to the one he himself had signed "to avoid endangering intelligence operatives who are still active." Several years later, Osborn became an official of the Organizing Committee for a Fifth Estate, the publisher of the magazine *Counterspy*, which freely and frequently exposes CIA operatives. In 1970 he had another reason for not revealing names: "There's no reason to identify them. The thing to do is to attack the thing at its source, which is at the policy-making level." This was in line with the official position of the CCI which, as one of its spokesmen stated at the end of the Washington hearing, sought to show

---

* My Lai was one of four hamlets in the village of Son My.

"that war crimes are a way of life in Vietnam; and that they are a logical consequence of our war policies."

The refusal to name names, and thus provide the kind of concrete information that would make possible an official investigation of charges, led at the time to sharp questioning of witnesses by correspondents covering the hearing. For instance, Michael McCusker of the First Marine Division declined to give the name of the commanding officer (CO) of one of the battalions allegedly involved in an atrocity. "The reason for not giving any particular names is once again we're going to lay it back on individuals. And the whole thing for this investigation is to take it away from individuals and not lay the blame back on them and make it as if it were isolated." This led a correspondent to ask: "You're absolving the CO of the battalion as just doing his duty, under standing orders, are you?" McCusker replied: "I'm absolving him as, in essence, the same way I'm absolving myself. That he was just as much a victim of the rigid structure in which he was involved.... And he was under orders as I was under orders. And I felt a great sense of powerlessness."

Another time, a spokesman for the inquiry put it this way: "We're not trying to find out who's guilty on an individual basis. If we did that we'd probably have to draw up a list with 2,500,000 names on it. What we're trying to do is find the responsibility for these actions and we say that the responsibility is at the highest levels of planning. That these tactical field policies emanate from these highest levels of planning and create a strain, a type of atmosphere in Vietnam, where these type of actions have to occur on a very frequent basis." That also meant, as an organizer of the CCI argued, that the trial of Lieutenant Calley had to be stopped. "The attempt, I suppose, is basically to...take the monkey off the individual's back, take it off Calley's back, and put it a step higher—let the generals do what they will with the monkey once it's on their back."

It may well be that certain "tactical field policies," such as the stress on body count, created an atmosphere conducive to atrocities. Yet, despite the pressure for a high enemy casualty toll, most soldiers in Vietnam did not kill prisoners or intentionally shoot unarmed villagers. Such violations of the law of war were committed by individuals acting against existing policy. With the exception of rare cases—themselves subject to legal prosecution—no orders were issued to commit atrocities; and when the plea of superior orders was introduced, as in the Calley case, courts-martial rejected it as a defense for the commission of war crimes.

Like other critics of the American command in Vietnam, the CCI erroneously assumed that the rules of engagement governing combat, with which it was not familiar, were in violation of applicable international law (of which it knew even less), and that individual atrocities therefore were committed in execution of standing orders. This charge is without foundation. Telford Taylor, a critic of many facets of U.S. Vietnam policy, has called the rules of engagement issued by the American command in Vietnam "virtually impeccable." So impeccable were they indeed, as measured by their encouragement of restraint, that Senator Goldwater, when he obtained several of these directives in 1975, exclaimed in anger: "It is absolutely unbelievable that any Secretary of Defense would ever place such restrictions on our forces. It is unbelievable that any President would have allowed this to happen.... I am ashamed of my country... for such restrictions to have been placed upon men who were trained to fight...."

The demand that men like Calley should be freed and that no other individual soldiers or officers be brought to trial in effect was a demand that nobody be held responsible for atrocities. It amounted to a repudiation of individual responsibility not unlike that made with regard to the German people after World War II. Yet while collective guilt, like the notion of original sin, may have a place in theology, it is no part of Anglo-American jurisprudence. If all are guilty, then in effect nobody is guilty—perhaps this was indeed the point which veterans relating tales of atrocities wanted to make. To cite again the candid acknowledgment of Michael McCusker: "I'm absolving him [the CO] as, in essence, the same way I'm absolving myself." Another veteran testifying to atrocities admitted that it was less difficult to live with such killings if one could convince oneself that one had been programmed to act in this way. "You know, maybe it wasn't 'GI Joe' who pulled the trigger to kill the baby, but in some very real way, it's the military who has made 'GI Joe' what he was then, who—quite obviously I think we all believe here—bear the responsibility for the act, if not the actual guilt itself."

The truth is that some individuals, under pressure and sometimes provocation, committed atrocities, while the vast majority successfully resisted such pressure and provocation. Rather than face up to the harsh fact of individual moral failure, some found it easier to place "the monkey" on the backs of the generals.

Another organization active in airing charges of American atrocities in Vietnam was the Vietnam Veterans Against the War (VVAW), which was founded in 1967 and by 1970 was said to have 600 members. From January 31 to February 2, 1971, the VVAW, with financial backing from the actress Jane Fonda, convened a hearing on American atrocities in Vietnam, known as the Winter Soldier Investigation in the city of Detroit. More than 100 veterans and 16 civilians testified at this hearing about "war crimes which they either committed or witnessed": some had given similar testimony at the CCI inquiry in Washington. The allegations included using prisoners for target practice and subjecting them to a variety of grisly tortures to extract information, cutting off the ears of dead VC's, throwing VC suspects out of helicopters, burning villages, gang-raping women, packing the vagina of a North Vietnamese nurse with grease, and the like.

Among the persons assisting the VVAW in organizing and preparing this hearing was Mark Lane, author of *Conversations with Americans*, a collection of interviews with Vietnam veterans about war crimes. In a highly critical review of *Conversations with Americans*, Neil Sheehan of the New York *Times*—himself a sharp critic of American policy—was able to show that some of Lane's "witnesses" had never even served in Vietnam while others had not been in the combat situations they described in horrid detail. To prevent the Detroit hearings from being tainted by such irregularities, all the veterans testifying there fully identified the units in which they had served and provided geographical descriptions of where the alleged atrocities had taken place.

Yet the appearance of exactitude was deceptive. Senator Mark O. Hatfield of Oregon, impressed with the charges made by the veterans, inserted the transcript of the Detroit hearing into the Congressional Record. Furthermore, he asked the commandant of the Marine Corps to investigate the numerous allegations of wrongdoing made against the Marines in particular. The results of this investigation, carried out by the Naval Investigation Service, are interesting and revealing. Many of the veterans, though assured that they would not be questioned about atrocities they might have committed personally, refused to be interviewed. One of the active members of the VVAW told investigators that the leadership had directed the entire membership not to cooperate with military authorities. A black Marine, who agreed to be interviewed, called the Vietnam war "one huge atrocity" and "a racist plot," but was unable to provide details of the outrages he had described at the hearing. He admitted that the question of atrocities had not occurred to him while he was in Vietnam and that he had been assisted in the preparation of his testimony by a member of the Nation of Islam. But the most damaging finding consisted of the sworn statements of several veterans, corroborated by witnesses, that they had in fact not attended the hearing in Detroit. One of them had never been to Detroit in his life.

Incidents similar to some of those described at the VVAW hearing undoubtedly did occur. We know that prisoners were tortured, corpses were mutilated, and hamlets destroyed. Yet these incidents either (as in the destruction of hamlets) did not violate the law of war or took place in breach of existing regulations. In either case, they were not part of a "criminal policy." The VVAW's use of fake witnesses, and the failure to cooperate with military authorities and to provide crucial details of the incidents, further cast serious doubt on its professed desire to serve the causes of justice and humanity. It is more likely that this inquiry, like others earlier and later, had primarily political motives and goals.

In the absence of corroborating evidence, the atrocity stories told by some Vietnam veterans should have been treated by the media with far more circumspection than they in fact were. But the tendency on the part of all too many reporters and editors was to see the war in Vietnam as an atrocity writ large, and specific incidents reported were therefore widely accepted as true. Some allegations were repeated so many times that they seemed to supply their own confirmation.

One such story was that of prisoners being pushed out of helicopters in order to scare others into talking. It is, of course, possible that some American interrogators engaged in this criminal practice, but not a single instance has been confirmed. We do know of at least one case where such an occurrence was staged with the use of a dead body. The Army's Criminal Investigation Division (CID) identified the soldier who had taken the photograph; it also identified a second soldier who acquired the picture, made up the story of the interrogation, and mailed it and the photograph to his girlfriend. She in turn gave them to her brother, who informed the Chicago *Sun Times*. On November 29–30, 1969, the picture and the story appeared in the Chicago *Sun Times* and the Washington *Post* and generated wide media interest. The lengthy investigation by the CID established that a dead North Vietnamese soldier had been picked up on February 15, 1969, after an operation in Gia Dinh province, and adduced other details of how the picture had been posed. The commander of the helicopter in question was reprimanded; the two crew members who had pushed the body out of the aircraft had already been discharged and therefore were beyond the Army's disciplinary jurisdiction. The professional manner in which the CID and the services' legal officers generally carried out their investigative and prosecutory mandate supports the credibility of the official Army account of this episode.

Reporters at times were so anxious to obtain pictorial proof of war crimes they had heard about that on at least one occasion they themselves actually incited the commission of atrocities. On October 9, 1967, the CBS evening news showed a young American soldier cutting off the ear of a dead VC soldier as a souvenir of battle. An investigation disclosed that the soldier and another man in the same unit had acted on a "dare" after being offered a knife by a CBS cameraman, who then filmed the sequence. The two soldiers were tried by special court-martial and convicted of conduct to the prejudice of good order and discipline and were sentenced to a reduction in grade and a fine. CBS News was informed of how the incident had been provoked, but refused to run a correction.

THE QUESTION OF GENOCIDE

In 1967, the second session of the Russell International War Crimes Tribunal adopted a statement on genocide that was formulated by Jean-Paul Sartre. The U.S. government, Sartre maintained, was engaged in "wiping out a whole people and imposing the Pax Americana on an uninhabited Vietnam." In the South specifically, American forces were conducting a "massive extermination" of the people of South Vietnam, killing men, women, and children merely because they were Vietnamese; this represented "genocide in the strictest sense."

The Russell tribunal was not alone in charging the U.S. with genocide. The new military technology used by America in Vietnam, wrote

Theodore Draper in 1967, "produces a dehumanized genocide"; American policy-makers, argued Daniel Berrigan, have, "for some time now, legitimated murder and expanded murder into genocide." According to Frances FitzGerald, although no one in the U.S. government consciously planned a policy of genocide, in fact the policy of the military commanders "had no other military logic, and their course of action was indistinguishable from it." The specific violations of the law of war, held Professor Richard A. Falk, may have "a cumulative impact that can fairly add up to genocide." Scorched-earth tactics and the use of cruel weapons against the civilian population "appears to me to establish a *prima facie* case of genocide against the United States."

A convention against genocide was adopted by a unanimous United Nations General Assembly on December 9, 1948; it came into force on January 12, 1951. The U.S. signed but so far has not ratified the convention; however, it probably can be assumed that the prohibition of genocide is today part of customary international law. In the convention, the crime of genocide was defined as committing, "with intent to destroy, in whole or in part, a national, ethnical, racial, or religious group, as such," acts such as "killing members of the group," "causing serious bodily or mental harm," "deliberately inflicting on the group conditions of life calculated to bring about its physical destruction in whole or in part." The prototype of genocide which inspired the convention was, of course, Hitler's attempted extermination of the Jews of Europe, designed to bring about "the final solution" of the Jewish question.

If genocide consists of the *destruction* of a people *in whole or in part*, the first place one should look in assessing this charge is at population statistics. According to figures compiled by the United Nations, the populations of both North and South Vietnam increased steadily during and despite the war, at annual rates of change roughly double the rate of the U.S. This fact alone makes the charge of genocide a bit grotesque.

In order to establish the crime of genocide, one must also be able to demonstrate *intent* to destroy a certain group of people in whole or in part. With regard to North Vietnam, as I have attempted to show, the bombing never deliberately aimed at the population and therefore cannot be adduced as evidence of genocide. As for the fighting in the South, the evidence available makes it similarly absurd to argue that the U.S. at any time in the war had the intent of destroying the people of that country. Indeed, quite the contrary can easily be shown to be true.

While the American way of war undoubtedly took the lives of many noncombatants, these casualties were never inflicted as a matter of policy. The concern of the American military command with the prevention of death or damage to the civilian population led to the promulgation of rules of engagement aimed at minimizing such casualties. American advisers, too, were told to "make every effort to convince Vietnamese counterparts of the necessity for preservation of the lives and property of noncombatants. Counterparts must be encouraged to promulgate and implement parallel instruction." In an instruction program established in 1965, newly arrived soldiers were taught that respect for civilian life was not only a matter of basic decency and legality, but was also essential for winning the "hearts and minds" of the people. The intelligence gained from a population willingly assisting in the war against the Communist insurgents, they were told, could save their own lives. It is true that until the My Lai incident, the rules of engagement were not as widely known as they should have been, and the American command can justly be faulted with failing to take all possible measures to enforce these rules. But such negligence is a far cry from having a genocidal intent to destroy the people of South Vietnam.

Moreover, American aid programs contributed substantially to the improvement of public health and the availability of medical care. Between the early 1960's and 1972, AID provided funds for the provision of 29 surgical suites, and for the construction of more than 170 district, 370 village, and 400 hamlet maternity-dispensaries. In addition, about 15 percent of occupied beds in American military hospitals were used by Vietnamese civilians. These measures gradually alleviated the overcrowded conditions created in the early years of the war by the load of civilian war casualties. Under contract with AID, 774 American physicians served 60-day tours of duty in a Vietnamese hospital; under the Military Provincial Health Assistance Program (MILPHAP), medical teams, each including three physicians, assisted Vietnamese provincial hospitals in the application of medical expertise; every American unit had its medical civic-action program (MEDCAP) which provided medical care in the villages and gave immunizations for polio, TB, tetanus, etc. The quality of medical care in Vietnam often left much to be desired. Yet whatever the shortcomings of the American medical-aid program, it surely does not fit into any kind of scheme to destroy the Vietnamese people.

All of this, together with the various aid programs aimed at improving the technological and economic development of South Vietnam, makes it understandable that the cumulative impact of the American presence in Vietnam was a substantial *rise* is the standard of living and a consequent population increase. The "good effects," a South Vietnamese oppositionist to Thieu wrote in late 1974, "were always intentional while the 'bad effects' were unintentional. They were the side-effects, the by-products of the war and the American presence."

Detailed calculations that cannot be reproduced here lead to the conclusion that the Vietnam war, during the years of active American involvement, was no more destructive of civilian life, both North and South, than other armed conflicts of this century and a good bit less so than some, such as the Korean war. Whereas the proportion of civilians killed in Korea may have been as high as 70 percent of the total death toll, in Vietnam it was about 45 percent. If we bear in mind that the battle for Korea leveled practically all major population centers, while much of the most severe fighting in Vietnam took place in uninhabited jungle terrain or in sparsely populated areas, this conclusion is hardly surprising. In any case, the cost of the Vietnam war in civilian lives does *not* justify the allegation that the U.S. was engaged in a conflict where an unusually and unacceptably high number of noncombatants was being killed.

In sum, the American record in Vietnam is not a succession of war crimes and does not support charges of a systematic and willful violation of existing agreements for standards of human decency in time of war. Such charges, leveled by many critics of the American involvement, were based on a distorted picture of the actual battlefield situation, on ignorance of existing rules of engagement, and on a tendency to construe every mistake of judgment as a wanton breach of the law of war. Furthermore, many critics had only the most rudimentary understanding of international law and freely indulged in fanciful interpretations of conventions and treaties so as to make the American record look as bad as possible. Finally, Communist propagandists unleashed a torrent of largely unsubstantiated charges with the hope that at least some of the lies would stick. This, indeed, occurred, for many publicists, journalists, and intellectuals in the West were only too well prepared to believe the worst about the conduct of the U.S. in Vietnam.

Much that happened during the American military effort in Vietnam was legal but could be criticized on other grounds. Some of the tactics used were certainly not calculated to help in winning the "hearts and minds" of the people, and were probably a contributory cause of the ultimate collapse of South Vietnam. There is reason to believe that the suffering inflicted upon large segments of South Vietnam's rural population during long years of high-technology warfare created a widespread feeling of resignation, war weariness, and an unwillingness to go on fighting against the resolute opponent from the North. Similarly, revulsion at the fate of thousands of hapless civilians killed and maimed by the deadly weapons of modern war undercut the willingness of America as a nation to prosecute the fight; this suggests that for a democracy, reliance upon such weapons may be counterproductive on still another level.

Insensitivity to political costs, rigidity of doctrine, and shortsighted and self-defeating tactics may lose wars, but they do not constitute war crimes or immoral conduct. Examined dispassionately, American actions in Vietnam lend no support to the accusations of criminality or of gross immorality with which America's conduct of the war was charged at the time, and of which it is still widely assumed to be guilty. Today it is more urgent than ever that this be understood, for the simple reason that Vietnam continues to haunt our minds and continues to exert a powerful influence on our conception of ourselves as a nation and of our role in the world. The task of clearing away the cobwebs of mythology which have helped to create the national trauma over Vietnam must begin—for the sake of historical truth as much as for our own self-confidence, our moral strength, and our future capacity to act responsibly in world affairs.

THREE

CONTROVERSIES AND CONSEQUENCES OF AMERICAN INVOLVEMENT

South Vietnam. A marine displays a communist flag found on patrol just south of the Demilitarized Zone (DMZ). OFFICIAL U.S. MARINE CORPS PHOTO

CHAPTER 8

Interpreting the War

All students of history eventually must try to explain why the United States got involved in Vietnam and why it stayed so long in the war; there are no more fundamental and important questions than these. Even as the war was going on, policy makers, scholars, and journalists were offering their interpretations of U.S. involvement. At first, some concluded the United States had been sucked into Vietnam: step by unthinking step, the well-intentioned but naive Americans had walked into a quagmire. Others (like James Thomson and Leslie Gelb, both of whom wrote before the American war had ended) argued that American presidents saw Vietnam as a test of American strength and will and thus did what they could, within the limits imposed by bureaucracy and public opinion, to keep South Vietnam out of Communist hands. Some (like Gabriel Kolko) argued that the demands of the U.S. economy compelled Americans to make a stand against revolution in Southeast Asia, though in the passage printed here Kolko emphasizes the commitment and resiliency of the Communists. Others (like Frances FitzGerald) asserted that American values and assumptions were inappropriate in Vietnam's cultural landscape and inescapably led to tragedy. In the late 1970s and early 1980s a "revisionist" interpretation of the war emerged. Led by Norman Podhoretz, the revisionists criticized the critics of the war and generally defended policy makers and military officials. Recently, a kind of postrevisionist anarchy has set in, characterized by a host of monographs that defy easy categorization.

Historical interpretation is always difficult, and the passions that continue to surround the Vietnam War make the work of its historians particularly hazardous. The various schools of thought on the U.S. intervention have different approaches to the evidence and different ideas about what is important and what is not, how to read a particular document, and how to weigh the importance of personality against that of the institutions or systems of policy making. It may be frustrating to confront the multiplicity of interpretations of the U.S. involvement in Vietnam, but it is also the first responsibility of students of history.

26
A Clash of Cultures
FRANCES FITZGERALD

Somewhere, buried in the files of the television networks, lies a series of pictures, ranging over a decade, that chronicles the diplomatic history of the United States and the Republic of Vietnam. Somewhere there is a picture of President Eisenhower with Ngo Dinh Diem, a picture of Secretary McNamara with General Nguyen Khanh, one of President Johnson with Nguyen Cao Ky and another of President Nixon with President Thieu. The pictures are unexceptional. The obligatory photographs taken on such ceremonial occasions, they show men in gray business suits (one is in military fatigues) shaking hands or standing side-by-side on a podium. These pictures, along with the news commentaries, "President Nixon today reaffirmed his support for the Thieu regime," or "Hanoi refused to consider the American proposal," made up much of what Americans knew about the relationship between the two countries. But the pictures and news reports were to a great extent deceptions, for they did not show the disproportion between the two powers. One of the gray-suited figures, after all, represented the greatest power in the history of the world, a nation that could, if its rulers so desired, blow up the world, feed the earth's population, or explore the galaxy. The second figure in the pictures represented a small number of people in a country of peasants largely sustained by a technology centuries old. The meeting between the two was the meeting of two different dimensions, two different epochs of history. An imagined picture of a tributary chieftain coming to the Chinese court represents the relationship of the United States to the Republic of Vietnam better than the photographs from life. It represents what the physical and mental architecture of the twentieth century so often obscures.

At the beginning of their terms in office President Kennedy and President Johnson, perhaps, took full cognizance of the disproportion between the two countries, for they claimed, at least in the beginning, that the Vietnam War would require only patience from the United States. According to U.S. military intelligence, the enemy in the south consisted of little more than bands of guerrillas with hardly a truck in which to carry their borrowed weapons. The North Vietnamese possessed antiaircraft guns and

From *Fire in the Lake: The Vietnamese and the Americans in Vietnam* by Frances Fitzgerald © 1972 by Frances Fitzgerald. By permission of Little, Brown and Company.

a steady supply of small munitions, but the United States could, so the officials promised, end their resistance with a few months of intensive bombing. In 1963 and 1965 few Americans imagined that a commitment to war in Vietnam would finally cost the United States billions of dollars, the production of its finest research and development laboratories, and fifty-five thousand American lives. They did not imagine that the Vietnam War would prove more politically divisive than any foreign war in the nation's history.

In one sense Presidents Kennedy and Johnson had seen the disproportion between the United States and Vietnam, but in another they did not see it at all. By intervening in the Vietnamese struggle the United States was attempting to fit its global strategies into a world of hillocks and hamlets, to reduce its majestic concerns for the containment of Communism and the security of the Free World to a dimension where governments rose and fell as a result of arguments between two colonels' wives. In going to Vietnam the United States was entering a country where the victory of one of the great world ideologies occasionally depended on the price of tea in a certain village or the outcome of a football game. For the Americans in Vietnam it would be difficult to make this leap of perspective, difficult to understand that while they saw themselves as building world order, many Vietnamese saw them merely as the producers of garbage from which they could build houses. The effort of translation was too great.

The televised pictures of the two chiefs of state were deceptive in quite another way: only one of the two nations saw them. Because of communications, the war was absurd for the civilians of both countries— but absurd in different ways. To one people the war would appear each day, compressed between advertisements and confined to a small space in the living room; the explosion of bombs and the cries of the wounded would become the background accompaniment to dinner. For the other people the war would come one day out of a clear blue sky. In a few minutes it would be over: the bombs, released by an invisible pilot with incomprehensible intentions, would leave only the debris and the dead behind. Which people was the best equipped to fight the war?

The disparity between the two countries only began with the matter of scale. They seemed, of course, to have come from the same country, those two figures in their identical business suits with their identical pronouncements. "The South Vietnamese people will never surrender to Communist tyranny," "We are fighting for the great cause of freedom," "We dedicate ourselves to the abolition of poverty, ignorance, and disease and to the work of the social revolution." In this case the deception served the purposes of state. The Chinese emperor could never have claimed that in backing one nomad chieftain against another he was defending the representative of Chinese civilization. But the American officials in supporting the Saigon government insisted that they were defending "freedom and democracy" in Asia. They left the GIs to discover that the Vietnamese did not fit into their experience of either "Communists" or "democrats."

Under different circumstances this invincible ignorance might not have affected the outcome of the war. The fiction that the United States was defending "freedom and democracy" might have continued to exist in a sphere undisturbed by reality, a sphere frequented only by those who needed moral justification for the pursuit of what the U.S. government saw as its strategic interests. Certain "tough-minded" analysts and officials in any case ignored the moral argument. As far as they were concerned, the United States was not interested in the form of the Vietnamese government—indeed, it was not interested in the Vietnamese at all. Its concerns were for "containing the expansion of the Communist bloc" and preventing future "wars of national liberation" around the world. But by denying the moral argument in favor of power politics and "rational" calculations of United States interests, these analysts were, as it happened, overlooking the very heart of the matter, the issue on which success depended.

The United States came to Vietnam at a critical juncture of Vietnamese history—a period of metamorphosis more profound than any the Vietnamese had ever experienced. In 1954 the Vietnamese were gaining their independence after seventy years of French colonial rule. They were engaged in a struggle to create a nation and to adapt a largely traditional society to the modern world. By backing one contender—by actually creating that contender—the United States was not just fighting a border war or intervening, as Imperial China so often did, in a power struggle between two similar contenders, two dynasties. It was entering into a moral and ideological struggle over the form of the state and the goals of the society. Its success with its chosen contender would depend not merely on U.S. military power but on the resources of both the United States and the Saigon government to solve Vietnamese domestic problems in a manner acceptable to the Vietnamese. But what indeed were Vietnamese problems, and did they even exist in the terms in which Americans conceived them? The unknowns made the whole enterprise, from the most rational and tough-minded point of view, risky in the extreme.

In going into Vietnam the United States was not only transposing itself into a different epoch of history; it was entering a world qualitatively different from its own. Culturally as geographically Vietnam lies half a world away from the United States. Many Americans in Vietnam learned to speak Vietnamese, but the language gave no more than a hint of the basic intellectual grammar that lay beneath. In a sense there was no more correspondence between the two worlds than that between the atmosphere of the earth and that of the sea. There was no direct translation between them in the simple equations of x is y and a means b. To find the common ground that existed between them, both Americans and Vietnamese would have to re-create the whole world of the other, the whole intellectual landscape. The effort of comprehension would be only the first step, for it would reveal the deeper issues of the encounter. It would force both nations to consider again the question of morality, to consider which of their values belong only to themselves or only to a certain stage of development. It would, perhaps, allow them to see that the process of change in the life of a society is a delicate and mysterious affair, and that the introduction of the foreign and the new can have vast and unpredictable consequences. It might in the end force both peoples to look back upon their own society, for it is contrast that is the essence of vision.

The American intellectual landscape is, of course, largely an inheritance from Europe, that of the Vietnamese a legacy from China, but in their own independent development the two nations have in many respects moved even further apart from each other. As late as the end of the nineteenth century Americans had before them a seemingly unlimited physical space—a view of mountains, deserts, and prairies into which a man might move (or imagine moving) to escape the old society and create a new world for himself. The impulse to escape, the drive to conquest and expansion, was never contradicted in America as it was in Europe by physical boundaries or by the persistence of strong traditions. The nation itself seemed to be less of a vessel than a movement. The closing of the frontier did not mean the end to expansion, but rather the beginning of it in a new form. The development of industry permitted the creation of new resources, new markets, new power over the world that had brought it into being. Americans ignore history, for to them everything has always seemed new under the sun. The national myth is that of creativity and progress, of a steady climbing upward into power and prosperity, both for the individual and for the country as a whole. Americans see history as a straight line and themselves standing at the cutting edge of it as representatives for all mankind. They believe in the future as if it were a religion; they believe that there is nothing they cannot accomplish, that solutions wait somewhere for all problems, like brides. Different though they were, both John Kennedy and Lyndon Johnson accepted and participated in this national myth. In part perhaps by virtue of their own success, they were optimists who looked upon their country as willing and able to right its own wrongs and to succor the rest of the world. They believed in the power of science, the power of the will, and the virtues of competition. Many Americans now question their confidence; still, the optimism of the nation is so great that even the question appears as a novelty and a challenge.

In their sense of time and space, the Vietnamese and the Americans stand in the relationship of a reversed mirror image, for the very notion of competition, invention, and change is an extremely new one for most Vietnamese. Until the French conquest of Vietnam in the nineteenth century, the Vietnamese practiced the same general technology for a thousand years. Their method of rice culture was far superior to any other in Southeast Asia; still it confined them to the river-fed lowlands between the Annamite cordillera and the sea. Hemmed in by China to the north and the Hindu kingdom of Champa to the south, the Vietnamese lived for the bulk of their history within the closed circle of the Red River Delta.

They conquered Champa and moved south down the narrow littoral, but by American or Chinese standards they might have been standing still, for it took them five centuries to conquer a strip of land the length of Florida. The Vietnamese pride themselves less on their conquests than on their ability to resist and to survive. Living under the great wing of China, they bought their independence and maintained it only at a high price of blood. Throughout their history they have had to acknowledge the preponderance of the great Middle Kingdom both as the power and as the hub of culture. The Vietnamese knew their place in the world and guarded it jealously.

For traditional Vietnamese the sense of limitation and enclosure was as much a part of individual life as of the life of the nation. In what is today northern and central Vietnam the single form of Vietnamese settlement duplicated the closed circle of the nation. Hidden from sight behind their high hedges of bamboos, the villages stood like nuclei within their surrounding circle of rice fields. Within the villages as within the nation the amount of arable land was absolutely inelastic. The population of the village remained stable, and so to accumulate wealth meant to deprive the rest of the community of land, to fatten while one's neighbor starved. Vietnam is no longer a closed economic system, but the idea remains with the Vietnamese that great wealth is antisocial, not a sign of success but a sign of selfishness.

With a stable technology and a limited amount of land the traditional Vietnamese lived by constant repetition, by the sowing and reaping of rice and by the perpetuation of customary law. The Vietnamese worshiped their ancestors as the source of their lives, their fortunes, and their civilization. In the rites of ancestor worship the child imitated the gestures of his grandfather so that when he became the grandfather, he could repeat them exactly to his grandchildren. In this passage of time that had no history the death of a man marked no final end. Buried in the rice fields that sustained his family, the father would live on in the bodies of his children and grandchildren. As time wrapped around itself, the generations to come would regard him as the source of their present lives and the arbiter of their fate. In this continuum of the family "private property" did not really exist, for the father was less of an owner than a trustee of the land to be passed on to his children. To the Vietnamese the land itself was the sacred, constant element: the people flowed over the land like water, maintaining and fructifying it for the generations to come.

Late in the war—about 1968—a Vietnamese soldier came with his unit to evacuate the people of a starving village in Quang Nam province so that the area might be turned into a "free fire zone." While the villagers were boarding the great American helicopters, one old man ran away from the soldiers shouting that he would never leave his home. The soldiers followed the old man and found him hiding in a tunnel beside a small garden planted with a few pitiful stunted shrubs. When they tried to persuade him to go with the others, he refused, saying, "I have to stay behind to look after this piece of garden. Of all the property handed down to me by my ancestors, only this garden now remains. I have to guard it for my grandson." Seeing the soldiers look askance, the old man admitted that his grandson had been conscripted and that he had not heard from him in two years. He paused, searching for an explanation, and then said, "If I leave, the graves of my ancestors, too, will become forest. How can I have the heart to leave?"

The soldiers turned away from the old man and departed, for they understood that for him to leave the land would be to acknowledge the final death of the family—a death without immortality. By deciding to stay he was deciding to sacrifice his life in postponement of that end. When the soldiers returned to the village fourteen months later, they found that an artillery shell had closed the entrance to the tunnel, making it a grave for the old man.[1]

Many American officials understood that the land and the graves of the ancestors were important to the Vietnamese. Had they understood exactly why, they might not have looked upon the wholesale creation of refugees as a "rational" method of defeating Communism. For the traditional villager, who spent his life immobile, bound to the rice land of his ancestors, the world was a very small place. It was in fact the village or *xa*, a word that in its original Chinese roots signified "the place where people come together to worship the spirits." In this definition of society the character "earth" took precedence, for, as the source of life, the earth was the basis for the social contract between the members of the family and the members of the village. Americans live in a society of replaceable parts—in theory anyone can become President or sanitary inspector—but the Vietnamese lived in a society of particular people, all of whom knew each other by their place in the landscape. "Citizenship" in a Vietnamese village was personal and untransferable. In the past, few Vietnamese ever left their village in times of peace, for to do so was to leave society itself— all human attachments, all absolute rights and duties. When the soldiers of the nineteenth-century Vietnamese emperors came to the court of Hue, they prayed to the spirits of the Perfume River, "We are lost here [*depaysée*] and everything is unknown to us. We prostrate ourselves before you [in the hope that] you will lead us to the good and drive the evil away from us."[2] The soldiers were "lost" in more than a geographical sense, for without their land and their place in the village, they were without a social identity. To drive the twentieth-century villager off his land was in the same way to drive him off the edges of his old life and to expose him directly to the political movement that could best provide him with a new identity.

During the war the village *dinh* or shrine still stood in many of the villages of the south as testimony to the endurance of the traditional political design of the nation. In prehistoric times, before the advent of national government, the *dinhs* referred to the god of the particular earth beneath the village. In assuming temporal power, the emperors of Vietnam took on the responsibility to perform the rites of the agriculture for all the Vietnamese villages and replaced the local spirits with the spirits of national heroes and genii. Under their reign the *dinh* contained the imperial charter that incorporated the village into the empire, making an ellision between the ideas of "land," "Emperor," and "Vietnamese." The French brushed away the sacred web of state, but they did not destroy this confluence of ideas. The Vietnamese call their nation *da nuoc*, "earth and water"—the phrase referring both to the trickle of water through one rice field and the "mountains and rivers" of the nation.

Like the Celestial Empire of China, the Vietnamese empire was in one aspect a ritual state whose function was to preside over the sacred order of nature and society. At its apex the emperor stood as its supreme magician-god endowed with the responsibility to maintain the harmonious balance of the *yin* and the *yang*, the two related forces of the universe. His success in this enterprise (like that of the villagers in the rites of ancestor worship) depended upon the precision with which he followed the elaborate set of rituals governing his relations with the celestial authorities and the people of the empire. To act in conformity with the traditional etiquette was to insure harmony and prosperity for the entire nation. In A.D. 1129 the Emperor Ly Than Tong proclaimed to the court: "We have little virtue; we have transgressed the order of Heaven, and upset the natural course of events; last year the spring was blighted by a long rain; this year there is a long drought.... Let the mandarins examine my past acts in order to discover any errors or faults, so that they may be remedied."[3] In analyzing these disasters the emperor blamed them on his deviation from Tao, the traditional way, which was at once the most moral and the most scientific course.

As Americans are, so to speak, canted towards the future, the traditional Vietnamese were directed towards the past, both by the small tradition of the family and the great tradition of the state. Confucianism—the very foundation of the state—was not merely a "traditional religion," as Judaism and Christianity are the traditional religions of the West. Originating in a society of ancestor worshipers, it was, like ancestor worship itself, a sacralization of the past. Unlike the great Semitic prophets, Confucius did not base his teachings on a single, contemporary revelation. "I for my part am not one of those who have innate knowledge," he said. "I am simply one who loves the past and is diligent in investigating it."[4] According to tradition, Confucius came to his wisdom through research into the great periods of Chinese civilization—the Chou empire and its predecessors in the distant past. Tradition presents the Master not as a revolutionary but as a true reactionary. Arriving at certain rules and precepts for the proper conduct of life, he did not pretend to have comprehended all wisdom, but merely to have set up guideposts pointing towards the Tao or true way of life. For him the Tao was the enlightened process of induction that led endlessly backwards into the past of civilization. The Tao may have been for him a secular concern, a matter of enlightened self-interest. ("The Master never spoke of the spirits," reported his disciples, leaving the question moot.) But for later Confucians it had a sacred weight reinforced by magic and the supernatural.

For traditional Vietnamese, formal education consisted of the study of the Confucian texts—the works of the Master and the later commentaries. To pass beyond the small tradition of the family and the village was therefore not to escape the dominion of the past, but to enter into it more fully. The mandarins, the literate elite, directed all their scholarship not towards invention and progress, but towards a more perfect repetition of the past, a more perfect maintenance of the status quo. When a French steamship was sighted off the shores of Vietnam in the early nineteenth century (or so the story goes) the local mandarin-governor, instead of going to see it, researched the phenomenon in his texts, concluded it was a dragon, and dismissed the matter.[5]

As long as Vietnamese society remained a closed system, its intellectual foundations remained flawless and immobile. Quite clearly, however, they could not survive contact with the West, for they were based on the premise that there was nothing new under the sun. But the coming of the French posed a terrible problem for the Vietnamese. Under the dominion of the old empire the Vietnamese were not members of a religious community (like the Christians of Byzantium or the Muslims of the Abbasid caliphate) but participants in a whole, indivisible culture. Like the Chinese, they considered those who lived outside of its seamless web to be by definition barbarians. When the Vietnamese conquered peoples of other cultures—such as the Chams—they included these people within the structure of empire only on condition of their total assimilation. The peoples they could not assimilate, they simply surrounded, amoeba-like, and left them to follow their own laws. The various montagnard tribes that lived beyond the zone of wet-rice cultivation retained their own languages, customs, and governments for thousands of years inside Vietnam. But with the arrival of the French forces in the nineteenth century the Vietnamese confronted a civilization more powerful than their own; for the first time since the Chinese conquest in the second century B.C. they faced the possibility of having to assimilate themselves. Confucianism was, after all, not merely a religion or an arbitrary morality, but a science that operated inside history. Confucius said, "If it is really possible to govern countries by ritual and yielding, there is no more to be said. But if it is not really possible, of what use is ritual?"[6] The rituals and the way of life they confirmed did not help the Vietnamese defend themselves against the French, and thus certain mandarins concluded they had to be abandoned. As the French armies swept across the Mekong Delta, Phan Thanh Giang, the governor of the western provinces, reconciled this logic with his loyalty to the nation by committing suicide and ordering his sons not to serve the French but to bring up their children in the French way.[7]

Similarly, those mandarins who decided to resist the French saw the foreign armies as a threat not only to their national sovereignty and to their beliefs, but to their entire way of life. The southern patriots warned their people:

> Our country has always been known as a land of deities; shall we now permit a horde of dogs and goats to stain it?
>
> The moral obligations binding a king to his subjects, parents to their children, and husbands to their wives were highly respected. Everyone enjoyed the most peaceful relationships.
>
> Our customs and habits were so perfect that in our country, in our ancestors' tombs, and in our homes, all things were in a proper state.
>
> But from the moment they arrived with their ill luck, happiness and peace seem to have departed from everywhere.[8]

And the mandarins were correct: the French occupation changed the Vietnamese way of life permanently. Since the Second World War the Vietnamese have been waging a struggle not merely over the form of their state but over the nature of Vietnamese society, the very identity of the Vietnamese. It is the grandeur of the stakes involved that has made the struggle at once so intense and so opaque to Westerners.

Just before the fall of the Diem regime in 1963 the American journalists in Vietnam wrote long and somewhat puzzling analyses of the Buddhist demonstrations, in which they attempted to explain how much the rebellion against Diem owed to "purely religious" motives, how much to "purely political" ones. Like most Westerners, these journalists were so entrenched in their Western notion of the division of church and state that they could not imagine the Vietnamese might not make the distinction. But until the arrival of the European missionaries there was never such a thing as a church in Vietnam. Shaped by a millennium of Chinese rule and another of independence within the framework of Southeast Asia, the "Vietnamese religion" was a blend of Confucianism, Taoism, and Buddhism sunken into a background of animism. More than a "religion" in any Western sense, it was the authority for, and the confirmation of, an entire way of life—an agriculture, a social structure, a political system. Its supernatural resembled one of those strange metaphysical puzzles of Jorge Luis Borges: an entire community imagines another one which, though magical and otherworldly, looks, detail for detail, like itself. In the courts of Hue and Thanglong, organization-minded genii presided over every government department and took responsibility for the success or failure of each mandarin's enterprise. (During a long period of drought in the seventeenth century the Emperor Le Thai Ton ordered his mandarins: "Warn the genii on my behalf that if it doesn't rain in three days, I will have their tablets boiled and thrown in the river so as to prevent my people from uselessly throwing away their money on them.")[9] In the villages the peasants recognized hosts of local spirits and ghosts as well as the official genii delegated by the mandarins. In Paul Mus's words, religion was the "spiritualization of the community itself" and "the administration of Heaven." The "religion," in some sense, was the state and vice versa—except that the emperor was not the representative of God on earth, but rather a collective moral personality, a representation of the sacred community to itself.

For the Vietnamese today as in centuries past, each regime—each state or political movement—has its own "virtue," its own character, which, like that of a human being, combines moral, social, and political qualities in a single form. Whether secular parties or religious sects, all modern Vietnamese political movements embrace a total design for the moral life of the individual and the social order of the nation. With Ngo Dinh Diem, for instance, this spherical Confucian universe showed up continually through the flat surfaces of Western language. He spoke of himself as the chosen of Heaven, the leader elected to defend Vietnamese morality and culture. The Buddhist leaders had much the same pretensions, and even for the Vietnamese Communists, the heirs to nineteenth-century Western distinctions between church and state, between one class and another, the society retains its moral impulse, its balanced Confucian design.

Never having known a serious ideological struggle in their history, many Americans persisted in thinking of the Vietnamese conflict as a civil war, as a battle between two fixed groups of people with different but conceivably negotiable interests. But the regional conflict existed only within the context of a larger struggle that resembled a series of massive campaigns of conversion involving all the people in the country and the whole structure of society. Owing to the nature of the old society, the struggle was even more all-encompassing than the European revolutionary wars. Americans, and indeed most Westerners, have lived for centuries with a great variety of institutions—with churches, with governments, with a patriarchal family, with industrial concerns, trade unions and fraternities, each of which offered a different kind of organization, different kinds of loyalties—but the Vietnamese have lived with only three: the family, the village, and the state.[10] As the family provided the model for village and state, there was only one type of organization. Taken together, the three formed a crystalline world, geometrically congruent at every level. The mandarins, for instance, were known as the "fathers of the people," and they stood in the same relationship to the emperor (himself the "son of Heaven") as the Vietnamese son stood to his father. Recruited by competitive examination, they moved closer to the emperor, that is, higher in the great imperial family, as they passed through the grades of the examination system. The village was a more informal organization—a Vietnamese deviation from the orthodox Chinese model—but it reflected a similar hierarchical design. The "government" of the family, the village, and the empire derived from one single set of instructions. Thus a change in one implied a change in all the others. [11]

To American officials throughout the war it seemed absolutely unreasonable that the non-Communist sects and political factions could not come to some agreement, could not cooperate even in their opposition to the Communists. But then the Americans had been brought up in a pluralistic world, where even the affairs of the family are managed by compromise between its members. In the traditional Vietnamese family—a family whose customs survived even into the twentieth century—the father held absolute authority over his wife (or wives) and children. The Vietnamese woman by custom wielded a great deal more power than her Chinese sister, but the traditional Chinese-based law specified that the patriarch governed his wife and children as he governed his rice fields. In theory, though not by customary practice, he could dispose of them as he wished, and they had no recourse against him.[12] The emperor held a similar power over the great family of the empire. By law the trustee of all the rice lands,[13] he held them for the villages on condition of their productivity and good behavior. Without a priesthood or independent feudal aristocracy to obstruct the unified field of his power, he exercised authority through a bureaucracy of mandarins totally dependent on him. Though Vietnam was often divided between warlord families, the disputes were never resolved by a sharing of power—by treaties such as the dukes of Burgundy made with the kings of France—but always by the restoration of an absolute monarch. Even after Vietnam had been divided for two centuries between the Trinh dynasty in the north and the Nguyen in the south, the Vietnamese would not acknowledge the legitimacy of both sovereigns. To do so would have been to assert that the entire moral and social fabric of the community had dissolved. As a family can have only one father, so the nation could have only one emperor to preside over its one Tao or way of life.

> Good conduct, then contentment; thus calm prevails. Hence there follows the hexagram of PEACE. Peace means union and interrelation.

In the *I Ching*, the ancient Chinese Book of Changes, lie all the clues to the basic design of the Sino-Vietnamese world. As the commentary to the verse explains, the Chinese character translated as "peace" implies not only the absence of conflict, but a positive union conducive to prosperity and contentment. To the Vietnamese of the twentieth century "peace" meant not a compromise between various interest groups and organizations, but the restoration of a single, uniform way of life. The Vietnamese were not interested in pluralism, they were interested in unanimity.

Since the Second World War one of the main reasons for the hostility of American intellectuals to Communism has been the suppression of intellectual freedom by Communist leaders in the Soviet Union and the Eastern European countries. In an attempt to rally Americans to the Vietnam War U.S. officials and their sympathizers took pains to argue that the Vietnamese Communists came from the same totalitarian mold. The difficulty with their argument was, however, that the non-Communist Vietnamese leaders believed in intellectual freedom no more than the Communists—a fact that would seem to indicate that their attitudes were founded not in ideology but in culture.

Intellectual freedom, of course, implies intellectual diversity. Westerners tend to take that diversity for granted, for the Western child, even of the narrowest background, grows up with a wide variety of authorities—parents, teachers, clergy, professional men, artists, scientists, and a host of other experts. The traditional Vietnamese child, however, grew up into a monolithic world composed of the family and its extensions in the state. For him there was no alternative to the authority of the father and no question of specialized knowledge. The education of a mandarin was greater, but hardly more diverse, than that of the rice farmer, for the Confucian tradition provided a personal philosophy, a religion, a technology, and a method of managing the state. For the mandarin there was no such thing as "pure science" or "knowledge for its own sake." There was (somewhere) a single correct answer to every question; the mandarin therefore studied in order to learn how to act.

The Vietnamese have lived with diversity for over a century, but the majority—including many of those brought up with French education—still perceive the intellectual world as uniform and absolute. While teaching at the Saigon university in 1957 one young American professor discovered at the second session of his course on comparative government that several students had memorized large sections of their first reading assignment. Pleased but somewhat bewildered, he asked them to finish their work on Machiavelli and turn to Montesquieu. The next day after class the students came to him in open rebellion. "What do you mean?" they asked angrily. "What do you mean by teaching us one thing one day and one thing the next?" The students could not conceive that government could be a matter of opinion. Either a government had worked or it had not, and if it had not worked, then it was not a proper subject for study. Ho Chi Minh said in answer to the question "What is the aim of study?": "One must study in order to remould one's thinking...to foster one's revolutionary virtues.... Study is aimed at action: the two must go hand in hand. The former without the latter is useless. The latter without the former is hard to carry through."[14]

In trying to teach comparative government, the American professor had, of course, assumed that his Vietnamese students possessed certain analytical tools: a conceptual framework, for instance, that allowed them to abstract the idea "government" from all the various instances of government that have existed in the world. In his course he would often be working from the general to the particular by a process of deductive logic. (A republic has certain characteristics, this state has the same characteristics, therefore it must be a republic.) What he did not realize was that his logic was hardly more universal than the forms of government he was discussing, and that most Vietnamese have an entirely different organization of mind.

The Chinese system of orthography, used by the Vietnamese until the mid-nineteenth century,[15] was not, like the Roman alphabet, composed of regular, repeatable symbols. It was built of particulars. The ideograms for such abstract notions as "fear" or "pleasure" were composed of pictures of concrete events (the pictures of a man, a house, and so on) and to the highly literate these events were always visible within the larger word. The writing was therefore without abstraction, for each word has its own atmosphere, impossible to translate into Western languages and irreducible to categories. Each word was a thing-in-itself.[16] Traditional Vietnamese education accorded with its medium. The child did not learn "principles" from his parents, he learned how to imitate his father in his every action. Confucius said, "When your father is alive, discover his project and when he is dead, remember his actions. If in three years you have not left the road followed by your father, you are really a son full of filial piety."[17] In his formal education the child encountered not a series of "disciplines" but a vast, unsystematized collection of stories and precepts. In the Confucian texts instructions on how to dress and write poetry were juxtaposed with injunctions to such virtues as patience and humility. Each precept, independently arrived at by a process of induction (the Confucian researches into the past), had its own absolute importance for the proper conduct of life. Phrased, perhaps, as a moral absolute, the precept still depended for authority on the success it was thought to have conferred in the past. Confucian logic was, in a sense, pure pragmatism applied over a vast distance in time. In reading the Confucian precepts the child arrived not at a theory of behavior but at a series of clues to the one true way of life.

At the end of his scholarly book, *Viet Cong*, Douglas Pike, an American official and the leading government analyst of the National Liberation Front, breaks out of his neutral tone to conclude: "The NLF and the people it influenced lived in a muzzy, myth-filled world of blacks and whites, good and evil, a simplistic world quite out of character with the one to which the Vietnamese was accustomed.... Here, one felt, was tomorrow's society, the beginning of 1984, where peace is war, slavery is freedom, the nonorganization is the organization."[18] American officials might, perhaps, legitimately criticize the National Liberation Front, but they have had, as in this instance, a curious tendency to criticize what is most typically and essentially Vietnamese. A world where there is no clear air of abstraction, no "principles" and no "theories," cannot but seem "muzzy" and "myth-filled" to Westerners. The Vietnamese Communist leaders differ from the non-Communists only in that they have successfully assimilated the Western conceptual framework and translated it into a form of intellectual organization that their less educated compatriots can understand. Like Mao's *Thoughts*, the NLF's "Three Silences" and "Six Duties of a Party Member" correspond exactly to the Confucian precepts. Taken together, they do not form an "ideology" in the Western sense, but the elements of a Tao, or, as the Vietnamese now call it, a "style of work," a "style of life." As for the NLF being "tomorrow's society, the beginning of 1984, where peace is war, slavery is freedom," it is not perhaps so different from the United States government—at least on the subject of Vietnam. In 1970, for instance, President Nixon called the American invasion of Cambodia a "step towards peace" and his firm stand behind President Thieu a firm stand "for the right of all the South Vietnamese people to determine for themselves the kind of government they want."[19] The difference between the two is simply that Americans have traditionally distinguished between objective truth and political persuasion, description and project, whereas the Vietnamese have not—at least not in the same manner.

Westerners naturally look upon it as sinister that the children of North Vietnam and the NLF zones of the South learn to read and do arithmetic from political material. But "politics," or "government" in the widest sense of the word, was also the basis for the traditional education. Confucianism was, first and foremost, a philosophy of social organization. The Confucian texts, for instance, provided the foundation for the imperial law. (Is not the law . . . true virtue? asked one of the nineteenth-century intellectuals. "In the law we can . . . find complete expositions of the three duties [of a prince, a father, and a husband] and of the five constant virtues [benevolence, righteousness, propriety, knowledge, and sincerity] as well as the tasks of the six ministries [of the central government]."[20]) As one historian has pointed out, the texts established a social contract between the government and the governed, for in order to claim legitimacy the emperor would have to echo Confucius's "I invent nothing, I transmit," thus acknowledging the limitations on his personal power. To learn how to read was therefore already to learn the management of the state. Because the Confucian texts formed the whole of civil education, the bias of the intellectuals was towards these "human sciences," towards practical instruction in the governing of society. To the traditional Confucian scholars all knowledge led back into the political and moral world of man. Mathematics and the physical sciences were no exceptions for, as scientists, the Confucians understood the universe as a unified "field" in which the movements of heaven and earth directly affect human society. The aim of the physical sciences was to plot these movements, these changes, so that man might put himself in tune with the world and with his fellow men. The mandarins, for instance, studied astrology in order to learn the political outlook for the nation: the appearance of comets or the fall of meteorites presaged the smaller disturbances of man. While man could do nothing by himself, he could with intelligence discern the heavenly movements and put his own smaller sphere in accord with the larger one. In China, after a dynastic struggle, the new emperor coming to power would break the instruments of the court musicians in the conviction that they, like the old dynasty, were out of tune with the universe—that they had in some sense caused the rebellion. Similarly, the new emperor would initiate the "rectification of names" so that the words he used for the affairs of state should (unlike those of his predecessor) perfectly accord with the magical etiquette governing the relations of man and nature.

At the time of the Buddhist struggle in 1966 the Buddhist leaders claimed, "Ninety percent of the Vietnamese are Buddhists . . . the people are never Communists," while the NLF leaders claimed by contrast, "The struggle of the religious believers in Vietnam is not separate from the struggle for national liberation." The two statements were mutually con-

tradictory, and an American might have concluded that one or both of
their proponents was telling an untruth. But neither the Buddhists nor
the NLF leaders were actually "lying," as an American might have been
under similar circumstances. Both groups were "rectifying the names" of
the Vietnamese to accord with what was no longer the "will of Heaven" but
"the laws of history" or "the spirit of the times." They were announcing a
project and making themselves comprehensible to their countrymen, for
whom all knowledge, even the most neutral observation, is to be put to
use.[21]

With this intellectual framework in mind it is perhaps easier to
see why the pilots of the People's Republic of China should read Mao's
Thoughts in order to learn how to fly an airplane. The Vietnamese Communists look upon technology as an independent discipline in certain
respects, but they insist that political education should be the basis for
using it. During the period of conflict and change in their society, this
emphasis on politics is not, perhaps, as unreasonable as it seems to most
Americans. Without political education it proved useless or destructive for
the cadets of the Saigon air force to learn how to fly airplanes.

For Americans the close relationship the Vietnamese draw between
morality, politics, and science is perhaps more difficult to understand now
than at any other time in history. Today, living in a social milieu completely
divided over matters of value and belief, Westerners have come to look
upon science and logic alone as containing universal truths. Over the past
century Western philosophers have worked to purge their disciplines of
ethical and metaphysical concerns; Americans in particular have tended
to deify the natural sciences and set them apart from their social goals.
Under pressure from this demand for "objective truth," the scholars of
human affairs have scrambled to give their own disciplines the authority
and neutrality of science. But because the social scientists can rarely attain
the same criteria for "truth" as physicists or chemists, they have sometimes
misused the discipline and taken merely the trappings of science as a
camouflage for their own beliefs and values. It is thus that many American
"political scientists" sympathetic to American intervention in Vietnam have
concluded that the NLF's subordination of science and "objective truth"
to politics has its origins in Communist totalitarianism.

For Westerners who believe in the eternal verity of certain principles
the notion of "brainwashing" is shocking and the experience is associated
with torture. But in such societies as those in Indonesia, China, and Vietnam, it is in one form or another an activity of every political movement.
Under the traditional Vietnamese empire there was only one truth, only
one true way. And all modern Vietnamese parties have had to face the task
of changing the nature of the "truth." Among people with an extremely
pragmatic cast of mind, for whom values depend for their authority upon
success, the task has implied a demonstration that the old ways are no
longer useful, no longer adapted to the necessities of history. During the
course of the war both the Saigon government and the NLF held "reeduca-

tion" courses for defectors and prisoners, with varying degrees of success. Those Americans who objected to the process (and most Americans singled out the NLF) saw it in European terms as the forcible destruction of personality, a mental torture such as Arthur Koestler described in *Darkness at Noon*. But to the Vietnamese, Communist and non-Communist, it did not imply torture at all, for the reason that they have a very different kind of commitment to society than do Westerners.

And it is this commitment that lies at the basis of intellectual organization. Unlike the Westerner, the Vietnamese child is brought up not to follow certain principles, but to accept the authority of certain people. The "Three Net Ropes" of the traditional society consisted in the loyalty of the son to his father, of the wife to her husband, and the mandarin to his emperor. The injunctions to filial piety and conjugal obedience were unconditional. Traditional Vietnamese law rested not upon the notion of individual rights, but the notion of duties—the duty of the sovereign to his people, the father to his son, and vice versa. Similarly, the Confucian texts defined no general principles but the proper relationship of man to man. Equal justice was secondary to social harmony. This particular form of social contract gave the individual a very different sense of himself, of his own personality. In the Vietnamese language there is no word that exactly corresponds to the Western personal pronoun I, *je, ich.* When a man speaks of himself, he calls himself "your brother," "your nephew," "your teacher," depending upon his relationship to the person he addresses. The word he uses for the first person (*toi*) in the new impersonal world of the cities originally denoted "subject of the king."[22] The traditional Vietnamese did not see himself as a totally independent being, for he did not distinguish himself as acutely as does a Westerner from his society (and by extension, the heavens). He did not see himself as a "character" formed of immutable traits, eternally loyal to certain principles, but rather as a system of relationships, a function of the society around him. In a sense, the design of the Confucian world resembled that of a Japanese garden where every rock, opaque and indifferent in itself, takes on significance from its relationship to the surrounding objects.

In central Vietnam, where the villages are designed like Japanese gardens, a young Vietnamese district chief once told this writer that he had moved a group of villagers from a Liberation village to his headquarters in order to "change their opinions." He had not lectured the villagers on the evils of Marxism and he did not plan to do so; he would simply wait for them to fall into relationship with his political authority. Had the villagers, of course, received an adequate political education, his waiting would be in vain. A "hard-core" NLF cadre would understand his community to include not only the village or the district but all of Vietnam. His horizons would be large enough in time and space to encompass a government-controlled city or years of a harsh, inconclusive war. But with regard to his refugees, the district chief was probably right: the old people and the children had left their NLF sympathies behind them in the burning ruins of a village only two miles distant.

In the old society, of course, a man who moved out of his village would find in his new village or in the court of Hue the same kind of social and political system that he had left behind him. During the conflicts of the twentieth century, however, his movement from one place to another might require a change of "ideology," or of way of life. In 1966 one American official discovered an ARVN soldier who had changed sides five times in the war, serving alternately with three NLF units and three GVN battalions. Clearly this particular soldier had no political education to speak of and no wider sense of community. But even for those that did, the possibility of accommodation and change remained open. When asked by an American interviewer what he thought of the GVN, one Front defector found it necessary to specify that "with the mind of the other regime" (i.e., that of the NLF) he felt it was bad for the people. At that point he was preparing himself to accept a new interpretation.

Such changes of mind must look opportunistic or worse to Westerners, but to the Vietnamese with their particular commitment to society it was at once the most moral and the most practical course. Indeed, it was the only course available, for in such situations the Vietnamese villager did not consider an alternative. In the old language, a man depended upon the "will of Heaven"; it was therefore his duty to accommodate himself to it as well as possible. In a letter to his subordinates of the southern provinces Phan Thanh Giang described this ethic of accommodation in the most sophisticated Confucian terms:

> It is written that he who lives according to Heaven's will is in the right way; he who departs from Heaven's will is wrong. To act according to Heaven's will is to act according to one's reason. Man is an intelligent animal created by Heaven. Each animal lives according to its proper nature, like water which seeks its own level or fire which spreads in dry places.... Man to whom Heaven has given reason should endeavor to live according to that reason.[23]

In conclusion Phan Thanh Giang requested that his officials surrender without resistance to the invading French forces. "The French," he wrote, "have huge battleships, full of soldiers and armed with powerful cannons.... It would be as senseless for you to assail [them] as for the fawn to attack the tiger. You would only draw suffering upon the people whom Heaven has entrusted to your care."[24] Loyal to the Vietnamese emperor, Phan Thanh Giang could not so easily accommodate himself to necessity. Branding himself as a traitor, he chose the same course that, throughout history, his predecessors had taken at the fall of dynasties. Suicide was the only resolution to the unbearable conflict between loyalty to the emperor and obligation to what he saw as the will of Heaven, to the will of the community as a whole.

But such protests against the will of Heaven were only for the mandarins, the moral leaders of the community. They were not for the simple villager, for as Confucius said, "The essence of the gentleman is that of wind; the essence of small people is that of grass. And when a wind passes over the grass, it cannot choose but bend."[25] In times of political stability the villager accommodated himself to the prevailing wind that clearly signaled the will of Heaven. Only in times of disorder and uncertainty when the sky clouded over and the forces of the world struggled to uncertain outcome, only then did the peasant take on responsibility for the great affairs of state, and only then did the leaders watch him carefully, for, so went the Confucian formula, "The will of Heaven is reflected in the eyes and ears of the people."

This ancient political formula clarified the basis on which twentieth-century Vietnamese, including those who no longer used the old language, would make their political decisions. Asked which side he supported, one peasant from a village close to Saigon told a Front cadre in 1963: "I do not know, for I follow the will of Heaven. If I do what you say, then the Diem side will arrest me; if I say things against you, then you will arrest me, so I would rather carry both burdens on my shoulders and stand in the middle." Caught between two competing regimes, the peasant did not assert his right to decide between them, rather he asked himself where his duty lay. Which regime had the power to claim his loyalty? Which would be the most likely to restore peace and harmony to his world? His decision might be based on personal preference (a government that considered the wishes of the people would be more likely to restore peace on a permanent basis). But he had, nonetheless, to make an objective analysis of the situation and take his gamble, for his first loyalty lay neither with the Diem regime nor the NLF but with the will of Heaven that controlled them both. At certain periods *attentisme* was the most moral and the most practical course.

As a warning to Westerners on the difficulties of understanding the twentieth-century conflict in Vietnam, Paul Mus told an ancient Chinese legend that is well known to the Vietnamese. There was trouble in the state of Lu, and the reigning monarch called in Confucius to ask for his help. When he arrived at the court, the Master went to a public place and took a seat in the correct way, facing south, and all the trouble disappeared.[26]

The works of Vo Nguyen Giap are but addenda to this legend, for the legend is the paradigm of revolution in Vietnam. To the Vietnamese it is clear from the story that Confucius was not taking an existential or exemplary position, he was actually changing the situation. Possessed of neither godlike nor prophetic authority, he moved an entire kingdom by virtue of his sensitivity to the will of Heaven as reflected in the "eyes and ears of the people." As executor for the people, he clarified their wishes and signaled the coming—or the return—of the Way that would bring harmony to the kingdom. For the Hoa Hao and the Cao Dai, the traditionalist sects of the south that in the twentieth century still believed in this magical "sympathy" of heaven and earth, political change did not depend entirely on human effort. Even the leaders of the sects believed that if they, like Confucius, had taken "the correct position," the position that accorded with the will of Heaven, all Vietnamese would eventually adopt the same Way, the same political system that they had come to.

Here, within the old spiritualist language, lies a clue as to why the Vietnamese Communists held their military commanders in strict subordination to the political cadres. Within the domestic conflict military victories were not only less important than political victories, but they were strictly meaningless except as reflections of the political realities. For the Communists, as for all the other political groups, the vehicle of political change was not the war, the pitch of force against force, but the struggle, the attempt to make manifest that their Way was the only true or "natural" one for all Vietnamese.* Its aim was to demonstrate that, in the old language, the Mandate of Heaven had changed and the new order had already replaced the old in all but title. When Ho Chi Minh entered Hanoi in August 1945, he made much the same kind of gesture as Confucius had made in facing south when he said (and the wording is significant, for he was using a language of both East and West), "We, members of the Provisional Government of the Democratic Republic of Viet-Nam solemnly declare to the world that Viet-Nam has the right to be a free and independent country—and in fact it is so already. The entire Vietnamese people are determined to mobilize all their physical and mental strength, to sacrifice their lives and property in order to safeguard their independence and liberty."[27] His claims were far from "true" at the time, but they constituted the truth in potential—if he, like Confucius, had taken the "correct position." For the Confucians, of course, the "correct position" was that which accorded with the will of Heaven and the practice of the sacred ancestors. For Ho Chi Minh the "correct position" was that which accorded with the laws of history and the present and future judgment of the Vietnamese people.

NOTES

1. Viet Hoai, "The Old Man in the Free Fire Zone," in *Between Two Fires: The Unheard Voices of Vietnam*, ed. Ly Qui Chung, pp. 102–105.

2. Léopold Cadière, *Croyances et pratiques religieuses des viêt-namiens*, vol. 2, p. 308.

3. Nghiem Dang, *Viet-Nam: Politics and Public Administration*, p. 53.

4. Confucius, *The Analects of Confucius*, p. 127.

---

* "The English word 'struggle,' a pale translation of the Vietnamese term *dau tranh*, fails to convey the drama, the awesomeness, the totality of the original." (Douglas Pike, *Viet Cong*, p. 85.)

5. Conversation with Paul Mus.

6. Confucius, *Analects*, p. 104. According to Waley, "The saying can be paraphrased as follows: If I and my followers are right in saying that countries can be governed solely by correct carrying out of ritual and its basic principle of 'giving way to others,' there is obviously no case to be made out for any other form of government. If on the other hand we are wrong, then ritual is useless. To say, as people often do, that ritual is all very well so long as it is not used as an instrument of government, is wholly to misunderstand the purpose of ritual."

7. Charles Gosselin, *L'Empire d'Annam*, p. 149.

8. Truong Buu Lam, *Patterns of Vietnamese Response to Foreign Intervention: 1858–1900*, p. 77. From an anonymous appeal to resist the French (1864).

9. Paul Mus, "Les Religions de l'Indochine," in *Indochine*, ed. Sylvain Lévi, p. 132.

10. There were also handicraft guilds and Buddhist and Taoist priesthoods, but these are details. The generalization is true enough for the purposes of contrast.

11. For the French, the emperor's persecution of French Catholic missionaries (though there were relatively few cases) served as a pretext for intervention in Vietnam. But to the French emperors conversion to Catholicism signified not just a religious apostasy, but alienation from the state itself.

12. The Gia Long code, promulgated by the early-nineteenth-century founder of the Nguyen dynasty, was a much more exact copy of the Chinese codes than the Le code that governed Vietnam from the fifteenth to the nineteenth centuries.

13. Le Thanh Khoi, *Le Viêt-Nam*. According to the French historian, Henri Maspero, the land did not belong to the emperor, but to the people, whose will was expressed by the mouth of the sovereign. This reflexive relation between the people and the sovereign is typical of the Vietnamese political philosophy derived from Mencius.

14. Truong Chinh, *President Ho Chi Minh*, p. 68.

15. In the seventeenth century a French missionary, Alexandre de Rhodes, transcribed the Vietnamese language into the Roman alphabet, using diacritical marks to indicate the different tones. His aim was to render the Bible and other Christian texts into Vietnamese. The first people to use *quoç ngu*, as his system was called, were therefore the Vietnamese Catholics. The Latin alphabet came into general use only after the French conquest.

16. A hypothesis: the spoken language with its five tones may also be more concrete (more allusive, less abstract) than Western languages because of the element of music in it. In the way that people recall particular situations and particular people from the sound of a familiar tune, so the Vietnamese may associate words more directly with particular events than do Westerners. Cf. A. R. Luria, *The Mind of a Mnemonist* (New York: Basic Books, 1968).

17. Gosselin, *Empire*, p. 27.

18. Douglas Pike, *Viet Cong*, pp. 379, 383.

19. *New York Times*, 8 October, 1970.

20. Nguyen Truong To, "Memorials on Reform," in *Patterns of Response*, ed. Truong Buu Lam, p. 98.

21. If the Buddhists were, for instance, to be proved wrong in the end, then their statement would be both untrue and useless.

22. Phan Thi Dac, *Situation de la personne au Viet-Nam*, pp. 137–156.

23. Phan Thanh Gian, "Letter on His Surrender," in *Patterns of Response*, ed. Truong Buu Lam, pp. 87–88.

24. Ibid., p. 88. Phan Thanh Gian may have been wrong in his assessment of the military situation. Other mandarins had behaved differently, many of them resisting the French to the last. Given his assessment, however, there was little else for him to do.

25. Confucius, *Analects*, p. 168.

26. Paul Mus, "Cultural Backgrounds of Present Problems," p. 13. In the *Analects* the Master recounts this story about one of the divine sages of the past.

27. Ho Chi Minh, *Ho Chi Minh on Revolution*, p. 145.

27
A Bureaucratic Tangle
JAMES C. THOMSON, JR.

As a case study in the making of foreign policy, the Vietnam War will fascinate historians and social scientists for many decades to come. One question that will certainly be asked: How did men of superior ability, sound training, and high ideals—American policy-makers of the 1960s—create such costly and divisive policy?

As one who watched the decision-making process in Washington from 1961 to 1966 under Presidents Kennedy and Johnson, I can suggest a preliminary answer. I can do so by briefly listing some of the factors that seemed to me to shape our Vietnam policy during my years as an East Asia specialist at the State Department and the White House. I shall deal largely with Washington as I saw or sensed it, and not with Saigon, where I have spent but a scant three days, in the entourage of the Vice President, or with other decision centers, the capitals of interested parties. Nor will I deal with other important parts of the record: Vietnam's history prior to 1961, for instance, or the overall course of America's relations with Vietnam.

Yet a first and central ingredient in these years of Vietnam decisions does involve history. The ingredient was *the legacy of the 1950s*—by which I mean the so-called "loss of China," the Korean War, and the Far East policy of Secretary of State Dulles.

This legacy had an institutional by-product for the Kennedy Administration: in 1961 the U.S. government's East Asian establishment was undoubtedly the most rigid and doctrinaire of Washington's regional divisions in foreign affairs. This was especially true at the Department of State, where the incoming Administration found the Bureau of Far Eastern Affairs the hardest nut to crack. It was a bureau that had been purged of its best China expertise, and of farsighted, dispassionate men, as a result of McCarthyism. Its members were generally committed to one policy line: the close containment and isolation of mainland China, the harassment of "neutralist" nations which sought to avoid alignment with either Washington or Peking, and the maintenance of a network of alliances with anti-Communist client states on China's periphery.

Another aspect of the legacy was the special vulnerability and sensitivity of the new Democratic Administration on Far East policy issues.

The memory of the McCarthy era was still very sharp, and Kennedy's margin of victory was too thin. The 1960 Offshore Islands TV debate between Kennedy and Nixon had shown the President-elect the perils of "fresh thinking." The Administration was inherently leery of moving too fast on Asia. As a result, the Far East Bureau (now the Bureau of East Asian and Pacific Affairs) was the last one to be overhauled. Not until Averell Harriman was brought in as Assistant Secretary in December, 1961, were significant personnel changes attempted, and it took Harriman several months to make a deep imprint on the bureau because of his necessary preoccupation with the Laos settlement. Once he did so, there was virtually no effort to bring back the purged or exiled East Asia experts.

There were other important by-products of this "legacy of the fifties":

The new Administration inherited and somewhat shared *a general perception of China-on-the-march*—a sense of China's vastness, its numbers, its belligerence; a revived sense, perhaps, of the Golden Horde. This was a perception fed by Chinese intervention in the Korean War (an intervention actually based on appallingly bad communications and mutual miscalculation on the part of Washington and Peking; but the careful unraveling of that tragedy, which scholars have accomplished, had not yet become part of the conventional wisdom).

The new Administration inherited and briefly accepted a *monolithic conception of the Communist bloc.* Despite much earlier predictions and reports by outside analysts, policy-makers did not begin to accept the reality and possible finality of the Sino-Soviet split until the first weeks of 1962. The inevitably corrosive impact of competing nationalisms on Communism was largely ignored.

The new Administration inherited and to some extent shared *the "domino theory" about Asia.* This theory resulted from profound ignorance of Asian history and hence ignorance of the radical differences among Asian nations and societies. It resulted from a blindness to the power and resilience of Asian nationalisms. (It may also have resulted from a subconscious sense that, since "all Asians look alike," all Asian nations will act alike.) As a theory, the domino fallacy was not merely inaccurate but also insulting to Asian nations; yet it has continued to this day to beguile men who should know better.

Finally, the legacy of the fifties was apparently compounded by an uneasy sense of a worldwide Communist challenge to the new Administration after the Bay of Pigs fiasco. A first manifestation was the President's traumatic Vienna meeting with Khrushchev in June, 1961; then came the Berlin crisis of the summer. All this created an atmosphere in which President Kennedy undoubtedly felt under special pressure to show his nation's mettle in Vietnam—if the Vietnamese, unlike the people of Laos, were willing to fight.

In general, the legacy of the fifties shaped such early moves of the new Administration as the decisions to maintain a high-visibility SEATO (by sending the Secretary of State himself instead of some underling to its first meeting in 1961), to back away from diplomatic recognition of Mongolia in the summer of 1961, and most important, to expand U.S. military assistance to South Vietnam that winter on the basis of the much more tentative Eisenhower commitment. It should be added that the increased commitment to Vietnam was also fueled by a new breed of military strategists and academic social scientists (some of whom had entered the new Administration) who had developed theories of counterguerrilla warfare and were eager to see them put to the test. To some, "counter-insurgency" seemed a new panacea for coping with the world's instability.

So much for the legacy and the history. Any new Administration inherits both complicated problems and simplistic views of the world. But surely among the policy-makers of the Kennedy and Johnson Administrations there were men who would warn of the dangers of an open-ended commitment to the Vietnam quagmire?

This raises a central question, at the heart of the policy process: Where were the experts, the doubters, and the dissenters? Were they there at all, and if so, what happened to them?

The answer is complex but instructive.

In the first place, the American government was sorely *lacking in real Vietnam or Indochina expertise*. Originally treated as an adjunct of Embassy Paris, our Saigon embassy and the Vietnam Desk at State were largely staffed from 1954 onward by French-speaking Foreign Service personnel of narrowly European experience. Such diplomats were even more closely restricted than the normal embassy officer—by cast of mind as well as language—to contacts with Vietnam's French-speaking urban elites. For instance, Foreign Service linguists in Portugal are able to speak with the peasantry if they get out of Lisbon and choose to do so; not so the French speakers of Embassy Saigon.

In addition, the *shadow of the "loss of China"* distorted Vietnam reporting. Career officers in the Department, and especially those in the field, had not forgotten the fate of their World War II colleagues who wrote in frankness from China and were later pilloried by Senate committees for critical comments on the Chinese Nationalists. Candid reporting on the strengths of the Viet Cong and the weaknesses of the Diem government was inhibited by the memory. It was also inhibited by some higher officials, notably Ambassador Nolting in Saigon, who refused to sign off on such cables.

In due course, to be sure, some Vietnam talent was discovered or developed. But a recurrent and increasingly important factor in the decision-making process was *the banishment of real expertise*. Here the underlying cause was the "closed politics" of policy-making as issues become hot: the more sensitive the issue, and the higher it rises in the bureaucracy, the more completely the experts are excluded while the harassed senior generalists take over (that is, the Secretaries, Undersecretaries, and Presidential Assistants). The frantic skimming of briefing papers in the back seats of limousines is no substitute for the presence of specialists; furthermore, in times of crisis such papers are deemed "too sensitive" even for review by the specialists. Another underlying cause of this banishment, as Vietnam became more critical, was the replacement of the experts, who were generally and increasingly pessimistic, by men described as "can-do guys," loyal and energetic fixers unsoured by expertise. In early 1965, when I confided my growing policy doubts to an older colleague on the NSC staff, he assured me that the smartest thing both of us could do was to "steer clear of the whole Vietnam mess"; the gentleman in question had the misfortune to be a "can-do guy," however, and is now [late 1960s] highly placed in Vietnam, under orders to solve the mess.

Despite the banishment of the experts, internal doubters and dissenters did indeed appear and persist. Yet as I watched the process, such men were effectively neutralized by a subtle dynamic: *the domestication of dissenters.* Such "domestication" arose out of a twofold clubbish need: on the one hand, the dissenter's desire to stay aboard; and on the other hand, the nondissenter's conscience. Simply stated, dissent, when recognized, was made to feel at home. On the lowest possible scale of importance, I must confess my own considerable sense of dignity and acceptance (both vital) when my senior White House employer would refer to me as his "favorite dove." Far more significant was the case of the former Undersecretary of State, George Ball. Once Mr. Ball began to express doubts, he was warmly institutionalized: he was encouraged to become the inhouse devil's advocate on Vietnam. The upshot was inevitable: the process of escalation allowed for periodic requests to Mr. Ball to speak his piece; Ball felt good, I assume (he had fought for righteousness); the others felt good (they had given a full hearing to the dovish option); and there was minimal unpleasantness. The club remained intact; and it is of course possible that matters would have gotten worse faster if Mr. Ball had kept silent, or left before his final departure in the fall of 1966. There was also, of course, the case of the last institutionalized doubter, Bill Moyers. The President is said to have greeted his arrival at meetings with an affectionate, "Well, here comes Mr. Stop-the-Bombing..." Here again the dynamics of domesticated dissent sustained the relationship for a while.

A related point—and crucial, I suppose, to government at all times— was *the "effectiveness" trap*, the trap that keeps men from speaking out, as clearly or often as they might, within the government. And it is the trap that keeps men from resigning in protest and airing their dissent outside the government. The most important asset that a man brings to bureaucratic life is his "effectiveness," a mysterious combination of training, style, and connections. The most ominous complaint that can be whispered of a bureaucrat is: "I'm afraid Charlie's beginning to lose his effectiveness." To preserve your effectiveness, you must decide where and when to fight the mainstream of policy; the opportunities range from pillow talk with your wife, to private drinks with your friends, to meetings with the Secretary of State or the President. The inclination to remain silent or to acquiesce in the presence of the great men—to live to fight another day, to give on this issue so that you can be "effective" on later issues—is overwhelming. Nor is it the tendency of youth alone; some of our most senior officials, men of wealth and fame, whose place in history is secure, have remained silent lest their connection with power be terminated. As for the disinclination to resign in protest: while not necessarily a Washington or even American specialty, it seems more true of a government in which ministers have no parliamentary back-bench to which to retreat. In the absence of such a refuge, it is easy to rationalize the decision to stay aboard. By doing so, one may be able to prevent a few bad things from happening and perhaps even make a few good things happen. To exit is to lose even those marginal chances for "effectiveness."

Another factor must be noted: as the Vietnam controversy escalated at home, there developed *a preoccupation with Vietnam public relations as opposed to Vietnam policy-making.* And here, ironically, internal doubters and dissenters were heavily employed. For such men, by virtue of their own doubts, were often deemed best able to "massage" the doubting intelligentsia. My senior East Asia colleague at the White House, a brilliant and humane doubter who had dealt with Indochina since 1954, spent three quarters of his working days on Vietnam public relations: drafting presidential responses to letters from important critics, writing conciliatory language for presidential speeches, and meeting quite interminably with delegations of outraged Quakers, clergymen, academics, and housewives. His regular callers were the late A. J. Muste and Norman Thomas; mine were members of the Women's Strike for Peace. Our orders from above: keep them off the backs of busy policy-makers (who usually happened to be nondoubters). Incidentally, my most discouraging assignment in the realm of public relations was the preparation of a White House pamphlet entitled *Why Vietnam,* in September, 1965; in a gesture toward my conscience, I fought—and lost—a battle to have the title followed by a question mark.

Through a variety of procedures, both institutional and personal, doubt, dissent, and expertise were effectively neutralized in the making of policy. But what can be said of the men "in charge"? It is patently absurd to suggest that they produced such tragedy by intention and calculation. But it is neither absurd nor difficult to discern certain forces at work that caused decent and honorable men to do great harm.

Here I would stress the paramount role of *executive fatigue.* No factor seems to me more crucial and underrated in the making of foreign policy. The physical and emotional toll of executive responsibility in State, the Pentagon, the White House, and other executive agencies is enormous; that toll is of course compounded by extended service. Many of today's Vietnam policy-makers have been on the job for from four to seven years. Complaints may be few, and physical health may remain unimpaired, though emotional health is far harder to gauge. But what is most seriously eroded in the deadening process of fatigue is freshness of thought, imagination, a sense of possibility, a sense of priorities and perspective—those rare assets of a new Administration in its first year or two of office. The tired policy-maker becomes a prisoner of his own narrowed view of the world and his own clichéd rhetoric. He becomes irritable and defensive — short on sleep, short on family ties, short on patience. Such men make bad policy and then compound it. They have neither the time nor the temperament for new ideas or preventive diplomacy.

Below the level of the fatigued executives in the making of Vietnam policy was a widespread phenomenon: *the curator mentality* in the Department of State. By this I mean the collective inertia produced by the bureaucrat's view of his job. At State, the average "desk officer" inherits from his predecessor our policy toward Country X; he regards it as his function to keep that policy intact—under glass, untampered with, and dusted—so that he may pass it on in two to four years to his successor. And such curatorial service generally merits promotion within the system. (Maintain the status quo, and you will stay out of trouble.) In some circumstances, the inertia bred by such an outlook can act as a brake against rash innovation. But on many issues, this inertia sustains the momentum of bad policy and unwise commitments—momentum that might otherwise have been resisted within the ranks. Clearly, Vietnam is such an issue.

To fatigue and inertia must be added the factor of internal confusion. Even among the "architects" of our Vietnam commitment, there has been persistent *confusion as to what type of war we were fighting* and, as a direct consequence, *confusion as to how to end that war.* (The "credibility gap" is, in part, a reflection of such internal confusion.) Was it, for instance, a civil war, in which case counter-insurgency might suffice? Or was it a war of international aggression? (This might invoke SEATO or UN commitment.) Who was the aggressor—and the "real enemy"? The Viet Cong? Hanoi? Peking? Moscow? International Communism? Or maybe "Asian Communism"? Differing enemies dictated differing strategies and tactics. And confused throughout, in like fashion, was the question of American objectives; your objectives depended on whom you were fighting and why. I shall not forget my assignment from an Assistant Secretary of State in March, 1964: to draft a speech for Secretary McNamara which would, *inter alia*, once and for all dispose of the canard that the Vietnam conflict was a civil war. "But in some ways, of course," I mused, "it *is* a civil war." "Don't play word games with me!" snapped the Assistant Secretary.

Similar confusion beset the concept of "negotiations"—anathema to much of official Washington from 1961 to 1965. Not until April, 1965, did "unconditional discussions" become respectable, via a presidential speech; even then the Secretary of State stressed privately to newsmen that nothing had changed, since "discussions" were by no means the same as "negotiations." Months later that issue was resolved. But is took even longer to obtain a fragile internal agreement that negotiations might include the Viet Cong as something other than an appendage to Hanoi's delegation. Given such confusion as to the whos and whys of our Vietnam commitment, it is not surprising, as Theodore Draper has written, that policy-makers find it so difficult to agree on how to end the war.

Of course, one force—a constant in the vortex of commitment— was that of *wishful thinking*. I partook of it myself at many times. I did so especially during Washington's struggle with Diem in the autumn of 1963 when some of us at State believed that for once, in dealing with a difficult client state, the U.S. government could use the leverage of our economic and military assistance to make good things happen, instead of being led around by the nose by men like Chiang Kai-shek and Syngman Rhee (and, in that particular instance, by Diem). If we could prove that point, I thought, and move into a new day, with or without Diem, then Vietnam was well worth the effort. Later came the wishful thinking of the air-strike planners in the late autumn of 1964; there were those who actually thought that after six weeks of air strikes, the North Vietnamese would come crawling to us to ask for peace talks. And what, someone asked in one of the meetings of the time, if they don't? The answer was that we would bomb for another four weeks, and that would do the trick. And a few weeks later came one instance of wishful thinking that was symptomatic of good men misled: in January, 1965, I encountered one of the very highest figures in the Administration at a dinner, drew him aside, and told him of my worries about the air-strike option. He told me that I really shouldn't worry; it was his conviction that before any such plans could be put into effect, a neutralist government would come to power in Saigon that would politely invite us out. And finally, there was the recurrent wishful thinking that sustained many of us through the trying months of 1965–1966 after the air strikes had begun: that surely, somehow, one way or another, we would "be in a conference in six months," and the escalatory spiral would be suspended. The basis of our hope: "It simply can't go on."

As a further influence on policy-makers I would cite the factor of *bureaucratic detachment*. By this I mean what at best might be termed the professional callousness of the surgeon (and indeed, medical lingo—the "surgical strike" for instance—seemed to crop up in the euphemisms of the times). In Washington the semantics of the military muted the reality of war for the civilian policy-makers. In quiet, air-conditioned, thick-carpeted rooms, such terms as "systematic pressure," "armed reconnaissance," "targets of opportunity," and even "body count" seemed to breed a sort of games-theory detachment. Most memorable to me was a moment in the late 1964 target planning when the question under discussion was how heavy our bombing should be, and how extensive our strafing, at some midpoint in the projected pattern of systematic pressure. An Assistant Secretary of State resolved the point in the following words: "It seems to me that our orchestration should be mainly violins, but with periodic touches of brass." Perhaps the biggest shock of my return to Cambridge, Massachusetts, was the realization that the young men, the flesh and blood I taught and saw on these university streets, were potentially some of the numbers on the charts of those faraway planners. In a curious sense, Cambridge is closer to this war than Washington.

There is an unprovable factor that relates to bureaucratic detachment: the ingredient of *crypto-racism*. I do not mean to imply any conscious contempt for Asian loss of life on the part of Washington officials. But I do mean to imply that bureaucratic detachment may well be compounded by a traditional Western sense that there are so many Asians, after all; that Asians have a fatalism about life and a disregard for its loss; that they are cruel and barbaric to their own people; and that they are very different from us (and all look alike?). And I *do* mean to imply that the upshot of such subliminal views is a subliminal question whether Asians, and particularly Asian peasants, and most particularly Asian Communists, are really people—like you and me. To put the matter another way: would we have pursued quite such policies—and quite such military tactics—if the Vietnamese were white?

It is impossible to write of Vietnam decision-making without writing about language. Throughout the conflict, words have been of paramount importance. I refer here to the impact of *rhetorical escalation* and to the *problem of oversell.* In an important sense, Vietnam has become of crucial significance to us *because we have said that it is of crucial significance.* (The issue obviously relates to the public relations preoccupation described earlier.)

The key here is domestic politics: the need to sell the American people, press, and Congress on support for an unpopular and costly war in which the objectives themselves have been in flux. To sell means to persuade, and to persuade means rhetoric. As the difficulties and costs have mounted, so has the definition of the stakes. This is not to say that rhetorical escalation is an orderly process; executive prose is the product of many writers, and some concepts—North Vietnamese infiltration, America's "national honor," Red China as the chief enemy—have entered the rhetoric only gradually and even sporadically. But there is an upward spiral nonetheless. And once you have *said* that the American Experiment itself stands or falls on the Vietnam outcome, you have thereby created a national stake far beyond any earlier stakes.

Crucial throughout the process of Vietnam decision-making was a conviction among many policy-makers: that Vietnam posed a *fundamental test of America's national will.* Time and again I was told by men reared in the tradition of Henry L. Stimson that all we needed was the will, and we would then prevail. Implicit in such a view, it seemed to me, was a curious assumption that Asians lacked will, or at least that in a contest between Asian and Anglo-Saxon wills, the non-Asians must prevail. A corollary to the persistent belief in will was a *fascination with power* and an awe in the face of the power America possessed as no nation or civilization ever before. Those who doubted our role in Vietnam were said to shrink from the burdens of power, the obligations of power, the uses of power, the responsibility of power. By implication, such men were soft-headed and effete.

Finally, no discussion of the factors and forces at work on Vietnam policy-makers can ignore the central fact of *human ego investment.* Men who have participated in a decision develop a stake in that decision. As they participate in further, related decisions, their stake increases. It might have been possible to dissuade a man of strong self-confidence at an early stage of the ladder of decision; but is is infinitely harder at later stages since a change of mind there usually involves implicit or explicit repudiation of a chain of previous decisions.

To put it bluntly: at the heart of the Vietnam calamity is a group of able, dedicated men who have been regularly and repeatedly wrong— and whose standing with their contemporaries, and more important, with history, depends, as they see it, on being proven right. These are not men who can be asked to extricate themselves from error.

The various ingredients I have cited in the making of Vietnam policy have created a variety of results, most of them fairly obvious. Here are some that seem to me most central:

Throughout the conflict, there has been *persistent and repeated miscalculation* by virtually all the actors, in high echelons and low, whether dove, hawk, or something else. To cite one simple example among many: in late 1964 and early 1965, some peace-seeking planners at State who strongly opposed the projected bombing of the North urged that, instead, American ground forces be sent to South Vietnam; this would, they said, increase our bargaining leverage against the North—our "chips"— and would give us something to negotiate about (the withdrawal of our forces) at an early peace conference. Simultaneously, the air-strike option was urged by many in the military who were dead set against American participation in "another land war in Asia"; they were joined by other civilian peace-seekers who wanted to bomb Hanoi into early negotiations. By late 1965, we had ended up with the worst of all worlds: ineffective and costly air strikes against the North, spiraling ground forces in the South, and no negotiations in sight.

Throughout the conflict as well, there has been *a steady give-in to pressures for a military solution* and only minimal and sporadic efforts at a diplomatic and political solution. In part this resulted from the confusion (earlier cited) among the civilians—confusion regarding objectives and strategy. And in part this resulted from the self-enlarging nature of military investment. Once air strikes and particularly ground forces were introduced, our investment itself had transformed the original stakes. More air power was needed to protect the ground forces; and then more ground forces to protect the ground forces. And needless to say, the military mind develops its own momentum in the absence of clear guidelines from the civilians. Once asked to save South Vietnam, rather than to "advise" it, the American military could not but press for escalation. In addition, sad to report, assorted military constituencies, once involved in Vietnam, have had a series of cases to prove: for instance, the utility not only of air power (the Air Force) but of supercarrier-based air power (the Navy). Also,

Vietnam policy has suffered from one ironic by-product of Secretary Mc-Namara's establishment of civilian control at the Pentagon: in the face of such control, interservice rivalry has given way to a united front among the military—reflected in the new but recurrent phenomenon of JCS unanimity. In conjunction with traditional congressional allies (mostly Southern senators and representatives) such a united front would pose a formidable problem for any President.

Throughout the conflict, there have been *missed opportunities, large and small, to disengage ourselves from Vietnam on increasingly unpleasant but still acceptable terms.* Of the many moments from 1961 onward, I shall cite only one, the last and most important opportunity that was lost: in the summer of 1964 the President instructed his chief advisers to prepare for him as wide a range of Vietnam options as possible for post-election consideration and decision. He explicitly asked that all options be laid out. What happened next was, in effect, Lyndon Johnson's slow-motion Bay of Pigs. For the advisers so effectively converged on one single option—juxtaposed against two other, phony options (in effect, blowing up the world, or scuttle-and-run)—that the President was confronted with unanimity for bombing the North from all his trusted counselors. Had he been more confident in foreign affairs, had he been deeply informed on Vietnam and Southeast Asia, and had he raised some hard questions that unanimity had submerged, this President could have used the largest electoral mandate in history to de-escalate in Vietnam, in the clear expectation that at the worst a neutralist government would come to power in Saigon and politely invite us out. Today, many lives and dollars later, such an alternative has become an elusive and infinitely more expensive possibility.

In the course of these years, another result of Vietnam decision-making has been *the abuse and distortion of history.* Vietnamese, Southeast Asian, and Far Eastern history has been rewritten by our policy-makers, and their spokesmen, to conform with the alleged necessity of our presence in Vietnam. Highly dubious analogies from our experience elsewhere—the "Munich" sellout and "containment" from Europe, the Malayan insurgency and the Korean War from Asia—have been imported in order to justify our actions. And more recent events have been fitted to the Procrustean bed of Vietnam. Most notably, the change of power in Indonesia in 1965–1966 has been ascribed to our Vietnam presence; and virtually all progress in the Pacific region—the rise of regionalism, new forms of cooperation, and mounting growth rates—has been similarly explained. The Indonesian allegation is undoubtedly false (I tried to prove it, during six months of careful investigation at the White House, and had to confess failure); the regional allegation is patently unprovable in either direction (except, of course, for the clear fact that the economies of both Japan and Korea have profited enormously from our Vietnam-related procurement in these countries; but that is a costly and highly dubious form of foreign aid).

There is a final result of Vietnam policy I would cite that holds potential danger for the future of American foreign policy: *the rise of a new breed of American ideologues who see Vietnam as the ultimate test of their doctrine.* I have in mind those men in Washington who have given a new life to the missionary impulse in American foreign relations: who believe that this nation, in this era, has received a threefold endowment that can transform the world. As they see it, that endowment is composed of, first, our unsurpassed military might; second, our clear technological supremacy; and third, our allegedly invincible benevolence (our "altruism," our affluence, our lack of territorial aspirations). Together, it is argued, this threefold endowment provides us with the opportunity and the obligation to ease the nations of the earth toward modernization and stability: toward a full-fledged *Pax Americana Technocratica.* In reaching toward this goal, Vietnam is viewed as the last and crucial test. Once we have succeeded there, the road ahead is clear. In a sense, these men are our counterpart to the visionaries of Communism's radical left: they are technocracy's own Maoists. They do not govern Washington today. But their doctrine rides high.

Long before I went into government, I was told a story about Henry L. Stimson that seemed to me pertinent during the years that I watched the Vietnam tragedy unfold—and participated in that tragedy. It seems to me more pertinent than ever as we move toward the election of 1968.

In his waning years Stimson was asked by an anxious questioner, "Mr. Secretary, how on earth can we ever bring peace to the world?" Stimson is said to have answered: "You begin by bringing to Washington a small handful of able men who believe that the achievement of peace is possible.

"You work them to the bone until they no longer believe that it is possible."

"And then you throw them out—and bring in a new bunch who believe that it is possible."

28
A Capitalist Imperative
GABRIEL KOLKO

Victory in war is not simply the result of battles, and nowhere in the twentieth century has this been truer than in Vietnam. To measure only the military balance of forces is misleading. To estimate the explicit designs of each of the contestants, while crucial, is by no means sufficient. Human goals and weaknesses are obviously critical, but in the social context which existed in South Vietnam between 1973 and 1975, far more was involved than conscious decisions. These were scarcely more than the sparks which led to the denouement neither side predicted, much less controlled. After the signing of the Paris Agreement, the fundamental change which occurred in South Vietnam was the general crisis of the entire social order the United States had installed. Its innumerable political, economic, and human consequences telescoped time and ended an epic, thirty-year war in a few stunning weeks in complete victory for the Communists.

The United States constructed a political and economic order in South Vietnam similar to the one it has repeatedly encouraged throughout the Third World. America's defeat was not merely a failure of its arms. Indeed, while partly successful in transferring military power to its surrogate, the Americans established institutional forms that were totally incapable of challenging the Revolution. The United States utterly failed to develop a credible limited-war doctrine and technical capability to intervene in the Third World, a crucial symbolic objective of the entire campaign for three administrations. Yet ultimately this was even less decisive than its intrinsic inability to create a viable political, economic, and ideological system capable of attaining the prerequisites of military success. This nonmilitary defeat makes Vietnam so significant for the limits of U.S. power in the Third World. America, locked into its mission to control the broad contours of the world's political and socioeconomic development, had set for itself inherently unobtainable political objectives.

Whatever the human and physical toll of the war on the Revolution throughout Vietnam, it was the myriad weaknesses of the foreign-sponsored society and the Communists' own strength which produced the decisive equation in the war. The individualism and egoism the Americans sought to implant were reflections of their own ideology and social system. Their encouragement of the private accumulation of possessions and wealth did not require an explicit counterrevolutionary ideology but only a lifestyle incompatible with the Revolution's essential values regarding personal behavior and social institutions. Washington's alternative, like its military doctrine, was capital intensive, since it purchased a corrupt, fragile, and fickle constituency, but it was also inherently self-destructive. The moment the amount of money to pay for the RVN system declined even slightly, the entire order began to tremble so that almost any challenge, military or political, would shatter it. Party decisions in 1974 and 1975 could operate only within this framework. Alone, they were important merely insofar as they created a confrontation of the two forces, in which the total power and disabilities of the two systems could be fully tested.

By 1974 the RVNAF [Republic of Vietnam Armed Forces] was disintegrating amid the ravages which inflation and the demoralizing prospect of interminable war imposed on its soldiers. The army was ready to capsize at the first significant challenge, and the RVN's collapse after over two decades of assiduous, costly American efforts to build its military says more about each side's human resources than about the Communist army's specific strategy or equipment.

No less critical was the role of the people in the RVN-controlled rural and urban areas. To the extent that a radicalizing process was again well under way among them by 1974, it assured the Revolution's eventual success with or without the test of arms. For had the PAVN [People's Army of Vietnam] not attacked in March 1975, the war would have ended in the very near future with economic and political upheavals from which the Revolution would have emerged victorious after a period of social chaos. When the attack came, it quickly upset a house of cards.

The United States had installed a military system as a mechanism for controlling the political structure and, above all, the American-subsidized economic order. Fear of a coup or rivalry colored every aspect of its organization and action under Nguyen Van Thieu, and the total failure of its leadership in March 1975 revealed that an initially successful political apparatus posing as an army will not suffice in the long run. Thieu's key generals, while politically reliable, proved incompetent and powerless as military leaders. The RVN was not, as some Americans later argued, a military machine with an annexed political structure. Rather, it was an intrinsically dysfunctional hybrid order that the United States had constructed both by default and by accretion: an army, in the final analysis, that could not make successful war or politics, much less operate an economy. Almost all Americans watching the RVN closely after 1973 knew that its ineluctable demise was not far off, and some of them were less surprised at the speed and form of the collapse than many of the Party's leaders. Wars often end when the social, human, and political conditions are ripe, and the nature and tempo of the Communist military triumph in Vietnam was primarily a consequence of them. The Communist Party was to inherit this social system's immense disorganization when it came to power.

America's losing the war had little to do with the crisis of its politics connected with Watergate. Given the dilemmas it confronted in the world economy, the administrations' problem in South Vietnam was one that would have arisen even if Nixon had been at the peak of his powers. It had to impose priorities on its global objectives in order to attain any of them. Economic difficulties at home and constraints on resources and manpower finally compelled the United States to make the RVN conform to American norms of efficiency—an obligation that merely triggered a crisis in Thieu's system.

Ultimately, the weakness of the RVN's social order was also the recurrent dilemma of the United States' relationship to all of its Third World clients, on which it has become fatally dependent as instruments for applying its foreign policy. The inevitable choice of Thieu as its surrogate made Washington's position increasingly precarious. It was impossible to meet this challenge, because the notion of an honest puppet was a contradiction Washington has failed to resolve anywhere in the world since 1945. In effect, while the White House had to cope with the problem of its own legitimacy and relationship to Congress after 1972, it still had to deal with this enduring, universal paradox of the relevance of the impotence of its dependents to the advancement of American power.

The Vietnam War was for the United States the culmination of its frustrating postwar effort to merge its arms and politics to halt and reverse the emergence of states and social systems opposed to the international order Washington sought to establish. It was not the first serious trial of either its military power or its political strategy, only the most disastrous. Despite America's many real successes in imposing its hegemony elsewhere, Vietnam exposed the ultimate constraints on its power in the modern era: its internal tensions, the contradictions between overinvolvement in one nation and its interests and ambitions elsewhere, and its material limits. Precisely because of the unmistakable nature of the defeat after so long and divisive an effort and because of the war's impact on the United States' political structure and aspirations, this conflict takes on a significance greater than that of either of the two world wars. Both of them had only encouraged Washington's ambition to guide and integrate the world's political and economic system—a goal which was surely the most important cause of its intervention in the Vietnam conflict after 1950.

While the strategic implications of the war for the future of American military power in local conflicts was the most obvious dimension of its defeat, it had confronted these issues often since 1946. What was truly distinctive was the collapse of a national consensus on the broad contours of America's role in the world. The trauma was intense; the war ended without glory and with profound remorse for tens of millions of Americans. Successive administrations fought the war so energetically because of these earlier frustrations, of which they were especially conscious in the early 1960s, scarcely suspecting that rather than resolving them, they would only leave the nation with a far larger set of military, political, and economic dilemmas to face for the remainder of this century. But by 1975 the United States was weaker than it had been at the inception of the war in the early 1960s, a lesson hardly any advocate of new interventions could afford to ignore.

The limits of arms and armies in Vietnam was clear by Tet 1968. Although the United States possessed nominally good weapons and tactics, it lacked a military strategy capable of overcoming its enemy's abilities and appropriate to its economic resources, its global priorities, and its political constraints in Vietnam, at home, and in the rest of the world. Although its aims in South Vietnam were never to alter, it was always incapable of coping with the countless political complexities that irrevocably emerge from protracted armed conflict. America's political, military, and ideological leaders remained either oblivious or contemptuous of these until the war was essentially lost. Even today they scarcely dare confront the war's meaning as Washington continues to assert aggressively its classic postwar objectives and interests in Latin America and elsewhere. America's failure was material, of course, but it was also analytic, the result of a myopia whose importance greatly transcended bureaucratic politics or the idiosyncrasies of Presidents and their satraps. The dominating conventional wisdom of American power after 1946 had no effective means of inhibiting a system whose ambitions and needs increasingly transcended its resources for achieving them. They remained unable and unwilling to acknowledge that these objectives were intrinsically unobtainable and irrelevant to the socioeconomic forms much of the Third World is adopting to resolve its economic and human problems, and that the United States' effort to alter this pervasive reality was certain to produce conflict.

That America's destiny in Vietnam should have been inextricably tied to two venal men is by itself a remarkable fact, but scarcely unique in the postwar era. Nor is it surprising that the nature and role of Thieu and the society he and the Americans fashioned became the critical variable in the war's astonishing end. Since there was no durable social, economic, and political basis for any of the French- or American-imposed regimes, their demise was inevitable despite the quite unforeseeable quality of the RVN's final weeks. In retrospect, it is extraordinary that four administrations attempted at immense cost to impose American hegemony on Vietnam while totally dependent on such vulnerable surrogates.

The United States had no way out of this hopeless trap short of a readiness to concede an early defeat of its aim to create an anti-Communist South Vietnam. It always favored erstwhile strongmen in the hope they would provide stability and an effective alternative. The size and the political and economic functions of the RVN military left no space for any of the largely ephemeral, disunited, non-Communist social forces. In every sense there was no serious option to the Revolution, and none would have emerged even if the United States had sought to encourage one. America's sponsorship of the military's central role in every dimension of the RVN system created a recipe for social, economic, and political disaster. In the end, this unavoidable policy was certain to produce a wholly artificial society which traumatized the masses and expanded the Revolution's objective potential, notwithstanding its large losses.

Linked to this problem of translating its armed might into political success was the fact that in the very process of fighting a war utilizing titanic firepower, the Americans created vast demographic and human upheavals, with their searing psychological and economic impact, resulting in an urbanized society that was not viable either economically or politically. The very consequences of its technological premises stretched South Vietnam's entire social fabric far beyond the control of the American surrogates in Saigon. It was the irony of the U.S. local-war strategy, and then of Vietnamization, that its intrinsic effects imposed intolerable and fatal burdens on the social order. These far outweighed the importance of its nominal victories in battles. It suggests, as well, why the American military cannot enter any society without accelerating the corrosive dynamics and problems sure to lead to political failure for its local allies.

Technology in the war played a profoundly different role for each side. Applying its existing weaponry and technological potential to define and develop a limited- and counterinsurgency-war strategy applicable to Third World contexts was far more complex then the United States had ever imagined in the early 1960s. America's leaders and generals substituted confidence in the quantity of their arms for cogent strategic and political analyses. They failed to make an accurate assessment of their prospects for success, or even of the economic costs of their doctrines, until well into the war, when symbolically important considerations, such as "credibility," paralyzed their thinking in additional ways. Only the Communists fully appreciated the larger context of the struggle. They overcame the most formidable array of arms in history with a protracted war based on decentralization, mass mobilization, and highly adaptive military tactics tailored to technology's specific vulnerabilities. Indeed, just as the United States hoped to develop a limited-war capability relevant throughout the globe, the Communists articulated political, organizational, and technical responses to American intervention and arms valuable to revolutionary forces everywhere. This fact is likely to compound the difficulties of America's self-appointed counterrevolutionary mission in the Third World for decades to come.

The Communist Party is the easiest contestant to understand in the Vietnam War. Its passion for theory and analysis was quite introspective, constant, and invariably public. Its role and decisions were always manifest both from its deeds and from its words. It is simpler to fathom because it succeeded, and the causes of a system's triumph are much more obvious than those of a system's failure. For the Party's victory is a testimony not only to the malleability of history as a general process but also to the wartime efficacy of the institutions and ideas of the winning side as well as those of the nation that lost.

The Party's power, especially before 1949, was intimately linked to the void which the breakdown of French colonialism and the nature of the class system do so much to create. The thread of its success by default, due largely to its existence and endurance and to its enemies' follies, weaves through the entire thirty-year war. The Party's carefully calculated political and military initiatives, of course, made it assume an increasingly activist leadership. But the disastrous structural impact of the actions of the United States and the RVN throughout South Vietnam meant that the Party would always be able to exploit the consequences of its enemy's innumerable weaknesses. The Party was highly creative and pragmatic in its attempt to make the most of the possibilities before it. The worst error anyone studying it can make is to try to explain its actions, policies, and resilience simply as a predetermined, deductive consequence of its Marxist-Leninist ideology. To a crucial extent, the diversity and richness of the Party's practice and success transcended its own formal theoretical system.

The Revolution had to organize large sectors of Vietnamese society. In the process it recorded errors as well as accomplishments. Most important, though, was its ability to survive both as an organization and, at the very least, as a cause in the minds of the people. It thereby retained the ability to reassert itself when there were new opportunities to do so. The Communist Party leadership's ability to analyze and adapt, to relate its resources to reality, and to avoid a sense of omnipotence as well as excessive caution was the essential link between its existing and potential forces and the future.

To a critical degree the Party's power to rally vast numbers was due to the corrosive impact of wars on the traditional rural order and to its own integrative role. The French-imposed land system and economy drove the masses to desperation by the time of World War Two, and the Communists offered them an organized revolutionary response to common social problems. It was from this assertion of community and class in the face of famine and war that the Party's organization became durable. And it was the economics of peasant discontent, more than any other single long-term issue, which gave the Party a capacity to mobilize the masses, its ultimate reservoir of power. Time and again the peasantry profoundly influenced the Party's grand strategy—most decisively during 1953–55 in the north, in 1959–61 in the south, and thereafter in various localities in the south. Adherence to the poor-peasant line made mobilization possible, and it was repeatedly the price of success.

Such concessions to pressures from below often conflicted with the Party's continuous advocacy of a united-front line against the French and Americans. Reconciling the tensions between class conflict and political unity was a perpetual challenge to it—one which it never wholly mastered and which compelled it at times to go against its preferences. Still the Party's ability to employ nonclass appeals like patriotism and to absorb better-educated revolutionaries of bourgeois origins at all levels proved an inestimable source of strength to it over the years. Although its united-front strategy was never as successful as the Party hoped after 1961, particularly in the cities, its minimal achievements were sufficient to provide the Party with the support it needed.

In coping with these and countless other challenges, the Party committed errors, but none, obviously, that were fatal to its entire effort. If the Party's leaders sought to portray themselves as performing a greater role on the road to power than they in fact played, their accomplishment as a guiding force was nonetheless exceptional in the twentieth century. Extremely careful students of social dynamics, essentially cautious, deliberative analysts both by inclination and because of the checks inherent in their collective decision-making structure, they were far more adept at making rational, logical assessments than any of their French and American enemies, whose penchant for illusions and symbolism made them the only total ideologists of the war. While ready to take risks to move toward their ultimate goals, the Party's leaders always carefully estimated the balance of forces they confronted at home and abroad and the long-range implications of various actions. Such realism prevented decisive mistakes.

The Party's leaders repeatedly responded to pressures from the masses, ostensibly to guide them along a coherent route but in reality sometimes only after recognizing that their demands were irresistible and would find expression with or without guidance. Given the immense length of the nation and the difficulties of communication, the process of both leading and following the people was an inherently slow one. Space and time imposed their own imperatives on both sides during the war, but particularly on the materially poorer Communists. While the Party leaders articulated an ideal organizational form, realities forced them repeatedly to conform in an ad hoc fashion to the local imperatives of economic underdevelopment and of protracted war. Their ultimate wisdom was to accept such inhibitions and define the nature of revolutionary commitment in a way that transcended predetermined organizational concepts but touched the essentials of revolutionary politics in a long war.

The Communist Party's genius was in its ability to survive and adapt to the most incredible challenges and reemerge sufficiently powerful to fill the vacuum that the United States and its dependents created. Its retention of the loyalty of its most committed members, who endured astonishing personal losses for long periods, was the core of this resiliency, and it could do so because of its ability to relate to the most pressing social problems facing the people. This effort after 1968 became far more complicated as the problems of peace and the preservation of a coherent society against the onslaught of the American presence and the traumas of war surpassed obvious class issues as the burning mobilizing questions. The Party's tasks in coping with this new, broader consciousness in both urban and rural areas posed a much more subtle challenge. It knew that the war's physical and psychological toll on the people had been profound, though most of its leaders failed to perceive that the true balance of forces had overwhelmingly shifted in their favor.

The Party therefore underestimated the distinctive transformation of political attitudes which was then taking place among the urban elements, quickly leading to an alienation and apathy fundamentally subversive to the RVN's cohesion and future. It understood the RVNAF's demoralization better, but, even here, the implications did not become apparent to most of its leaders until December 1974, when they realized resistance to an offensive might be minimal and ineffective. That a large and growing vacuum existed, which any concerted effort could fill, seemed possible to the Communists, but little did they imagine the monumental occurrences of March and April. To the degree that these were the outcome of Thieu's priorities and commitments to himself, they were predictable, however, and the precedents of Lam Son 719 and the 1972 offensive were powerful indicators of his incompetence and of the fragility of his soldiers and officers when confronted with danger.

To some extent, then, although the astounding events of the final chapter of the war were unforeseeable to the Communists, their results were the inexorable and predictable outcome of their own efforts and of the nature of the forces arrayed against them. When the moment came, they seized the opportunity and entered the enormous void during the most remarkable seven weeks in the entire history of the war. But that astonishing drama was merely the culmination of a political, social, and human struggle that had begun two decades earlier and that the Revolution had used to build its ranks and establish its legitimacy in a slow, patient, and painfully cumulative process. It could only predict that this vast, interminable chain of sacrifices and efforts would produce total victory. And at times it offered those who stayed with it throughout the long ordeal only the often abstract and all-too-distant proposition, grounded in its Marxism, that people and social processes can intersect and interact to determine their own future and shape the outcome of their history.

The Vietnam War, in the final analysis, was a contest between the U.S. with its abundantly subsidized, protected surrogate and a Revolutionary movement whose class roots and ideological foundations gave it enormous resiliency and power. The way individuals behaved both in war and in peace reflected the social norms and the nature of the two competing systems. The Communist Party's most important source of strength over thirty-five years was its conception of a socialist and revolutionary morality and its insistence on the primordial significance of radical values and conduct to the achievement and implementation of a socialist society. Its capacity to develop an organization whose members' lives conformed sufficiently to these principles attained this objective functionally, if never perfectly. This notion of the critical role of the individual was Vietnamese Communism's most distinctive and fundamental addition to Marxist-Leninist theory and an implicit major revision of the relative importance of leaders and purely organizational forms. No one can comprehend how countless tens of thousands of men and women struggled for decades—usually under conditions of extreme privation and often in isolation, demanding extraordinary personal commitments, patience, and sacrifices—without appreciating the influence of such revolutionary commitments and values as well as the attraction of its social and political program. For while the Party's tactics and strategy throughout the war had to be correct far more often than not, that was a necessary but not sufficient condition of success. In a protracted struggle in which a multidimensional crisis affected in a manner exceeding the capacity of anyone—including its leaders—to anticipate, the Party's ultimate power was its ability to endure and thereby, either wisely or erroneously, to continue to relate to events. The very existence of its persistent, devoted members gave the Party the freedom to assume mastery of the nation's future and to fill the void the French and American experience left in Vietnam.

Revolutionary morality postulated the consciousness affects the historical process by its very being. It did not, lest it become radical mysticism and romanticism, ignore the material balance of forces, but it asserted the critical role of personal responsibility and action. Whatever the exact internal nature of a party, which requires discipline in some measure to address itself to difficult circumstances, the very existence of such a degree of optimism assumes an element of freedom in social processes. A conception of the masses' role in great events and history produced a self-consciousness which itself became an ingredient of power. However strict Party control, the very existence of the Party is an affirmation of the role of will and choice in history, and its cohesion became the precondition of eventual freedom from the constraints of a historical process which makes the need for unity and morality essential in the first instance. Conscious of the risks of excessive discipline as well, the Party sought to minimize them with an essentially institutionalized antibureaucratic campaign which, though far from solving the problem, lessened it significantly.

In analyzing the Communist Party's remarkable and often unique efforts on behalf of a revolutionary morality and personal socialist values, one must make a clear distinction between total success and sufficient attainment of its goals. It never became a Party of revolutionary saints, nor did it proclaim total triumph for its efforts to achieve its ideal standards, but it did manage to bring together a great number of men and women whose morals and dedication to a cause were very high, who made monumental sacrifices and underwent incredible deprivation, and who alone made the Party play its role in history. These people, as well as a substantial number who were not so devoted, were the objects of a constant effort at self-renewal and reinvigoration. The Party was, after all, a group of mortals who possessed many of the weaknesses of humankind, but also a great share of its all-too-rare strengths. One could ask little more. The very drive for personal morality was seen as a part of the process to overcome the freely acknowledged faults of its members, and the attempt to deal explicitly with their limitations resolved many of them. In a word, the system worked, thereby confirming revolutionary optimism's relationship to historical change.

It is the extent of the Party's success which is all the more interesting, as if the constant pressure of the lone struggle strengthened many of its members and made it easier for them to dedicate their lives to the cause. Underlying the commitment of the Party's best and strongest members was a synthesis of belief and confidence in the future, based on a merger of their own required action with a rational assessment of the nature of social reality and historical materialism—a synthesis of the personal and impersonal that made belief all the more plausible and action all the more necessary. Each could attain personal fulfillment by seeking to change history, but it would be through and for the people—and for a cause in which each person's destiny was linked with that of the revolution. The impact of this conception made the seemingly impossible victory over France and America possible, and the strongest proof of its efficacy is that, in the end, experience vindicated it.

The role of freedom and constraint in historical processes and great events intrudes perpetually into mankind's ideas. The real question in this search for primary explanations is the extent to which both choice and necessity operate over time and, above all, how, when, and why one becomes more important than the other. The significance of these issues, fundamental for understanding the modern historical experience, resists simplifications and does not permit the evasion of contingent conclusions, for living with the tensions of complexity and partial insight is superior to the false security of pretentious final solutions to the inherent, but creative, dilemmas of knowledge.

For the activist the extent of freedom in the face of historical forces is a fundamental question about the meaning of action and about a life's commitments. The comprehension of the limits *and* possibilities of reality is the essence of political strategy and the precondition for optimal social change. Over time, risks of error are constant, their consequences to the destinies of conscious people being easily capable of defining their lives and crucial experiences. The effort to master one's environment and world is integral to the nature and extent of rationality and freedom in modern life. That constraints have and will always operate on people's desires is less contentious than understanding that social change in this century has been astonishingly rapid and traumatic. The external crises of war and multiple internal developments will sustain this transformation of the world in the future. The very inevitability and the impact of such monumental events create both the potential and the need for directed change, making the possibilities of freedom and mastery integral to the human condition.

The interaction between reality and ideals, in Vietnam but also in many other nations throughout this century, has been a critical element in those successes that proponents of deliberate changes have attained. Whatever the precise validity of various socialist diagnoses of the nature of capitalism and the Third World, their ultimate intellectual and political strength has been their keen appreciation of the profound importance of change and crisis in the modern historical experience and of the ability and obligation of organized forces to attempt to influence them. It is this fixation that has renewed socialism's significance time and again after sometimes enormous political failures and errors in analysis, for change is also predicated both on the ability and on the need of people to respond to real opportunities in defining society's affairs. The comprehending of social forces and guiding them in a resilient and patient manner is relevant when existing orders become unstable or fail. The costs of protracted wars to national economies and their social and ideological cohesion have been the most important source of change, especially in accelerating the decolonization of the European and American imperialist orders, but there have been others as well. As the longest conflict of the modern era, the Vietnam War offers a vast panorama for assessing the origins and components of a crisis affecting two major Western nations and for exploring the significance of action and organizations in consciously defining the final outcome of a major historical event.

War is generally the transcendent element in all societies that compels choices and action. Parties of change at such times relate to the masses, attempting to impose ideas and roles on those now increasingly likely to act with or without leadership. When large numbers of people realize that they are unable to evade the personal consequences of their action or inaction—and may indeed pay a much higher price for their passivity—they become a social force, all the more durable to the extent they take an organized form. Evasion is, however, the normal response of most people to the risks about them, and it usually is far less the party with claims of leadership than the breakdown of the traditional order that stimulates their initial consciousness and discontent, conditioning them to act. Evasion will tend to recur as the society's crisis is alleviated, though not without the persistence of residues of earlier ideas and values in mass consciousness. But stability is so rarely permanent that a party's main role in this process is to provide the continuity and linkage between periods of crisis and relative tranquillity, along with such leadership as the masses will accept when their readiness for action returns. In this sense, though a party must not make too many errors, it is less important that it always be correct than that it be able to sustain its existence and relationship to social dynamics and forces so that its influence reemerges with the growth of society's crisis. Its capacity to persist is a critical measure of the potential of freedom and rationality in history.

This commitment to activism as a way of extracting maximum change from given social conditions becomes integrated with institutional processes and also accelerates them. It does not passively wait for such processes to culminate impersonally at some desired, hypothetical point. To the extent that social forces and movements are underdeveloped, they are galvanized through a merging of objective conditions in the economy and society with the activity of a party. A party's significance may range from utter futility at one period to decisive relevance at another, or to all the intermediate stages possible. Activism, along with organization, is a risk that the assumption of freedom to measurably affect historical forces requires—and one that has produced success so often in this century, and in so many nations, that the numerous occasions on which it has failed in whole or in part should never occlude our comprehension of the parameters of human possibilities and change in our age. This degree of accomplishment does not eliminate all limitations on freedom, but only those which would result if there were no concerted efforts at controlled change. The general Marxist tradition has not, in any event, minimized the domain of impersonal institutional and social inhibitions. But precisely because the Left is aware of the reality of the absence of total liberty, it has also acknowledged the existence of opportunities to transform, and the obligation to exploit, historical processes.

Yet when all of these contingencies are taken into account, events in the twentieth century, in Vietnam and in countless other nations, have shown that those who have pursued the route of action for social change and paid their price in time, passion, and commitments are also those who have most defined the extent to which human choice and freedom affect social developments. The residual legacies and problems of past institutional and social experiences exist throughout the world, of course, and no nation, even when the old regime is totally eliminated, is able easily or quickly to transcend them. Historical experiences are complex and often problematical, and that successes are never total or victories truly final is less important than that they occur often as a consequence of human will and action, with coveted social changes often resulting from combinations of freedom and necessity, desire, action, and insight, but never from apathy and indifference.

The Vietnam War was a monumental event which transcends one nation or time and reflects, in the most acute form, the basic dynamics and trends in the historical experience since 1946. It was scarcely accidental but rather the logical outcome of contemporary U.S. ambition, strength, and weakness. The war once again confirmed the inevitability of social transformations and social movements in the world today, their real vulnerabilities as well as their enormous force, and the awesome potential of men and women to define their own future against overwhelming opposition. To weigh both American resources and ultimate impotence against the capabilities of those adversaries it may very well confront in some other hapless nation in the Third World, this year or in the future, is to gauge the true nature of power and the components of change in today's world. For given all the social and human dimensions which will affect the outcome of warfare between the United States and radical movements and nations, it is scarcely imaginable that another massive encroachment in some recalcitrant revolutionary nation would have an end different from that in Vietnam.

All that the United States has the ability to accomplish today is to impose immeasurable suffering on people whose fates its arms and money cannot control. To do so once more would also demand from the American public a price it eventually refused to pay in Vietnam and is even less likely to give willingly in the future. Profound social change in the modern historical experience is irresistible. But the nature of that process and the manner it affects the lives of the masses in developing countries over the coming decades are inextricably linked to the question whether its defeat in the Vietnam War constrains the United States from interventions elsewhere and the people of the world to develop their own future.

29
A Defense of Freedom
NORMAN PODHORETZ

Here then we arrive at the center of the moral issue posed by the American intervention into Vietnam.

The United States sent half a million men to fight in Vietnam. More than 50,000 of them lost their lives, and many thousands more were wounded. Billions of dollars were poured into the effort, damaging the once unparalleled American economy to such an extent that the country's competitive position was grievously impaired. The domestic disruptions to which the war gave rise did perhaps even greater damage to a society previously so self-confident that it was often accused of entertaining illusions of its own omnipotence. Millions of young people growing to maturity during the war developed attitudes of such hostility toward their own country and the civilization embodied by its institutions that their willingness to defend it against external enemies in the future was left hanging in doubt.

Why did the United States undertake these burdens and make these sacrifices in blood and treasure and domestic tranquillity? What was in it for the United States? It was a question that plagued the antiwar movement from beginning to end because the answer was so hard to find. If the United States was simply acting the part of an imperialist aggressor in Vietnam, as many in the antiwar movement professed to believe, it was imperialism of a most peculiar kind. There were no raw materials to exploit in Vietnam, and there was no overriding strategic interest involved. To Franklin Roosevelt in 1941 Indochina had been important because it was close to the source of rubber and tin, but this was no longer an important consideration. Toward the end of the war, it was discovered that there was oil off the coast of Vietnam and antiwar radicals happily seized on this news as at last providing an explanation for the American presence there. But neither Kennedy nor Johnson knew about the oil, and even if they had, the would hardly have gone to war for its sake in those pre-OPEC days when oil from the Persian Gulf could be had at two dollars a barrel.

In the absence of an economic interpretation, a psychological version of the theory of imperialism was developed to answer the maddening question: *Why are we in Vietnam?* This theory held that the United States was in Vietnam because it had an urge to dominate—"to impose its national obsessions on the rest of the world," in the words of a piece in the *New York Review of Books*,[1] one of the leading centers of antiwar agitation within the intellectual community. But if so, the psychic profits were as illusory as the economic ones, for the war was doing even deeper damage to the national self-confidence than to the national economy.

Yet another variant of the psychological interpretation, proposed by the economist Robert L. Heilbroner, was that "the fear of losing our place in the sun, of finding ourselves at bay,...motivates a great deal of the anti-Communism on which so much of American foreign policy seems to be founded." This was especially so in such underdeveloped countries as Vietnam, where "the rise of Communism would signal the end of capitalism as the dominant world order, and would force the acknowledgment that America no longer constituted the model on which the future of world civilization would be mainly based."[2]

All these theories were developed out to a desperate need to find or invent selfish or self-interested motives for the American presence in Vietnam, the better to discredit it morally. In a different context, proponents of one or another of these theories—Senator Fulbright, for example—were not above trying to discredit the American presence politically by insisting that *no* national interest was being served by the war. This latter contention at least had the virtue of being closer to the truth than the former. For the truth was that the United States went into Vietnam for the sake not of its own direct interests in the ordinary sense but for the sake of an ideal. The intervention was a product of the Wilsonian side of the American character—the side that went to war in 1917 to "make the world safe for democracy" and that found its contemporary incarnations in the liberal internationalism of the 1940s and the liberal anti-Communism of the 1950s. One can characterize this impulse as naive: one can describe it, as Heilbroner does (and as can be done with any virtuous act), in terms that give it a subtly self-interested flavor. But there is no rationally defensible way in which it can be called immoral.

Why, then, were we in Vietnam? To say it once again: because we were trying to save the Southern half of that country from the evils of Communism. But was the war we fought to accomplish this purpose morally worse than Communism itself? Peter L. Berger, who at the time was involved with Clergy and Laymen Concerned About Vietnam (CALCAV), wrote in 1967: "All sorts of dire results might well follow a reduction or a withdrawal of the American engagement in Vietnam. Morally speaking, however, it is safe to assume that none of these could be worse than what is taking place right now." Unlike most of his fellow members of CALCAV, Berger would later repent of this statement. Writing in 1980, he would say of it: "Well, it was *not* safe to assume.... I was wrong and so were all those who thought as I did." For "contrary to what most members (including myself) of the antiwar movement expected, the peoples of Indochina have, since 1975, been subjected to suffering far worse than anything that was inflicted upon them by the United States and its allies."[3]

To be sure, the "bloodbath" that had been feared by supporters of the war did not occur—not in the precise form that had been anticipated. In contrast to what they did upon taking power in Hanoi in 1954 (when they murdered some 50,000 landlords), or what they did during their brief occupation of Hué during the Tet offensive of 1968 (when they massacred 3,000 civilians), the Communists did not stage mass executions in the newly conquered South. According to Nguyen Cong Hoan, who had been an NLF agent and then became a member of the National Assembly of the newly united Communist Vietnam before disillusionment drove him to escape in March 1977, there were more executions in the provinces than in the cities and the total number might well have reached into the tens of thousands. But as another fervent opponent of the war, the New York *Times* columnist Tom Wicker was forced to acknowledge, "what Vietnam has given us instead of a bloodbath [is] a vast tide of human misery in Southeast Asia—hundreds of thousands of homeless persons in United Nations camps, perhaps as many more dead in flight, tens of thousands of the most pitiable forcibly repatriated to Cambodia, no one knows how many adrift on the high seas or wandering the roads."[4]

Among the refugees Wicker was talking about here were those who came to be known as "the boat people" because they "literally threw themselves upon the South China Sea in small coastal craft...."[5] Many thousands of these people were ethnic Chinese who were being driven out and forced to pay everything they had for leaky boats; tens of thousands more were Vietnamese fleeing voluntarily from what Nguyen Cong Hoan describes as "the most inhuman and oppressive regime they have ever known."[6] The same judgment is made by Truong Nhu Tang, the former Minister of Justice in the PRG who fled in November 1979 in a boat loaded with forty refugees: "Never has any previous regime brought such masses of people to such desperation. Not the military dictators, not the colonialists, not even the ancient Chinese overlords."[7]

So desperate were they to leave that they were willing to take the poor chance of survival in flight rather than remain. Says Nguyen Cong Hoan: "...Our people have a traditional attachment to their country. No Vietnamese would willingly leave home, homeland, and ancestors' graves. During the most oppressive French colonial rule and Japanese domination, no one escaped by boat at great risk to their lives. Yet you see that my countrymen by the thousands and from all walks of life, including a number of disillusioned Vietcongs, continue to escape from Vietnam; six out of ten never make it, and for those who are fortunate to make it, they are not allowed to land."[8] Adds one of the disillusioned who did make it, Doan Van Toai: "Among the boat people who survived, including those who were raped by pirates and those who suffered in the refugee camps, nobody regrets his escape from the present regime."[9]

Though they invented a new form of the Communist bloodbath, the North Vietnamese (for, to repeat, before long there were no Southerners in authority in the South, not even former members of the NLF and the

PRG) were less creative in dealing with political opposition, whether real or imagined. The "re-education camps" they had always used for this purpose in the North were now extended to the South, but the result was not so much an indigenous system of Vietnamese concentration camps as an imitation of the Soviet Gulag. (*The Vietnamese Gulag*, indeed, was the name Doan Van Toai gave to the book he published about the camps in 1979.) The French journalist Jean Lacouture, who had supported the Communists during the war to the point (as he now admitted) of turning himself into a "vehicle and intermediary for a lying and criminal propaganda, [an] ingenuous spokesman for tyranny in the name of liberty,"[10] now tried to salvage his integrity by telling the truth about a re-education camp he was permitted to visit by a regime that had good reason to think him friendly. "It was," he wrote, "a prefabricated hell."[11]

Doan Van Toai, who had been in the jails over which so much moral outrage had been expended in the days of Thieu, describes the conditions he himself encountered when he was arrested by the Communists: "I was thrown into a three-foot-by-six-foot cell with my left hand chained to my right foot and my right hand chained to my left foot. My food was rice mixed with sand.... After two months in solitary confinement, I was transferred to a collective cell, a room 15 feet wide and 25 feet long, where at different times anywhere from 40 to 100 prisoners were crushed together. Here we had to take turns lying down to sleep and most of the younger, stronger prisoners slept sitting up. In the sweltering heat, we also took turns snaching a few breaths of fresh air in front of the narrow opening that was the cell's only window. Every day I watched my friends die at my feet."[12]

Toai adds: "One South Vietnamese Communist, Nguyen Van Tang, who was detained 15 years by the French, eight years by Diem, six years by Thieu, and who is still in jail today, this time in a Communist prison, told me ... 'My dream now is not to be released; it is not to see my family. My dream is that I could be back in a French prison 30 years ago.'"[13]

No one knows how many people were sent to the Vietnamese Gulag. Five years after the fall of Saigon, estimates ranged from 150,000 to a million. Prime Minister Pham Van Dong, who so impressed Mary McCarthy with his nobility in 1968, told a French magazine ten years later that he had "*released* more than one million prisoners from the camps,"[14] although according to the figures of his own government he had arrested only 50,000 in the first place.

These prisoners naturally included officials of the former government of South Vietnam, but many opponents of the Thieu regime could also be found among them, some of whom were by 1981 known to have died in the camps. One such Thic Thien Minh, "the strategist of all the Buddhist peace movements in Saigon, ... who was sentenced to 10 years in jail by the Thieu regime, then released after an outpouring of protest from Vietnamese and antiwar protesters around the world," and who died after six months of detention by the Communists in 1979. Another was Tran

Van Tuyen, a leader of the opposition to Thieu in the Saigon Assembly. A third was the philosopher Ho Huu Tuong, "perhaps the leading intellectual in South Vietnam," who died in a Communist prison in 1980. All these—along with other opponents of Thieu possibly still alive, like Bui Tuong Huan, former president of Hué University; Father Tran Huu Thanh, a dissident Catholic priest; and Tran Ngoc Chau, whose own brother had been a North Vietnamese agent—were arrested (and of course held without trial) "in order," says Toai, "to preempt any possible opposition to the Communists."[15]

Before the Communist takeover, there had been a considerable degree of political freedom in South Vietnam which manifested itself in the existence of many different parties. After the North Vietnamese conquest, all these parties were dissolved: as for the NLF, "they buried it," in the bitter words of Truong Nhu Tang, "without even a ceremony," and "at the simple farewell dinner we held to formally disband the NLF in late 1976 neither the party nor the government sent a representative." The people of Vietnam, who "want only the freedom to go where they wish, educate their children in the schools they choose and have a voice in their government" are instead "treated like ants in a colony. There is only the opportunity to follow orders strictly, never the opportunity to express disagreement. Even within the [Communist] party, the principle of democracy has been destroyed in favor of the most rigid hierarchy. Stalinism, discredited throughout most of the Communist world, flourishes under the aged and fanatic Vietnamese leadership."[16]

Reading these words, one recalls Susan Sontag, Mary McCarthy, and Frances FitzGerald expending their intellectual energies on the promulgation of theories of Vietnamese culture calculated to deny that the people of Vietnam cared about freedom in the simple concrete terms set forth by Tang. One recalls Sontag saying that "incorporation" into a society like that of North Vietnam would "greatly improve the lives of most people in the world." One also recalls that both Sontag and McCarthy were troubled by the portraits of Stalin they saw all over the North; they were there, Sontag thought, because the Vietnamese could not bear to waste anything. Perhaps that is also how she would explain why portraits of Soviet leaders began appearing in public buildings, schools, and administrative offices throughout South Vietnam after 1975, and why the following poem by To Huu, president of the Communist Party Committee of Culture and a possible successor to Pham Van Dong,[17] was given a prominent place in an anthology of contemporary Vietnamese poetry published in Hanoi in the seventies:

> *Oh, Stalin! Oh, Stalin!*
> *The love I bear my father, my mother, my wife, myself*
> *It's nothing beside the love I bear you.*
> *Oh, Stalin! Oh, Stalin!*
> *What remains of the earth and of the sky!*
> *Now that you are dead.*[18]

Written on the occasion of Stalin's death, this poem no doubt earned its place in an anthology twenty years later by virtue of its relevance to the spirit of the new Communist Vietnam. For if the Vietnamese Communist party is Stalinist, so is the society over which it rules. "Immediately after the fall of Saigon, the Government closed all bookshops and theaters. All books published under the former regimes were confiscated or burned. Cultural literature was not exempt, including translations of Jean-Paul Sartre, Albert Camus and Dale Carnegie [!]....The new regime replaced such books with literature designed to indoctrinate children and adults with the idea that the 'Soviet Union is a paradise of the socialist world.'"[19]

As with books, so with newspapers. Under the old regime, under constant attack throughout the world for its repressiveness, there had been *twenty-seven* daily newspapers, three television stations, and more than twenty radio stations. "When the Communists took over," writes the political analyst Carl Gershman, "these were all closed down, and replaced by two official dailies, one television channel, and two radio stations—all disseminating the same government propaganda."[20]

All the other freedoms that existed, either in full or large measure, under the Thieu regime were also eliminated by the Communists. Freedom of movement began to be regulated by a system of internal passports, and freedom of association was abolished to the point where even a large family gathering, such as a wedding or a funeral, required a government permit and was attended by a security officer.

Freedom of religion, too, was sharply curtailed. The Buddhists, who were so effective an element in the opposition to Diem, soon learned that there were worse regimes than his. A Human Rights Appeal drafted by the Unified Buddhist Church and smuggled out by the Venerable Thich Manh Giac when he escaped by boat, charged that the government, "pursuing the policy of shattering the religious communities in our country,...has arrested hundreds of monks, confiscated hundreds of pagodas and converted them to government administration buildings, removed and smashed Buddha and Bodhisattva statues, prohibited celebration of the Buddha's birthday as a national holiday,...and forbidden monks to travel and preach by ordering restrictions in the name of 'national security.'"[21]

Unlike demonstrations by Buddhists in 1963, this appeal fell on deaf ears; whereas a raid on a Buddhist temple led directly to the overthrow of Diem, a similar raid by the Communist police in April 1977 went unnoticed; and whereas the self-immolation of a single Buddhist monk in 1963 attracted the horrified attention of the whole world, the self-immolation of twelve Buddhist nuns and priests on November 2, 1975, in protest against Communist repression, received scarcely any notice either in the United States or anywhere else.

When all this is combined with the terrible economic hardships that descended upon Vietnam after 1975—hardships that were simultaneously caused by the new regime and used by it to justify resettling millions of people in the so-called New Economic Zones, remote jungle areas where they worked "in collective gangs at such tasks as clearing land and digging canals,"[22] under primitive living conditions with little food and rampant disease—it is easy to see why a sense of despair soon settled over the country. Truong Nhu Tang: "The fact is that today Communism has been rejected by the people and the even many party members are questioning their faith. Members of the former resistance, their sympathizers and those who supported the Vietcong are disgusted and filled with bitterness. These innocent people swear openly that had they another chance their choice would be very different. The commonly heard expression is: I would give them not even a grain of rice. I pull them out of their hiding holes and denounce them to the authorities."'[23]

The Buddhist human-rights appeal conveyed much the same impression: "Since the liberation thousands have committed suicide out of despair. Thousands have fled the country in small boats. Hospitals are reserved for cadres: civilians hardly have a chance to be hospitalized in case of sickness, while more than 200 doctors remain in detention. Schoolchildren under fourteen have been assigned to collect pieces of scrap material in big garbage heaps and other places during the summer vacation....A country that used to export rice has no rice to eat, even though the number of 'laborers' has now increased about ten times." The government, the appeal went on to say, prohibits "creative thinking and participation of independent groups. Totalitarianism destroys all possibility of genuine national reconciliation and concord."[24]

Some years after these words were written, a great and angry dispute broke out in the United States over the question of whether there was any practical validity or moral point in the distinction between authoritarianism and totalitarianism. Not surprisingly, those who dismissed the distinction as academic were in general veterans of the antiwar movement, who still refused to see that (as Gershman said in 1978) "for the Vietnamese, the distinction between a society that is authoritarian...and one that is totalitarian" turned out to be anything but academic.[25]

Peter L. Berger, one of the few former members of the antiwar movement who recognizes that "the transformation of Saigon into Ho Chi Minh City now offers a crystal-clear illustration of the difference between authoritarianism and totalitarianism, both in terms of political science and political morality," expresses amazement at "the persistent incapacity of even American professors to grasp a difference understood by every taxi driver in Prague." He believes that this incapacity derives in large part from a strong ideological interest in hiding "the fact that totalitarianism today is limited to socialist societies"—a fact that "flies in the face of the socialist dream that haunts the intellectual imagination of the West...."[26]

I have no doubt that Berger is right about this. But where Vietnam in particular is concerned, there is a strong interest not only in protecting the socialist dream in general but, more specifically, in holding on to the sense of having been on the morally superior side in opposing the American struggle to prevent the replacement of an authoritarian regime in the South with a totalitarian system. The truth is that the antiwar movement bears a certain measure of responsibility for the horrors that have overtaken the people of Vietnam; and so long as those who participated in that movement are unwilling to acknowledge this, they will go on trying to discredit the idea that there is a distinction between authoritarianism and totalitarianism. For to recognize the distinction is to recognize that in making a contribution to the conquest of South Vietnam by the Communists of the North, they were siding with an evil system against something much better from every political and moral point of view.

Some veterans of the antiwar movement have protected themselves from any such acknowledgment of guilt by the simple expedient of denying that there is any truth in the reports by refugees like Toai, Coan, and Tang or journalists like Lacouture. Noam Chomsky, for example, speaks of "the extreme unreliability" of these reports,[27] and he is echoed by William Kunstler, Dave Dellinger, and other inveterate apologists for the Vietnamese Communists. Peter Berger compares such people to "individuals who deny the facts of the Holocaust" and rightly considers them "outside the boundaries of rational discourse."[28]

There are, however, others—like the editors of the Socialist magazine *Dissent*, Irving Howe and Michael Walzer—who are fully aware of the horrors that have followed the American withdrawal and the Communist conquest, and who are at least willing to ask, "Were We Wrong About Vietnam?" But of course their answer to this question is No. They were right because they were against both Saigon *and* Hanoi: they were right "in refusing to support the imperial backers of both." What then did they support? "Some of us...hoped for the emergence of a Vietnamese 'third force' capable of rallying the people in a progressive direction by enacting land reforms and defending civil liberties." But since, as they admit, there was very little chance of any such alternative, to have thrown their energies into opposing the American effort was tantamount to working for the Communist victory they say they did not want. Nevertheless, they still congratulate themselves on being against the evils on both sides of the war: "Those of us who opposed American intervention yet did not want a Communist victory were in the difficult position of having no happy ending to offer—for the sad reason that no happy ending was possible any longer, if ever it had been. And we were in the difficult position of urging a relatively complex argument at a moment when most Americans, pro- and antiwar, wanted blinding simplicities."[29] This is not moral choice; this is moral evasion—irresponsible utopianism disguised as moral realism. Given the actual alternatives that existed, what did the urging of "a relatively complex argument" avail for any purpose other than to make those who urged it feel pleased with themselves? If it served any purpose at all for the people of South Vietnam, it was to help deliver them over to the "blinding simplicities" of the totalitarianism Howe and Walzer so piously deplore and whose hideous workings they are now happy to denounce and protest against, even though there is no one in Ho Chi Minh City or Hanoi to listen or to hear.

Another veteran of the antiwar movement, Professor Stanley Hoffmann of Harvard, who also sees "no reason not to protest the massacres, arbitrary arrests, and persecutions perpetrated by the regimes that have taken over after our exit," nevertheless urges "those who condemned the war...to resist all attempts to make them feel guilty for the stand they took against the war." It was not, says Hoffmann, the antiwar movement that contributed to these horrors, but rather the people (led by Nixon and Kissinger) who were supposedly fighting to prevent them. True as this was of Vietnam—where "a monstrously disproportionate and self-destructive campaign" only added "to the crimes and degradation of eventual Communist victory"—it was even truer of Cambodia. "All those who, somehow, believe that the sufferings inflicted on the Cambodian people, first by the Pol Pot regime, and now by the Vietnamese, retrospectively justify America's attempt to save Phnom Penh from the Reds" were instructed by Hoffmann in 1979 to read a new book "showing that the monsters who decimated the Cambodian people were brought to power by Washington's policies."[30]

The book Hoffmann was referring to, *Sideshow: Kissinger, Nixon and the Destruction of Cambodia*, by the English journalist William Shawcross, sought to demonstrate that those Americans who fought to stop the Communists from coming to power in Cambodia were responsible for the crimes the Communists committed when the fight against them was lost. They can be held responsible, not as one might imagine because they did not fight as hard as they should have, or because in the end they deserted the field, but on the contrary because they entered the field in the first place. By attacking—first by bombing, then by invading—the North Vietnamese sanctuaries in Cambodia, the Americans (that is, Nixon and Kissinger) not only drove the Communists deeper into Cambodia, thereby bringing the war to areas that had previously been at peace. They also intensified the rage and bitterness of the Khmer Rouge (as the Cambodian Communists under Pol Pot were called), thereby turning them into perhaps the most murderous rulers ever seen on the face of the earth.

Sideshow is a brilliantly written and argued book. Indeed, not since Hannah Arendt's *Eichmann in Jerusalem*—which shifts a large measure of responsibility for the murder of six million Jews from the Nazis who committed the murders to the Jewish leaders who were trying to save as many of their people as they could—has there been so striking an illustration of the perverse moral and intellectual uses to which brilliance can be put.

There are, for example, the clever distortions and omissions that enable Shawcross to charge the Nixon Administration with having destabilized the neutral government of Prince Norodom Sihanouk by bombing the sanctuaries (when in fact Sihanouk welcomed these attacks on the Communist military bases within his own country which he himself was not powerful enough to banish) and with causing large numbers of civilian casualties by the indiscriminate pattern of the bombing raids (when in fact care was taken to minimize civilian casualties). But what is fully on a par of perversity with Hannah Arendt's interpretation of the Jewish role in the genocidal program of the Nazis against them is the idea that Pol Pot and his followers needed the experience of American bombing and the "punishment" they subsequently suffered in the war against the anti-Communist forces of Cambodia to turn them into genocidal monsters.

This idea about the Khmer Rouge can easily enough be refuted by the simple facts of the case. Thus according to Kenneth Quinn, who conducted hundreds of interviews with refugees from Cambodia, the Khmer Rouge began instituting the totalitarian practices of their revolutionary program in areas they controlled as early as 1971.[31] So too Father Francois Ponchaud, who was in Phnom Penh when the Communists arrived and whose book *Cambodia: Year Zero* Shawcross himself calls "the best account of Khmer Rouge rule":[32] "The evacuation of Phnom Penh follows traditional Khmer revolutionary practice: ever since 1972 the guerrilla fighters had been sending all the inhabitants of the villages and towns they occupied into the forests to live, often burning their homes so they would have nothing to come back for."[33]

Indeed, as Shawcross himself points out, this revolutionary program was outlined in uncannily clear detail in the thesis written at the University of Paris in 1959 by Khieu Samphan, who would later become the Khmer Rouge commander in chief during the war and the head of state afterward. But Shawcross, in line with his own thesis that it was the war that made "the Khmer Rouge...more and more vicious,"[34] stresses that "the methods this twenty-eight-year-old Marxist prescribed in 1959 for the transformation of his country were essentially moderate."[35] In support of the same thesis, he quotes Quinn to the effect that "the first steps to change radically the nature of Khmer society" that the Khmer Rouge took in 1971 were "limited."[36]

What Shawcross fails or refuses to see is what Ponchaud understands about such moderate methods and limited steps—namely, that they remained moderate and limited only so long as the Khmer Rouge lacked the power to put them into practice. "Accusing foreigners cannot acquit the present leaders of Kampuchea," Ponchaud wrote (before the Vietnamese invaded Cambodia and replaced the Khmer Rouge Communists with a puppet Communist regime of their own); "their inflexible ideology has led them to invent a radically new kind of man in a radically new society." Or again: "On April 17, 1975, a society collapsed: another is now being born from the fierce drive of a revolution which is incontestably the most radical ever to take place in so short a time. It is a perfect example of the application of an ideology pushed to the furthest limits of its internal logic."[37]

The blindness to the power of ideas that prevents Shawcross from recognizing ideology as the source of the crimes committed against their own people by the Khmer Rouge is his greatest intellectual sin. It is a species of philistinism to which many contemporary intellectuals (who, as intellectuals, might be expected to attribute a disproportionate importance to the role of ideas) are paradoxically prone, and it takes the form of looking for material factors to account for historical developments even when, as in this case, the main causal element is clearly located in the realm of ideas.

But this sin is exceeded in seriousness by the moral implications of Shawcross's book. As Peter W. Rodman (who has been an aide to Henry Kissinger both in and out of government) says in concluding a devastating critique of Shawcross's scholarship: "By no stretch of moral logic can the crimes of mass murderers be ascribed to those who struggled to prevent their coming into power. On hopes that no craven sophistry will ever induce free peoples to accept the doctrine that Shawcross embodies: that resistance to totalitarianism is immoral."[38]

Yet it is just this "craven sophistry" that Stanley Hoffmann reaffirms in the very face of the horrors that have befallen the peoples of Indochina under Communist rule: "As Frances FitzGerald put it," he writes,"our mistake was in creating and building up 'the wrong side,' and we were led by that mistake to a course of devastation *and* defeat."[39] One can almost forgive Anthony Lewis for asking "What future possibility could be more terrible than the reality of what is happening to Cambodia now?"[40] since he asked this question before the Khmer Rouge took over. One can almost forgive the New York *Times* for the headline "Indochina Without Americans: For Most, A Better Life" on a piece from Phnom Penh by Sydney H. Schanberg[41] since it was written before the Khmer Rouge had begun evacuating the city and instituting a regime that led to the death of nearly half the population of the country. Such writers should have known enough about the history of Communism to know better, and they should now be ashamed of their naivete and of the contribution they made to the victory of forces they had a moral duty to oppose. Nevertheless, they were not yet aware of what Hoffmann already knew when he *still* described the Communists as the right side in Indochina and still denounced those who resisted them as immoral and even criminal. This is almost impossible to forgive.

In May 1977, two full years after the Communist takeover, President Jimmy Carter—a repentant hawk, like many members of his cabinet, including his Secretary of State and his Secretary of Defense—spoke of "the intellectual and moral poverty" of the policy that had led us into Vietnam and had kept us there for so long. When Ronald Reagan, an unrepentant hawk, called the war "a noble cause" in the course of his ultimately successful campaign to replace Carter in the White House, he was accused of having made a "gaffe." Fully, painfully aware as I am that the American effort to save Vietnam from Communism was indeed beyond our intellectual and moral capabilities, I believe the story shows that Reagan's "gaffe" was closer to the truth of why we were in Vietnam and what we did there, at least until the very end, than Carter's denigration of an act of imprudent idealism whose moral soundness has been so overwhelmingly vindicated by the hideous consequences of our defeat.

NOTES

1. Jason Epstein, "The CIA and the Intellectuals," *New York Review of Books*, Apr. 20, 1967.

2. Robert L. Heilbroner, "Counterrevolutionary America," *Commentary*, Apr. 1967.

3. "Indochina and the American Conscience," *Commentary*, Feb. 1980.

4. Tom Wicker, *New York Times*, July 8, 1979. Quoted in Charles Horner, "America Five Years After Defeat." *Commentary*, Apr. 1980.

5. Carl Gershman, "After the Dominoes Fell," *Commentary*, May 1978.

6. Nguyen Cong Hoan, Hearings Before the Subcommittee on International Organizations of the House Committee on International Relations, July 26, 1977, pp. 145–67.

7. Truong Nhu Tang, "Vietnam, the Myth of a Liberation," unpublished ms., 1981.

8. See note 6 above.

9. Doan Van Toai, "A Lament for Vietnam," *New York Times Magazine*, Mar. 29, 1981.

10. Jean Lacouture, interview with Francois Fejto, in *Il Giornale Nuovo* (Milan), quoted in Michael Ledeen, "Europe—The Good News and the Bad," *Commentary*, Apr. 1979.

11. Jean Lacouture, quoted in "After the Dominoes Fell," *Commentary*, May 1978.

12. "A Lament for Vietnam," *New York Times Magazine*, Mar. 29, 1981.

13. *Ibid.*

14. Quoted in "A Lament for Vietnam," *New York Times Magazine*, Mar. 29, 1981.

15. "A Lament for Vietnam," *New York Times Magazine*, Mar. 29, 1981; "After the Dominoes Fell," *Commentary*, May 1978.

16. Truong Nhu Tang, "Vietnam, the Myth of a Liberation," unpublished ms., 1981.

17. *Foreign Report*, July 16, 1981.

18. To Huu, quoted in "A Lament for Vietnam," *New York Times Magazine*, Mar. 29, 1981.

19. "A Lament for Vietnam," *New York Times Magazine*, Mar. 29, 1981.

20. "After the Dominoes Fell," *Commentary*, May 1978.

21. Quoted in "After the Dominoes Fell," *Commentary*, May 1978.

22. "After the Dominoes Fell," *Commentary*, May 1978.

23. Truong Nhu Tang, "Vietnam, the Myth of a Liberation," unpublished ms., 1981.

24. Quoted in "After the Dominoes Fell," *Commentary*, May 1978.

25. "After the Dominoes Fell," *Commentary*, May 1978.

26. "Indochina and the American Conscience," *Commentary*, Feb. 1980.

27. Quoted in "After the Dominoes Fell," *Commentary*, May 1978.

28. "Indochina and the American Conscience," *Commentary*, Feb. 1980.

29. Irving Howe and Michael Walzer, "Were We Wrong About Vietnam?," *New Republic*, Aug. 18, 1979.

30. Stanley Hoffmann, "The Crime of Cambodia," *New York Review of Books*, June 28, 1979.

31. Peter W. Rodman, "Sideswipe," *American Spectator*, Mar. 1981.

32. William Shawcross, "Shawcross Swipes Again," *American Spectator*, July 1981.

33. Francois Ponchaud, *Cambodia: Year Zero*. New York: Holt, Rinehart & Winston, 1978, p. 21. Quoted in "Sideswipe," *American Spectator*, Mar. 1981.

34. "Shawcross Swipes Again," *American Spectator*, July, 1981.

35. William Shawcross, *Sideshow*. New York: Pocket Books, 1979, p. 243.

36. Kenneth Quinn, quoted in "Shawcross Swipes Again," *American Spectator*, July 1981.

37. *Cambodia: Year Zero*, pp. xvi, 192. Quoted in "Sideswipe," *American Spectator*, Mar. 1981.

38. "Sideswipe," *American Spectator*, Mar. 1981.

39. "The Crime of Cambodia," *New York Review of Books*, June 28, 1979.

40. Anthony Lewis, *New York Times*, Mar. 17, 1975. Quoted in "Sideswipe," *American Spectator*, Mar. 1981.

41. *New York Times*, Apr. 13, 1975. Quoted in "Sideswipe," *American Spectator*, Mar. 1981.

30
A Systemic Success
LESLIE GELB

The story of United States policy toward Vietnam is either far better or far worse than generally supposed. Our Presidents and most of those who influenced their decisions did not stumble step by step into Vietnam, unaware of the quagmire. U.S. involvement did not stem from a failure to foresee consequences.

Vietnam was indeed a quagmire, but most of our leaders knew it. Of course there were optimists and periods where many were genuinely optimistic. But those periods were infrequent and short-lived and were invariably followed by periods of deep pessimism. Very few, to be sure, envisioned what the Vietnam situation would be like by 1968. Most realized, however, that "the light at the end of the tunnel" was very far away—if not finally unreachable. Nevertheless, our Presidents persevered. Given international compulsions to "keep our word" and "save face," domestic prohibitions against "losing," and their personal stakes, our leaders did "what was necessary," did it about the way they wanted, were prepared to pay the costs, and plowed on with a mixture of hope and doom. They "saw" no acceptable alternative.

Three propositions suggest why the United States became involved in Vietnam, why the process was gradual, and what the real expectations of our leaders were:

First, U.S. involvement in Vietnam is not mainly or mostly a story of step by step, inadvertent descent into unforeseen quicksand. It is primarily a story of why U.S. leaders considered that it was vital not to lose Vietnam by force to Communism. Our leaders believed Vietnam to be vital not for itself, but for what they thought its "loss" would mean internationally and domestically. Previous involvement made further involvement more unavoidable, and, to this extent, commitments were inherited. But judgments of Vietnam's "vitalness"—beginning with the Korean War—were sufficient in themselves to set the course for escalation.

Second, our Presidents were never actually seeking a military victory in Vietnam. They were doing only what they thought was minimally necessary at each stage to keep Indochina, and later South Vietnam, out of

Communist hands. This forced our Presidents to be brakemen, to do less than those who were urging military victory and to reject proposals for disengagement. It also meant that our Presidents wanted a negotiated settlement without fully realizing (though realizing more than their critics) that a civil war cannot be ended by political compromise.

Third, our Presidents and most of their lieutenants were not deluded by optimistic reports of progress and did not proceed on the basis of wishful thinking about winning a military victory in South Vietnam. They recognized that the steps they were taking were not adequate to win the war and that unless Hanoi relented, they would have to do more and more. Their strategy was to persevere in the hope that their will to continue—if not the practical effects of their actions—would cause the Communists to relent.

Each of these propositions is explored below.

I. ENDS: "WE CAN'T AFFORD TO LOSE"

Those who led the United States into Vietnam did so with their eyes open, knowing why, and believing they had the will to succeed. The deepening involvement was not inadvertent, but mainly deductive. It flowed with sureness from the perceived stakes and attendant high objectives. U.S. policy displayed remarkable continuity. There were not dozens of likely "turning points." Each post-war President inherited previous commitments. Each extended these commitments. Each administration from 1947 to 1969 believed that it was necessary to prevent the loss of Vietnam and, after 1954, South Vietnam by force to the Communists. The reasons for this varied from person to person, from bureaucracy to bureaucracy, over time and in emphasis. For the most part, however, they had little to do with Vietnam itself. A few men argued that Vietnam had intrinsic strategic military and economic importance, but this view never prevailed. The reasons rested on broader international, domestic, and bureaucratic considerations.

Our leaders gave the *international* repercussions of "losing" as their dominant explicit reason for Vietnam's importance. During the Truman Administration, Indochina's importance was measured in terms of French-American relations and Washington's desire to rebuild France into the centerpiece of future European security. After the cold war heated up and after the fall of China, a French defeat in Indochina was also seen as a defeat for the policy of containment. In the Eisenhower years, Indochina became a "testing ground" between the Free World and Communism and the basis for the famous "domino theory" by which the fall of Indochina would lead to the deterioration of American security around the globe. President Kennedy publicly reaffirmed the falling domino concept. His primary concern, however, was for his "reputation for action" after the Bay of Pigs fiasco, the Vienna meeting with Khrushchev, and the Laos crisis, and in meeting the challenge of "wars of national liberation" by counterinsurgency warfare. Under President Johnson, the code word rationales became

Munich, credibility, commitments and the *U.S.* word, a watershed test of wills with Communism, raising the costs of aggression, and the principle that armed aggression shall not be allowed to succeed. There is every reason to assume that our leaders actually believed what they said, given both the cold war context in which they were all reared and the lack of contradictory evidence.

With very few exceptions, then, our leaders since World War II saw Vietnam as a vital factor in alliance politics. U.S.-Soviet-Chinese relations, and deterrence. This was as true in 1950 and 1954 as it was in 1961 and 1965. The record of United States military and economic assistance to fight Communism in Indochina tells this story quite clearly. From 1945 to 1951, U.S. aid to France totaled over $3.5 billion. Without this, the French position in Indochina would have been untenable. By 1951, the U.S. was paying about 40 percent of the costs of the Indochina war and our share was going up. In 1954, it is estimated, U.S. economic and technical assistance amounted to $703 million and military aid totaled almost $2 billion. This added up to almost 80 percent of the total French costs. From 1955 to 1961, U.S. military aid averaged about $200 million per year. This made South Vietnam the second largest recipient of such aid, topped only by Korea. By 1963, South Vietnam ranked first among recipients of military assistance. In economic assistance, it followed only India and Pakistan.

The *domestic* repercussions of "losing" Vietnam probably were equally important in Presidential minds. Letting Vietnam "go Communist" was undoubtedly seen as:

- opening the floodgates to domestic criticism and attack for being "soft on Communism" or just plain soft;
- dissipating Presidential influence by having to answer these charges;
- alienating conservative leadership in the Congress and thereby endangering the President's legislative program;
- jeopardizing election prospects for the President and his party;
- undercutting domestic support for a "responsible" U.S. world role; and
- enlarging the prospects for a right-wing reaction—the nightmare of a McCarthyite garrison state.

U.S. domestic politics required our leaders to maintain both a peaceful world and one in which Communist expansion was stopped. In order to have the public support necessary to use force against Communism, our leaders had to employ strong generalized, ideological rhetoric. The price of this rhetoric was consistency. How could our leaders shed American blood in Korea and keep large numbers of American troops in Europe at great expense unless they were also willing to stop Communism in Vietnam?

Bureaucratic judgments and stakes were also involved in defining U.S. interests in Vietnam. Most bureaucrats probably prompted or shared the belief of their leaders about the serious repercussions of losing Vietnam. Once direct bureaucratic presence was established after the French departure, this belief was reinforced and extended. The military had to prove that American arms and advice could succeed where the French could not. The Foreign Service had to prove that it could bring about political stability in Saigon and "build a nation." The CIA had to prove that pacification would work. AID had to prove that millions of dollars in assistance and advice could bring political returns.

The U.S. commitment was rationalized as early as 1950. It was set in 1955 when we replaced the French. Its logic was further fulfilled by President Kennedy. After 1965, when the U.S. took over the war, it was immeasurably hardened.

There was little conditional character to the U.S. commitment— except for avoiding "the big war." Every President talked about the ultimate responsibility resting with the Vietnamese (and the French before them). This "condition" seems to have been meant much more as a warning to our friends than a real limitation. In every crunch, it was swept aside. The only real limit applied to Russia and China. Our leaders were not prepared to run the risks of nuclear war or even the risks of a direct conventional military confrontation with the Soviet Union and China. These were separate decisions. The line between them and everything else done in Vietnam always held firm. With this exception, the commitment was always defined in terms of the objective to deny the Communists control over all Vietnam. This was further defined to preclude coalition governments with the Communists.

The importance of the objective was evaluated in terms of cost, and the perceived costs of disengagement outweighed the cost of further engagement. Some allies might urge disengagement, but then condemn the U.S. for doing so. The domestic groups which were expected to criticize growing involvement always were believed to be outnumbered by those who would have attacked "cutting and running." The question of whether our leaders would have started down the road if they knew this would mean over half a million men in Vietnam, over 40,000 U.S. deaths, and the expenditure of well over $100 billion is historically irrelevant. Only Presidents Kennedy and Johnson had to confront the possibility of these large costs. The point is that each administration was prepared to pay the costs it could foresee for itself. No one seemed to have a better solution. Each could at least pass the baton on to the next.

Presidents could not treat Vietnam as if it were "vital" without creating high stakes internationally, domestically, and within their own bureaucracies. But the rhetoric conveyed different messages:

- To the Communists, it was a signal that their actions would be met by counteractions.
- To the American people, it set the belief that the President would ensure that the threatened nation did not fall into Communist hands—although without the anticipation of sacrificing American lives.

- To the Congress, it marked the President's responsibility to ensure that Vietnam did not go Communist and maximized incentives for legislators to support him or at least remain silent.
- To the U.S. professional military, it was a promise that U.S. forces would be used, if necessary and to the degree necessary, to defend Vietnam.
- To the professional U.S. diplomat, it meant letting our allies know that the U.S. cared about their fate.
- To the President, it laid the groundwork for the present action and showed that he was prepared to take the next step to keep Vietnam non-Communist.

Words were making Vietnam into a showcase—an Asian Berlin. In the process, Vietnam grew into a test case of U.S. credibility—to opponents, to allies, but perhaps most importantly, to ourselves. Public opinion polls seemed to confirm the political dangers. Already established bureaucratic judgments about the importance of Vietnam matured into cherished convictions and organizational interests. The war dragged on.

Each successive President, initially caught by his own belief, was further ensnarled by his own rhetoric, and the basis for the belief went unchallenged. Debates revolved around how to do things better, and whether they could be done, not whether they were worth doing. Prior to 1961, an occasional senator or Southeast Asian specialist would raise a lonely and weak voice in doubt. Some press criticism began thereafter. And later still, wandering American minstrels returned from the field to tell their tales of woe in private. General Ridgway as Chief of Staff of the Army in 1954 questioned the value of Vietnam as against its potential costs and dangers, and succeeded in blunting a proposed U.S. military initiative, although not for the reasons he advanced. Under Secretary of State George Ball raised the issue of international priorities in the summer of 1965 and lost. Clark Clifford as Secretary of Defense openly challenged the winnability of the war, as well as Vietnam's strategic significance, and argued for domestic priorities. But no systematic or serious examination of Vietnam's importance to the United States was ever undertaken within the government. Endless assertions passed for analysis. Presidents neither encouraged nor permitted serious questioning, for to do so would be to foster the idea that their resolve was something less than complete. The objective of a non-Communist Vietnam, and after 1954 a non-Communist South Vietnam, drove U.S. involvement ever more deeply each step of the way.

II. MEANS: "TAKE THE MINIMAL NECESSARY STEPS"

None of our Presidents was seeking total victory over the Vietnamese Communists. War critics who wanted victory always knew this. And so, more minimal steps were always necessary.

Our Presidents were pressured on all sides. The pressures for victory came mainly from the inside and were reflected on the outside. From inside the administrations, three forces almost invariably pushed hard. *First*, the military establishment generally initiated requests for broadening and intensifying U.S. military action. Our professional military placed great weight on the strategic significance of Vietnam; they were given a job to do; their prestige was involved; and of crucial importance (in the 1960's)—the lives of many American servicemen were being lost. The Joint Chiefs of Staff, the MAAG (Military Assistance Advisory Group) Chiefs and later the Commander of U.S. forces in Vietnam were the focal points for these pressures. *Second*, our Ambassadors in Saigon, supported by the State Department, at times pressed for and often supported big steps forward. Their reasons were similar to those of the military. *Thirdly*, an ever-present group of "fixers" was making urgent demands to strengthen and broaden the Saigon government in order to achieve political victory. Every executive agency had its fixers. They were usually able men whose entire preoccupation was to make things better in Vietnam. From outside the administration, there were hawks who insisted on winning and hawks who wanted to "win or get out." Capitol Hill hawks, the conservative press, and, for many years, Catholic organizations were in the forefront.

The pressures for disengagement and for de-escalation derived mostly from the outside with occasional and often unknown allies from within. Small for most of the Vietnam years, these forces grew steadily in strength from 1965 onward. Isolated congressmen and senators led the fight. First they did so on anticolonialist grounds. Later their objections developed moral aspects (interfering in a civil war) and extended to non-winnability, domestic priorities, and the senselessness of the war. Peace organizations and student groups in particular came to dominate headlines and air time. Journalists played a critical role—especially through television reports. From within each administration, opposition could be found: (1) among isolated military men who did not want the U.S. in an Asian land war; (2) among some State Department intelligence and area specialists who knew Vietnam and believed the U.S. objective was unattainable at any reasonable price; and (3) within the civilian agencies of the Defense Department and isolated individuals at State and CIA, particularly after 1966, whose efforts were trained on finding a politically feasible way out.

Our Presidents reacted to the pressures as brakemen, pulling the switch against both the advocates of "decisive escalation" and the advocates of disengagement. The politics of the Presidency largely dictated this role, but the personalities of the Presidents were also important. None were as ideological as many persons around them. All were basically centrist politicians.

Their immediate aim was always to prevent a Communist takeover. The actions they approved were usually only what was minimally necessary to that aim. Each President determined the "minimal necessity" by trial and error and his own judgment. They might have done more and done it more rapidly if they were convinced that: (1) the threat of a Communist takeover were more immediate, (2) U.S. domestic politics would have been more permissive, (3) the government of South Vietnam had the requisite political stability and military potential for effective use and (4) the job really would have gotten done. After 1965, however, the minimal necessity became the maximum they could get given the same domestic and international constraints.

The tactic of the minimally necessary decision makes optimum sense for the politics of the Presidency. Even our strongest Presidents have tended to shy away from decisive action. It has been too uncertain, too risky. They derive their strength from movement (the image of a lot of activity) and building and neutralizing opponents. Too seldom has there been forceful moral leadership; it may even be undemocratic. The small step that maintains the momentum gives the President the chance to gather more political support. It gives the appearance of minimizing possible mistakes. It allows time to gauge reactions. It serves as a pressure-relieving valve against those who want to do more. It can be doled out. Above all, it gives the President something to do next time.

The tactic makes consummate sense when it is believed that nothing will fully work or that the costs of a "winning" move would be too high. This was the case with Vietnam. This decision-making tactic explains why the U.S. involvement in Vietnam was gradual and step by step.

While the immediate aim was to prevent a Communist victory and improve the position of the anti-Communists, the longer term goal was a political settlement. As late as February 1947, Secretary of State Marshall expressed the hope that "a pacific basis of adjustment of the difficulties" between France and the Vietminh could be found.[1] After that, Truman's policy hardened, but there is no evidence to suggest that until 1950 he was urging the French not to settle with the Vietnamese Communists. Eisenhower, it should be remembered, was the President who tacitly agreed (by not intervening in 1954) to the creation of a Communist state in North Vietnam. President Kennedy had all he could do to prevent complete political collapse in South Vietnam. He had, therefore, little basis on which to compromise. President Johnson inherited this political instability, and to add to his woes, he faced in 1965 what seemed to be the prospect of a Communist military victory. Yet, by his standing offer for free and internationally supervised elections, he apparently was prepared to accept Communist participation in the political life of the South.

By traditional diplomatic standards of negotiations between sovereign states, these were not fatuous compromises. One compromise was, in effect, to guarantee that the Communists could remain in secure control of North Vietnam. The U.S. would not seek to overthrow this regime. The other compromise was to allow the Communists in South Vietnam to seek power along the lines of Communist parties in France and Italy, i.e. to give them a "permanent minority position."

But the real struggle in Vietnam was not between sovereign states. It was among Vietnamese. It was a civil war and a war for national independence.

Herein lies the paradox and the tragedy of Vietnam. Most of our leaders and their critics did see that Vietnam was a quagmire, but did not see that the real stakes—who shall govern Vietnam—were not negotiable. Free elections, local sharing of power, international supervision, cease-fires—none of these could serve as a basis for settlement. What were legitimate compromises from Washington's point of view were matters of life and death to the Vietnamese. For American leaders, the stakes were "keeping their word" and saving their political necks. For the Vietnamese, the stakes were their lives and their lifelong political aspirations. Free elections meant bodily exposure to the Communist guerrillas and likely defeat to the anti-Communists. The risk was too great. There was no trust, no confidence.

The Vietnam war could no more be settled by traditional diplomatic compromises than any other civil war. President Lincoln could not settle with the South. The Spanish Republicans and General Franco's Loyalists could not have conceivably mended their fences by elections. None of the post-World War II insurgencies—Greece, Malaya, and the Philippines—ended with a negotiated peace. In each of these cases, the civil differences were put to rest—if at all—only by the logic of war.

It is commonly acknowledged that Vietnam would have fallen to the Communists in 1945–46, in 1954, and in 1965 had it not been for the intervention of first the French and then the Americans. The Vietnamese Communists, who were also by history the Vietnamese nationalists, would not accept only part of a prize for which they had paid so heavily. The anti-Communist Vietnamese, protected by the French and the Americans, would not put themselves at the Communists' mercy.

It may be that our Presidents understood this better than their critics. The critics, especially on the political left, fought for "better compromises," not realizing that even the best could not be good enough, and fought for broad nationalist governments, not realizing there was no middle force in Vietnam. Our Presidents, it seems, recognized that there was no middle ground and that "better compromises" would frighten our Saigon allies without bringing about a compromise peace. And they believed that a neutralization formula would compromise South Vietnam away to the Communists. So the longer-term aim of peace repeatedly gave way to the immediate needs of the war and the next necessary step.

III. EXPECTATIONS: "WE MUST PERSEVERE"

Each new step was taken not because of wishful thinking or optimism about its leading to a victory in South Vietnam. Few of our leaders thought that they could win the war in a conventional sense or that the Communists would be decimated to a point that they would simply fade away. Even as new and further steps were taken, coupled with expressions of optimism, many of our leaders realized that more—and still more—would have to be done. Few of these men felt confident about how it would all end or when. After 1965, however, they allowed the impression of "winnability" to grow in order to justify their already heavy investment and domestic support for the war.

The strategy always was to persevere. Perseverance, it seemed, was the only way to avoid or postpone having to pay the domestic political costs of failure. Finally, perseverance, it was hoped, would convince the Communists that our will to continue was firm. Perhaps, then, with domestic support for perseverance, with bombing North Vietnam, and with inflicting heavy casualties in the South, the Communists would relent. Perhaps, then, a compromise could be negotiated to save the Communists' face without giving them South Vietnam.

Optimism was a part of the "gamesmanship" of Vietnam. It had a purpose. Personal-organizational optimism was the product of a number of motivations and calculations:

- Career services tacitly and sometimes explicitly pressured their professionals to impart good news.
- Good news was seen as a job well done; bad news as personal failure.
- The reporting system was set up so that assessments were made by the implementors.
- Optimism bred optimism so that it was difficult to be pessimistic this time if you were optimistic the last time.
- People told their superiors what they thought they wanted to hear.
- The American ethic is to get the job done.

Policy optimism also sprang from several rational needs:

- To maintain domestic support for the war.
- To keep up the morale of our Vietnamese allies and build some confidence and trust between us and them.
- To stimulate military and bureaucratic morale to work hard.

There were, however, genuine optimists and grounds for genuine optimism. Some periods looked promising: the year preceding the French downfall at Dienbienphu; the years of the second Eisenhower Presidency when most attention was riveted on Laos and before the insurgency was stepped up in South Vietnam; 1962 and early 1963 before the strategic hamlet pacification program collapsed; and the last six months of 1967 before the 1968 Tet offensive.

Many additional periods by comparison with previous years yielded a sense of real improvement. By most conventional standards—the size and firepower of friendly Vietnamese forces, the number of hamlets pacified, the number of "free elections" being held, the number of Communists killed, and so forth—reasonable men could and did think in cautiously optimistic terms.

But comparison with years past is an illusory measure when it is not coupled with judgments about how far there still is to go and how likely it is that the goal can ever be reached. It was all too easy to confuse short-term breathing spells with long-term trends and to confuse "things getting better" with "winning." Many of those who had genuine hope suffered from either a lack of knowledge about Vietnam or a lack of sensitivity toward politics or both.

The basis for pessimism and the warning signals were always present. Public portrayals of success glowed more brightly than the full range of classified reporting. Readily available informal and personal accounts were less optimistic still. The political instability of our Vietnamese allies—from Bao Dai through Diem to President Thieu have always been apparent. The weaknesses of the armed forces of our Vietnamese allies were common knowledge. Few years went by when the fighting did not gain in intensity. Our leaders did not have to know much about Vietnam to see all this.

Most of our leaders saw the Vietnam quagmire for what it was. Optimism was, by and large, put in perspective. This means that many knew that each step would be followed by another. Most seemed to have understood that more assistance would be required either to improve the relative position of our Vietnamese allies or simply to prevent a deterioration of their position. Almost each year and often several times a year, key decisions had to be made to prevent deterioration or collapse. These decisions were made with hard bargaining, but rapidly enough for us now to perceive a preconceived consensus to go on. Sometimes several new steps were decided at once, but announced and implemented piecemeal. The whole pattern conveyed the feeling of more to come.

With a tragic sense of "no exit," our leaders stayed their course. They seemed to hope more than expect that something would "give." The hope was to convince the Vietnamese Communists through perseverance that the U.S. would stay in South Vietnam until they abandoned their struggle. The hope, in a sense, was the product of disbelief. How could a tiny, backward Asian country *not* have a breaking point when opposed by the might of the United States? How could they not relent and negotiate with the U.S.?

And yet, few could answer two questions with any confidence: Why should the Communists abandon tomorrow the goals they had been paying so dear a price to obtain yesterday? What was there really to negotiate? No one seemed to be able to develop a persuasive scenario on how the war could end by peaceful means.

Our Presidents, given their politics and thinking, had nothing to do but persevere. But the Communists' strategy was also to persevere, to make the U.S. go home. It was and is a civil war for national independence. It was and is a Greek tragedy.

IV. AFTER TWENTY-FIVE YEARS

A quick review of history supports these interpretations. To the Roosevelt Administration during World War II, Indochina was not perceived as a "vital" area. The United States defeated Japan without Southeast Asia, and Indochina was not occupied by the allies until *after* Japan's defeat. FDR spoke informally to friends and newsmen of placing Indochina under

United Nations trusteeship after the war, but—aware of French, British and U.S. bureaucratic hostility to this—made no detailed plans and asked for no staff work prior to his death. For all practical purposes, Truman inherited *no* Southeast Asia policy.

In 1946 and 1947, the U.S. acquiesced in the re-establishment of French sovereignty. Our policy was a passive one of hoping for a negotiated settlement of the "difficulties" between Paris and the Vietminh independence movement of Ho Chi Minh. To the south, in Indonesia, we had started to pressure the Dutch to grant independence and withdraw, and a residue of anticolonialism remained in our first inchoate approaches to an Indochina policy as well.

But events in Europe and China changed the context from mid-1947 on. Two important priorities were to rearm and strengthen France as the cornerstone of European defense and recovery in the face of Russian pressure, and to prevent a further expansion of victorious Chinese Communism. The Truman Doctrine depicted a world full of dominoes. In May 1950, before Korea, Secretary of State Acheson announced that the U.S. would provide military and economic assistance to the French and their Indochinese allies for the direct purpose of combating Communist expansion.[2] After years of hesitating, Truman finally decided that anti-Communism was more important than anticolonialism in Indochina.

Acheson admits that U.S. policy was a "muddled hodgepodge":

> The criticism, however, fails to recognize the limits on the extent to which one may successfully coerce an ally.... Furthermore, the result of withholding help to France would, at most, have removed the colonial power. It could not have made the resulting situation a beneficial one either for Indochina or for Southeast Asia, or in the more important effort of furthering the stability and defense of Europe. So while we may have tried to muddle through and were certainly not successful, I could not think then or later of a better course. One can suggest, perhaps, doing nothing. That might have had merit, but as an attitude for the leader of a great alliance toward an important ally, indeed one essential to a critical endeavor, it had its demerits, too.[3]

Several months after the Korean War began, Acheson recalled the warning of an "able colleague": "Not only was there real danger that our efforts would fail in their immediate purpose and waste valuable resources in the process, but we were moving into a position in Indochina in which 'our responsibilities tend to supplant rather than complement those of the French'." Acheson then remembers: "I decided however, that having put our hand to the plow, we would not look back."[4] He decided this despite the fact that he "recognized as no longer valid an earlier French intention to so weaken the enemy before reducing French forces in Indochina that indigenous forces could handle the situation."[5]

V. THE EISENHOWER ADMINISTRATION

President Eisenhower inherited the problem. Although, with Vietminh successes, the situation took on graver overtones, he, too, pursued a policy of "minimum action" to prevent the total "loss" of Vietnam to Communism. Sherman Adams, Eisenhower's assistant, explains how the problem was seen in the mid-1950's:

> If the Communists had pushed on with an aggressive offensive after the fall of Dienbienphu, instead of stopping and agreeing to stay out of Southern Vietnam, Laos and Cambodia, there was a strong possibility that the United States would have moved against them. A complete Communist conquest of Indochina would have had far graver consequence for the West than a Red victory in Korea.[6]

Apparently the President felt he could live with Communist control in the restricted area of North Vietnam, away from the rest of Southeast Asia.

Eisenhower did not take the minimal necessary step to save *all* of Indochina, but he did take the necessary steps to prevent the loss of most of Indochina. He paid almost all the French war cost, increased the U.S. military advisory mission, supplied forty B-26's to the French, and continued the threat of U.S. intervention, first by "united action" and then by forming SEATO. In taking these actions, Eisenhower was deciding against Vice-President Nixon and Admiral Radford, Chairman of the Joint Chiefs of Staff, who favored U.S. intervention in force, and against General Ridgway, Chief of the Army Staff, who opposed any action that could lead to an Asian land war. He was treading the well-worn middle path of doing just enough to balance off contradictory domestic, bureaucratic, and international pressures. The Vietnamese Communists agreed to the compromise, believing that winning the full prize was only a matter of time.

In public statements and later in his memoirs, President Eisenhower gave glimpses of his reasoning. At the time of Dienbienphu, he noted, "...we ought to look at this thing with some optimism and some determination...long faces and defeatism don't win battles." [7] Later he wrote, "I am convinced that the French could not win the war because the internal political situation in Vietnam, weak and confused, badly weakened their military position." [8] But he persevered nevertheless, believing that "the decision to give this aid was almost compulsory. The United States had no real alternative unless we were to abandon Southeast Asia." [9]

The Geneva Conference of 1954 was followed by eighteen bleak and pessimistic months as official Washington wondered whether the pieces could be put back together. Despite or perhaps because of the pessimism, U.S. aid was increased. Then, in the fall of 1956, Dulles could say: "We have a clean base there now, without a taint of colonialism. Dienbienphu was a blessing in disguise." [10] The years of "cautious optimism" had begun.

President Eisenhower kept the U.S. out of war because he allowed a territorial compromise with the Communists. More critically, he decided to replace the French and maintain a direct U.S. presence in Indochina. With strong rhetoric, military training programs, support for Ngo Dinh Diem in his refusal to hold the elections prescribed by the Geneva accords, and continuing military and economic assistance, he made the new state or "zone" of South Vietnam an American responsibility. Several years of military quiet in South Vietnam did not hide the smoldering political turmoil in that country nor did it obscure the newspaper headlines which regularly proclaimed that the war in Indochina had shifted to Laos.

VI. THE KENNEDY ADMINISTRATION

The Administration of John F. Kennedy began in an aura of domestic sacrifice and international confrontation. The inauguration speech set the tone of U.S. responsibilities in "hazardous and dangerous" times.

Vietnam had a special and immediate importance which derived from the general international situation. Kennedy's predictions about dangerous times came true quickly—and stayed true—and he wanted to show strength to the Communists. But it was also the precarious situation in Laos and the "neutralist" compromise which Kennedy was preparing for Laos that were driving the President deeper into Vietnam. In Sorensen's words, Kennedy was "skeptical of the extent of our involvement [in Vietnam] but unwilling to abandon his predecessor's pledge or permit a Communist conquest...." [11]

Kennedy had to face three basic general decisions. First, was top priority to go to political reform or fighting the war? On this issue the fixers, who wanted to give priority to political reform, were arrayed against the military. Second, should the line of involvement be drawn at combat units? On this issue the fixers were more quiet than in opposition. The military and the Country Team pushed hard—even urging the President to threaten Hanoi with U.S. bombing. Some counter-weight came from State and the White House staff. Third, should the President make a clear, irrevocable and open-ended commitment to prevent a Communist victory? Would this strengthen or weaken the U.S. hand in Saigon? Would it frighten away the Communists? What would be the domestic political consequences?

Kennedy's tactics and decisions—like Eisenhower's—followed the pattern of doing what was minimally necessary. On the political versus military priority issue, Kennedy did not make increasing military assistance definitively contingent on political reform, but he pointed to the absence of reform as the main reason for limiting the U.S. military role. On the combat unit issue, according to biographer Sorensen, "Kennedy never made a final negative decision on troops. In typical Kennedy fashion, he made it difficult for any of the pro-intervention advocates to charge him privately with weakness." [12] On the third issue, he avoided an open-ended commitment, but escalated his rhetoric about the importance of Vietnam. While he did authorize an increase of U.S. military personnel from 685 to 16,000, he did so slowly, and not in two or three big decisions. He continually doled out the increases. He gave encouragement to bureaucratic planning and studying as a safety valve—a valve he thought he could control. He kept a very tight rein on information to the public about the war. In Salinger's words, he "was not anxious to admit the existence of a real war..." [13] By minimizing U.S. involvement, Kennedy was trying to avoid public pressures either to do more or to do less.

The President would make it "their" war until he had no choice but to look at it in a different light. He would not look at it in another light until Diem, who looked like a losing horse, was replaced. He would not gamble on long odds. But it is not clear what he expected to get as a replacement for Diem.

With the exception of much of 1962, which even the North Vietnamese have called "Diem's year," the principal Kennedy decisions were made in an atmosphere of deterioration, not progress, in Vietnam. This feeling of deterioration explains why Kennedy dispatched so many high-level missions to Vietnam. As Kennedy's biographers have written, the President was not really being told he was winning, but how much more he would have to do.

Writing in 1965, Theodore Sorensen summed up the White House view of events following the Diem coup in November 1963:

> The President, while eager to make clear that our aim was to get out of Vietnam, had always been doubtful about the optimistic reports constantly filed by the military on the progress of the war....The struggle could well be, he thought, this nation's severest test of endurance and patience.... He was simply going to weather it out, a nasty, untidy mess to which there was no other acceptable solution. Talk of abandoning so unstable an ally and so costly a commitment 'only makes it easy for the Communists,' said the President. 'I think we should stay.'[14]

VII. THE JOHNSON ADMINISTRATION

Lyndon Johnson assumed office with a reputation as a pragmatic politician and not a cold war ideologue. His history on Southeast Asia indicated caution and comparative restraint. And yet it was this same man who as President presided over and led the U.S. into massive involvement.

Three facts conspired to make it easier for Johnson to take the plunge on the assumed importance of Vietnam than his predecessors. First, the world was a safer place to live in and Vietnam was the only continuing crisis. Europe was secure. The Sino-Soviet split had deepened. Mutual nuclear deterrence existed between the two superpowers. Second, the situation in Vietnam was more desperate than it ever had been. If the U.S. had not intervened in 1965, South Vietnam would have been conquered by the Communists. Third, after years of effort, the U.S. conventional military forces were big enough and ready enough to intervene. Unlike his predecessors, Johnson had the military capability to back up his words.

In sum, Vietnam became relatively more important, it was in greater danger, and the U.S. was in a position to do something about it.

At Johns Hopkins in April 1965, the President told the American people what he would do: "We will do everything necessary to reach that objective [of no external interference in South Vietnam], and we will do only what is absolutely necessary." But in order to prevent defeat and in order to keep the faith with his most loyal supporters, the minimum necessary became the functional equivalent of gradual escalation. The Air Force and the Commander in Chief, Pacific (CINCPAC) pressed hard for full systems bombing—the authority to destroy 94 key North Vietnamese targets in 16 days. Johnson, backed and pressured in the other direction by Secretary McNamara, doled out approval for new targets over three years in a painstaking and piecemeal fashion. Johnson accommodated dovish pressure and the advice of the many pragmatists who surrounded him by making peace overtures. But these overtures were either accompanied with or followed by escalation. Johnson moved toward those who wanted three-quarters of a million U.S. fighting men in Vietnam, but he never got there. Guided by judgments of domestic repercussion and influenced again by McNamara, the President made at least eight separate decisions on U.S. force levels in Vietnam over a four-year period.[15] For the "fixers" who felt that U.S. conduct of the war missed its political essence and for the doves who wanted to see something besides destruction, Johnson placed new emphasis on "the other war"—pacification, nation-building, and political development—in February 1966. Johnson referred to this whole complex of actions and the air war in particular as his attempt to "seduce not rape" the North Vietnamese.

The objective of the Johnson Administration was to maintain an independent non-Communist South Vietnam. In the later years, this was rephrased "allowing the South Vietnamese to determine their own future without external interference." As the President crossed the old barriers in pursuit of this objective, he established new ones. While he ordered the bombing of North Vietnam, he would not approve the bombing of targets which ran the risk of confrontation with China and Russia. While he permitted the U.S. force level in Vietnam to go over one-half million men, he would not agree to call up the Reserves. While he was willing to spend $25 billion in one year on the war, he would not put the U.S. economy on a wartime mobilization footing. But the most important Johnson barrier was raised against invading Cambodia, Laos, and North Vietnam. This limitation was also a cornerstone in the President's hopes for a compromise settlement. He would agree to the permanent existence of North Vietnam—even help that country economically—if North Vietnam would extend that same right to South Vietnam.

In order to sustain public and bureaucratic support for his policy, Johnson's method was to browbeat and isolate his opponents. To the American people, he painted the alternatives to what he was doing as irresponsible or reckless. In either case, the result would be a greater risk of future general war. The bureaucracy used this same technique of creating the bug-out or bomb-out extremes in order to maintain as many of its own members in "the middle road." The price of consensus—within the bureaucracy and in the public at large—was invariably a middle road of contradictions and no priorities for action.

President Johnson was the master of consensus. On Vietnam this required melding the proponents of negotiations with the proponents of military victory. The technique for maintaining this Vietnam consensus was gradual escalation punctuated by dramatic peace overtures. As the war was escalated without an end in sight, the numbers of people Johnson could hold together diminished. The pressures for disengagement or for "decisive military action" became enormous, but with the "hawks" always outnumbering and more strategically placed than the "doves."

Johnson knew he had inherited a deteriorating situation in Vietnam. Vietcong military successes and constant change in the Saigon government from 1964 to 1966 were not secrets to anyone. Throughout the critical year of 1965, he struck the themes of endurance and more-to-come. In his May 4, 1965, requests for Vietnam Supplemental Appropriations he warned: "I see no choice but to continue the course we are on, filled as it is with peril and uncertainty." In his July 28, 1965, press conference he announced a new 125,000 troop ceiling and went on to say: "Additional forces will be needed later, and they will be sent as requested."

Talk about "turning corners" and winning a military victory reached a crescendo in 1967. At the same time a new counterpoint emerged— "stalemate."[16] The message of the stalemate proponents was that the U.S. was strong enough to prevent defeat, but that the situation defied victory. Hanoi would continue to match the U.S. force build-up and would not "cry uncle" over the bombing. The Saigon government and army had basic political and structural problems which they were unlikely to be able to overcome. Stalemate, it was urged, should be used as a basis for getting a compromise settlement with Hanoi.

These arguments were not lost on the President. At Guam in March 1967, while others around him were waxing eloquent about progress, the President was guardedly optimistic, speaking of "a favorable turning point, militarily and politically." But after one of the meetings he was reported to have said: "We have a difficult, a serious, long-drawn-out, agonizing problem that we do not have an answer for."[17] Nor did the President overlook the effects of the 1968 Tet offensive, coming as it did after many months of virtually unqualified optimism by him and by others. He stopped the bombing partially, increased troop strength slightly, made a peace overture, and announced his retirement.

In November 1963, Johnson is quoted as saying: "I am not going to be the President who saw Southeast Asia go the way China went."[18] In the spring of 1965, Lady Bird Johnson quoted him as saying: "I can't get out. I can't finish it with what I have got. So what the Hell can I do?"[19] President Johnson, like his predecessors, persevered and handed the war on to his successor.

VIII. WHERE DO WE GO FROM HERE?

If Vietnam were a story of how the system failed, that is, if our leaders did not do what they wanted to do or if they did not realize what they were doing or what was happening, it would be easy to package a large and assorted box of policy-making panaceas. For example: Fix the method of reporting from the field. Fix the way progress is measured in a guerrilla war. Make sure the President sees all the real alternatives. But these are all third-order issues, because the U.S. political-bureaucratic system did not fail; it worked.

Our leaders felt they had to prevent the loss of Vietnam to Communism, and they have succeeded so far in doing just that. Most of those who made Vietnam policy still believe that they did the right thing and lament only the domestic repercussions of their actions. It is because the price of attaining this goal has been so dear in lives, trust, dollars, and priorities, and the benefits so intangible, remote, and often implausible, that these leaders and we ourselves are forced to seek new answers and new policies.

Paradoxically, the way to get these new answers is not by asking why did the system fail, but why did it work so tragically well. There is, then, only one first-order issue—how and why does our political-bureaucratic system decide what is vital and what is not? By whom, in what manner, and for what reasons was it decided that all Vietnam must not fall into Communist hands?

Almost all of our leaders since 1949 shared this conviction. Only a few voices in the wilderness were raised in opposition. Even as late as mid-1967, most critics were arguing that the U.S. could not afford to lose or be "driven from the field," that the real problem was our bombing of North Vietnam, and that this had to be stopped in order to bring about a negotiated settlement. Fewer still were urging that such a settlement should involve a coalition government with the Communists. Hardly anyone was saying that the outcome in Vietnam did not matter.

There is little evidence of much critical thinking about the relation of Vietnam to U.S. security. Scholars, journalists, politicians, and bureaucrats all seem to have assumed either that Vietnam was "vital" to U.S. national security or that the American people would not stand for the loss of "another" country to Communism.

Anti-Communism has been and still is a potent force in American politics, and most people who were dealing with the Vietnam problem simply believed that the Congress and the public would "punish" those who were "soft on Communism." Our leaders not only anticipated this kind of public reaction, but believed that there were valid reasons for not permitting the Communists to take all of Vietnam by force. In other words, they believed in what they were doing on the national security "merits." The domino theory, which was at the heart of the matter, rested on the widely shared attitude that security was indivisible, that weakness in one place would only invite aggression in others.

What can be done?

The President can do more than Presidents have in the past to call his national security bureaucracy to task. He can show the bureaucracy that he expects it to be more rigorous in determining what is vital or important or unimportant. Specifically, he can reject reasoning which simply asserts that security is indivisible, and he can foster the belief that while the world is an interconnected whole, actions can be taken in certain parts of the world to compensate for actions which are not taken elsewhere. For example, if the real concern about Vietnam were the effect of its loss on Japan, the Middle East and Berlin, could we not take actions in each of these places to mitigate the "Vietnam fallout" ?

None of these efforts with the bureaucracy can succeed, however, unless there is a change in general political attitudes as well. If anti-Communism persists as an overriding domestic political issue it will also be the main bureaucratic issue. Altering public attitudes will take time, education, and political courage—and it will create a real dilemma for the President. If the President goes "too far" in re-educating public and congressional opinions about Communism, he may find that he will have little support for threatening or using military force when he believes that our security really is at stake. In the end, it will still be the President who is held responsible for U.S. security. Yet, if our Vietnam experience has taught us anything, it is that the President must begin the process of re-education despite the risks.

NOTES

1. *New York Times*, February 8, 1947.

2. Department of State Bulletin, May 1950, p. 821.

3. Dean Acheson, *Present at the Creation* (New York: W. W. Norton, 1969). p. 673.

4. *Ibid.*, p. 674.

5. *Ibid.*, p. 676–7.

6. Sherman Adams, *Firsthand Report* (New York: Harper & Row, 1961), p. 120.

7. Public Papers of the Presidents, Eisenhower, 1954, p. 471. This remark was made on May 12, 1954.

8. Dwight D. Eisenhower, *Mandate for Change* (New York: Doubleday, 1963), p. 372.

9. *Ibid.*, p. 373.

10. Emmet John Hughes, *The Ordeal of Power* (New York: Dell, 1962), p. 182. Eisenhower himself wrote that in 1954 "The strongest reason of all for United States refusal to respond by itself to French pleas was our tradition of anti-colonialism," (in *Mandate for Change*, p. 373).

11. Theodore Sorensen, *Kennedy* (New York: Harper & Row, 1965), p. 639.

12. *Ibid.*, p. 654.

13. Pierre Salinger, *With Kennedy* (New York: Doubleday, 1966), pp. 319–329.

14. Sorensen, *op. cit.*, p. 661.

15. See the Chronology in U.S. Senate Foreign Relations Committee, *Background Information Relating to Southeast Asia and Vietnam*, March 1969.

16. R. W. Apple, "Vietnam: The Signs of Stalemate," *New York Times*, August 7, 1967.

17. Quoted in Henry Brandon, *Anatomy of Error* (Boston: Gambit, 1969), p. 102.

18. Tom Wicker, *JFK and LBJ* (New York: Penguin Books, 1968), p. 208.

19. Lady Bird Johnson, *A White House Diary* (New York: Holt, Rinehart and Winston, 1970), p. 248.

November 17, 1965. Peace demonstrators along Pennsylvania Avenue, in front of the White House. UPI BETTMANN NEWSPHOTOS

CHAPTER 9

The War at Home and the Media

The Vietnam War was not the first American war to attract domestic protest, but by the late 1960s the war had almost certainly become the most unpopular in the nation's history. (The slight qualification is needed because there were no public opinion polls at the time of the War of 1812 or the Civil War.) Americans opposed the war for a variety of reasons. Some felt that the United States was immorally engaged in imperialism in Vietnam. Others continued to have faith in the rectitude of American foreign policy generally but held that the intervention in Vietnam was a terrible mistake, a departure from the necessary (or generally benign) foreign involvements of the past. And there is no question that some marched in antiwar demonstrations out of fear that if the war dragged on they or someone they loved would be sent off to fight. The readings in this chapter address these and other concerns. The piece by Lawrence Baskir and William Strauss studies the draft and notes the ease with which the privileged escaped it. Sociologist Nigel Young places the antiwar movement in the larger context of the New Left and offers a critical analysis of the policy of the organization Students for a Democratic Society (SDS). The first part of this chapter concludes with a look at women who resisted the war, an excerpt from Myra MacPherson's book *Long Time Passing*. Implicit in the selection of this excerpt is the question of whether gender conditioned an individual's reaction to the war.

Dissenters, indeed most Americans, learned about the war in Vietnam by reading newspapers and magazines, watching television, and listening to the radio. As Michael J. Arlen wrote in 1969, "probably the largest and most valued single export from South Vietnam these days is American journalism." The speed of international communication and the immensity of the media's presence in Vietnam combined to give Americans wide and nearly up-to-the-minute coverage of the war. From 1965 to 1973 the war dominated the news. There were those who wondered, however, just what kind of coverage they were getting. Obviously, reporters selected items they believed newsworthy, but, as Arlen points out, they were constrained by the need to file stories quickly (and presumably with some journalistic punch), and thus failed to convey much in the way of context or analysis. Images and "facts" had to stand by themselves. To this argument Daniel Hallin adds another: at the time of Tonkin Gulf incident in 1964, journalists implicitly allowed President Johnson to control information because they endorsed the U.S. position in the Cold War and they observed certain canons of what they termed "professionalism." The Vietnam War caused much soul searching within the media, with the result that some reporters, at least, now seem more inclined to be suspicious of official sources of information.

31
The Draft and Who Escaped It

LAWRENCE M. BASKIR AND WILLIAM A. STRAUSS

When John F. Kennedy was inaugurated on January 20, 1961, the new President told the nation and the world that "the torch has been passed to a new generation of Americans," under whose leadership America would "pay any price, bear any burden...to assure the survival and the success of liberty." These were brave words, very well received.

This "new generation," described by Kennedy as "tempered by war, disciplined by a hard and bitter peace," consisted of World War II veterans then in their late thirties and forties. Their "best and brightest" would later steer the nation through a very different, much more controversial war in Vietnam. Yet this time it was not they who had to do the fighting. Fewer than five hundred members of this generation died in Southeast Asia, most from accidents, diseases, and other causes that had nothing to do with combat. The rest paid the taxes to finance this $165 billion venture. It was their children, the baby-boom generation—the product of an enormous jump in the birthrate between 1946 and 1953—who paid the real price of Vietnam.

Fifty-three million Americans came of age during the Vietnam war. Roughly half were women, immune from the draft. Only six thousand women saw military service in Vietnam, none in combat. But as sisters, girl friends, and wives, millions of draft-age women paid a heavy share of the emotional cost of the war.

For their male counterparts, the war had devastating consequences. As Figure 1 illustrates, 26,800,000 men came of draft age between August 4, 1964, when the Tonkin Gulf Resolution marked the nation's formal entry into the war, and March 28, 1973, when the last American troops left. Fifty-one thousand died—17,000 from gunshot wounds, 7,500 from multiple fragmentation wounds, 6,750 from grenades and mines, 10,500 from other enemy action, 8,000 from nonhostile causes, and 350 by suicide. Another 270,000 were wounded, 21,000 of whom were disabled. Roughly 5,000 lost one or more limbs in the war. A half million were branded as criminals, more than two million served in the war zone, and millions more had their futures shaped by the threat of going to war.

These were the sons of parents reunited after a long but victorious war, parents who, in columnist George Will's description, "were anxious

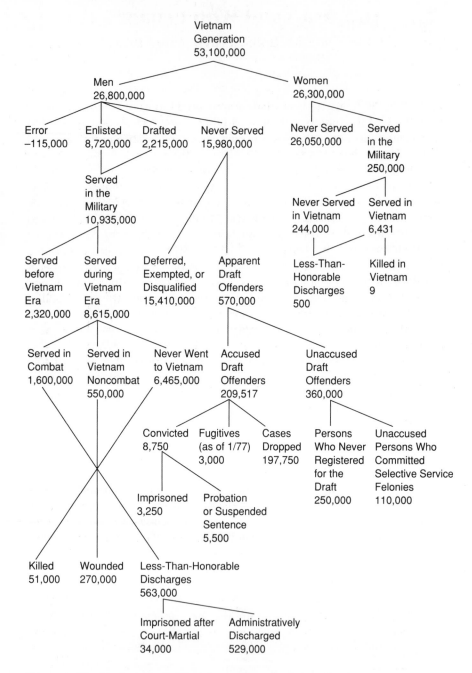

Figure 1. The Vietnam Draft: The Channeling of a Generation

to turn from the collective task of history-making to the private task of family-making. Like Studebakers and toothpaste, the next batch of children would be 'new and improved.'" Having faced depression and war, they wanted their children to know nothing but peace and prosperity.

As William Manchester noted in *The Glory and the Dream*, their offspring would be "adorable as babies, cute as grade school pupils, and striking as they entered their teens. After high school they would attend the best colleges and universities in the country, where their parents would be very, very proud of them." They were the Dr. Spock generation, the Sputnik generation, the Pepsi generation, and eventually the Woodstock generation. But above all else, they became the Vietnam generation.

As children and teenagers, they had grown accustomed to the existence of the draft. Some looked forward to military service as an exciting and potentially valuable experience—a chance to demonstrate their manhood, serve their country, and get some adventure before settling down. Others saw the draft as an unpleasant but nonetheless tolerable demand on two years of their lives. Many, especially those from well-to-do families, looked upon the draft as something to avoid, an unwelcome interference with their personal plans. But most never thought much about it. Consciously or unconsciously, they put the draft out of their minds; it was something that happened to someone else, never to them.

But when the generation and the Vietnam war collided, the draft became a preeminent concern. In 1966, a survey of high-school sophomores found that only 7 percent mentioned the draft or Vietnam as one of "the problems young men your age worry about most." But when the same question was asked of the same individuals after their high-school graduation in 1969, that number had grown to 75 percent. Few nineteen- to twenty-six-year-olds were eager to risk their lives in Vietnam.

Although only 6 percent of all young men were needed to fight, the Vietnam draft cast the entire generation into a contest for individual survival. The draft was not, however, an arbitrary and omnipotent force, imposing itself like blind fate upon men who were powerless to resist. Instead, it worked as an instrument of Darwinian social policy. The "fittest"—those with background, wit, or money—managed to escape. Through an elaborate structure of deferments, exemptions, legal technicalities, and noncombat military alternatives, the draft rewarded those who manipulated the system to their advantage.

Among this generation, fighting for one's country was not a source of pride; it was misfortune. Going to Vietnam was the penalty for those who lacked the wherewithal to avoid it. A 1971 Harris survey found that most Americans believed that those who went to Vietnam were "suckers, having to risk their lives in the wrong war, in the wrong place at the wrong time."

Much of the sentiment reflected the public's growing disenchantment with American involvement in Vietnam. The outspoken antiwar views of many young people helped sway public opinion and turn around the nation's policies. Their activism involved moral courage, but little concrete sacrifice. Except for occasional individuals who, on principle, abandoned deferments and exemptions to go to prison or take exile, opposing the war was in every draft-age man's self-interest. The sooner the war ended, the less likely it was that he would bear personal hardship.

This sense of self-interest was best illustrated by the attitude of anti-war collegians toward their student deferments. Harvard College graduate James Glassman recalled that in 1966, before the draft calls began to rise, "students complained that the system was highly discriminatory, favoring the well-off. They called the II-S an unfair advantage for those who could go to college." But as the war escalated, "the altruism was forgotten. What was most important now was saving your own skin." In 1967, when graduate-school deferments were abolished, the Harvard *Crimson* published an editorial entitled "The Axe Falls," accusing the government of "careless expediency" which was "clearly unfair to students."

Many students defended their deferments—and their draft avoidance—with a measure of class arrogance. A Rhodes scholar, now a corporate lawyer, observed that "there are certain people who can do more good in a lifetime in politics or academics or medicine than by getting killed in a trench." A University of Michigan student commented that "if I lost a couple years, it would mean $16,000 to me. I know I sound selfish, but, by God, I paid $10,000 to get this education." These attitudes were shared by millions of draft-age men with other deferments and exemptions. "I got a good steady job," a Delaware defense worker said. "I'm making good money and having a ball every weekend. Why the hell should I want to go?" Why should he have wanted to go? Vietnam veterans were held in no esteem, and the fate of the nation hardly lay in the balance.

"The result," as Yale University president Kingman Brewster noted, was "a cynical avoidance of service, a corruption of the aims of education, a tarnishing of the national spirit . . . and a cops and robbers view of national obligation." Avoiding Vietnam became a generation-wide preoccupation. According to the Notre Dame survey, approximately 15 million (60 percent) of the draft-age men who did not see combat took positive steps to help fate along. More than half of all men who escaped the draft, and almost half of all servicemen who escaped combat, believe today that the actions they took were wholly or partly responsible for keeping them away from the fighting.

Avoiding Vietnam did not necessarily mean emerging unscathed. For one in four, it meant hurried marriages, unwanted children, misdirected careers, or physical impairments. But millions emerged untouched, triumphant in what New Orleans draft counselor Collins Vallee called a "victory over the government." They never went to war, and they never faced the costly alternatives of prison, exile, or court-martial.

Avoidance was available to everyone. Ghetto youths sidestepped the draft by failing to register. High-school dropouts married and had children. But by far the greatest number of escape routes were open to youths from privileged backgrounds. Through status deferments, physical exemptions, or safe enlistments, they had little difficulty staying far from Vietnam. Even doctors, who were subject to special draft calls, were seldom involved in the war. Fewer than one of every ten medical-school graduates was drafted; many of the rest found refuge in the National Institute of Health, Public Health Service, or the reserves.

The draftees who fought and died in Vietnam were primarily society's "losers," the same men who get left behind in schools, jobs, and other forms of social competition. The discriminatory social, economic, and racial impact of Vietnam cannot be fairly measured against other wars in American history, but the American people were never before as conscious of how unevenly the obligation to serve was distributed. Few of the nation's elite had sons or close friends who did any fighting. Leslie Fiedler, commenting about his university community, wrote that he

> had never known a single family that had lost a son in Vietnam, or indeed, one with a son wounded, missing in action, or held prisoner of war. And this despite the fact that American casualties in Vietnam are already almost equal to those of World War I. Nor am I alone in my strange plight; in talking to friends about a subject they seem eager not to discuss, I discover they can, they must, all say the same....

The racial inequities became a major scandal of the late 1960s. General S. L. A. Marshall commented that he had seen

> too many of our battalions come out of line after hard struggle and heavy loss. In the average rifle company, the strength was 50% composed of Negroes, Southwestern Mexicans, Puerto Ricans, Guamanians, Nisei, and so on. But a real cross-section of American youth? Almost never.

At the end of World War II, blacks comprised 12 percent of all combat troops; by the start of the Vietnam war, their share had grown to 31 percent. In 1965, blacks accounted for 24 percent of all Army combat deaths. The Defense Department undertook a concerted campaign to reduce the minorities' share of the fighting. That share was reduced to 16 percent in 1966, and 13 percent in 1968. In 1970, the figure for all services was under 9 percent.

Over the course of the war, minorities did more than their share of the fighting and dying. Yet the most serious inequities were social and economic. Poorly educated, low-income whites and poorly educated, low-income blacks together bore a vastly disproportionate share of the burdens of Vietnam. The Notre Dame survey found that men from disadvantaged backgrounds were about twice as likely as their better-off peers to serve in the military, go to Vietnam, and see combat. (See the table below.) These were the men President Eisenhower once called "sitting ducks" for the draft.

The government did not undertake any wartime studies of the social and economic incidence of military service. The only contemporary evidence was scattered and anecdotal. A 1965–66 survey discovered that college graduates made up only 2 percent of all draftees. Congressman Alvin O'Konski took a personal survey of one hundred inductees from his northern Wisconsin district. Not one of them came from a family with an annual income of over $5,000. A Harvard *Crimson* editor from the class of 1970 tallied his twelve hundred classmates and counted only fifty-six who entered the military, just two of whom went to Vietnam. By contrast,

Likelihood of Vietnam-Era Service

	Military Service (%)	Vietnam Service (%)	Combat Service (%)
Low-Income	40	19	15
Middle-Income	30	12	7
High-Income	24	9	7
High-School Dropouts	42	18	14
High-School Graduates	45	21	17
College Graduates	23	12	9

thirty-five men from the Harvard class of 1941 died in World War II, and hundreds more saw combat duty. Not many Vietnam-era troops were college graduates, and even the relatively few who joined the service had a better-than-normal chance of avoiding Vietnam.

After the war was over, however, the evidence began to mount. Postwar Army records showed that an enlisted man who was a college graduate had a 42 percent chance of going to Vietnam, versus a 64 percent chance for a high-school graduate and a 70 percent chance for a high-school dropout. Surveys in Long Island, Wisconsin, and Salt Lake City found a very heavy incidence of combat deaths among disadvantaged youths. In the most significant study thus far, Gilbert Badillo and David Curry analyzed casualties suffered by Chicago neighborhoods with different socioeconomic characteristics. They discovered that youths from low-income neighborhoods were three times as likely to die in Vietnam as youths from high-income neighborhoods. They also found youths from neighborhoods with low educational levels to be four times as likely to die in Vietnam as youths from better-educated neighborhoods.

During World War II, conscription and combat service were matters of personal honor. Men bent the rules to get into military service. Patriotism knew no class boundaries; Winthrop Rockefeller and the president of the New York Stock Exchange volunteered to be among the first ten thousand to submit to induction. Returning veterans were public heroes. Prisoners of war were more an embarrassment than the object of national pride. But among the tragic ironies of Vietnam, the only real heroes of the war were POWs. Ordinarily, they were not members of the younger generation; they were Air Force and Navy pilots, officers well beyond draft age. The youths returning as combat veterans were easily forgotten.

America was not winning the war, and many people were ashamed of what was happening. With the war calling into question so much of America's self-esteem, and with so many young men resisting the war, the nation needed assurance that patriotism still had meaning. Draft resisters and deserters thus became the folk villains of the times. John

Geiger of the American Legion spoke for a great many Americans when he called them "a mixture of victims of error, deliberate conspirators, and professional criminals." Their detractors insisted that their numbers were small—Richard Nixon referred to them as "those few hundreds"—and that the judicial system dealt with them swiftly and severely. None of this was true, but it helped reaffirm traditional values.

The national conscience was also salved by comparing the cowardice of draft resisters and deserters with the courage of combat soldiers. This helped blind the nation to the fact that 25 million men of military age did not serve in Vietnam, and that relatively few were touched directly by the sacrifices of those who did.

After the fighting was over, draft resisters and deserters served one last, tragic purpose. They became scapegoats, much like Eddie Slovik, the only soldier executed for desertion in World War II. Slovik was a misfit totally incapable of being a combat soldier. He performed so poorly in basic training that his commanding officer tried, without success, to get him discharged or transferred to a noncombat unit. Slovik never actually ran away, but he confessed to desertion as a way of staying out of the fighting. On the day of his execution, a few months before the end of the war, Slovik told a reporter, "They are not shooting me for deserting the U.S. Army. Thousands of guys have done that. They just need to make an example out of somebody, and I'm it."

Those who feel a deep, unarticulated resentment about what happened to America in Vietnam have made whipping boys of the draft resisters and deserters. They are the ones to blame for the tragedy of a lost war and lost illusions, symbols of the nation's lack of resolve to win. For those who condemn the antiauthoritarian values of the generation, the resisters and deserters represent the worst of a bad lot. For those who suffered personal tragedies in the war, these are the men who should have gone in place of loved ones.

As important a symbol as the draft resisters and deserters have been, Americans know little about them. They are, like the draftees who saw combat, society's "losers"—disproportionately black, poorly educated youths from low-income families. Had they been better advised or more clever, most could have found one of the escape routes used by so many others. The disadvantaged not only did more than their share of the fighting; they also paid too much of the penalty for not fighting.

Vietnam-era draft and military offenders number more than a million. An estimated 570,000 men committed draft violations that could have sent them to prison for five years. Yet fewer than half were reported to federal prosecutors, only some 25,000 were indicted, and fewer than 9,000 convicted. Just 3,250 went to prison, most of whom were paroled within a year. In the military, a quarter of a million men were punished with Undesirable, Bad Conduct, or Dishonorable Discharges, branding them as deserters or military criminals of other sorts. Yet only 13 percent of them were convicted by court-martial, and even they seldom spent more than a few months in prison. Another 300,000 servicemen were sent home with General Discharges, which are technically given "under honorable conditions," although they are nonetheless a handicap in these men's search for jobs.

A great many escaped the brunt of the law because of legal or administrative problems. More than 100,000 draft cases were dismissed because of draft boards' failure to obey court-imposed rules. The over burdened military justice system gave 130,000 servicemen undesirable discharges as plea bargains, sparing the armed forces the expense of trying and imprisoning them. But, in part, this leniency reflected the views of many prosecutors, judges, and military officers that these individuals did not deserve the stiff punishments the public thought they were getting.

It is inaccurate to assume that the "evaders," as a group, did anything fundamentally worse than their 24 million peers who also escaped Vietnam, but by legal means. The term "evader" says little about each individual's attitude toward his responsibility to serve in the military. A great many men who legally avoided combat service would have been evaders had the necessity arisen; the Notre Dame survey found that 15 percent of all draft avoiders would have seriously considered breaking the law if that had been their only recourse. As one resister commented, "Almost every kid in this country [was] either a draft evader, a potential draft evader, or a failed draft evader." According to Michael Brophy, a Milwaukee draft counselor, the epithet has been misapplied:

> To evade is to avoid something by deceitful means. The draft evaders are in the Reserves and the National Guard, and other educational institutions. ...A man who [breaks the law] may do so to avoid the draft, but he is not deceiving anyone.

The opprobrium of "evader" is inappropriate for large categories of Vietnam-era offenders. About one-third of all draft resisters could have avoided the draft through deferments, exemptions, and legal loopholes, but they insisted on accepting exile or punishment as the consequence of their beliefs. One-fifth of all deserters never actually evaded Vietnam service. They finished full combat tours before running afoul of military discipline back home, often because of postcombat readjustment problems.

The law has worked its will on these men. By the mid-1970s, all but a few thousand had paid the legal penalty. They were prosecuted, punished, and officially forgiven. Still, the question remains whether the American people will continue to condemn them.

Until Americans evaluate the conduct of these men in the context of the entire generation's response to the war, there can never be any real understanding of the tragedy of Vietnam. The memory of the war may be too bitter for any to be cast as heroes. But perhaps the American people can begin to understand the extent to which so many young men, veterans and law breakers alike, were victims. And, with the passage of time, critics of the generation may stop setting victim against victim, fixing blame that only exacerbates the tragedy of the war.

Vietnam wrought havoc on millions of lives in a manner that most Americans may never understand. The war was, at root, the personal calamity of the generation called upon to fight it. They are the ones who faced the terrible choices, and they are the ones who suffered. "You were damned if you did go and damned if you didn't," said Ursula Diliberto, whose son was killed in Vietnam two weeks before the end of his tour. "My son was a victim, my family was a victim, all boys of draft age were victims in one way or another."

Beating the draft was by no means a lonely endeavor; in fact, it became more of a status symbol than did fighting for one's country. "If you are I-A, you are a nobody," observed Congressman Alvin O'Konski. "You happened to get caught because you didn't know any better. If you are not I-A, you have status." President Johnson's daughter Luci defended student efforts to keep their deferments: "Some of the students are fighting just as hard to get their education as...you could expect them to." A mother of a draft-deferred son spoke the minds of millions when she boasted of him as "a boy who knows how to take advantage of his opportunities." One of every four Notre Dame survey respondents had parents who openly encouraged him to avoid the draft. Outside the family, people from the most respected elements of society—teachers, employers, doctors, and lawyers—provided important help, without which millions of men might never have stayed out of the military.

Colleges were the main sanctuary from the draft, and many teachers and administrators did what they could to help their students. College grades were referred to as "A, B, C, D, and Nam," and antiwar professors sometimes adjusted their grading policies accordingly: "It's a rotten, stinking war, and I'll be damned if I'll help it along by sending over more cannon fodder. Unless he's clearly an idiot,...I intend to pass every able-bodied man in my class." Some professors even gave all A's in their courses, since even a B or C could affect a student's draft status.

The well-connected working man could stay away from Vietnam by getting timely help from the right people. Farmers often convinced draft boards that their sons were essential to the continued operation of the family farm. Plumbers, electricians, and other craftsmen lobbied local boards for automatic deferments for union apprentices. Employers could guarantee deferments for favored employees by designating them as supervisors of four or more full-time workers, making them "indispensable" according to the draft system's rule-of-thumb. Employers wrote letters like the following to local boards: "Braking systems for railroads and mass transit systems have been judged as essential to the welfare and safety of the nation, and our contribution as a primary supplier [is] vital for Selective Service purposes." Rural draft boards regularly granted deferments to truck drivers, laborers, and others whose employers were close friends of board members. A presidential commission reviewing the files of 199 local boards around the country in the late 1960s found that "about half" of all registrants with occupational deferments "were in neither a critical occupation nor an essential industry as defined by the Department of Labor."

Family doctors contributed to the exemption of many long-time patients. Anyone who had seen the same doctor for years had a medical history that was likely to document some kind of physical defect, and most doctors were inclined to cooperate. They gave extra tests to find heart murmurs or other minor conditions that qualified for IV-F or I-Y exemptions. As one doctor commented, "The traditional doctor-patient relationship is one of preserving life. I save lives by keeping people out of the Army." However, some doctors were staunchly against helping patients avoid the draft, even those with grounds for legitimate physical exemptions. One Bloomington, Indiana, doctor promised his patients he would write letters in their behalf, but he confidentially alerted their local boards that they were physically fit, and he urged that they be drafted as punishment.

The primary source of help came from an unprecedented network of counselors, lawyers, and other professionals with special expertise on the draft. More than one-fourth of all Notre Dame survey respondents consulted with experts, many of whom flatly guaranteed that anyone who followed their advice could avoid military service. By the late 1960s, the only real challenge left to the draft was to find the right advice in time.

Draft counseling had its roots in the pacifist movement of earlier wars. Conscientious objectors were the pariahs of the First and Second World Wars; sometimes they were jailed, sometimes they were isolated in special work camps, but always they were looked upon with suspicion by their draft boards and most of the public. Pacifist religious organizations gave them counseling and protected their rights, an unpopular task at the time.

In the early 1960s, these same groups helped establish conscientious objection as a commonly sought alternative to military service. CO exemptions were generally limited to Jehovah's Witnesses, Quakers, and members of other recognized pacifist religions, but a growing number of young people were citing personal, nonsectarian reasons for refusing to take arms. In 1965, the Supreme Court declared in the *Seeger* case that CO exemptions had to be granted to all confirmed pacifists, regardless of their religious backgrounds. To qualify, an individual's beliefs had to conform to legal standards, and he had to convince his local board of his sincerity.

Religious organizations like the Catholic Peace Fellowship and American Friends Service Committee provided the bulk of counseling in the early war years. At first, they concentrated on helping confirmed pacifists, but the growing unpopularity of the war brought an increasing number of "selective objectors" to their offices. These individuals objected only to the Vietnam war and did not qualify for exemption under the law. However, every counselor knew that CO status was only one of several ways of staying out of the military, and they rarely turned away people without giving some helpful advice.

As the war progressed, draft counseling became increasingly comprehensive, expanding well beyond conscientious objection. By the late

1960s, churches, colleges, high schools, and antiwar groups were offering a variety of counseling services. Most cities and university towns had at least one full-time counseling center. The typical center had one bona fide expert on the draft, aided by a number of paraprofessionals who relayed advice to walk-in clients. Some were volunteers, and others were paid out of church funds or donations from people they helped. A few universities hired their own full-time draft counselors, gave them clerical help, and paid for their office space. Through its legal assistance program, the Office of Economic Opportunity provided federal funds to pay salaries of lawyers engaged in draft counseling.

From the earliest days, counselors were enormously successful. Through newsletters and word of mouth, they learned each others' tactics. It was rare for a counselor to have a success rate of under 90 percent. The Catholic Peace Fellowship in New York City advised thousands of draft-age men, and all but a handful received deferments or exemptions. Even in the South and other parts of the country where public sentiment was strongly in favor of the war, counselors did extremely well.

Attorneys made especially good draft counselors. In San Francisco, Los Angeles, and other cities, lawyers' committees steered clients to participating attorneys while providing backup legal services to keep the local bar well ahead of draft boards in its knowledge of the law. Fees were fairly reasonable—usually about $200, and rarely more than $1,000. For anyone who found a competent lawyer, avoiding the draft was virtually assured. William Smith, the chairman of the Los Angeles draft attorneys' panel, told the local press that "any kid with money can absolutely stay out of the Army—with 100 percent certainty." A local prosecutor agreed with him: "If you got the dough, you don't have to go." Attorneys who charged nominal fees could represent hundreds of clients. All that was generally required was a quick interview, a standard letter, and one or two follow-up phone calls.

Expert advisers were not hard to find. They were cross-referenced with local service agencies, covered by the press, and known to most community leaders. Every state except North Dakota had at least one walk-in center, and more than half of all draft-age men had a center within a two-hour drive of their home. At the peak of the war, thousands of lawyers and paraprofessionals were doing draft counseling, serving about a million clients every year.

Most of the clients were surprisingly ill-informed about the draft and unaware of their most fundamental rights under the law. Some knew nothing about deferments or exemptions for which they were obviously qualified. Others were discouraged from filing legitimate claims by draft board clerks who misunderstood the law. Some youths were even mistaken about what their lottery numbers were. Without a visit to a draft counselor, these men might have been drafted or pressured into enlisting in the service.

Frequently, the first question a counselor heard was, "Can I qualify for a CO exemption?" Many draft-age men knew that conscientious objection was one way to avoid the war, but they had little idea about how to apply or how to qualify. The counselors' main role was to help CO applicants articulate and document their beliefs in a way that would convince draft boards of their sincerity. One organization advised people to

> sit down and think about why you are against killing people in war. Write down short sentences or ideas (for instance: love...brotherhood...peace... equality...personal responsibility...). Let your mind work freely, and you will probably get down on paper most of the ideas that will make a good CO case.

CO applicants were encouraged to get people they knew, especially clergymen, lawyers, or educators, to discuss their beliefs with them, and then write letters of reference attesting to the firmness of their convictions. Clients were sometimes referred to clergymen who were adept at writing letters supporting CO claims. Through schools like the Jane Addams Peace Center in Philadelphia, CO applicants were prepped on the questions that were commonly asked by local draft boards in personal interviews.

Most counselors who specialized in conscientious objection believed that no one could fabricate sincerity, but some draft board members were not so sure. Over time, CO applications became so standardized that it was hard for draft boards to tell who was sincere and who was not. As the chairman of a Denver board complained, "So many of these CO's—you could tell they were so cleverly coached. We could tell outside forces were directing these boys."

In the view of most draft counselors, almost all conscientious objectors were spurred by deep principle, not by a shallow desire to avoid going to war; some even did their alternative service by working for civilian agencies in Vietnam. A large number of CO's were Jehovah's Witnesses, Quakers, Mennonites, Muslims, and others whose churches preached total pacifism. Many others were Catholics who had to overcome their draft boards' knowledge that the Catholic church was not pacifist. One Samoan was exempted by his California draft board because of his sincere belief that if he killed anyone, his pagan god would cause a volcano to erupt. Others belonged to no established religion, but convinced their boards of their moral and ethical opposition to all wars.

However, a few saw conscientious-objector status as nothing more than a convenient way to avoid the draft. They copied examples of successful personal statements, falsified ministers' names, and wrote their own letters of reference. Draft boards rarely had time to check up on them.

Most draft counselors knew there were better ways to avoid the draft and refused to prepare a fraudulent CO claim as a matter of principle. They tried to discourage the insincere by describing CO status as a bleak alternative to military service. The Central Committee for Conscientious Objection published a handbook which *Newsweek* magazine described as "enough to convince all but the most determined malingerer that only confirmed, absolute pacifists need apply for the dirty details, civilian volunteer work, or jail terms that conscientious objection invites."

Conscientious objection did involve considerable hardship. Almost all of the 172,000 Vietnam-era conscientious objectors were asked to do alternative service in lieu of induction. CO's had to work for two years in low-paying jobs beyond commuting distance from their homes. Many worked as hospital orderlies or as conservation workers in wilderness camps. However, most draft boards were so overloaded with inductions and reclassifications that they kept only very loose contact with CO's, and alternative service was often very casually supervised. "Many of these local boards couldn't stand the sight of CO's and wanted nothing to do with them," recalled a top-level Selective Service official. "They didn't realize that they were doing these boys a favor." Almost fifty thousand CO's dropped out and were never certified as having fulfilled their obligations. Refusing to do alternative service was a federal crime, punishable by up to five years in prison, but only about a thousand individuals were convicted of this offense.

For a number of persons, a conscientious-objector claim was only the first step in a long procedural tangle with the draft system. Even a CO application that had no chance of succeeding could tie up a draft board for months or sometimes years. By pyramiding claims and appeals, a skillful counselor could enable his client to outlast his draft vulnerability. After years of exchanging paperwork with draft boards, clients turned twenty-six, received high lottery numbers, took advantage of the lottery loophole, outlasted the draft itself, or goaded their local boards into procedural errors that made induction orders unenforceable. Stalling tactics were often expensive and always the cause of great personal anxiety, making them usually the strategy of last resort. According to New Orleans counselor Collins Vallee, "The system was full of escape valves, and all we had to do was try one tactic after another until something finally worked."

By far the biggest escape valves were the preinduction and induction examinations. Every prospective draftee had to be examined twice, once before his draft board could classify him I-A and again when he reported for induction. On either occasion, he could be given a IV-F or I-Y exemption for mental, physical, psychological, or "administrative" reasons. The mental exam was hard to fake, and examiners were quick to question anyone with a peculiarly low score. But other aspects of the examination process were extremely vulnerable to manipulation and fabrication.

Young men could qualify for an administrative exemption by admitting membership in any subversive organization listed on the Armed Forces Security Questionnaire. If a person refused to fill out the questionnaire, Army regulations required that he undergo further investigation before he could be drafted. Sometimes these men were exempted without further inquiry. As one official at Selective Service headquarters admitted, "As long as there are plenty of men available, no one's going to spend any time investigating hippies." One youth was exempted simply because he claimed that his father was a member of the Communist Party.

A person could also get what one handbook called a "draft immunization" by developing a history of petty criminal behavior. Notwithstanding the movie *Alice's Restaurant*, dumping trash by a roadside was not enough—but cattle rustling, killing an eagle, or engaging in what the rules called "sexual misconduct" could qualify a person for a I-Y exemption on the grounds of "questionable moral character." In New York City, one arrest for marijuana possession was sometimes enough to keep a person home from the war. Some men were rejected for administrative reasons upon nothing more than a subjective determination that they would not make good soldiers. "The I-Y classification is sort of a dumping ground," explained one draft counselor. "It's a place for guys the Army just doesn't want, and it's often very hard to find out why they were put there."

The physical part of the exam was easy to fake. The military knew this was a serious problem, yet it was never able to solve it. According to Colonel William G. Peard, head of the Army department which set medical standards for induction:

> Even when we suspect malingering, to prove it is very difficult. A registrant may play upon some defect which might be minor, and it's almost impossible for a physician to say he's lying....Only when fakery is flagrant is...any detective-type investigation of a registrant's claimed defect undertaken.

To help registrants fail the preinduction physical, many draft counseling centers organized special clinics, often staffed by antiwar medical students or doctors at university health centers. A careful examination by a knowledgeable specialist and an equally careful choice of a preinduction physical site guaranteed an exemption for nine clients out of ten.

The military's stringent standards required that each inductee meet the physical requirements of an infantryman under stress. This precluded the induction or enlistment of anyone with a defect that might impair training, be aggravated by military duty, or interfere with military routine. Trick knees, flat feet, skin rashes, even excessive or obscene tattoos were enough to qualify for a IV-F or I-Y exemption. As Los Angeles attorney David Caplan explained, "There are thousands of disqualifying physical and mental conditions, and it's a rare case that someone does not have *one* of them." Roughly half of all draft-age youths failed to meet physical standards, two to three times the rejection rates for other NATO countries.

Even well-conditioned athletes in apparent good health could qualify for physical exemptions, since many of them had some history of bone or joint injuries. As described in the House Armed Services Committee's 1967 report on the draft, many military experts believed that "the chronically injured, deferred athlete is not physically able to meet the full demands of service in a combat zone....[Without] quick access to whirlpool baths and other modern and elaborate therapeutic devices,...[he] would become a quick liability to a military unit." The public's attention focused on Joe Namath and his IV-F knees, but thousands of hometown high-school athletes got similar exemptions.

Medical counselors stretched the rules as far as their imaginations allowed. "I just followed the Army's own standards," one commented sarcastically. "I'm sure the Army appreciates my help in screening out unsuitable prospects." They helped document disqualifying conditions, and sometimes advised clients of the necessary symptoms. Some conditions had symptoms that no civilian or military doctor could disprove if a person complained of them convincingly. Ménière's syndrome, for example, could be faked by attesting to persistent dizziness, nausea, ringing in the ears, and an inability to concentrate.

A determined individual with strong fortitude could fake a gastrointestinal ulcer. A few hours before his preinduction physical, he had to borrow a syringe and extract a pint of his own blood, making sure that the needle mark was in an inconspicuous place. Just before entering the examination center, he had to drink the blood. This induced vomiting a few minutes later, ideally in the presence of a military doctor. He then had to complain of severe stomach pains. When tests confirmed that his blood pressure was down and the vomited blood was his own, a IV-F exemption was guaranteed.

One draft manual, *IV-F: A Guide to Exemption,* described how a number of people could "very likely" be exempted for a defect that only one of them actually possessed:

> Since civilian doctors know their patients only by the names they give, a registrant bent on fraud with a bona fide disqualifying defect which was either intermittent (such as asthma) or unverifiable by objective tests (such as Ménière's syndrome) might receive treatment from several doctors using the names of several conspirators.

The law provided an exemption for anyone under orthodontic care, and almost every draft-age person had teeth sufficiently crooked to give braces some therapeutic value. In the Los Angeles area alone, ten dentists willingly performed orthodontic work for anyone who could pay a $1,000–$2,000 fee. Wearing braces was a common last-minute tactic for registrants who faced immediate call-up. According to one youth who wore unneeded braces, this "dental cop-out" was "very expensive and very uncomfortable. But it sure beat KP, getting up at 4 A.M., and going to Vietnam."

One could also look to a sympathetic psychiatrist or psychological therapist for another costly escape from the draft. Through a series of visits, a patient could translate his anxiety about being drafted into a psychological trauma that qualified him for an exemption. Mindful of military standards, therapists probed for a variety of mental problems: "You could theoretically be rejected for any neurotic trait from bedwetting to nail-biting." Sometimes, therapists coached patients about the necessary symptoms. "I had only one patient who was denied a psychiatric exemption," a psychiatrist recalled. "He wanted me to say he was crazy, but he wouldn't take the responsibility of acting crazy." A Washington, D.C., psychologist recalled writing a letter for one of his patients:

I described his anxiety and periods of deep depression, but there wasn't any reason why he couldn't have served in Vietnam. The day before his interview, he accidentally cut his wrist opening a jar of pickles. He went to the examination center with my letter and a bandage on his wrist, but he never told anyone how it happened. He got an exemption.

Homosexuality was a common ground for a psychiatric exemption, and one antidraft pamphlet advised how to fake it:

Dress very conservatively for the Army shrinker. Act like a man under tight control. Deny you're a fag, deny it again very quickly, then stop, as if you're buttoning your lip. But find an excuse to bring it back into the conversation again and again, and each time deny it and quickly change the subject. And maybe twice, no more than three times over a half hour interview, just the slightest little flick of the wrist. But above all, never admit it. Even after they're hooked, keep up the denials.

San Francisco draft counselor Paul Harris recalled that "all of my clients who faked it got their exemptions, but they drafted the one fellow who really was gay." One antiwar protester in Chicago was exempted as a homosexual, but he later married and was threatened with induction. He replied that if drafted, he would demonstrate his tendencies beyond any possible doubt at his induction physical. No one called his bluff.

The preinduction physical was a highly regimented process, with long lines of men receiving very brief attention from military doctors. Anyone who drew special attention to himself improved his chances of getting an exemption, if only because he slowed the process down. Peter Simpson suffered from a minor skin rash which he knew was, at best, borderline grounds for an exemption. While everyone else was walking around undressed, he kept wearing his business suit and carried a *Wall Street Journal* under his arm. Simpson displayed so much confidence in his claim that the examiners gave him an exemption.

One way to get special attention was to disrupt the process. Radical draft counselors often encouraged this tactic, "not only because it obstructed the smooth operation of the criminal war machine, but also because it might impress the examiners with your undesirable character traits." One San Francisco youth, tentatively stamped I-A, made a desperate visit to a draft counselor during the lunch recess from his physical. He was advised to "piss on the table" when he saw the psychiatrist. He did, and he got an exemption. In Chicago, an antiwar activist brought seventy-five demonstrators to picket outside during his examination. To keep them from storming the building, examiners summoned the military police, gave the activist a I-Y exemption, and asked him to leave.

Documenting a disqualifying condition or disrupting the process was not necessarily enough to guarantee exemption. Every preinduction examination center interpreted official standards differently, and some were alert to tricks that were popular in their areas. For these reasons, counselors often advised their clients to take advantage of a major loophole in the draft law which existed throughout the war: the right of every registrant to choose the site of his preinduction physical.

The examination process had a built-in bias which favored out-of-state examinees. Examiners had no quotas of their own, but they knew if they failed an unusually large percentage of local youths, they would draw a reaction from nearby draft boards, which did have quotas to fill. However, examiners almost never heard complaints when they disqualified out-of-state youths. Besides, many of the latter were politically oriented students whose disruptive tactics could be avoided if they got what they wanted. At the Boston examination site, for example, graduate students from Harvard and MIT were told, "If you cooperate with us, we'll cooperate with you."

The counselor network kept an up-to-date "book" on which centers were receptive to particular claims. For most of the war, Butte, Montana, was considered an easy mark for anyone with a letter from a doctor, and Little Rock, Arkansas, for anyone with a letter from a psychiatrist. Beckley, West Virginia, was well-known for giving exemptions to "anyone who looked freaked out." A number of famous rock stars avoided the draft by going to Beckley incognito with beads, bare feet, and long hair. By far the most popular place to go for a preinduction physical was Seattle, Washington. In the latter years of the war, Seattle examiners separated people into two groups: those who had letters from doctors or psychiatrists, and those who did not. Everyone with a letter received an exemption, regardless of what the letter said.

The preinduction examination process rewarded careful planning, guile, and disruptive behavior. But if a person came without a letter from his doctor, he was very likely to be declared fit for induction, regardless of any actual medical problem. All but the most obvious physical defects were easy to overlook in the confused environment and mass processing of the examination center, and disadvantaged youths who had not received adequate medical care were often classified I-A. One draftee from a low-income family spent three months in the Army before it was discovered that he was an extreme diabetic. At his preinduction physical, his urine sample had been confused with that of another person, who got the exemption. Blacks and members of other minority groups were the most common victims. In 1966, the only year for which racial data was published, a mentally qualified white youth was 50 percent more likely than his black counterpart to fail the preinduction physical.

Many doctors, dentists, and psychiatrists who specialized in draft avoidance now feel a sense of disquiet about their role during the war. The people they most wanted to help—blacks, low-income youths, and conscientious war resisters who had been denied CO status—were rarely the ones who came to see them: "The people we saw were all middle class. It wasn't that the others didn't have the money. They just never thought of going for professional help." Even at the draft-counseling medical clinic of predominantly black Fisk University, walk-ins were overwhelmingly well-educated, middle-class whites. At a large Chicago clinic, doctors refused to help any white who failed to bring at least one black with him for a medical interview.

Professionals were especially discouraged by the self-centered attitudes of many of the young men who came for help. Dr. Peter Bourne, a psychiatrist working at the time in Atlanta, commented that "some people acted as though all doctors had a moral obligation to help them dodge the draft for nothing." Dr. Bourne counseled people for free, but he sometimes had to refer them to specialists who knew more about certain disqualifying conditions. Later, he heard complaints when the specialists charged $25 to write letters to draft boards. Dr. Herbert Schwartz of Hartford, Connecticut, refused to do draft counseling after consistently encountering "opportunists who felt threatened by the war, but did not oppose the war. They were people without ideals or principles who were just looking for an easy way out."

Yet a number of the professionals were themselves opportunists. Many were far too willing to bend professional principles to help clients connive their way out of the draft. Others had a false view of what they were accomplishing. One counselor said that his goal was to encourage draft avoidance until the government could be provoked into rescinding all deferments and exemptions. "When that happens," he commented, "the sons of the rich will be drafted right along with those of the poor. And then the shoe will begin to pinch the wrong foot." But the impact of draft counseling was exactly the opposite. The burdens of war were shifted even more to the socially and economically disadvantaged.

32
The SDS and Vietnam
NIGEL YOUNG

In the origins of the New Left, both in Britain and America, radical pacifists occupied influential positions and played key roles, but during the 1960s they were faced with the choice of either retaining influence at the expense of their pacifism (the case in the USA) or retaining their pacifism with a consequent loss of influence. Had a nonviolent critique of the spread of national liberation movements been developed early enough, things might have been different, not only in the peace movement, but in the New Left as a whole, including the civil rights movement and political groups like Students for a Democratic Society (SDS). But such was not the case: the result of this theoretical vacuum, the deep compassion for those suffering the rigours of colonial rule or American bombardment, and the lack of effective nonviolent strategies to alleviate these situations was the typical defensive pacifist double-standard position of the later 1960s; nonviolence at home, but tacitly endorsed 'just' violence abroad.

The peace movement's crises of the later 1960s can thus be analysed substantially in terms of the inter-relation between its internal weaknesses and such external factors as the events of 1968, the Third World movements, and identification with groups either promising revolutionary change outside America (like the National Liberation Front, or NLF) or those apparently offering a revolutionary lead at home.

One can trace this capitulation back to the early years of the decade and the response to the Algerian and Cuban revolutions by peace movement leaders. Faced with similar choices in relation to Vietnam in the mid-1960s, the attempt to avoid the roles of victim or executioner became an anguished one.

In the USA, pacifist activists like David Dellinger, (editor of *Liberation* magazine), the historian Staughton Lynd, the veteran peace leader A. J. Muste, Tom Hayden of the newly forming student movement, and David McReynolds of the War Resisters International, each contributors to *Liberation*, were influential on SDS. These movement spokespersons gave prestige to a position on Vietnam (already declared in regard to Cuba) that came close enough to an endorsement of armed struggle; had they held the line at this point, there would have been fewer openings in the movement to the crude anti-imperialist, pro-militarist positions that developed later. Early in 1965 Lynd and the rest of the *Liberation* collective played a key role in generating the Vietnam war protests.

But it was SDS, filling the gap left by the Student Peace Union, which became, almost by accident, first the foremost student peace organization (although foreign policy issues had not been a predominant theme in SDS hitherto) and then, during the course of 1965, the vanguard of a revived national student movement. The SDS decision to hold a demonstration just after the beginning of routine bombing on North Vietnam (February 1965) was fortuitous—taken without foreknowledge of US escalation of the war. It grew rapidly as a result.

Before this, community themes had come prior to campus organizing in SDS, and its involvement in generating the Vietnam war movement was almost an afterthought; but it was in part its involvement with the initial 'Teach-In' movement that focused these protests on the universities and the student constituency.

However, the fact that it was primarily the issue of the Vietnam war that made SDS a major national movement, an issue that SDS was not well equipped to deal with, was not without its political costs. The inter-relation between campus, community, and peace issues was often obscure and uneasy, reflecting the fragility of the early SDS coalition.

As the Vietnam situation deteriorated, and following SDS's April demonstration, Lynd and others, including Muste, Dellinger, and Bob Moses (then secretary of the Student Nonviolent Coordinating Committee) had initiated the ad hoc Assembly of Unrepresented People at Washington, fusing participatory democracy, trans-national initiative, and radical anti-militarism. From this Lynd hoped to develop a full-scale civil disobedience campaign. Three hundred and fifty were arrested in the August civil disobedience; despite SDS's earlier opposition to this method it continued to participate in such protests against the war. As the anti-war movement revived on the issue of Vietnam, it was the symbolism of individual direct action, in some cases the most desperately dramatic and personal kind of self-sacrifice, which expressed the movement's internationalist concerns.

But an early crisis developed and preoccupied SDS as the movement against the war grew during 1965. A split occurred between many of the organizers on the question of relationship to the Vietnam issue and the dangers it posed to long-term grassroots work.

The peace movement as a whole nevertheless related to an alternative counter-institutional strategy; with the Assembly of Unrepresented People of 1965, draft-resistance and tax-refusal projects and local community-based peace groups and centres were moving towards re-possessing aspects of decision-making on key issues of war and peace.

The idea of participatory democracy and counter-institutions fused with the Peace Movement and nonviolent traditions in America in the anti-Vietnam War resistance of 1965. The call for a "people's peace," negotiated by the movement directly with the Vietnamese at the Assembly of Unrepresented People in Washington in August 1965, clearly exemplified the influence of ideas of direct democracy. The Assembly met without 'organization structure or established discipline'; no 'single policy was predetermined and imposed; all policies could be established or modified by the participants'.

Muste and Lynd demonstrated the continuities of nonviolent civil disobedience and a movement's right to resist injustice, even at the risk of undermining respect for the rule of law.

The development of the anti-war movement and SDS involvement was a major factor in the recession in the community projects after 1965, and some argued for shifting the focus to the role of the poor as white and black mercenaries in Asia and the Asian victims of these American executioners. They also stressed the diversion of funds, 'from welfare to warfare'.

Tension mounted between those who focused mainly on anti-war action, using the campus as a base, and those who focused on student power, student issues, and organizing that constituency per se; these two tendencies were fused in many of the anti-draft actions and opposition to army and navy recruiters. The SDS anti-draft exams of 1966 did not herald a forthright SDS leadership of the draft resistance movement but did emphasize the needs and interests of students.

SDS became less clearly 'interest oriented' in the demonstrations against Dow Chemicals (then the main napalm manufacturer), the Central Intelligence Agency (CIA), and government representatives. In addition, encouraged by Progressive Labor (PL), SDS was involved in increasing opposition to the Reserve Officer Training Corps (ROTC), taking up where radical pacifists had left off in the early 1960s; substantial confrontations with the military occurred at Berkeley and Chicago in 1966 and 1967. Following these, SDS chapters and other campus groups launched a call for the severing of university ties with the military.

SDS participation in the growth of draft-resistance opened up major debates within the whole of the New Left, and specifically between the resistance and anti-resistance wings of SDS. A draft-resistance movement represented both a political and moral revulsion to the war and war in general, with specific objections to Vietnam policy and the Selective Service. In it, individual conscientious resistance was combined and contrasted with collective solidarity and organized civil disobedience.

But despite its apparent militancy, SDS was still nervous of direct action; the leadership initially was chary even of civil disobedience: in 1965 its National Council had turned down Lynd's Washington civil disobedience proposals.

The Resistance alone among the anti-war groups and tendencies retained its morale, unity, and integrity in this period of movement crisis. This was largely because it was rooted in undramatic, morally based, personal action and a nonviolent ethic. It combined mutual aid with individual responsibility and local organizing. It is significant that, from the start, it had least need of identification with a foreign military force, such as that of the NLF or North Vietnamese, and did not in fact concern itself with supporting them.

It may well be, as one commentator (Howard Zinn) suggested, that some Resistance members would have equally resisted the oppressive conscription systems of both the Vietnamese combatants, in the North and South, even though the penalty for such resistance was often—as from both sides during the 1968 Tet offensive—summary execution; they may well have identified with the actions of their Buddhist counterparts, resisting even to the death the forcible conscriptions of Thieu and the NLF and deserting from both armies.

Yet it is a tragic irony that despite this potentially common identity, the Resistance failed to make stronger trans-national links with those resisters in Vietnam closest to them in spirit and action, e.g. the young, militant and neutralist Buddhists, often monks, using nonviolent techniques against successive Saigon regimes. Calling for immediate ceasefire, the 'Third Way' monks, nuns and social workers encouraged draft-resistance against both armies, refusing to fight themselves and sheltering thousands of deserters. Their fearless opposition to the militarism of both Saigon and Hanoi led to often fatal results; the destruction of pagodas, assassination and execution or mass imprisonment of Buddhist workers, or else wounding or involuntary exile.

Yet even Resistance leaders like Lynd, with his Quaker background and his long record of civil disobedience, failed to publicly identify with this thoroughgoing and massive anti-militarism by ordinary Vietnamese, and instead juggled with inaccurate formulae that endorsed the 'just struggle' of 'the Vietnamese'.

That the Western anti-war movements failed to identify with these forces until it was far too late[1] can only partly be explained away by their ignorance of these groups' existence and activities, and the fact that the National establishments and the Left establishment both presented the war as a simple dichotomy between polar military formations. It was a symptom of the tragedy of nonviolence in the late 1960s[2] that those Vietnamese of similar style and politics should actually be consistently excluded or eliminated from peace movement platforms in the West, or even accused of CIA links....

That this occurred, it has been suggested, had a great deal to do with the changing leadership role of *Liberation*, its entanglement with SDS and influence on New Left attitudes to the Vietnam war. Of those associated with the magazine, Muste, Lynd, and Dellinger and later even McReynolds, drifted away from absolute pacifism in the critical years after Cuba; of the four, only Lynd, the least absolute to begin with, maintained some elements of a genuine pacifist critique. *Liberation* itself flirted with the cult of violence surrounding both the Cuban revolution and the NLF; and those caught up in this process, like Dellinger and McReynolds—who had initially been closer to absolute pacifism—moved away from it; Dellinger in 1965 significantly refers to both the 'heroic forces' of the 'Fidelistas' and 'the Viet Cong.'

Reactionary or oppressive roles by other groups than the USA were increasingly and flagrantly ignored, as the growing anti-imperialism of SDS in turn reinforced these double-standard tendencies. Tom Hayden, bridging SDS and *Liberation*, although not a pacifist, had also at the outset been ostensibly opposed to 'militarism and nationalism',[3] but he quickly and easily came to terms with both the militarism and nationalism of the NLF; the visits of most of the *Liberation* group and Hayden to Cuba and North Vietnam appeared to affirm and take this identification one stage further.

It is ironic that it was this very weakening of their pacifism that was a factor in enabling such erstwhile pacifists around *Liberation* (Muste, Dellinger, Lynd and McReynolds) to take decisive leadership roles in the American peace movement during the following years.[4] Muste's concern with 'neutralization' of potential world flash points led him naturally to urge a unilateral US ceasefire in Vietnam, negotiations and re-unification, independent of his general 'Third Camp' politics. Lynd's appearance in the leadership of an alliance of SDS and *Liberation*, forming in 1965 the first major anti-Vietnam war coalition, was a significant early indication of this new development. Whilst most older Pacifist groupings and traditional peace groups tended to keep aloof from this SDS-initiated coalition, some Old Left groups, such as the Socialist Workers' Party (SWP) with their slogan 'Bring the Boys Home Now', as well as Muste and some of the radical pacifists round *Liberation*, joined.

Having been involved with this initial Vietnam coalition during 1965, by 1966 and right up to his death at eighty-two in 1967, Muste played a leading role in both the National Co-ordinating Committee against the War, and the Spring Mobilization Committees—a mantle that was to pass on to the shoulders of Dellinger, Muste's chief lieutenant. But no one walked the knife-edge closer than Lynd; calling himself a 'personal' pacifist, he made distinctions enabling him to adopt positions on the Vietnam war in which his political pacifism became highly selective, since it was not derived from any overall analysis of war and militarism, but from personal religious preference.

Lynd's equivocation on the Vietnam war primarily stemmed from the common belief that the USA were altogether more culpable than the NLF, the DRVN (North Vietnamese) and their allies. Thus the outcome of the 'struggle' was 'not a matter of indifference'. As a result he took a stretcher-bearer attitude to one of the armies, maintaining that his personal pacifism was compatible with non-combatant participation in a 'just war'.

This standpoint, adopted by several *Liberation* editors, endorsing both the 'just war' thesis, and a non-combatant role in that war, re-occupied positions previously rejected by radical pacifists. In so doing it left any anti-militarist analysis in tatters, and a truly pacifist movement virtually leaderless. This subsequently had enormous implications both for the Vietnam war movement itself and the NL generally.

However, unlike some of his colleagues, Lynd did not thereby abandon all his critical senses in relation to the armed solutions of the NLF/DRVN, and he showed this in dissociating himself from the bias and selectivity of the 'War Crimes Tribunal' when it refused to entertain substantial evidence of terror and atrocities by the NLF and the North Vietnamese Army. Lynd also insisted on sending medical aid to *all* civilians and combatants (unlike the Medical Aid Committees) and condemned terror on both sides although he wrote that one should not 'absolutely condemn revolutionary terror' (no reasoning given). At the same time, he expressed the hope that we would react to torture by the NLF 'exactly as to torture by the other side',[5] here again the fatal ambiguity, if not contradiction, that characterized Muste's position was also evident in Lynd.

Muste, like the others, expressed a surprisingly simplistic view of the relationship between a nonviolent revolution and the attempted military revolution by some sections of the Vietnamese people. He almost implied that they might only differ over means. Yet Muste had, over the years, consistently criticized various revolutionaries and political sectarians for separating means and ends, or believing that after a military victory or after 'the revolution' 'things' would be different.

The *démarche* that began with the *Liberation* pacifists and later briefly included Daniel Berrigan accelerated, each new convert finding some reason for identification with the NLF, and fewer taking note of the non-NLF, non-Communist resistance groups in Vietnam, such as the Buddhists. By 1966, Muste had clearly qualified his previously non-aligned and fairly consistent pacifist position, elaborating on the Vietnam issue an apparently contradictory stance; on the one hand he claimed that he still 'rejected all war and organised violence regardless of who or what nation or movement resorts to it', and that he did 'not accept and condone violence on the part of any people, any group'. On the other hand, he believed that a 'distinction between the violence of liberation movements' (i.e. the NLF) and 'imperialist' violence has to be made and allowed the pacifist to 'support some who are engaged in violent action' because their violence was morally superior. This elusive distinction between refusal to condone violence and yet willingness to support those who used it laid the fatal, if ambiguous, foundations for a shift from an anti-militarist analysis into an anti-imperialist one. It was a drift that moved not only *Liberation*, but substantial sections of the movement, across Camus's 'tragic dividing line', from pacifism to militarism.

This change of position was reflected in the evolution of two distinct policy positions on how the war could be brought to an end (as distinct from a third calling for an unambiguous NLF military victory—which few in the New Left, at this stage, were yet prepared to do).[6]

The first more general position was to call for a ceasefire with the slogan 'Stop the Killing Now' and implied an agreed or unilateral cessation of military activity by the USA, pending withdrawal. The second position, taken by Lynd, Dellinger and McReynolds, was that since the USA had no right to be in Vietnam it should just unilaterally withdraw, even if this led to an eventual end to the war by Communist victory. This latter position either did not call for a ceasefire *at all*, or called for it only after unconditional troop withdrawal or an agreement to so withdraw. Though these subtleties were largely lost on the larger peace movement, it became clear that those who held out for unilateral and unconditional withdrawal by the USA without ceasefire gave overwhelming political and military advantage to a specific armed formation in taking over the South Vietnamese, with heavy support continuing from its big-power allies. The arguments amongst pacifists centred on whether any self-styled pacifists could take positions either way which actually meant the continuation of killing, and thus implicit support for a military solution.[7]

The parallel argument over 'realism' was as to whether, on the one hand, the USA would in any case accept a withdrawal *without* a prior ceasefire, and whether, on the other, the NLF and the North Vietnamese (DRVN) would ever accept a ceasefire without agreement on withdrawal; this was of course eventually the nub of the Paris peace negotiations, but even before that, it provided a sort of watershed for the peace movement both in the West and in Vietnam itself.

Though many in the movement did not firmly commit themselves or make their position plain (this was largely true, for example, of the generalized Trotskyist call for troop withdrawal, without calling for NLF victory), it opened the way for an eventual and substantial identification with what in 1965 was still the slogan of only a handful of Maoists: 'Victory to the NLF'....

In 1966, both SNCC and SDS issued statements entirely uncritical of the 'other side' (also referred to as 'forces for liberation').[8] From then on, an increasingly one-sided view of the war developed, which concealed the deep contradiction between, for example, support for participatory democracy at home, and support of indisputably authoritarian regimes and movements abroad—formations that were quite clearly not dedicated to the principle of 'let the people decide'. In the long run, this identification helped not only to undermine the belief in participatory democracy, but also to tempt many to jump out of the frying pan of US imperialism into the fire of a new oppositional Stalinism.

Thus almost from the start, criticism of the Vietnam war by the New Left excluded critiques of authoritarian leftism.[9] One of the left social democrats critical of SDS—Bayard Rustin—prophetically characterized the Lynd-SDS coalition of 1965 as being one between those giving covert, and those giving explicit, support to the NLF.

In 1965, SDS went so far as to vote to remove any 'anti-totalitarian' statements or criticism of the NLF from its constitution, and restrict its criticism to the policy of the USA. From this moment, SDS's attack on 'anti-Communism', as Kahn pointed out, failed to differentiate between criticism of, for example, the NLF by democratic libertarian socialists, and criticism by people in the establishment or on the far Right [10]

The New Left failed in this context to create criteria by which to judge either the ideas or the methods of such movements and regimes. The very word or concept 'totalitarianism' was rejected because of its previous deployment as a convergent Cold War term. New Left leaders also argued, with some substance, that since Communism was no organized force in American politics, then domestically the question of pro- or anti-Communism was irrelevant.

But whilst in domestic terms this was possibly true, in international terms, particularly in relationship to Hanoi, and the NLF, and to a lesser degree China and Cuba and Russia, it created deep ideological ambiguity. Popular front politics was no longer an organized phenomenon associated with a strong Communist Party, but rather an atmosphere or milieu in which adulation of Communist leaders and movements could grow unchallenged. Double standards in the Vietnam war, an uncritical attitude to the concept of 'liberation', and a failure to condemn excesses by America's opponents inevitably ensued. All this indicates the growth of an extensive, emotive and predominant anti-Americanism that was a principal basis for the growing unwillingness to criticize any authoritarian regimes and movements on the Left, including the NLF. After all, even if 'national liberation' turned out to be the same type of double-talk phrase as 'free world', at least it represented an effective stick to beat America with.

But equally, this shift represents the revival, encouraged by [Che] Guevara and mentors such as [Herbert] Marcuse and [Jean Paul] Sartre (and to a lesser degree [Franz] Fanon), of a revolutionary morality that is selective in its criticism and uses relative standards for judging 'liberation'. Sartre had defended revolutionary regimes at the War Crimes Tribunal, arguing that opposition to them is a form of treason, just as criticism of bourgeois states is morally necessary. The standards of individuals (e.g. freedom) are irrelevant; in such a debate, it was argued that these formations could not be judged by the same moral criteria as bourgeois states; whereas the errors of the former can be rectified, the crimes of the latter spring from their inherent evil. Indeed such was the horror at the American presence, and the much greater destructive capacity of Western militarism, that undoubted evidence of Communist excesses was neither sought out, nor countenanced.

The stunning success of North Vietnamese propaganda amongst young radicals[11] is not entirely to be explained in terms of public relations. Some within the New Left not only wished to believe certain things—they were as willing to distort, select, omit and exaggerate the facts of the war, as part of their dedication to the cause it represented. Such a conscious development was nothing new in the history of the Left, but it did represent a departure for the New Left, and re-enacted the deception and self-deception of the Comintern years.

Probably when the New Left identified with the NLF and the 'whole Vietnamese people', and argued that their resort to arms had *only* occurred after all other channels had been blocked, this was sometimes sincere. On the other hand, many were undoubtedly encouraged by both the Maoist and post-Marcusian views that propaganda must be met with counter-propaganda, lies by lies, distortions by distortions; it was certainly a view that the Cuban and Vietnamese regimes seemed to share in practice; 'truth' was whatever served the cause of the revolution.

The New Left's precipitate descent into propaganda, largely born out of compassion and frustration, was partly based on the felt need to counter-balance biased information with slanted material on the other side. If any radicals still wondered whether more than two parties were involved in the Vietnam conflict, their doubts had to be removed and the 'David and Goliath' image reinforced. When in December 1966 SDS first used the formulation 'Vietnamese people in their struggle for self-determination', it may well have been an unselfconscious, well-intentioned phrasing. But such resolutions helped to eliminate the greys from the Indo-China situation,[12] and actively discouraged alternative modes of resistance.

The newspeak of 'people's war' would probably have been challenged by the early New Left; however, by the later 1960s, such formulae were not. The consideration of third or fourth choices in Vietnam (i.e. involving the millions of progressive Buddhists and others) was thus discounted. The majority disappeared, as in other wars, between two forces, two pro-paganda machines. Much of the New Left consequently became aligned with one of them as a lesser evil,[13] purveying images, symbols and slogans direct from Vietnamese materials, and making any balanced or accurate view of the war increasingly elusive.

It became typical for radicals to hold up Vietnam as an exception to any generalized criticisms of 'revolutionary degeneration'; traditional 'class analyses' of the peasant role proved inadequate, however, since they ignored the conscious nationalist manipulation of the rural masses by party cadres. As one radical critic put it:

> the NLF is controlled by an incipient bureaucratic ruling class. The fact that the mass base of the NLF lies among the peasantry does not mean that the NLF is controlled by the peasantry, nor that an NLF victory will establish peasant control of the state.[14]

The charge of 'Stalinism' regularly levelled against both the North Viet-namese and the NLF had to do with the reproduction of the Stalinist organizational imperatives and an apparatus based on deception, relent-less regimentation and precisely managed terrorism that recalled similar excesses in China and Russia.[15]

Yet the imagery of a popular, spontaneous and decentralized 'strug-gle' in which the NLF and the 'people of Vietnam' were synonymous, persisted long after the TET offensive of 1968. The anti-war movement had accepted an imagery of the war drawn from the early 1960s, and preserved it long after the reality had become transformed. Indeed there was plenty of evidence around in the early 1960s to suggest that Ho Chi Minh's regime (like the NLF) probably had one of the more brutalized and repressive, as well as highly bureaucratized, leaderships in the history of Communism.[16] Its strong links to Stalin and Stalinism in the past and its reproduc-tion of Stalinist ideals and models in the present were beyond doubt.

The 'Titoist' interpretation of the DRVN was harder to sustain after Tet; by 1968 there was substantially less autonomy; the war became firmly situated in an international power struggle (where it was 'solved') and its continuation depended critically on Russian and Chinese arms.[17] Even while the image of NLF independence from the North was being accepted in the New Left, it was becoming less true (i.e. from 1960 onward). Equally, the independence of both NLF and DRVN from Russian and China was being accepted on the Left, at a time when this too was in rapid decline.

But whilst the New Left was initially partly accurate in stressing a relative national autonomy of the NLF—e.g. independence of direct control by Hanoi before the early 1960s (let alone by Peking or Moscow)—its analysis of the internal structure of the war, and of its relationship to those external models, was always wholly inflexible and inadequate.

To say that at one stage the NLF and DRVN were not 'puppets' of the great powers, and had interests of their own, independent of one another, was one thing. It was quite another to deny influences and similarities, or to deny that the war steadily drew the North, and subsequently Russia and China, into deep involvement; increasingly the context altered the nature of the internal struggle until finally it could only be sustained or halted at their will.

Indeed, the increasing conventional fire-power of the NLF/DRVN forces and the degree to which the North, armed by its great power allies, took over the main operations of the war, made almost any kind of 'guerilla' analysis factually irrelevant. On the other hand, this development merely confirmed processes—bureaucratic and militarist tendencies for example—that had already clearly existed in the first Indo-China war, and lay at the foundation of the Hanoi regime.

Rather than allow the original illusion to be shattered, the 'David and Goliath' imagery of the Vietnamese war was maintained, enabling Western radicals to identify with an Asian pygmy struggling against the imperialist giant. This version of the war, e.g., an ill-equipped peasantry brutally oppressed and spontaneously struggling against monstrous odds, documented by pictures of black pyjamas and old rifles pitted against long-range artillery and napalm, projected an 'underdog' image which went down well with the New Left and liberals alike. At one point, significant of this, Lynd used the extraordinary phrase 'the oppression of Vietnamese guerillas'.

The myth springing from all this, that the struggle was a spontaneous, mass-based upsurge against Saigon and the USA, that half-a-million troops of the most advanced military-industrial power were stalemated by popular heroism, obscured the tragic reality of a North Vietnamese numerical superiority on the ground enabling an appallingly profligate use of life in combat (almost as careless as the Communists in Korea); that it was essentially *the pattern of control*—over masses of men and resources—that had emerged North and South that was able to meet and check American power on its own terms. Although at hideous costs, the growing political infrastructure and expanding industrial and armed strength of the North, together with substantial Eastern-bloc aid, reinforced the immense organizational effort in the South, and marked the increasingly 'conventional' nature of the struggle. The guerilla armies, far from the romantic image of decentralized spontaneity, turned out to be small versions of the military machines of the great empires, East and West; carefully wrought bureaucratic, military apparatuses.[18]

Thus the image (never the whole truth) was overtaken by the reality of the increasing conventionalization of the war. Such imagery had depended on a notion of voluntary, majority support and sympathy for military struggle; after 1968, and probably a good deal earlier, evidence to sustain this was also lacking.

Between 1960–3, in the last three years of Diem's regime, military resistance, although Communist-led, had been clearly widespread and often spontaneous. But it was mass Buddhist opposition that had actually led to Diem's overthrow. However, in the first years of the military rising (1957–60) and again after 1963, this kind of unified resistance did not appear; thereafter the NLF increasingly depended on force and terror rather than consent in mobilizing opposition (as Tet confirmed, much later).

The evanescent nature of the NLF's mass popularity also created major dilemmas and problems for that informed section of the New Left which now openly supported the NLF. On the one hand, it could accept the necessity for terror and accept the subordination of means to ends, justified by the same 'revolutionary morality'. Or, on the other hand, it could deny that this terror existed and maintain an imagery of the war as a 'spontaneous' people's struggle. The first 'realistic' position was taken by a militant minority (e.g. PL) and eventually was used to justify terror in America itself: the second, that adopted by sections of the more liberal, mainstream Vietnam war movement, was reinforced by Eastern bloc propaganda.[19]

Many in the New Left seemed unwilling to relinquish an idealized image of the NLF, a force 'respecting and respected' by the 'people'. This impression even survived the events of Tet and the use of civilians as hostages; Oglesby could still call the protracted militarized insurrection in Vietnam 'as honest a revolution as you can find anywhere'. Since the movement leaders had become unwilling to adapt their theory to the facts (i.e. that the NLF *was* top-down, élitist, centralizing, bureaucratic and often brutalized, and the DRVN very deeply influenced and imbued by Stalinism), the facts were adapted to the theory, an anti-bureaucratic movement from the bottom up. Thus it was continually claimed that the 'struggle' had developed not as a planned strategy of armed takeover, but only as a heroic and instinctive resistance to US aggression....[20]

But even before open identification, it had been easy enough to interpret anti-militarist activity as 'anti-imperialist'; indeed leaders were often glad to sophisticate simple anti-war activity with that title; after all, was not anything which hurt the war-machine hurting American imperialism? Many Left papers were glad to write up events as anti-imperialist, even if the main impulse of those who took part was anti-militarist, outraged opposition to sophisticated methods of killing, or hatred of war as an institution; but Marxists claimed to know its 'real' meaning. Even if the motivation of the demonstrators was closer to pacifist instincts than Old Left ones, the 'historical significance' of their action lay in its contribution to the success of the military opponent in Asia. Such interpretations raised many questions: was napalm 'neutral'? If 'anti-imperialists' started using the same 'oppressive means', then would these protests against them then cease (as they tended to after 1969)? Or would anti-war groups reject usage of such weapons by either side (as a principled radical pacifism might be expected to do)?[21]

In such moral and ideological confusion, it was those New Left groups least obsessed with anti-imperialist analysis which retained their identity longest; draft-resistance had a myriad of motivations, but endorsement of 'anti-imperialist struggle' was the last and least of them. This is not to say that among the groups like the Resistance there was any lack of awareness of the oppressive role of American world power, but there was a sense that *all* imperialisms—and not just imperialism, but militarism and authoritarianism as well—were being opposed. The concept of 'imperialism' was viewed by them as yet another slogan—an inevitable oversimplification; it was enough to oppose the war-machine where it stood; if that made an impact abroad, it was a welcome, but subordinate, dimension to their activity.

Certainly for a considerable time there had been an awareness throughout the New Left of the inevitability of further wars after Vietnam, and a belief, expressed in the then current phrase 'the seventh war from now', that a U.S. peace movement would only actually prevent the US involvement in such conflicts in the very long term. The point is that initially this had *not* implied any one-dimensioned imperialist analysis, nor had it called for 'one, two, three...(let alone seven)...Vietnams'—the slogan that emerged, however briefly, in 1968 and 1969....

The one-sided view of the revolutionary movements of the underdeveloped countries, the unwillingness, or inability to see them as they really were, was perhaps, as an erstwhile SDS leader charged, a reflection of the New Left's own restless search for a 'revolutionary tradition which would give it memories and spirit'.

As Lasch argues, under the influence of imported ideologies, models and myths of imminent revolution, the New Left eventually 'loses sight of its own peculiar traditions of local autonomy and democratic decision-making'.[22] Libertarian instincts fail to be translated from the campuses, communities and ghettoes of America or Europe to a systematic appraisal of Third World movements, free of guilt, self-repudiation and self-delusion. Thus the gut anti-élitism of the New Left organizers becomes aligned with the self-conscious élitism of organizers of the Third World's poor and peasantry. The democratic praxis of the movement becomes fatally intertwined with the bureaucratic and even pacifists and libertarians in the movement had not capitulated to propagandized versions of the war. The pronouncements by Dellinger, McReynolds, Hayden and the radical philosopher, Noam Chomsky in particular, made this possible (even Muste's early visit to North Vietnam was easy to misinterpret). The key importance of these identifications with élitist or bureaucratic military leaderships of the Third World guerilla armies is revealed by their reflexive impact on the domestic movement of the New Left. Openly organized support for wars of liberation did not fully emerge till 1967; in that year, the small 'revolutionary contingent' with miniature Viet Cong flags appeared on the April marches in New York; during the next three years, however, they became a sizeable and assertive minority on demonstrations.

Had NLF styles in organization and leadership entered the Movement in 1965, they would have faced immediate rejection; but the transition in two or three years is dramatic. The NLF flags and portraits of Ho or other rather superficial symbolic identifications with revolutionary war remained a fringe element in 1966 and 1967. But tolerated by a 'non-exclusionary' movement in these years, and in the context of a growing shame and anger focused on Vietnam, by 1968 and 1969 such styles and identifications became the predominant tone of many demonstrations, along with all the paraphernalia of pseudo-militarism or the attempts to create a revolutionary 'discipline'....

The anti-imperialist stance had its most significant impact on the New Left through the changing nature of the Vietnam war movement. Initially the New Left attitude to 'liberation wars' in Asia was the liberal one, of minimizing the military potential of such communist regimes and movements. Typical was the SDS critique of 1966, which reassured the establishment that the domino theory was a myth and that US withdrawal was safe because there would be no expansion of China or North Vietnam in South East Asia if South Vietnam was abandoned.[23]

By 1969, this position was almost entirely reversed; not only was such extension of the war admitted as likely, it was welcomed as the impending victory of the Indo-China 'People's War'. The proliferation of liberation wars throughout Laos, Thailand, and Cambodia was endorsed as a form of radical domino theory. The slogan 'one, two, three, many Vietnams' taken up by many militants, expressed this *volte-face* into an 'anti-imperialist' militarism: the imperialist powers must be met on their own terms, on their own ground.

This tended inevitably to the situation where a political blank cheque was written for any 'anti-imperialist' movement that happened along, and large sections of the peace movement had shuffled off the complicated and often unrewarding burdens of non-aligned internationalism in favor of this open-ended call for 'national self-determination'. Oglesby, a key figure in this transition to an anti-imperialist stance, traces the route from a 'peace movement' in the traditional sense, towards an 'anti-peace' movement favoring continued armed struggle, rather than a ceasefire agreement (SDS in 1969).[24]

By this time the very word 'peace' had become suspect. From sympathy for the NLF, the New Left evolved through anti-imperialism to support for sundry Third World armies; it was a transition aided and abetted of course by a scatter of Marxist-Leninisms, official and unofficial: Maoists—the Progressive Labor Party (PLP) and its front organization on the campus (1964–5), proved the earliest and most effective anti-imperialist, 'pro-liberation war' groups within the 'anti-war' movement.

Whether on the basis of guilt, misinformation, physical distance, wishful thinking or double standards, this identification with Third World liberation movements became widespread by the end of the decade. It was based on what the movement commentator James Weinstein called self-repudiation and had 'the implicit idea of redemption through identification with one of the true, or key revolutionary agents', whether 'ghetto-blacks, freaks, youth-as-a-class (students), industrial-workers or colonial-revolutionaries'. It was a result of the unresolved dilemma of agency (previously analysed)[26] and the apparent failure to communicate to the more immediate constituencies and communities. For SDS, 'students and déclassé intellectuals became strictly appendages or tutors to the "real" social forces'[27] For some it was an excuse not to organize at all.

There were, however, many in the Movement who resisted these tendencies; an underground paper editorialized:

> The sooner SDS gets back to white America and changes that [the better]... forget about Mao, China, Ho, the NLF: forget about Che, Debray and even forget about Fanon, Malcolm, Huey....

James Weinstein maintained that the effect of such identifications had jettisoned some major tenets of the movement; for example that 'radicalism is based on awareness of one's own oppression' and that 'popular participation in the process of decision-making is central to radical politics'. This abandonment meant their replacement by the Leninist élite-vanguard model of revolutionary politics (at least in theory), older versions of class, or the prime emphasis on military action.[28] Accompanying this, as can be argued in the case of the Weatherman faction, for some in the New Left the only political role available to Western white radicals was as *francs tireurs* for the Third World struggles or commandos behind enemy lines.

Strong parallels exist between such positions and those adopted by writers such as Fanon, Marcuse and Sartre, not least in their abandonment of the Western proletariat in favour of other agencies,[29] and their faith in the outcasts and lumpen proletarians of the Third World. These analogies, imitations and transplants were all rooted in a belief—or a hope—that the post-industrial and pre-industrial struggles could somehow link hands, merge, or become a unified cause. But such a scenario created thoroughgoing ambivalence as to the role of the metropolitan movement. Was it a revolutionary movement in its own right or merely a support group for the Third World? 'The rootless detached shock troops of other peoples' revolutionary movements' following programmes designed for fundamentally different societies?[30] Either way, did it merely imitate Third World movements, or did it actually pursue the same tactics?

Some of the worst failures of the Movement can be traced to this kind of mimicry, or implementation of the programme of another movement outside the realities of its own time and place. As the black critic Julius Lester pointed out, 'Ho and Mao and Fidel, each used Marxist-Leninism to suit his own particular problems'.[31] But exaggerated versions of military action, over-emphasizing the role of militarism in politics, whilst it reproduced the press version of Che Guevara's ideas, bore little or no relationship to those of ordinary Americans, and their needs.

The switch in Movement language from the term 'freedom' to the more negative 'liberation'[32] represents in part the growing identification with liberation struggles abroad. But more than this, it is symptomatic of the growing crises relating to internal attitudes to freedom; glorification of the Third World is associated with increasing self-censorship within the Movement as far as national liberation wars or 'progressive' regimes are concerned. In the unwillingness to criticize Chinese or Vietnamese policies, in the apparent indifference to the degeneration of the Cuban revolution, its émigrés and 40,000 political prisoners, or its cultural and sexual persecutions, this one-dimensional attitude to freedom in 'revolutionary' contexts betrays a further reversion to standard Old Left procedure.

This, a failure of intellect and imagination by the New Left in relation to the people of the Third World, presages its increasing internal crisis. Just as it settles for an Old Left solution in the Third World, it begins to turn to Old Left solutions at home. Slowly but steadily, the Movement itself begins to aspire organizationally, and even resemble or imitate, 'the autocratic bureaucracies of the Stalinist period against which SDS and other groups had originally rebelled'. The Movement becomes more centralist, more militarist, and in those organizations which leant towards a more disciplined para-Leninist organization, or for those joining existing Leninist organizations, more bureaucratic.

These authoritarian tendencies in the Movement, were in part an attempt to 'catch up with' an authoritarian reality in the Third World movements; since the initial identification had been made on the basis of a libertarian ideal—and compassion for the mass-base from which these armies were recruited—profound adjustments were necessary. In this way, the prevailing guilt about imperialism, and the militarism of America, together with compassion for Third World peasant peoples opens a trap. Guilt and shame, as the sociologist Todd Gitlin argued, although an antidote to privilege, become poisonous in large doses. Compassion on its own proved a snare that had led much of the Old Left into inhumanity, and Vietnam in cumulative intensity now threatened to do the same for the New.[33]

NOTES

1. Daniel Berrigan and the FOR both strongly identified with the Buddhists but only at a late stage did this become widespread in the peace movement (Adam Roberts had advocated this even in the early 1960s in the pages of *Peace News*).

2. See Thich Nhat Hanh *et al.* and other Buddhist writers on this exclusion: *Peace News Fellowship* and also in *Le Lotus* (their overseas peace newsletter). McReynolds both supported their exclusion and opposed even a temporary ceasefire to enable humanitarian tasks to be performed.

3. E.g. in the Port Huron Statement.

4. As well as A. J. Muste, Dellinger, Lynd and McReynolds, the *Liberation* group also involved Paul Goodman, Barbara Deming, Sid Lens, Nat Hentoff, Mulford Sibley and (until 1966) Bayard Rustin, who were all more sceptical of the Cuban and Vietnamese revolutions. It also maintained contact with older socialists like Fromm, Norman Thomas, and Irving Howe; as well as with the younger Leftists from SDS, like Tom Hayden. McReynolds, initially critical of communism and totalitarianism, was pragmatic and even reformist (he once lined up with Rustin) yet seems to have shifted the most sharply on these issues.

5. See S. Lynd in J. Finn (ed.), *Protest, Pacifism and Politics*, p. 223. Presumably implying that he would not absolutely condemn either. See also Lynd's letter to *Liberation* about the War Crimes Tribunal. As an example of the propagandistic role of 'Medical Aid', see the *Newsletter* of the British Medical Aid for Vietnam group.

6. Nevertheless, SDS's utter naïveté about the war at this stage is symbolized by a song about 'Strategic Hamlets' (written by Al Haber's wife in 1965): 'Before I'll be fenced in, I'll vote for Ho Chi Minh and go home to the north and be free' (cited in K. Sale, *History of SDS*, p. 178).

7. Since 1945, pacifism has undoubtedly found itself profoundly compromised by successive wars of liberation, faced by the armed strategies of the FLN in Algeria, of Castro and Guevara, the Biafran and other African military struggles, Bangladesh, the Palestinian guerillas and the IRA in Northern Ireland, etc. In this last case the arguments around the 'British Withdrawal' campaign run somewhat parallel to those on the Vietnam issue, i.e. simple withdrawal vs. ceasefire and negotiated withdrawal.

8. See SNCC/SDS statement on NLF in Sale, op. cit. In adopting such a strong stance, SDS was probably marginally influenced by the formation of M2M on an anti-imperialist, pro-Chinese, pro-Cuban (Maoist-Castroite) ticket in 1964.

9. An exception was Gail Kelly of the SPU—'Who are the Viet Cong?', *Peace News*, 1966.

10. See Clecak's remarks, op. cit. pp. 304–5, and T. Kahn, 'The Problem of the New Left, *Commentary*, 1966.

11. The evidence suggests that Ho was, after 1968, much more effective in deceiving the Western NL than Vietnam's peasantry about the nature of the war. The propaganda from Hanoi and its allies certainly played a role in the earlier development of the movement against the American presence, e.g. 1964–6.

12. As I argued elsewhere at the time 'War, National Liberation and the State',

> The war is being sustained by two rather large coalitions of groups of Vietnamese 'people' fighting against each other with outside help, and with a third rather larger group (mainly peasants) indifferent to the outcome or preferring neither. There is a relationship between leaders and led to be examined, and a reality which is much more complicated than the formula: struggle between the *people of Vietnam* and the American government.
>
> Such a formula clearly begs the question of the identification of the NLF with the 'people of Vietnam' (a slogan not a description).

13. In understanding the emergence of this Manichean choice, it is worth recognizing that most NL activists do not seem to have known that other popular options even existed, because of the degree to which the establishment and the Old Left alike presented the war as a simple military struggle between two sides. But one of the more sinister elements in the Vietnam tragedy was that this essentially *third force* option was not even allowed to enter radical debate between 1965 and 1968. Here again those libertarian pacifists, aware of the Buddhist struggle against Diem, and of the continuing size of the Buddhist movement, have something to explain. In new contexts, largely unaware of its nature and the immense difficulties of developing strategies that were appropriate or realistic, the radical pacifist wing of the NL still had few justifications for this apostasy.

14. M. Oppenheimer, *Urban Guerrilla*, p. 39 and I. Howe, *The Radical Papers*, p.322. The NL was correct in so far as, like other peasants in other revolutions and wars, some Vietnamese were persuaded to support the intermediate aims of the revolutionary élites. But building a centralized, industrial state—the implied objective of new leadership groups—is not the preference of any peasant people; indeed it amounts to conscious self-elimination in fact (certainly in a cultural if not physical sense). Vietnam, a traditionally fragmented society whose disparate groups had shown little support for central authority of any kind, initially supported this decentralist impulse which worked strongly in favor of opposition groups like the Communists, who were seen to be opposing Saigon. The war thus grew on a decentralist basis in alliance with regional and ethnic groups, but this support became decreasingly voluntary as the NLF and later the PRG began to construct its own system of authority—including eventually an alternative central authority—in the countryside. See also Bob Potter, 'Vietnam: Whose Victory?', *Solidarity*, 1973, for a somewhat belated libertarian socialist analysis.

15. See Potter, ibid., on Ho's close links with Stalinism.

16. See Bernard Fall, *The Two Vietnams*, Pall Mall Press, 1965.

17. In the early stages of the second Vietnam war there was some evidence that weapons used by the NLF (as distinct from the divisions from North Vietnam) were American, captured from the Saigon army. This gradually changed, however, as Chinese and Russian support increased, and supplies from the North intensified.

18. Oppenheimer, op. cit., and Roszak, op. cit., p. 77; cf. also Thich Nhat Hanh, *The Lotus in the Sea of Fire*, SCM, 1967. Since these are revolutions that liberate the forces of modernity, the mobilization and organization of men and resources, and the centralization of control in a context of nationalism and technological development linked to military action, they must be imposed from outside—by conquest, by the transformation of feudalism, the intervention of state or urban-trained revolutionary cadres—working as military organizers (see Appendix). Recent history argues that such patterns cannot create or sustain political orders of freedom.

19. The term 'Vietnam war' rather than 'peace' or 'anti-war' is appropriately used to describe the movement of the later 1960s, since these other terms only accurately describe the majority of the movement before 1967—after that only the draft-resistance and pacifist organizations fit such labels. In 1967, the VSC in England was, for example, in effect, a *'pro-war'* organization—favoring not

ceasefires or settlements but further intensified military 'struggles' against 'imperialism' everywhere (very much the mood of 1968–9).

20. Typical of this argument, which fails to take seriously the influence of Giap's 'protracted-war' theory in the DRVN leadership even before Dien Bien Phu, is the view of NLF militarism as the violence of the last resort, e.g. see Fall, op. cit., chapter 15. This was Malcolm Caldwell's position whilst chairman of CND in this period. But the disciplined ranks of the Viet Minh and later the Viet Cong armies, were structures imported externally to peasant cultures. Various hierarchies of struggle—the combat parties, cadres, terrorist structures, guerilla or peoples' militias like the political arm of the war; the provisional Revolutionary Government and the central bureaucracies—arose and were officered from outside the peasantry itself; it is hard to persuade peasants to fight, or stay fighting for long in such a process (as is implied by Cabral, 'Liberation of Guinea', *Monthly Review*, 1972; B. Davidson, *Liberation of Guinea*, Penguin, 1967; and E. Wolf, *Peasant Wars in the 20th Century*, Faber, 1969).

33
Women at the Barricades, Then and Now

MYRA MACPHERSON

Women in the antiwar movement became media stars—from singer Joan Baez and actress Jane Fonda to extreme radicals and anarchists who advocated violent revolution, like Weathermen Bernardine Dohrn and Kathy Boudin. Others, less visible among the bomb throwers, like Jane Alpert, blew up their buildings, then became wanted fugitives who traveled underground and surfaced in the eighties to write about their experiences. Yet all along there were other women—nameless and faceless to the press— who threw themselves into the antiwar movement with dedicated passion. They were the reasonable, the caring, who did not make headlines. Like many veterans, some feel they were war casualties who lost time. They got off the track, but the train kept going. Curiously, while veterans feel they were discriminated against for having gone to war, many of these women feel they were also discriminated against because of their far-left credentials—especially as the country moved more to the right.

For most involved in antiwar work, writing a résumé in the mid-seventies became a game of artful dodging. "Only the top leaders landed jobs with the Carter administration. On the West Coast, the welcome mat was not out," recalls a former activist who wants to remain anonymous. "Frankly, I'm not at all anxious to portray myself as the agitator I was." She is in her late thirties and has been "trying to get legitimate for three years." Friends told her to rewrite her résumé when she came to Washington. She played up her skills—she was a superb editor of a sizable magazine—but deemphasized that they were acquired on a left-wing publication. She told her prospective bosses, "You might not agree with the content, but you have to admit I have the skills and experience." She attended both Harvard and Berkeley graduate schools but never acquired a master's, dropping out for antiwar work. She is now overqualified for her current researcher's job. "I'm doing the kind of work I used to *assign*," she says ruefully.

In many ways, she epitomizes the best of the women of her generation. Intelligent, gentle, thoughtful, she pursued antiwar activism with passionate and sincere intensity. She uses the constant phrase of many who sided with the NLF: "We were naïve. We idealized the 'noble Vietnamese.'" She sighs. " 'If America was wrong, then they *must* be right.' There was no in-between. There was a real lack of ambiguity. Still, even if we had known it would turn out *exactly* as it did, our job was to get the U.S. *out*."

Some of her friends still work with causes. One female friend slogged through years of postwar schooling to catch up and become a doctor. Others, like herself, had not reckoned with either the shifting tides of conservatism or the heavy psychological toll of being an outsider all those years. "A lot have never left. The more their vision of the world isn't validated, the more they are convinced they are right. Getting an establishment job is still viewed as anathema to them."

During the war there had been a wrenching separation from parents and a brother in the Army. If her brother went to Vietnam and she continued to march in the streets, her mother warned she would not be welcome at home. She told her daughter, "I will never speak to you again." There was intense conflict; *she* could not understand how her mother could let a son go to Vietnam. Her brother did not go, but it took years to reunite the family.

For her, a demonstration was no Saturday-night revelry. "I took it terribly seriously." There is a touch of envy for those younger, less committed, who went on with their lives. "Even now, in their early thirties, they are young enough to start careers and families." She is approaching forty and knows that she will never have children. A marriage she has had, though not a documented one. She lived for a decade with an antiwar activist. When they parted it was, for her, like a divorce.

For women like her, Vietnam put her personal life on hold. "It didn't just interrupt your career, it could screw it up." During the early part of the seventies, she continued to speak out against the war—for a leftist radio network, newsletters, magazines—and became a foreign-policy analyst. By the late seventies, leftist views were out of fashion; few places would give her the benefit of believing she could separate her expertise from her beliefs. "Dropping out and spending ten years of your life very *actively* against the war doesn't seem the best résumé for a job."

She lacks both a strident self-promotion and the arrogance of some in her age group. "You talk about people who thought we acted superior. I'm sure we *acted* that way—but I felt I was the 'enemy.'"

They were the outsiders—the hunted, the chased, the beaten. The women would dress for demonstrations; would wear heavy work boots and jackets to catch the blows, wetted handkerchiefs to cover the face and eyes when the tear gas came. It was an experience women in the generation before and those in college now, with their designer labels and sorority pins, could never know.

Polls consistently show that demonstrators had little backing in the country. Middle America eventually tired of the war, but they disliked student demonstrators even more. Those who viewed them as troublemakers seldom saw the confrontation through the eyes of students. Some drove police to a frenzy, true, but many of the dedicated rank and file were victims of nonprovoked attacks—chased into corners of alleys or buildings and then beaten. Many still recall the terror of being trapped by police swinging wildly with their clubs.

"I remember a demonstration when Dean Rusk was speaking at the Mark Hopkins [hotel]. It was the first time the police used *attack* techniques to stop us. They just started chasing us. *Anyone caught was beaten.*" The concept of free speech and assembly was gone. "They chased us into a little chapel. I knew they could get in and beat the crap out of us, and we couldn't get out. A priest came out and talked to the police, and they let us out. They shot a demonstrator in People's Park. At Berkeley, they had to rotate the National Guard constantly. They were our age, and they didn't want them fraternizing with us." The police on attack were fearsome to this woman, barely 5'2". "They wore masks, helmets, and came down fiercely."

Mollie Ivins recalls the same reaction, the unleashed rage. "I had great admiration for good cops and great loathing for bad cops. There was that whole class thing, that generational hostility. Older cops would eye these long-haired kids, certain they were 'getting a lot of pussy.' I saw some ugly stuff—cops deliberately going after women. It happened to me in a couple of demonstrations."

Being an "enemy" of the establishment provoked a sense of lawlessness in the California activist who was clubbed and chased into the chapel. "Why was I bothering to stop at a red light? Why do I obey the law when they would beat the crap out of me if they could? We were outlaws in America. We assumed our phones were tapped, assumed half our friends were agents. It affected me for a long, long time."

Reentry into the establishment world was frightening. A wariness remains. It is vastly ironic that veterans and some women who fought so hard against the war would turn up in the eighties as survivors. They lived through a searing period as unwanted outsiders.

"I'm not saying it is anything as bad as veterans who can't find jobs, but believe me it has been hard. For a lot of people, taking up your life again was not easy. *Almost no one talks about it!* Imagine what we believed! For a long time we thought and were told, 'You're all privileged. You can do this and pop back in, whenever you want.' It just wasn't true. You had to be almost irresponsible—turn away from your personal goals."

After the war, she staked everything on a nonestablishment magazine that might have remained rewarding if it had ever become solvent.

She realizes now that she "never thought through what I was going to do with the rest of my life. The movement was an all-absorbing thing. I didn't stop to think *ever* what plans I should have. *Thinking personally wasn't highly regarded.* Living in a commune, working on the war . . . There wasn't much time for yourself." Her voice gets a bit firmer. "I feel I gave a whole bunch of the best years of my life to that. Now I do not think of myself as an activist or an organizer. Now I have to put my own life together."

Jane Fonda remains the point-woman for the wrath of many veterans. The right, incorrectly, blame the whole antiwar movement for her actions. In any gathering of veterans there will always be an expletive for her. Even some who turned antiwar cannot forgive her for embracing Hanoi, for posing on one of their tanks. Dean Phillips, a much-decorated antiwar veteran, explodes, "Fonda did irreparable damage to the antiwar movement. She pissed off 80 percent of Americans not on the fringes.

People needed to hear it from the guy who fought it—not those assholes at Yale whose biggest decision was getting Daddy's Mercedes and Fonda, who was not in danger of starving to death. There she was criticizing the capitalistic system—which is the hallmark of hypocrisy."

In the late seventies, Fonda further created discord by refusing to join Joan Baez and other antiwar activists in lending her name to an ad decrying the fate of Vietnam's boat people and those oppressed in Vietnam.

Today Fonda has moved on to making more millions as she deflabs the overweight women of America with her "Work-Out" books, records, and video cassettes. Most of the women who went through her regimen in 1982 have no idea that they were in fact subsidizing the political career of former SDS leader Tom Hayden. Fonda contributed handsomely to her husband's 1982 million-dollar-plus campaign for an insignificant state assemblyman seat.

When Hayden was deriving fame and power through antiwar leadership, women were discovering a cruel truth. Lip service to equality did not mean they joined the council of decision makers. Often excluded from meaningful roles at the top, many turned to the feminist movement. The civil rights and antiwar movements emphasized a heightened sense of injustice and—at least in rhetoric—created a more receptive climate for the women's movement. The rebirth of feminism was a welcome niche for those who had been burned by chauvinism in male antiwar ranks.

Margery Tabankin was a University of Wisconsin activist from 1965 to 1969 and later visited Hanoi. The first woman president of the National Student Association since 1947, she was elected on an antiwar platform. She recalls that "Hayden was my hero. We revered these guys. It was like 'what could we do for them?' When Hayden got off the plane to make a speech in Wisconsin, the first thing he handed me was his dirty laundry and asked if I would do it for him. I said, 'I'll have it for you by tonight.'"

Tabankin became one of the few women organizers, joined SDS, and helped coordinate the 1969 Moratorium. "Part of being a woman was this psychology of proving I was such a good radical, 'better than the men.' We felt we were motivated by something higher because we didn't have to go to war ourselves. Most guys didn't take women seriously, however. They were things to fuck. We once did a questionnaire to check reasons why students were drawn to antiwar rallies and demonstrations. One reason frequently checked was 'to make social contacts.' You went through this intense experience, and you went back and had sex." People forget that the women's movement was fledgling at the time. "It [sex] was much more on men's terms."

Despite such aspects of second-class citizenship, the antiwar movement gave Tabankin a sense of heightened consciousness: "You had the right to have opinions about anything—including your government.

"I got beaten up badly covering one of my first civil disobedience rallies for the University of Wisconsin paper. Seventy people were hospitalized," says Tabankin. "We were protesting Dow Chemical on campus. Kids were sitting in a building, refusing to move, and the cops walked in and shouted, 'Everybody out—we'll give you three seconds.'

"They started busting heads, and everyone just totally freaked out, running to get out, clustering in panic at two doors. I got hit in the stomach with a club. Because I was injured, I was the only reporter to get into the emergency room. I ended up being the person the New York *Times* was calling in the hospital to tell them what was going on, how many were injured." Her eyes still shine, recalling the moment. "I was, like, ecstatic—but on the other hand, my friends were hurt." The experience radicalized her. "I remember saying, 'I've had it with writing about things. I'm going to *do* it.'"

Tabankin abandoned everything for antiwar work. There are great gaps in her education. "For two semesters I literally never went to classes. Borrowed notes and took the tests. We were really self-righteous. We knew a better world, and we were going to make it. That wasn't even negotiable. Our demands were to stop the war, to guarantee the poor an annual income and racial equality. We really created in our minds what the world should be like. *It was my whole reason to live.* I found a passion in my life I never knew was there. Realistically, there were about 100 major activists out of 40,000 on campus. The rest were like soldiers who marched."

Like some other women who threw themselves totally into the movement, she is somewhat envious of those who did not. "They had a much more integrated life. They still came to the demonstrations, but they were graduating and going on. The guy I was in love with—I really think one reason he would not marry me was because of my Vietnam politics—went on to law school and is with a very establishment firm. He really changed."

Tabankin recognized the less committed for what they were. "People get emotional when self-interest is at stake. Young people didn't care enough when their lives weren't on the line. I'd say 5 percent felt intensely passionate about the issue."

She recognizes the deep schisms between some antiwar leaders and the radical left. She agrees with those who view Sam Brown and Tom Hayden as pragmatic manipulators thrust into prominence by the movement. "Some were only for stopping the war, but one faction of SDS got so caught up in being against the system and for economic and racial change. They saw this as totally interrelated. Then you had crazies splitting off, anarchists, and terrorists. I was between the SDS and the student government type. Although a little more to the left of student government, I wasn't totally an SDS person. Many in the Mobe viewed Sam Brown and Al Lowenstein as sell-out pigs. We just didn't see it, the polarization, then. We were so caught up, we didn't see how destructive it was."

Tabankin was arrested seven times and finally became a burned-out casualty. She dropped out of activism and went home. "The greatest luxury was having my mother's housekeeper do my laundry." She became a community organizer for youth projects, raised money for foundations, worked on two union-reform efforts for miners, and became head of VISTA when Sam Brown became Carter's director of the Action agency. She defends the activists of the sixties and sees ongoing commitment. "The same 5 percent *then* are the same 5 percent of our generation still working for causes—toxic waste, nuclear freeze, trying to get progressives elected. Much of it is grassroots."

The attempt of some in the media to lump "the generation" as idealistic causists was a mistake. "There never *was* a 'generation' that really meant it. Many didn't give a shit, then and now. Most got caught up in the time period—but it wasn't based on ideology, it was based on events. They weren't socialized then and they aren't now."

Today Tabankin, in her mid-thirties, is herself opting for profits while working for causes on the side. In 1981 Tabankin and Bill Danoff, author of the song "Country Roads," formed Danoff Music Company. They represent twenty-four Washington-area songwriters, plugging them to Los Angeles and Nashville producers and singers. They also manage a few bands. Tabankin's biggest coup was selling a song by Jon Carroll, Washington rock musician and songwriter, to Linda Ronstadt. Carroll's "Get Closer" became the title track of an album that went gold in 1982. The single made the Top Twenty. Tabankin tries to make a vague connection between yesteryear's activism and today's entrepreneurship. You need "commonsense networking skills" in both fields, she says—whom to contact and how, what will be effective. One difference, however, is the "profit motive."

Tabankin feels she acquired strength and self-confidence during the sixties and has been able to transfer organizing skills into business. The negatives? "It became my whole life, and I lost out on normal, lasting personal relationships."

The negatives for the generation? "People want to make it more than it was. Civil rights didn't change the fact that blacks still have problems, the women's movement doesn't mean women have equal rights, the antiwar movement doesn't mean our foreign policy isn't going to go totally crazy in the near future."

As women activist recall that era, it is striking how negatively they regarded American soldiers. "As we turned against the government, we turned against them as symbols," said Tabankin. "That was our biggest mistake. That was stupid tactically. The compassion wasn't there; the expressed view was that 'I don't want to get killed, and I don't think *they* should go do that.' Instead of the government, we blamed the foot soldier. If I have any regret, it's the way we treated them." At the time, reviling soldiers was part of the tactic—such as war-crime tribunals—to heighten the perception that the war had to be stopped. "You had to be for the North if you wanted the people to win."

Tabankin looks back with some chagrin at her naïvety. In 1972, as part of a delegation to Hanoi, she was imbued with the concept that the war was nationalistic in origin and had remained so. "I was witnessing destruction of civilian life. I saw their hospital forty-five minutes after it had been totally demolished. The ambulance was taking out the dead and living. That was in May 1972—the scariest time of my life. There were bombing attacks at all times of day and night. We brought the first footage out of North Vietnam and sold it to '60 Minutes.'

"The North Vietnamese didn't want us to meet with POWs. We pushed and pushed and made ourselves obnoxious, and we saw ten of them," recalls Tabankin. "They looked pale but healthy. One black had heard that Wallace had been shot and was interested in that. Another asked me to go back and tell his wife he was all right."

The prisoners said little about their treatment; it did not even occur to Tabankin at the time that they would have major difficulty expressing themselves with North Vietnamese officials in the room. The accounts of torture that emerged after POWs' return demolished reports of those who had seen them under such carefully controlled conditions. We talked of Susan Sontag's ecstatic descriptions of the "gentle captors" of the North. Tabankin winces slightly, then reiterates, "It was so easy to be naive."

The range of opinions among those twenty-seven million women who came of age during the Vietnam Generation was clearly vast.

Some dropped the sixties with a vengeance, like those who populate Jerry Rubin's Manhattan mix-and-mingle salons. Rubin, yesteryear's Yippie trying to make it in the eighties as an example of the "Me" Decade Meets Wall Street phenomenon, is a "networking" party giver. He talks about money, power, and "leveraged" women. "Leverage in financial terms is when a small amount of money controls a larger amount of money. Leverage is therefore power. I'm into leverage. Now Barbara Walters is leveraged. She speaks, you know, and people listen. Right? Huh? You get it? The leveraged woman."

Those serious in the movement always viewed Rubin as a member of the comic fringe, much overplayed by the media. They are not surprised that he shed his antiwar activism like an old worn overcoat and speaks without a scintilla of idealism about past motivation. "I get very nervous talking about the sixties. Who wants to live in the past?" More than anyone from the sixties antiwar, antiauthoritarian movement, Rubin epitomizes the view of one cynical observer: "Money is the long hair of the eighties." One evening incipient leveraged men and women—eager imitations of high-fashion gloss—moved around at one of his "networking" salons, handing out business cards as they used to pass around joints. Pat Frazer, who said she is a "commercial actress," spoke in a super-modulated voice and seemed to epitomize the women present. What was she doing? "Anything I can."

In the sixties, "Jerry was my ideal. At college I was involved. Now I'm involved in the eighties. You're on your own—and all of a sudden it's 'getting for yourself.' I'm interested in taxes." She had no quarrel with cutting social programs for the poor and disadvantaged. "That's okay. My priorities are now in defense and space." And in the sixties? "Then I was anti-American." Because it was chic? "Partly."

Of course there are other sixties women who wouldn't spend a minute at Rubin's mixers or embrace his values. They may be involved in careers or motherhood rather than issues—but they do not negate their past. Others remain active in causes. For some, a need for personal peace followed radical commitment. In 1983 a bright college graduate in Washington summed up the feeling of many taking time off to be a full-time mother. "I gave my *all* to the movement, but now it is time for myself." ...

The class division of the war created friction between some in the emerging women's movement and returning veterans. Leaders in the women's movement had little or no firsthand experience with anyone who went to Vietnam. For them it was simple to cavalierly dismiss veterans' preference in civil service as discriminatory. In the early seventies, when returning veterans needed all the help they could get, various women's groups, particularly NOW, opposed laws which gave extra points to wartime veterans applying for civil service jobs. For example, the Federal Women's Program Committee of the Denver Federal Executive Board questioned whether the law was consistent with equal-employment rulings—acknowledging that those who were drafted "may have suffered disruptions in their normal lifestyles." That understatement enraged combat veterans since draftees comprised 60 percent of U.S. Army dead from 1967 through 1970.

Dean Phillips, special assistant to the VA director (1977–81), said, "Women were not beating down doors to demand entrance into the armed services during Vietnam." Phillips noted that women who served did not make up the 2 percent quota then established for females. They too would have been entitled to veterans' preference if they had entered the service. "Treatises on sex discrimination often ignore perhaps the most blatantly sexist policy in our country's history," said Phillips, "the limitation of the drafting of those who will die and be crippled in combat exclusively to the male sex. At no time during the war did any women's organization file any lawsuit claiming that restrictive draft or enlistment laws injured female employment opportunities by making it more difficult for women to serve in the armed forces. After virtually ignoring the issue of the male-only draft during the veterans' preference debate in the late seventies, NOW president Ellie Smeal made a fool out of herself in 1981 by claiming that past exclusion from the draft had discriminated *against women*. Feminists, who *avoided* service during Vietnam, were now saying that their younger sisters are discriminated against by not being included in draft registration—something *they* wanted no part of during Korea or Vietnam."

Phillips, an ex-paratrooper who went on long-range patrols in enemy-controlled areas with the 101st Airborne Division in 1967–78, won numerous decorations, including the Silver Star, Purple Heart, and two Bronze Stars. During law school in Denver in the early seventies, he had a compatible relationship with NOW. He even received letters of appreciation from them for his active support of the ERA. That union was shattered when NOW refused to alter its 1971 position of opposing *any* and *all* government laws or programs giving special preference to veterans, even those badly maimed in combat. Phillips points to a letter from NOW's national headquarters confirming in 1979 that the 1971 resolution—with no modifications—was still their official position. Phillips assisted in the defense of the constitutionality of veterans' preference—which was ultimately upheld by the Supreme Court in June of 1979.

Phillips contends that NOW's opposition to all forms of veterans' preference was a tactical error that helped defeat the ERA in several crucial states. "The two-million-member VFW passed a resolution opposing the ERA in *direct* response to the NOW resolution opposing all forms of veterans' preference. Then VFW people worked effectively against the ERA through their contacts with state legislators. Sure, they would not have been *for* the ERA in any case—but they wouldn't have even gotten involved to oppose it if it hadn't been for NOW's position."

Other veterans, less active than Phillips, also felt that the women's movement should have left veterans' preference alone. "In one way I felt the government was back to pitting all of us minorities against one another in a fight for jobs," said one combat veteran, "but we felt the women didn't understand what we had been through."

Today, in urban centers like Boston, New York, and Washington, there are curious permutations of friendships from the Vietnam Generation. Ann Zill, who helps spend millions in liberal causes for Stewart Mott, had a brother who was injured in Vietnam. One of her closet friends is a Marine combat veteran who argues vehemently that the United States should have been in Vietnam and could have won. Zill herself was an antiwar activist.

Ann Broderick Zill, the oldest of four children, grew up in a small town in Maine. Her father was a "corporate mogul" who worked for Chevrolet. At Barnard College in New York, she was among the early war protesters. Zill had violent arguments with her brother, Peter Broderick, five and a half years younger, about the war, and was devastated when he joined the Army in 1968 and became an officer. Two months into Vietnam, he was "literally blown up" and spent nearly fifteen months recuperating. "He lost a whole lot of his intestines and had a colostomy for a while and has 60 percent permanent disability, and he basically does nothing with his life," Zill said in 1981. "He's a town janitor and plays a lot of tennis." For a man loaded still with shrapnel, she says, "He's in very good shape."

The wounded brother and the "knee-jerk peacenik" sister were forced to confront each other's views. There was a night in 1981 when their mother died. The Irish Catholic family had always been able to drink and fight and laugh together. The drinks came heavily that night. "Peter was sobbing and reliving the Vietnam War, and this is 1981." Did he come to a political point of view? "He views it through a very small slit of consciousness. He does not deal with the larger moral questions. Yet I suspect that if pressed to the wall now he would be able to say some things were fundamentally wrong with the war—but he's never been able to in the past. He's scarred by the war.

"We don't fight now, but we used to back then. He was a young kid, and I could *not* believe that he believed in this war. I argued that it was stupid and wrong for us to be involved."

All the time her brother was in Vietnam, all the time he lay in the hospital, Zill marched and worked for peace. "I felt very conflicted. I watched this man of six feet two, who now weights 190, go to something just over 100 pounds. Skin and bones and could barely walk. He kept getting pneumonia." His agony reinforced her feeling that the war was wrong. "But I couldn't talk about that with Peter. He didn't want to hear that. He liked to tell war stories and make us laugh, and I had to laugh at the damn fucking war stories whether I wanted to or not. I will *always* believe that war was senseless."

Her brother tells a story of a marine whose injuries were so overwhelming that he was encased in a plaster cast. For nights he kept begging for a knife. Broderick was convinced the man wanted to commit suicide. Then one night the marine, whose face was bandaged except for his face and mouth, yelled, "I can't see, I'm caught in a net and can't get out." Broderick felt "deep elation. He *didn't* want to kill himself." He was trying to see. "I sensed a great pride in that marine; he hadn't given up. He didn't let my faith down. He was a fighter...never quitting the struggle or relenting an inch...I never saw him again, although he remains with me forever."

It is this emphasis on personal bravery and courage that fills the memory of many veterans, not the ideological rights and wrongs of the war. Ann Zill, unlike many women in the movement, was able to broaden her perspective through her brother, to understand the motivation of some who went. "He was a very good antidote for my overall sense that if you were for the war, you were crazy. He forced me to realize that a lot of perfectly reasonable people had been trained to believe it was your patriotic duty to defend your country—and that they believed this war was about protecting Vietnam from the Communists."

Zill is now divorced from the husband who "used to joke that he made love, not war, because that's how he got out. By having babies." As a father he was deferred. In 1981 she was dating a Mexican American who was too young for Vietnam and now organizes against the draft, arguing that blue-collar and lower-class youths would still be the ones to go. "The inequities would still be there."

Zill loved growing up in the sixties. "The spirit of liberation and of questioning authority. Vietnam shaped my life. One of my closet friend's lifework grew out of war protest. She now does analytical think-pieces about Indochina and Southeast Asia. And I haven't changed my basic view—although I like to think I'm more effective now. I work for a man who gives away about a million a year, and his first interest is to prevent nuclear annihilation. Trying to prevent another going-to-war exercise is a very sobering, humbling exercise. The peace movement today is *meshuggina*. It's a terrible failure, completely inadequate. The selling of the Pentagon was brilliant. They played to the psychological needs of this country to be strong and protected after Vietnam—even as life is crumbling all around." Zill was talking in 1981, before public sentiment had shifted to some degree against the government's excessive defense budget.

She is asked to assess the sixties movement.

"I'm somewhat critical by nature. There were a lot of arrogant kids. Sam Brown so turned me off that I have never been able to like him to this day, and I used to run into him at the same parties when he ran Action."

Like many dedicated antiwar activists, she tried to overlook personalities. "My allegiance remained with the people who were trying to stop the war. And my efforts in that regard got more sensible as time went on. It never occurred to me to side with the North, but I can't blame those who did. Still, that is part of my brother's story. He was really rejected when he showed up on campus in his Army outfit one day because he had to wear it to get some discount on the cost of something—I've forgotten what. But how vilified he was!" She points up an important psychological reaction of many veterans in similar situations. "That made him cling to the *need* to defend that war longer, I think, than he would otherwise have done. And so that's an example of one of those great ironies about how much campus condemnation exacerbated and helped polarize an already tough situation. Yet I understand those people who did it."

Zill is not too optimistic about generational reconciliation. "You need to bring the extremes together, and I'm not sure that can happen. I doubt that I would ever to able to say that my sympathies are with my brother, who believed in it as he did. On the other hand, I will defend to the death his right to think that way. Maybe if more people can understand someone like I can my brother, there *will* be a coming together."

One of the problems of the Vietnam Generation was a tendency to stereo-type, to divide into monolithic clumps of "them" and "us." Vestiges of that thinking remain. One female antiwar activist enjoys a close friendship with a veteran—but irreconcilable differences cloud it.

"We all viewed each other back then as some faceless mass. To the veterans, we were a faceless mass who treated them like shit. Just as I criticize people for not seeing *us* as individuals, we didn't see *soldiers* as people. We just wanted to stop the war. We felt so defensive, a minority of college kids clustered together. I remember being angry at the soldiers. It was good to say, 'Fuck you,' to let them know people didn't like it—that there were people who passionately *did not want this war.* We had a real macro view—do anything to stop it. We were more oblivious than arrogant about the classness."

She pauses to reflect. "We were lucky to live in a time when there was a social movement. As a generation it set us apart in an irreconcilable way—even as it caused huge divisions within the generation. Maybe as time goes by, and people don't know where Vietnam is once again, maybe it will bring us together. The fact that we lived through it, on one hand, is all of our touchstone with reality. For us it will always be—and for the veterans it will always be. And yet on another level, we are on opposite sides."

She sighs. "I'm still emotional about it, and so are they. One friend thinks he's better because he faced death and we haven't. I think there is something more important to life than being on a battlefield—I don't see it as the highest value of life, and yet I appreciate his feeling.

"People who fought and people who fought against the war were at loggerheads—but it changed our lives forever." She sighs. "Still, there is no settling of accounts.

"No one can lay it to rest."

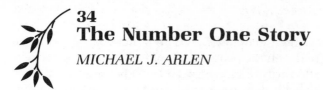

34
The Number One Story
MICHAEL J. ARLEN

There's still rubber, of course—the rubber that finds its way from the large French plantations in the south and in the Central Highlands into Michelin and other Free World tires—but, aside from that, probably the largest and most valued single export item from South Vietnam these days [1969] is American journalism. The stuff pours out of Saigon each day in a torrent of television film, still photographs, and words—the film and the photographs heading east toward relay stations in Tokyo or San Francisco on the now daily jet flights out of Tan Son Nhut Airport, and the words rushing along the new cable that links Siagon, Guam, Honolulu, and the West Coast and that makes a phone conversation between Saigon and Chicago infinitely clearer than anything that can usually be managed between one Saigon hotel room and another. General William Westmoreland has a telephone in his quarters that enables him to speak instantly with the Commander-in-Chief in Washington. Simmons Fentress, of *Time-Life*, has a telephone that enables *him* to communicate instantly with the *Time-Life* news bureau in Rockefeller Center. Most bureaus are not quite that up-to-the-minute; in fact, many bureaus, the *Times* among them, borrow the Reuters lease line, the *Times* men trudging up to their small office on Tu-Do Street after dinner in order to file their three or four daily stories by one or two in the morning, which is one or two in the afternoon (the previous afternoon) in New York, and thus get them there in time for the next morning's edition. All the same, there is a staggering amount of communication going on in Vietnam: the military, with all its field radios and private telephones and teletype machines, communicating within the military; the embassy and the CIA and USAID and so forth communicating within "the mission"; all of them communicating, when they choose to, with the journalists; the journalists communicating with their editors, and the editors with the public—hundreds of teletypes and Telexes clackety-clacking away all over the bloody country, roughly five-hundred working journalists (and working pretty hard for the most part, too), and where it all ends up, where it all ends up is Fred leans forward in his chair at eleven-thirty in the evening, stares briefly and intensely at the floor, sticks his chin out a bit, adopts a thoughtful look, and, speaking somewhere in the direction of his left shoe, declares, "Well, it's certainly, um, you have to say ah,... a very... *complex* situation."

After even a little time in Vietnam, a couple of things seem fairly clear. One is that although in a certain sense one can hardly avoid calling the situation in Vietnam "complex" (for that matter, the cell structure of the Arizona tree frog is complex), on a number of possibly more useful levels (for instance, the level of operable communication, of what can be sent out and what can be received) it isn't so complex after all. (The word "complex" tends to be one of our contemporary talismans; whatever you touch with it becomes somehow embalmed and unreachable, and the "complexity" itself is likely to become more interesting or important than the subject it is supposed to enfold.) The situation in Vietnam is obviously composed of many different parts—parts involving such seemingly disparate elements as power politics, South Vietnamese peasant life, the United States Congress, military firepower and tactics, local politics, and corruption—but the parts themselves are relatively simple, or, at any rate, relatively comprehensible. One will never know everything there is to know about politics in the United States. One will never know everything there is to know about politics in Vietnam. Still, if one had the time, or took the trouble, to get in touch with a certain number of reliable Vietnamese political authorities and ask them what was actually happening as a result of such-and-such a power alignment, or what might happen if such-and-such a Cabinet change was effected, they could probably tell one enough so that one could put together a fairly concrete, useful analysis of the subject, so that, for example, in the aftermath of the recent Vietnamese elections, with the Buddhists marching and the students getting beaten up and the Assembly threatening to throw out the vote, one wouldn't get stuck, as most of the American television stations and newspapers got stuck, with trying hastily to explain to the public at the end of September what it was that had been going on for more than a month and had been pointing in the direction of such an outburst (and for the most part not even trying to explain, just giving the bare facts or running around trying to illustrate them), and with the public, responding to yet another overquick, undercooked explanation, once again nodding its head and muttering, "I told you so. Another mixed-up South American republic."

Vietnam may be the Number 1 story, but journalists don't have that smooth a time covering it. Virtually none of them speaks Vietnamese. Most newspapermen and TV men are here nowadays on only six-month tours of duty, which is hardly enough time to find out the name of the province chief in Binh Dinh, let alone ask him how the corruption situation is coming along—and, in any case, most of the six months is usually spent in chasing Vietnamese fire engines for the New York desk. When somebody gets on to a story, as CBS did with Con Thien early in September, then everyone goes chasing after it—wire services, newspapers, rival networks—the Saigon bureau chiefs receiving "rockets" from New York to get competitive (not really much different from the way the papers and TV cover a fast-breaking news event back home). The trouble is, Vietnam isn't a fast-breaking news event most of the time. The papers back home have their deadlines; the TV stations have their scheduled news broadcasts. The journalists here try to feed the stuff back—there's usually some kind of stuff to feed back, some of it technically useful, and now and then it's good (R. W. Apple had a fine long piece in the *Times* this August on the "stalemate" in the war); sometimes it's ridiculous (as are the solemn transmissions of enemy casualty figures that are often obtained by a pilot looking down from a spotter plane a couple of thousand feet in the air)—and a lot of chatter comes out of the newspapers and picture tubes, but sometimes nothing really happens. Or, when it does happen, it happens in a time and space that often isn't very meaningfully evoked in terms of standard hard-news copy. People have this feeling that they're not getting the "true picture" of Vietnam from daily journalism. (Just about the first thing anyone asks a returning visitor from Vietnam is "What's *really* going on there?") People are, on the whole, right, and what makes the failure of the press to communicate the reality of the Vietnam war something well worth looking into is that the Vietnam war isn't such an isolated phenomenon as many people seem to think it is. "Not like the Second World War," people say. Indeed it isn't: no formal front lines, no supportive religious illusions about a Holy War, no happy embrace of propaganda ("We're all in this together, Fred. Hang the Kaiser. Down with Tojo. Here's a toast to Winnie, Uncle Joe, and Madame Chiang"). A different world now, a different war. The Detroit riots of 1967 are qualitatively, not just chronologically, different from the Detroit riots of 1943. The waves of energy emanating from the hippies in California are qualitatively different from those that emanated from the Lindy Hoppers that short while ago. It isn't, perhaps, that the world is deeper in chaos than it used to be, but that the element of chaos which has always been there in life, which really *is* life (after all, there were minority groups and emerging nations in the eleventh century too), is now coming more and more out from under wraps: Father has left the house, and the children have some new toys and are threatening to knock the house to pieces, and that would be all right, it would be manageable, if we could somehow get inside the house and really find out what was going on, could sit down and try to understand the children, listen to them, at any rate if we could confront what it was that they were doing (let alone thinking about), but, as things are, we make this big thing about how we know everything that's going on—*nothing* escapes us, because we too have new toys, which tell us things—but what really happens is that we sit outside the house and every now and then a maid comes out onto the porch and stamps one foot lightly for attention and then reads us a brief announcement, and we sit there looking thoughtful or impatient and listening to the sounds of breaking furniture from somewhere on the second story. We have this great arrogance about communications. We've given up much of our capacity for first-hand experience—certainly for first-hand sensory experience—cheerfully sitting at home shrouded in plastic, film, magnetic tape, peering out at the world throught lenses, electronic tubes, photographs, lines of type. And we've also, at a time when the ability of a people to order and enhance its existence depends increasingly on its ability to know what is really going on (no more just getting the word from Father or the King; no more milling around in front of Whitehall to find out what really gives with Kitchener in the Sudan)—we've also given up the ideal of knowing firsthand about ourselves and the world in favor of receiving sometimes arbitrary and often nearly stenographic reports through a machine system we call "communications," which for the most part neither recognizes the element of chaos in the world for what it is nor is able to make contact with it except on a single narrow-beam wavelength.

It's ironic, maybe, that, among the methods men have devised for usefully reflecting the world back to themselves, only those methods that the population at large doesn't really take very seriously—one thinks especially of the novel and the film—have made any significant attempt to cope with the evolving human experience. Not so long ago, in the nineteenth century, when the world was held in place by nuts and bolts, when the doors to all the upstairs rooms were locked up tight, when Father was home and brooked no nonsense—in those days, because it seemed relevant and interesting to find out about the things in people's lives, what work they did, what trolley car they took from where to where, and whom they married, novelists wrote book after book after book that covered these things in an orderly way, and that often appeared to describe the universe largely in terms of stationary articles of furniture. Nowadays it seems more relevant to write about the inside of people's heads (or at least the writers' heads) and about how they really live—about how life doesn't always go in a straight line from here to there but moves forward, backward, upside down, inside the head, and outside. The nervier writers—the Mailers, the Pynchons, the Updikes—go reaching out and grabbing at how things seem to be right now. A book by Mailer, or a film by Antonioni, may not define the world, and you may not like it, but, taken all in all, the novels and films being turned out today seem to attempt to reflect more of the shifting dynamism of present-day life than does even the best of daily journalism (both press and television), which we take *very* seriously and defer to for most of our public and private impressions of the world and, one imagines, of ourselves. Daily journalism, in fact, seems to have changed very little over the last few decades—as if nobody quite knew what to do with it (except for adding more white space, syndicating Clayton Fritchey, and "livening up" the women's page), as if its conventions were somehow eternal. The *Times*, which has editors and reporters with sufficient imagination and sense of history to recognize that there is more to be reflected upon in our evolving experience in Vietnam than the daily bombing reports, continues for the most part to treat the war as an accounting exercise—and "treat" is right, for the hurly-burly of the world emerges in the pages of the *Times* somehow ordered and dignified, a bit the way a man's ridiculous life emerges as so splendidly established (all those "estate"s and "issues"s and so forth) when he listens to the lawyer read him out his will. Television, with all its technical resources, with all the possibilities of film and film-editing for revealing fluid motion, continues for the most part to report the war as a long, long narrative broken into two-minute, three-minute, or four-minute stretches of visual incident. Now, it's obvious that there are plenty of events in the war, or anywhere, that ought to be treated in an accountant's manner, and also that there are plenty of incidents that are inherently visual and can most accurately be revealed on film. If there's an important battle, it ought to be put down, covered—just that. The thing is, though, that it doesn't take one very long in Vietnam to realize—perhaps "feel" would be closer than "realize"—that there is a crucial difference between what seems to be *here* and what is reflected of it back home on television and in newspapers. It isn't so much a matter of the press distorting the picture (one of the favorite themes of our embassy in Saigon), because, although there's a certain amount of that—a certain amount of deferring to official pronouncements that one knows are biased, a certain amount of translating battles in which we lost a cruel number of men into gallant actions that were "gallant" because we took so many losses—somehow the concept of press distortion implies a demonology that for the most part just doesn't exist. What really seems to be standing in the way of an accurate reflection of Vietnam right now isn't that the press is "lying" or not telling all it knows. It's partly that much of the press, especially the wire services and television, just doesn't have either the time or the inclination to investigate the various parts of the Vietnam picture—what's the true military situation, what's being done with new technology, what can't be done, how solid is the government's hold on the villages, how solid is the government, how good or bad is the ARVN, and so on. And, more important, when they do get hold of one of these parts, neither most of the newspapers nor most of television seems to be able to do anything more with it than to treat it as an isolated piece of detail—maybe an important piece of detail, maybe unimportant, but isolated in any case, cut off by the rigors and conventions of journalism from the events and forces that brought it into being, cut off, too, from the events and forces that it will in turn animate. The other week, as a small example, a crew from ABC flew in here to do an interview with Ambassador Ellsworth Bunker. The ambassador sat behind his desk and, in response to questions gently shoved at him by ABC's John Scali, discoursed at length on such matters as the "new stability" that would, he said, result from the Thieu-Ky election, and on the fine prospects for Thieu and Ky to work well together in the new government ("They have worked together very well in the last two years"). The program was presented a few days later in the United States—presented, naturally, at face value. At the end of the next week, Buddhists were marching in the streets here, students were getting clubbed by the police, reporters and TV crews (including ABC's) were tearing around Saigon trying to cover a situation that was, after all, a fairly predictable result of the unpopularity of the recent elections, of the fact that the "new stability" we are so hopefully committed to in many instances seems to depend largely on the ability of General Loan to hold down the lid on the kettle, even of the fact that Thieu and Ky have trouble staying in the same room with each other, let alone in the same government. The point isn't that Mr. Bunker shouldn't have said what he said, or that journalists shouldn't have been chasing after riot coverage, but that in life, after all, events don't sit stiffly, separately upon a page, don't take place in terms of three-minute narrative slices of film; they push and jostle and flow and mix against one another, and the process of this mixing is often a more important and revelatory part of what is really going on (this continuing reality that we so proudly call history when it has gone past us) than the isolated announcements that we usually have to make do with. It's obviously not fair—or, at any rate, not realistic—to expect a consistent re-sourcefulness in writing, political analysis, and so forth from a profession (journalism) that has traditionally been longer on energy than on anthing else. But it seems true to say that most journalists here convey a more firmly realized picture of Vietnam in a couple of hours of conversation in the evening (with all those elisions made, the separate parts connected) than they've achieved sometimes (in complicity with their editors and their public) in six months of filing detached, hard-news reports. And it seems even truer to say that one of the notable results of all this has been the almost tangible inability of people back home to pay any very rigorous attention to Vietnam. It obsesses people, certainly, but more as a neurosis (which it's become, it often seems, largely as a result of this inability to confront it) than as a very real, evolving attempt of a large, important nation to relate outward to a large, important sector of the world, which, whether one finds the attempt good or bad, moral or immoral, useful or useless, is what it's all about.

People often refer to television's coverage of Vietnam as "television's war" (as one could probably describe television's coverage of civil rights as "television's civil war"), and although it seems fair to say that in general television has done very well strictly in terms of what it has set out to report about Vietnam—in terms of those usually combat-oriented film clips that appear on the morning and evening news programs—it also seems fair to say that for the most part television in Vietnam has operated on a level not much more perceptive than that of a sort of illustrated wire service, with the television crews racketing around the countryside seeking to illustrate the various stories that are chalked on the assignment boards in Saigon ("4th Div. Opn.," "Chopper story," "Hobo Woods Opn.," "Buddhist march"), constantly under pressure to feed the New York news programs new stories (ideally, combat stories), moving in here, moving out, moving in there the next day. Recently, the major effort of the military war has been taking place up north in the I Corps area, and, as a result, many of the television and newspaper correspondents are now working out of the Danang press center. Ordinar-

ily, though, much of the work is done almost in bankerish fashion from
Saigon, and one says "bankerish" not to disparage the factor of risk-taking
in their covering of various operations (a factor that ranges from slight to
very considerable), but as an indication of how difficult it is to get close to
a strange war in an unfamiliar country by a process that more often than
not consists in your having breakfast at the Hotel Caravelle at seven-thirty,
driving out to a helicopter base, going by chopper to where some military
operation is occurring (say, a search of an area where a Vietcong ammunition dump supposedly exists, the possible picture value being in the
blowing up of the ammo dump), wandering around in the woods taking
pictures until three-thirty, maybe getting shot at a bit and maybe not, then
taking the chopper back, doing all your paperwork and film-shipment arrangements, and meeting friends in the Continental bar at seven o'clock.
The correspondents tend to have mixed feelings about all this themselves.
Many of them, to be sure, are older men with families and are not crazy
about spending more time than necessary out in the field, and, doubtless
like journalists everywhere, they complain of not having enough time to
cover the "right stories," and of the pressure from New York to provide
combat coverage. Of the newspapermen and magazine correspondents,
in fact, except for a couple of people like Peter Arnett and Henri Huet of
the AP, and David Greenway of *Time*, and Dana Stone of UPI, virtually none
are doing the combat work that television is now doing almost on a routine basis (a seemingly routine basis, anyway). And although it's true that
the Vietnam story is more than the story of men shooting at one another
(the television people themselves refer to it as "bang-bang" coverage, and
have a healthy respect for what goes into the getting of it), it's also true
that American men (and Vietnamese men) are indeed getting shot and
killed, and are shooting and killing others, and one would have to be a
pretty self-indulgent pacifist to say that it wasn't somebody's job to record
and witness something of that. The trouble is that television doesn't do
much more than that. It doesn't try. There are the highly structured news
programs, with correspondents from around the world coming on for a
few minutes at a time. And then, as a way of circumventing this limitation, there are the "news specials," which up to now have generally been
done with the same hasty, unfeeling, technically skillful professionalism
that (more justifiably) characterizes the shorter film clips. For the most
part, "television's war" is a prisoner of its own structure, a prisoner of
such facts as that although television is the chief source of news and information for the majority of the people, the News & Information act is
still just another aspect of the world's greatest continuous floating variety show; that the scope and cost of television news require an immense
weight of administrative managing from above; that for TV the newsworthiness of daily events is still so restrictively determined by visual criteria.
For example, people watching an evening news show about an ammo
dump being blown up in the Hobo Woods might reasonably conclude,
on a day, say, when a nationwide strike was averted in San Diego, when a

rebel army was captured in Nigeria, when the Pope fell sick, and when Indonesia broke relations with Red China, that there was some special significance to the blowing up of this particular ammo dump, or not even anything special about it, just some significance—that its presentation on the screen in front of one said something useful about the war. In all too many cases, though, what the blowing up of the ammo dump says is that when you blow up an ammo dump it goes boom-boom-boom and there is a lot of smoke, and that is about it. Daily journalism in general seems to be virtually rooted in its traditional single-minded way of presenting the actuality of daily life, as if some invisible sacred bond existed between the conventional structures of daily journalism and the conventional attitudes of so many of the people whom daily journalism serves. This has been increasingly noticeable in journalism's severely conventional covering of most of the major matters of our time—covering civil rights, for instance, with its technically proficient battle-action accounts of rioting, and its distracted, uncomprehending, essentially uninterested sliding over of the dark silences that fill the empty spaces in between the riots. It is now especially evident, and damaging, in Vietnam, where, for the most part, American journalism has practically surrendered itself to a consecutive, activist, piecemeal, the-next-day-the-First-Army-forged-onward-toward-Aachen approach to a war that even the journalists covering it know to be nonconsecutive, non-activist, a war of silences, strange motions, where a bang on the table gets you nothing and an inadvertent blink causes things to happen in rooms you haven't even looked into yet, where there is no Aachen, and "onward" is a word that doesn't seem to translate very well into the local language. The journalists reorder the actuality of Vietnam into these isolated hard-news incidents for the benefit of their editors. The editors say that that's what the public wants, and, to a great extent, the editors are right about that. The public does indeed want and need hard news, something concrete amid the chaos, something you can reach out to over the morning coffee and almost touch—a hill number, for example. Hill 63. Hill 881. It's a truism, especially among wire-service reporters in Vietnam, that if you can somehow get a hill number attached to a military operation (most operations start at one latitude-longitude point and move to another), regardless of the number of casualties, regardless, especially, of the relevance of this operation to the rest of the war, the story will run on for days, particularly in the pages of the small-to-medium-circulation newspapers that buy most of the wire-service copy. The public also presumably wants and needs a sense of progress, and since this is a public that tends to measure progress numerically—so many yards gained rushing, so many villages pacified, earnings per share up, body counts down, carloadings steady—there is a tendency on the part of the dispensers of information, the military and the government, to scour Vietnam for positive statistics and dole them out to newsmen, who are always under pressure to supply copy, and who know that there is nearly always a market back home for these firm-sounding stories that seem to be about numbers, which in turn seem to mean something, but in fact are often just about the numbers. One of the better *Catch-22* effects over here is to pick up the daily *Stars & Stripes* and read the wire-service lead, datelined Saigon—"Hurtling out of an overcast sky, warplanes of the United States Seventh Fleet delivered another massive air strike against the port city of Haiphong," and so on—and try to recall the atmosphere and the phrasing when the source information was delivered in the course of the daily briefing, the famous "five-o'clock follies" held each day at the Mission Press Center. A couple of dozen correspondents are slouched in chairs in the briefing room, a bored Air Force major is reading aloud in a flat, uninflected voice the summary of the various air strikes conducted that morning and earlier that afternoon: "Airplanes of the United States Seventh Fleet flew 267 missions against targets in the south.... Airplanes of the 12th Tactical Fighter Wing flew 245 missions and 62 sorties against selected targets, including the warehouse system outside Hanoi and bridges in the Loc Binh area.... " Everybody has been dozing along, except that now someone asks, "Say, Major, isn't that Loc Binh just five miles from the Chinese border?" The major will acknowledge that it is. "Say, Major, isn't that the closest we've yet come to the Chinese border?" The major will acknowledge that it is. "Major," another voice will ask, "wouldn't you say that was a 'first'—I mean in proximity terms?" The major looks thoughtful for a moment. "In proximity terms," he will reply, "I would say 'affirmative.' "

Television correspondents try to get around the limitations, not of their medium but of what they are structurally required to cover (at least, the more political and thoughtful among them do), by inserting some sort of verbal point of view in the taped narrative they send off with their brief film reports, as though to say, Okay, fellows, here's your bang-bang footage, but if I put a little edge in my voice maybe it will come out a bit closer to the way things were. Morley Safer used to do this with a vengeance on CBS, and CBS's David Schoumacher and NBC's Dean Brelis do it to a certain degree now, and in some ways it's effective—it sharpens a point of view, if there should be one to begin with, and it allows for a slight intrusion of irony into a war that most news organizations are attempting to report without irony. (Trying to report a war without irony is a bit like trying to keep sex out of a discussion of the relations between men and women.) The fact is, though, that if you show some film of, say, half a dozen helicopters whirring in onto the ground, our men rushing out with rifles at the ready amid sounds of gunfire here and there, a platoon commander on the radio, men running by with stretchers amid more gunfire, what you are really doing is adding another centimeter or millimeter to what is often no more than an illusion of American military progress (our boys rushing forward, those roaring helicopters, the authoritative voice of the captain). And to stand up there afterward, microphone in hand, and say, with all the edge in your voice you can muster, as Safer used to do, "Another typical engagement in Vietnam.... A couple of battalions of the Army went into these woods looking for the enemy. The enemy was gone. There was a little sniper fire at one moment; three of our men were hit, but not seriously. It was pretty much the way it usually goes," doesn't pull the picture back quite straight—or perhaps, to be a bit more accurate, it focuses one's eyes on a picture that may not really have any useful connection with the situation it claims to be communicating about. Communications. One is so terribly serious about some things. One has a direct circuit installed between Rockefeller Center and the Hotel Caravelle. One can whoosh eight cans of 16-millimeter film two-thirds of the way around the world in less than twenty hours. For around seventy-five hundred bucks, one can buy thirty minutes' worth of satellite time and relay the film in from Tokyo. The television people work like hell in Vietnam—Saturdays, Sundays, all the time, really. Many of the journalists there work like hell—able men, responsible men, pasting detail upon detail into some sort of continuing scrapbook of stories about bombing raids, and pacification programs, and bombing raids, and about the Buddhist march, and the new infrared searchlight, and bombing raids, and about the fact that forty thousand Vietcong defected in the last six months. And the detail accretes, day in, day out; paragraphs clatter out over the cable, film by the bagload heads home for processing, detail, detail, detail, and people back home, who have been fed more words and pictures on Vietnam than on any other event in the last twenty years, have the vague, unhappy feeling that they still haven't been told it straight. And, of course, it's true. When President Johnson stands behind the podium in the East Room, looks into the cameras, and declares that he has "read all the reports" and that the reports tell him "progress is being made," it isn't that he's lying. He doesn't need to lie for the situation to be potentially disastrous; all he needs to do is defer to the authority of a reportorial system (one is thinking especially of the government's) that, in terms of the sensitivities, the writing skill, and the general bias of the reporters, is unlikely to be automatically accurate, or anywhere near it. Patriotism doesn't have much to do with it, any more than inaccuracy or distortion has much to do with whatever it is that gives old Fred—after three years in which he has read 725,000 words about Vietnam—the feeling that he couldn't write three intelligible sentences about the subject on a postcard to his mother.

35
Covering the Gulf of Tonkin

DANIEL C. HALLIN

Aside from a fleeting awareness of the Buddhist crisis of 1963, Vietnam probably entered the consciousness of most Americans for the first time in August 1964. On August 5 the lead story in the *New York Times* began:

> President Johnson has ordered retaliatory action against gunboats and "certain supporting facilities in North Vietnam" after renewed attacks against American destroyers in the Gulf of Tonkin.
>
> In a television address tonight, Mr. Johnson said air attacks on the North Vietnamese ships and facilities were taking place as he spoke, shortly after 11:30 P.M.....
>
> This "positive reply," as the President called it, followed a naval battle in which a number of North Vietnamese PT boats attacked two United States destroyers with torpedoes. Two of the boats were believed to have been sunk. The United States forces suffered no damage or loss of lives.
>
> Mr. Johnson termed the North Vietnamese attacks "open aggression on the high seas."
>
> Washington's response is "limited and fitting," the President said, and his administration seeks no general extension of the guerrilla war in Southeast Asia.

In the *Washington Post* that day the headline ran, "AMERICAN PLANES HIT NORTH VIETNAM AFTER 2D ATTACK ON OUR DESTROYERS; MOVE TAKEN TO HALT NEW AGGRESSION." The right-hand lead, which like the *Times*'s lead focused on the president's address, termed the incident "the gravest military confrontation since the Cuban missile crisis of 1962." It was accompanied by an analytic article, by Chalmers Roberts, under the head "Firm Stand Is Warning to Hanoi":

> The United States turned loose its military might on North Vietnam last night to prevent the Communist leaders in Hanoi and Peking from making the mistaken decision that they could attack American ships with impunity.
>
> But the initial United States decision was for limited action, a sort of tit-for-tat retaliation, and not a decision to escalate the war in Southeast Asia.
>
> Those views came last night from official American sources who would not let themselves be otherwise identified. But there was no doubt they reflected the views of President Johnson and what was described as the unan-

imous decision of all the American policy makers meeting in the Security Council.

No one was prepared to say where the President's decision might lead. Yet no one doubted the historic immensity of the step and its possible vast consequences.

The great mystery here was whether the attacks by North Vietnamese PT boats on the American vessels were part of some larger scheme on the Communist side to escalate the war. It was said by American sources that the attacks, clearly not accidental, could be part of some over-all plan.

On virtually every important point, the reporting of the two Gulf of Tonkin incidents (two days before the second incident, which led to American bombing, the destroyer *Maddox*, backed by carrier aircraft, had fought off an attack by three North Vietnamese PT boats, sinking two) was either misleading or simply false.[1] On August 3, following the first incident, the *Times* reported,

> The incident was announced here in an official statement by the Defense Department.... The statement said that the destroyer...was on a routine patrol when an unprovoked attack took place in the Gulf of Tonkin.... Officials here...said there was no ready explanation why the PT boats would in effect attack the powerful Seventh Fleet.[2]

In fact, the *Maddox* was on a highly sensitive intelligence-gathering operation, mapping North Vietnamese coastal and air defenses. The day before, two attacks on North Vietnam, part of a campaign of increasing military pressure on the North that the United States had been pursuing since early 1964, had taken place.[3] South Vietnamese patrol boats had carried out an attack on the North Vietnamese island of Hon Me, and Laotian Air Force T-28s had bombed and strafed two villages in North Vietnamese territory near the "Ho Chi Minh Trail." Intercepts of North Vietnamese communications prior to the attack had indicated that the North Vietnamese were speculating about the connection of the destroyer with the South Vietnamese naval operations.

The second attack, which served as the rationale for U.S. retaliation and the passage of the Gulf of Tonkin resolution, probably did not take place at all. The *Maddox* had been joined by a second destroyer, the *Turner Joy*. On the night of August 4 the two destroyers detected unidentified signals on their radar which they interpreted as hostile naval craft. A furious "battle" followed, including aircraft from a nearby carrier, under conditions of great confusion. The sonarman on the *Maddox* detected torpedo after torpedo; but his experience was limited, and many of the crew thought afterwards he was probably picking up the sound of the ship's own propellers, or of water on its hull as it turned to avoid the previous "torpedo." The *Turner Joy* fired furiously, while the *Maddox* had great difficulty finding any targets on its fire control radar. The crew of the *Turner Joy* believed they had sunk one North Vietnamese craft and damaged another, but a search the next morning turned up no physical evidence—no debris, survivors, or oil slicks. Several hours after the engagement the commander of the task force, Captain John J. Herrick, cabled to Pacific headquarters:

> Review of action makes many reported contacts and torpedoes fired appear doubtful.... Freak weather effects and overeager sonarman may have accounted for many reports. No actual visual sightings by *Maddox*. Suggest complete evaluation before any further action.[4]

The Pentagon spent a frantic afternoon trying to get confirmation of the attack, and they were still trying when Secretary McNamara gave the order to carry out the retaliatory air strikes. At 8:00 P.M. Washington time, about three and a half hours before the president's address, Herrick cabled:

> *Maddox* scored no known hits and never positively identified a boat as such. ...Weather was overcast with limited visibility.... Air support not successful in locating targets.... There were no stars or moon resulting in almost total darkness throughout action.... No known damage or personnel casualties to either ship.... *Turner Joy* claims sinking one boat and damaging another.... The first boat to close *Maddox* probably fired torpedo at *Maddox* which was heard but not seen. All subsequent *Maddox* torpedo reports were doubtful in that it is supposed that sonarman was hearing ship's own propeller beat.[5]

The most significant inaccuracy in the news of the first acknowledged American combat operation in Vietnam, however, had to do not with events in the Tonkin Gulf but with American policy. Johnson was not lying outright when he reported to the nation that the United States "sought no wider war" in Vietnam. He and his advisors were reluctant to get involved more deeply in Vietnam, and they had not yet firmly decided on the massive escalation that would take place beginning in February 1965. But it certainly was not the case that the first air strike against North Vietnam was merely a "tit-for-tat" retaliation. The administration had been moving throughout 1964 toward a fundamental change in American policy.[6] The covert operations begun in February were part of a systematic program of "increasingly escalating pressure" on North Vietnam. (The document approving this program includes "communications intelligence missions."[7] The *Maddox* was on one of these missions, known as a DESOTO patrol.) In March, following intelligence reports of "dramatic Communist gains" in South Vietnam, the Joint Chiefs of Staff were directed to begin planning for possible "retaliatory actions" and "graduated overt military pressures." In April North Vietnam was warned through a Canadian intermediary that "in the event of escalation the greatest devastation would of course result for the DRV itself." And in late May and early June, as specific plans for escalation were reviewed, policymakers discussed obtaining a joint resolution from Congress authorizing increased military involvement in Southeast Asia. Decisions on these plans were deferred in mid-June. "[A] consensus," as one analyst puts it, "was slowly emerging on the eventual need for greater pressures on the North, [but] there was no consensus over how to exert those pressures."[8] When the Gulf of Tonkin incident occurred, however, the draft of the joint resolution was revised and sent to Congress. It was passed—with two dissenting votes in the Senate and none in the House—in an atmosphere of national unity comparable to that of the Cuban missile crisis.

It does not appear that policymakers deliberately provoked the Tonkin Gulf incidents in order to provide a rationale for escalation. Their motivations were no doubt complex. It was an election year, and Johnson may have felt he had little choice but to take some action, lest he hand Goldwater a useful campaign issue: American ships are attacked on the high seas, and the president does nothing. But planned or not, the incidents clearly did give the administration an invaluable opportunity to deepen American commitment without arousing political controversy. "The net effect of the swift U.S. reprisals and the Congressional Resolution," as the *Pentagon Papers* put it, "was to dramatically demonstrate, publicly state and formally record the commitments to South Vietnam and within Southeast Asia that had been made internal U.S. policy" in the spring, when the National Security Council had reaffirmed the aim of preserving an "independent, non-Communist" South Vietnam and approved increased pressures on the North. The *Pentagon Papers* continue:

> They were also conceived and intended as a clear communication to Hanoi of what it could expect if it continued to pursue its current course of action. They were portents of the future designed to demonstrate the firmness of U.S. resolve and the direction its policy was tending. The psychological impact of the raids on the Administration and the American public is also significant. They marked the crossing of an important threshold in the war, and it was accomplished with virtually no domestic criticism. . . . The precedent for strikes against the North was thus established and at very little apparent cost.[9]

The Gulf of Tonkin incident was a classic of Cold War news management. Through its public statements, its management of information, and its action (there was no "grave military confrontation" until the decision was made to retaliate), the administration was able to define or "frame" the situation in such a way that its action appeared beyond the scope of political controversy.[10] The opening line of the president's address (the text of the speech was printed on page 1 of both the *Times* and *Post*) illustrates well the implications of the package of images the administration had invoked. "My fellow Americans," Johnson began, "as President and Commander in Chief, it is my *duty* to the American people to report that the renewed hostile actions against U.S. ships on the high seas in the Gulf of Tonkin have *required* me to order the military forces of the United States to take action in reply" [emphasis added]. By presenting both the air strikes and the joint resolution as responses to an attack on U.S. forces by a Communist power, the president could claim that events "required" him, in the nonpolitical role of commander in chief, to take the action he did. Many in Congress were nervous about the broad wording of the resolution, which authorized the president to take "all necessary measures to repel any armed attacks against forces of the United States and to prevent further aggression." But the administration argued that any display of disunity would only encourage further North Vietnamese aggression. And in the midst of "the gravest military confrontation since the Cuban missile crisis," few were willing to take the political risk of opposing the president.

An American president, as Richard Neustadt observed in 1960, exercises most of his power indirectly.[11] He does not command; he bargains. He uses his unique structural position, his ability to do things other politicians need done, to induce them either to support or not to oppose his actions. But in foreign affairs, in the early 1960s, presidential power was often exercised in a much more one-sided way. Lyndon Johnson did not have to bargain with anyone to get the Gulf of Tonkin resolution passed. He was, of course, commander in chief of the armed forces. But if it were not for a certain symbolic context that surrounded that role, it would have been nothing more than another source of bargaining power. The president's power in foreign affairs lay in his ability to manipulate symbols, to define events in such a way that he would be considered to have the authority to act not as one politician among others, but as the representative of the nation. What modern scholars sometimes call the "public presidency" existed in an extraordinarily pure and potent form in the Cold War politics of the early 1960s.[12]

The exercise of this kind of symbolic power naturally depended to a large degree on the president's control of the news. But the media are private institutions, protected by constitutional injunctions against government interference, and hence are especially far removed from the president's direct authority. How is it that a president is able to control them as effectively as Lyndon Johnson seems to have done in August 1964?

In the case of the Gulf of Tonkin incident, control of information was clearly an important factor. Journalists had no direct access to any of the details of the incident. They could not talk with the crew or see the cables. They also had relatively little information about what was happening behind the scenes in the administration itself—no way of knowing, for instance, that the text of the joint resolution had been written in the spring, as part of a scenario for a step-by-step escalation of the war. This would change, at least to a degree, later on. Divisions within the administration would increase, and officials involved in bureaucratic conflicts would "leak" much more information about internal policy debates. But in 1964 policy debates were tightly contained, and this greatly enhanced the ability of the president and his top advisors to place any action they took within a context that would guarantee maximum public support.

Control of information by itself, however, by no means explains the effectiveness of their efforts. There was, in fact, a great deal of information available which contradicted the official account; it simply wasn't used. The day before the first incident, Hanoi had protested the attacks on its territory by Laotian aircraft and South Vietnamese gunboats.[13] It was generally known, moreover, and had been reported in the *Times* and elsewhere in the press, that "covert" operations against North Vietnam, carried out by South Vietnamese forces with U.S. support and direction, had been going on for some time.[14] But neither the *Times* nor the *Washington Post* mentioned them at all, either at the time of the incidents or in the weeks that followed, aside from inconspicuous sidebars on Hanoi's "allegations" and a passing reference in James Reston's column.

On the second incident *Le Monde* provides a striking contrast to the U.S. press. "Now that the first armed clashes and the threats have passed," the paper reported on August 8, "it is time to explore the . . . circumstances in which the 'incidents' in the Gulf of Tonkin took place. As our correspondent in Washington has reported, the American 'dossier' contains serious gaps. Even if Hanoi and Peking need to be taken with a grain of salt in their presentation of the facts, it is nevertheless useful to consider their claims, at least to reexamine the facts such as they can be known."[15] The article went on to review the public statements of Washington, Peking, and Hanoi (Hanoi had acknowledged the first attack on the *Maddox*, but called the second a "fabrication"), concluded that the evidence was fragmentary, and speculated that the incident might have been the product of tension and confusion. Neither the *Times* nor the *Post* made any such analysis of the record. There was even, despite the administration's fairly tight control of information about policy debates, a good deal on the public record that suggested that a change in U.S. policy toward North Vietnam was in the offing, for the administration had at times been using the press to warn North Vietnam of this fact.[16] As we shall see, it is only in the context of a certain political climate and a certain conception of what journalism is about that an administration's control of information can give it this kind of control over the content of the news.

There are, of course, ways an administration can apply direct pressure against journalists and news organizations. It is well known that presidents and other well-placed officials will often use the carrot of access and the stick of its denial to influence coverage; it is a significant punishment to deny a reporter the favors—interviews, "leaks," access to *Air Force One*—granted to his or her competitors. News organizations can also be vulnerable to legal and economic pressures, particularly when they are involved in the government-regulated field of broadcasting, as most now are. In the 1970s the Nixon administration made an effort to mobilize the local affiliates against what it saw as excessively critical coverage by the networks, offering them longer periods between license renewals while warning that local stations would be held responsible in license hearings for the content of network news. It also, through a company headed by Nixon associate Bebe Rebozo, initiated a license challenge against a Miami television station owned by the parent company of the *Washington Post*.[17]

The argument is often made, too—though somewhat vaguely—that personal connections tying top executives in the media to political elites keep the media subservient. This was part (but by no means the strongest part) of C. Wright Mills's classic critique of the media in *The Power Elite*.[18]

There is no evidence, however, that any of these forms of direct influence were at work at the time of the Gulf of Tonkin incident, and in general they are little help in explaining the docility of the press during the years of escalation in Vietnam. Pressures on individual journalists were certainly exercised by the Johnson and Kennedy administrations. But they are far too frail a mechanism to account for the consistent pattern of support for the official perspective that we will trace in the following pages. As for economic and legal pressures against news organizations, these were an innovation of the Nixon administration and were less a source of power (though they were not entirely without effect) than a sign of its erosion; by the Nixon period presidential management of the news was becoming substantially more difficult.

As for the "power elite" model, it rests on a fundamental misunderstanding of the nature of the news organization. There are certainly occasions when top executives intervene in day-to-day news decisions. The publisher of the *New York Times* was involved in a decision to downplay an advance story on the Bay of Pigs;[19] William Paley, chairman of the board of CBS, intervened in 1972 to cut back the second half of a lengthy two-part report CBS News was preparing on the Watergate affair.[20] These interventions and others like them probably have "halo effects," reinforcing among journalists a sense that their autonomy is bounded. They also, however, have important costs.

It is worth pausing for a moment to consider the story of the *Times* report on the Bay of Pigs, for it says a good deal about the nature of social control in American journalism. Early in April 1961 *Times* correspondent Tad Szuelc visited Miami on personal business. The coming invasion was an open secret in the Cuban exile community there; there were even pictures of the training bases in the Spanish-language press. And Szuelc, who had excellent Cuban sources, was easily able to piece together a story detailing the preparations. This is how Harrison Salisbury recounts the events that transpired in New York:

> The *Times* bullpen, that is, the major news editors, Theodore Bernstein and Lewis Jordan, two skilled professionals who approached the daily task of "laying out" page one of *The Times* with the solemnity of open-heart surgeons, placed the Szulc story in column eight of page one and assigned it a four column head. This . . . signified in the typographical symbolism of *The Times* that it was a story of exceptional importance. . . . The layout of page one was a ritual performed in Bernstein's monastic cubicle at the southeast corner of the third-floor newsroom. . . . Bernstein and Jordan sat down to their task after a general news conference held by managing editor [Turner] Catledge. They worked swiftly and in virtual silence, their minds and news judgments so finely attuned that rarely was there disagreement, and in these rare cases Jordan . . . quickly deferred to Bernstein, his senior. . . . Catledge was, in theory, of course, free to attend and participate in the process but almost never did. It went forward in what some witnesses felt was the holy hush of the communion, with a subaltern editor or two sitting silently at the table, never uttering a word, drinking in what the participants felt was the ultimate ecstasy of the news process.[21]

But Orvill Dryfoos, the publisher, had meanwhile been on the phone to James Reston, the Washington bureau chief. He and Reston had agreed, he told Catledge, that the story should at least be toned down, lest the *Times* be "blamed for tipping off Castro." All references to the imminence of the invasion and the involvement of the CIA were excised, the size of the head was reduced from four columns to one, and the story was bumped from the right-hand lead to column four. Bernstein and Jordan, Salisbury recounts, were "stunned" by what they saw as an extraordinary intrusion of politics into the news process. "To them the news evaluation process was sacred and they were its high priests. This process had been contaminated by infidels."[22]

The modern American journalist thinks of himself as an autonomous professional. No fact is more central to understanding the politics of the news. The ideology of the "professional" journalist, as Salisbury's shifting metaphors suggest, is ambiguous and contradictory. At one moment Salisbury compares the journalist to a heart surgeon, at another to a priest. He also likens Bernstein and Jordan's decision on the *Times* layout to a "judgment ... of the Joint Chiefs of Staff in assessing a degree of military alert."[23] We shall see as well that the ideology of the journalist as professional is in important ways a "false consciousness." Based on the idea that "news judgment" can be politically neutral, it not only conceals the process by which the news is shaped politically, but is itself a part of that process. It is, in short, a "myth"—but in a particular sense of that word. Far from being a mere lie or illusion, it is a deeply held system of consciousness that profoundly affects both the structure of the news organization and the day-to-day practice of journalism.

When executives of a news organization intervene directly in editorial decisions, they threaten the very basis of authority within it. This is particularly true when they seem to be bowing to political pressure—or anticipated political pressure—from outside. Modern journalism is a collective enterprise in which the contribution of any individual to the final product is relatively small. It is also an enterprise dedicated, in theory, to the pursuit of truth, in which authority cannot be legitimated by property or political sovereignty. Journalists accept as legitimate the many accommodations they must make in the bureaucratic production of news because they see them as accommodations not to economic or political power, but to the collective standards of journalism. Journalistic autonomy is also the basis of the media's public claim to legitimacy: when questions are raised about the right of "a small group of men" (as Sprio Agnew would later put it) to manage a good part of the society's flow of political information, the media's defenders answer that news judgments are made on the basis of "purely journalistic" standards. Violations of journalistic autonomy disrupt the internal functioning of a news organization, sully its prestige within the larger journalistic community (incidents like the *Times*'s decision on the Bay of Pigs are often publicized extensively within that community), and potentially threaten its public image.

It is rare, therefore, to find power, in the traditional sense of the word, being exercised in the news-making process—rare to find some identifiable person or group, either inside or outside the news organization, making a political decision and enforcing his or her or its will directly on those who produce the final product. Power is exercised indirectly, through the manipulation of symbols and routines of working life that those subject to it accept as their own.[24] Often it simply does not *have* to be exercised: the mechanisms that maintain "control" or "consensus" are strong enough that the media simply do not come into conflict with other established political institutions. Often, too, it seems to have no author, but to lie in structures of consciousness and organization that are larger than all the individuals involved, impelling them forward in ways they cannot control. Johnson and Kennedy both possessed great power of manipulation, but, as we shall see, their freedom of action was sometimes limited by the very factors that gave them their power. The forces that compelled the journalists often compelled the policymakers as well.

The president's power to control foreign affairs news in the early 1960s rested primarily on two factors. The first was the ideology of the Cold War: the bipartisan consensus, forged during the Truman and Eisenhower administrations, that had identified foreign policy with "national security," and hence removed most foreign policy decisions from the agenda of political debate. There were differences, of course, about what exactly "national security" meant and what it required, both in terms of tactics abroad and politics—or the suppression thereof—at home. Kennedy was furious at the *New York Times* for printing the advance story on the Bay of Pigs at all.... Many journalists in turn were furious when they were asked to suppress information that was clearly no secret to "the enemy" (Castro's sources in Miami were certainly as good as those of Tad Szulc). But on the broad outlines of the Cold War consensus, the journalists and government policymakers were united. It took no arm-twisting to induce reporters to treat mockingly "scare headlines about...alleged invasion plans" in the Cuban press, as a *Times* article put it late in 1960, [25] just as it took none to induce them to ignore Hanoi's charges of provocation and fabrication in August 1964. The "responsible journalist" did not give credence to "Communist propaganda"; neither did he quibble when the leader of the "Free World" announced to the nation that "aggression" had occurred. These were core symbols of the journalists' world view, just as deeply held as they were for anyone else in the political establishment....

Now we can return to the *Times*'s reporting of the Gulf of Tonkin incident, which we have already encountered....[The Times reported the incident] precisely how the administration wished its action to appear, as a "positive" but limited "reply" forced upon the president by the actions of the enemy, *not* related to any change in U.S. *policy* which might require public debate. This was also objective journalism: Wicker merely presented "the facts"—in this case primarily facts about what the president said in his television address; he took no position on the truth or falsity of the president's remarks or on the policy itself. A right-hand lead on a major event, Wicker explained looking back on this story, was "supposed to be almost dead-pan...as near absolutely—'objective' is too strong—it's supposed to have no content other than what is documentable and quotable fact. No interpretation of any kind. If the president says, 'Black is white,' you write, 'The president said black is white.' "[26] Of course, the reporter is doing more here than simply excluding interpretation. He is exercising "news judgment" according to several of the basic conventions of objective journalism, conventions which here make the *New York Times* essentially an instrument of the state. These conventions include the following:

1. *The use of official sources.* The injunction to present "just the facts" leaves the journalist in a difficult position, for in politics the facts are almost always to some degree in dispute. As many studies of newsmaking have shown, American journalism resolves the problem, most of the time, by taking its facts from official sources.[27] This was certainly the case on August 5, 1964. Wicker's story contained official sources exclusively. Most were administration officials; the only sources outside the administration were Senators Mike Mansfield, the majority leader, and Barry Goldwater, Johnson's opponent in the approaching 1964 election, both of whom supported his action. Indeed, every *Times* story on the Gulf of Tonkin incident that day was based on official U.S. sources exclusively, with the exception of a two-paragraph "shirttail" reporting Hanoi's contention that the naval battle of August 4 was "sheer fabrication" (as we have seen, there is strong evidence that in fact there was no battle that night). One study of the *Washington Post* and the *New York Times* found not only that most of the sources in the two papers were official, but that most stories were based on government/press contacts initiated by officials rather than journalists, especially press conferences and press releases. And, indeed, each of the *Times's* three front page stories on the Tonkin Gulf incident on this day centered around officially initiated events: the right-hand lead, around the president's address; the other two stories, around two Defense Department press conferences.

   The use of official sources, as many have pointed out, is convenient for reporters. The government is organized to provide a timely flow of information, geared to the demands of daily journalism; it is extremely efficient for news organizations to locate their personnel at the channels provided by government. But the use of official sources also fulfills another, perhaps more important function for the media: it fills a vacuum of authority left by the rise of "disinterested realism." Journalists cannot, without stepping outside the role of disinterested observer, decide on their own authority to favor one version of the facts over another because it seems to them, for instance, closer to the truth or more desirable in terms of its effect on public opinion. The principle of balance is no solution. The decision to weight equally conflicting accounts of political reality is no less a political act than the decision to report only one. For the *Times* to have given prominent play to Hanoi's version of the Tonkin Gulf incident would, in the political context of the time, have been a significant and highly controversial political statement, a challenge to the structure of political authority. The solution American journalism has adopted is to defer to authority, justifying that choice as a decision to "let things be what they are," and hence a choice compatible with objectivity. Whether they are true or not, statements by top administration officials are unquestionably "newsworthy" because they come from people of power and authority.

2. *Focus on the president.* Whenever the president acts publicly, he is the focus of coverage; his "newsworthiness" overrides all other priorities. On the day of the Tonkin raids the right-hand lead was constructed around Johnson's address, the address itself was printed next to it, and above the address, beside the headline on the right-hand lead, was a photograph of the president speaking behind the presidential seal, with the caption, "DECISION: President Johnson, in a nationwide broadcast, tells of action he ordered taken against North Vietnam." The personal leadership of the president occupied the foreground of the coverage. Judging from what we know about public response to international events, this is probably very significant. People generally know little about policy, and their attitudes on foreign policy options tend to be ambivalent and unstable. But when a president appeals for unity in a crisis situation, popular support is generally forthcoming.[28]

3. *Absence of interpretation or analysis.* The principles of objectivity forbid editorializing in the news columns. But the status of interpretation, what journalists call news analysis, has been ambiguous since the rise of the ethic of objectivity.[29] Its role was particularly circumscribed during the early 1960s.

Here we encounter another important dilemma which the principle of objectivity creates for the journalist. Journalists are supposed to report the news "straight"—"just give the facts." At the same time they are inevitably teachers and storytellers: they must place events in some kind of framework that will make them meaningful to the news audience. Journalists have generally resolved this dilemma by focusing on the only sort of fact which really does "speak for itself"— facts about what people—in the case of political reporting, generally official people—*say*. Wicker's Tonkin story is a perfect example. All he does is to report what the president said. The president's words, however, are more than mere data being transmitted to the audience: they serve to place the day's events within a context the public can easily understand. American ships were attacked on the high seas; the president, as commander in chief, responded to the Communist challenge with military force; the United States seeks no wider war. Good and evil and cause and effect are clear—yet the journalist has remained strictly objective. Here again official sources fill an important void left by the ethic of objectivity: they fill the vacuum of meaning left by the journalist's renunciation of the role of interpreting reality.

This renunciation of the role of interpretation is not, of course, required of all journalists all of the time. Coverage of a major story like the Tonkin Gulf incident would normally include a number of "news analysis" pieces, though these were less common, less extensive, and less prominently played in the early 1960s than they are today. And none had more prestige in American journalism in the 1950s and early 1960s than the columnists whose job it was, much more exclusively at that time than now, to put the news in perspective—Alsop, Reston, Krock, Lippmann, Sulzberger, and others. But the line between analysis and "straight" reporting was drawn so rigidly in this period that, as we shall see, even at times when the columnists and editorial writers were all but screaming that things were not as they appeared, the front pages continued to report as fact official assurances of "no change in policy." And there is good reason to believe that front page reporting, not the views of columnists or editorialists, is the most important influence, at least on mass public opinion.[30]

In many ways, moreover, analytic journalism was not so different from "straight" journalism. It was, after all, the Alsops, two of the most prominent columnists of the time, who quipped, "His feet are a much more important part of a reporter's body than his head."[31] The columnists, too, were above all gatherers of facts. And what gave them their prestige was primarily their "access": they were not less, but more closely tied than the average journalist to the highest policymakers, though the range of their contacts often made them more independent in relation to any given official or branch of the bureaucracy than reporters who covered only a single beat, at the State Department, for instance, or the White House. Their reputation for influence derived in large part from the fact that they were seen as a kind of semiofficial voice, reflecting the private thinking of the very highest levels of government.

In foreign affairs coverage during this period, a "news analysis" was generally a story based on background briefings or other not-for-attribution contacts with officials, rather than public press conferences, in which the reporter would present, either in the officials' words or in his or her own, the rationale behind the policies announced in public. When officials were unified, therefore, as they were at the time of the Tonkin Gulf incident, analytic reporting generally served as one more channel for the transmission of the official view. Thus Reston reported in one *Times* analysis:

> Had Washington hesitated, or left the retaliation to the South Vietnamese, the President is understood to have felt, the North Vietnamese might then have been encouraged to believe that they could commit their main forces to the war and win a military victory without United States intervention.... The objective of his policy is not to widen the war but to convince the communists that they cannot win the war, and that their sensible course is to negotiate an honorable peace.[32]

4. *Focus on immediate events.* Closely related to the low priority American journalism places on analysis and interpretation is a strong tendency to focus on immediate events. The definition of *news*, as the term implies, involves a time dimension. In principle, journal-

ists could report on phenomena of any duration, as long as demographic changes unfolding over decades or as instantaneous as individual deaths in battle. In practice, news is normally defined in terms of discrete "events" which unfold over the course of a day or less[33]—the period of time between one broadcast or issue of a newspaper and the next—and the historical or structural context of these events, unless it is made an issue by the newsmakers themselves, is relegated to the ambiguous realm of analysis—and generally to the back pages. A presidential speech or press conference is news; a gradual change in policy is not. A clash between Buddhists and the South Vietnamese government is news; the power relations or cultural tensions that lie behind it are not.

The news on August 5, 1964, was the president's address and the raids on North Vietnam, which were described in great detail in the *Times*—the nature of the targets, the damage to them, and so on. Officials had described those raids as a response to the North Vietnamese attacks on U.S. destroyers, and those events were mentioned prominently in the *Times*. Beyond that, the *Times* contained only the slightest fragments of historical context. And this was true not only on the day of the event, but in the days that followed as well, as attention first turned to the passage of the Gulf of Tonkin resolution and then fell off. The *Times* contained, for example, only a few brief and ambiguous allusions to the intensification of covert operations against North Vietnam which had preceded the previous clash in the Gulf of Tonkin, the North Vietnamese attack—this one acknowledged by North Vietnam—of August 2. Little was said either about the implications the incident might have for the future, aside from the official statement that the United States sought no wider war. The closest thing to an independent assessment of the significance of the event was an ambiguous comment buried deep in Wicker's August 5 story, and stated virtually without elaboration: " . . . despite Mr. Johnson's assurances that the U.S. sought no 'wider war,' it was plain that the situation in South Vietnam and the surrounding area had reached new gravity." The absence of these elements of historical context cannot be explained by simple lack of information. The *Times* had reported in some detail on the covert operations against the North as recently as July 23;[34] and although the administration was giving out little information about its policy deliberations, it had, as we shall see, frequently gone public in the months preceding Tonkin with warnings to Hanoi that it might well expand its involvement—among other things by air action against the North—if North Vietnam did not cease its "aggression." By the conventions of objective journalism, however, none of this was news in August 1964.

NOTES

1. The account of the Gulf of Tonkin incident which follows is based primarily on Joseph C. Goulden, *Truth Is the First Casualty: The Gulf of Tonkin Affair—Illusion and Reality* (New York: Rand McNally, 1969), and Eugene V. Windchy,

Tonkin Gulf (Garden City, N.Y.: Doubleday, 1971). See also Wallace J. Thies, *When Governments Collide: Coercion and Diplomacy in the Vietnam Conflict, 1964–1968* (Berkeley: University of California Press, 1980), pp. 41–52.

2. Arnold H. Lubasch, "Red PT Boats Fire at U.S. Destroyer on Vietnam Duty," *NYT*, Aug. 3, 1964, p.1.

3. Thies, *op. cit.*, p. 43.

4. Goulden, *op. cit.*, p. 152.

5. *Ibid.*,p. 156. Herrick recently told the *Los Angeles Times* he thought probably no torpedo was fired. Robert Scheer, "Tonkin—Dubious Premise for a War," *Los Angeles Times*, April 28, 1985, p. 1.

6. *Pentagon Papers*, Senator Gravel, ed. (Boston: Beacon Press, 1971), Vol. III, pp. 106–251; Thies, *op. cit.*, pp. 21–41.

7. *Pentagon Papers*, III, p. 150.

8. Thies, *op. cit.*, p. 30.

9. *Pentagon Papers*, III, p. 109.

10. On the concept of "frame," see Todd Gitlin, *The Whole World Is Watching: Mass Media in the Making and Unmaking of the New Left* (Berkeley: University of California Press, 1980), pp. 6–7.

11. Richard E. Neustadt, *Presidential Power: The Politics of Leadership with Reflections on Johnson and Nixon* (New York: Wiley, 1976).

12. Samuel Kernell, *Going Public* (Washington: Congressional Quarterly Press, 1985).

13. "Raid from Laos Alleged by Hanoi" (AP), *NYT*, Aug. 2, 1964, p. 1.

14. Peter Grose, "Sabotage Raids on North Confirmed by Saigon Aide," *NYT*, July 23, 1964, p. 1. And see Georges Chaffard, "Des commandos sud-vietnamiennes entrainéîes par les Americains opèrent depuis longtemps au Tonkin," *Le Monde*, Aug. 7, 1964, p. 1.

15. Jean Planchais, "Les circonstances du second combat naval demeurent imprécises," *Le Monde*, Aug. 8, 1964, p. 2. See also I. F. Stone, "What Few Know about the Tonkin Bay Incidents," *In a Time of Torment* (New York: Random House, 1967).

16. Thies, *op. cit.*, pp. 40, 42.

17. William E. Porter, *Assault on the Media: The Nixon Years* (Ann Arbor: University of Michigan Press, 1976). These were only two elements of a multifaceted campaign against the media.

18. "[S]ome of the higher agents of these media are themselves either among the elites or very important among their servants." C. Wright Mills, *The Power Elite* (New York: Oxford University Press, 1956), p. 315.

19. The story of press coverage of the Bay of Pigs, and of the *Times* decision specifically, has been told many times: Harrison Salisbury, *Without Fear or Favor: An Uncompromising Look at The New York Times and Its Times* (New York: Ballantine, 1980); Tom Wicker, *On Press* (New York: Viking, 1978); Neal D. Houghton, "The Cuban Invasion of 1961 and the U.S. Press in Retrospect," *Journalism Quarterly* 42:3 (Summer 1965); Victor Bernstein and Jesse Gordon, "The Press and the Bay of Pigs," *Columbia University Forum*, Fall 1967; Gay Talese, *The Kingdom and the Power* (New York: World Publishing, 1969), pp. 4-5.

20. David Halberstam, *The Powers That Be* (New York: Knopf, 1979), pp. 651–61.

21. Salisbury, *op. cit.*, pp. 153–54.

22. *Ibid.*, pp. 155–56.

23. *Ibid.*, p. 154.

24. See Steven Lukes, *Power: A Radical View* (London: Macmillan, 1974); John Gaventa, *Power and Powerlessness: Quiescence and Rebellion in an Appalachian Valley* (Urbana, Ill.: University of Illinois Press, 1980); Murray Edelman, *The Symbolic Uses of Politics* (Urbana, Ill.: University of Illinois Press, 1967); and the large literature employing Gramsci's concept of hegemony: Antonio Gramsci, *Selections from the Prison Notebooks*, ed. and trans. Quintin Hoare and Geoffrey Nowell Smith (New York: International Publishers, 1971); Perry Anderson, "The Antinomies of Antonio Gramsci," *New Left Review* 100 (Nov. 1976–Jan. 1977); Raymond Williams, *Marxism and Literature* (Oxford: Oxford University Press, 1977); Stuart Hall, "Culture, the Media and the 'Ideological Effect,' " in James Curran, Michael Gurevitch, and Janet Woollacott, eds., *Mass Communication and Society* (Beverly Hills: Sage, 1979); and Todd Gitlin, *op. cit.*

25. R. Hart Phillips, "Havana Drums Up Fear of Invasion," *NYT*, Oct. 28, 1960, p. 10.

26. Wicker interview.

27. Sigal, op. cit., ch. 6.

28. Robert Weissberg, *Public Opinion and Popular Government* (Englewood Cliffs, N. J.: Prentice-Hall, 1976), 234–37.

29. See Schudson, op. cit., pp. 144–59.

30. About 25% of the public reads the average editorial, according to a study commissioned by the American Newspaper Publishers' Association, and about 20% the average political column. The general average for all types of content in this study was 25%. Assuming that readership of the front page is much higher than average, readership of the front page is obviously much greater than readership of editorials and columns. The data are from Galen Rarick, ed., *News Research for Better Newspapers* (Washington, D.C.: ANPA Foundation, 1975), Vol. 7, pp. 35–39. Studies of the impact of news on public opinion have generally found front page content a powerful predictor, though none have compared it directly with the editorial page. See Richard A. Brody and Benjamin I. Page, "The Impact of Events on Presidential Popularity: The Johnson and Nixon Administrations," in Aaron Wildavsky, ed.; *Perspectives on the Presidency* (Boston: Little, Brown, 1975); Arthur H. Miller, Lutz Erbring, and Edie N. Goldenberg, "Type-set Politics: Impact of Newspapers on Public Conference," *American Political Science Review* 73:1 (1979). Given what we know about the effects of mass communication on political beliefs in general, it makes sense that the front page should have greater impact than columns or editorials: people are less affected by media messages they perceive as attempts to persuade than by messages they perceive as informational. See Carl I. Hovland, Irving L. Janis, and Harold H. Kelly, *Communication and Persuasion* (New Haven: Yale University Press, 1953).

31. Joseph and Stuart Alsop, *The Reporter's Trade* (New York, Renal and Co., 1958), p.5.

32. James Reston, "North Vietnam's Motives," *NYT*, Aug. 6, 1964, p. 8.

33. Johan Galtung and Marie Ruge, "The Structure of Foreign News: The Presentation of the Congo, Cuba and Cypress Crises in Four Foreign Newspapers," *Journal of International Peace Research* 1 (1965).

34. Peter Grose, "Sabotage Raids on North Confirmed by Saigon Aide," *NYT*, July 23, 1954, p. 1.

Photograph taken at the traveling Vietnam Veterans' War Memorial in Houston, Texas, May 21, 1987. UPI/BETTMANN NEWSPHOTOS

CHAPTER 10

The Legacy of the War

This chapter offers a necessarily sketchy view of an enormous subject: the impact of the war on Vietnam and the United States. When North Vietnamese and National Liberation Front forces captured Saigon in April 1975, they faced the daunting tasks of unifying and rehabilitating their shattered country. Professor William Duiker describes the beginning of these processes, as the Communists, convinced of the need for nationwide socialism, started to consolidate the country politically and nationalize its economy, despite the skepticism or resistance of many southerners. In the United States, the results of the war were hardly so cataclysmic, but many individuals were deeply affected by the Vietnam experience. There were those who deserted from the military because they could not countenance the possibility of participation in the war. One of these was Richard Perrin, whose story is told here by Gloria Emerson. And of course, there were those who did go to war, and who came back with wounds both physical and psychic; Emmett, a character in Bobbie Ann Mason's novel *In Country*, is one of these. At the end of the novel (and this excerpt), Emmett goes to visit the Vietnam Veteran's Memorial—the Wall—in Washington. With him are his niece, Sam Hughes, and Mawmaw, Sam's paternal grandmother, whose son Dwayne—Sam's father—was killed in Vietnam. The last scene is a reminder of the pain caused by the war, but it carries with it hope of redemption.

36
The Aftermath of Communist Victory
WILLIAM J. DUIKER

Our mountains will always be, our rivers will always be, our people will always be. Once the American invaders have been defeated, we will rebuild our land ten times more beautiful.

Ho Chi Minh. *Testament*

On the morning of April 30, 1975, communist tanks rumbled down the leafy avenues of downtown Saigon and up onto the spacious green lawn of the Presidential Palace. A North Vietnamese soldier mounted the roof of the Palace, lowered the red and yellow striped flag of the Government of Vietnam (GVN) and hoisted the standard of the Provisional Revolutionary Government (PRG) in its place. Two hours earlier, in a radio broadcast from the Palace, President Duong Van Minh had called on all South Vietnamese forces to lay down their arms. Then he and his cabinet awaited the inevitable and with the arrival of the first communist units, surrendered meekly. After a generation of bitter struggle, the long Vietnamese conflict had ended, not with a bang, but with a whimper.[1]

IDEOLOGICAL PERSPECTIVE

In Hanoi, where communist leaders of the North Vietnamese regime (formally called the Democratic Republic of Vietnam, or DRV) had directed the revolutionary struggle in the South since the 1950s, the news of the triumph was undoubtedly greeted with satisfaction. There would be little time for jubilation, however, for with victory came new challenges and new responsibilities. Power must be consolidated over the South, and the remnants of the opposition eliminated. The national economy, badly damaged by a generation of civil conflict, must be restored to a peacetime footing, and productive forces put back to work. A new revolutionary program must be drafted to broaden the base of support for the new order. South and North must be reunified and prepared for the final advance to socialism. Finally, the nation must be ever vigilant, and prepare for the possible defense of the revolution from its external enemies.

Excerpted from William J. Duiker, *Vietnam Since the Fall of Saigon,* Updated Edition, (Athens, Ohio: Monographs in International Studies, 1989), pp. 3–27. Copyright 1989 by the Center for International Studies, Ohio University. Reprinted by permission.

Communist parties are well drilled in the ways of waging revolution, of course, and there is ample literature in the library of Marxism-Leninism on what they must do once power is in their grasp. Even here, however, the challenges were formidable. In the first place, Vietnam was not, in the classical Marxist sense, an advanced capitalist society ripe for a socialist revolution. To the contrary, it was a relatively backward society with a primitive industrial base characterized by small-scale production. Marx had assumed that communism would only have to distribute existing material wealth; in Vietnam the Party would have to create it first.

Secondly, the population in the South did not possess the political sophistication necessary to provide the communists with the solid base necessary for the advance to socialism. Party leaders had recognized this problem during the war. Although popular support for the revolutionary forces in the South was relatively widespread, it was based less on communist ideology than on a simple desire for political and economic reforms and social justice. This fact had been reflected in the program of the Party's front organization, the National Liberation Front (NLF), which had been deliberately designed to appeal to Southern moderates in the struggle against the Saigon regime. Politically, the program of the NLF promised to ensure broad democratic freedoms. In the economic sphere, it made no mention of communism and called simply for the confiscation of the property of the American imperialists and their puppets. The right of public ownership of the means of production and distribution would be protected. In rural areas, a program of "land to the tiller" would be instituted, and the new government would "confirm and protect the peasants' ownership of lands allotted to them by the revolution." The program was deliberately vague on the issue of national reunification, in deference to separatist feelings in the South. At some unspecified point in the future, the reunification of the two zones would be achieved on the basis of peaceful negotiations.[2]

In facing such challenges, the Party was not without precedents and ideological guidelines. The basic documents had come from Lenin and Mao Zedong (Mao Tse-tung). Lenin had provided affirmation of the need for a Dictatorship of the Proletariat led by its vanguard element, the Communist party, until the power of the class enemies had been totally destroyed. But he had also come to realize that when communists come to power in a backward society in which the industrial revolution has not yet been completed, they must undertake themselves the task of leading society through the capitalist stage, and thence on to socialism.[3] During the first stage after seizing power, the Party would nationalize only the major industries, banks, and utilities, while encouraging local capitalists to increase production. Under this so-called "New Economic Policy" (NEP), the land of the feudal landowning class would be divided among the poor, but the bulk of private farmers would be left alone to encourage them to increase grain production. Nationalization of commerce and industry, and the collectivization of agriculture, would be postponed until the second, or proletarian stage of the revolution.

The Chinese Communist Party (CCP), on coming to power in China in 1949, was faced with similar problems and had found the Leninist model useful. In its first few years after seizing power the CCP had refrained from adopting measures to transform the economy to socialist forms, and in a program entitled "New Democracy" had permitted the continued operation of the private sector in the hope of increasing production and speeding up economic recovery from the long years of war. Socialist transformation, including the transformation of private farming to collective ownership, began in earnest only in the mid-1950s.[4]

But Mao Zedong had carried Lenin's ideas a step further. Like the Vietnamese, the CCP had been faced with the fact that its support in China was broad but shallow, based on its reformist public program rather than its long-term radical intentions. To broaden and deepen the Party's constituency, Mao not only called for the adoption of "mass line" policies, which would appeal to the broad mass of the population while gradually preparing it for the next stage of socialist transformation, he also replaced the Leninist Dictatorship of the Proletariat with the concept of a "People's Democratic Dictatorship" composed of the Leninist four-class alliance of workers, peasants, petty bourgeoisie, and national bourgeoisie. This approach would carry society through to the stage of communism and the final withering away of the state. While the Communist party, as the sole organization possessing a true understanding of doctrine and the determination to carry it out, would naturally be the dominant force in government, other parties representing the various progressive classes in the revolutionary alliance would be allowed to participate in the political process as well. Popular participation also would be realized through the creation of mass organizations formed on the basis of religion, sex, ethnic background, or economic occupation, and operating through the national united front directed behind the scenes by the Party. In effect, Mao was gambling that the overwhelming bulk of the Chinese population—workers, peasants, and urban middle class alike—could be brought to support the goals of the revolution. Only a handful of reactionary feudal elements and the "comprador bourgeoisie" (those within the local manufacturing and commercial sector whose fortunes were closely tied to the foreign imperialists) were viewed as inveterate class enemies who would be pitilessly eliminated.

The Vietnamese communist leadership was well aware of these precedents and had already applied them in the North following the Geneva Conference in 1954. Power was consolidated in the hands of the Party—then known as the Vietnam Worker's Party (VMP)—but a Maoist "mass line" program was put into effect which operated through a series of mass organizations under the direction of the Party's united front, the Fatherland Front. During its first years in power, the VMP followed Soviet and Chinese practice and refrained from radical measures to do away with the system of private ownership.[5] Banks, utilities, and major commercial and manufacturing enterprises were nationalized, but many small businesses were permitted to remain temporarily under private ownership in order to encourage production. In rural areas land reform was instituted, with over half of all peasant families in the North receiving some land under the program. Only in 1958 did the regime begin to move directly toward socialism with the institution of small collective farms in the countryside.

The results were mixed. From a purely economic point of view, performance did not match expectations, for the regime had only meager success in increasing production and building the technological foundations of an advanced socialist society. Little progress was achieved in transforming the economy from small-scale to large-scale production. Labor productivity remained low, and few of the regime's production targets were met. Grain output lagged, and with a burgeoning population, the ratio of man to land in the countryside increased at an alarming rate.[6] From a political and ideological standpoint, however, the program was a qualified success. Within a few years, state-owned enterprises gradually became dominant in the urban sector while the bulk of the rural economy was placed under collective ownership without the violence that had accompanied the liquidation of the rich peasant class in the Soviet Union in the 1930s.[7] On that popular base the Party was able to wage, with considerable success, its revolutionary war in the South.

THE CONSOLIDATION OF REVOLUTIONARY POWER

It was from this ideological perspective that the Party leadership approached the challenges of peace. Not only must the regime consolidate revolutionary rule, eliminate the remaining enemy forces from the South, and promote the recovery of the economy of the entire country from the devastating effects of two decades of war; it must also bring about a cultural transformation of the capitalist South and an integration of the two zones into a single state while preparing for the transition to an advanced socialist society.

The immediate task was to fill the vacuum left by the virtual disintegration of the previous regime. The rapidity of Saigon's collapse had caught the Party leadership by surprise. During the last years of the war, Party strategy had been based on the assumption that victory would probably not be realized through a direct military takeover of the South by revolutionary forces, but as the result of a negotiated settlement resulting in the creation of a coalition government including both communist and non-communist elements. The program of the NLF had referred in general terms to the formation of a "democratic government of national union" composed of representatives from all progressive sectors of South Vietnamese society. In the Party's plan, this transitional regime would gradually be replaced by a government under total Party control and finally reunited with the North.

It was one of the many ironies of the long war that when the end came, it did not come as the Party leadership had expected. The final triumph was achieved by military means, and the communists did not have to share power. The decision to seek a total military solution appears to

have been made in late 1974 or early in 1975, in response to the unexpected weakness of the Saigon regime and the apparent inclination of the
Ford administration in Washington not to re-enter the conflict.[8] During
the final days of the war, as regular units of the North Vietnamese army
struck ever closer to Saigon, high political figures in South Vietnam maneuvered frantically in an effort to arrange a negotiated settlement with
Hanoi, or with the PRG, its surrogate in the South. To the last there were
tantalizing rumors that even at that late date the communists might be
willing to settle for a negotiated agreement. But the Party's longtime strategy of a transitional regime was overtaken by events. With total military
victory at hand, Hanoi now decided to dispense with the stage of a coalition regime. As an article in the December 5, 1975, issue of the Party's
newspaper *Nhan Dan* later put it, a coalition government "was only necessary on the condition that the revolutionary forces, with the proletariat
serving as a nucleus, did not possess an absolute advantage." As it turned
out, "victory was so great that there was no need for the formation of a
coalition administration."

The North did not relent even after Hanoi's nemesis Nguyen Van
Thieu stepped down as president, ultimately to be replaced by General
Duong Van Minh—long rumored to be an acceptable figure to the North
Vietnamese. Hanoi's response to Minh's final desperate appeal, in the form
of a directive from the Politburo to the Southern military command, was
terse and to the point:

> Continue the attack on Saigon according to plan, advancing in the most
> powerful spirit, liberate and take over the whole city, disarm enemy troops,
> dissolve the enemy administration at all levels, and thoroughly smash all
> enemy resistance.[9]

During the last few weeks of the war, Hanoi hurriedly attempted to fill
the gap that would appear with the collapse of the Saigon regime. During
the final campaign, as the hammerblows of the People's Army of Vietnam
(PAVN) were striking ever closer to the capital, a Military Management
Committee was set up under the chairmanship of General Tran Van Tra,
veteran commander of revolutionary forces in the South.[10]

The obvious purpose of preceding civilian with military rule was to
facilitate the restoration of order and the elimination of forces loyal to
the previous regime. There were indications that this task would not be
difficult. Most of the leading members of the GVN, including ex-President
Thieu, had already fled the country in ships, planes, or the American helicopters that had hovered like gigantic birds over the sky of Saigon during
the war's final hours. Of the civilian and military officials who remained,
a few fled to the hills or the swamps to continue the struggle, but most
accepted the inevitable and awaited their destiny. As for the Southern
population as a whole, there were undoubtedly many who welcomed the
victory of the revolutionary forces but, if reports by foreign observers who
were in Saigon at war's end are reliable, most accepted their new masters less with enthusiasm or with fear than with resignation. If there was a

sentiment that united most Southerners, it may have been sheer relief at the end of the long war. If this proved to be the case, the communists would have time to work their miracle.[11]

The new ruling authorities immediately set out to bring order out of chaos. In the first weeks, the only visible power in the conquered South was in the hands of the eleven-man Saigon Military Management Committee under general Tran Van Tra. In June, a civilian government under PRG president Huynh Tan Phat formally took office, and a month later, a fifty-nine-member Advisory Board was created from among members of the PRG and other elements from the "third force" group which had opposed the Thieu regime. Actual power, however, continued to rest with the Military Management Committee and with the Party, represented behind the scenes by Pham Hung, a Politburo member and in charge of Party operations in the South since 1967.[12] . . .

One of the primary tasks of the new revolutionary administrations at the local level was to maintain order and locate possible sources of opposition to the new regime. Normally this task was to be handled by locally organized self-defense forces called the people's militia and described as "dictatorial tools of revolutionary administration" with the authority to "directly suppress counter-revolutionaries on the spot." Where necessary, units of the PAVN in the vicinity could be assigned to provide backup support. In most areas, resistance was light or nonexistent, although there were reports of opposition in the Central Highlands, and near the city of My Tho in the Mekong Delta, an area with a substantial Hoa Hao population.[13]

In general, individuals whose loyalty to the new order was suspect, such as officials of the previous regime or members of the South Vietnamese armed forces, were simply instructed to report to the authorities. They were then classified in various categories. Those not considered a source of potential opposition were instructed to return home to await further instructions. Most would later attend brief indoctrination sessions in Marxism-Leninism. Others were directed to report to reeducation camps, usually for a few weeks of political indoctrination. The most serious offenders were sent to isolated work camps, where they were expected to remain for an extended period of time.[14]

The total number of Southerners requiring reeducation was well over a million persons. Fewer than 150,000 supporters of the old regime had left in the final weeks of the war. At first, many did not report as instructed, and either fled to join resistance units in the countryside, or waited at their homes. In June, the PRG reported that one-third had not registered. As the establishment of local revolutionary order proceeded, however, most were located, and by the end of the year, at least one million supporters or employees of the Saigon regime had presented themselves for registration.[15]

In general, revolutionary rule had been established with little evidence of widespread bloodshed. Several hundred thousand potential opponents of the regime had been placed in reeducation camps, and reports began to filter back to their families that conditions in the camps were primitive and sometimes brutal, but there were few trials of public figures or public executions. Duong Van Minh himself was reported to be living under surveillance.[16] The regime did make an effort to round up "undesirable elements" such as beggars and street urchins, bargirls, and prostitutes. But to avoid panic all signs of a campaign of mass arrests or the widely feared "bloodbath" were avoided. In a few cases, revolutionary zealots ranged throughout downtown Saigon—now renamed Ho Chi Minh City—attacking local youths in Western dress. According to press reports, some were dragged from buses to have their long hair sheared and their Western-style clothing ripped to shreds. Government directives soon appeared in the press, however, warning that such revolutionary excesses would be severely punished.

On the other hand, the new regime moved expeditiously to eliminate or at least reduce the "poisonous weeds" of Western bourgeois culture and plant the seeds of a new and beautiful socialist culture. Books reflecting Western influence were removed from bookstores and libraries. The playing of the most obnoxious forms of Western music, such as rock and roll, was banned. According to one report, Saigon radio stations, now under Party control, were permitted to play Western music for only two hours each day, and the beat and lyrics were toned down. The key vehicle for controlling behavior and transmitting cultural values to the young, of course, was education. For a brief period, the entire school system was shut down, and teachers were given reindoctrination courses before being certified to teach under the new regime. When the schools reopened, students were issued new textbooks hurriedly sent from the North to replace the existing ones, which were withdrawn from circulation. A new curriculum was instituted based on the system in use in the North.[17]

Finally, the regime took a number of measures to control potential sources of independent or hostile political activity. All political parties established during the previous regime were banned, and a number of quasi-political "third force" organizations, many of which had been sympathetic to the revolutionary cause, were disbanded or integrated into new mass organizations controlled by the government. The authorities announced that freedom of religion would be protected, but it soon became clear that the secular activities of religious organizations such as the Catholic Church, the Unified Buddhist Association, and the Hoa Hao and the Cao Dai sects would be placed under careful supervision or prohibited. In the case of the Hoa Hao, long considered one of the organized groups most hostile to the revolution, the central organization of the church was disbanded, and a number of key leaders arrested. Worship was permitted, but only at the personal level.[18]

PROMOTING ECONOMIC RECOVERY

A second challenge of importance for the regime was to stimulate economic recovery from the long years of war. During the final years of the conflict the economy in the South, long propped up by American largesse, had gradually deteriorated. Industrial growth was stagnant. Hindered by the war in the countryside, grain production was well below the level needed for self-sufficiency in food. Unemployment was rife. During the last years of the war thousands of peasants had fled to the cities from their native villages to escape the fighting in the countryside. The flood of refugees from the villages added to an already serious problem of unemployment among urban residents who had been in service occupations connected to the American presence. With the departure of their clients and the cutting of the umbilical cord to the American economy, the source of their livelihood had been eliminated. According to communist estimates, by the end of the war some eight million Vietnamese, comprising 34 percent of the total population in the South, were living in the cities. In the process, the population of Saigon increased from less than one million in the 1950s to over four million in 1975.[19]

For the new regime, the logical answer was to reverse the flow and encourage the refugees to return to their homes in the countryside. The effects of the exodus from rural areas were clearly evident. Entire villages virtually had been abandoned and agricultural production had declined significantly. According to one communist estimate, agricultural production in 1975 represented only about 10 percent of the entire gross national product of South Vietnam.[20] With the overcrowded North chronically short of food, the restoration of the rice-rich South to its historic role of rice bowl of Vietnam was undoubtedly a matter of high priority to the Party leadership.

The primary means utilized to repopulate the countryside was the formation of so-called New Economic Zones (NEZs). The concept had originated during the first five-year plan in the early 1960s when planners in the DRV had called for the construction of middle-sized urban centers encompassing both food production and manufacturing. Set up at the district level, these new population centers (described as the "urbanization of the countryside") were to be located, wherever possible, in underdeveloped areas in the mountains and plateau regions, thus bringing virgin lands into cultivation and providing new foci for industrial development, or at least local industrial self-sufficiency, in the countryside. The plan was initiated in 1961. Though hampered by poor planning and the peasants' reluctance to depart from their native villages, by the end of the war it had resulted in the transfer of nearly one million peasants from the crowded Red River Delta to the mountains or foothills, thus creating several hundred new agricultural cooperatives and clearing over one hundred thousand hectares of virgin land.[21]

With the return of peace, the concept of the New Economic Zones was resuscitated as a means of resolving the economic crisis in the South. Plans were drafted hurriedly to set up NEZs in underpopulated provinces throughout South Vietnam. While a few were located in the Mekong Delta or along the Central Coast, most were established in the sparsely settled Central Highlands or in the piedmont regions along the Cambodian border, where the effects of war had been particularly severe. Theoretically, the locations were to be selected on the basis of their economic potential, but it is likely that political and security factors were often involved. Once the areas had been given on-the-spot preparation by teams of cadres, they were considered ready for settlement and the government would recruit volunteers who would be provided with seed, farm implements, building materials, and sufficient food for several months. In preparation for its eventual transformation into collective farms, much of the land was held in common, but each family was allotted a private plot for its own use.

Government sources indicate that the ultimate objective was to settle up to two million people in the new settlements. According to regulations, recruitment was supposed to be on a voluntary basis, but complaints soon appeared in the press that certain categories of citizens—members of the previous regime, the minorities, the poor, and the unemployable— were being recruited forcibly. The problem was exacerbated when reports began to filter back from the new settlements of poor cadre preparation, lack of facilities, and economic hardship. The problem was frequently particularly difficult for urban residents, often overseas Chinese, who were unaccustomed to the rigors of rural life. Nevertheless, by the end of the year the government announced that half a million Vietnamese had been transferred under the new program.[22]

A second major task for the new regime was to stimulate industrial production and increase the flow of goods into the economy. To a degree, this was simply a matter of instilling confidence within the business sector. One of the first acts of the new administration in Saigon was to call on merchants and manufacturers to open their shops and factories and to assure them that their profits would be guaranteed by the new government "as long as it benefits the national economy and the welfare of the people." Several large-scale construction projects owned and operated by the government (and, in some cases, operated by units of the PAVN) were announced to help relieve the unemployment problem and help set the economy back on its feet. Actions were taken to stabilize wages, and the old trade unions were abolished and replaced by new "liberation unions."[23]

The matter of encouraging the productive capacity of the urban economy, however, had to be handled with some delicacy, for the Party's long-term objective was to eliminate the influence of the private sector in the South. So long as the bulk of the manufacturing and commercial sector was under private control, the regime would be unable to stabilize prices and the distribution of goods or to establish centralized planning procedures. Yet the process of undermining the power of private capital must be undertaken in such a way as to minimize disruptive economic and political effects in the cities.

The first cautious moves to establish control over the urban economy in the South were taken almost immediately after the establishment of revolutionary rule. All property owned by the GVN was confiscated, and private banks and a number of enterprises belonging to foreign capitalists were seized. In order to reduce the power of major industrialists and traders, the government launched a campaign to confiscate the property of the so-called comprador bourgeoisie (described in one article as bankers, war contractors, ex-imperialists, investors, and speculators). Contending that these elements were guilty of speculation, hoarding, and related efforts to sabotage the efficient functioning of the market, the government moved quickly to eliminate them by seizing their businesses and confiscating their property in a campaign described in the leading Saigon newspaper as "difficult, violent, and extremely complex." Several individual entrepreneurs, described as "the pharmaceutical king" or "the barbed wire king," were placed on trial and charged with serious crimes against the people.[24] A few were executed after show-trials, presumably as a means to *encourager les autre*. The purpose of the campaign, according to the Party's theoretical journal *Hoc Tap* (the journal was renamed *Tap Chi Cong San* in early 1977), was "to eliminate the traces of neo-colonialism, the comprador bourgeoisie, bureaucratic and militaristic remnants of the feudal system." In order to prevent panic from spreading throughout the business sector, the regime used the time-tested united front approach and encouraged the Southern commercial middle class (in Marxist jargon, the national bourgeoisie, whose own "positive aspects" were to be encouraged) to "enthusiastically take part in the struggle" against reactionary elements.

The practical effect of the campaign was to undercut the economic power of the overseas Chinese community in South Vietnam. Under the Saigon regime, Chinese controlled half of all retail trade in the South, and were dominant in the export-import sector. According to one source, forty-two of the sixty largest firms in the GVN were in the hands of Chinese.[25] Although the regime vigorously denied that the campaign had racial connotations, many in the Chinese community were convinced that the action was directed specifically at eliminating their role in the economy.

A second measure to reduce the influence of private business in South Vietnam was the establishment of a new currency. The old piaster was abolished as a medium of exchange and replaced by a new Southern *dong*. The new currency was not to be interchangeable with the dong in use in the North, and was described as a temporary expedient until final unification of the two zones. In theory, all piasters held by private citizens in the South were to be exchanged for the new currency (at a rate of one dong for five hundred piasters) but in reality each family possessing less than one million piasters was allowed to exchange up to one hundred thousand piasters (approximately U.S. $1,000) for four hundred dong and deposit the remainder in the Central Bank.[26]

In rural areas, the new authorities were faced with even more intimidating problems. Increasing food production in the South would have to be a matter of highest priority. With nearly 50 percent more arable land and a more salubrious climate than the North, the Southern provinces were targeted to become the rice bowl of the unified Vietnam. But the ravages of the war had reduced agricultural production in the GVN severely. Between 1969 and the signing of the Paris Agreement in January 1973, the United States had provided the Saigon regime with an average of 650,000 million tons of food annually....

During its first months in power, the new regime was in effect taking the first tentative steps toward building socialism in the South while for the time being tolerating a significant degree of private enterprise in most sectors of the economy. This policy was formalized in the announcement that for the foreseeable future the Vietnamese economy would be divided into five separate sectors: (1) state owned, (2) collective, (3) joint state-private enterprises, (4) private capitalist, and (5) individual ownership. Because of the strength of the socialist system in the North, observed one commentator, the presence of capitalist elements in the South could be tolerated temporarily.[27] This cautious approach undoubtedly reflected the Party's hope that state control over the Southern economy could be achieved gradually without unnecessarily disrupting production and arousing the anxiety of the mass of the population.

POLITICAL REUNIFICATION

The program of the NLF had declared that after the victory of revolutionary forces in the South, the two zones would retain their separate administrations for a period of time before embarking on the road toward peaceful reunification. In the immediate aftermath of the fall of Saigon, it appeared briefly as if reunification would indeed be delayed for a considerable period of time. During the spring, regime spokesmen commented that a five-year period of separate development was under consideration while the South completed its national democratic revolution. As a formal indication of such intentions, the PRG and the DRV applied for separate membership in the United Nations. One source speculated that Party leaders felt that a separate Southern administration, suitably sprinkled with representatives of the "third force" elements from the Saigon regime, could win substantial international support.[28]

By late summer, however, signs began to appear which suggested that the Party leadership had begun to re-evaluate its plans. At the twenty-fourth plenary session of the Central Committee held at the mountain resort of Dalat in the Central Highlands in July and August, the Party decided to bypass a period of separate administration and move rapidly toward socialism and unification with the North. As the resolution issued at the close of the plenum pointed out, reunification would "create a new strength and new advantages for developing the economy and culture and consolidating national defense. National reunification will further enhance Vietnamese influence in the world arena."[29]

Why did the Party decide to accelerate the process of economic and political change in the South? In his address to the Political Consultative Conference, Truong Chinh had relatively little to say about the issue, noting only that while there were a few differences between the two zones— notably within the economic sector and in the class system—they were similar in their essential characteristics. Specifically, he noted that both zones were under the firm rule of the Party.

Comments in the official press following the close of the conference amplified Truong Chinh's remarks and provided additional insight into the reasons for the decision. Several editorials pointed out that the situation in the South in 1975 differed in several major respects from that of the North after the close of the Geneva Conference, when the New Democratic stage had remained in operation for several years (thus implying that opponents of the decision may have pointed to the post-1954 situation as a precedent). In 1954, the primitive state of the Northern economy had compelled an extended period of economic construction to raise the technical level of the economy prior to an advance toward socialist production relations. By contrast, in 1975 the urban economy in the South was relatively advanced (a grudging admission of one of the advantages of the capitalist system) and thus more capable of moving directly toward socialist forms of ownership. In particular, the consumer industry already was well developed in the South and many towns and cities possessed a relatively advanced commercial and manufacturing sector. Moreover, the technological level of the population was high, and there was a large and dynamic petty bourgeoisie. Transportation and communications were quite sophisticated. Thus, conditions for rapid material and technological development were already present in the South, where they had not been two decades earlier in the North.

As for conditions in rural areas, unlike the situation in the North in 1954, where the remnants of the "feudal production system" had still existed, in South Vietnam the power of feudal landowners in rural areas had already declined. Most of the arable land was already in the hands of private landowning peasants, and a comprehensive land reform program similar to that undertaken in the North in the mid-1950s would not be required as a preliminary step to collectivization.[30] In addition, resistance to the new regime collapsed more rapidly than had been anticipated. By late fall, armed opposition was limited to scattered groups operating in remote areas.

In a number of respects, then, Party leaders must have been favorably surprised by the conditions they encountered in the South. On the other hand, the overall political and economic situation was sobering, to say the least. The early moves to reassure the private economic sector in the South had only limited effect in raising production and reducing unemployment. The campaign against the comprador bourgeoisie had eliminated some of the more flagrant disruptive forces in the marketplace, but had not substantially reduced the problems of speculation and hoarding that created shortages and drove up consumer prices. Private farmers in the South were not selling their surplus grain to the state purchasing organizations, but placing it on the private market or feeding it to their livestock. In effect, much of the Southern economy remained outside government control, and relatively immune to its influence.

At the same time, the regime encountered problems in coping with the "corrupt and parasitic" lifestyle of South Vietnamese society. Despite efforts to stamp it out, Western influence continued to exude its noxious fumes and even threatened the revolutionary purity of Northern cadres and soldiers stationed in the South. Journals abounded with comments about drug addicts, decadent habits, and a hedonistic lifestyle. The authorities appeared to voice particular concern over indications that it had begun to affect the attitudes of Party members and cadres. The latter were warned against corrupt habits, selfish individualism, laziness, and addiction to the pleasures of the decadent West. One report in a Hanoi publication even complained that soldiers returning from South Vietnam brought with them tape cassettes and then played loud Western rock music at all hours of the night, disturbing the repose of decent citizens.

To some, such disturbing trends may have suggested the need for caution. To others, it apparently represented convincing proof that the nation's political and economic problems could only be resolved when the government had successfully removed what one commentator labelled the "harmful neo-colonialist garbage of the U.S. imperialists" and established firm control over the commercial and manufacturing sector in the South. It is hardly surprising that most Party leaders, convinced believers in the virtues of central planning, reacted to problems encountered in the South by concluding that the solution lay in the exercise of tighter government control.

Ideology, then, had won the first battle in the intra-Party struggle over the direction of postwar strategy in the South. In retrospect, the decision to move rapidly to socialism and reunification reflected the Party's confidence in its own leadership and in the industriousness, talent, and resilience of the Vietnamese people, who would now be expected to recover rapidly from twenty years of armed conflict and launch immediately into an arduous and complex period of socialist construction. Spokesmen for the regime frequently commented that although Vietnam was a poor nation in comparison with the advanced countries of the world, its great strengths lay in the talent and character of the Vietnamese people, and in the quality of Party leadership. These qualities had led the revolutionary movement to victory in the long struggle for national liberation. They would now be called upon to lead the nation to a bright socialist future.

One obvious risk posed by the decision to move rapidly toward the integration of the two zones into a unitary state was the impact it would have on popular attitudes in the South. Regional differences between Northerners and Southerners in Vietnam ran deep and predated the ideological cleavage of the post-1954 period. In the North, where Vietnamese civilization had originated, the vagaries of weather and crowded conditions in the Red River Delta made life a constant challenge, and the influence of tradition was strong. The Southern provinces were absorbed hundreds of years later, after the Vietnamese state conquered the coastal trading state of Champa and seized the Mekong Delta from the declining Angkor empire. Vietnamese settlers moving down from the North found plentiful land and a favorable climate, contributing to a more easygoing attitude and a "frontier village" atmosphere.

Such cultural differences were accentuated during the colonial era, as the French economic presence was significantly stronger in the South, and during the post-Geneva period, when American culture and capitalist practices rapidly permeated the South. Southern suspicion of Northern dominance was a factor in the civil conflict of the 1950s and 1960s and rapidly surfaced after the fall of Saigon in 1975. The Hanoi regime was undoubtedly conscious of such problems and apparently hoped to rule the South from behind the scenes. But the shortage of Southern cadres and an apparent lack of trust in their reliability compelled the regime to dispatch thousands of cadres from the North to assume positions of responsibility in the southern administration.

To allay suspicions of Northern domination, the regime appointed a number of Southerners to prominent positions within the administration, but the widespread presence of Northerners in positions of authority, and their propensity to treat the local population with arrogance or contempt, led to growing criticism, even among Southerners who had served in the revolutionary movement. Reports in the press noted that Northern cadres and government officials frequently did not understand the situation in South Vietnam, and failed to "respect the rights and freedoms of the masses." Some did not appear to realize that the transformation to socialism in the South "must be well prepared and carried out gradually and methodically." Others demonstrated an unreasonable suspicion of anyone of bourgeois extraction and did not realize that some individuals of reactionary class background could overcome their political weaknesses and transform themselves into useful and progressive members of society.[31]

The decision to accelerate the process of reunification undoubtedly exacerbated such feelings. Although official statements declared that the Southern population had greeted the announcement with jubilation and satisfaction, privately regime spokesmen conceded that the decision had not met with universal rejoicing in the South, and that the issue had been hotly debated in the conferences held in November. Still, the process of administrative reunification was achieved with relative ease. In December, the decision was given final ratification in both North and South, in the former by the National Assembly of the DRV and in the latter by a conference of people's representatives of the PRG.[32] In January 1976, the South returned formally to civilian rule as the military management committees were disbanded and the Saigon committee handed over power to a fourteen-member People's Liberation Committee under the chairmanship of Vo Van Kiet, formerly vice-chairman of the Saigon-Gia Dinh Military Management Committee.[33] Then, in April, elections were held for a new National Assembly composed of representatives of both zones. The new unified Assembly, slightly over half of whose members represented the North, convened in June and approved the formation of a new unified Socialist Republic of Vietnam (SRV), formally promulgated in early July, and adopted a resolution to draft a new constitution to take the entire country to socialism.[34]

NOTES

The following abbreviations frequently occur in the notes: AFP (Air France Press), FBIS (Foreign Broadcast Information Service), FBIS-EAS (Foreign

Broadcast Information Service–East Asia Service), FEER (Far Eastern Economic Review), IC (Indochina Chronology), JPRS (Joint Publications Research Service), SWB/FE (Survey of World Broadcasts/Far East), VDRN (Vietnam Documents and Research Notes), VNA (Vietnam News Agency).

1. I have decided not to include a discussion of the last weeks of the war in this study, in the interests of saving space. Two excellent accounts based on personal observation are Frank Snepp, *Decent Interval* (New York: Random House, 1977) and Tiziano Terzani, *Giai Phong! The Fall and Liberation of Saigon* (New York: Ballantine Books, 1976).

2. *South Viet Nam National Front for Liberation: Documents* (Saigon: Giai Phong Publishing House, 1968).

3. Lenin's most detailed exposition of his views on the subject came in *The State and Revolution*, written on the eve of the Bolshevik seizure of power in 1917. These views were revised after the end of the civil war in 1920 when Lenin launched the New Economic Policy. Marx and Engels had dealt with the issue of the Dictatorship of the Proletariat, but only in general terms.

4. Mao Tse-tung, "On New Democracy," in *Selected Works of Mao Tse-tung* vol. 3 (London: Lawrence & Wishart, 1954).

5. There is no definitive study of this period. For a useful analysis, see David W. P. Elliott, "Revolutionary Reintegration: A Comparison of the Foundation of Post-Liberation Political Systems in North Vietnam and China" (Ph.D. diss., Cornell University, 1976). On agricultural policy, see Edwin E. Moise, *Land Reform in China and North Vietnam* (Chapel Hill: North Carolina Press, 1983).

6. Much of the problem, of course, could be attributed to the resumption of the revolutionary war in the South during the 1960s. For over a decade, the Northern economy was geared primarily to provide rear support in the struggle for reunification. Its industrial base was badly damaged by intensive American bombing. Much of the working-age population was drafted into the armed forces, and the nation became increasingly dependent upon food imports from China and the Soviet Union. Whatever the reasons, at war's end, the North Vietnamese economy was badly in need of attention.

7. There was some violence associated with the land reform program in 1955 and 1956, but not on the scale of the 1930s in the Soviet Union. See Moise, *Land Reform*.

8. The decision is discussed in Van Tien Dung, *Our Great Spring Victory* (New York and London: Monthly Review Press, 1977), p. 20. For a brief discussion of earlier plans for a transitional regime, see my *The Communist Road to Power in Vietnam* (Boulder: Westview Press, 1981), p. 207.

9. Cited in Van Tien Dung, *Our Great Spring Victory*, p. 242.

10. Tran Van Tra, born in 1918 in South Vietnam, joined the Indochinese Communist Party in the 1930s and, after spending most of World War II in a French prison, was released in March 1945 and reportedly participated in the famous Ba To uprising in Central Vietnam which preceded the August Revolution a few weeks later. During the Franco-Vietminh War he rose rapidly in the PAVN and in the late 1950s became deputy chief of staff. During the 1960s he served the Party in the South and eventually became the ranking military officer in the People's Liberation Armed Forces. After the fall of Saigon, he served as commander of the Seventh Military Region, but was dropped in 1982, report-

edly for his candid comments in his autobiography, *Ket Thuc Cuoc Chien Tranh 30 Nam* (The Thirty Years War). The general's book was translated in Joint Publications Research Service (hereafter JPRS), 82,783, February 2, 1983, Labelled Volume 5 of a series, it is apparently the only one in print.

11. For an account of the immediate postwar period, see Terzani, *Giai Phong!*

12. Pham Hung, born in 1912 in a scholar-gentry family in Vinh Long province, South Vietnam, joined the Party as one of its founding members in 1930. Arrested during May Day riots in 1931, he was not released from prison until 1945. In 1951, he was assigned as a member of the Central Office of South Vietnam (COSVN), which directed Party affairs in the South, and became second in command to chairman Le Duan. After the Geneva Conference he returned to the North and in 1957 was elected to the Politburo. In 1967, he replaced Nguyen Chi Thanh as head of the Southern branch of the Party and chairman of COSVN.

13. According to one Western source, most organized resistance came from Hoa Hao areas in Soc Trang province. See John C. Donnell, "South Vietnam in 1975: The Year of Communist Victory," *Asian Survey* 16/1 (January 1976), p.7.

14. In general, civilian members of the GVN were considered potentially more dangerous than members of the South Vietnamese armed forces. See the article in *Saigon Giai Phong* (Liberated Saigon), November 8, 1975, translated in JPRS 66,574. According to this article, inmates in the camps needed the sponsorship of "revolutionary families" before being released.

15. Carlyle A. Thayer, "Building Socialism: South Vietnam Since the Fall of Saigon," in *Vietnam Since 1975: Two Views from Australia* (Center for the Study of Australian-Asian Relations, Research Paper No. 20, February 1980), p.9. By mid-1976, nearly 95 percent of the 1.5 million people required to register had done so. See Douglas Pike, "Vietnam During 1976: Economics in Command," *Asian Survey* 17/1 (January 1977), p. 38.

16. *Il Giorno*, January 10, 1976, in JPRS 66,574.

17. Hoang Ngoc, "General education in South Vietnam," *Hoc Tap* (Study), December 1976.

18. For an article describing the official policy on religious freedom, see Tran Huu Tien, "Social revolution and freedom of religion," *Tap Chi Cong San* (June 1977), translated in JPRS 69,480. Regime policy towards the Buddhists was discussed in Patrice De Beer, *Le Monde*, May 19, 1977, in JPRS 69,123. For official policy towards the Hoa Hao, see Nguyen Khac Vien, "Pilgrimage to Hoa Hao land," *Vietnam Courier* (October 1983), pp. 7–9. A more critical view is located in Ginetta Sagan and Stephen Denney, *Violations of Human Rights in the Socialist Republic of Vietnam* (Atherton, California: Aurora Foundation, 1983), pp. 11–12. Also cf. Nguyen Van Canh, *Vietnam Under Communism, 1975–1982* (Stanford: Hoover Institution Press, 1983), pp. 183–84. Relations between the Party and the Hoa Hao had been strained since the assassination of sect founder Huynh Phu So by Vietminh orders in 1947.

19. Che Viet Tan, "Redistribute labor and population, develop our people's abundant labor and strength in national construction," in *Tap Chi Cong San* (February 1977), translated in Foreign Broadcast Information Service (FBIS), vol. 4, March 30, 1977.

20. Che Viet Tan, "Redistribute Labor."

21. For a brief discussion, see Le Duan, *The Vietnamese Revolution: Fundamental Problems and Essential Tasks* (New York: International Publishers, 1971), p. 93.

22. *Nhan Dan* (The People), November 20, 1975. According to *Saigon Giaiphong*, October 4, 1975, "forced" or "volunteered" "depends on your attitude." See JPRS 66,638.

23. For an official decree on the subject, see *Saigon Giaiphong*, September 10, 1975, in JPRS 66,543. In cases where the owners had fled the country, workers' committees were reportedly set up to run the factory. See John C. Donnell, "South Vietnam," p. 9.

24. See the article on the campaign against the "barbed wire king" in *Nhan Dan*, September 18, 1975.

25. Thayer, "Building Socialism," p. 16.

26. For the regulations, see Nguyen Tien Hung, *Economic Development of Socialist Vietnam, 1955–1980* (New York: Praeger, 1977), appendix, pp. 167–70.

27. Ho Liem, "A number of matters."

28. Thayer, "Building Socialism," p. 7, citing *The Economist* (June 14, 1975), "Two into One Won't Go Yet."

29. Chui Thuy, "Our nation's historic victory," *Quan Doi Nhan Dan* (People's Army), first in a series beginning November 27, 1975, translated in JPRS 66,594. According to Carlyle Thayer, top Party officials may have begun discussing the possibility of rapid reunification in May. See his "North Vietnam in 1975: National Liberation, Reunification and Socialist Construction," *Asian Survey*, 16/1 (January 1976), p. 17.

30. Nguyen Khac Vien, interview in *Rinascita*, April 30, 1976. For additional comments, see Ho Liem, "A number of matters."

31. For example, see the article in *Nguoi Xay Dung* (The Builder) (November 1978). Refugee accounts often noted that there was frequent favoritism toward revolutionary families, and discrimination against those with a middle-class background. For one such comment, see Bruce Grant, *The Boat People: an 'Age' Investigation* (Harmondsworth: Penguin, 1979), p. 103.

32. Saigon Domestic Service, December 28, 1975.

33. Vo Van Kiet was born in Can Tho province in the Mekong Delta in 1922, probably in an educated family. He took part in the August uprising in Saigon in 1945 and reportedly worked in the Party's Southern apparatus during the war of resistance against the French. By the early 1970s he had become a member of the Standing Committee of COSVN. Later he would become a vice premier and a member of the Party Politburo.

34. The new government included several native South Vietnamese among its ranks, including Huynh Tan Phat, formerly chairman of the PRG, as vice president. According to a news report, 20 percent of the members of the National Assembly were peasants, 18 percent were intellectuals, 10 percent were soldiers, 9 percent were officials, and 1.6 percent were workers. One quarter were women. See *New York Times*, June 25, 1976. Other decisions added five new ministries and reduced the total number of provinces in the country from sixty-one to thirty-five.

37
A Deserter and His Family
GLORIA EMERSON

Rennie Perrin, a middle-aged Vermont barber, was sound asleep when his wife, a nurse, came home from her shift at the Veterans Administration Hospital, so she thought it wiser to wait until the morning to tell him their son, Richard, had deserted. Mrs. Perrin heard it on the radio at the hospital, where she had night duty. The next day—it was in September 1967—Mr. Perrin had to be told, for there was a story on their son, a nineteen-year-old private, in the local paper, the Springfield *Times-Reporter*. Mr. Perrin, a veteran of World War II who had been discharged after a year in the Army because he had tuberculosis, listened to his wife, Betty. Then he began to cry. She stayed very calm.

"Somebody had to," Mrs. Perrin said.

Five years after Richard Perrin made that choice, his parents were still anxious and shy about talking about the son who had so much changed their lives, as if they still feared he might be hurt. For quite some time Mrs. Perrin thought certain Americans might go to Canada and try to kill the deserters living there.

The couple live in a mobile home in Sharon, Vermont, off Route 14, about ten miles north of White River Junction. They moved here in 1972 from North Springfield, where they lived for fifteen years and raised three children. Springfield is a factory town with not more than ten thousand people, known for its machine tools and often called "precision valley," Mr. Perrin said. He had his own barbershop, called Ray's, but he left it at the age of sixty-three. He only says of all this that business was slow because men were letting their hair grow longer and that he wasn't trained to do the hair styling that younger customers wanted. He does not give his son's notoriety as a reason for leaving. They moved to Sharon to be nearer the V.A. hospital where Mrs. Perrin has worked since 1966 in the orthopedic and neurosurgical wards.

It was in December 1973 when I saw them. They are not cheerful now at Christmas. Mr. Perrin speaks with effort, as if his words were little roots that had to be pulled up carefully from hard ground.

"We had a terrible time for a long time," Mr. Perrin said. "As long as he is in Canada, it will never really be over for us." He thought that people whose sons had been killed in Vietnam might find it easier to accept their loss, find it easier to go on with life, than he and his wife did. Their boy was always missing. "You make up your mind they're gone now and you can't bring them back," he said. "But with Dick, he's alive and can't come back."

The unspoken fear of Mr. and Mrs. Perrin was quite clear. It was that one of them—he at sixty-four, or she at fifty—might fall ill and not be able to see Richard before death. The other children would come to them, of course, but without Richard there was always a space and a longing.

"You'd be surprised at how fast things can happen to people," Mrs. Perrin said, meaning the heart-can-go, the lungs-can-go, the-kidneys-or-liver-can-go, just like that. She looked at Mr. Perrin; he looked at her. They did not want to complain about how they had been treated or tell me the names of people who had snubbed or wounded them. They did not want to be considered whiners.

Mr. Perrin was still a member of the American Legion because he paid his dues, but he had stopped going to their meetings. Mrs. Perrin was a member of the Daughters of the American Revolution.

I've never been back because I know how they would feel. It would be hard for me to listen to them talk—oh, I know how they talk." Mr. Perrin said, "You know they all went to war, and anybody who doesn't do that—well, I feel I'm just as good a legionnaire as they are. I believe in this country. I love this country. Even if Dick did desert, he said himself that he loved this country. There was the time when they asked him if he wanted to become a C.O. and he said no. He wasn't against all wars, just this one. If someone came to attack this country, he'd fight for the defense of it...

In the beginning it was terrible for us. I was very patriotic, like most men are. I used to make statements like those I've heard people say in front of me since Dick deserted. People saying "Anyone who deserts should be shot." It's awful hard for people to understand. When this first happened we didn't go along with Dick because we didn't understand it. Like most people don't. But when you're involved in it you start asking yourself questions, why all this happened. Now that we know, we feel a lot better. In the beginning it was terrible.

Mr. Perrin was born in France, in Vosges above Nancy; he remembered his parents talking, with bitterness, about World War I. He came to Vermont as a child, growing up in Barre, but no one could pronounce his real first name, Rene. They called him Re-en, or Rinay, or Rin, so he called himself Rennie, for everyone could pronounce that.

Richard Perrin was nineteen, a tank mechanic in the 1st Battalion of the 64th Armored Brigade stationed in Kitzingen, West Germany, when he deserted and went to Paris to begin an organization called RITA, which stood for "Resist Inside the Army." It was an underground antiwar group of GIs trying to encourage dissension. Perhaps the most shocking time for his parents was December 11, 1967, when they saw their son on CBS television from Paris with the black radical Stokely Carmichael, who had recently called for the defeat of the United States in Vietnam.

I remember the deserters who came to Paris. A very tall boy from Florida who liked scrambled eggs slept on my living-room floor for three nights, but we thought it better if I did not know his last name. He went on to Sweden, he could not bear being in Paris. None of them were sure if the French government would not turn them over to the Americans, if there would not be a knock on the door at midnight, and the door kicked down. The deserters had pledged that they would engage in no political activity while in France, but their existence was a political act, their being in a room meant the war and the Army were in the room too.

The notorious interview took place at midnight in Paris after long, secret arrangements which took the CBS television crew and a *New York Times* reporter to a middle-class apartment. White bedsheets were hung in one room to shield a Dutch activist who had arranged everything. He stayed behind the sheets as he spoke of increasing desertions. Private Perrin walked through the sheets to sit down and face the camera, which rested on him like a huge, unblinking eye. He was calm and spoke quietly of his life, recalling how at fifteen he had joined a march in Chicago in 1964 led by the Reverend Dr. Martin Luther King, Jr.

"About this time I began thinking that, maybe, everything I was told in school, maybe, wasn't all like that," the private said.

In Springfield, Vermont, his parents were horrified. Mr. Perrin told a reporter: "We don't go along with what this boy did but we realize he has been brainwashed." He insisted that his son had been a "good soldier" when he first enlisted. Local people, who considered Carmichael a Communist if not something even more evil, were very critical and let their opinions be known. A picture of Richard Perrin appeared on the front page of the town newspaper with the headline AWOL GI RECALLED AS AVERAGE STUDENT.

Mrs. Perrin was worried that the two younger children, David and Nancy, would be bullied or taunted. "That day when I sent them off to school—it was David's twelfth birthday—I remember telling the kids to hold your head high," she said. "When David went in his classroom one of the kids said 'Is that your brother?' and David said 'Shut your big fat mouth.' That's the way he handled it."

She is dark-haired, small, quicker to smile than her husband. Both speak softly. Their son once said of them, in an interview with another American in exile, that his parents were outwardly conservative people but more liberal than their Vermont friends.

"With my folks there is a sort of basic humanism which stuck in my head," Richard Perrin said. "They wouldn't tolerate me saying nigger, Polack, anything like that...I was always truthful with them, anything I did, I would always go home and tell them about it."

The word "deserter"—the ancient, horrid word with its dreadful picture of a cringing, failing man who flees—made them feel sick. It is a word they still do not like. It makes most Americans nervous, too, for they think of a battlefield and a soldier running from it, leaving other men in a lurch. No one thinks of courage or convictions.

It took Mr. and Mrs. Perrin nearly three years to accept what Richard had done and to see his reasons, although they always defended him even when they disapproved. Her husband was ahead of her on that, Mrs. Perrin said.

After graduating from high school, Richard had been unable to find a job because of his draft status. He went to California to visit his half brother, Ronald, the child of Mr. Perrin's first marriage, who was fifteen years older and always had a stunning and gentle influence on the younger boy. It was he who had worked for civil rights and made Richard see its importance. That year Ronald, who was teaching at the University of California, was in the antiwar movement, but nothing about Vietnam seemed to reach Richard Perrin until after he enlisted and was in advanced infantry training.

While sitting in a PX cafeteria at Fort Leonard Wood, Private Perrin, an E-2 squad leader at the armored vehicles repair shop, overheard two sergeants reminiscing about Vietnam. One described how he had gotten a confession from a captured Vietnamese by pushing the naked prisoner against the very hot engine of a tank so his genitals would burn. The sergeant was talking in a normal voice, not as if he was telling a secret. From then on, Richard Perrin began to pay attention to everything about the war. At the end of June 1967 he was sent to Fort Sill, Oklahoma. Ronald, who had earlier told him not to desert, had heard that a Private Andy Stapp, also at Fort Sill, was organizing GIs to protest the war. Richard later described his good friend Andy, who formed the American Servicemen's Union, as "anticapitalist, antiimperialist" while saying of himself that at Fort Sill he was just "antiwar." But he was that, and he worked hard.

"He was learning and reading about Vietnam. He was really tore up. He called home, very upset, and begged us to see it the way he did," Mr. Perrin said.

"But of course we didn't," Betty Perrin added, "we believed what we were reading in the papers at that time. We wanted him to just get the three years over and get home."

At Fort Sill, during a press conference of antiwar GIs, Private Perrin handed out his own statement, which received considerable attention in the press. He was eighteen.

"I was being trained as a truck mechanic and was on my way to Fort Sill to work on armored trucks and self-propelled artillery," the statement said. "I realized I was being trained to support these atrocities. At this point I decided to find out for myself whether there was any justification for the war. Everyone said there was, but they couldn't tell me what it was."

He ended the statement by saying that he hoped the people in the United States would wake up to the fact that they were being led through a period that would one day "be called the darkest in our history."

For his failure one night to sign out on the pass register, shortly after the press conference, Private Perrin was arrested, handcuffed and taken to the city jail in Lawton, before being turned over to the military authorities. He was charged with an article 15, nonjudicial punishment, which he refused to sign. He demanded a court-martial. It was clear to him he was only being punished for his antiwar activities, not for neglecting to sign the pass register.

Mr. and Mrs. Perrin were flown down to see their son and told by officers to try to bring the boy around to a reasonable point of view, that the military only wanted to straighten him out. They talked to a captain, then to a general, who explained the domino theory to them and the importance of South Vietnam being protected. When they saw Richard, who was in the stockade, they could hardly believe it.

"It was an awful shock," Mrs. Perrin said. "His head had been shaved but they wouldn't let him shave his face or change his clothes."

"He didn't look like our boy," Mr. Perrin said.

"He said he was ashamed to wear the uniform," Mrs. Perrin said.

Richard Perrin said later that when the Army assumed he repented, they offered to shorten his sentence of thirty days' hard labor. If he stopped his antiwar work, the Army said, they would send him to Germany, not Vietnam. Perrin agreed, but in Germany the racism on the bases— much more acute than in the United States—the memory of the stockade, his fatigue and disgust with the military led him to desert. He refused, in all ways, to be a soldier any more. In Paris he wanted RITA to inspire soldiers to challenge and harass the military.

"I was sort of hanging on to the old liberal myth: There's nothing wrong with the U.S.... The war is just a mistake...We can stop this and elect a new administration," Richard Perrin said of himself in 1968.

In Springfield nothing was quite the same for his parents, or ever could be. Some people wrote letters to the paper protesting what Richard Perrin had done.

"One letter, I remember, said that we or the schools had failed in not having the Perrin boy read the story *The Man Without a Country*," Mrs. Perrin said. A disabled World War II veteran wrote in his letter that deserters like their son should be shot. The man's wife was a friend of Mrs. Perrin's; they were both nurses. "We never talked about it, we just never even mentioned it," she said.

A lot of people asked his parents about Richard, including some whose own sons had been in Vietnam.

"You've heard me say this, Betty, but sometimes I had the feeling that some people, not all of them, would ask me about Dick because some of them were pumping me and that deep down they were probably hoping he was having a hard time," Mr. Perrin said, shaking his head.

But there were a few people who tried to tell him when he was still puzzled and sorrowful, that his son had done the right thing. The couple were encouraged to keep in touch with their son, not to turn their backs on him, by Phillips B. Henderson, pastor of the North Springfield Baptist Church, who had known Richard and had liked him.

Mrs. Perrin felt as if she and her husband had lost a child. "If they were mean, it made me mad. If they were kind, it almost brought me to tears," she said.

She was more often on the verge of tears. When Richard wrote from Canada for a grade transcript, the Springfield school board refused to send it to him. One board member was the father of Richard's closest friends in high school. He told his own children never to associate with their classmate again and he forbid them to write the deserter. When I asked them about the reaction of relatives in Vermont and New Hampshire, Mr. and Mrs. Perrin looked at each other but said nothing.

Richard moved to Canada in January 1969, working for a year and a half operating two hostels and a counseling service for the Union of American Deserters in Regina, Saskatchewan. He married a Canadian girl and both worked at a center for retarded children in Moose Jaw. At twenty-two Richard Perrin said that he did not think he would plan on returning to the United States and that he would be of no use there. At twenty-five he was in Regina working as a garage mechanic. He had always loved working on cars, that was one reason he never let his hair grow long, for he couldn't stand having it get in his eyes when he worked. His two-year-old son was named Shayne.

"He was the quietest of the children," Mrs. Perrin said. "There was a wide streak of idealism in Richard, together with an impatience with hypocrisy. Richard was the most quiet, I didn't always know what he was thinking because he didn't talk much, but when he did open up to talk you better be ready to listen . . . "

They are stubborn people, refusing to give in to the strain and isolation they had felt for so long. Perhaps they had not even known how taxing it had been until the Perrins went to an amnesty conference in Vermont in the fall of 1973. It was so new for them to be surrounded by people like themselves, people who were proud of their sons for escaping the draft or leaving the Army. One young man went up to Mr. Perrin to shake his hand because he had a son in Canada. It was a man who had gone to jail rather than to Vietnam. Mr. Perrin spoke of that handshake, and the encounter, as if he had suddenly received an award.

"Even if they did let them come back, maybe it wouldn't be very pleasant for them—there would always be someone saying something and pointing them out as deserters," Mr. Perrin said. "Dick wouldn't want to come back to live."

The couple had visited their son and his family five times in Saskatchewan. The visits had been happy. David, the youngest son, had spoken often of the brother who went to Canada, for he was proud of him. Richard did not become a ghost. Mrs. Perrin showed me some color photographs of their reunions in Canada; there was Richard Perrin, a tall dark-haired man with a face that was a little blurred in the photographs.

"He doesn't look like a criminal, does he?" Mrs. Perrin asked.

38
Agent Orange, and the Wall at Home

BOBBIE ANN MASON

...Sam had seen a bumper sticker in town: SPRAYED AND BETRAYED. When she told Emmett, he grunted and kept digging. He had Clearasil on his face. She realized that not every soldier who came back from Vietnam was as weird as Emmett. She knew of veterans—relatives of classmates—who had adjusted perfectly well. They had nice houses and wives and kids. They didn't wear skirts, even for a joke, and they didn't refuse to get a job or buy a car. Allen Wilkins was one of them. He owned a menswear store and coached Little League. His daughter was a teen model in a Glamor Barn TV ad on Channel 6. Sam wondered if it was just her own crazy family rather than Vietnam.

The next morning, she decided to go along with Emmett to McDonald's instead of taking her usual run. She was curious about the veterans he hung around with. She had known them for years but had never thought much about them as vets.

At McDonald's, Emmett's buddies weren't there yet. A small bald man who worked with Lonnie's father at the hardware store stopped at their booth and teased Emmett about his "new girlfriend." He meant Sam.

"She keeps me in line," Emmett said, elbowing Sam.

"Emmett, I heard they're hiring at the cookie factory," the man said.

"Fuck the cookie factory," Emmett said, with his mouth full of Egg McMuffin.

The man winked at Sam. "Do you let him use that language at home, Sam?"

She shrugged. "It's on HBO."

"Does he let you watch HBO?"

"He don't care," she said, irritated.

"If I had HBO, I wouldn't let my wife watch it."

"Don't pay no attention to him, Sam," Emmett said as the man walked away. "He's got shit for brains."

Pete Simms and Tom Hudson joined them then. They had Cokes and little apple pies. Pete worked on a highway crew, and Tom was an auto mechanic with his own body shop. Sam knew Tom had been wounded in the war, but she couldn't tell, except that his posture was a little stiff. He sat down beside Emmett.

"Do you care if I set next to you, Sam?" asked Pete. "I won't bite."

"I'll let you set here if you show me your tattoo," Sam said impulsively. Emmett had once told her about Pete's tattoo. When Pete was in Vietnam, he had had a map of the Jackson Purchase region of western Kentucky tattooed on his chest.

"You want me to show you right here?" Pete asked flirtatiously. "I might get arrested. Come on out to my truck and I'll show you."

"What kind of truck you got?"

"A Ford Ranger. Why?"

"I need a car," Sam said.

"You need a hole in the head," said Emmett.

"I wonder if anybody ever tattooed his own face on his chest," Sam said. "Like a face on a T-shirt."

"I tell you one thing," Pete said. " I wish I had a goddamn T-shirt with this map on it instead of having it on my chest." He ate a bite of apple pie. "Ow! That's hot! Emmett, how come this long-legged little niece of yours is here? What's her trouble?"

"She's got ants in her pants," said Emmett.

"*He's* got Agent Orange," said Sam. "Look at his face."

"*I* got Agent Orange," said Pete jokingly. "In the head." He laughed and blew on his pie. "I had a place come on my leg, all brown and funny? But it went away. Reckon it ate on down to the bone?"

"Nothing can hurt you, Pete," said Tom. "You're like that guy on TV that ate a bicycle."

"That was on *That's Incredible*," said Sam. "I saw that."

"Don't you know that was bound to mess that guy up?" Pete said with a grin.

"Did either one of you get sprayed with Agent Orange?" Sam asked pointblank.

Pete and Tom sucked their Coke straws simultaneously.

"I don't think so," Tom said slowly. He tapped a cigarette from a wrinkled pack.

Emmett snapped his Egg McMuffin box shut. "Sam's got Nam on the brain," he said. "She's been reading a bunch of history books and pestering me."

"What do those books tell you, Sam?" asked Tom, staring at her.

"Nothing. They're just dull history books." She was embarrassed. The books didn't say what it was like to be at war over there. The books didn't even have pictures.

Pete said, "Hell, I remember when they used to spray it. They'd tell us to get inside because they were going to spray, but it wasn't any big deal. It smelled sweet. It smelled like oranges."

"Buddy Mangrum can't even drink half a beer without getting sick," Tom said. "They say that's Agent Orange."

There was a racket in the back of McDonald's. A kid's birthday party was beginning. Sam tried to imagine these men fighting in the jungle. She had never been able to picture Emmett with a gun, but Granddad had talked offhandedly about shooting the dog. Emmett had told her Granddad wasn't serious.

"I think my problem's I might be allergic to fleas," Emmett said with a shiver. "My cat's got fleas. And he sleeps right on my head."

"If I had a car, I'd take you to the V.A.," Sam said. "I'd march you right in there and show them your face. Boy, I'd give anything for a car."

"Tom's got a car he wants to sell," Pete said.

"That bug? Yeah, I'll sell you my VW bug." Tom and Pete looked at each other and laughed. "I'll have to fix it up some, but you can have it for six thousand dollars."

Pete laughed. "Don't let him rip you off, Sam. It's a seventy-*three.*"

"I'll give you a bargain," Tom said. "You can have it for six hundred. It runs good. I just have to fix it up a little."

"I don't have that much." She had three hundred dollars in the bank, but she had to live on it for the summer.

"You can come and see it."

Tom was looking straight into her eyes, and she looked away, punching her straw in her drink. Something about him excited her, but she didn't know what it was. He looked at her as though he really wanted her to have that car. She knew her face must be red.

Emmett flattened his Egg McMuffin box and went to the men's room.

"Do you want to see my tattoo, Sam?" Pete said with a wink.

"Sure."

"That's my street," Pete said, lifting his T-shirt and pointing to his chest. "And that little red thing that looks like a ladybug is my old Corvette. My wife sold it while I was gone. It would be a classic now."

Hairs sprouted from the heart of the Jackson Purchase. The tattoo was the size of a *National Geographic*, outlined in blue, with the towns in red.

He said, "I look at it upside down, and in the mirror it's backwards. This was maybe the stupidest thing I ever did in my life." He laughed.

Tom laughed with him. "When you're that age, you do some of the stupidest things you could ever think of, and you think, Oh, wow, ain't this the funniest thing in the world!" He shrugged. He wasn't bad-looking, Sam thought. He was about Emmett's age.

"You think about that car, Sam," Tom said when he left. "Come over and see it if you want to."

On the way home, Sam asked Emmett, "Are your friends always that goofy?"

"They just like to have fun. They're good guys."

"I wish I had that Volkswagen," she said. Her mother used to have one, and Sam had learned to drive on it.

"I don't think you can buy a car. You're underage."

"I could if you sign for me."

"Since I'm so responsible and have so much money? Yeah, anybody suing me would strike it rich!"

"Would you sign for me if I bought a car?"

"You get the money first and ask me again."

Sam saw a blue Volkswagen Beetle down the street, in front of a funeral parlor. She wouldn't mind having a VW bug.

Sam suddenly remembered something she had heard about Pete. Cautiously, she asked, "Hey, Emmett, is it true that Pete chased his wife out of the house once with a shotgun?"

"No, she was chasing him. He was out in the yard shooting—not at her. He was just shooting. Cindy wouldn't put up with his foolishness, though. She told him he had to quit it or she was walking."

"What was Pete shooting at?"

They crossed the street before he would answer. On the corner was the dental clinic where her mother used to be a receptionist. Sam asked him again, "What was Pete shooting at?"

"He said it was just an urge that come over him, and he got rid of it by going out and shooting off his gun."

When they were a block from the house, Emmett said suddenly, "He had a map of Vietnam in the den, and his wife tore it down because it didn't fit her decorating scheme. It sounds crazy, but I think he'd rather be back in Nam."

"Did you ever wish that?"

"No. Hell, no! Are you kidding?"

At the corner of their block, Emmett paused to look at something off in the field down by the waterworks, perhaps a bird, but he seemed to be listening for something, and Sam thought of the way Radar O'Reilly on M*A*S*H could always hear the choppers coming in with wounded before anyone else could.

Emmett could look at anything—a rosebush, a stop sign, an ordinary bird, or even a circular from Kroger's—and get absorbed in it as though it were the most fascinating thing on earth. That was how he was so good at *Pac-Man*, and it was the way he watched his birds, stalking them and probably imaging a full-feathered bird based on nothing more than a glimpse of wing, a bright patch of crest or throat. Emmett reminded Sam of James Stewart in *Harvey*, an old movie they had seen on Channel 7's Midnight Theatre. Harvey was an imaginary rabbit who went everywhere with James Stewart. Sometimes it seemed that Emmett had somebody invisible along with him, too, some presence that guided him. But it probably wasn't a rabbit. It was probably a cat.

When Sam was seven or eight, she and Emmett had a stamp collection. They spent hours together poring over cellophane packets of exotic stamps sent on trial each month from stamp companies. Their stamp album was old and the countries were wrong—old colonial countries like Ceylon and the Belgian Congo. Vietnam was Indochine. While they played with the stamps, Emmett told Sam war stories, sprinkled with M-60s and grenade launchers and C-130 transport planes, and Sam's favorite—the amtrac, which Emmett laughingly described as a "yellow submarine." Sam ant countryside, something like Florida, with beaches and palm trees and watery fields of rice and green mountains. The sky was crowded with wonderful aircraft—C-47s with Gatling guns, Hueys, Chinooks, Skytrains, Bird Dogs. Emmett even made plastic models of helicopters and jet fighters, and he used them to act out his stories.

Irene stopped the stories. It upset her to be reminded of the war, but the reality of it didn't register on Sam until one day soon after they got their first color TV set. She was eight or nine. On the evening news, a report from Vietnam—it was during the fall of Saigon, in 1975, she thought— showed some people walking along a road with bundles on their backs. Some were carrying babies in their arms. Army jeeps chugged along the road. The landscape was believable—a hill in the distance, a paved road with narrow dirt shoulders, a field with something green planted in rows. The road resembled the old Hopewell road that twisted through the bottomland toward Paducah. For the first time, Vietnam was an actual place. As Sam watched, a child in a T-shirt and no pants ran down the road, and its mother called after it, scolding it. . . .

As they drive into Washington a few hours later, Sam feels sick with apprehension. She has kept telling herself that the memorial is only a rock with names on it. It doesn't mean anything except they're dead. It's just names. Nobody here but us chickens. Just us and the planet Earth and the nuclear bomb. But that's O.K., she thinks now. There is something comforting about the idea of nobody here but us chickens. It's so intimate. Nobody here but us. Maybe that's the point. People shouldn't make too much of death. Her history teacher said there are more people alive now than dead. He warned that there were so many people alive now, and they were living so much longer, that people had the idea they were practically immortal. But everyone's going to die and we'd better get used to the notion, he said. Dead and gone. Long gone from Kentucky.

Sometimes in the middle of the night it struck Sam with sudden clarity that she was going to die someday. Most of the time she forgot about this. But now, as she and Emmett and Mamaw Hughes drive into Washington, where the Vietnam Memorial bears the names of so many who died, the reality of death hits her in broad daylight. Mamaw is fifty-eight. She is going to die soon. She could die any minute, like that racehorse that keeled over dead, inexplicably, on Father's Day. Sam has been so afraid Emmett would die. But Emmett came to Cawood's Pond looking for her, because it was unbearable to him that she might have left him alone, that she might even die.

The Washington Monument is a gleaming pencil against the sky. Emmett is driving, and the traffic is frightening, so many cars swishing and merging, like bold skaters in a crowded rink. They pass cars with government license plates that say FED. Sam wonders how long the Washington Monument will stand on the Earth.

A brown sign on Constitution Avenue says VIETNAM VETERANS MEMORIAL. Emmett can't find a parking place nearby. He parks on a side street and they walk toward the Washington Monument. Mamaw puffs along. She has put on a good dress and stockings. Sam feels they are ambling, out for a stroll, it is so slow. She wants to break into a run. The Washington Monument rises up out of the earth, proud and tall. She remembers Tom's bitter comment about it—a big white prick. She once heard someone say the U.S.A. goes around fucking the world. That guy who put pink plastic around those islands should make a big rubber for the Washington Monument, Sam thinks. She has so many bizarre ideas there should be a market for her imagination. These ideas are churning in her head. She can hardly enjoy Washington for these thoughts. In Washington, the buildings are so pretty, so white. In a dream, the Vietnam Memorial was a black boomerang, whizzing toward her head.

"I don't see it," Mamaw says.

"It's over yonder," Emmett says, pointing. "They say you come up on it sudden."

"My legs are starting to hurt."

Sam wants to run, but she doesn't know whether she wants to run toward the memorial or away from it. She just wants to run. She has the new record album with her, so it won't melt in the hot car. It's in a plastic bag with handles. Emmett is carrying the pot of geraniums. She is amazed by him, his impressive bulk, his secret suffering. She feels his anxiety. His heart must be racing, as if something intolerable is about to happen.

Emmett holds Mamaw's arm protectively and steers her across the street. The pot of geraniums hugs his chest.

"There it is," Sam says.

It is massive, a black gash in a hillside, like a vein of coal exposed and then polished with polyurethane. A crowd is filing by slowly, staring at it solemnly.

"Law," says Sam's grandmother quietly. "It's black as night."

"Here's the directory," Emmett says, pausing at the entrance. "I'll look up his name for you, Mrs. Hughes."

The directory is on a pedestal with a protective plastic shield. Sam stands in the shade, looking forward, at the black wing embedded in the soil, with grass growing above. It is like a giant grave, fifty-eight thousand bodies rotting here behind those names. The people are streaming past, down into the pit.

"It don't show up good," Mamaw says anxiously. "It's just a hole in the ground."

The memorial cuts a V in the ground, like the wings of an abstract bird, huge and headless. Overhead, a jet plane angles upward, taking off.

"It's on Panel 9E," Emmett reports. "That's on the east wing. We're on the west."

At the bottom of the wall is a granite trough, and on the edge of it the sunlight reflects the names just above, in mirror writing, upside down. Flower arrangements are scattered at the base. A little kid says, "Look, Daddy, the flowers are dying." The man snaps, "Some are and some aren't."

The walkway is separated from the memorial by a strip of gravel, and on the other side of the walk is a border of dark gray brick. The shiny surface of the wall reflects the Lincoln Memorial and the Washington Monument, at opposite angles.

A woman in a sunhat is focusing a camera on the wall. She says to the woman with her, "I didn't think it would look like this. Things aren't what you think they look like. I didn't know it was a wall."

A spraddle-legged guy in camouflage clothing walks by with a cane. Probably he has an artificial leg, Sam thinks, but he walks along proudly, as if he has been here many times before and doesn't have any particular business at that moment. He seems to belong here, like Emmett hanging out at McDonald's.

A group of schoolkids tumble through, noisy as chickens. As they enter, one of the girls says, "Are they piled on top of each other?" They walk a few steps farther and she says, "What are all these names anyway?" Sam feels like punching the girl in the face for being so dumb. How could anybody that age not know? But she realizes that she doesn't know either. She is just beginning to understand. And she will never really know what happened to all these men in the war. Some people walk by, talking as though they are on a Sunday picnic, but most are reverent, and some of them are crying.

Sam stands in the center of the V, deep in the pit. The V is like the white wings of the shopping mall in Paducah. The Washington Monument is reflected at the center line. If she moves slightly to the left, she sees the monument, and if she moves the other way she sees a reflection of the flag opposite the memorial. Both the monument and the flag seem like arrogant gestures, like the country giving the finger to the dead boys, flung in this hole in the ground. Sam doesn't understand what she is feeling, but it is something so strong, it is like a tornado moving in her, something massive and overpowering. It feels like giving birth to this wall.

"I wish Tom could be here," Sam says to Emmett. "He needs to be here." Her voice is thin, like smoke, barely audible.

"He'll make it here someday. Jim's coming too. They're all coming one of these days."

"Are you going to look for anybody's name besides my daddy's?"

"Yeah."

"Who?"

"Those guys I told you about, the ones that died all around me that day. And that guy I was going to look up—he might be here. I don't know if he made it out or not."

Sam gets a flash of Emmett's suffering, his grieving all these years. He has been grieving for fourteen years. In this dazzling sunlight, his pimples don't show. A jet plane flies overhead, close to the earth. Its wings are angled back too, like a bird's.

Two workmen in hard hats are there with a stepladder and some loud machinery. One of the workmen, whose hat says on the back NEVER AGAIN, seems to be drilling into the wall.

"What's he doing, hon?" Sam hears Mamaw say behind her.

"It looks like they're patching up a hole or something." *Fixing a hole where the rain gets in.*

The man on the ladder turns off the tool, a sander, and the other workman hands him a brush. He brushes the spot. Silver duct tape is patched around several names, leaving the names exposed. The names are highlighted in yellow, as though someone has taken a Magic Marker and colored them, the way Sam used to mark names and dates, important facts, in her textbooks.

"Somebody must have vandalized it," says a man behind Sam. "Can you imagine the sicko who would do that?"

"No," says the woman with him. "Somebody just wanted the names to stand out and be noticed. I can go with that."

"Do you think they colored Dwayne's name?" Mamaw asks Sam worriedly.

"No. Why would they?" Sam gazes at the flowers spaced along the base of the memorial. A white carnation is stuck in a crack between two panels of the wall. A woman bends down and straightens a ribbon on a wreath. The ribbon has gold letters on it, "VFW Post 7215 of Pa."

They are moving slowly. Panel 9E is some distance ahead. Sam reads a small poster propped at the base of the wall: "To those men of C Company, 1st Bn. 503 Inf., 173rd Airborne who were lost in the battle for Hill 823, Dak To, Nov. 11, 1967. Because of their bravery I am here today. A grateful buddy."

A man rolls past in a wheelchair. Another jet plane flies over.

A handwritten note taped to the wall apologizes to one of the names for abandoning him in a firefight.

Mamaw turns to fuss over the geraniums in Emmett's arms, the way she might fluff a pillow.

The workmen are cleaning the yellow paint from the names. They sand the wall and brush it carefully, like men polishing their cars. The man on the ladder sprays water on the name he has just sanded and wipes it with a rag.

Sam, conscious of how slowly they are moving, with dread, watches two uniformed marines searching and searching for a name. "He must have been along here somewhere," one says. They keep looking, running their hands over the names.

"There it is. That's him."

They read his name and both look abruptly away, stare out for a moment in the direction of the Lincoln Memorial, then walk briskly off.

"May I help you find someone's name?" asks a woman in a T-shirt and green pants. She is a park guide, with a clipboard in her hand.

"We know where we are," Emmett says. "Much obliged, though."

At panel 9E, Sam stands back while Emmett and Mamaw search for her father's name. Emmett, his gaze steady and intent, faces the wall, as though he were watching birds; and Mamaw, through her glasses, seems intent and purposeful, as though she were looking for something back in the field, watching to see if a cow had gotten out of the pasture. Sam imagines the egret patrolling for ticks on a water buffalo's back, ducking and snaking its head forward, its beak like a punji stick.

"There it is," Emmett says. It is far above his head, near the top of the wall. He reaches up and touches the name. "There's his name, Dwayne E. Hughes."

"I can't reach it," says Mamaw. "Oh, I wanted to touch it," she says softly, in disappointment.

"We'll set the flowers here, Mrs. Hughes," says Emmett. He sets the pot at the base of the panel, tenderly, as though tucking in a baby.

"I'm going to bawl," Mamaw says, bowing her head and starting to sob. "I wish I could touch it."

Sam has an idea. She sprints over to the workmen and asks them to let her borrow the stepladder. They are almost finished, and they agree. One of them brings it over and sets it up beside the wall, and Sam urges Mamaw to climb the ladder, but Mamaw protests. "No, I can't do it. You do it."

"Go ahead, ma'am," the workman says.

"Emmett and me'll hold the ladder," says Sam.

"Somebody might see up my dress."

"No, go on, Mrs. Hughes. You can do it," says Emmett. "Come on, we'll help you reach it."

He takes her arm. Together, he and Sam steady her while she places her foot on the first step and swings herself up. She seems scared, and she doesn't speak. She reaches but cannot touch the name.

"One more, Mamaw," says Sam, looking up at her grandmother—at the sagging wrinkles, her flab hanging loose and sad, and her eyes reddened with crying. Mamaw reaches toward the name and slowly struggles up the next step, holding her dress tight against her. She touches the name, running her hand over it, stroking it tentatively, affectionately, like feeling a cat's back. Her chin wobbles, and after a moment she backs down the ladder silently.

When Mamaw is down, Sam starts up the ladder, with the record package in her hand.

"Here, take the camera, Sam. Get his name." Mamaw has brought Donna's Instamatic.

"No, I can't take a picture this close."

Sam climbs the ladder until she is eye level with her father's name. She feels funny, touching it. A scratching on a rock. Writing. Something for future archaeologists to puzzle over, clues to a language.

"Look this way, Sam," Mamaw says. "I want to take your picture. I want to get you and his name and the flowers in together if I can."

"The name won't show up," Sam says.

"Smile."

"How can I smile?" She is crying.

Mamaw backs up and snaps two pictures. Sam feels her face looking blank. Up on the ladder, she feels so tall, like a spindly weed that is sprouting up out of this diamond-bright seam of hard earth. She sees Emmett at the directory, probably searching for his buddies' names. She touches her father's name again.

"All I can see here is my reflection," Mamaw says when Sam comes down the ladder. "I hope his name shows up. And your face was all shadow."

"Wait here a minute," Sam says, turning away her tears from Mamaw. She hurries to the directory on the east side. Emmett isn't there anymore. She sees him striding along the wall, looking for a certain panel. Nearby, a group of marines is keeping a vigil for the POWs and MIAs. A double row of flags is planted in the dirt alongside their table. One of the marines walks by with a poster: "You Are an American, Your Voice Can Make the Difference." Sam flips through the directory and finds "Hughes." She wants to see her father's name there too. She runs down the row of Hughes names. There were so many Hughes boys killed, names she doesn't know. His name is there, and she gazes at it for a moment. Then suddenly her own name leaps out at her.

SAM ALAN HUGHES PFC AR 02 MAR

49 02 FEB 67 HOUSTON TX 14E 104

Her heart pounding, she rushes to panel 14E, and after racing her eyes over the string of names for a moment, she locates her own name.

SAM A HUGHES. It is the first on a line. It is down low enough to touch. She touches her own name. How odd it feels, as though all the names in America have been used to decorate this wall.

Mamaw is there at her side, clutching at Sam's arm, digging in with her fingernails. Mamaw says, "Coming up on this wall of a sudden and seeing how black it was, it was so awful, but then I came down in it and saw that white carnation blooming out of that crack and it gave me hope. It made me know he's watching over us." She loosens her bird-claw grip. "Did we lose Emmett?"

Silently, Sam points to the place where Emmett is studying the names low on a panel. He is sitting there cross-legged in front of the wall, and slowly his face bursts into a smile like flames.

August 13, 1987. Two of the refugees—"boat people"—who have
fled Vietnam in the years since liberation, this ethnic Chinese
woman and her child wait at a processing center in Hong Kong
REUTERS/BETTMANN NEWSPHOTOS

CHAPTER 11

Afterword

The "Afterword" is an excerpt from a book written by a Vietnamese woman named Le Ly Hayslip. The book is a memoir of her life in Vietnam, from her birth in 1949 to her departure for the United States (with an American husband) in 1969. The memoir is intercut with a description of Le Ly's return to Vietnam in 1986, an attempt to come to terms with her past. Hers was a harrowing life: she joined the Viet Cong when she was twelve, was jailed and tortured several times by the South Vietnamese government, then falsely accused of treachery and raped by two of her comrades. She fled her village for Saigon and Danang, had a child out of wedlock, and became embroiled in the black market, selling Americans "souvenirs," including marijuana. Her father committed suicide. Determined to leave Vietnam for the United States, Le Ly fell into a series of unhappy relationships with Americans, who feigned tenderness and exploited her mercilessly. Finally, she met Ed Munro, a lonely old man who wanted "a good oriental wife who knows how to take care of her man." Practicality overcomes romance in the following, melancholy passage.

39
Letting Go
LE LY HAYSLIP

...I found it very hard to concentrate at work after Ed made his proposal. He said that in return for marrying him and coming to America and taking care of him as his wife, he would see to it that I would never have to work again; that my little boy, Jimmy, would be raised in a nice neighborhood and go to an American school; and that neither of us would have to face the dangers and travails of war again. It was the dream of most Vietnamese women and the answer to my prayers—except—

I was still a young woman. The proper time to care for a sixty-year-old husband is at the end of a long and happy marriage, not the beginning. I knew I was attractive to young men and wanted a husband my own age—as my mother and Ba Xuan and Sister Hai all had. On the other hand, I did not especially want to wind up like my sister Lan, who had many lovers, both Vietnamese and American (and now a child by one of them) and no prospects for marriage and a better life at all. Those friends in whom I confided about this problem weren't much help. Some were jealous of my golden opportunity to flee the war, or at least to enjoy the easy life of an American housewife. Others only ridiculed me for even considering a union with someone old enough to be my father. It seemed an unsolvable dilemma.

Of course, Ed was as persistent as he was kind. Because I did not want to be disrespectful, I kept putting him off by saying. "It's too far away," meaning the idea was "so distant" that I didn't even want to think about it, although he took it to mean that I thought America was too far away, so he redoubled his efforts to assure me that it was a wonderful place to live. At the core of my problem, I knew, was the Vietnamese distinction between *duyen* and *no*—the components of marriage that every child learns when he or she becomes engaged. *Duyen no* together denotes a married couple's karma—the destiny they share and what they owe to each other to achieve it. *Duyen* means love—physical attraction and affection; *no* means "debt"—the duty that goes with the office of husband or wife. In a marriage without *no*, the flames of emotion run too high and the couple risks burning up in too much passion or despair. In a marriage without *duyen*, which is the union I would face with Ed, there would be no passion at all—no affection beyond good manners—and nothing to look forward to but the slow chill of a contract played out through all its clauses. Worse, marriages of *no*—quite common in Vietman—often led to the abuse of one spouse by the other, through extramarital affairs, wife-beating, and the thousand other games perfected by cheated souls.

It took me many months to come to grips with this problem and learn my own mind. Young men, I decided, were for marriageable young women—not unwed mothers, black marketeers, and Viet Cong fugitives. By trying to do my duty to everyone in my life—parents, Communist cadremen, rich employers, corrupt officials—I had wound up failing in my duty to myself and the child of my breast, who depended on me. I decided to read the handwriting on the wall. Younger men valued me as a companion, an ornament, and a plaything—that was true enough; but not as a partner for their lives. And why should they? For any American to want me for a wife, he would have to have an extraordinary need—not for a party girl or bedmate or crutch to support his weaknesses, or for someone to help him pretend the times were normal when they were not—but as a companion for the completion of his own life's circle. For me to trust myself again to an American, that man must be such an extraordinary person. In Ed Munro, who was completely unlike the other men I had met in my life, perhaps I—and my fatherless son—had discovered such a man.

In August 1969, when Ed's contract in Vietnam was into its final year, I agreed to become his wife. It was a decision that turned out to be filled with many unexpected costs.

For example, instead of rejoicing wholeheartedly with me, my friends began to warn me about the many legal and practical roadblocks established to discourage Vietnamese-American marriages and emigration to the United States. To make matters worse, the detailed investigations that went into certifying every applicant for a visa made it almost inevitable that my previous arrests (for everything from aiding the Viet Cong to selling illegal drugs) would be discovered and I would quickly be branded an "undesirable alien." What such revelations might mean to my fiancé, I couldn't even think about.

Fortunately, Ed was a man of the world as well as a man of his word. He didn't ask about my past and said that as far as he was concerned, our new life began on the day we met and I could make of it anything I chose; that nothing in my past should stand between us and our future happiness. He said he would be willing to pay whatever was necessary to ensure that our paperwork was approved. Because he had never before dealt with the corrupt Republican machinery, he had no inkling of how costly this blank check might be. Because I had never tried to pull off anything this big either, I was in no position to tell him.

My first step, then, was to return to the landowner—the "dragon lady," Sister Hoa—who had helped me before. Our first meeting was not too productive because she only wanted to talk about the niceties of marriage and how wonderful life was in America; how happy she was that I had found a nice, mature American and how lucky I would be to live in Southern California. When we finally got around to talking turkey, I discovered this particular goose would take a lot of stuffing!

"What you want is very, very expensive!" she admonished me, as if she found the profit she was going to make distasteful. "You'll need permission from government agencies at the city, district, provincial, and national levels. You'll need a marriage certificate and favorable reports from both the Vietnamese and American counselors you'll have to visit. Do you plan to take your little boy with you?"

"Of course! He's my son!"

"That's too bad," she said, smiling pleasantly. "You'll need a birth certificate stating he's *con hoan*—a child without father—and we'll have to get an exit visa for him as well. Tsk!" She shook her head. "The best way to approach it is to tell me how much you and your man are prepared to spend, and I'll try to negotiate the best deal I can at each step, taking my fee from what's left over. That way, you'll know I'm not trying to cheat you."

"How much do you think all this will cost?" I asked.

"It's hard to say without knowing the problems I'll run into. When the war's going well, everything gets cheaper. When there's bad news from the front, everyone gets worried and wants more money for everything. I'd say the basic package should run about a hundred and fifty thousand *dong*—"

"I'll go to America with the caskets!" I start to get up. She was talking almost *double* the amount Ed and I had discussed. Even with my own savings, it would be impossible to pay what she asked.

"Hold on, take it easy!" She put her long-nailed fingers on my arm. "I said that's how much it *should* cost, now how much you will actually have to pay! Remember, you'll have *me* as your adviser. Now, let's talk things over like businesswomen, shall we? Would you care for some tea?"

By the end of the interview, we had agreed upon thirty to fifty thousand *dong* as a reasonable price—but this was for "guarantees" only, and did not include the official fees or gratuities (such as whiskey and cigarettes) that customarily went to decision makers at each level. Despite my earlier remark, I was glad I did not have to buy my way into the illegal transportation network out of the country, such as the occasional Vietnamese who, as rumors had it, rode empty American caskets to Guam or to the Philippines or Honolulu. Even an American's resources would be hard-pressed to fund such desperate and costly schemes.

While we waited for Sister Hoa to grease the proper wheels, I began to live with Ed—to become the kind of wife that he desired. At first, our jobs kept us apart a good deal of the time, which was okay with me. My shift at the Navy EM club ended about eleven, which was when Ed's night shift at the outlying camps was beginning. Although this didn't bother me at all (the idea of ministering to an old, fatherly man as a husband was still too queer to appeal to me), it was not what Ed had in mind for our relationship, so, shortly after we moved in together, he told me to quit my job. Ed's conception of a wife was not someone who worked shoulder to shoulder with her man "in the fields," which was the Vietnamese way, but a queen on a pedestal who spent her days at the beauty shop or overseeing the full-time maid he hired to do all the housework and so kept her long, red fingernails from getting broken. It was a curious role for Phung Thi women, who, for a thousand years, had never been without a day's work before them. Although I tried to please him and play the role he had in mind (idleness was infectious, I discovered—as though every day was New Year's!), I felt more guilt than pleasure. It was as if I had become Lien—an icy princess who seemed to have nothing better to do than read magazines and lord over her servants. Nevertheless, the gift of time was one I could now pass on to my son, and Jimmy began to rediscover his mother just as I began to rediscover what families were all about. Shortly after I accepted Ed's proposal, in fact, I was told by the doctor that my family was about to get a little bigger.

One Sunday, after my clothes began getting tight again at the belly, Sister Hoa came with the one-eyed policeman, an armful of papers—including a marriage certificate and a birth certificate for little Jimmy—and a justice of the peace, to the nice house Ed had rented. While we filled out the forms, Ed sent for his friends, who had agreed to be our witnesses, and told our maid to prepare for a little party to celebrate our marriage. To mark the occasion, I had borrowed one of Lan's fancy cocktail dresses, which (with a few pins and a short veil cut from a sun hat), I quickly turned into a makeshift, Western-style bridal gown.

Within an hour Ed and I were married in a civil ceremony. I had invited my sisters Ba and Lan to come, but they refused; so Hoa cried on behalf of my absent relatives. Although Lan's objections to my marriage seemed more to do with envy than principle (her American boyfriend, Robert, was a friend of Ed's and I think it nettled her that I received a marriage proposal first), Ba's complaints were more traditional. Custom demanded that a bride wait three years after the death of her father before she gives herself to a man, and even in wartime many people thought I was acting too rashly.

"*Phan boi,*" Ba Xuan said one day after a particularly heated discussion of my situation. "You betray your ancestors!" She then sang a little song for my benefit, which I remembered singing myself with other girls in derision of a woman who left the village to marry a man in the city:

> *Da Da birds live only in Da Da trees,*
> *They sing: Why do you marry and go far away,*
> *Instead of loving a man nearby?*
> *Your father gets weak;*
> *Your mother gets old;*
> *Who will be around*
> *To bring them a bowl of rice,*
> *Or serve them tea?*

"Do you see now what you're doing?" Ba asked, genuinely concerned for my soul. "Americans are *thu vo thuy vo chung*—they have no beginning and no end. They don't care about their ancestors. Because they don't know what reincarnation is, they think they're free to do any cruel thing they want in this life—no matter how much it hurts others."

"Can't I be married to Ed without becoming an American myself?" I replied sincerely. "Can't I keep an altar in my house and pray to our father and to Sau Ban and to Grandma and Grandpa Phung, even if Ed doesn't believe in it himself?"

"Sure you can—of course you can—" Ba was really angry. "But secretly, he'll scorn you—and that scorn will come out later in cruelty and disrespect. I'm older than you, Bay Ly. I've been married a long time and know how men act. Why do you think all those little Amerasian bastards are shunned by our people, eh? Not because we don't think they're cute or need help, but because they're tainted with the invader's karma. You don't have to be Viet Cong to know that and hate them for it. Now you want your next child to become one of them! Honestly, Bay Ly—what gets into your head sometimes? And what will our mother think?"

That, of course, is what I regretted most: that my mother could not be with me anymore, even in spirit. Although I did not have the courage to speak to her directly about my plans, I believed the simple fact that I was marrying outside my race, let alone to an American invader, was enough to threaten her motherly love. Sadly, Lan kept me well apprised of my mother's black moods:

"*Dua con hy*, she calls you, Bay Ly," Lan told me shortly before the wedding. "A spoiled rotten child! She says you're acting ungrateful toward your parents and soiling the family name. She says that even though our father's dead, you have made him sad with your decision. It's not too late to call things off, you know."

I felt like challenging Lan—for her years of ignoring our customs herself and her own easy ways with Americans—but I knew it would be fruitless. Our mother usually sided with Lan because Lan had money and was a mature woman and was not the "baby of the family," which is how I gradually realized I would always be viewed, no matter what I did in life. Although Vietnamese are raised to respect their ancestors and love their nation, they are not above civil war. In the triangle formed by our family's sad situation—Lan's contest with me for our mother's affection, our struggle against the tide of a changing society, and our different feelings about Americans—I could almost see a fishpond version of the Viet Cong war itself. If I could not make peace with my family in such matters, how could the real fighters on both sides expect to resolve their differences?

When the short ceremony was over, Ed shook the officials' well-greased palms and complimented them on their sense of duty—working on a Sunday just to help an American get married! Their attitudes, he said innocently, were what Vietnamese-American cooperation was all about. We then had a fine party with Ed's friends, but they, too, left quickly, as if embarrassed by their old friend's child bride. Later, my little niece Tinh, Hai's daughter, came over with sweet rice to wish me good luck and tell me that she loved me. We hugged and cried and I told her I would never forget her.

Unfortunately, our quest, which had begun so hopefully, soon bogged down in obstacles thrown up by destiny or luck—or the government.

First, there was the problem of marriage counseling, a requirement mandated by the American consulate in Danang. Now that his own child was on the way, Ed said he wanted to adopt Jimmy, which was fine with the Americans; but the Vietnamese counselor—a short, fat, greedy woman about Ed's age—raised a long list of objections. While Ed was at work, I attended sessions with this woman and negotiated a price for each objection. Unfortunately, the more I paid, the more she wanted, and each dispensation cost more than the last. After several of these "conferences," I was running out of money Ed allotted for our paperwork. (He gave me two hundred dollars a month to run our household, fifty of which went to pay rent. The rest was to buy food and wrap up our affairs with the government.) Because Ed didn't want me to work after we were married, I had nothing to draw on for the difference but my savings—most of which I had already given to my mother. For several weeks, the officials at the chief district headquarters dined well while my mother and Jimmy and I practically starved. Still, I made sure my husband never suspected our situation. His plate was always full and our refrigerator was always stocked with cold beer. I didn't want my American savior to know the depth of corruption into which my homeland had sunk.

Finally, just when the counselor was getting ready to sign our release, she paused, and said, "Oh, yes, about my bonus—"

"What bonus are you talking about?" I asked, amazed. "I've already paid you almost every dollar to my name—including every cent my husband gives me to run our house. What more could you possibly want?"

"Oh, it's not for me," she said, as if she were asking for church donations. "It's for our 'coffee fund' here at the office. You know, we have lots of volunteers who come in and help us with our cases. We can't afford to pay them, so we offer them coffee and tea and meals when they work overtime—the way they had to work for your application. And you know how long *that's* taken us!"

I couldn't believe what I was hearing. "So—how much coffee are we talking about?" I asked guardedly.

"Well, to tell you the truth," she gazed pensively out the window, tapping her yellow teeth with the end of the pencil, "cash loses its value quickly these days, have you noticed? Even American greenbacks. I was thinking more in terms of merchandise—something that holds its value. You know, like diamonds—"

"*Diamonds!*"

"Now, don't get excited." She opened her desk drawer and produced a page torn from a Sears catalogue. "I don't mean raw gemstones or anything like that. Just something nice that will keep its value better than paper money. Like this nice diamond watch, for example"—she pointed to a pretty lady's watch on a much-handled page—"or maybe a nice dinner ring—like this!" While she shopped from the catalogue, I wondered how many other poor applicants had spent their life savings just to furnish this greedy lady's home, wardrobe, or office on the eve of their departure. We finally decided that a genuine pearl necklace would be just what the volunteers needed for breakfast, so I used up my last favors from old black market partners and obtained one for half-price. I had now completely exhausted my reserves and prayed there would be no more surprises.

In the world's shortest adoption ceremony, I slid the black velvet jewelry case across her desk, received Jimmy's papers in return, and was out of the office before the price could go up again.

Unfortunately, like a frog trying to jump from a table by leaping half the distance remaining on each try, my victories always fell just short of my goal. When I brought the signed papers back to Hoa, she informed me that my plans had hit another snag.

"Of course," she said, as if it were nothing, "we'll need your mother's signature. You're still under age, and even if you're married, you'll need your parents' consent before leaving the country."

Up to this point, I had been able to avoid the whole issue of what to do about my mother. As far as she was concerned, Ed was just another American "boyfriend" (marriage to an outsider was not valid in her eyes) and my life and future, whatever they would be—as well as the life and future of my son—would always be in Vietnam. Although I knew my mother must eventually learn what was going to happen to me, I was not so sure that I had to be the one to tell her; or that she should even know before I left. Now, my procrastination had caught up to me. I would have to be either an exceptionally brave and honest daughter or a very skillful liar. Like many young girls that age, I decided to be the latter.

"Here, Mama *Du*," I said casually, shoving a form and a pen at her one day after lunch. "You have to sign this."

"What is it?" I knew she couldn't read or write, although, like many peasants, she had been taught to make her mark when it was required on legal papers.

"It's nothing; just an application for a bank account. You've probably wondered where all our savings sent, right? Well, I deposited them in a safe place. What if the house burned down? All our money would go up in smoke! With my second baby on the way, I have to be more responsible."

She looked at the mysterious form a long moment, and for a guilty instant, I thought that maybe she had learned to read and would discover what I was up to. As independent as I had become over the last few years, I knew I could never stand up against my mother if she made a really big fuss over things. If the choice came down to leaving the country or destroying my mother's love for me, I knew I would have no options— even if it meant raising a hated Amerasian baby as an outcast among our people. Fortunately, I had a lifetime of peasant's habits on my side.

"Okay, if you really think it's wise." She made her mark and gave me the form. "I still wouldn't trust anyone outside the family with my money, though. Why don't you just give it to Uncle Nhu's son? He's helped us before—"'

I gave her a long, tight hug and kissed the top of her graying head. "Thanks, Mama *Du*. You won't regret it!"

On February 11, 1970, my second son was born in a clean hospital run by Americans for U.S. dependents. Although Ed already had two grown sons he greeted the arrival of this new spirit like a brand-new father. He passed out cigars to his friends and told them how proud he was of

"Thomas"—a good Christian name for a strong and spirited little boy. Alone in the hospital room, I sang a song of welcome to the little soul I called "Chau"—one who was destined to wander—who lay nursing at my breast:

> Go out every day and you will learn,
> Each step that you take will make you wiser.
> Go here, go there, go eveywhere—
> How can you be smart by staying home?
> In the world you will find many nations
> And many people all over the land;
> You'll cross deep oceans and tall mountains,
> And roads that crisscross the sand.
> You'll find people that come in four races:
> Yellow, white, red, and black;
> You'll float through the sky in four directions:
> East,west, north, and south'
> But you will never know all these things, my son,
> Unless you get out of your house.

When I got out of the hospital, my mother came to stay with us at Ed's house and help me through my period of *buon de*. Although Ed always tried to treat her kindly, she was content to behave like a servant when he was around—grunting only when spoken to and showing indifference to his favors. She was mostly concerned about how little Tommy (she always called him Chau) would get by when the war was over. If the Communists won, she knew his invader's blood—*con lai*—would put all of us in danger. If the Republicans won, she knew that same foreign blood— his light skin and American features—would cause him to be shunned in the village as soon as the Americans withdrew. As a result, she spent hours pressing his nose against his face, hoping to flatten it like a Vietnamese. she fed him dark juice and rubbed the juice on his body and kept him outdoors in hopes that his skin would darken like ours. I didn't know if these things would work or not, but I could see in them the desperation that was rising inside my mother; desperation that made it harder for me even to think about telling her the truth: that Ed and I and my two fine boys would one day step on an airliner and, very likely, never be seen by her again.

A few months after Tommy was born, Ed's overseas contract expired and it was time for him to return to the States. The plan was for Ed to go to San Diego first and prepare his home and local relatives for our arrival. After seeimg him off at the airport, I moved my things to Lan's apartment where I would live until my own departure, now less than a week away.

During my last few weeks in Danang, when word of my marriage spread through the neighborhood and I dealt with people as "Mrs. Ed Munro" rather than Phung Thi Le Ly, the world around me began to change. Certainly, I was the same person I had always been, but now I was labeled in a different way. I was no longer completely Vietnamese, but I was not quite American either. Apparently, I was something much worse. Even people I had expected to understand me, to be sympathetic to my dreams, looked down on me and called me names—not always to my back: *Di lay My! Theo de quoc Ve My! Fai choi boi!* Bitch! Traitor! American whore! During many endless hours spent standing in line or sitting in waiting rooms or by desks of minor officials, I found myself on the receiving end of dirty glances from Vietnamese clerks, secretaries, errand boys, and janitors. No citizen of Danang was so poor or humble that he or she was not superior to Le Ly *Munro*—turncoat to her country. Teenagers and a few Republican soldiers who lived in our neighborhood gave me cat-calls and sang derisive songs when I passed and, on two occasions, threw stones at me when I appeared on the street alone. In one instance our home was broken into, burglarized (which was understandable), and vandalized (which was not).

Even people who forgave me my new American name could not excuse me for accepting an older man as my savior. On many occasions Ed and I were openly cheated—charged two or three times more than even the black market price for food or supplies—just so people could show us their indignation. It seemed as though the more we accepted their wrath, the more contempt they showed us. In private conversations, I was often pleasantly (and sometimes not so pleasantly) reminded that in America, people hated anyone—even other Americans—who came from Vietnam, and quoted the war protestors' slogans. They were a gallery of sullen, unforgiving faces that I often saw in my sleep: tattered victims on Vietnam's foundering ship of state watching jealously as I abandoned them for the lifeboat of America. I was experiencing, I discovered, not only what foreigners had faced in my own land for generations; but the ultimate price of my own independence. It made sister Hoa's demands seems paltry by comparison.

In any event, after paying more bribes to obtain my passport, I was finally ready to depart Danang for Saigon; to get a visa at the American embassy—the last hurdle standing between my sons and me and our flight to a better life.

On March 20, 1970, Jimmy, Tommy, our maid, and I boarded the shuttle flight for Tan Son Nhut. All through the flight, I thought about my mother and how she would react when my maid (she drew the short straw—none of my sisters would do it!) returned to Danang and broke the news of our departure to my mother. Part of me wanted to believe she already knew the truth—learning it, perhaps, from a neighbor or by that intuition through which every mother knows her daughter—and that the truth had been in her eyes the last time I looked into her face: a benediction for my new life. Of course, unless I was to come back someday, I would probably never know.

During the two-month stay before our overseas flight, I had no trouble saying farewell to Saigon. As the capital of our country as well as Anh's home, it had become the symbol of everything I wanted to leave behind—to let go of and cut loose from my life. In the three years since I had been here, Saigon had become even bigger and noisier and dirtier and more wealthy and more wealth-driven and more cosmopolitan than it had ever been before. Rather than being less Vietnamese, which is how the Viet Cong described it, Saigon now seemed to be more and more what the Vietnamese people themselves were becoming: vicious, grasping, estranged, desperate, and dangerous—mostly to themselves. Still, I had one last piece of business to attend to before these chains were broken.

The great U.S. embassy was busy as a marketplace—full of staff and visitors. After a long wait, a junior American clerk received me only to tell me that Vietnamese citizens seeking visas were supposed to report to a different building, where such requests were processed by the Vietnamese Immigration and Naturalization Department. This distressed me greatly—not just for the extra step—but because dealing with Vietnamese bureaucrats always meant more cost and trouble.

The emigration office was located in a two-story white apartment building that was near the main post office and the Nha Tho Duc Ba Catholic Church. I was not encouraged when I walked through the door. Instead of a businesslike office, the apartment was the residence of a well-heeled Republican woman who had refined the art of administrative extortion to a science.

"How badly do you want to go to America?" she asked, cutting right to the heart of the matter. "You'll need documentation from the Vietnamese embassy in Washington. It's going to be expensive. How much do you have to spend?" Perhaps she phrased it this way so that if anybody ever challenged her, she could say she was simply separating the charity cases from those who could pay the government's fee.

I replied with a good, cheap guess.

"That's not enough," she said flatly. "Come into my house. We'll have to discuss your case."

After brief negotiations, accelerated by my early admission that my American husband was no longer around to pay my bills and that I could only raise more cash by selling my airline ticket, which would defeat the purpose of a visa, we agreed upon a price.

"Okay," she said, ushering me back outside. "You'll have to wait out here while I prepare your letter. My house isn't a bus station, you know. And by the way, there'll be a small surcharge for our tea fund—"

I spend the next few hours hoping that tea was cheaper than coffee—even at Saigon's inflated prices. By the end of the day, though, I went home with the all-important letter.

On May 27, 1970, my sons and I stood in line to board the big American jetliner to Honolulu. As the passengers shuffled forward, juggling their carry-on bags and jackets, they showed their tickets to one last Republican official. The Americans passed quickly. The Vietnamese, however, usually had to stop and delay the line while they fumbled through their purses or pockets. When my turn came, the official did not ask for passports or visas or certificates of any kind. He asked only a single question—the last phrase I would hear in my native tongue on the soil which held my father's bones:'

"Are you carrying Vietnamese money? If so, please drop it in the basket before you go."

A Chronology of the Vietnam War, 1945–1975

1945

Sept. 2   Ho Chi Minh proclaims the Democratic Republic of Vietnam.

26   A. Peter Dewey, head of the OSS mission in Saigon, is shot by Vietminh troops, becoming the first American to die in the Vietnam War.

1946

Mar. 6   Franci-Vietnamese Accords signed.

June 1   The Fontainebleau Conference convenes.

Nov. 23   The French shell Vietnamese neighborhoods in Haiphong, killing an estimated 6000 Vietnamese.

Dec. 19   The Vietminh attack French forces in Tonkin, formally beginning the First Indochina War.

1948

June 5   The French name Bao Das head of state of Vietnam.

1949

Mar. 8   Élysée Agreement signed.

Oct. 1   Mao Zedong proclaims the People's Republic of China.

1950

Jan. 14   Ho Chi Minh again proclaims establishment of the Democratic Republic of Vietnam.

May 1   President Harry S. Truman announces U.S. economic and military assistance to Vietnam.

Aug. 3   United States Military Assistance and Advisory Group arrives in Saigon.

Dec. 30   United States signs a Mutual Defense Assistance Agreement with France, Vietnam, Cambodia, and Laos.

1952

Nov. 4   Dwight D. Eisenhower is elected president.

1953

July 27   Korean War armistice is signed.

1954

Mar. 13	Vietminh attack the French fortress at Dienbienphu.
20	Admiral Arthur Radford proposes Operation Vulture to assist the French in defending Dienbienphu.
Apr. 7	President Dwight D. Eisenhower uses the domino analogy to explain the political significance of Indochina.
25	Winston Churchill and the British refuse to participate in Operation Vulture.
29	President Eisenhower announces that the United States will not provide air support to the French garrison at Dienbienphu.
May 7	The Vietminh conquer Dienbienphu.
8	The Geneva Conference opens.
July 20	France signs a cease-fire ending hostilities in Indochina.
Aug. 1	The first of nearly one million refugees from North Vietnam cross into South Vietnam.
Sept. 8	United States signs the Manila Treaty forming the Southeast Asia Treaty Organization.

1955

Mar. 28	Ngo Dinh Diem attacks the Binh Xuyen.
June 5	Ngo Dinh Diem attacks the Hoa Hao.
July 6	Ngo Dinh Diem repudiates the Geneva Agreements and refuses to plan for open elections throughout the country. He is backed by the Eisenhower administration.
Oct. 26	Ngo Dinh Diem proclaims the Republic of Vietnam with himself as president.

1957

May 5–19	Ngo Dinh Diem visits the United States.

1959

Apr. 4	President Eisenhower makes his first commitment to maintain South Vietnam as a separate nation.
22	Christian A. Herter replaces John Foster Dulles as secretary of state.
July 8	First American servicemen (Major Dale Bius and Master Sergeant Chester Ovnard) killed by Vietcong attack at Bien Hoa.
Dec. 1	Thomas S. Gates, Jr., replaces Neil H. McElroy as secretary of defense.
31	Approximately 760 U.S. military personnel in Vietnam.

1960

Dec. 20	National Liberation Front established.
31	Approximately 900 U.S. military personnel in Vietnam.

1961

Jan. 21	John F. Kennedy succeeds Dwight D. Eisenhower as president. Dean Rusk succeeds Christian A. Herter as secretary of state. Robert S. McNamara succeeds Thomas S. Gates, Jr., as secretary of defense. McGeorge Bundy succeeds Gordon Gray as national security adviser.
28	Kennedy approves a Vietnam counterinsurgency plan.
Mar. 23	Kennedy insists that a Laotian cease-fire must precede negotiations to establish a neutral Laos.

May 9–15   Vice President Lyndon Johnson visits South Vietnam and recommends a strong American commitment there. Geneva Conference on Laos opens.

June 9   President Ngo Dinh Diem asks for U.S. military advisers to train the South Vietnamese Army.

July 1   General Maxwell Taylor is appointed military adviser to president John F. Kennedy.

Nov. 3   General Maxwell Taylor concludes that U.S. military, financial, and political aide will bring victory without a U.S. takeover of the war. He advises Kennedy to send 8,000 U.S. combat troops to Vietnam.

Dec. 15   Kennedy restates U.S. commitment to an independent South Vietnam.

31   U.S. military personnel in Vietnam now number 3,205.

1962

Feb. 6   MACV (U.S. Military Assistance Command, Vietnam) established in Saigon under the command of General Paul Harkins. The major buildup of American forces begins.

14   Kennedy authorizes U.S. military advisers in Vietnam to return fire if fired upon.

Mar. 22   United States launches the Strategic Hamlet (rural pacification) Program.

July 23   Geneva Accords on Laos signed.

Oct. 1   General Maxwell Taylor replaces General Lyman Lemnitzer as chairman, Joint Chiefs to Staff.

Dec. 31   U.S. military personnel now in Vietnam number 11,300.

1963

Aug. 21   South Vietnam troops attack Buddhist pagodas.

22   Henry Cabot Lodge replaces Frederick Nolting as U.S. ambassador to Vietnam.

Nov. 1   Military coup overthrows the government of President Ngo Dinh Diem.

2   Diem and his brother Ngo Dinh Nhu assassinated.

22   President John F. Kennedy assassinated.

Dec. 31   U.S. military personnel in Vietnam now number 16,300.

1964

Feb. 7   Johnson removes American dependents from South Vietnam.

June 20   General William Westmoreland replaces General Paul Harkins as head of MACV.

23   General Maxwell Taylor replaces Henry Cabot Lodge as U.S. ambassador to South Vietnam.

Aug. 2   U.S. destroyer *Maddox* allegedly attacked by North Vietnamese patrol boats in the Gulf of Tonkin.

4   U.S. destroyer *Turner Joy* claims attack by North Vietnamese patrol boats.

7   U.S. Congress passes Gulf of Tonkin Resolution.

Oct. 1   U.S. Army Fifth Special Forces Group arrives in Vietnam.

Nov. 1   Vietcong attack Bien Hoa Air Base. Six U.S. B-57 bombers destroyed; five American service personnel killed.

2   Johnson defeats Senator Barry Goldwater in presidential election.

Dec. 24   Vietcong kill two U.S. soldiers in an attack on the Brinks Hotel in Saigon.

31   U.S. military personnel in Vietnam now number 23,300.

1965

Feb. 7   Vietcong launch a widespread attack on American military installations in South Vietnam.

Mar. 2   Operation Rolling Thunder begins.

8   First American combat troops (U.S. Third Marine regiment) arrive in Vietnam to defend Danang.

24   First teach-in held at the University of Michigan.

Apr. 6   Johnson permits U.S. ground combat troops to conduct offensive operations in South Vietnam.

17   Students for a Democratic Society hold antiwar rally in Washington, D.C.

May 15   National Teach-In held throughout the country.

June 8   State Department reports that Johnson has authorized the use of U.S. troops in direct combat if the South Vietnamese Army requests assistance.

July 8   Henry Cabot Lodge succeeds Maxwell Taylor as U.S. ambassador to South Vietnam.

Oct. 15–16   Antiwar protests in forty American cities.

Nov. 14–16   Battle of the Ia Drang Valley.

Dec. 25   Johnson suspends bombing of North Vietnam (Operation Rolling Thunder) and invites North Vietnam to negotiate.

31   U.S. military personnel in Vietnam now number 184,300. 22,420 Allied troops in Vietnam.

1966

Jan. 31   Bombing of North Vietnam (Operation Rolling Thunder) resumes.

Feb. 4   Senate Foreign Relations Committee opens televised hearings on the Vietnam War.

6   President Lyndon Johnson convenes the Honolulu Conference.

Mar. 1   Senate refuses to repeal the Gulf of Tonkin Resolution.

20   President Lyndon Johnson convenes the Guam Conference.

Apr. 1   Walt Rostow replaces McGeorge Bundy as national security adviser.

7   President Lyndon Johnson offers the Johns Hopkins Speech.

May 1   U.S. forces bombard Vietcong targets in Cambodia.

June 29   United States bombs oil facilities in Haiphong and Hanoi.

Oct. 26   Johnson visits U.S. troops in Vietnam.

Dec. 31   U.S. military personnel now in Vietnam number 385,300. 52,500 Allied military personnel in Vietnam.

1967

Jan. 8   Operation Cedar Falls begins.

26   Operation Cedar Falls ends.

Feb. 22   Operation Junction City begins.

Apr. 15   One hundred thousand antiwar protesters rally in New York.

May 1   Ellsworth Bunker replaces Henry Cabot Lodge as U.S. ambassador to South Vietnam.

14	Operation Junction City ends.
19	U.s. planes bomb a power plant in Hanoi.
July 7	Congressional Joint Economic committee estimates the war will cost $4 to $6 billion more in 1967 than the $20.3 billion requested by Johnson.
Sept. 3	Nguyen Van Thieu elected president of South Vietnam.
29	Johnson offers to stop bombing of North Vietnam if the North Vietnamese will immediately come to the negotiating table (San Antonio Formula).
Oct. 21	Fifty thousand antiwar activists protest at the Pentagon.
Dec. 31	U.S. military personnel now in Vietnam number 485,600.

1968

Jan. 3	Senator Eugene McCarthy announces his decision to seek the Democratic presidential nomination.
21	NVA siege of Khe Sanh begins.
30	Tet Offensive begins.
31	Vietcong and NVA capture Hue.
Feb. 1	Richard M. Nixon announces his candidacy for the presidency.
25	ARVN and U.S. troops reconquer Hue.
27	Westmoreland requests 206,000 more troops.
	CBS anchorman Walter Cronkite predicts over the evening news that the war cannot be won.
Mar. 12	Eugene McCarthy wins the New Hampshire Democratic presidential primary.
16	Senator Robert Kennedy announces his decision to seek the Democratic presidential nomination.
	My Lai massacre takes place.
25–26	Senior Advisory Group on Vietnam recommends deescalation of the American commitment in Vietnam.
31	Lyndon Johnson announces his decision no to run for reelection.
Apr. 23	Columbia University demonstrations begin.
26	Two hundred thousand people in NYC demonstrate against the war.
27	Vice President Hubert Humphrey announces his decision to seek the Democratic presidential nomination.
May 3	Johnson announces that formal peace talks will take place in Paris.
12	Vietnam peace talks open in Paris.
June 6	Robert Kennedy is assassinated.
July 1	General Creighton Abrams replaces General William Westmoreland as head of MACV.
3	General William Westmoreland replaces General Harold Johnson as chief of staff, U.S. Army.
Aug. 28	Antiwar protests and riots in Chicago during the Democratic National Convention.
Oct. 31	Johnson announces end of bombing of North Vietnam.
	Operation Rolling Thunder ends.
Nov. 5	Richard Nixon defeats Hubert Humphrey in the 1968 presidential election.
Dec. 31	U.S. military personnel in Vietnam now number 536,000. 65,600 Allied troops in Vietnam.

1969

Jan. 22	Richard Nixon inaugurated as president; William Rogers becomes secretary of state; Melvin Laird becomes secretary of defense; Henry Kissinger becomes national security adviser.
Mar. 18	Operation Menu begins.
26	Women Strike for Peace demonstration in Washington, D.C.
Apr. 30	The number of U.S. military personnel in Vietnam reaches 543,300.
May 14	Nixon proposes peace plan for Vietnam involving mutual troop withdrawal.
June 8	Nixon announces the removal of 25,000 troops from Vietnam.
July 25	Richard Nixon proclaims the Nixon Doctrine.
Aug. 27	U.S. Ninth Infantry Division withdraws from Vietnam.
Sept. 3	Ho Chi Minh dies.
Oct. 15	National Moratorium antiwar demonstrations staged throughout the United States.
Nov. 15	The New Mobilization committee to End the War in Vietnam sponsors a demonstration of 250,000 in Washington, D.C.
16	My Lai massacre described in the press.
Dec. 31	U.S. military personnel strength in Vietnam declines to 475,200. Allied personnel in Vietnam totals 70,300.

1970

Feb. 20	Henry Kissinger opens secret peace negotiations in Paris.
Mar. 18	Prince Norodom Sihanouk of Cambodia deposed by General Lon Nol.
Apr. 29	Operations in Cambodia begin.
30	United States invades Cambodia.
May 4	National Guard troops kill four students at Kent State University during demonstrations against the Cambodian invasion.
June 30	Operations in Cambodia end.
Nov. 21	Unsuccessful raid on the Son Tay Prison in North Vietnam.
Dec. 22	U.S. Congress prohibits U.S. combat forces or advisers in Cambodia and Laos.
31	U.S. military personnel strength in Vietnam declines to 334,600. Allied military personnel declines to 67,700.

1971

Jan. 30	Operation Lam Son 719 begins.
31	Winter Soldier Investigation begins in Detroit.
Mar. 29	Lt. William L. Calley, Jr., found guilty of murder.
Apr. 6	Operation Lam Son 719 ends.
20	Demonstrators in Washington, D.C., and San Francisco call for an end to the war.
May 3–5	People's Coalition for Peace and Justice demonstrates against the war in Washington, D.C.
June 13	*New York Times* starts publishing the Pentagon Papers.
30	Supreme Court allows publication of the Pentagon Papers.
Nov. 12	Nixon confines U.S. ground forces to a defensive rule.
Dec. 26	Nixon orders resumption of bombing of North Vietnam.
31	U.S. military strength declines to 156,800. Allied military personnel in Vietnam declines to 53,900.

1972

Feb. 21	Nixon seeks detente with the People's Republic of China by visiting Beijing.
Mar. 23	United States suspends Paris peace talks until North Vietnam and the NLF enter into "serious discussions."
30	Eastertide Offensive begins.
Apr. 7	Battle of An Loc begins.
15	U.S. bombing of Hanoi begins again.
15–20	Widespread antiwar demonstrations across the United States.
27	Paris peace talks resume.
May 1	North Vietnamese conquer Quang Tri.
4	United States suspends the Paris peace talks.
8	U.S. Navy mines North Vietnamese ports.
June 18	NVA forces an end to the battle of An Loc.
22	Watergate break-in and arrests.
July 13	Paris peace talks resume after ten weeks.
Sept. 15	ARVN forces recapture Quang Tri.
26–27	Henry Kissinger conducts secret talks with North Vietnamese diplomats in Paris.
Oct. 11	Kissinger and North Vietnamese negotiator LeDuc Tho reach substantial agreement on a settlement.
16	General Creighton Abrams becomes chief of staff, U.S. Army.
17	Peace talks begin in Laos.
19–20	Kissinger meets with President Nguyen Van Thieu in Saigon to secure South Vietnamese support for the pending Paris Peace Accords. Thieu is unconvinced.
Nov. 7	Nixon is reelected president in a landslide over Senator George McGovern.
Dec. 13	Paris peace talks stall.
18–29	Operation Linebacker II—the Christmas bombing—conducted.
31	U.S. military strength declines to 24,000. Allied personnel drops to 35,500.
	SVNAF personnel killed in action to date numbers 195,847.

1973

Jan. 8–12	Kissinger and Le Duc Tho convene more private negotations.
15	Nixon halts all U.S. offensive action against North Vietnam.
27	Peace pact signed in Paris by the United States, South Vietnam, North Vietnam, and the National Liberation Front.
30	Elliot L. Richardson becomes secretary of defense.
Feb. 12	First of American POW's released by North Vietnam.
21	Peace agreement signed in Laos.
Mar. 29	MACV headquarters removed.
	Last of American POWs released by North Vietnam.
June 13	Implementation accord signed in Paris by the United States, South Vietnam, North Vietnam, and the National Liberation Front.
24	Graham Martin becomes U.S. ambassador to South Vietnam. Congress prohibits all bombing in Cambodia after August 15.
July 2	James Schlesinger becomes secretary of defense.
Aug. 14	All direct American military operations end in all of Indochina.

Sept. 22   Henry Kissinger becomes secretary of state.

Nov. 7   War Powers Resolution becomes law despite a presidential veto.

Dec. 31   American military personnel in South Vietnam drops to 50.

1974

Aug. 9   Nixon resigns the presidency.

Gerald Ford is inagurated as president of the United States.

20   Congress reduces aid to South Vietnam from $ 1 billion to $700 million.

Sept. 16   Ford offers clemency to draft evaders and military deserters.

Dec. 13   Combat between NVA and ARVN is conducted in Phuoc Long Province.

31   U.S. military strength in Vietnam remains at 50.

1975

Jan. 6   NVA troops take control to Phuoc Long Province.

8   North Vietnam decides on a massive invasion of South Vietnam.

Mar. 10   NVA captures Ban Me Thuot.

14   President Nguyen Van Thieu withdraws ARVN forces from central Highlands.

19   NVA captures Quang Tri Province.

26   Hue falls to the NVA.

30   Danang falls to the NVA.

Apr. 1   Cambodian President Lon Nol flees Cambodia in face of Khmer Rouge invasion.

South Vietnam abandons the northern half of the country to North Vietnam.

8–20   Battle of Xuan Loc.

11–13   Operation Eagle Pull removes U.S. embassy personnel from Phnom Penh, Cambodia.

12   President Nguyen Van Thieu resigns.

17   Cambodia falls to Khmer Rouge troops.

29–30   Operation Frequent Wind evacuates all American personnel and some South Vietnamese from Vietnam.

NVA captures Saigon.

30   Vietnam war ends.

Glossary

AID: Agency for International Develoment (U.S.)

AIRBORNE: People or material delivered by helicopter

ARVN: Army of the Republic of Vietnam

Base area: An area of installations defensive fortifications, or other physical structures used by the enemy

Base camp: A semipermanent field headquarters and center for a given unit, usually within the unit's tactical area of responsibility

Battalion days in the field: Days when battalions are patrolling in the field; a standard measure of battalion productivity

Body bags: Plastic bags used for transport of bodies from the field

Charlie, Charles: Nickname used by American troops to identify the Vietcong.

Chieu hoi: An amnesty program offered to the Vietcong by the government of the Republic of Vietnam

CIA: Central Intelligence Agency (U.S.)

CIDG: Civilian Irregular Defense Group, South Vietnamese nationals recruited and trained by U.S. Special Forces

CINCPAC: Commander in Chief, Pacific (U.S. Navy)

Clear and hold: An American military tactic in which U.S. troops tried to capture and permanently hold an area

CORDS: Civil Operations and Revolutionary Development Support, created in 1967 to direct the U.S. pacification effort

COSVN: The North Vietnamese Central Office of South Vietnam

CTZ: Corps tactical zone, South Vietnam (numbered I–IV from north to south)

DEROS: Date of expected return from overseas for U.S. soldiers in Vietnam

DeSoto: U.S. Navy destroyer patrols in the South China Sea

DMZ: Dimilitarized zone on either side of the 17th parallel

DRV: Democratic Republic of Vietnam (North Vietnam)

Fire base: A temporary artillery firing position often secured by infantry

Fire fight: An exchange of small-arms fire between opposing units.

IV Corps: Southernmost military region in South Vietnam, located in the Mekong Delta

Frag: To kill or attempt to kill one's own officers or sergeants

Free fire zone: Any area in which permission was not required prior to firing on targets

Gooks: Derogatory term, brought to Vietnam by Korean War veterans, for anyone of Asian descent

Green Berets: U.S. Special Forces troops

Guerrila warfare: Military operations conducted in hostile territory by irregular, primarily indigenous forces

Hedgehogs: Isolated outposts in which the French high command concentrated troops

Hot pursuit: Policy allowing American troops to chase Vietcong and NVA soldiers across the border into Cambodia

I Corps: Northernmost military region in South Vietnam

JCS: Joint Chiefs of Staff (U.S.)

Khmer Rouge: Cambodian Communists

Light at the end of the tunnel: Term used to describe the imminent demise of the Vietcong and North Vietnamese

LRRPs (lurps): Long-range reconnaissance patrols

MAAG: Military Assistance and Advisory Group

MACV: Military Assistance Command, Vietnam (Mac-Vee); the commander of MACV was known as COMUSMACV

Main force: Vietcong and North Vietnamese military units

M-16: The standard American rifle used in Vietnam after 1966

Napalm: A gelatinous incendiary used by French and Americans as a defoliant and as an antipersonnel weapon

NLF: National Liberation Front, the political organization of the Vietcong until 1969

NVA: North Vietnamese Army

Pacification: Several programs of the South Vietnamese and the U.S. governments to destroy the Vietcong in the villages, gain civilian support for the Republic of South Vietnam, and stabilize the countryside

Pathet Lao: Laotian Communists

PAVN: People's Army of Vietnam (North Vietnamese Army, NVA)

PLVN: People's Liberation Army of Vietnam (Vietcong troops)

POWs: Prisoners of war

PRGVN: Provisional Revolutionary Government of South Vietnam (political organization of the Vietcong after 1969)

Punji stake: A razor-sharp bamboo stake sometimes coated with poison or feces and usually hidden under water, along trails, at ambush sites, or in deep pits

ROKs: Troops from the Republic of Korea (South Korea)

Ruff-Puffs: South Vietnamese Regional Forces (RFs) and Popular Forces (PFs); paramilitary forces usually of squad or platoon size recruited and utilized in a hamlet or village

RVN: Republic of Vietnam (South Vietnam)

SAM: Soviet-made surface-to-air missiles

Sappers: North Vietnamese or Vietcong demolition commandos

Search and destroy: Offensive operations designed to find and destroy enemy forces rather than establish permanent government control

Seventeenth Parallel: Temporary division line between North and South Vietnam

Sortie: One aircraft making one takeoff and landing to conduce a mission for which it was scheduled

Special Forces: U.S. soldiers, best known of which were the Green Berets, trained in techniques of guerilla warfare

SRV: Socialist Republic of Vietnam

Tet: Vietnamese lunar new year holiday period

III Corps: Military region between Saigon and the Central Highlands

II Corps: Central Highlands military region in South Vietnam

Vietcong: Communist forces fighting in South Vietnam

Vietminh: Communist and nationalist forces fighting the French before 1954

Vietnamization: President Nixon's program to turn the war gradually over to the South Vietnamese while phasing out American troops